Rydal. Edited by Willingham F. Rawnsley

Mary L Armitt, Willingham Franklin Rawnsley

Nabu Public Domain Reprints:

You are holding a reproduction of an original work published before 1923 that is in the public domain in the United States of America, and possibly other countries. You may freely copy and distribute this work as no entity (individual or corporate) has a copyright on the body of the work. This book may contain prior copyright references, and library stamps (as most of these works were scanned from library copies). These have been scanned and retained as part of the historical artifact.

This book may have occasional imperfections such as missing or blurred pages, poor pictures, errant marks, etc. that were either part of the original artifact, or were introduced by the scanning process. We believe this work is culturally important, and despite the imperfections, have elected to bring it back into print as part of our continuing commitment to the preservation of printed works worldwide. We appreciate your understanding of the imperfections in the preservation process, and hope you enjoy this valuable book.

RYDAL

RYDAL

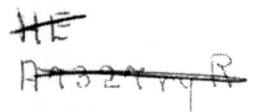

BY

THE LATE MISS ARMITT

Author of the "Church of Grasmere."

EDITED BY

WILLINGHAM F. RAWNSLEY, M.A.

AUTHOR OF

"Early Days at Uppingham." "Introductions to
the Poets," and "Highways and Byways
in Lincolnshire."

ILLUSTRATED

Kendal
Titus Wilson
Printer and Publisher

1916

DA
670
W5 A75

EDITOR'S PREFACE.

Most people in the neighbourhood of Rydal, and all in the County who take pleasure either in Archaeology or Natural History have long known Miss M. L. Armitt's writing and valued it. Her observations were painstaking and her statements accurate.

It was my privilege to be a frequent visitor at Rydal Cottage when all the sisters were alive, and I question if since the days of the Brontes in the parsonage at Haworth any small roof-tree ever covered so interesting a triad Each in her own line had so much first-hand information, and each was so ready in the simplest manner to impart it and to make it attractive. The survivor of this remarkable family, Mrs Stanford Harris, in spite of ill-health, has written with vigour and with no ordinary charm a very considerable amount both in prose and verse, and her sound critical judgment has been of great service to me in editing the present volume.

Though all were fond of things Antiquarian and especially of old buildings, and though in the days before they kept school together at Eccles (and what a delightful school it must have been with those young, enthusiastic teachers!)—they had been students of Literature, Painting and Music, I think that the chief interest latterly of the other sisters was some branch of Natural History. Sophia, who died first (June 12th, 1908), was a genuinely scientific botanist, not only a lover of plants and flowers, as many of us are, but a real authority on all that concerned the vegetable world. She regularly contributed papers to a Botanical Society to which she belonged, and her excellent notes on flowers, together with those of her sister on birds were reprinted continuously between December, 1911—December, 1912 in the *Parents Review*, edited by Charlotte M. Mason. She loved to go on archæological excursions, and all the way she would be ready to point out the habitat of some rare plant or the geological conditions which favoured certain flora.

On one occasion, in July, 1907, when we went with the Cumberland and Westmorland Society to Crosby Ravensworth, she seized the opportunity to take us to the place where she had always hoped to find a rather rare plant, the Alpine Bistort (*Polygonum Viviparum*), and where we indeed quickly found it. At another time she pointed to the outcrop of the Coniston limestone by the road side, with its own peculiar flora. Or she would gather samples of the foreign plants which had taken root on the sea bank near the little port of Silloth on the Cumberland side of the Solway Firth. At home she once showed me the specially interesting arrangement for the fertilization of the Grass of Parnassus, of which she was watching the daily development, or she would be painting with admirable fidelity the smaller funguses or lichens; and her garden, tended entirely by herself, was a treasury of interesting plants. Her sister, M. L. Armitt, known to her intimates as "Louie," was for years more or less of an invalid; but she managed to do a surprising lot of reading and research in matters archæological, and especially in all that pertained to the life of the early dwellers in the Rydal Valley and neighbourhood. But I think her keenest enjoyment was in the little expeditions, some of which we had together, in search of some rare or notable bird. Every bird was known to her, his habitat, his dates of migration, his note, his method of nesting, and all that a bird would be at most pains to conceal, was to her an open book. The Pied Flycatcher, the migratory Wagtails, the Dipper, his song, his singular habits and the discovery of his nest were an annual delight to her. The circling Buzzards were, I might almost say, her familiar friends. Together we went to call on the black and white "Tufted Duck," and found him at home without fail on "Priests Pot" near Hawkshead; and the crested Grebe, though not so easy to see, was not far off on Esthwaite, near which Miss Armitt noted with satisfaction the increasing number of Redshanks, reported by that very "rara avis" a Naturalist gamekeeper to be nesting thereabout. Her face lit up with pleasure when I described to her the Woodcock who alighted close to me on the lawn at Loughrigg Holme in order to get a firmer hold of the young one she was carrying in her claws, and who tried to wriggle away from her grasp. But the greatest delight of all was the sight, early in the spring, of a Mother Snipe and her three young ones on the Little Langdale road. We pulled up close to them, and when the mother flew into the grass on one side of the road the little ones ran back to the other side and in a moment, squatting close, were so hidden that we could not find a trace of them, though all the time they were within a few feet of us.

A full report of the birds of the Lake District, from her pen, forms the opening chapter in Part II. [Natural History and Sport] of Prof. Collingwood's delightful *Lake Counties*, one of the series of Dent's County Guides; and her special list of the birds of Rydal, published in *The Naturalist* in August, 1902, is given in the Appendix at the end of the volume, by kind permission of the Editor.

But though the Natural History of Birds was Miss Armitt's chief delight, and the subject in which she most excelled, her hard close work extending over several years was given to the History of Rydal and Grasmere. Her Grasmere book was published in 1912, a year after her death, and the Rydal Book, about which I had had a good deal of conversation with her at various times, and had gone through the MS. of several chapters, was left practically finished at her death, on July 31st, 1911, and

I could not help feeling that it was a duty I owed to her valued friendship that, according to her wish, I should do what was necessary to prepare it for the press. The task for many reasons has not been a very easy one ; but the result will, I think, be found to be a very full and in many directions an extremely interesting account of the History, not only of Rydal, but of all the neighbourhood, and also of the whole county, and in some respects of the whole realm. The chapters on trade and husbandry and on domestic life and fashions in the seventeenth century will be found most interesting : and the life and times of Sir Daniel Fleming are described with great fullness and much humour.

The work all through seems to me to exhibit an amazing deal of research, often of a most laborious kind, and to be a monument of what the old writers called " painful " industry, resulting in an accuracy which was the Author's constant aim. The interest mostly centres in Rydal Hall and its owners, and the uniquely interesting Rydal Hall MSS. have of course been the main source of information for several of the chapters : and it is chiefly owing to the free access to them which the owner, Mr. Stanley le Fleming, has permitted, that Miss Armitt was enabled to begin and encouraged to continue this main work of her later years. Help, too, she undoubtedly received, and that of a very valuable kind, from Dr. Magrath, Provost of Queen's Coll., Oxford, whose two vols. *The Flemings in Oxford*, contain so much information, mostly derived from the same fountain-head.

By her will Miss M. L. Armitt left her own and her sister Sophia's books to form a students' library in Ambleside. This was opened in November, 1912, under the name of the Armitt Library, the excellent Ruskin Library, which had been in existence for 30 years in Ambleside, being joined to it and the balance of the funds of the old " Ambleside Book Society," founded in 1828, of which

W. Wordsworth was a member, handed over to it. Portraits of the founders and of their Rydal home are on the walls, and among other things a copy of a sonnet, by one who knew them well. This, which was written at the time of the opening of the Library, may I think fitly find a place at the end of this Preface.

W. F. RAWNSLEY.

SONNET.

As in some inland solitude a shell
Still gently murmurs of its home, the deep,
So in the world of being beyond all sleep
Where those two happy sister spirits dwell,
This book-lined room, this simple Students' cell
Shall, in the silence, pure memorial keep
Of those who sowed that other minds might reap
Their wisdom won from lake and wood and fell :
And as we gather up their gentle lore,
Made rich by jewels from their treasury,
The whispers grow " Behold ! These souls had power
Because with patient heart and loving eye
They learned that man and bird and beast and flower
Were in God's purpose friends for evermore."

H.D.R.

POSTSCRIPT.

The editor had hoped to complete long ago the task left him to do. But the war, which has everywhere borne heavily on printer and publisher, has caused one delay after another. Still, if such Antiquarian studies as Miss Armitt had spent the latter years of her life over are worth anything, I must agree with Professor Haverfield that, " even in war-time, it does not seem necessary or desirable to drop all intellectual work on them save in the direst need." Hence he argues that we do well to keep up, within due limits, both the holding of regular meetings and the issuing of publications, and thus continuing our more serious intellectual activity. With this strong opinion to uphold me I have thought it best to bring this book out at once, hoping that it will be found of permanent interest far beyond the immediate neighbourhood of Rydal, rather than wait for the end of the war, an event whose date lies yet upon the knees of the gods.

It was not until a good deal of the book was already in type that I first saw the sketch of George Banks, the Rydal clerk. The Banks family is described on pages 363 to 368. John Banks, having come to Rydal in 1669, was for twenty years the agent and factotum at the Hall. Two centuries went by before George took up the duties of parish clerk in Rydal chapel. He was the last of his kind, and used to give out the hymns and tunes, start the orchestra with his pitch-pipe, and then play his part on the flute. There are still some living who remember how some boys stopped his pipe with cobbler's-wax. A Lincolnshire clerk in similar difficulties gave it up, saying aloud, " pick-pipe weànt speàk, she's full o' muck." but George would not be beaten, and when the clergyman (Mr. Fleming) said " I think, George, we'll have a prayer," the old fellow declined this fictitious aid and said, " neà prayer! neà prayer! We'll hev t' hymn"

From a sketch in possession of Mary Tyson, Rydal.

CONTENTS.

PART I.

Chapter 1.—Introductory.
,, 2.—The days of the Celt and Roman.
  Appendix—The Roman Camp and Borrans Field.
,, 3.—The Angles, Danes and Norsemen.
,, 4.—Norman Administration. The making of Westmorland.
,, 5.—The Barony of Kendal.
,, 6.—The Land and the People.
,, 7.—The Institution of the Manor.
,, 8.—The Lord's Demands. Fines, etc.
,, 9.—The Heriot.
,, 10.—Yearly Dues
  Appendix—Rights of Common.
,, 11.—The Law of Greenhew.
,, 12.—The Courts.
  Appendix—Witheburne Court-Baron.
,, 13.—Military Service and Border Warfare.
  Appendix—Calls on the County for Service and Contributions.
,, 14.—The Lord's Deer Parks.
  Appendix—Summons for Forest trespass.

PART II.

THE DE LANCASTERS.

Chapter 1.—Roger the Hunter.
  Two Appendices—Deeds and Agreements.
,, 2.—The Flemings in Rydal.
  Appendix—Military Service.
,, 3.—Trade in the Valleys.
  Appendix—Kendal Cloth.
,, 4.—The Lords of Rydal.
  Three Appendices—Letters and Agreements.
,, 5.—The Lord's Seat.
  Appendix—Sir Daniel's Alterations.

PART III.

AGRICULTURE AND FISHERIES.

Chapter 1.—Husbandry in Rydal.
" 2.—Cattle Grazing and Marketing.
" 3.—Corn-growing.
" 4.—Sheep.
" 5.—The Fisheries.

PART IV.

A LAKELAND TOWNSHIP AND ITS FOLK.

Chapter 1.—The Typical House.
" 2.—Husbandry.
" 3.—The Farmholds.
" 4.—The Smithy.
" 5.—The Cornmills.
" 6.—The Inns.
" 7.—The School.

PART V.

UPHEAVALS IN MANOR AND KINGDOM.

Chapter 1.—Sir John Fleming.
" 2.—The Rydal Household.
" 3.—The Troubles.
" 4.—The Struggle for Rydal.

PART VI.

THE GREAT SQUIRE OF RYDAL.

Chapter 1.—Rydal House.
" 2.—Dress and Fashion.
" 3.—Sir Daniel's Public Life.
" Appendix.
" 4.—Later Days.

PART VII.

"THE NAB."

Home of De Quincey and Hartley Coleridge
Unpublished Letters of De Quincey

APPENDIX.

THE BIRDS OF RYDAL

LIST OF ILLUSTRATIONS.

	Page
Miss Armitt's garden, Rydal Cottage	*Frontispiece*
G. Banks	xi.
Rydal	9
The Author	15
Sophia Armitt	157
Site of the Old Hall	237
"Hartshead" in Rydal	331
Nab Cottage	356
View of a Rydal Homestead about 1822	362
Pelter Bridge, Rydal	387
The Smithy and White Lion Inn, Ambleside	394
Old Inn called "Davids," Rydal	435
Cottage in Rydal, "Hare and Hounds"	441
Coniston Old Hall	475
Daniel Fleming	561
Pedigree—Fleming of Rydal	At end.

ERRATA.

On page 43, line 2, *for* Marsh, *read* March
,, 52, ,, 14, *for* Penwardyn, *read* Pedwardyn
,, 119, ,, 7, *for* part vi, *read* part vii.
,, 171, ,, 11, *for* one of his descendants, *read* Sir John de Lancaster.
,, 181, ,, 25, *for* Ed. VI., *read* Ed. IV
,, 214, ,, 9, *for* 1686, *read* 1486.
,, 215, ,, 4, *for* Huddlesden, *read* Hudleston.
,, 475, ,, 13, *for* Greys, *read* Grays.
Pedigree —*for* A. F. Hudleston d. 1883, *read* 1861.

PART I

CHAPTER I

INTRODUCTORY

The Parish of Rydal; the Dawn; the Manor, Township and Vill.

THE parish of Rydal is modern, its boundaries having been laid down in 1826, when a district apportioned to the chapel, built by Lady le Fleming in 1825, was made independent of the mother parish of Grasmere. But Rydal, as manor and as township, has a history reaching back into ancient times. Manor and township were never, however, identical, their boundaries being different, and each being different again from the parish. All possess a common boundary from the summit of Nab Scar round the amphitheatre of heights that close in Rydal Head and drop thence by the Scandale Beck to the Rothay; but there they part company. The ancient manor boundary (according to a deed of 1274) turns up stream with the Rothay, and from the southern shore of Rydal water crosses the lake to ascend the face of Nab Scar. The parish boundary on the other hand turns for a short distance down the Rothay, ascends the face of Loughrigg by a tiny rill near Gilbert Scar, continues along the tops to Huntingstile, drops by a rill to Grasmere Lake, girdles the lower end of the lake to the grounds of the Prince of Wales Hotel and runs up the field by the foot-path to the higher White Moss road; then, when Dunna Beck is reached, climbs by that stream to the summit of Nab Scar. The township is still larger; it follows the Rothay down to the union of this river with the Brathay, and goes up by the Brathay to Elterwater, whence it strikes by means of a runnel up to Huntingstile, to join the parish boundary again. It thus embraces the whole of the low mountain mass of Loughrigg that lies between the converging rivers, while the parish takes only that half of Loughrigg that slopes down to the Rothay and Rydal Water.

The township, however, parts company again with the parish on the road over White Moss, and skirts round and below the ancient common. It descends to the Rothay at the foot-bridge, embracing a field at the swampy lake-head; and at the promontory of Swan Stone turns to run directly up the face of Nab Scar; thus coinciding with the ancient manor in its final outlines.

Another small divergence is where the parish follows the old road (since altered, about 1830) and embraces Miller Field which the township handed over to Ambleside about 1880. We will now deal with the parish more fully.

The parish of Rydal (as distinct from the manor and township) contains 3,020 acres. Its mountainous character is evident from the one fact alone, that within this small area lie the summit of a mountain nearly 3,000 feet high and a lake only 180 feet above sea-level. It is drained by the river Rothay, flowing through its main valley, and by the Rydal Beck, a considerable stream rising within its boundaries, which joins the Rothay below Smithy Bridge. Its boundaries follow in general the sky-line of the heights which hem in its lake and its streams. A line ruled along the rugged and much deflected summits of Loughrigg, rising to a general altitude of 1,000 feet, represents its boundary to the south. Where the mass of Loughrigg falls to the dip of Red Bank (which alone separates it from the neighbour-height of Silver How), the boundary cuts down in an arbitrary and almost straight line to the shore of Grasmere Lake; it follows the shore downwards—passing the exit of the river Rothay from the lake-foot—and completely round the lower end of the lake, till it reaches the grounds of the Prince of Wales Hotel. Thence it turns, after crossing the high-road, along a wall within the grounds of How Foot that borders the drive, and so reaches the older, higher road between Rydal and Grasmere. This it follows upward, mounting with a still higher and older road till the summit is reached at White Moss Tarn, believed by some to be the scene of Wordsworth's Leech-gatherer,* and now a tame, domestic duck-pond. Thence, leaving all tracks, it strikes up the rough fell-side to Dunna Beck, a small stream draining the back of Nab Scar. With the beck it rises and curves round the Scar, till, leaving the source behind, it reaches the bold height of Lord Crag, 1,500 feet high. Thence it follows the summits of those heights that form so remarkable an amphitheatre round the upland valley of Rydal Head (or Fairfield basin), touching as it runs northward Heron Crag (2,000 feet), Great Rigg (2,500 feet), and stopping a little short of the actual summit of Fairfield (2,862 feet). At this point it meets the boundary of Barton parish, and turning with it follows the sky-line still, but now southward and downward (though with little drop at first) to Hart Crag (2,598 feet), and still on, after the Barton boundary strikes away to skirt Scandale, along the gradually lessening heights to High Pike (2,155 feet), to Low Pike (1,656 feet), until, with the shoulder of the fell, it drops abruptly to the main stream of the Scandale Beck ; with this it crosses the highway at Scandale Bridge, and the flat meadows of the bottom, till it reaches the Rothay itself. The boundary should now keep with the river, but in actual fact does not. A wide deflecting curve is made by it about the meadows towards the new church of Ambleside and Cross Syke. And this curve represents the old course of the river, for which a shorter and artificial channel was cut some time back ; so that

---

* A reedy-pool lower down also claims this honour, and more fitly

it may be said that the river has left the boundary, rather than the boundary the river. It regains the river just past the grounds of Miller Bridge, follows it to the house called Gilbert Scar Foot, and thence strikes straight up Gilbert Scar, to reach the heights of Loughrigg : and so completes its circuit in some fourteen miles

The area thus circumscribed falls into three natural divisions :—

(1) A mountain basin which holds Rydal Water, the smallest mere of the country, scarcely over a mile long and a quarter broad. It was described by Hawthorne as a flood in a field, and yet it possesses in miniature every property of a true glacial lake, in sloping rocky shores, wooded islands, and rocky islets. And small as it is, the mountain basin that holds it is no larger. The water brims to the slopes, and Loughrigg and Nab Scar rise at either hand without a perch of flat meadow between ; while the scant pasture and meadow land of this division has altogether an Alpine character, on steep, thin-soiled inclines. The Rothay, flowing into the lake from Grasmere, rounds the projecting arm of White Moss by a rough little pass at full speed ; then, slackening speed as it enters the lake, forms a very small marsh at the head. On leaving the lake it again finds but a narrow passage, and rounds the outstanding spur of Loughrigg in rapids, leaving the mere shut in completely.

(2) The second natural division embraces the rise and course of the Rydal Beck up to its union with the Rothay. The stream is enclosed by the amphitheatre of heights enumerated above, and—their wild and desolate slopes rising sheer above it—forms as typical an Alpine valley as Lakeland possesses. Springs supply its source, and intermittent rills that flow down the northern face of Fairfield, often crowned with snow ; it starts fairly at a height of 1,500 feet, and pursues a tolerably level course on a valley bottom that drops imperceptibly till it reaches a point

almost parallel with Lord Crag on one hand and Low Pike on the other. Here it meets with a wall of rock that lies right across its path—a massive, pyramidal wall, not high, but even and smooth and regular as a breakwater made of concrete. No better instance of the action of ice in a former age can be offered than this wall of rock, ground and polished to an even height by the glacier that no doubt once filled the valley and poured its volume downward and over the obstacle with irresistible force. Now the little stream turns sharp against the wall and runs behind it, till it finds the crack itself has worn at floodtimes or when perhaps at a higher level than now. And by this it flings itself over the wall in a long fall, to settle at the base in a deep pool known to natives by the strange name of Buckstones Jum. Once beyond this natural lock, that has kept its level high, the beck knows no quietude, but leaps down the sloping screen that shuts off Rydal Head from the Rothay valley in a series of waterfalls that are among the shows of the county.

(3) When Rydal Beck has entered the Rothay, the last natural division of our parish is reached. This division consists of a flat and fertile valley bottom, enclosed on three sides by moderate heights. Cut off completely from Rydal Water, it seems to form a basin, filled in with alluvial matter, to itself. But it is in fact only the head of the Windermere basin; and the great lake, shut off by rocky knolls, is at present only half a mile beyond our boundary limit, while once, no doubt, it reached further up the flat. This valley bottom, formerly a marsh, has been carefully drained by the farmer, and its water-channels walled and guarded; and it forms the only deep arable land of the parish. Its smooth, green surface is diversified by hummocks of rock that stud it like islands; and once maybe they were islands in the wide stream of ice that has ground their up-valley sides into pyramidal and smooth contours, and left their down-valley sides sharp and broken.

All of them are crowned with trees, remnants of a forest that was older than the age of man's settlement and his careful tillage of the soil

It is not known certainly when Loughrigg was united to the old manor of Rydal as a township. It would be hardly safe to place the date further back than the reign of Elizabeth, when the Poor Law of 1601 was passed, and provision for its administration was made through the townships, whether by existing ancient ones, or new ones created for the purpose. Rydal and Loughrigg stood in different manors and were owned by different lords from the time of William de Lancaster III, who died without heirs in the early part of the thirteenth century.

Nicolson and Burn (*Hist of Westmorland*) describe these adjacent lands as being two manors, making one village, united by a bridge. But this is hardly correct. Three or four of the homesteads that nestle under Loughrigg are indeed fairly contiguous to Rydal village, but they make no part of it ; and Loughrigg besides possesses a true hamlet of its own, at Clappersgate, where the once important wharf for freight-boats on Windermere was situated. Neither Rydal nor Loughrigg can in fact be termed manors in the strictest sense of the word, which signifies a complete territorial unit dating from Saxon times, ruled by a resident lord exercising jurisdiction through courts of his own, and which is identical often with parish and township. For both Rydal and Loughrigg in ancient times were merely parts of much larger holdings, that were settled late ; and for ages they were but loosely associated with the more firmly established manorial lands about Kendal. Loughrigg especially, being but a rocky mass hemmed in by waters, must have had little territorial importance at first. We know it to have been part of the lands carried by Alice de Lancaster to her husband, when, on the death of her brother William de Lancaster III., the Barony of Kendal was divided between herself and her sister Helwise.

Yet in an inquisition of 11 Edward I., describing the properties left by her grandson William de Lindsay, it is not even mentioned by name. We can only suppose that the settlers on the Rothay side of Loughrigg were so few as barely to count, while those on the Brathay side were classed as in Langdale, for this inquisition of 1273, after enumerating tenants of Langdale, its forest and its mill, mentions a fishery belonging to it called Routhamere, worth 18d. yearly, thus bringing the district of Langdale right over Loughrigg down to the shores of Routhamere, as Rydal Water was then called. Nor does the name of Loughrigg appear in a rental of the year 1375, nor in several succeeding ones preserved at Levens. It first appears in a rent-roll of uncertain date, though apparently of the next century, wherein are enumerated by name nineteen tenants in Loughrigg, who paid their dues to the Lord of the Manor holding that portion of the Barony of Kendal that was subsequently called the Richmond fee.

Rydal seems to be first mentioned in a deed of 1275, which shows it to have been apportioned, when the Barony of Kendal was divided between the two sisters, to Helwise, as Loughrigg was apparently to Alice. But of this later. It is to the Barony of Kendal therefore that we must look if we would know anything of the history of our parish in ancient times.

But to tell the tale of our village without reference to the larger world outside it, would be much as if an attempt were made to describe a tiny twig that was wantonly broken from the tree that bore it. The twig in its place is a continuation of the branch, the branch is joined to the mighty trunk, and the trunk—through which the sap courses—is sustained by the millions of roots that suck moisture from mother-earth. So our village, whether viewed as a present entity or as an historic survival, belongs to the corporate body of the nation, and is linked on to the governmental centre, from which it receives the impulse of a national life.

The *vill* is enclosed in the manor, the manor is associated with the township; both belong to the county, as the county to the kingdom. So, if the history of our village and manor is traced backward into the dim receding past, we find them in the first instance to have been a parcel of the Norman Barony of Kendal, which was part of the newly constituted county of Westmorland; next, and a little earlier, classed in Doomsday Book as Stirkland in a nameless district of Yorkshire; earlier still to be part of Deira, which (before England was corporate) made the southern half of the powerful kingdom of Northumbria; and, still earlier, to belong to the Celtic land of Teyrnllwg, which was wrested from the Britons by the victorious Angles in the seventh century

Something of all these parcels and states must be known (in as far as they are revealed in record) if we would understand the little community of men, who clustered their simple dwellings on the slope of the mountain, above the river and the fords, and called the place Rydal.

But the scant tale is not an easy one to tell; for many skeins, criss-crossed by historic events, entangle the little place with neighbouring lands. Only as a *vill* had it an individual entity. It was but one half of the township called Rydal and Loughrigg, while even the manor slipped in places over the river that made the division between the two place-names. And three townships were needed to make up the parish of Grasmere, to which it was ecclesiastically attached from time immemorial Parish, township, manor, all have their history, which also is in great part that of the little *vill* dependent on them.

If we would seek to understand the place, to learn the secret of its origin, we must look to the primeval forces of nature, and study its geography. And there is no better spot for the study than the rock that rises abruptly from

RYDAL.

From a Photograph by Walmsley Bros., Ambleside.

the valley flat, and is now known as Old Hall Hill. The head of the great lake, that stretches its sinuous length twelve miles southward towards the great Bay of Morecambe, is but a bare mile from here; but it cannot be seen, for the rising ground between, while the river that flows towards it, disappears too, swerving under the steep slope of Loughrigg, in order to round that rise. The rock or " how " stands in the centre of what seems a small flat, but which is in reality a cup-like hollow that catches the water that pours down from the mountains north and east, and which was of old a marsh. The mountains close in abruptly, as we look north across the strip of green, the last spur of the Fairfield range advancing to meet Gate Crag, the outpost of Loughrigg, while between the two as between half-closed doors the fretted Rothay runs in rapids, slackening in a curve of rest at our very feet, where it meets its confluent beck from Rydal Head.

Here is the veritable gateway of the mountains, locked by the river. Yet, once through the gateway, a chamber opens beyond, in which the lake—Routhamere of old—reposes; and beyond that again, a second more spacious chamber, with lake and rich flat lands. At the head of the second chamber, indeed, lies the water-shed, from which streams flow north and south; but so low and easy is it, that it presents the appearance of a gap, cleft between the mighty flanks of the Helvellyn and Scafell ranges on either side of it. It is a natural and obvious northward road through the heart of the mountains.

Here then we have the very spot to promote events: a fitting theatre for invasion and battle. First and farthest the water-shed, that makes the natural line between kingdom and kingdom; next the lake-chambers, hemmed in by sudden mountains, fit refuge for a harassed race; then the gap that beckons an invading foe; with the closed gate, so easily defended, that guards the gap; and finally the rock in the marsh that watches the gate

CHAPTER II

THE CELT AND THE ROMAN

The Borrans Field; "Cotes"; Appendix—The Roman Camp.

THERE are not wanting evidences, that even in the dim ages, the valley of the Rothay knew stirring events. It was the marching line of armies, the wrestling ground of opposing races, the scene even of a known great battle, fought upon that watershed which was for so long the boundary between the kingdoms of the Celt and the Angle.

In those pre-historic days, when the Briton roamed as master over the land (having crushed maybe an earlier race), the valley would be a place impenetrable to the stranger, where morasses filled the bottoms, and thick tangled forest clothed the steep slopes of the mountains. But the hunter would have his paths, simple "trods" though they might be, worn and kept open by use. The lake below, on which he floated his wicker-work coracle, would furnish him with ample store of fish; and upwards he would follow the red deer, that grazed in boundless freedom over vale and crag and mountain-top. The tributary "glen" of Rydal Head, remote and high, would have peculiar attractions for the deer. Its rocky hummocks that flank the beck—polished smooth by the glacier of yet earlier ages—are still known as Beckstones, and there no doubt the monarchs of the herd were wont to foregather Hart Crag is not far away, over in Scandale. Other quarry too there was for the hunter—the wolf, the fox, the wild cat, the pine-marten, all of which, as well as hawks and eagles, were themselves preying on the smaller life of the forest. The brock, or badger besides was there, that has left its name at several spots. Erne Crag (degraded now to Heron Pike) that lifts a precipitous face above the glen, records the former nesting place of the eagle.

And not by the nomad huntsman alone, who slept beneath an easily planted shelter of boughs, may the vale have been peopled A settlement, a group of huts surrounded by walls, where a family or tribal division associated themselves and pastured their flock of cattle in common,* may early have existed here. If so, it was lifted well above the marshes of the bottom, and placed so as to have an outlook over the approaches to the valley Such a spot we may find above the later village, where the sunny slope of Nab Scar rounds itself to Rydal Head, and a slightly terraced flat has a wide southward view over the river gate below and the great shining lake of Windermere beyond. Here are gathered many little stones, as if the refuse of walls which the villagers of late times may have cleared away for their houses. And it is suggestive to find that the highest of the village fields is named Burn Mire ; for Borran, with its contraction Burn, was a name that clung hereabouts to the ruined stony sites of a forgotten people.

The Celt indeed has left few tangible traces behind him in the country round. A few clusters of hut-circles, a few rude fortifications, a few dropped stone-implements, two or three so-called Druidical circles, as at Keswick, and an apparently vanished one on Kirkstone Pass ; with a few place-names, to be mentioned later, are all the record of his race that peopled the valleys for so long.

There came a time when his mastery of even these remote mountain lands was disputed. The Roman legions had not long gained footing in the south before they pushed onward to conquer (if they might) the whole island of Britain. When Agricola in the year 79 led his army from

---

* See Vinogradoff's *Growth of the Manor*

Chester northward, he avoided, it is supposed, the more direct routes up the narrow wooded valleys that open upon Morecambe Bay, regarding them as dangerous traps where the hostile natives would have great advantages of attack, and chose instead the more circuitous but open route across the estuaries and round the coast.* But when the land beyond the great barrier of the Cumbrian mountains was conquered, and a great Wall was built from shore to shore to define the limits of the Roman empire to the north, a new and quicker route as also a sounder one was required by which to forward supplies for it from the military base at Chester. The easy waterway by the great lake, and the tempting gap in the mountains at the head of the Rothay, over which the far summit of Cumbrian Skiddaw beckoned, were not overlooked, since they led straight to their town of Carlisle; while the Wry-nose Pass, at the head of Rothay's twin valley Brathay, though higher by 500 feet (1281 against 782) was seen to form a convenient route to their Cumbrian sea-port of Ravenglass. The Romans thereupon proceeded to lay a military base, on a small scale, at the head of the great lake, which they approached from Kendal by a road trending somewhat north of the present road to the modern town of Windermere, passing by Gilthroton, the site of the old "chapel in the wood" † behind Bannerrigg and Orrest Head, by Broadgate, and thence dropping down to Troutbeck Bridge, and so by the lake-shore to Ambleside. Here their camp was laid out as a parallelogram, close by where the united streams of Rothay and Brathay, called Birdhouse Mouth, flow into the lake, upon very flat ground hemmed in by marsh, which they crossed on a corduroy road.

---

* See *Transactions* of the Cumberland and Westmorland Antiquarian and Archæological Society, vol iii, o s, which show that Chancellor Ferguson and Mr W Jackson arrived at this conclusion independently

† For a suggestion of a dedication here to the Irish St Rodan, see "Lost Churches in the Diocese of Carlisle," *Transactions*, C & W A & A Society, vol xv, o s

We know that during the late excavations for the sewerage in the Borrans Road at Ambleside, some rather interesting evidences of the old Roman road were discovered. The site is about 500 feet north of the northwest angle of the station, and the finds were in the following order —(1) Oak stakes placed alongside big stones. (2) transverse oak beams laid as a "corduroy" road apparently across a moss. These were observed for 85 feet, The beams were four to five feet below the present road, and were covered with some six inches of metalling ; the old road surface. From here north for about 130 feet there was no corduroy, but at a similar depth there was what appeared to be a roughly made pavement, and at one place the points of upright posts or piles were found at intervals. In the way of relics nothing but the usual potsherds were discovered. It seems possible, though the evidence is very fragmentary, that the roads from Ravenglass, Keswick and Brougham united somewhere above Rothay Bridge, and a single road led across an intervening moss to the main gate at the east front of the castrum. Since the lake and the river protected the west and south sides, and mosses the northern side, the site strategically was well chosen.

But it seems certain, from turn-overs of the soil in the last half century, that an extensive suburb stretched over the rising ground to the north and east of the camp,* where all but the soldiers were lodged The place, when Camden saw it towards the close of the sixteenth century, was strewn with the wreckage of an ancient city, amongst which could be traced paved approaches, ramparts, and ditches. But with the growth of the little modern town on the adjacent hill-slope, the site was gradually stripped. It is certain that the Brathwaite family of Ambleside Hall, who owned the Borrans, or Borrans-

---

*See "Ambleside Town and Chapel," *Transactions*, C & W A & A. Society, vol vi , n s

Ring, as it came to be called, made from the spot the collection of coins which Gawen bequeathed in 1653 to his son Thomas as family heirlooms, and which had been stored apparently in the " Box wth drawers in it for antiquies " that figures in the inventory of his furniture   Thomas in his turn bequeathed his " ancient medals and Roman Antiquities " to the University of Oxford, through the Provost of Queen's, but they appear never to have been handed over by either claimant of the disputed will. The antiquary Machel saw this collection, which was said to have numbered 6 gold, 66 silver, and 250 brass or copper coins , and Clarke in his *Survey of the Lakes* (1789) stated that they had lately been in the possession of the Countess Dowager of Lichfield : but nothing further is known of a collection that might, if preserved intact, have thrown considerable light on the history of the camp. The place was not entirely denuded in Clarke's time ; for after mention of the Castle at Ambleside, he goes on to speak of " another place called the Borrans, a square fort, more remains of which may be seen than of the other." He tells how, not very long before, the inhabitants had dug up there several pieces of freestone, which were probably altars or the like ; and greatly valuing such stone, which was not to be had within twenty-five miles of Ambleside, had broken them small " for scowring sand ! " West, who published his *Antiquities of Furness* in 1774, found some slight remains, for he says, in speaking of the place " it is evident that the stones made use of in the walls of the said castrum have been carried thither from the neighbourhood of Dalton in Low Furness, where only freestone of the same kind and colour is found " Probably they were brought by boat and landed on the adjacent wharf.*

When the Romans proceeded to lay down their road northward through Rydal, they did not apparently keep

---

* Some of this stone was found when the site of the camp was dug in 1913. See Appendix —ED on the level by the Rothay, which—studded as it then was by *holms* and *dubs*— must have offered but treacherous ground. The road, whether it came through Ambleside or not, crossed the rise between Ambleside and Rydal known as Scandale Hill, much on the line of the present road. This was proved when the turnpike road was engineered between the years 1763 and 1768; and Colonel Thornton* was clearly repeating what he had either seen or had heard on his visit in 1786 to Sir Michael le Fleming (who was responsible for the construction of the road through his demesne) when he wrote " it is evident that the ancient Roman road took the same direction as the present turnpike road through Rydal." The excellent antiquary West, in his Guide (1821) gives further particulars, and says " in forming the turnpike-road through Rydal, an urn was lately taken up, which contained ashes and other Roman remains, and serves to prove that the tract of the ancient road laid (*sic*) that way."

Several old people speak of traces of it having been discovered some thirty years back, when alterations at the side of the road were being made near Old Orchard, which is the strip of flat between Scandale Hill and the Old Hall rock. It was found at some depth below the surface, and no doubt it had sunk in the marsh that once filled this basin, as did the road close to the camp which is now five feet below the surface.

The watch-fires of the Romans, in the time when they first held the valley in the face of the hostile natives, and later when they constructed the road, must have blazed from Old Hall Hill. Their paved way came straight for it, skirting it possibly on its south-western side And next? For here they were confronted by the locked gateway of the mountains, through which they had to push. Across the river, curving almost at their feet, was the

---

* See his Sporting Tour.

rising ground about Gate Crag, that offered firm soil to the pavior and an excellent, open out-look forward for the sentinel. The river, shallow except after rains, was easily forded at this point, and had but a narrow marge of flat on either side. Once through the water, the ground was hard and solid. It is difficult, indeed, standing on the spot not to credit the Roman engineer with forging straight ahead by Gate Crag and Cote How and so debouching on the lake ; and there is an interesting tradition that a Roman way once crossed this very strip of land, which would be wholly inexplicable if they did not ford the river. A ford existed here from ancient times, it is certain. Only cattle use it now, and one side of it was partly walled up in 1903. But the ancient stepping-stones, that seem now to lead no whither in particular, and are the joy of the young, are really a relic of it ; for they carried the foot-passenger across the water a little lower than the ford, where the higher banks landed him dry-shod from shore to shore. That a paved way led down to the ford and stones from Old Hall Hill even in comparatively recent times is certain, for Sir Daniel Fleming in his account-book for 1685 enters 3s. od. for nine days work " paveing ye Cawsey in Berkitmoss." Cote How too on the farther side must have received its name from the shelter placed there for passengers through the ford, who might be detained by storm and flood, or for a guard to watch the way. We find the word " cote " lingering by many a now forgotten ford or crossing of the waters ; and the actual shelter or shanty is mentioned in deeds concerning the Ferry over Windermere. For Cote means a covering or shelter. We have it in Salt Cotes by the Esk mouth in Cumberland and in Sea Cote near St. Bees both probably indicating the site of some salt pans with a cover for the workers. Again near Carnforth we find Coat Stones, and Cote How at Ambleside, a rise just outside the town which held a shelter possibly for a guard to watch the approach.

Pigeon or dove-cote remains, while the frequent peat-cote (the shelter used for storing peats on the moss and mentioned in old wills and documents) has died out with the use of peat. In 1789 the " shedd or coathouse " on Ferry Nab, Windermere, was rebuilt. In 1707 Wil. Rawlinson, Esq., bought the right of Ferry on Windermere with boats, &c. and " all that House, shelter, harbour or coat for passengers on ye Nab "

It is true that the Romans, by carrying their road over the ford, would have later to re-cross the river, whereas if they pursued the line of the present road they would have to cross Rydal Beck, just above its union with the Rothay There is evidence however that this spot was a dangerous one even down to recent times. In floods, the waters of the beck and its confluent sike were forced back by the overcharged river into a far-reaching deep morass ; and to skirt this, paths from Old Hall to the village of Rydal made a wide detour The ground by the beck was broken up into islands, about which the waters meandered in ever-changing channels, or *allans*. To encompass this slough, the Romans would have to turn sharply to the right and trend upwards, almost as far as the present Hall ; and thence pursue their way under the frowning precipices of Nab Scar, a route that would lay them open, in troublous times, to ambuscades both from Rydal Head, and the broken ground of the Scar. On the other hand, the more direct line of the ford and the southern shore of the lake would enable them to pursue their march on safer as well as firmer ground.

The name of this old ford, which was the key that unlocked the river-gate between the rock-posterns that led into the mountains, we do not know, unless the Celt's simple significant term of Ry, = the ford, clung to it, and spread to all parts adjoining. The Old Hall of Rydal truly stood in front of the ford ; the *how* that goes by the name of Rydal rises from its brink ; the beck so-called flows into the river there; while the village or the slope above may have caught a nomenclature, which as we know did not spread to the lake till about the sixteenth century. However that may be (and another derivation has to be considered), this ancient ford must have played a considerable part in the early history of the place and valley. The other, at the head of the lake, represented by the present foot-bridge, which the Romans would also use, if they marched on the southern lake-shore, we have fortunately recovered the name of, from an old deed in which it is spoken of as Bath-wath.

There is no doubt of the line of the Roman road from Bathwath. It struck upward over the projecting arm of White Moss in a direct line for Grasmere. It exists yet, in the highest line of road; but the ground here has been so much mauled, first by quarries, and then by the Manchester water-works, which planted during the period of pipe-laying a row of workmen's sheds and offices on the common land about it, that no trace of it is now recognizable. Mr. Herbert Bell remembers the large slab of stone that paved it, totally different from the round cobble later used for " causage "; and the late Mr. Dawson, of High Close, hard by, considered that its workmanship proved it to be Roman.

Along this road then, which leaves the boundary of Rydal at this point, the Romans marched, pushed troops and stores, and conducted the business of governing the country and its wild tribes for almost three centuries. Whether they built a permanent fort on Old Hall Hill is not certain, though it is probable. A route that would lead from it over Loughrigg to join their road to Ravenglass (whose guardian fort is still in evidence) bears to this day the suggestive name—foreign to these parts, of Fox Gill *Street.*

But the time came (410) when the great administrative rule of Rome over Britain drew to an end; and her legions were withdrawn, to defend her borders nearer home. The Celt was left again to the mastery of the land; left with the roads, the camps, the forts, and above all the great Northern Wall, all of them constructed by a great civilizing force and all too big for his hands. Something he had learned from Rome, of art, and civilization and perhaps Christianity; but something too he had lost, in primæval strength and independence of character. His own tribal system of government had been overlaid by the urban rule of the Romans which he was unequal to carry out. He was left to fight unaided the enemies that soon swarmed upon him, the Pict and the Scot, the Angle and the Dane, and the vale after three hundred and fifty years of Roman rule, fell back into silence and the undisputed occupation once again of the Celtic huntsman.

APPENDIX

From Camden's *Britannia* (1st edition 1586) trans with additions. 1695

"At the upper corner of this Lake *Winandermere*, lyes the carcaes, as it were, of an ancient City, with large ruins of walls, and scatter'd heaps of rubbish without the walls. The Fort has been of an oblong figure, fortify'd with a ditch and rampire, in length 132 Ells, and in breadth 80. That it was the work of the Romans, the British bricks, the mortar temper'd with small pieces of bricks, the little Urns or Pots, the Glass Vials, the Roman coins commonly met with, the round stones like Mill-stones (of which soder'd together, they us'd formerly to make Pillars) and the pav'd ways leading to it; are all undeniable Evidence But the old name is quite lost, unless one should imagine from the present name *Ambleside*, that this was the *Amboglana* mention'd by the *Notitiæ*"

Additions to *Westmorland* made by " Mr Thomas Machel " He discourses on the question of Ambleside being " Amboglana," speaks of " several medals " found here, and in collection of Mr T " Brathwate " left to Queen's Coll.

"A little north of Ambleside, is *Ridal*-hall, a convenient large ancient house: in which Lordship is a very high mountain call'd *Ridal* head." . . . " The present owner being Sir Daniel

Fleming, a great lover of ancient Learning, to whom we are particularly oblig'd for several useful informations in this County and Lancashire." Speaks of Camden travelling fr Lancaster, through the Barony of Kendal, to Workington in Cumb and so neglecting the *bottom* of Westmorland

Camden in *Lancashire* says: " Upon this lake (Windermere) stands a little town of the same name, where in the year 791 *Euthred*, King of the Northumbrians, slew the sons of King *Elfwold*, after he had taken them from York, that by his own wickedness and their blood he might secure himself in the Kingdom."

It is said in a volume-published by C Bates in 1895, that they were drowned in the lake This seems quite probable because Windermere would be on the route from York to the Isle of Man, which was then used as a place of refuge.

The Latin original runs thus :—

Anno DCC XCI filii Elfwaldi regis ab Eboraca civitate vi abstracti, et de ecclesia principali per promissa fallacia abducti, miserabiliter sunt perempti ab Ethelredo rege in Wonwaldremere* quorum nomina Oelf et Olelwine fuere

Symeonis Dunelmensis,
Historia Regum.

EDITOR'S NOTE.

The Roman camp, in the Borrans field spoken of above as the head of lake Windermere, being in imminent danger of being built over, was happily acquired in the autumn of 1912, and vested in the National Trust. Digging was begun in 1913 and continued the two following years under the superintendence of Mr R. G. Collingwood; the whole of the wall of the camp, enclosing 2 75 acres, and the top of which was mostly within six inches of the surface, was laid bare The form was a parallelogram, measuring about 420 feet by 300, the longest axis being east and west, with corner turrets The largest of the four gates was on the east side, on the south the threshold stone, 10½ by 4¼ feet, with socket holes was in situ In the middle of the camp was found the commandant's house, the Principia and the Granary A double outer ditch was traced on the north side. The finds were more numerous than valuable, a couple

---

* " Winandermere, or Windermere " Note by John Hodgson Hinde, F S A , Surtees Society Edition p 30

of ladies' shoes, fragments of Samian and other ware, lead, glass, bronze nails, sling bullets, roof slates, a silver spoon, a few silver and bronze coins, one of the Emperor Valens (d. 375) which would show that the camp which probably dates from Hadrianic times, cir. 135 A.D., was occupied for some 240 years at least. Like those on Hardknott and at Ravenglass, it was one of the chain of strategic sites garrisoned by the Romans in order to keep the natives quiet along the frontier; but the soil in one of the turrets, and elsewhere, showed evidence of more than one burning, which if done by hostile hands would point possibly to some successful raids by our barbarian ancestors.—ED.*

CHAPTER III

THE CELT AND THE ANGLE

The Danes in Northumbria; Athelstan; Norsemen Colonists.

THE natives of these parts, though peculiarly liable to incursions from northern foes, were however secure for a far longer period than their tribal relatives of the south and east from the inroads of the Saxon and the Angle. It was the southern and eastern coasts that were first attacked by the pirates, who came and went across the sea; and some hundreds of years were to elapse before those first settlements, made along the shore by handfuls of fighters under a leader of prowess, grew into little states or kingdoms. One of the foremost of these kingdoms from the beginning was Bernicia, traditionally founded in the sixth century by Ida on the rock of Bamborough, which later became Northumbria; and it was to this alien power after it had absorbed its neighbour kingdom Deira that the Celts of the district round the great Bay of Morecambe were ultimately forced to submit. For long indeed they valiantly held

---

* A full account with photographs and diagrams is given in *Transactions*, C. & W. A. & A. Society, vol. XV, N.S., 1915.

their own in the west, and their dominion stretched unbroken down the western shores through Cumbria or Cumberland, Cambria or Wales, to west Wales or Devon and Cornwall. But the time came when the bleak Pennine chain, flanked by barren lands, which protected this dominion from the conqueror in the north, was to be crossed. It was Ethelfrith, King of Northumbria, who first broke the line, and by the battle of Chester (fought according to the Saxon Chronicle in 607, but according to Welsh Annals in 613) extended his kingdom to the western sea, cutting off for ever the Britons of Cambria from those of Cumbria. He is reputed to have gained more territory than he could well govern, so while he colonized a portion with his Anglian followers, he left the rest in the hands of the natives on payment of tribute by them It is doubtful if his successes affected our parts He was himself killed in battle in 617 ; and it was left to his successor Edwin, who was mighty enough to proclaim himself overlord of England, to conquer in 620 the British state of Elmet, in western Yorkshire, by which Westmorland would be most easily accessible.* Again, Edwin was slain in 633 by the great Celtic leader Cadwallan or Caedwalla, who regained not only the lands recently lost by the British, but the whole of Northumbria, till he was himself slain at Hexham in 635 by King Oswald of saintly memory. It is difficult therefore to assign an exact date to the conquest by the Angle of that large western district, including the later north Lancashire, south Westmorland, and a piece of Cumberland by the coast, which appears to have been nameless to the conqueror, while the Briton called it Teyrnllwg ; but if we place it as late as King Oswy's victory over the old heathen Penda, Saxon king of Mercia, who for so long had been the constant enemy of Northumbria, and the ally of the

---

* See Mr Collingwood's story of Cumbrian independence in "*Early Sculptured Crosses*" of the Diocese of Carlisle.

Celt, at Winwaed, we get it no later than 650. Of this conquest Professor Rhys says* " The disgrace the Kymry felt at losing the crown of Britain . . . was probably nothing in comparison with their bitterness at being robbed of one piece after another of their country. We have already alluded to Eadwine annexing Lordes and Elmet to his own kingdom of Deira, but far more fatal to Kymric independence was the appropriation by the Angles of the district of Teyrnllwg, described by Welsh tradition as reaching from the Dee to the forests of Cumberland and the neighbourhood of the Derwent, which was once the boundary of the diocese of Chester: the tract consisting of the level part of Cheshire and south Lancashire must have been taken from the Kymry soon after, possibly before, the battle of Chester."

When the western sea was gained, near the estuary of the Dee, and the mountain passes at the head of the west Yorkshire dales were open, there was little indeed to check the conquerors till the mountains of Cumbria were reached. The lands round the great frith of Morecambe that lay to the west would soon be over-run, the fertile valleys that opened upon it would tempt them onward ; and the great lake whose foot was barely five miles from the sands would lead them forward still, to the Roman fort at its head, standing silent now after 250 years of abandonment, and to the open road beyond, running due north. Truly, if the Angles pushed further than the deserted fort, our mountain gateway at Rydal would soon give them pause. With forests filled with retreating Celts, it would hardly be safe to hazard the passage of the ford and the narrow gorge, to be overwhelmed possibly in the closed mountain chambers beyond.

And as a matter of fact, the boundary of the Anglian kingdom is found, when it emerges into the light of history,

---

* Celtic Britain

to lie hereabouts. It is defined, to the west, by the water-shedding line of the Brathay and the Rothay, with their tributaries, as it is to the north-west by that of the Kent and by the forest of Inglewood. Beyond the moors of Shap, beyond the high slate hills of Rydal, the Celt held his own in the kingdom of Cumbria for nearly 500 years longer; and for that period our mountain Fairfield rose as a bulwark between lands of the Englishman and the Briton.

The position of this newly acquired province (the British Teyrnllwg) must have rendered it peculiarly difficult for the Angle to govern. It lay beyond the barren moorlands of the Pennine chain, and could only be reached from Deira, to which it was annexed, by long passes at the head of the Yorkshire dales. The main road from York, the capital of Deira, was the Roman one connecting that city with Carlisle, and it led over the high and dangerous Stainmoor, then, and for long after, the battle-field of races. Safer and more direct routes might be made up Wensleydale and the Aire, to emerge at Kirkby Lonsdale and Sedbergh. And there is evidence that within seventy years after the battle of Chester an effort was being made to colonize this district to the west by means of the Church, which was becoming a powerful agent among the recently converted English. A monastery had been founded at Ripon by the pious King Alchfrid, who ruled Deira under his father, Oswy of Northumbria, about 660; and some four years later he handed it over to Wilfrid, the great churchman and prelate of the north. Wilfrid proceeded to build there, in a fashion new to the English, whose churches hitherto had been of wood or wattle, a basilica of polished stone, sustained by columns and vaults, and furnished with rich accessories, in the manner of the western church. The consecration of this splendid building was an affair of state, attended by King Egfrid the successor of Oswy, and his brother

Alfwin, by sub-kings, reeves, and abbots of other monasteries, and at the close of a gorgeous ceremony Wilfrid, with his face turned towards the people, recited the names of the lands, recently as well as formerly, bestowed upon Ripon, together with some holy places of the British Church. Through the garbled version of these names that have come down to us, several at least are clear, and they refer to the lately conquered district. Parts about the Ribble are mentioned, and Amounderness, the district between the Ribble and the Cocker. Cartmel seems to be referred to on the peninsula between the estuaries of the Leven and Kent, and in the name " Duninga " may possibly be recognized Dunnerdale, about the river Duddon, where we still find the hamlet of Old Dunning Well.*

This consecration took place after the deaths of Kings Oswy and Alchfrid in 670; and before Wilfrid's dispute with King Egfrid, and his banishment in 678, which must have checked the great scheme of church colonization for a time. But Egfrid himself clearly recognized the political uses of the new church, and invited Archbishop Theodore from the south, for the purpose of arranging his unweildy kingdom of Northumbria into bishoprics. To the saintly Cuthbert, appointed Bishop of Lindisfarne, he gave over, we are expressly told, the district of Cartmell, with all the Britons in it; and Cuthbert, finding it no doubt too distant for his immediate supervision, handed it over to the care of the " good Abbot Kineferth." † The restless Egfrid, whose conquest of the city of Carlisle was likewise given over to Cuthbert, met his death in 685, when fighting the Picts north of the Wall; and with him vanished for ever the supremacy of Northumbria over the rest of the English kingdoms. Incessant war

---
* See Edde's *Life of Wilfrid*, *Memorials of Ripon*, Surtees Society Raine's *Historians of the Church of York*, and *Victoria History of Cumberland*.
† See Simson's *Life of Cuthbert*

between weak claimants to the throne paralyzed the State for the next hundred years, when the ravages of the Danes began on the eastern coasts. Yet through all the anarchy and mis-rule, the church seems to have spread and flourished; and where her sacred buildings and monasteries were planted, and pious priests officiated and taught, there the Anglian rule must have swayed the subject Celt. The late seventh and eighth centuries seem to have been a great cross-erecting era*, and the fragment of one ascribed by experts † to Anglian workmen is to be seen at Heversham. Indeed it is supposed that a monastery may have been founded at Heversham in the reign of Osred, who was slain in 717.

It is in this century that we hear of a connection between Northumbria and the Isle of Man and Ireland via the coast of Cumberland. St. Bega is reputed to have been travelling from Ireland in order to visit the holy places of the Anglian church when she was shipwrecked at St. Bees. The Isle of Man became a refuge for claimants to the throne of Northumbria, or for expelled rulers of Bernicia or Deira. Later, Irish and Norse allies came over by way of Cumberland to help the decrepit kingdom to withstand the power of the Wessex kings. Now this route of travel crossed our district, and came very near to Rydal. The landing was doubtless at Ravenglass, the haven of the Romans, and the only natural one on the Cumbrain coast, which was within the lines of the old land of Teyrnllwg, wrested from the Celt by the Angle. The route probably (and almost certainly at an early date), followed the straight Roman Road over the Wrynose and Hardknott passes, dropping to the deserted camp at Ambleside, and continuing by

---

* The magnificent cross erected at Bewcastle to the memory of King Alchfrid still stands One stated to be of great beauty was placed at Lindisfarne by Bishop Ethelwold (724-40), and was later mutilated by the Danes

† *The Lake Counties,* by W. G Collingwood

Kendal to cross one of the passes of the Pennine chain into Yorkshire.

There is another route which may have been pursued at a later time, less direct but less mountainous and exposed. It started perhaps, near the easy landing at Waberthwaite, on the east branch of the Ravenglass harbour, crossed Burn moor to the Duddon, dropping by Ulpha Old Hall (which has been hitherto something of a puzzle), and thence by Walna Scar to Coniston where some minor king may once have held sway; thence by Hawkshead Hill, (where we find the name of High Cross) and along the shore of Esthwaite to Windermere, which would be crossed by the Ferry, and so to Kendal. On this route we find evidence of traffic in the number of holy places of unknown date upon it; the chapel on Mary-holme; St. Martin's on the lake shore; St. Catharine's on the brow above the lake; crosses higher still; then the site of the old chapel in the wood by Hugill,* as well as the old manor house on the island of Langholme.

It is impossible to overlook, in the history of these parts, the existence from an early time of this manor-house on the lake of Windermere. It is mentioned as early as 1272, when Walter de Lindesay died, as well as in the various Inquisitions of his followers, where it is always spoken of as ruined and derelict, and as being of no worth, since the houses had gone to decay. (See Appendix.) There is no indication indeed of it being in use, in Norman times, as a centre of manorial life, where a resident lord might hold sway over the neighbouring lands. Yet there are signs that seem to show that it once occupied such a position, and that there was concourse and traffic in its neighbourhood. The church on the shore of the lake was its companion, and was to remain as the parish church of a wide district. On the

---

* See "Lost Churches of the Diocese of Carlisle," *Transactions* C & W. A & A Society, vol xv., o s.

other hand sacred spots hard by were, like it, when we first obtain a glimpse of them, going to decay. The uses of the little Chapel of St. Catherine, of which some vestige remained till the eighteenth century, have never been recorded. Those of St. Mary's on the island appear from the time of their first mention in 1272 to 1350, when they appear to have lapsed for a time, to have been gradually sinking

The fact that the chantry was affiliated to the Augustinian House of Segden, at Berwick in Scotland, suggests a possibility that it was a foundation of the early Anglo-Scottish church, whose invariable habit it was, where possible, to place their sacred buildings on an island, both for peace and for security against heathen attack. St. Herbert, the hermit of the island of Derwentwater, is known to us through his friendship with St. Cuthbert, as narrated by Bede But of this island fane, sometimes called a hermitage, but apparently of greater importance and standing, since it was served by two chaplains till the time of Edward III , the origin is unknown.

The occupation of Langholme may likewise have been early From the fact that remains of a former building were found at a depth of six feet, when Mr. English built the present house there in 1774, as well as " a beautiful pavement curiously paved with pebbles of a small kind " * it has been conjectured that a Roman villa stood upon the island It is not impossible But it is more probable that the conquering Angles planted foot here When they pushed up the lake, to find the Roman city at the head, they would, if they acted in their usual manner, reject the site, preferring a fresh and rural settlement. The island would offer, in the face of a hostile and only partially subjugated foe, safe ground whereon a thane or lord might plant his capital dwelling, which was to serve

---

* Nicolson and Burn, vol 1 Addenda

as a centre to the manor which his followers would form on the annexed lands round about, and where the infant church, protected by him, would give him support in the work of colonization. And if the old manor house on the island were actually of Anglian origin, it must have seen stirring events, connected with Northumbrian history. In 788 King Alfward the Just was slain in battle near the Roman wall, and his body, conducted by a long procession of monks and clergy singing dirges, was carried for burial to Hexham. His sons, Alf and Alfwin, were infants, so Osred was called to power. A year later, when an insurrection took place in favour of Ethelred I. (who had occupied the throne before) he was obliged to fly to the Isle of Man. Ethelred, embittered perhaps by eleven years of life in a dungeon, behaved with great barbarity to the rival royal house.* The High-Reeve, Erdwulf, he caused to be executed before the monastery of Ripon; and the kindly monks prepared to bury him, when he was discovered to be living, and escaped to become (in 800) king himself. Alf and Alfwin had likewise been placed by their friends in sanctuary, in the Minster of York, where the tyrant dared not touch them. By some specious promise however, he beguiled them thence, and caused them (says Symeon of Durham) to be drowned in Winwaldremere—a name that has generally been supposed to mean Windermere.†

If an Anglian burh or manor-house did exist on the Island, this story becomes more explicable. Under pretext of carrying the children to a safe place, Ethelred would have an easy opportunity of getting rid of them, by causing the boat which conveyed them to the stronghold across the lake to be sunk. Horror of the crime, it

---

* See Appendix to Chapter II
† See note by J Hodgson Hinde to Bates' *Northumberland* In connection with the likeness yet unlikeness of the two names, it may be mentioned that for Wansfell, the mountain at the head of the lake, the derivation Wodensfell has been found To the whole side of the mountain the name Groves still clings, suggesting a place of heathen rites

is said, caused Osred to be recalled from the Isle of Man ; but he was captured by his enemies on the coast of Cumberland, and there slain.

The first descent of the Danes on Northumbria followed soon on this murder. Lindisfarne was desecrated and robbed, and the lands accessible from the Danish ships were over-run and pillaged. The distracted country was in no position to withstand the claim of Egbert, king of Wessex, to the position—so long held by its own kings—of over-lord of Britain ; and when he marched north in 827 the men of Northumbria did homage to him. Then once more, in 835, after fifty-three years of absence, the Danes poured in upon England, ravaging, destroying, and this time settling upon the lands they had wrested from the Angles. The House of Wessex had much ado, for years to come, to hold its own precariously against them in the south, and in Northumbria they swamped the frail government and put an end to the race of effete kings. The slaughter of Osbert and Ella at York, (867) may be said to have put the close to the kingdom founded by Ida 320 years before.*

A Danish king, Hulfden, son of Ragnas, became ruler at York, while other sons of Ragnas raided the coasts of Ireland and Scotland, and set up a kingdom at Dublin. In 875 Hulfden crossed the Tyne and invaded Bernicia, hitherto unharried, and destroyed churches and monasteries. This was the death-blow to the Christian civilization of Northumbria.

It is probable that in this time of confusion and bloodshed, our district suffered less on account of its position west of the Pennine chain which checked the Danish advance, than the older province to which it was attached. There may have been indeed a considerable influx of Angles at this time into these parts, fleeing west in the

---

* *History of Northumberland*, by J. Hodgson Hinde.

face of the Danes ; for it is unlikely that the monks of Lindisfarne (who did not await a second attack) were the only ones who resorted to this plan of safety. The district, unlinked from its old centre of government—both in church and state—which lay over the passes eastward, would drift for a time in a kind of chaotic independence ; and the Celt, always numerically strong, would rise in power as the Angle weakened. Eugenius, king of the old British state of Cumbria, now took occasion to spread his bounds, which are said to have extended in 904 from the Clyde to the confines of Lancashire.*

But the Wessex kings, who had been making slow but sure headway against the Danes, now stepped forward as over-lords, for the control of the distracted and dismembered north ; and in 923, Edward the Elder (great Alfred's son) compelled the submission of Ragnas, King of Northumbria, and Ealdred, ruler at Bamburgh, as well as the kings of Scotland and Strathclyde, with all their mixed peoples—Scots, Angles, Danes, Norwegians and Britons. It seemed, for the moment, as if England were united under one strong ruler. But such turbulent elements could not be held long in control, especially by a government whose centre was fixed in the distant south coast. Almost as soon as Athelstan succeeded his father Edward in 925, he came north to settle matters with recalcitrant rulers. On the death of the Danish king of Deira, he deposed Guthred, the son of Sihtric and took over this great state to govern without a subordinate. With Constantine king of the Scots, however, and Eugenius or Oswain king of Cumbria he made a treaty. Their meeting with him took place in 926, and is severally recorded by William of Malmesbury—who says it was at Dacre—and by the Anglo-Saxon Chronicle, which speaks of the river Eamont. Now at Dacre, which stands on

---

* *History of Northumberland*, by J Hodgson Hinde

the little river of that name about 8 miles above its confluence with the Eamont, there was a monastery in Bede's time, and it may well have been in the security of its sacred precincts that the two northern rulers chose to stand face to face with the great southern king. The place of the meeting is significant. The Eamont indeed, curving eastward on its outflow from the lake of Ullswater, to its junction with the Eden, has ever played a great part as a boundary or " mere " stream. It is now the dividing-line between Cumberland and Westmorland. From the earliest times of church history the wide parish of Barton, which touches Rydal on the summit of Fairfield, stopped against its current. At different times Celt and Angle, Scot and English have looked with alien eyes across its waters, claiming or acknowledging it as the line past which they might not move. To this day its banks, fertile though they are, are strewn with the defences of combatants of all ages. The Roman reared his fort over against the ford at Brougham, where Norman lords eventually followed him. The earth-work at Eamont Bridge is possibly an ancient burh that guarded the crossing; and Mayborough the work of the Briton. Mediæval castles and pele towers abound along its line; for every gentleman had need to fortify his house till the days of Elizabeth, against the raiding Scot. It seems as if Athelstan, marching up to this river of strife by York and across Stainmoor, and meeting there the northern kings, regarded it also as a boundary for his kingdom of England, and as a line up to which he meant personally to govern.*

Of the district round the Bay of Morecambe we hear nothing, in treaty or in subsequent conflicts. Amounderness indeed, part of the old British province won by the

---

* There is in Dacre Church, a carved stone which possibly bears witness of this meeting of the three kings C. & W A & A Society's Extra Series, vol xi.

Angles, Athelstan gave over in 930 to the metropolitan church of St. Peter at York.

This grant we find quoted from the original Latin in *Historians of the Church of York,* by James Raine, &c., vol iii.

A Grant of Lands in Amunderness by King Athelstan to Walstan, Archbishop of York.

Nottingham, June 7, 930   (Preamble)

Ego Adelstanus Rex Anglorum, per Omnipotentis dextram, quae Christus est, totius Britanniae regni solio sublimatus, quandam non modicam telluris particulam Deo Omnipotenti et Beato Petro Apostolo ad ecclesiam suam in civitate Eboracensi tempore quo Wulfstanum archiepiscopum illuc constitui, in loco quem solicolae Aghemundernes vocitant, sub Dei timore libenter attribuo, ut ille episcopus ea sine jugo exosae servitutis, cum pratis pascuis, silvis, rivulis, omnibusque ad eam utilitatibus rite pertinentibus, quamdiu aura in naribus spiritali ocellorumque convolatu cernibili utatur, ac satius heredibus post se semper illius ecclesiae in aeternam hereditatem derilinquat. Hanc praefatam donationem propria, et non modica, emi pecunia, [I have bought with the money of my own and no small sum] non solum illam quin potius cuncta illius praetitulatae praedia

Pr . autem a mare sursum in Cocur usque ad fontem illius fluminis, ab illo fonte directe in alium fontem qui dicitur Saxonice Daleshope ; sic per descensum rivuli in Hodder, ipso dirigamine in Ribbel, et sic in illo flumine per dimidium alveum iterum recursus in mare . . .

This is a huge area, and in later times, in 1233 we find that Archbishop Gray having set the difficulties arising for the too large parishes in his Diocese before Gregory IX., the latter writes bidding him build oratories and chapels where he sees need. CX. 1244. Licence from Innocent IX. to Arch. Gray, to confirm and consecrate Bishops of Man.

This measure no doubt was intended to promote peaceable colonizations in an imperfectly governed district, as well as to protect the Christian establishments within it ; and it served to bind our lands still more closely to Deira, and its church.

But peace was not possible yet, nor for long after, with the turbulent mixed races of the north. Athelstan was soon after fighting Constantine and Eugenius, and their defeat only produced a brief breathing-space. For now all the northern rulers drew together in one vast effort to withstand and overthrow the English king. The dethroned king of Deira got his Danish relative, Anlaf, King of Dublin, to come to his aid with another Anlaf Eugenius, the King of Strathclyde, joined with his Britons from the west, and Constantine from the north came both by sea and land with his Scots. At a place in Deira called Brunanburh the allies were met by Athelstan and his brother Edmund, and in a mighty battle—in which five Danish sea-kings and seven earls, as well as Eugenius and the son of Constantine, are said to have been killed—they were defeated. This terrific conflict, and the foregathering for it, which took place in 937, must have affected our district, though it was not fought upon the ground.* From all sides forces were drawn for it. The Celts of Cambria would pour over the pass at the head of the Rothay, marching through the valley by the Roman road to Kendal, being joined doubtless as they marched by their kinsmen who had unwillingly suffered the domination of the hated English. The Danes of Dublin under Anlaf would land at Ravenglass, and pursue the road over Wrynose or the lower one across Duddon to reach the battle-field in the East. With shattered forces he doubtless returned the same way, carrying news of the disaster through all the country-side.

For a time there was peace. But soon after Athelstan's death in 940 an insurrection broke out in Northumbria, and a Danish king was placed upon the throne. Edmund,

---

* The spot has not been definitely fixed Aldborough by Boroughbridge, on the Ouse has been suggested (Skene's *Celtic Scotland*) and as several of the chief combatants escaped to their ships lying in the Humber, it must have taken place in eastern Yorkshire [or in north Lincolnshire near Barton.—ED]

as successor to his brother on the throne of Wessex, had again to subdue the province, and expel two minor kings from it Wearied with a struggle that Northumbria continually renewed by the help of the Danes of Dublin, who passed to and from Deira through the friendly state of Cumbria, he determined to chastise Cumbria ; and in 945 he advanced to the west, and overthrew Dunmail (or Donald) king of Cumbria, son of Eugenius, and handed over the little state (extending from the Clyde to the Duddon) to Malcolm, King of Scotland, who undertook to do fealty to him for it. The battle took place, according to tradition, at the head of the Rothay, on the pass ever since called Dunmail Raise, where a great cairn of stones marks the grave—if not of the British king (for some accounts say that he escaped, and afterwards went to Rome) at least of his followers, and of the English who fell on that day. Through the forest of Rydal then the great Edmund marched with his army by the Roman way ; and on the rock by the ford, afterwards called Old Hall Hill, he might well set a watch to guard his return, and erect a burh in the vale to hold its Britons in awe.

A year after he died, by the hand of an assassin, and his brother Eadred had at once the work to do over again. He did it more brutally however, and when Northumbria rebelled, and set up again a Danish king, he devastated it, not sparing even churches and monasteries, and destroying Ripon by fire. This was in 947. The last Danish king of Northumbria and his son were slain, "in a lonely region called Stainmoor (954). Eadred, after some further trouble, in 954 entrusted the government of Northumbria to an earl, Osulf, and its days of kingship finally closed. Uchtred acted as Earl in the days of King Ethelred, who, finding the Danes again troublesome, attacked and vanquished them, apparently in the west , for in 1000 he " went into Cumberland, and ravaged it well nigh all." Eadulf, who was earl in the reign of Hardicnut, is remembered as acting with great barbarity to the Celts or Britons, whose territory he invaded. He ruled in partial independence, but submitted to Hardicnut in 1041. Next came Siward who died at York, 1055.* He ruled Northumbria as its earl under Edward the Confessor, last king of the royal line of Wessex, then Tosti, son of the great earl Godwin. The wide lands which he owned in Amounderness and Furness are conjectured to have been wrested from the Celts by his predecessor Eadulf.† His own oppressions ended in revolt, and Morcar was chosen in his place. Tosti played a dire part in the last tragedy of the old English kings, for when he landed in Deira with a hostile force, he fell at Stamford Bridge, fighting his brother Harold, 1066. Harold then had to return in haste to to meet Duke William on the field of Hastings, where he also fell.

In all this varied and bloody history of the state to which our district was so long attached, through all the attacks it endured from foreign foes, coming east and north and south, we hear not one word of an invasion that is generally allowed to have taken place from the west. Not the valley of the Rothay alone, but the dales of the whole of Cumberland and Westmorland are studded with names that betray a Norse origin; and the sturdy tall folk who inhabited these dales are believed to have come from Norway. The silence of this invasion perhaps bespeaks its character. The Norsemen came, not as conquering warriors, nor as raiding pirates, but as colonists landing from their long boats with wives and children and cattle to form peaceful settlements on the more fertile slopes of the fells. The rugged country, so like their own, would appeal alike to their sense of home and of husbandry; and it is thought that the hardy race of

---

* His rule seems to have been benificent See Mr Wilson's judgment in *Victoria History of Cumberland*

† *History of Northumbria*, J Hodgson Hinde

Herdwick sheep that graze on these mountains, and which have formed for hundreds of years the main wealth of the farmer, was brought in by them. They must by this inroad it is true, have dispossessed the Celt of his lands to a large extent; but their settlements, or setas, would be small, and with their different methods of husbandry, the two races might after a time fit in together in tolerable amity. The fact that the Welsh numerals have been found in use for the counting of sheep in some parts of the district up to recent times, is considered to show that the older race was used by the new-comers for menial service and for herding the sheep.* The settlement of the Norsemen may have been favoured by the Danish kings who were in the ninth and tenth centuries ruling at York and at Dublin.†

These far-off days of conflict and final settlement have left scarce a tangible trace in our valley. It is harder to certify the mark of the Celt and the Angle within it than even that of the Roman, for all alike have been slowly wiped out by the dalesman, whose utilitarian mind and unsuperstitious temper causes him to set his hand to everything he finds. But one or two sites must be mentioned. The sunny slope above the village of Rydal, is perhaps a shadowy one, whence the keen-eyed Celt, from a safe retreat in the upland valley behind him, could watch the mountain gate through which the river flowed below and the open road from the south, by which his enemy always advanced; another site is by Dunna

---

* The Celtic system of counting sheep still lingers in Lincolnshire; 4, 5, 10, 11, 15, 16, being—pethera, pimp, dik, yan-a-dik, bumpit, yan-a-bumpit : the Welsh equivalents being pedwar, pump, deg, un-ar-deg, pymtheg, unarbymtheg Both systems start again at 15, and do not go further than 20, when a "score" was cut on the tally, and the counting commenced over again. See Mansel Sympson's *Lincolnshire,* p 63 —ED

† It has been suggested by Mr. Collingwood (*Book of Coniston*) that the immigration was caused by Harold Fairhair, King of Norway, who sailed (880-890) to do battle with the Vikings settled in Ireland, Galloway, Man and the Western Islands, which caused these incontinently to flee and take refuge in the mountains of Cumbria.

Beck, where in our lake recess (looking southward too) he guarded the further ford and the arm of Whitemoss.* But there is another, just over the line of our manor and on the Ambleside side of Scandale beck, that may well have been an outpost of the Angle after he had conquered the district. It too, like the Celt's post, from elevated and secure ground, with a valley (Scandale) behind, watched the ford below; but, unlike the Celt's which looked south, it had a northern out-look towards the narrow mountain gate through which the Celt might come. It is called the Castle field. Not a vestige of building or of mound shows upon it. Yet this is probably the place which, so recently as 1789 Clarke in his *Survey of the Alps*, casually mentions as a Roman station, called the Castle, where he says, the remains are less apparent than at another place called the Borrans—which is the certified Roman station at the head of the lake.

And in the village itself is an artificial mound of prehistoric age. It stands in the old row of homesteads dotting the slope, and has given the modern name of Rydal Mount and Undermount to those next above and below it. It is flat-topped, with sloping sides, which drop to a terrace—bounded now by the garden wall, beyond which again in the field below, there are appearances of a second terrace. No story of the past is connected with the spot, nor is it known for what purpose it was reared upon this rocky slope. Could it have served, for the last northern settlers, who pitched their group of homesteads (as ever) on the dry sunny slope, out of reach of floods, as a place of council and of village government? Was it a little moot-hill or Thing-mount, where the body of free and equal townsmen discussed not only the *dails* or

---

* Mr W H Hills has found here, in the White Moss intake, a number of great stones, apparently artificially placed. They are too incoherent however, for any kind of identification. The habit, prevalent to this day, of breaking up large stones and boulders for building purposes, must have destroyed many a mark of history

divisions of the land which they owned in common,* and which they held in a yearly rotation, but where they themselves administered justice and the unwritten laws of their race? If this were so, the sacred well, a temple by a stream, said always to be associated with such a spot, and to be connected with it by a straight path leading east, can be found here readily. For the way from the mound by the field gate, if followed across the road and continued by the one in the park, would lead to a spot sought after to this day, where the Rydal beck plunges down in its last long fall. Here there exists a summer-house, built by Squire Daniel Fleming, in 1668, at what he calls the "Caw-weel," meaning perhaps the well with the paved way (*caw* or causey); the bridge above being likewise called the Caw-bridge. (See appendix following).

APPENDIX.

From D. F's Account Book.

1668. Dec. 19   Payment for walling " ye Sumer house at ye Caw weel " at 5^d a day.

1669 April 30   " Paid unto Jo. Green, Slater for 12 load of Slate 3^s, and 4 dayes slating ye Grot in ye Mill-Orchard 2^s."

,,   July   2.   "for plastering ye Grott" and other work

£   s.   d.
00. 14. 00.

,,   ,,   "Paid by J. B. unto ye Kendall Joyner for Wainscotting of my Grott-House ye sum of   ..   ..   ..   03. 00. 00.

,,   July 15.   "for glassing of ye Grott &c" the sum of 15^s 0^d is paid.

---

* Hence the term "dalesman"

CHAPTER IV

NORMAN ADMINISTRATION

The making of Westmorland.

THOUGH nominally conqueror of England in 1066, it was years before William forced the wild north to his yoke. Northumbria—now to the east divided into the counties Northumberland, Durham and Yorkshire—again and again defied him. He tried at first to keep terms with the men in power there, of whom Gospatric was chief. Gospatric was a great personage. A large land-owner like Tosti, he was moreover grandson to King Ethelred, and was allied to the royal house of Scotland; besides which he claimed an hereditary right to the earldom of Northumbria through his mother Aldgotha, who was daughter of Earl Uhelred.* William in 1067 allowed this claim, but by next year the earl had fled into Scotland, being implicated in all probability in the rebellion of Edwin and Morcas. William, while he separated Yorkshire from Northumbria, and ruled it as a county through a sheriff, yet thought well to receive Gospatric's submission for a time; but in 1072 he deprived him of all power, on the grounds that he had connived at the murder of Robert Cumen, the Norman administrator at Durham, as well as at the slaughter of the Normans at York. For these two outbursts of the men of the north, William's revenge was terrible. Marching north himself, he devastated the country, and left the awful peace of desolation behind him.

From sharing in this great disaster, our position west of the Pennines seemingly saved us. But a little later William's land surveyors and tax-layers crossed the chain for their great survey, written down in Doomsday Book

---

* *Victoria History of Cumberland*

and completed in 1086. No Westmorland truly is mentioned in it, nor Cumberland, a matter once considered mysterious, until the historians discovered that these counties did not at that time exist. Cumbria, the shrunken hold of the Britons, was no part of England, but a fief in the hands of the king of Scotland; while the district round the great bay of Morecambe, extending to Kendal and our own parts, was yet without an official name. It was classed in the Survey along with north *Lancashire,* Yorkshire (Eurvicscire), being still regarded as a part of the Northumbrian province of Deira. In Mr. Farrer's examination of the Doomsday Survey of this old conquest of the Angles,* he says

"The discovery that Furness, Kendal and North Lancashire, bounded on the north by the river Duddon, Dunmail Raise, Kirkstone Pass and Borrow Beck, and on the south by the river Ribble, formed a complete fiscal area of five hundred team-lands for the levying of Danegeld, is of great importance, not only in proving the identity of certain obscure names in Furness, Cartmel, and Millum, but also in demonstrating the distinct tribal separation of that territory from Cumbria in Strathclyde on the north, and Mercia on the south. This area was, in fact, a rateable district within the kingdom of Northumbria, while the land between the Ribble and the Mersey was a rateable area with Cheshire within the kingdom of Mercia."

The district immediately round Kendal is called in the Survey Stircaland, which is accounted as "The land of the King" and nine manors, of which Cherchebi, or Kirkby Kendal, is one, are entered as belonging to it. The list finishes with the laconic statement, "These Gilemichel† had. In these there are 20 teamlands to geld."

Stircaland then was the Anglian name of a lordship, or *goderd,* of which no doubt the centre was Kendal; and to

---

* See Lancashire and Cheshire Antiquarian Society's *Transactions,* vol xviii.
† It has been pointed out that Gilmichel is an Irish name. This is another fact favourable to the suggestion that our district was largely open, in the later times of Northumbria, to intercourse with the west

this centre the people of the various *vills* within its radius would assemble for their hundred—moot or court. How many *vills* or townships there were at that time we have no means of knowing. It is possible that some of the small Norse settlements in the forest beyond the great lake (self-governing communities) were overlooked in this tax survey. Mr. Farrer considers that the nine manors reckoned as Stircaland embraced as many as twenty-two present townships, and among them Grasmere, Langdale, and Rydal-and-Loughrigg.* The name Stircaland became Strickland, and has survived as Strickland Roger and Strickland Ketel, two small townships near Burneside. The later name was once applied to the valley of the Brathay, for as late as the close of the fourteenth century the manor of Little Langdale is stated to be in " Strickeland Kettyll " † It seems probable therefore that the valley of the Rothay was also within it, and that at a period later than the Doomsday book it was ruled by some sub-lord whose name was Ketel. The name is also found at Ketilthorp, near Lincoln.

William Rufus it was, as is well known, who finally fixed the boundary of England to the north-west. Marching north in 1092, he took from Dolpin, son of Gospatric, the land of Carlisle, which the latter had been ruling under the protection of the King of Scotland, and joined it to England. The ancient British kingdom of Cumbria, much shrunk, was soon to become the modern Cumberland.

But the evolution of the counties of Cumberland and Westmorland is not an easy one to follow. The administration of these incoherent districts and lands to the

---

* A great number of these were estates which had been granted out after the date of the survey, but never assessed to Danegeld, being originally pasture and waste, and only constituted townships by a gradual process of enclosure and settlement, partly from wastes nominally belonging to the nine manors, but largely by purpresture made in the Forest of Kendal This explains the reason that the yearly levy, called Noutgeld, *in lieu of cattle*, was rendered to the Crown from Kendal . in place of money service from each *vill* or manor.

† Rental at Levens Hall.

north-west, either for purpose of peace or taxation, was from their character as Marsh or border-land, different, and the first attempts were tentative. Both William Rufus and Henry I.—who carried on the work of re-construction begun by his brother—relied at first on their father's method of placing Districts or Honours under the lordship of some foreign noble, whom they believed they could trust. The barony of Kendal when it emerged from the old Stircaland, was given over as a fief by William to Ivo Taillebois, a native of Anjou who had been married (in the summary fashion of the time) to an English heiress named Lucia Ivo had only one daughter, who married Ranulf Meschin. Now Ranulf was a Norman of great possessions. Henry I. had given to him the land of Carlisle, where he had built a castle. Moreover, on the death of his cousin in the White Ship in 1120, he succeeded to the great earldom of Chester

On this last acquisition, however, Ranulf resigned his more northern fiefs to the king, who possibly feared he might become too great a subject to rule, and Henry appears to have held the administration of them in his own hands between 1120 and 1130. It is probably to some unfixed year within these dates that we may assign the great reconstruction of these parts, and the formation of the county of Westmorland.* It is in 1130, that "Westmarieland" (a very poetic name, if it means the land of the western sea) appears as a definite area, ruled over by a sheriff. It was made up in the main of two distinct parts, which had come to be known under the Norman kings as the barony of Appleby and the barony of Kendal The latter, or more southerly portion, whose waters flow into the Bay of Morecambe, had been part of the Anglian conquest of the seventh century, annexed to Deira. The former, whose waters flowed west to Carlisle and the

---

* *Victoria History of Cumberland.*

Solway Firth (and which seems to have fixed the wandering name of Westmorland) had been part of the alien kingdom of Cumbria, long struggled over, and ruled by Celt or Scot, till the days of the Red king. Thus a political boundary line, 500 years old, was summarily wiped out, on the formation of the county; and it is interesting to note that the church preserved this line for 700 years longer. For while the bishopric of Carlisle created by Henry I. in 1133, embraced Appleby, Kendal was left to her old diocese of York. And even when Henry VIII. created the see of Chester, and caused Kendal to be added to it, the barony still remained within the archdeaconry of Richmondshire, which repeated in so remarkable a manner the contour of the old British land of Teyrulwyg, that now was broken up into parts of Cumberland, Westmorland, Lancashire and Yorkshire. It was not till 1856, when the new archdeaconry of Westmorland was formed, and Kendal as part of it was handed over to the diocese of Carlisle, that this district and our valley finally lost that connection with Yorkshire that had been begun 1200 years before.

The two districts, or baronies, lying on two sides of a watershed, there summarily united to form a county by Henry I., have never cohered. Westmorland is practically a county without a centre or county-town. Appleby, that wears that dignity, a little place that grew about a great Norman stronghold, has had no other importance or influence. Kendal, a busy trading town, is the centre of its own district, and troubles not at all with Appleby, except when a criminal has to be carried thither for justice in the higher Courts.

THE AUTHOR.

TO FACE P. 45.

CHAPTER V

THE BARONY OF KENDAL

Its Divisions and its Lords; Will de Lancaster and his daughter Helwise.

THE confusion that characterized the tenure of the lands of Appleby and Kendal during the reign of Henry I., Stephen, and Henry II. is not easy to penetrate, and the reader who desires to wrestle with all the details of the subject is referred to those authors who have studied the Pipe Rolls in the original *

It seems sufficient for this small history to say that during this period our district of Stircaland seems to have been held, not directly of the crown by a tenant in chief, but by a subsiduary lord who paid suit and court for it to the chief lord. That chief lord was in the days of Henry I, Nigel de Albini, of the house of Mowbray, who held it by grant of the king as subsequent charters show, and he was followed by his son Roger de Mowbray. Roger de Mowbray handed it over to an under tenant between 1150-1153, giving "all my land of Lonsdale, and of Kendal, and Horton of Ribblesdale" to one William, son of Gilbert de Lancastre, to hold by service of four knights. The lordship of Kendal however, seems to have been lost to Mowbray in 1154; and Henry II., when restoring order after the anarchy that prevailed in Stephen's time, seems to have united it to "Westmarieland" (which he gave over to Hugh de Morville) as a mesne lordship held by service of rendering neatgeld.† Hugh de Morville ceased to enjoy it at the time of the rebellion of 1173-4, with which he was probably connected; and after the

---

* See *Pipe Rolls of Cumberland and Westmorland*, Hodgson-Hinde, and *Pipe Rolls of Lancashire*, W Farrer; also the latter's "Tenure of Westmorland" *Transactions*, C & W A & A Society, vol vii N S

† Mr Farrer's *Tenure of Westmorland*.

sheriff had accounted for it for three years, it was handed over to Henry's chief justice, Ranulf de Granvill.

We thus arrive at a family calling themselves de Lancastre, who held the lands of Kendal successively under Roger de Mowbray, Hugh de Morville and Ranulf de Granvill as chief lords in rapid succession.

William, son of Gilbert, first of the family to acquire the lands of Kendal, was a man of affairs, who acted probably as seneschal to William Earl Warren, the Lord of Lancaster.* He stood high in favour with the earl, married a relative of his, and by licence took the surname of Lancaster.

He was followed by his son, likewise William, who dying in 1184, left a daughter and heiress only, named Helwise. Helwise was given in marriage to Gilbert fitz Reinfred, whom the king styles in the grant as "our Dapifer." Gilbert had acted occasionally as Justiciar, and on Richard I.'s accession he as well as his father Roger were employed in the administration of justice and peace in the district. There was room for them, for Richard had at once deprived his father's chief justice, Ranulf de Granvill of all his appointments, and likewise robbed him of the lordship of Westmarieland Gilbert, who under Ranulf had held Kendal, by right of his wife Helwise, now secured the fee by a freer and higher tenure. Hitherto the holder of it had rendered to his superior the annual rent of £14 6s. 3d., which was a money equivalent of the old Nout or Neatgeld, a tax formerly paid in cattle. Gilbert gave the king 600 marks to exchange this service of neatgeld for the nobler one of military service, which placed him in the higher feudal position of tenant in chief, responsible to no man but the king. Richard's charter, which indelibly fixed the lands of Kendal as a barony, is dated April 15, 1190, and of the

---

* Mr Farrer's *Lancashire Pipe Rolls*

same date is a confirmation to Gilbert of the forest of Westmorland, of Kendal, and of Furness, as William de Lancaster the son of Gilbert had held it; and that he should hold the forest in Kendal which the king had given him along with six librates of land " as fully and freely as Nigel de Albini had ever held it." When King John came to the throne, Gilbert proffered him a fine of £100 for arrears of cornage charged him, and for a confirmation of the charters he held, including the " holding in peace the land in Kendal which he had by the gift of King Richard."

Gilbert and his wife Helwise had three children who came to be concerned in the barony of Kendal and our own parish; William, Alice, and Helwise They all, as well as a half brother Roger, took the surname of de Lancaster. Gilbert died some time between 1217 and June of 1220. In the former year he is instructed by mandate to meet the king of the Isles, who comes to do homage to Henry III., at Sulewad, or Carlisle, or Lancaster or some other place in those parts *; and in the latter William de Lancastria is bidden to deliver up a young girl " whom King John our father entrusted to the nurture of Gilbert son of Reinfrid, thy father." It is evident therefore that the wardship of this heiress had been closed by the probably recent death of Gilbert.

William de Lancaster, who succeeded, was the third of that name. He is said to have fought in the Barons' war against King John † and to have been taken prisoner in 1216. Certainly one of the name was a prisoner at Chester in 1217, and by the king's mandate was despatched under safe conduct to Gloucester ‡ No doubt he was pardoned; and as baron of Kendal and great land-owner in Westmorland and Lancashire he played his due part.

---

* *Patent Rolls*, Henry III
† West's *Antiquities of Furness*
‡ Patent Rolls 1 Henry III

Like other great people of his time, he was the benefactor of religious houses His great-grandfather William had given lands by the Cocker to a distant establishment at Leicester,* and his grandfather William had interested himself in the formation of an abbey there, called Cockersand. He himself endowed the new Priory of Conishead on the shore of Morecambe Bay (which had taken the place of the hospital of St. John of Jerusalem at Bardsey) with much land about Ulverston, and many perquisites ; and besides these, with a small remote corner of his barony of Kendal, viz , the " land of Basebrune " in Little Langdale, which is in the parish of Grasmere He likewise conferred some lands on Furness Abbey, which was now taking the lead of all other houses in Furness and Amounderness. This was in 1240, when he expressed his wish to be buried there as his grandfather had been. He died in 1246, without issue, and bequeathed certain lands to other than his heirs. To the religious men of Conishead he left meadow lands at Elterwater, adjacent to their settlement at Baisbrowne. Above all he enfeoffed

" Roger de Lancastre of 220 acres of land of his demesne in Patricdale [Patterdale] worth 4 li yearly, and of one mill worth 60s yearly, and of the farm of free tenants to the value of 18s 10d

The said Roger has the service of Gilbert de Lancastre, who holds by knight's service by the tenth part of one knight's fee.

And the service of Walter de Lancastre, who holds by knight's service, by the tenth part of one knights' fee " " Also the said Roger d Lancaster of the whole forest of Westmorland, except Fensdale and S Cartefel, and the head of Martindale, which the said Roger held before of ancient feoffment "†

Through three November days William dictated the charter of his gifts, and at midnight of the 21st, his death seeming imminent, his seal (we are told) was solemnly broken He revived however, but only for a few days.

---

* W Farrer's *Lancashire Pipe Rolls*
† Mr Farrer's Lancashire Inquests, Extracts, &c

The king took over his lands, as the custom was, and after an Inquisition, held by worthy men, and after assigning a reasonable dower to William's widow (Agnes de Brus) he handed them over to his true heirs.

These heirs were declared to be Peter de Brus and Walter de "Lyndeseye," the nephews of the dead man. For, in default of right male heirs, the inheritance of the barony now reverted to his sister, the daughter of Helwise de Lancaster and Gilbert fitz Reinfred, and Alice de Lancaster had been married to William de Lindesey, and Helwise to Peter de Brus, lord of Skelton. In these two lines (with a further division of the Brus portion) the lands of the barony remained till they were united under the crown in Queen Elizabeth's days; and the crown in Charles II's time leased them to the Lowther family, whose chief member has been lord of the manor ever since.*

This division between the de Lancaster sisters and their heirs, that took place in the middle of the thirteenth century, affected not only the parish of Grasmere, but even our little domain of Rydal. The wide lands were parted in a fashion that, to our simpler modes of land tenure, seems strangely complicated and confused. Instead of one clear line being drawn across the barony with all the lands on one side assigned to Alice, and all on the other to Helwise, the partitions were scattered and minute, and struck through existing town, parish, township, or hamlet alike. For this reason the manorial rights in the barony have always been peculiarly involved; and dalesmen who have been neighbours on their little estates owed suit and service and paid dues to different lords of the manor.

The original land-tenure of these parts, before the manorial methods were somewhat loosely applied to them, must be briefly considered later. At the time that this

---

* See Mr Farrer's Lancashire Inquests, Escheats, &c

division was made, the Forest of Kendal, as it was called, stretched along the eastern shores of Windermere and on into the valleys of the Rothay and the Brathay (meeting at the lakes' head) with breaks here and there where settlements had been made, and clearings, that would ensure pasture and plough-land to the little village communities that had sprung up around the first settlements of the conquering race. These settlements are generally called, in the early rentals, hamlets; but they seem to have been already locally governed as townships. Several townships were grouped together for church government in one parish; the parish of Windermere, with its church by the lake for a centre, embracing Undermilbeck, Applethwaite, Troutbeck, with part of Ambleside; and that of Grasmere embracing the township of that name (lying within the last chamber of the Rothay where the mother church stands) with its neighbour "Langdesse" at the head of the Brathay, and Rydal with part of Ambleside—to which latter township was united the scattered homesteads on Loughrigg—the rocky mass separating the lower parts of the valleys. That this ecclesiastical division was made at a very early time, is certain, for we find that the natural boundary of Stockgill which it followed, cuts in two a little settlement that was later to become the thriving town of Ambleside, now in the division.

The stretch from the middle of the lake to its head, belonging to the parish of Windermere (which came to be more exclusively considered a forest for game) was handed over intact to Alice de Lindesey; it included the townships or hamlets of Applethwaite and Troutbeck and crossed the church boundary at Stock-gill in order to include the whole of Ambleside likewise. Beyond that, within the parish of Grasmere, Rydal with its hamlet and subsidiary valley fell to the lot of Helwise de Brus. Beyond that again, Grasmere, Langdale and Loughrigg seem each to have been divided equally between them, the two taking half the holdings in the three settlements. Nor was even little Loughrigg divided by one clear line ; for though Helwise certainly got the majority of the holdings that stood opposite to Rydal, on the further bank of the river, even here a few important ones—such as Cockstone, Fox-gill, Loughrigg Brow, and Miller Bridge—were assigned to her sister, Alice de Lindesey, and broke up into many parts what might have been an even stretch of demesne, rising to the watershed.

The fisheries—then an important source of revenue to the manorial lord—were likewise divided in a complicated fashion. Alice had the whole lake of Windermere with its islands, except Roger Holme, which fell to her sister. She had also Routhmere (Rydal Water) with the plentiful " dubs " or pools of the Rothay, also a part of the fishing of Grasmere, and the Brathay as far as the " on' brygge " at Skelwith.

Helwise appears to have taken "Skelefwater" elsewhere called Bratha lake (by which Elterwater is probably meant) and the greater share of the Grasmere fishing. She obtained the balance of Alice's rich possessions in the great lake by the fisheries of the Kent, then of high value ; though even here her sister had a fraction, as *she* had in Windermere.

Helwise took half the town of Kendal as her portion ; and Alice, who also had half of Ulverston in Lancashire, the other half.

And the king in confirming this division of lands between the two ladies and their heirs, assigned to each " a chief messuage," that of Peter de Brus, son of Helwise, being at Kirkby [Kendal] and that of Walter de Lindesey, Alice's son, at Warton in Lancashire

The Lindeseys therefore, as long as they were in residence in these parts, lived at Warton, and thence controlled their manorial possessions in our valleys ;

while the line of Brus or Bruce ruled at the nearer stronghold of Kendal Castle.

That line changed its name in the next generation. Helwise's son Peter died without issue in 1272, and his possessions fell to his four sisters. With one, Ladarina, who married John de Belle Aqua, we have nothing to do, for she received of Kendal lands only Kentmere. Lucy another sister married Marmaduke de Twenge; and her son Marmaduke eventually took a large share of Grasmere and some of Langdale; and this share, after being enjoyed by his three sons, William, Robert, and Thomas, passed to his daughter Margaret. Margaret's daughter Matilda married a de Hothorne, and her daughter Isabella (who was married to Walter Penwardyn) and her son John de Hothorne shared it. A rental of the year 1375, at Levens Hall, accounts for their receipt from some thirty tenants at Grasmere and eleven at Langdale The Hothornes were seated at Staveley, where they likewise had a share of the barony, and in later times, when their possessions in our valleys seem to have shrunk, these were claimed as belonging to the manor of Staveley. When an Inquisition * was held on the possessions of the late Sir John Hothorne in 1434, only three messuages or farmholds were accounted for in the " hamlet of Grysmere," and three in the " hamlet of Skelmeser and Langdene† "; and this attenuated portion passed by purchase from a John de Hothorne in 1570, along with Staveley ‡ to Allan Bellingham.

A third daughter of Helwise is a factor in the history of Rydal not to be forgotten. Her name was Margaret; she was married to Robert de Ros of Wick, whose father, likewise Robert, had married Isabel, daughter of the king of Scots. As her husband died in 1274, two years after

---

* See Chan Inq. p m 14 Ed. III (1st num) 31 and No. 68 (1st num) 48 Ed III.

† See Chan. Inq p m 12 Henry VI No. 16

‡ Nicolson and Burn.

her childless brother Peter, we hear of her often, for she not only held large landed possessions, but seems to have enjoyed considerable power in the disposal of them. On the great partition of Peter's property, she and her husband had received " the castle of Kirkeby in Kendale, with all Kendale, whatever pertained to Sir Peter de Brus in demesnes, villeinages, rents and service of freemen and others, except the dale of Kentmere, which is assigned to Sir John de Bella Aqua and to " Luderana " (*sic*) his wife, and with the advowson of Konigesheved priory." * And Margaret, on her husband's death does fealty to the king for these lands, and takes oath not to marry without his licence. In 1281, some re-distribution of Peter's lands took place. Margaret was declared not to have received her full share, and three-quarters of a fee held by William de Stirkeland which had been assigned to the fourth sister Agnes (married to Walter de Faucumberg) was transferred to her. Her lands clearly included almost the whole of her mother Helwise's half of the barony, as stated; and one half of Grasmere, Langdale and Loughrigg. With Rydal she parted the very next year; and the charter by which she granted it to her kinsman, Sir Roger de Lancaster, gives us our first record of the place, and of its boundaries (See Appendix). The rest of her property she divided between her son William and her nephew Marmaduke de Twenge: so that when an inquisition was held at her death in 1307, the jurors declared that she then held nothing. They continued

" but she sometimes held the moiety of the Barony of Kendal —except the vale of Kentmere—of the King in chief by the service of one knights fee. Of which moiety the said Margaret enfeoffed Roger de Lancaster of the vale of Ridale, to hold of the King in chief by the service of the fourth part of one knight's fee, whereof he has the King's charter; it is worth £20 in all issues. The said Margaret also enfeoffed William de Ros, her

---

* See Cal of Close Rolls, Ed.I.

son, of the Castle of Kyrkeby in Kendal, with the fourth part of the town of Kyrkeby, and the hamelets of Hoton Haye, Scalthaybrige, Stirkeland Randolfe, and Greurige, with 45 acres of land of the demesnes of Helsington, and with the holdings of William, son of Adam and Henry de Wytfalhend in Hogayl, with the mills of the Castle, Hoton, Greurige, Strykeland Randolfe, and Dillaker; the moiety of the mills of Patton, Grarige, and Respton, worth £40 yearly, to hold to the said William and the heirs begotten of his body (in default to remain to Marmaduke de Thwenge and his heirs) of the lord the King by the service of the third part of one knight's fee . . . .

The said Margaret also enfeoffed Marmaduke de Thweng of the manor of Helsington—except 40 acres of land of the demesne of Helsington—and of the fourth part of the *vill* of Kyrkeby-in-Kendal, with the hamelts, of Crosthayth, Gresmer, and Langden with the appurtenances, and of the mill of Helsington, with moiety of the mills of Crosthayth, Respton, Gresmer, and Langden, worth £40 yearly in all issues; to hold of the said Marmaduke and the heirs begotten of his body (in default to remain to William de Ros and his heirs) of the King in chief by the service of the moiety of the third part of one knight's fee, whereof the said Marmaduke has the Kings charter of confirmation." . . *

It will be seen that (according to this inquisition) no portion of her Grasmere and Langdale lands went to her son. Yet her son's line is eventually found in possession of almost the half of these two townships; and we can only conjecture that it was re-acquired from the Pedwardyns, since after 1375 we hear no more of that branch of the Twenge line in either of the places. Margaret's line ran through William, Thomas, and John de Ros, and through John's daughter Elizabeth, (who married Sir William Parr) into the Parr family, till it ceased with Sir William, who rose into high favour with Henry VIII., and was created by him Earl of Essex and Marquis of Northampton. His possessions in the barony of Kendal, including half of Grasmere and Langdale, came to be known as the Marquis Fee, and will be called so in the

---

* Mr Farrer's Lancashire Inquests, Escheats, &c.

following pages they represent, roughly speaking, the share given over to Helwise de Lancaster and her heirs in 1246.

Alice's share passed through Walter and William de Lindesey, and by William's heiress Christiana, to the French family of de Gynes, who were lords of Coucy. From 1284, onward, Christiana's husband, Ingram or Ingelram was playing his role in these parts as chief tenant to the king, being summoned to council and parliament, and bidden to advance with the other northern knights (of whom his connection Marmaduke de Twenge was one) against the Scots.* His journeys thither were sometimes of a more peaceful character; one was taken in 1284 with his wife and mother-in-law, who was daughter of John de Balliol, when both he and the latter appointed attorneys to act for them during their absence Christtiana survived him ten years, dying in 1335, and she was followed by their son William, though another son Robert took a portion of the lands in east Westmorland for life. On William's death in 1343 an Inquisition declared Ingelram his brother to be his heir. Ingelram's claim however was set aside by the king, who wished to reward John de Coupland (who married William de Coucy's widow Joan) for his prowess in battle, and his capture of the king of Scots alive at the battle of Neville's Cross; and so granted to him and his wife, for their joint lives William's possessions in the barony, with reversion to Ingelram de Gynes and his heirs. This Ingelram, the sire of Coucy was a great man, though more French in his interests than English. That he was in favour with Edward III.—at least for a time—is certain, for he married his daughter Isabella, and was created Earl of Bedford. But when the boy Richard came to the throne, Ingelram haughtily renounced his allegiance to the English king,

---

* See Close Rolls, 1307 and 1313.

and returned the Order of the Garter which had been bestowed on him ; and his confiscated lands in England were assigned to the support of his wife. The children of Ingelram and Isabella were Philippa and Mary ; and while to Mary were assigned her father's possessions in France, Philippa (who married Robert de Veer, Earl of Bedford, and Duke of Ireland) took the English ones, including apparently those of Kendal, with which we are concerned These last remained from that time in the hands of the royal house. They were granted to John, Duke of Bedford, son of Henry IV., and on his death in 1436 fell to his nephew Henry VI., a third however being portioned to his widow Jaquetta (who married Sir Richard Woodville) as a dower. Next they were assigned to John, Duke of Somerset ; and he, dying in 1444, left only a little daughter Margaret, afterwards to be the mother of Henry VII., who carried them to her husband the Earl of Richmond. After a temporary deprivation of them during the ascendency of the House of York, in favour of its adherents the Parrs of Kendal, Margaret, Countess of Richmond resumed them , and it was from her (it is said) they gained their name of the Richmond Fee. Through Henry VII. they passed to Henry VIII., who endowed his natural son, the Duke of Richmond, with them. When they fell to Elizabeth, she not only kept them in her own hands, but with the widow of the Marquis of Northampton she exchanged lands, so that the Marquis Fee became hers likewise. The bulk of the lordship of Kendal thus became re-united, and passed down the line of sovereigns—James I allowing it as a portion to his son Prince Charles, and Charles II. settling it as a dower on his queen—till it was leased and ultimately sold to the Lowther family.

Such, briefly put, is the roll of the lords of the manor who ruled conjointly over the lands of Kendal. This descent will be more clearly scanned in a table. Two of the lines branching from Helwise remained as residents in the neighbourhood, at Kendal and at Staveley. The third passed through local de Lindeseys and French Coucys to mighty warriors and kings; and it is with this line we are chiefly concerned, because half Loughrigg belonged to it.

The Inquisitions that were held when these lords died, and from the rentals and accounts made out for them by the steward, are our only materials for reconstructing the history of our valleys and their villages till the line of Elizabeth; and these unfortunately are incomplete and scanty. Of court rolls, in which the proceedings of the village courts were written, but one specimen appears to exist, which is in the Record Office.

The descent of the manor of Rydal through Sir Roger de Lancaster will be given later.

CHAPTER VI

The Land and the People

Meaning of " Dalesman," " Dales " and " Meres "; " stinted " pastures; Appendix; " Boundering."

IT is with the rulers that history first concerns itself, and thus it is through the lords of the manor who held them that we first hear of the lands of the Rothay and Brathay. But there was an ownership other than theirs in those lands, older, closer, and more lasting; that of the people who lived upon and by the soil. Reaching far back into the past, silent, yet tenacious, the character of this occupation and possession can only be guaged by later evidences, and by the customs that were found to prevail when record begins.

Along the valleys, making gaps here and there in the ancient forest, were little communities of men, each bearing a name and constitution, as *vill* or township. The open spaces surrounding these villages, where forest had been cleared for pasture of cattle and sowing of corn were no doubt of immemorial age; and if the Celt had not anywhere planted on them his permanent "vicus," he would certainly have erected on them the summer dwellings that belonged to his more nomad state. The conquering Angle or the Norseman had but to seize the ground, erect with a few of his fellows their houses, and to begin, along with them and some slaves or dependents, that life of common possession and joint interest that made each village community an autonomy, self-governing and independent.

From the rocky nature of the soil, which made arable land hard to find, these communities were small. Three of them—Troutbeck, Ambleside, and Rydal, occupied similar sites, close upon the banks of subsidiary streams just above where these streams fell into the main valley, with their houses clustered pretty thickly together on the dry sunny slope. Here they were not only lifted above the morasses of the bottom, but behind them on the fell was good grazing for their cattle, while below them was to be found that scanty patch of flat alluvial land that yielded a soil deep enough for the plough to turn. In Grasmere, with its circular vale, the homesteads were more scattered, as they were in Langdale, but there too, while each man held his *toft* and *croft*, or allotment on which his house actually stood, as his own by private right, the rest was open field, which he held jointly with his neighbour and tilled and controlled by common council. The town field, towards Easdale, is known, and yet unenclosed in parts, while the mere-stones, which divided, etc., one man's balks or strips from his neighbour's, are not all gone. On the other side of the valley, the little meadows —like those of Rydal—were found early last century (though then enclosed) to be in possession of several statesmen, relic of the time when every part of the village land was held jointly and interchangeably. In Loughrigg indeed, where of arable land there was practically none, the men of the few homesteads on the pastures by the Rothay were joined on to Rydal as a township; for the hamlet of Clappersgate, within the Loughrigg division, never was a *vill*, but appears to have sprung up late about the wharf on the Brathay, that was used for landing goods brought by Windermere.

Around the houses of each village community there lay then the open fields, of which each member owned a certain share, fixed in quantity, but changing in position, This he held as *alad*, his indeed unalienably and by inheritance, yet held by witness of the community only. He tilled his apportioned strip each year with the plough and team of oxen he held in common with his fellows; he reared his temporary hedge or fence round his apportioned pasture while the hay grew upon it. His cattle, drawn in to the village for winter, roamed in summer the wide common pasture. In the forest, which lay between village and village unenclosed, and grew densely up to the clearings, he had his apportioned strip upon the edge, called his wood-mire, where he cut all the *elding* wanted for his fire-hearth, and all the timber needed for his house and implements. On the fell, he had his bracken-dale, where he could gather the fern for bedding of his cattle; and in the moss, his dalt or dale for the cutting and drying of his peat. These shares or dales,* in which all his property, excepting house and cattle, was held, gave him his name of dalesman; though he was later known, when property in land had become more individual and consolidated, as statesman or estatesman too. When he died, his house and his share of village

---

* Dale = to divide, share The word occurs in many wills and deeds of the 17th and 18th century. A deal a part or portion See appendix to this chapter

land passed to his family, to his widow first for her life (who held it for his children) and then in general to his eldest son. That however, it had originally been property vested in the family, and not in the individual, seems likely.

In an Ambleside rental of 1505-6, Christopher Partrygge and James Partrygge are charged 6s. 8d. rent " for a tenement and 5 cattle, to hold of one of them according to the custom of the manor, and the other is bound to agree for his part upon view of his years." Some settlement between the two was clearly made. And in what late wills we possess, the testator endeavoured to compensate his younger sons for their heritage by causing the inheritor to pay to them a certain sum in money (generally out of the estate). Also if there were an idiot in the family (as in the case of the Parks of the Nab less than a hundred years ago) there was a charge laid upon the estate for his maintenance.*

But written wills were a very late device. In the primitive community when a man died his fellows drew together, and a selected number of them, called a Jury, examined his affairs, declared what his communal portion amounted to, and to whom it passed. This declaration developed after lands became fixed and enclosed, into the practice of " boundering " of which we have an example written out for the benefit of Sir Daniel Fleming, after he had inherited a small estate at the Wray in Grasmere. (See Appendix to this chapter).

The village law in fact was custom ; a custom founded on ages of usage : and that law was declared by the older and more revered men of the community. All indeed, gathered together for the village moot or council, for all in these small communities—except the few landless

---

* Both these claims of the family were set down by the jury who were called to declare the customs of the dalesmen of Furness in 1583 West's *Antiquities of Furness*

men or cottars—seem to have been equal. There was so much to be arranged and settled in village affairs. Besides the extraordinary ones of restraining an unruly member or witnessing to a dead man's share, there were the current and very pressing ones of fixing and apportioning the dales, when these were yearly interchangeable in the arable field and the meadow; there was the question to be settled—if the common were a " stinted " one *—as to how many cattle each member was entitled from the size of his holding to put upon it and, above all, there were certain men to be appointed out of their number, who would undertake that this village law should be carried out, and the approved custom upheld throughout the year, in every department of the village and its lands. Whether all these offices were ancient is not certain. Some of them may have originated when the village moot passed into the lord's court. The *reeve*, or grave as he was here called,† was the chief village officer; and he was bound to represent it at the higher court of the hundred, which for these parts was held at Kendal. He came later to collect the lord's rents, and to be called bailiff; but it remained an unwritten law that no man could fill the office who was not a land holder in the township, and most of his duties eventually passed to the constable. Then there were the two hedge-lookers of whom we hear at Wythburn, and whose duties no doubt were to supervise those hedges which must be made by all at the right time; the *moss-lookers*, who were responsible for the *peat-mosses*, where no unfair advantage must be taken by one cutter over another; and above all, the *house-lookers* and *bier-law men*,‡ who had to see that no man exceeded his right to lopping in the forest, and who later (when their office became a

---

* Limited *i.e*, to a certain head of cattle
† The name occurs in many documents
‡ Perhaps the " Wood-Linchers " of W. were the same.

most difficult one as we shall see) had to view a man's house, and declare how much timber it required for its repair and then (in company with the lord's officer) to mark out such trees in the common wood as he might cut. The *frithmen* * were responsible for the common and the cattle put upon it during the summer; and for Rydal, where the pasture was a "stinted" one, these officers appear in the Agist-books and papers of the manor down to the eighteenth century. They are stated also, in the seventeenth century, to have the care of the "Pairable Hedge." They seem to have been elected in rotation, each village land-holder taking his due turn; as were the *grave*, the constable, the churchwarden, and the later overseer of the poor and the surveyor of the highways. Only for the eighteen men who represented the whole parish of Grasmere in church council, six from each township (and so six from Rydal-and-Loughrigg) was there permanence of office. The grave, however, who originally served for one year only, as early rentals show, came later—when he degenerated into a mere collector of the lord's rents—to hold office for life; such was Edwin Green of Rydal.

The village moot or council was held at first, there is no doubt, in the open air, upon some mound or by some prominent stone that served as a convenient centre.† The mount at Rydal may have served such a purpose. A stone now immersed by the raised water of Thirlmere was known traditionally as the Steady-stone, because to it gathered the Wythburn men, to settle the number of their cattle to be put on their stinted common. The suggested law-ting ‡ at Fell Foot in Little Langdale just within the barony of Kendal may have served for a wider

---

* Frith seems to mean a wood or a clearing in a wood. To Frith = to cut underwood. Also to drive or clear off cattle. See end of chapter x.

† Such a stone still exists near Spalding. It is called the Elloe Stone from the Hundred of Elloe in the County of Lincoln.—Ed.

‡ Thing (Dan and Swed ting) = a council.

concourse where the Norsemen of the coast could meet those of the valleys to discuss larger matters of policy and war.

APPENDIX —RYDAL MSS

Outside in Sir Daniel Fleming's hand   "A Verdict concerning Wray—Tenement in Gresmere, May 1683."

Gresmere

Whereas wee the Queen's Majesties Jureors of the manor of Grasmer [*sic*] in the county of Westmorland being comanded by our bailif according to our Ancient Custome to vew & Bounder A Tenament of her Majesties Land Called the Richmond Fee of the yearly Rent of sixteen pound halfepeny farthing stuate lying & being at wrey in Grasmer within the said county of Westmorland, hereto belonging unto Daniell Fleming of Rydall in the said County, Esq, (now Sir Daniel Fleming, knight) & now appertaining unto William Fleming, Esq his son & heire apparent, wee the said jureors whose names are here under writen being duly empaneld & sworne; &; haueing vewed euery particualer parcell of ground belonged to the said Tenement haueing lately seen & perused a former verdict or Award Concerning the said tenement bearing daite the 21 day of July Anno Domi; 1668; haueing set divers marks & meerstones upon the said Land belonging to the tenement aforesaid wheire any was needful to bee set, & haueing heard the Evidence of diuers old men & of our owne knowledge; wee according to our Antcient Custome doe verdict order & Award as ffoloweth First that one poll of medow lying at welfoot bridge, Another parcell of medow ground lying on the north side of stonydaill in the wrey feild A parcell of towne ground Caled little Broad Croft Another parcell of Cornland & medow Lying under Rantry Cragg A Road of Corne ground Caled Catsend; Another Rood of Corn ground lying under Regnald Close. A parcell of medow lying in the Broad Ing being the 16th part of the said closes; which was Rente (?) for Robertt wilsone ground at wray And was afterwarde in the posesion of John Rawson A little parcell of Corn ground Caled pyottnest, A litte Intack of pasture ground adjoining to the wrey gill, & an House & ylard lying at wrey upon the south side of the way between the highway And the gill; A parcell of Corn ground Caled Thisel Leyes A wall, standing upon the said daill of ground which said wall mayde by John

Jackson or done for him wee order to bee Removed & noe way to be made at any time hereafter by him or any other persons ouer the said daill, in Testimoiny where off wee the said Juriors haue here subscribed our names & marks; the 16th day of may Anno Domini, 1683.

John Haukrigg	John Hird H
Rowland Atkinson	Robert Greene
Michell Watson	Edwin Green
Robert Hird	John Hawkrigg
Michaell Knott K	Robert Hird R
John Haukrigg ∧	John Walker ⊥
Gerall Clork H	John Benson ⊲

CHAPTER VII

The Institution of the Manor

"Bokland", Bainbrigg; Various rentals; Courts in Moothall or Church.

UPON the once self-governing village community the manorial system came to be superimposed, by which it was linked on to the state, and furnished its share to the state's maintenance * At what time the men of our little settlement first acknowledged a feudal lord, rendering him suit and service for the protection he gave them, and marching under his banner to the wars, is not known. The system was in force in Anglo-Saxon times, and the Angles, when they colonized the region round Morecambe Bay, certainly laid that region out in manors. The "capital messuage" or manor-house found upon the island of Windermere (Langholme) in the very first rental of these parts, but always spoken of as ruined or waste, may have been a centre of theirs, where a lord or thane administered the park around. Certain it is that as late as 1376, when an Inquisition was made on the death of

---

* The reckoning would be so many cattle for each stead or holding. In Ambleside the value of the stead was given in cattle

Joan de Coupeland, she is declared to have held for her life " the manor of Wynandermer with its members, namely, the hamlets of Langeden, Loghrigge, Grismer, Hamelsate, Troutebek, Appelthwayte, Crosthwayt, Stirkeland-kells and Hoton "*; and from time immemorial the villages of Troutbeck and Ambleside attended a court held twice a year at Windermere, as belonging to that manor.

But the Anglian government could never have been strong in the valleys, that were filled largely with a Celtic population till the Norsemen made their settlements; and during the period of Danish inroad and the anarchy that resulted, its force must have declined. Our little mountain settlements, buried in forest, would be left pretty much to their own independent ways; and it is doubtful how much they furnished by way of suit and service, to that Gilmichael of whom we hear in Doomsday Book, or whether the sturdy dalesman did him homage for their lands as lord.

But with Norman rule, and the settlement of the counties by Henry I. and Henry II., the feudal system was put into effectual force. The plan of the manor could never indeed be carried out completely and satisfactorily in these valleys, from the restricted character of the ground occupied by the settlements; but the machinery of the manor was applied to them, and each little township—though without a lord's seat or manor-house with its indispensable adjuncts—came to be loosely called a manor. The great barons of Kendal, who owned all the county, and more, were for long the sole lords of the manor of our valleys, until the grant of Rydal to William de Lancaster, and there was nothing between the lord and the free land-holding ceorl † of those village-settlements, which he may never have visited, unless he happed upon

---
* Inq. p m. No 29, 49 Ed III. pt. 1.
† A S. form of churl = man.

F

them in some long day's hunting. Still there were his officers who could apply the system and see that it was carried out: and the free ceorl became in legal language, the lord's man, or tenant at will of the lord, paying heavy dues for that lord's protection while the village moot passed into the Court-baron, The forest too, lying unenclosed between *vill* and *vill*, became the lord's, and the dalesman had to pay as a tax or acknowledgment for continuing to make use of his old privileges within it. If the lord did not reserve it for the chase, he was very apt to grant a large portion of it to some stranger who had rendered him a service, thus creating a new species of land-tenure, called *bok-land*, because the grant was written down in a book, and that writing gave possession, in place of the older method of witness by the community. This new tenure created a new class of men, who were called free tenants, and took rank higher than the " tenants at will," because the suit and service they paid to the lord was—beyond the indispensable and most honourable service in arms—light and even complimentary in character. The rent being paid in the form of a hawk, a pair of spurs, a pair of gloves, a barbed arrow,* a rose even, though more generally of a pound of cummin, which was a spice used in noble households. Without a certain number of these free tenants, it was technically considered that a Court Baron could not be held.

Of *Bok-land* we have one well certified instance in our valley. It is the stretch of woodland called Bainrigg, lying in what must have been the primeval forest that separated the settlements of Grasmere and Rydal. It was a " free " holding, and is stated as late as the early seventeenth century, to have been held " by ancient charter."

---

* The Inq p m of Walter de Lindesay 56 Hen. III. No 61, whose free tenants in the barony furnished him with all these.

Bainriggs.

Manorium de Staueley. } John Fleming, Esqre holdethe off S^r Ja Bellingham knight off his manor off Staueley, by doinge suite off Court yearly, & paying yeerly one pound off Comyn, or two pence in monye, Tho^e Tenne Acres off Land or thereaboutes lying & being in Gresmire, nye unto or adioying unto gresmire Tarne, And holdeth ye premisses by an Ancyent Charter; And it is called Baineriggs; Late in ye Tenure of Robt Bainerigge,

A family of de Bainrig or de Baynbrig held it in the fourteenth century, when they were already divided into two branches, represented by Henry, who paid to the Lindesey Fee a " free " rent of 2d and a pound of cummin, and Richard, who paid in 1375 to the Hothom and Penwardyn Fee 30s. 6d. and a pound of cummin.* It is probably the former branch that is referred to in William de Lindesey's Inquisition of 1283 † as " a certain free tenant " of Grasmere who holds about four acres of land and renders half a pound of cummin. Later, an Inquisition of 1335 † speaks of four free tenants of Grasmere, paying 2s 8½d. besides the half-pound to the same Fee. In the 1375 rental of the other fee there appears the name of Beatrix de Wyresdale, who owned a " place " (of higher status than a tenement) now held by someone else. We hear also of a freehold held in Loughrigg (probably " Field Foot ") being held by rental of " 2d. and a peppercorn paid at the Feast of St. Michael to the chief lord of the Fee if lawfully demanded, with all other services and dues." Besides these, the family of Alan Pennyngton, knight, are found to be " free " holders of the manor of Lyttyl-Langdall in Strickeland Kettyll by homage and fealty and an annual gift of venison, this was in the middle of the thirteenth century; at which time William de Lancaster, the last baron who possessed the lands of Kendal undivided, likewise chartered the religious men

---

* Rentals at Levens Hall
† Inq p m. No. 36, 11 Ed I and No 74 (12) 8 Ed III

of Conishead Priory with adjacent lands at Baisbrowne and Elterwater. These two grants of *Bok-land* remain intact to this day, and are dignified by the names of manor though they consist only of the barren slope of Lingmoor, facing severally north and south with the few farmholds and fields that fringe the two river banks. But the " free " tenant of these valleys, if he had not greater possessions elsewhere, was not much higher in actual status than the dalesman or tenant at will ; and he was apt (like those of Grasmere) to drop into the latter's class. In the township of Rydal and Loughrigg as a rule there was no free tenant.

These settlements at the heads of the twin valleys, whose individual existence can be expressed only as *vills* or townships, can never have been closely attached to Windermere in a manorial sense The distance was too great for their men to attend a bi-yearly court at Windermere, or to obtain thence the supplies that were a lord's monopolies We find indeed, in the earliest record that gives details, that Grasmere was then serving, though without a lord's seat or manor-house, as a manorial centre for herself and her sister townships of Langdale and Loughrigg, as, probably, before the grant to Roger de Lancaster separating it finally from the surrounding lands, she had done for Rydal also. The fact that there the church was situated, whose boundaries embraced these neighbouring townships, gave to her a natural pre-eminence over them. The men of Langdale, Rydal and Loughrigg every Sunday set their faces for Grasmere, and entered its church for worship ; it was easy therefore to go thither for the Lord's Court, which was not improbably held in the church too, for want of another building, as it was at Windermere, as late as 1443.* The Levens' rental (about 1400) when accounting for the proceeds of that

---

* Court Roll 188/21 Hen VI.

roll of Grasmere which belonged to the Lindesey fee, explains " Half the hamlet there belongs to the lord, the other half belongs to the lord Hothom, knight. The aforesaid will hold a court together, the profits whereof ought to be equally shared between them." The Inquisition of the Duke of Bedford mentions that it was then the custom to hold a court in Grasmere thrice a year; and a roll for the court held there October 3, 1604, for the two fees or lordships, exist at the Record Office, though in the previous year (the first of King James') the men had been called to a court held at the moot-hall in Kendal.*

The Inquisition of 1283,† which is the first to furnish any particulars of the townships, shows that certain indispensable adjuncts to a manor existed then at Grasmere besides the " four acres of meadow in demesne " accounted for as worth 2s. 6d. yearly. While Langdale likewise possessed a corn-mill, Grasmere alone had a fulling mill, where the cloth, spun and woven in the homesteads, was bound to be carried for the dressing. There was a brewery there too, for which (and the monopoly attending it) a brew-wife (braceatrix) paid 6d yearly to the lord. It seems to have been the practice at that time to let out the right of brewing to women, who were perhaps considered more expert in the art, or to have more time than men. For King Edward I., in 1250, considering with his council sitting at Westminster certain complaints of faulty administration of justice in Westmorland which were brought before him, ends his edict thus :—" For the rest, the king wills that women brewers (braceresses) in that county may not for one amercement brew and sell all the year contrary to the assize and to their profit and to the damage of the people, but that they shall be punished according to the award of the county ‡ [court]

---

* Court Roll ???.
† On the death of William de Lindesay. Inq. p.m. No 36ᵇ 11 Ed I.
‡ Calendars of Close Rolls

as is done elsewhere in the realm." From which it appears that the canny wives of Westmorland, after paying a fine for brewing beer of a quality inferior to that presented by the "assize," went gaily on with the same profitable course, as do many modern defiers of the law.* The next brewer we hear of in Grasmere was a man.

The Hothom half of the lordship of Grasmere likewise possessed a brewery, situated at Kelbergh (Kelbarrow), for which 2s. 0d. was paid in 1375; and it appears later to have been held in partnership by several tenants there, who no doubt saw that the beer brewed was up to quality.† This half also possessed the monopoly of a forge (perhaps as a balance to the walk-mill), for which Richard Smith paid 12d. and 1d.

At a later date, these privileges of a walk-mill, a brewery, a shop and a forge—at first like the corn-mill, the exclusive property of the lord—came to be extended to each township; and to the growth of the walk or fulling industry, a chapter must be subsequently devoted. Thus Loughrigg came to possess a corn-mill and a brewery.

We hear too, of a shop in Grasmere, which furnished 2d. to the lord. For no more than one accredited trader, who bartered the very few necessities of life which the dalesman could not produce from his land and within his homestead, was tolerated on the manor.

About the shop, or stores, we hear from the subsidies of later times, for all persons owning goods above a certain value were taxed; and the ordinary dalesman's property not coming up to the fixed sum, only the storekeeper paid. In 1626-7 John Knott in Grasmere paid on goods; George Jackson in Ambleside; Edward Benson of High Close in Rydal and Loughrigg; and in Langdale

---

* The fines of brewers for breach of assize, paid to the Lindesay Fee in Ulverston, amounted to 25s 0d. yearly in 1347. Inq. pm., No 63 (2 Nrs) 20 Ed III.

† This portion of the Levens document is too mutilated to be consecutively legible.

two men (probably allowed because of the scattered nature of the township), viz. Charles Middlefell and Regnald Willson. This limit is maintained down to the subsidy of 1675, the names only of the accredited shop-keepers changing from time to time.* The traders of Rydal village (of which we shall hear later) seem to have escaped taxation. There was a little shop down to recent times.

CHAPTER VIII

The Lord's Demands

Inquisition of Queen Elizabeth; Suit and Service; The Godpenny; "Old" and "New" Tenants; Arbitrary and Extortionate Fines in the manor in the Seventeenth, Eighteenth and Nineteenth Centuries; "General" and "Dropping" Fines; The Income Fine.

THE lord of the manor's receipts did not stop with his monopoly of industries, and his profits on courts and assizes. Many and various were the obligations by which the dalesman was bound to him. But though his steward wrote down the Tenant on the court roll, as "tenant at will" of his lord, "ad voluntatem domini," he had no power to dispossess him of the holding he had inherited, except for felony or murder. But he could tax him. And this he did, upon every occasion possible, both on the extraordinary occasions of death and inheritance, and on annual ones. The dalesman paid not only fines and heriots, but a yearly tax, called rent, on his holding: he paid yearly for the increase of his flock, for the hewing of timber and the grazing of his cattle in the forest; if he enclosed and worked a little garden on his own land by his homestead,

---

* Rydal Hall MSS

he paid upon that, and if he kept fowls, he was obliged to furnish the Hall larder with a hen every year. Besides all this he had not only to serve in war if required, under his lord, but he had to assist when a hunt was forward, and at the harvesting of the lord's crops.

Originally no doubt the dalesman's dues were all paid to the lord in kind, or by boon-service The dues differed in different places according to the character of the place and of the lord's pursuits ; and some strange ones survived down to recent times.

These no doubt had their origin in some ancient bargain struck between lord and tenant, which growing fixed as "custom" became the law of the village communities, and tenaciously held by as a right But many dues in kind were exchanged gradually for small payments in money. These were fixed in sum, as was the annual rent upon the holding. The lord, having no power to raise these, sought as time went on, to raise the fine or gressum and heriot due when the tenant died and his next-of-kin inherited, or when he himself succeeded to the lordship. Such attempts were stoutly contested by the tenants, on the plea of custom and tenant-right, with varying success ; and the smaller and weaker communities, and those that came more directly under the personal influence of the lord, were forced to yield, as we shall see. The question had become such a burning one in the time of the Tudors, that Queen Elizabeth, when the main portion of the lordship of Kendal came into her hands, (including both the Richmond and Marquis Fees), caused an Inquisition to be held at Kendal, when a jury of landowners sworn for the purpose, declared before her commissioners, the Customs of the Lordship, as they had been handed down from times beyond the memory of man.

This verdict, written down, and confirmed in 1574, served as a useful text. Many copies of it were made, and were carefully preserved by such customary tenants in the lordship—of which there were not a few—as had become large land-holders. The copy used here is from the Phillipps MSS.

Another, in the possession of Mr. Pollitt, is essentially the same, but for difference of wording and spelling. It seems to have been made for a Mr. H. Crossfield of Godmond Hall in Strikeland-Roger. Mr. Gawen Braithwaite, of Ambleside Hall, who was a large customary holder, had a splendid copy of the customs made up on a parchment roll, which (in its original case) was possessed by Mr. George Browne up to the time of his death.

In spite of this settlement of vexed questions for those fortunate holders (including those of Grasmere, Langdale, Ambleside and part of Loughrigg) who were in the royal lordship, King James tried to completely upset the land-tenure of these parts. On the pretext that border-warfare had ceased with the Union of the two kingdoms, and that the customary tenant was no longer called to serve in it, he claimed that the whole bargain between him and his lord broke down, and that the land reverted to the lord.

At this threatened deprivation, the tenants drew together, prepared to make a stubborn defence of their rights ; but there is no doubt that the £2,700 which some of them collected and offered to the crown as a fine or bribe, was a main factor in procuring a settlement and confirmation of those rights. The matter was only concluded, indeed, on the death of James ; and even then, the proposed settlement by the court of star chamber, of the disputes between lord and tenant of adjoining lands which naturally had arisen at this juncture seems never to have taken place. Upon some manors it is said that the dalesman compounded with his superiors as to the amount of the fines exacted ; and it is to be feared that the lord, who here had his opportunity, in many cases pressed hard on his poorer tenants.*

---

* See Nicolson and Burn for a complete account of the long proceedings that resulted from James' action.

These fines and rents and taxes, of whose amounts we have little evidence before the date of Queen Elizabeth's Inquisition, we may now consider more particularly, taking those first in order which were due on extraordinary occasions, as on inheritance and on death of the lord, and the widow's heriot ; and next the annual ones, such as " boon " service and rents.

The Gressum or Fine

On the death of a land-holder, his successor, whether he was classed as a free or a customary tenant, was bound to appear at the court of the lord and claim admission to the inherited holding. When the court had ceased to perform any other functions but the exaction of extraordinary fines, it was called together specially, even in places as small as Rydal, for the admission of a tenant. This was no doubt a relic of the freer times of the village community, when each member received his lands by witness of the whole community assembled at the moot. No document was needed for the holding of folk-land, since the testimony of a holder's fellows proved his right of possession Title-deeds indeed began to be written in the seventeenth century when a holding was sold and passed into strange hands ; but the majority of the village lands were still held by the simple and formal admission at the court. The deeds of the Field Foot estate in Loughrigg, which had become freehold, go no further back than its sale in 1773 ; and within the last twelve years an estate in Grasmere passed into the hands of its purchaser without a single document but the immediate contract

The tenant on his admission paid in the " open face of Court " a piece of silver known as a God's penny. Originally this would be the old English silver penny, set down as a token or confirmation of a transaction which secured to the new holder his inherited land " according to Ancient Custom, known as Tenant Right." The God's penny came, however, for the customary tenant, to bear a relative value to the value of the land so passed over ; and that value, exacted as a gressum or fine to the lord, tended ever to increase.

There seems to be some slight ground for supposing this fine to have been fixed for the whole of the barony of Kendal in time of the Norman settlement, at double the annual rent paid to the lord. We have no means of guaging the proportion of the gressums that appear in the accounts of 1515-6,* when John Gyrrigge pays 66s 8d for a messuage with lands inherited from his father William, in Langdale and another 20s for property in Loughrigg, and Henry Coke pays 6s. 8d. in Loughrigg, because their rents are not told. But an agreement which was drawn up in 1572, between the tenants and lord of the little manor of Braisbrowne (long held by the Priory of Conishead, but now in the hands of the Benson family) reveal to us the old custom in that remote quarter of the barony. It states that the tenants there

holding " acordinge to th annciannte and laudable custome of the countrie called Tenn't-riyghte commonlye used within the baronye of Kendall withoute memorie of man always payed to the said John [Benson] and all other persons for the tyme beinge Lord thereof onlie the double rente and no more for and in the name of a gresshume or ffyne." Now, however, as certayne debaite and variannce before this time hathe happenyed and growne " between the two, " sundry frendes " have brought about an agreement, by which John Benson undertakes on the receipt of a certain sume of money tendered to him by these tenants, to claim no more from them in future than twice the rent for any fine on change of lord and tenant †

The Inquisition of 1574 states indeed that in the Richmond Fee of the barony every old tenant pays on change of lord or tenant a fine equal to two years rent, but a new tenant pays a sum equal to three times the rent, except

---

* Ministers Account, Henry VII 877.
† Rydal Hall MSS.

in the " forests of Troutbecke and Ambleside," where the old tenant pays but once the rent and the new tenant twice the rent. But the rental of customs for the Marquis Fee given in the same Inquisition declares that at change either of lord or tenant every tenant ought to pay double the rent only, adding that if larger sums were paid to the late marquis or marchioness (as is apparent by the acquittances), these sums were given only of the good-will of the tenant or by the persuasion of the lord's officers, and such payment " is not hurtful to the custom."

It is difficult to understand the distinction made between " old " and " new " tenant in the customs of the Richmond Fee.* Perhaps the old was one who could claim by long descent, going back beyond certain " new rental " which was made out in the year 1500. At any rate we find at a court held for the Marquis Fee on September 12, 1602, the following admissions made. Robert Richardson, for fine and entry into one tenement in Grasmere inherited from his father, rent 10d.; fine 2s. 6d., being three times the rent. Thomas Richardson, inheriting likewise a tenement from his father, the same. John Knott, for fine and entry into a tenement inherited from his father, Edward, rent 2s. 6d. and ⅓ of a penny; fine " at the rate of two annual rents (for this time only) because he paid to the Receiver of the lord the king aforesaid at the general survey the fine for his said father thereupon, at the rate of the three yearly rents which he ought to pay, for him only at the rate of two yearly rents, because he was an ancient tenant " 5s. 0d. John likewise paid for admission to another tenement, rent 4s. 5d., a fine of 8s. 10d. And John Hunter inheriting from his father John, as well as Reynold Thomson from Robert Grigge, and John Wrenn from Peter Wrenn all pay " at the rate aforesaid," that

---

* The tenants presentment of their case against James I, state *old tenants* to imply a change of lord and *new tenants* a change of holder by death or alienation See Nicolson and Burn.

is, at double the rent; though again in the final entry the words occur " for this time only," as if the lord reserved a right to set the fine higher.*

The fine appears to have remained fixed, from that time at three times the rent, at all events for the whole of the Richmond Fee, except Ambleside and Troutbeck which was twice the rent; and this irrespective of " old " and " new " tenants.† For admissions show that John Forrest, when inheriting in 1597, from Henry, paid a fine of 26s. 8d. on a rent of 13s. 4d., and Edward Forrest when inheriting in 1626 from John, 40s. on a rent of 20s., though the tenure of the Forrests went back to ancient times. And at a court held at Ambleside in 1707, George and Richard Cumpston were admitted to the many parcels of lands inherited by them from George Mackereth at almost the same rate; namely, a fine of £3 17s. 2d., on a rent of £1 18s. 7d., another of £1 11s. 2d. on a rent of 15s. 10d., and others of 13s. 4d., on a 6s 8d. rent.

For Cockstone (now stepping-stones) in Loughrigg, a customary holding of the Richmond Fee, a God's penny and 5s. 0d. was paid as admission in full court by Lancelot Fleming inheriting from his father John, in 1785, and again in 1819 by Thomas Fleming inheriting from Lancelot; the sum being exactly three times the rent of 8d.

The internal economy of the small " manor " of Rydal is unknown for almost four centuries after it fell to the lordship of Roger de Lancaster, because for that period no manorial records have been preserved Originally its customs must have been almost identical with those of the neighbouring villages and lands, at all events as far as obligations to their joint lord were concerned. But

---

* Public Record Office, Court Roll ²⁴⁷.

† At Courts held at Kendal, 1625 to 1641 for the marquis Fee, tenants of the other side of the barony—Helsington, Hutton in the Hay, Underbarrow, &c., are all charged on admission a fine of three times the rent.

‡ Rydal Hall MSS.

they emerge, after the dark epoch, as considerably altered from those of the Richmond and Marquis' lands adjoining. The isolation of the village from those lands, under the rule of a separate lord who owned a seat in the place had not been favourable to the freedom of the community. While the Loughrigg men across the river, and the men of Langdale and Grasmere on one side and those of Ambleside on the other, were free with their graves or reeves to manage the affairs of their *vills*, on the old lines, little disturbed by the occasional visits of the distant lord's officers, and stoutly resisting any increased demands of those officers, the men of Rydal fell under the restraints of a personal connection with their lord, whose claims they had little power to contest Isolated as they were, they had to submit to encroachments on their village common lands and to the rise of the gressum; for there was no joint sufferer in other *vills* with whom to join hands so as to offer their lord a strong united opposition and along with it a seasonable bribe collected from among their richer members

Perhaps it was in the convulsion, created by King James' action, that the Rydal fines were raised; since no general confirmation of old customs was secured at the end of it by the tenants of resident lords in the barony, as was the case with the tenants of the royal lord At all events, on the succession of Daniel Fleming to the manor of Rydal in 1655, we find the fines much higher than in the neighbouring places. This energetic and able man left not only an account of the manorial customs of Rydal, in writing, but papers showing the fines he exacted from the tenants on his entry as lord. He declares that they are bound to pay

"such Arbitrary Fines of Gersumes as their Lord shall be pleased to assess and demand, upon ye change of every Lord of ye said Manor by death, and upon ye change of every Tenant there, by death or Alienation."

THE LORD'S DEMANDS

The tenants however never acknowledged this arbitrary fine for both occasions, as we shall see; and they personally "compounded" with their new lord when he held his court, seeking as large an abatement in the sum of the fine as they could secure from him.

Accordingly, we find that the fines were fixed at a varying proportion to the rent, but all at a figure that is astonishing when we consider the basis of a two and three years rent obtaining in all the lands around. The lowest of them stand at a ten years rent, as when Thomas Hobson pays £6 13s. 4d. on a rent of 13s. 4d. From that they rise through a varying ratio to fifteen and twenty times the rent, the latter being possibly considered the normal limit; though it is twice exceeded, Elizabeth Gregg paying thirty times (or 15s. 0d. on a 6d. rent) for what was probably the village shop, and the wealthiest statesman Edward Walker, who possessed several holdings, as much as thirty-three times the rent. It is clear that the lord wrung from each what he thought the holder could pay, the husbandman Edward Grigg's fine being fixed at £4 10s. 0d. on a 7s. 3d. rent, and Thomas Fleming's—husbandman, carpenter and inn-keeper as well—at £7 0s. 0d. on a 7s. 2d. rent. Graduated as they were, it is to these fines, imposed upon men who often had not the ready money to pay with, that we can trace the ruin of several statesman-families in the place. John Thompson, for instance, whose fine in 1655 was fixed at £5 10s. 0d. on a 6s. 8d. rent, was already two years in arrears. The fines were kept up after this to about the twenty-multiple of rent, with a general tendency to rise upon any opportunity.

At a court held September 24 1760, George Parke inheriting from John, paid a *dropping fine* of £5 16s. 8d. on a rent of 5s. 10d., and another of £2 10s. 0d. on one of 2s. 6d., while Matthew Fleming, purchasing from John Grigg, paid £7 8s 4d. on a rent of 7s. 5d.

In 1778 William Park was admitted to Nab for £11 0s. 0d. on an 11s. 0d. rent, and to a "parcel" for £1 13s. 4d. on 1s. 8d. John Grigg had been admitted in 1746 for £7 8s. 4d. on a rent of 7s. 5d., and in 1748 William Robinson was admitted to Kittsgill in Loughrigg for 15s. 0d. on a rent of 9d.

When Mr. George Knott died in 1785, the customary holdings in Rydal which his family had possessed since the ruin of Walker carried a rent of £1 6s. 10d. The steward proceeded to fix the fines due from Mr. Knott's trustees " on the different parcels " at £40 10s. 0d., but agreed not to insist on the payment before writing for Sir Michael le Fleming's directions, " because tho' the Tenants agree the *General Fine* [on death of lord] is arbitrary, they acknowledge the Dropping Fines [on death of tenant] are twenty penny Fines only and are not subject to variation." And on this latter basis the fine was finally settled.

The General Fine, which the lord claimed to be able to fix on an arbitrary basis, seems to have been leniently laid when the bishop of Carlisle inherited from his brother Sir William, to judge from the £6 6s. 0d. charged to William Grigg on a rent of 7s. 5d. It did not, as we shall see, much exceed a twenty-multiple on the death of Lady Dorothy Fleming in 1788. It rose however on the death of Sir Michael le Fleming in 1806 to an unprecedented figure.

There grew up a tendency too, when village holdings became disintegrated, and were sold on the ruin of their inheritor, and when a statesman added a piece of what had formerly been his neighbour's land to his own, to charge a separate fine (and often at a higher rate) for the "parcel." A counsel's opinion was asked on this practice by a tenant on the Lowther manor in 1731, who was disposed to contest the various fines demanded from him by the lord's steward when the latter, in order to increase his own fees (it was stated) made out these separate admissions. Counsel replied ambiguously, that the custom of the place was to be considered, though his opinion leant against the steward. The practice certainly obtained in Rydal. At a court held on August 30, 1769, Jane Wilkinson, daughter of John Wilkinson and Agnes Harrison " both of Loughrigg " married, 1729, was admitted tenant, with the following fines for the principal holding (the old " Davids " which she had inherited from the Harrisons) and for parcels.

Rent.		Fine.		
s.	d	£	s	d.
3	0	3	10	0
0	4	0	6	8
0	8	0	13	4
0	4	0	6	8

And John Parke at the same time paid a 6s 8d fine on a parcel that carried 4d. rent. In 1807, George Birkett's admittance to one half the close called Dockey Tarn, of which the rent was 4d., cost him 8s. 7d., and he paid on it for Sir Michael's death 10s. 0d.

Then too there was the " Income " fine, which Daniel Fleming claimed for the lord.

" If any stranger (viz. one who is not Tenant within ye said Manor) shall *Buy* any House, Land, or Tenement, within the said Manor, he is obliged by custom to pay forty shillings to ye Lord as an "*Income*" over and above his fine, or so much thereof as his Lord pleaseth to take."

Accordingly, when John Birkett, a carpenter of Rydal, bought in 1707 a little house for himself carrying a rent of 6d. he not only compounded with his lord (Sir William Fleming) for an admission fine of 10s. 0d., but he paid also an income fine of £2. 0s. 0d. It was not always pressed so hardly. John Bateman, buying only half a tenement in 1769, paid £2. 18s. 4d. on a 2s. 11d. rent, with an additional " Income " fine of 15s. od. and William Richardson paid, on his purchase of the old smithy in 1769, besides his fine of £1. 0s 0d. on a 1s. 0d. rent, only 5s. 0d. as " income " fine.

CHAPTER IX

THE HERIOT

An Odious Tax; Difficulty of Compounding; Cottage Restrictions.

THE tax of the heriot is said to have existed only in those parts of England that were settled by Scandinavians or Danes,* and to have had its origin in the military service demanded of the freeman, whose lord furnished him with horse or with weapons when he was called to the war. Subsequently it came to be the custom on the death of the landowner for his widow (if he left one) to furnish the lord with the best beast of which he died possessed " in ye name of an harriott," (Inquisition of 1574) and by this the holding is confirmed to her for life. In times when record is forthcoming, this claim to the best beast was compounded for and paid in money. The stewards of the Richmond Fee, in such early accounts as have been preserved, invariably enter the assets, or non-assets, from this source; but no particulars are given. The courts held at Kendal, indeed, in Stuart times, furnish more particulars for the other side of the barony. In 1625 a widow's heriot is appraised at 26s. 8d., on a yearly rent of 19s.; another at 24s. 8d. on a rent of 20s., and a third and fourth at 40s., and £3, rent unquoted. The sum appears to have been proportionate to the rent. The Rydal Hall account-books show for 1646

---

* See Vinagradoff's *English Society in Eleventh Century*. On the other hand the Church originally claimed the best beast.

"Rec. of Anthonie Harrison wife for a Herriott, 20 Jan.
1^l 10^s 0^d

This was upon a rent of 7s. 8d. Daniel Fleming demanded more; and in 1662 agreed with "Simon Park wife for a Hariot" at £3 10s 0d on a rent of 11s. 6d. Two neighbour statesmen stood surety for her, as no money was immediately forthcoming, her husband having only shortly before his death finished the payments of his own "general" fine on entrance of a new lord, and that due on the death of his father; which amounted in all to £13.

Next year a Rydal widow did better, for the lord entered in his April accounts

"Tho. Hobson's wife is to pay me betwixt (*sic*) and Martinmas 1663, for her Hariott, ye sum of 02^l 10^s 00^d The rent was 13s 4d.

In 1671 Thomas Fleming undertook—perhaps on his mother's account—to pay £2. 2s. 4d. for "A Heriot-sow of his Father's," which surely at the price must have been a superior animal for breeding In 1697, widow Agnes Harrison and her son David are found giving the lord a bill for £20, "for 5 Heriots sold her." This entry seems to imply that this tax was sometimes farmed.

In 1759, £1. 11s. 6d. was paid as "Heriot for John Johnson's Tenement in Rydal Manor," and as the expenses concerning the same are set down as 2s. 0d., there must have been some difficulty in securing it. Next year "2 Hariots of Widow Birkets" stand at the high figure of £9; and one of Otley's in 1763 at £2. This shows that the demand for a separate heriot on each "parcel" like the fine, had begun to be demanded. In 1791 George Rigg of Clappersgate died, who had inherited the old Harrison or "David" holding in Rydal. In order to secure payment of the four heriots demanded, the steward of the manor (Thomas Harrison, lawyer of Kendal) despatched an officer to the premises, and he seized a horse, a cow, a clock, and a feather bed, "well worth together" the steward gleefully writes, "the £15 demanded." Whether the abatement upon this claim, which the widow begged, was made, we have no information. The "tenement" carried a rent of 3s. 6d., and the "parcels" could not have been more.

On the death of Mr. Blakeney in 1522, who had bought the Fox How estate in the Rydal manor, his trustees refused to pay the heriot demanded from his widow, whereupon the lord's officer rode off to Whitehaven (where he had lived) to seize a horse or some other animal that had been his.

By this time the Gressum and the Heriot had become as odious to the people as they seemed to be unreasonable. Their meaning had in fact been lost. That personal connection with the lord, which had been deemed of so sacred a character that in Alfred's laws treachery towards him had been the one uncompoundable sin, and which had been loyally sustained so long as the men of the village had ridden out with him to the wars, was now a thing of nought. Through slow ages the bondage of an effete "custom" had been borne, and with a dignity and fine temper that had done credit to the dalesman; for indeed his relations with his lord had almost always been excellent; and even when there was discontent, friction and rebellion, he was disposed to blame not so much his superior, but that superior's officer, whose own fees were increased by all he could squeeze from the manor. The fine on admission to the family holding might still have been cheerfully borne, even on a twenty multiple basis, as is the legacy duty now exacted by the government; but the arbitrary fines on the death of a lord were severely felt. They came unexpectedly, and often at times when the little holding had not recovered from the drain of the last demand.

The Knott estate for instance had had to bear a fine, on death of the holder in 1785, of over £20; and, on the death of Lady Dorothy Fleming in 1788, another of £30 was exacted. The decease of this old lady, widow of the first Sir William, who for long had not resided in Rydal but who was reckoned as "an admitting lord" or one who had held courts of admission, wrung a large sum from the few struggling statesmen of Rydal, which went into the pockets of Sir Michael's tradesmen in London and into those of his steward. Only eight years later the death of Sir Michael himself gave opportunity to the steward to demand the arbitrary fine of forty times the rent, which from the Knott estate would produce over £40 *

From this terrible imposition of the arbitrary fine in 1806 the tenants had no legal redress. A letter was addressed to Miss le Fleming, by one Thomas Ellis, who was trustee for six orphans to whom the little estate of Fox How had descended, praying that, as the fine would deprive them of all source of income from the estate for three years, she would grant a little relief. Probably the young heiress had no power of interference, and the estate was sold to Mr. Blakeney. The opposition aroused by this fine was so strong, that some of the tenants— William Park of the Nab, and Thomas Fleming and James Backhouse among them refused to pay their lord's rents, hoping no doubt to force from the manor some concession

Efforts after enfranchisement from the lord's claims had indeed long been made by the statesmen of the valleys. Though those who held in the Richmond and Marquis Fees had enjoyed the fixed low fines confirmed by Elizabeth and James, they desired to be able to free themselves from those by the payment of a reasonable sum of money. Besides this, the heriot, as exacted by the Lowther family (after its purchase of these fees) came to be a source of discontent. Its unreasonableness was apparent in the case of the school lands of Ambleside, left by John

---

* Mr Michael Knott appears also to have paid a fine in 1803 of £25 16s 0d., perhaps on his coming of age

Kelsick to the town. For when Mr. John Knott died, who had acted as trustee for the endowment, a heriot was demanded by the lord, because he had left a widow; and as the injustice of charging her with it was manifest, it was suggested that the remaining trustees should pay. Then the mode of collecting the heriot, when an officer of the lord entered a dead man's premises, and forcibly seized any valuable beast or piece of furniture, that should cover the sum demanded (often exorbitant), was peculiarly irritating. `We find therefore, when a strong effort was being made in 1711 by the customary tenants of the barony of Kendal to bring their difficulties before parliament, and to obtain an Act for a just settlement of their relations to their lord, that, of the eight articles proposed, the one which should fix the heriot to a sum only three times the rent was considered the most pressing.*
Nothing, unfortunately, seems to have come of this effort.

In 1789, George Birkitt of Rydal freed his holding of the heriot that would have been due from his widow, by the payment of a certain sum during his life, which reached the high figure of £32. 10s. 0d., this did not affect his fine.

The Knotts, who were not only well-to-do customary tenants of Rydal, but for two generations had acted as stewards to the manor, and were connected by marriage with the lord, made several efforts for freeing their land, first from the fines and heriots, and then from all rentals. It was a difficult matter; but from the following undated statement, it is clear that Mr. Michael Knott was willing to compensate, not only the present lord (Bishop of Carlisle) and his heir, but all members of the family who might have a possible future claim on the manor.

---

* Correspondence of Lady Otway and Benjamin Browne MSS. of Mr. G Browne

THE HERIOT

MEMORANDUM; no name or date attached.

"I propose to give for purchasing only the Fines & Heriots of my small Estate at Rydall, being willing to Continue the Rent, Boons, & Services, the Rent being 19s 2d, & 12 Boon Days yearly, that is 4 days mowing, 4 Days Shearing, & 4 Days Leading Manure; The sd Small Estate was purchased by my Grand-father & only cost him £100

To my Lord Bishop for Conveying his Right to the Fines &c	20. 0. 0.
To Mr Archdeacon Fleming for Conveying his Right	20. 0. 0
To Lady Fleming for Conveying Her Right	10. 0. 0.
To Mr Wm Fleming for Sealing	5 0. 0
To Mr Danl Fleming for Sealing	5. 0. 0.
To Mr Fletcher Fleming for Sealing	5. 0 0
	65 0 0.

However on Mr Knott's death, the proceedings had not terminated. Mr. George Knott wrote in 1774 to one of the officials of the manor, asking for an answer regarding Rydal Enfranchisement

"as I could wish to know whether it would be agreeable to you to confirm what your Father and the rest of the Remainder men has executed and the consideration Money paid by my Father & whether I may be permitted to gett fresh Deeds Drawn for your Inspection there is one very small Tenement called Banks' Tenement" (this the writer had inherited from his uncle Edward) "which is not included in the old Enfrancht but could wish to have it on the same Footing as the other it being so intermixed with the other Land."

When George's son, Michael Knott, sold in 1803 or 1804 the whole estate to Mr. Ford North, no terms of enfranchisement had been settled, and the negotiations continued by the new tenant were finally broken off in 1812, when he was required to pay up arrears of fines, rents, and boons. Disgusted and wearied by the whole proceedings, Mr. Ford North consented to sell the estate out and out to the Rydal manor, and bought property that should be a home in Ambleside.

In 1820, the refractory Rydal tenants—who for the last six years had been joined by George Birkitt in their refusal to pay rent—were brought to a stand. A court was held by the Revd. Thomas Jackson (then acting as steward) and a lawyer, on August 15, to insist on the payment of arrears, and to consult (it was stated) as to the " sale of Allotments " At this court John Fleming and William Park were compelled to produce respectively £14. 11s 0d. and £8. 6s. 0d. for fourteen years arrears, and George Birkitt £5. 17s 0d James Backhouse—less well-to-do than they—had weakened, and had already paid his eleven years arrears (£1. 2s. 10d.) in 1817. Perhaps some hope was held out to these indignant statesmen that reasonable terms would be granted for the enfranchisement of their holdings At any rate through the following year a good deal of discussion as to terms took place , and Mr. Robert Blakeney, holder of Fox How, offered £28. 0s. 0d. to free his estate, which was rented at 3s. 4d. But no settlement could be effected, except by James Fleming, who freed his small property for £25.

The restriction of the number of souls to a cottage and the rule against taking a lodger shows how the landlord was able to interfere with the liberty of his tenant in what to us would seem an unwarrantable manner , but in the eighteenth century the lord of the land gave the Cottage a privilege which he subsequently lost and has often vainly tried to recapture. For the following Act of parliament was passed in the 31st of Elizabeth, 1588.

" For the avoiding of the great inconvenience which are found by experience to grow by the erecting and building of great numbers and multitude of Cottages, which are daily more and more increased in many parts of this Realme Be it enacted by the Queans most excellent Majesty, *and the Lords Spirituall and Temporall,* and the Commons in this present parliament Assembled and by Authority of the same, that after the end of this session of parliament no person shall within this Realme of England make, build, or erect or cause to be made builded or erected, any maner of Cottage for habitation or dwelling, nor convert or ordaine any building or housing made or hereafter to be made, *to be used as a Cottage for habitation or dwelling, unless the same person do assigne and lay to the same Cottage or building, foure acres of ground at the least,* to be acompted according to the Statute or ordinance de terris mensurandis, being his or her own freehold and inheritance, lying near to the said Cottage, to be continually occupied and manured therewith, so long as the same Cottage be inhabited, upon pane that every such offendor shall forfeit to our Sovereigne Lady the Queen's Majesty, her heires and successors x li of lawfull money of England, for every such offence "

1686 April 16th At a General Sessions held at Kirkby Kendal by adjournment—present Daniel Fleming, Kt., Edward Wilson Sen[r], William Fleming, Edward Wilson Jun[r], and John Fisher, Esquires,

John Cookson late of Troutbeck, was *Indicted for having built & maintained a Cottage for habitation, without having assigned sufficient Land to the same* (according to the above statute). The cottage in question is what is now the farm house at *Low Skelgil*, Troutbeck.

1737. Easter Sessions—*John Birkett* presented for having, &c , *a Cottage without assigning 4 acres of land to it.* The following presentment of the jury.

Westmorland to wit
The Jurors for our Sovereign Lord the King, upon their Oaths p'sent that John Birkett late of Troutbeck in the county aforesaid gentleman, on the fourth day of July in the year of our Lord one thousand seven hundred and thirty four at Troutbeck aforesaid in the County aforesaid, did support, uphold, maintain and continue, one cottage house lying in Troutbeck aforesaid in the County aforesaid, for the Inhabitation of one Will[m] Wilson, when in truth and in fact the said John Birkett never laid or assigned to the said Cottage Four Acres of Freehold land according to the ordination of measureing & computing land, to be so near the said Cottage that the same four acres of land might be continually occupied with the said Cottage so long as the said Cottage should be Inhabited, to the great contempt of our Sovereign Lord the King, and against the peace and against the form of the Statute in that case made and provided. And the said Jurors

further upon their Oaths present, that the said John Birkett the same Cottage so as aforesaid converted for habitation, from the said fourth day of July one thousand seven hundred and thirty four, untill the first day of April one thousand seven hundred and thirty seven at Troutbeck aforesaid in the County aforesaid, willingly sustained, maintained, upheld and continued, to the great contempt of our sovereign Lord the King, and against the peace and against the form of the Statute in that case made and provided

                  Will Wilkin Cl. of the peace

It was also enacted the Statute 31 Elizabeth Cap. VII.

" that from and after the feast of All Saints next coming *There shall not be any Inmate or more famlies or housholds than one, dwelling or inhabiting in any one Cottage* made or to be made or erected, upon paine that every Owner or occupier of any such Cottage placing or willingly suffering any such Inmate, or other family than one, shall forfeit and lose to the Lord of the Leet, within which ye cottage shall be, the same summe of ten shillings, of lawfull money of England for every moneth, that such any Inmate, or other family than one, shall dwell or inhabit in any one Cottage as aforesaid " &c , &c.

The Act of the 31st *Eliz. Cap. VII.* was *repealed* 15th *George the* 3rd (1774) by an Act setting forth,

" that the said Statute of 31st Eliz had laid the industrious poor under great difficulties to procure habitations, and tended very much to lessen population, and in divers other respects was inconvenient to the labouring part of the nation in general."

            Cottages with less than 4 acres.

In 1735, the Great-House Estate, Troutbeck, was sold in parcels. The house, out-buildings and a small portion of land was sold to James Birkett of Calgarth, who sold a field off it to John Cookson in 1735—whom the lord refused to admit tenant of the said field, as will be seen from the following endorsement of Cookson's deed—

| Manor of Troutbeck parcel of the Manor of Windermere &c | 20th June 1730 This Deed was presented But be it remembered that this deed was rejected, tho' presented in due Time |

by reason that there was not sufficient Land left with the Messuage and Tenement called Great House, whereof the Premises within Mention were parcel, but as there is now another parcel of the said Great House Tenement repurchased to it, the within-named John Cookson is now admitted to it

At a Court there holden for the said Manor."
           Before
            Hu Holme
             Dep Steward.

CHAPTER X

YEARLY DUES

Boon Service; Yeld; Walking-silver; Geld-wether; Forest-silver; The Common Pasture; Appendix; Rights of Common.

OF the various annual dues exacted by the lord, the Boon services take precedence, as being most ancient in character. They were never severe in these parts, and in fact appear to have been non-existent in most of the village communities of the valleys When the barons of Kendal ruled the wild fell lands without an intermediate lord, it would have been hopeless to try to draw men from the sources of Rothay and Brathay to help at the getting in of the manorial hay or corn. Once indeed we hear of demesne land in Grasmere, but no tradition of boon labour there has come down to us. The boon service of the fields hereabouts was a late importation, introduced by the few lords who, after the break up of the barony, took up their seat in their small manors. It is probable—nay almost certain—that the Norman lords did impose service on such tenants as lived within the deer forests, when the hunt was forward, in warding or turning back the deer [see later]. And such service may have been performed for Sir Roger de Lancaster and his followers by the Rydal men on this side of the mountains, as they were certainly performed on the other.* They may afterwards have been exchanged when the deer were no longer hunted, and the lord became resident on a demesne farm, for that boon service in the seventeenth century. Sir Daniel Fleming summarized these when he wrote out a list of the tenants in 1655 as " yearly 1 day mowing, 1 day shearing, & 1 day leading of manor (= manure), but Grasmer tenants are excepted, haveing no Calve grasses in y^e Nab. Yearly 2 Tenants by Turne are to helpe to wash ye sheep." Afterwards, in his account of the manor, he is more expansive and more ambiguous. They are to do, he says, so many days mowing and shearing " as they are named in ye Rental excepting onely for Baneriggs, which payeth yearly two of either."

Only when the old freehold of Bainrigg passed into the manor of Rydal in Squire John Fleming's time could it have been brought into the line of " customary tenure " by boon service. The service of sheep-shearing was perhaps late, for we find it separately insisted on in the admission of one of the tenants.

In a MS. at Rydal Hall, we have the following —

" And likewise each of them the same number of dayes *Leading of Manure* (haveing onely a dinner) for so many Calves grasses in ye Nab " This last bargain and obligation is supposed not to be older than the reign of Dame Agnes Fleming, who introduced improved methods of agriculture on the demesne Sir Daniel also cites another boon labour. " All the said Tenants, upon warning or summons from their Lord's Sheepheard, or other servant, are obliged by their custom to helpe yearly to make ye Wash-Pool, and to Lait, or look for, the Lords sheep for washing, clipping, and putting ye Ewes to Tupp, or Ram , And ye said Tenants are, upon Sumons to assist ye Lord's Sheepheard in all *Snows and other Storms* , and two of them yearly by turn, are to help to wash the Lord's Sheep within ye said Manor."

---

* Inquisition of 17

That the tenants faithfully performed service in the hay-fields, in person or by deputy, is shown in the carefully kept lists of boon-mowers, which reach down to the year 1733.

They were willing also to give their lord that help which they always furnished each other on the extraordinary occasion of a house or barn "raising," as Sir Daniel's Account Book shows [see later]. Indeed, boon-service rendered each to each was a main feature of the village community, which survived a century ago in the small dalesman's hay meadows, as it survives to-day in the annual sheep-clipping.

The boon-hen, which was in some parts of the barony demanded by the lord after poultry was introduced, (with the reduction of a 1d. from the green-hew rent) was not required from the Rydal tenants. The Coniston tenants however each supplied one; and as many as 43 or 44 arrived at Rydal Hall.

The Rydal papers show that one tenant is called on to pay the arrears for three half-year's rent, besides 5s. 6d. for the pasture of his cattle on the common; total £1. 10s. He does what he can in payment of this debt by producing for his lord, one fat calf, valued at 7s. 0d., two sheep, valued at 12s. 0d., by his wife's labour in the Hall hay-field, at 6d. a day and his own in greasing the lord's sheep at 6d. a day. But in a very few years his name has dropped from the roll of the manor.

The early Inquisitions and Rentals account for, as dues paid yearly to the lord by the tenants of the barony, Forest-silver, Gold or Geld-wether, Yeld, and Walking-silver.

Yeld. It is not certain what the tax called yeld covered. It is mentioned in the Levens Rental of 1375, as "a gressum called yeld," which was due from the Grasmere and Langdale men who held under the Hothom Fee.

Walking (or Walkyn) *silver*. There has been some discussion as to what this tax covered; but it seems clear that it refers to the fulling of cloth. This was done at the walk-mill, a term still known.

In a MS. of 1389, of Wycliffe's translation of St. Mark IX., 3 (The transfiguration). We have " And his clothes ben maad schynynge and white ful moche as snow, and which maner clothis a fullere *or walker of cloth* may not make white on irthe." [and his raiment became shining exceeding white as snow; so as no fuller on earth can white them]. The words in italics in Wycliffe's version are given by him as an alternative reading.—*Note communicated by Mr. J. A. Martindale.*

It was not exacted from every *vill* or township. The Loughrigg men paid it, as we learn from the Levens Rental of the Richmond Fee (1379-1403) and so did the men of Ambleside, each township furnishing then 6s. 8d. to the lord; while in the Sizergh Rental of 1493-4, Loughrigg paid 4s. 5½d., and Ambleside an unknown sum merged in the general rents. Loughrigg paid again 4s. 5½d. in 1453 and in 1493-4. Burneside outside our district likewise paid this due. It may have originated in some compromise, by which the tenants were free to do their fulling other than at the lord's mill. Ambleside and Loughrigg, it may be mentioned, both became considerable centres of the cloth trade.*

Gold-wether, or geld-wether. This was probably a tax on the dalesman's increase in sheep. It is mentioned for Langdale in the 1283 Inquisition, when the tenants furnished 5s. 0d. Afterwards it dropped to quite a nominal sum. In the Levens Rental (c. 1400), Grasmere paid 13d., Langdale 6d., and Loughrigg 3d.; in 1453 Langdale paid 4d. and Loughrigg 5d., and in 1493-4 Grasmere paid 7¾d., Langdale 4d., and Loughrigg 3¼d.

---

* See Notes and Queries.

In *Notes and Queries*, III-170, it is said to have been a payment by the tenants for the service of Rams kept by the lord.

Forest-silver and Pasture-dues. The heaviest annual due paid to the lord at the time of the first Inquisitions was *forest-silver*. This was demanded from the dalesman as compensation for the agistment or pasturage of his cattle in the wide mark or forest lands, which the lord had come to claim as his own. We do not know how the tax was laid or collected, but its amount came to a high figure under the Plantagent lords, successors to those Norman rulers who had laid so heavy a burden on the people by their enclosures of deer forests [see later]. Accordingly we hear in 1283, under the heading of Grasmere in the Lindesay Fee, or half of the barony, of a certain forest there " rendering yearly for herbage 3li 6s 8d., and for pannage * 5s." and another in Langdale "whereof the herbage is worth 50s. yearly." The forest of " Skamdal " is mentioned separately from Ambleside, and is entered at the high figure of £17. 6s. 8d.

Gradually the tax lessened. In 1324, indeed, the forest of Grasmere is declared to be worth nothing yearly to its lord, Ingelram de Gynes. But this must have been temporary. In 1335 its agistment is set down as 40s. In 1375, the rental of the Hothom Fee mentions that the tenants pay forest-silver, but, unfortunately, without specifying the amount. In the Levens Rental of the Lindesey Fee, (c. 1400) the Grasmere forest-silver returns to the £3. 6s. 8d of 1283, and Langdale to the 50s. In 1453 the two places stand at 44s. 5½d. and 33s. 4d., which is exactly repeated in 1493. The forest-silver collected from Loughrigg is mentioned for the first time in 1453, when

---

* From Lat., pastum; Fr. pain. A term still in use in the New Forest, meaning the feeding of pigs at large on the oak and beech mast. The "pannage month," being about eight weeks, beginning fifteen days before Michaelmas. (See Manwood's Forest Laws.)—Ed.

it amounted to 12d. only ; and in 1493 it had dropped to 8¼d.

Besides which there was in Langdale a separate pasture, with a name variously spelt, that was probably Whelpstrath.* At the end of the fourteenth century it realized 5s. 0d., for both the Hothom and Lindesey lords. To the latter it realized in 1453 and 1493, 3s. 4d.

From this time the term forest-silver is dropped.

In *Notes and Queries*, tenth series iii., 170, we read that forest-silver was a payment by the tenants in certain hamlets (*e g.* Applethwaite) for the agistment of their animals *in the forest*. This expression is explained thus, viz. that these hamlets had been "purprestures" or encroachments made in the Forest of Kendal in the twelfth century with the approval of the lords of Kendal. These encroachments were legalized by a royal charter in 1190.

We hear no more indeed of the "lord's forest" at the heads of the valleys ; and the growth of the communities of Grasmere, Langdale and Loughrigg, which was rapid in the fifteenth century, must have absorbed all the unoccupied ground at a low and fertile level ; while the rents accruing from the new holdings would more than compensate to the lord for the clearing of low-lying woodland. The case was different with Ambleside and Troutbeck. The forest about them had from the first been carefully preserved and guarded as hunting-ground for the lords, and it remained the home of the deer until Tudor times [see later]. The dalesmen of the low *vills* were consequently more restricted in their use of it both for timber and for the pasture of their cattle within it. Their holdings or tenements were rented according to the number of beasts they were allowed to keep in the forest, and the scale was rigid. Perhaps it was re-adjusted at the time

---

* 1375-1400, Whelpstrocke, Whelpstroth, Qwelpstrathe ; 1453 and 1493, Whelptreth. The name is now lost.

of that " new rental " which is stated to have been settled between the Countess of Richmond's commissioners and (at least) the men of Grasmere and Langdale in 1500.* For from 1505, onwards we find the holdings of these two *vills* classed as five and ten cattle tenements, the larger paying a rent of one mark (13s. 4d.) and the smaller half a mark (6s. 8d.)† each " cattle-gate " (as the phrase went), representing the pasturage of one cow or ten sheep. And in the Court Rolls of Windermere for 1442 and 1443, most of the fines chronicled were exacted from the tenants for their having exceeded their grazing rights in the forest.

When we reach the only court roll known to exist for our head valleys—that recording the court held at Kendal for Grasmere and Langdale in 1603,‡ it is the common pasture that is spoken of, and not the lord's forest. Certain dalesmen are fined for driving sheep and cattle on the common pasture against the village law or custom.

The Common Pasture. From primæval times each village community must have possessed its common pasture, independently of the lord's forest. The pasture was a cleared ground, always in these parts situated upon high fell land, on to which the village cattle were driven in summer, while upon the carefully fenced-in meadow and field below, the village crops of hay and oats grew and ripened. The fixing of a barrier, temporary and easily adjustable with "yeats," (= gates) between their pasture and the village, was the work of all the dalesmen. The Frithmen superintended the drawing of the cattle within it at a certain fixed time, and saw what " Gist "§ goods each man put upon it. And any offence against the common

---

* Min. Account, Henry VII. 877.

† The Ministers Account of 1505-6 adds 4d and 8d. to these two sums, doubtless including one or more of the small annual taxes due to the lord.

‡ Public Record Office Court Roll, 207

§ A corruption of the word " agist " which Manwood derives from agito (= to drive) "Agistment" means both the herbage eaten by the cattle and also the money paid for the same (*Forest Laws*, 4th edition, p 1)—Ed

law or custom, as to the number or time, was dealt with and punished in the village court.

The commons in these parts were in general large ones, because they occupied the mountain tops, which were otherwise of little value. Inter-commoning also took place. That is to say, two *vills*, separated by wide waste or fell lands, would drive their cattle from either side on to that fell-land, without attempt at discussion of it between the two Such an instance Rydal afforded, as Margaret de Brus's deed of 1275 affirms.

" Moreover, I have given and granted to the said Sir Roger, the whole of my part of Amelsate and Loghrigg, with all the appurtenances, by their right bounds, without any retention, with common of pasture within the bounds of Gressemere, for all manner of his beasts. Also I have granted, for me and my heirs, that the aforesaid Sir Roger and his heirs, and their men dwelling within the aforesaid bounds of Rydale, shall have common of pasture everywhere with my men of Gressemere "

The statement is perfectly clear. The " men . . . . of Rydale " were not to be shut within the new bounds made by this grant, but were to share the wide common of Grasmere, as no doubt they had always done. Accordingly, when a boundary was set up about the manor of Rydal, running from the precipitous crest of Nab Scar, round the water-shedding line of the mountains about Rydal Head, a way was left for the passage of cattle through it, called a Ley-gate. The gate exists to this day.

The Rydal right of inter-commoning on the mountain-range that stretched between Fairfield and Helvellyn was never lost sight of, but it became unfortunately absorbed by the lord of the manor, and lost to the dalesmen. And so we read the following statement in Sir Daniel Fleming's hand.

Ry. Hall M S S.

1683 *Rights of Common*

[Scrap of paper in Sir D's hand.]

"In Gresmere there are 4 Ley-yates and 4 Gaps of ease.

YEARLY DUES

"The Lords of ye Manor of Rydal and their Assignes have right to put every year three score Heiffers or other Beasts in at any of ye 4 Ley-yates or ye 4 Gaps of Ease, and to go upon Gresmere Comon all ye Sumer, or as long as they please Witness thereof Rich. Nicholson Ap 15 1683"

The witness was a Rydal statesman who was completely under the influence of his lord.

By the time indeed that we obtain any clear knowledge of the Rydal customs in regard to the common pasture, that pasture had become extremely limited in extent. Starting where the arable land ceased, just above the top houses of the village, it extended along the right bank of Rydal beck to the boundaries of the manor on the watershed. The whole of the left side of the valley must have been reserved as park-land from the time of Sir Roger ; and after the deer were killed, and it was used for pasturage, the Rydal dalesman, if he put cattle upon it, had to pay the same rate for agistment as any stranger.

The Rydal pasture was moreover a "stinted" one While the happier dalesmen of Grasmere Langdale and Loughrigg possessed an "unstinted" right of grazing on the common and had in the case of the two first an almost limitless acreage on which to freely turn their cattle the Rydal man could but put thirty sheep and a horse (no cow) free upon his small common and for the rest pay a tax to his lord. The amount of the tax is clearly stated by Daniel Fleming when he became lord ; and was recapitulated by his successor in the following terms.

"The Tenants of Rydall are yearly (by their custome) on or before the 14th day of May to give in upon oath unto such as ye Lord shall appoint, all such Horses, Beasts, and Sheep as any of them shall putt unto, or have on ye said day ; all wch are to be entered in the Lord's Book, and for which ye s^d Tenants are yearly to pay unto the L^d at Michaelmas following, according unto these Rates, viz , For every Cow, Twelvepence, for every Horse or Mare above one, two shillings, for every sheep above Thirty, two shillings and so proportionably for all, tho' under a score, for every three year old Beast eight-pence, and for every two year old Beast sixpence.* Also two of the Tenants are then to be sworne yearly to be Frythmen by Turne, who are to look unto ye Pasture and the Painable Hedge.

Another recapitulation of 1754 adds the oaths taken by tenants and frithmen on the annual occasion of driving in the cattle.

" You sware to give in a True and just acc^t of all such Goods as y^u have or shall have upon ye pasture of Rydal this year, 1754. Except 30 Sheep and a Horse, for each Tenem^t according to ye Custome of this Manor, So help y^u God "

" You Sware well and truly to Execute the Office of Frithmen for this year 1754 to the best of y^r Knowledge and skill. According to ye Custome of this Manor. So help y^u God."

The Agist or " Gist " book of the manor, carefully kept from 1655 to 1700, gives an account not only of the cattle put on the common, but of all that were taken into the park to graze, from far and near. The rules for this privilege, which occasionally the Rydal statesman in his shortage of ground, was obliged to make use of, were for a cow 7s. 6d and 8s. 0d., a heifer 7s. 0d., sheep 5s. 0d. or 5s. 6d. the score, mare and foal £1, stag (= colt) 9s. 0d. and 10s. 0d., or by the week, an ox 1s. 0d., a cow 6d. and 7d., a stot 5d., a calf 4d., horse or mare 9d. and 10d., foal 4d.

The richer Rydal man often, too, rented from the manor those manor closes that lay among the village fields, on which to graze his flocks. For Frith in the Nab, £1. 16s. 8d. was annually charged, though it once dropped to £1. 13s. 4d., for the Allans 12s. 0d., Old Hall 15s. 0d., and for the two with Adam How £1. 16s. 8d. The crafty miller however securing all three, after times got bad in Rydal, for 15s. 0d. New Close commanded the steady rent of £2. 10s. 0d.

---

* The Agist-booke of 1655 enters these as the *twinter*, 6d , the *thurntor*, 8d , and there is likewise the *duntor*, 6d The cow is *key*, pl *keyne*, a young heiffer *why*. *Twinter* and *twinter why* is used as late as 1754

Birket Moss was sometimes let at £1. 0s. 0d., and Low Park How at £1. 16s. 8d. and £1. 12s 6d.

It may be mentioned, in connection with the stinted pasture and its rates, that the Ambleside and Troutbeck men, who were likewise stinted, paid for each " cattle-gate " or " grass " on certain pastures 1½d. a year.

There was in Rydal, on the slope of the Nab, a small close or garth held by the tenants in common, where they could pasture their calves in summer. This, though not an unusual adjunct to the *vill* or manor * is always stated by the lord's officers to have been granted to them so late as the time of Mrs Agnes Fleming (who died 1631), and in exchange for the boon service performed by the holders of sixteen tenements of leading manure to the demesne fields one day in the year. From the appended document that concerns it, which was written at a time when many of the old families of dalesfolk had fallen in the struggle with bad times and lord's fees and exactions, it will be seen how easily imposts sprang up after the village court' which could protect old rights, became defunct. Through-steps in the wall still lead over from the high-way into this old common field, while its present gate is above.

The other document on common rights, made out in 1663, and probably enforced, (since it was signed by a majority of the tenants), shows how doubly restricted the Rydal man became in the number of cattle he could keep. He not only paid a tax on all he placed on the common beyond one horse and thirty sheep, but he was limited in these, by the imposition of a further prohibitory fine, to such a number as he could support through the winter on his own ground, on his dales or in his byre and hog-house.

By 1751, five statesmen only were putting cattle on

---

* The name Calgarth or Calfgarth by Windermere must have originated from such an enclosure

the common ; and aged memory speaks of four village flocks of sheep that had the run of the now lost common.

APPENDIX.—RYDAL HALL MSS

(Paper in hand of John Banks). *Right of Common.*

"May (or Maij) the xi[th], 1663. It is Ordered by Daniel Fleming, Esq., Lord of the manor of Rydall, together w[th] the Consent of the Customary Tenants of the sayd mannor ; that if any of the sayd Tenants, shall put to the pasture any more goods, of what sortt soever, then they can well winter upon there owne Tenement or other Lands any of them shall take w[th]in the s[d] mannor (excepting one beast) ; That then Every tenant for euery Sheepe above the number of ffoure-score then they can winter as affore s[d], w[ch] they shall put to the sayd Pasture Shall pay to the Lord Twelve pence And for every beast Two Shillings and Sixe pence, And that the sayd goods may be put and kept in the Pinfould till the same bee payed.

In witness whereof they have hereunto put theire hands and markes the day and yeare above written.

       Dan : Fleming
       Willi Walker
(fine, old fashioned letters) Richard Nicholson
       Charles Wilson his m[r]ke +
       Thomas Fleming his m[r]ke 8
       Gawen Greigg his m[r]ke +
       Daniel Harrison sen[r] A
       Daniel Harrison Ju[r] H
       Edwin Greene his ma[r]ke H
       John Thompson ma[r]ke T

RYDAL HALL MSS.

Nab.
(Fragment in 17th cen. handwriting). *Common Field.*

"Whereas there is a close or pcell of ground in Rydall in the Co. of West : comonly known by the name of nabbe holden of S[r] Dan : Fleming, Kn[t] Lord thereof w[ch] doth belong and is appurtenant to the severall and respective Tenements in Rydall aforesaid, And wch for the most part hath been kept for the grazeing of calves, in wch every Tenement hath one belonging to it amounting in all to the number of sixteen. And Whereas the said Nabbe for several years last past hath been possessed by Widdows, Infants or Farmers, soe that the same hath been neglected and is overgrown with Bryers, Brabons(?), and other offensiue matter For the better settleing the same for the future, wee the present Tenants widdows and farmers and occupiers of the several and respectiue Tenements in Rydall aforesaid, haue agreed to pay one shilling for every Tenem^t this present year for dressing the same, and likewise to pay an equal and proportionable share towards the walling and repairing the fences in the scar-foot adjoyning on the high side of the said nabbe from the Frith-railes, to John Nicholson intacke And for the future that the same be mown and dressed att an equal charge according to the number of calfe gates there And wee doe Likewise agree that every calfe gate shall be rated att 2s 6d amongst ourselves and that none shall be let or farmed to strangers if any Tenante in ye said Ry-dall have need The same to be frithed or driven at mid-Aprill day in every year and stinted the tenth of May at wch time every pson therein concerned shall give in one calfe a year old or under for every Tenem^t, and for want of such calfe or calves a Cow or heifer for three calves That every Tenant shall haue liberty to weane his lambs in ye same that every Tenant shall put in at the same time, and haueing kept y^m there tenn dayes shall at the same time take y^m out againe dureing wch time they shall put their calues or other beasts in scar foot. And wee doe further agree to frith or drive the same att Michaelmas in euery year and soe keep the same clean till wee put our Ewes and Rams together and then every occupier of any Tenem^t shall for every Tenem^t put in Tenne Ewes and soe keep the same for a month or six weekes at the least for their Rams and Ewes onely and from the time of takeing out the same shall lye in Com̃on till Mid-Aprill-day then next following and the aforesaid agreements to be looked to by the sworn men for the pastures In witness whereof wee the present Tenants widdowes Farmers and occupiers of the said respective Tenem^ts haue hereunto set our hands the (   ) day of August Anno Domino 1695

          (Unsigned)

CHAPTER XI

THE LAW OF GREEN-HEW

Forest and Timber rights, their constant restrictions; Bierlaw (or Byre Law) men; Greenhew strife; Scott v. Fleming, quarrel over the Oaks of Bainbrigg.

"M^d y^t every tenant payeth 1^d green-hew."

SUCH is the legend written alongside the names of the Grasmere tenants of the Marquis Fee in the great Inquisition of 1574, which declared the customs of the barony of Kendal as they had been preserved to that time

Accordingly, if we scan the few court rolls that are at present known, those of 1442, 1443, and 1603, we find that the men of Applethwaite, Troutbeck, Ambleside, Grasmere and Langdale all lay down their pennies—or in some cases two-pence—in open court for "vert." This seems indeed to have been the first business of the court, and if any man wished to be exonerated from the payment he swore a solemn oath that he had cut no wood of any kind since the last court. In fact, on some manors within the barony he swore in any case, that he had cut no woods of warrant.* That is oak, ash, holly, or crab-tree†—without consent of the lord, before he paid the green-hew penny, which was his acknowledgment of his lord's right to the forest, as well as of his own in the same, to cut underwood‡ or elding for his hearth-stone.

But the tenant or dalesman had also rights to timber in the forest besides underwood which it was the continual effort of the lord to control, and in later days to curtail.

---

* = of a certain quality. In the N Forest, a deer of a certain age is called a warrantable deer —Ed.

† To these, in Wythburn, birch and white thorn seem to have been added

‡ The Wythburn list gives this as hazel, wyth (willow), elm, ram-tree (= rowan), yew and eller (= alder).

In the old free days of settlement, when a man cleared the wild ground with his axe for his homestead, and built it of the cut wood, no question of rights in timber could arise. There was enough and to spare; it was a civic virtue to fell. But a growing population that lived by husbandry gradually pushed back the wood-land that had once grown close up to the settlement, and the forest shrank. As it shrank, its value grew. When the Anglo-Saxon noble or lord took over the government of the *vill* as a manor, he claimed jurisdiction over the forest marsh and—after making exception to certain prior claims of the villagers—even the direct ownership of it. And when we consider the vital necessity of woodland to the community, we can understand the struggle of the claimants over it, which began in those early times, and lasted here in Rydal till the early years of last century. It furnished wood for the hearth, for every common implement of daily use, and for the structure of the house; it was used for the smelting of iron, and it supplied the pleasures of the chase to the rich man.

So valuable had the woodland become by the ninth century, that a law of Alfred's meted out death as the punishment for the man who cut down the lord's forest without license. But in the wild mountain lands, the abundant native forest and its timber must have been free and open for some hundreds of years after restrictions had grown up in the south. Till the Norman barons built their castles at Kendal and Appleby there would be little talk of rights and of limitations. They, indeed, soon began to mark out districts for the chase, and we hear as early as 1225 of the complaints of the people that had reached the ears of the king, of the afforesting that had taken place, to the detriment of "Bongate and other honest men."[*] The woods of the eastern slopes of

---

[*] Calendar of Patent Rolls, Hen III, vol 1

Windermere, between Kendal and the lake-head, were devoted to the deer, and the men of the *vills* upon those slopes suffered restrictions in consequence. The homesteads of Troutbeck and Ambleside, paying a lord's rent of 6s. 8d. were allowed only fuel for one fire, and if another were lighted, a fine of 12d. was imposed.* An order of the court of Windermere forbade strictly the burning of charcoal. The deer-park of Sir Roger de Lancaster closed more than half the woodlands of Rydal at the end of the thirteenth century.

Yet, powerful as the lords became, they could not altogether extinguish the earlier rights of the dalesmen in the woodland. Nor was it in their interest to do so. The dalesman paid tribute to, and fought under his lord; therefore the maintenance of his holding must be made possible to him. The waste homesteads that we read of in Langdale, in one Inquisition, were bringing in no rent. It was, indeed, an offence punishable in the court if he let his house or his barns fall into decay. In the court roll of Michaelmas of 1442, several tenants of Troutbeck are " presented " for having their tenements (house or mill) defective or ruinous, and a fine of 6s. 8d. imposed, if they are not put in repair before the following Christmas.

What then were the rights of the villager within the forest, beyond the right of underwood to maintain his hearth-fire? That he had rights in it, conjointly with his lord, seems certain For, though the lord might claim for his own uses all of it that was not required for the uses of the tenants, he had no right to destroy it, or to sell it. This was made clear by the action of Charles II., who, when lord of the manor of the lands of the barony, proceeded to sell to Richard Kirkby, squire of Kirkby, all such timber standing upon them as might not be useful

---

* In 1443 Roger Fysher of Ambleside was presented in the courts at Windermere for having two fires upon one tenement His fine was only 6d Hugh de Birkehed of Troutbeck the same Christopher Birkehed was also presented for the like offence.

for his navy. The commissioners who viewed the wood, found standing in Loughrigg, 537 such trees, valued at £39 11s. 0d. (a higher figure than any other township but Applethwaite), as well as other timbers, valued at £115 11s. 0d., which it was proposed to sell to Mr. Kirkby. But there were able and powerful men among the tenants who refused to brook this clearance. An opposition was formed, whose representatives went to London to prefer their claims, and Charles lost his case.

It is difficult to determine these unforgotten but unwritten rights of the past The assertions of them are all of late date, when old men mouthed traditions, and evidence is conflicting, according to the side from which it comes. And it comes almost all from the lord's side.

"Item . That such Tenn[t] and Tennants soe admitted (to the manor) and allowed as is afforesayd is or ought to have by the appoyntment and delliverie of the Lord or his Bayliffe beeinge Tennant and ffower other Tenn[ts] sworne sufficient Timber to bee had of the same Lands for repayringe of theire buildings and for Hedge-boote, Plough-boote and Harrow-boote And for other necessaryes to bee imployed about their Husbandry." *Inquisition of* 1574

This claim of the dalesman for "sufficient timber" for the requirements of his holding was large and elastic. His own ground might furnish him with timber enough; for the scattered homesteads, like the Nab, often had a little patch of old forest trees left upon it. And indeed in the more closely compacted *vills* or hamlets, each holder had his own appointed dale of woodland, or wood-mere, somewhere on the fields where a few trees grew on a rocky strip, or along the border of a meadow.* But these meres, as a rule, furnished him only with elding and hedge sticks, and not sound old timber for repairs.

---

* The apportioning of these meres or dales, on the enclosure of the common fields, was eventually productive of the greatest confusion, and, finally of strife among the townsfolk, for they were assigned where they could be found, and often lay against, if not upon, another man's ground

If, therefore, timber for building was not to be found on his own holding, he could demand it from other parts of the township, even upon the lord's demesne.*

" And Whereas the respective Customary Tenants of the several Manors of Rydal, Conistone . . claim a Right to fell, cut down and take away Timber and other wood from off the Demesne Lands for the repairs of their respective Customary Houses situate within the Manor where the timber and other wood is cut down." . .

So runs a document of agreement concerning the felling of old timber within the park which was drawn up by those members of the le Fleming family who had possible claims to the estate after the death of George, Bishop of Carlisle To prevent this invasion of the demesne, a patch of woodland was often set aside for the uses of the villagers Or in the words of the old document, if their tenements do not supply them with enough wood

" the Landlord may and doth usually make Springs or Coppices or such Woody grounds within the Tenants grounds, as have been anciently Coppices or Sprung, And these after the Lord have sufficiently fenced them, then they are to be meantaned and kept by the Tenants, according to the Statute in that case made and provided "

Such a common wood was Nab wood, which stretched unenclosed down the slope behind the house of Rydal village to the shores of the lake, and which may have existed from the time when Sir Roger shut out the men from his newly-made park. Its uses are past, but its ancient oaks (now fast rotting away) show what those uses were. Another common woodland for Loughrigg was on the steep slope behind Field Foot called Lanty Scar. This too, may have been early apportioned by a lord of Rydal to the uses of the tenants of his manor within the township of Loughrigg, who were very much mixed up with the tenants of the Lindesey manor.

---

* This, however, is denied in MS.

The remnant of the old trees in these common woods, as well as those at the Nab, and a few at Bainrigg's, spread fantastic arms from the crown of an ancient trunk at the highest some ten feet from the ground. This height marks the limit of the tenants power to cut ; for he might not anywhere fell a tree entirely, but only use its branching wood above the crown. Also, from all oak cut, even on his own ground, the lord claimed the bark as a perquisite.

There were—or grew up—other limitations to the tenant's use of timber. He might not even use timber for the erection of a new house or byre, but only for the repair of an old one, though the old one might be rebuilt from the ground, so long as it rose again on the old site. It is probably this law that produced the extraordinary permanence of the sites of the village houses, which date back to immemorial times * He might not enlarge his premises, but only take timber for " a Convenient dwelling house, Barn, Byer or Cow house," and the writer of the old document goes on to say that his old father who had acted as Lord's steward on some manor used, in his charge to the jury at the court, to specify particularly the parts of the frame work of a building allowed, restricting the " barn or bier " to three pairs of supports, or even fewer on small tenements.

In this matter of mutual, entangled, and closely-watched rights, each side had for long its representative watchers or guardians. The lord had his bailiff, acting under the steward ; the dalesmen their elected fellows, to act on their behalf. Four sworn men are spoken of in 1574 ; but two bierlawmen † or house-lookers was the general number appointed. On this point the document says :—

---

* When the writer entered Rydal, in 1896, not a single house stood on a new site, while many ancient sites were empty Since then the new building impulse has invaded the place and houses have been erected on new sites.
† See Whittakers' *History of Craven*.

"That once a year, when the Lord kept his Court, Two of the most Substantial Tenants in the Lordship were elected by the Jury and the Court, and those they called Bierlawmen, and their office was this. If any Tenant complain'd for want of Timber to repaire his houses, then these Bierlawmen were to view the decay, and see whether it came by the Tenants default or by accident; and they were also to view what trees would be needfull and sufficient for the repair; and if it came not through the Tenants default, then the Lord's Bailiff Upon the Bierlawmen's presentment was to sett out for the Tenant upon his own Tenement such and so many trees as the said Bierlawmen did or should say to be sufficient"

An order of the Windermere court, agreed upon by Mr. Christopher Philipson, deputy steward, and the tenants, on November 30, 1630, stands.

"Itm —It is ordered by the Consent as above said that noe Tenant in Troutbecke or Ambleside Shall have any Timber Delivered to his building but upon his own Tenement, without the Consent of the Owner of the Ground, and the same to be Assigned by the Houselookers, and Delivered by the Bayliffe according to the Custome, upon paine of every Default, 6s 8d

At what time the dalesmen lost their acting representative, and house-lookers or bierlawmen ceased to be elected in court, is not apparent. There is no evidence of any such village officers existing in Rydal from the time when particulars of the manor are extant, which is 1654. Yet Rydal needed them; for while the cordon was drawn even more tightly round her tenants' rights of timber, those of the men of the townships surrounding her, in the royal manor, became even more free and unfettered. The men of Ambleside were indeed quarrelling among themselves by this time about the law of greenhew, and were seeking to make their own judges or umpires, outside the court, as a document of 1633 shows.*

A short reign of freedom came to Rydal with the interregnum, when not only king and church were deposed,

---
* See Appendix.

but her own manorial lord. Her townsmen clearly made use of it, cutting timber unrestrained, while they might. An order was therefore issued in 1654, or the previous year, which is alluded to in a letter from William ffleminge

" John Banks
upon Munnday last I receaved a letter from Mr Wharton (the agent) as alsoe a Coppie of a petiton wch hee hath p^rferred and already passed the same Comittees, and he likewise writes that their was then an order granted, but not signed against the cuttinge downe and spoyleinge of the woodes, wch hee would send down by the next post, wch if already sent away then soe, if not then hasten it wth all possible speed for that daylie greate spoyle is done in the woddes "

When the new lord of the manor was firmly fixed in his seat, he made it clear to his tenants that there should be no tampering with timber, except by his license. Three of the most prominent and wealthy of them appear to have defied him, or at least to have refused to acknowledge his undisputed power in the matter. Whereupon, appealing to no village or manor court—where a jury of townsmen would have declared the customary law of greenhew and pronounced judgment—he promptly summoned them to appear before the next Quarter Sessions at Kendal (on whose bench he sat) to answer for their actions. Their surrender is shown in his account book for 1658.

" May 14. Received of David Harrison for felling   lb   s.   d
     a tree in ye Nab, and for carrying of wood out of
     ye Parke, by his children and servants   ..   00.   05.   00
more of Thomas Fleming for ye like offence   ..   00.   10.   00
22 more of Simond Parke for ye like   00   10.   00

Satisfied with his victory, he gives back to the three 2s. 6d., 1s. 0d., and 2s. 0d. respectively. And therefore we hear only of his own sale of timber-trees on the manor, to the carpenters of the neighbourhood, of whom there were three at least among the tenants of his manor.

By the time that the eighteenth century opened, the ancient law of greenhew had hopelessly broken down. But the results of the old village community remained—even after a fixed tenure and enclosure had taken the place of a system of rotatory possession in open fields—and showed in the scattered closes and dales and woodmeres of which a man's holding was made up. Each man and his successor had to remember what was his, and to stick as closely to it as he could. There was no longer the regularly kept village court, where the voice of the aged declared the customs, and a responsible jury " boundered " a man's holding, or decided a dispute about the cutting of wood * Where there was no resident lord to hold all in check, a species of anarchy prevailed, the strong holding their own, and the mean and crafty seeking to encroach on their neighbour.

Nor was the law of greenhew simple, even for the honest. Timber needed time to grow. That a man's trees—allotted as the wood-mere of his holding in long past time—grew on another man's land, promoted both confusion and complications, when there was no court of appeal. As a striking instance of the confusion and strife that might and sometimes did ensue, we may quote the records of Ambleside, though out of our boundary. Benjamin Browne, a prosperous statesman of Troutbeck, was between the years 1705 and 1717 acting as agent for the absent Lady Otway, who had inherited the large and mixed customary lands accumulated by the Brathwaites of Ambleside Hall His letters constantly refer to the greenhew difficulties he had to contend with. For instance, George Ellis claims a wood-mere in the lady's field called Old Helmes ; and has not only proceeded to cut down several great oaks within the close, but several

---

* It is interesting to note that while Sir Daniel called no court in his manor for the settlement of timber disputes, he called upon the Grasmere court to bounder his tenement there, that his rights might be confirmed in it.

others that stood within her wall, pulling down a great deal of it to get to them, and leaving the close open to the common fields. In reply she can only suggest an appeal against this outrage on her rights to the neighbours, or to the court of Windermere. Again, an old man informs the agent that the Ambleside Hall property possessed a wood-mere in a close of John Mackereth's; and John's son James now succeeding to the property, proceeds to cut down wood in it, nor does an attempted arbitration succeed. Then widow Kelsick makes a most unwarrantable claim on the wood growing on Batesmerhow, and even proceeds to offer it for sale; this claim is an invention slowly pushed, the Kelsicks never having ventured to cut wood there themselves, but sending poor people to do so, who have begged from them, and have not known the rights of the matter. It is cheerful to record one straightforward attempt to straighten matters. Robert Partridge states that Lady Otway has a wood-mere on his land called Roughsides, and desires to purchase it. As to Lady Otway's extensive woods at the Pull, within Lord Montague's manor of Hawkeshead, the agent is at his wits end. He can get no timber set out by the bailiff or lawyer, acting for the manor, even for the repair of her property there, while trees are felled within them by his leave for other tenants. A "tip" or a friendly glass are resorted to in vain as persuaders; a "guinea or two" is even spoken of. She grants five or six oaks for the rebuilding of the Hawkeshead school "mansion house," because she is pressed for them; but this has to be done, "quietly, and without a noise," while she dare not cut for herself. "Crooked trees" for certain repairs the agent reports as not to be had, except at Rydal: he buys some, however, at Baisbrowne.

Timber, indeed was getting scarce, for the lively state of the iron trade was tempting everyone who could, to "coal" their wood for its manufacture [see later].

Even the customary tenants of Ambleside, regardless of the ancient forest law, were busy lopping such " springs " or coppice as they could command, and rearing on the pit-steads those cones of burning sticks that came out as charcoal.

Green-hew matters were running no more smoothly in Rydal, and with a far greater risk of ultimate disaster to the tenants, whose duel of rights was with lord instead of neighbours. Discord centred itself for a time in Bainrigg, the fine stretch of woodland once freehold, that covers the arm of White Moss. It was held at this time as customary land under the manor of Rydal by William Scott, who bought it in 1739 from his father-in-law, Robert Harrison of Church Stile, Grasmere. William was apparently a cantankerous man, separated from his wife and unloved by his neighbours; but his letters of complaint to the heads of the manor, who were acting for the young heir, Sir Michael, reveal an extraordinary state of affairs, in which he seems not the only one to blame. According to his own account, he had had a passage of arms with the late Sir William, who had served him with a writ " for taking customary rights " of wood in Bainrigg; but upon his appearing in (presumably) the Kendal court, and claiming freehold right, the case had dropped, and the plaintiff had to pay the expenses. This emboldened William to stop his lord, both when the latter's servant next came to cut wood, and to order firewood for Mr. Wilson, the Grasmere parson. So the matter seems to have stood, at a breather in the contest, rather than a conclusion, when William in 1751, sold some wood from his estate to John Fleming, and the latter—warned that Scott's right to sell might be disputed—failed to conclude the bargain and carry off the wood. Whereupon Scott served him with a writ, and the dispute blazed forth afresh.

Unfortunately, the Revd. John Wilson fanned the

flames of discord that now broke out from the smouldering of woodland grievances. He advised the steward (Mr. Moore) to bring up a counter action on Scott, and thought this might be made good on the ground of his " cutting down and coaling several large oaks, and bringing others home, some of which he had sold." He proposes a notice being read out in the church, prohibiting Scott's felling of timber—a measure, he adds, which will deprive the man of his winter fuel, " as he is so detested, that upon the least whisper no person will work for him." The notice ran as follows.—

" Whereas great quantities of wood have been un-lawfully cut down in a field or fields called Bainriggs, parcell of ye manor of Rydal, which is a great injury to the tenants of the said manor —This is to therefore give notice, that if any person whatsoever shall presume, contrary to ye custom of ye said manor to cut down, or peel any wood in the said Bainriggs, they shall be immediately prosecuted."

Counsel's opinion, however, when appealed to, was not in favour of bringing a case against Scott ; and Mr Michael Knott of Rydal, whose written opinion on the customs was asked for, he having been " many years steward to old Sir Wm Fleming," replied in the usual manner. He believed .

" that the Wood on the Tenants Ground within the Manor of Rydal is Chiefly in the Lord of the said Manor ; The Tenants are by Custom Entitled to House, Fire, Plough and Hedge [paper torn] ought not to Cutt any Timber Wood even for the [   ] Repairs or Rebuilding their Houses, till obtain'd (at) the Consent of the Lord, and to be Sett Out by his Steward or Bailif "

We next hear Scott's side. For in 1759 he was driven to appeal to Mr Moore, the acting agent in Sir Michael's minority, concerning the abuses of the wood on his ground at Bainrigg. The tenants of Rydal, he said, though they had sufficient wood in their own ground for building or repair, get the lord's officers " to sett forth large quantities every year in Bainrigs ; then, after letting it lie several years, convert it to other uses." He particularizes with a backward eye to grievances. "Mr. Knott when he built his House Cutt down above Sixty Trees, in order to spaire his own, then thinking to gett it a Freehold as he did quickly afterwards, he hez coal'd it" Then again, "He hez cutt down wood in Bainrigs Twice since the former time," in particular cutting down "five or six years ago eleven trees for building An Ass (ash) House To ly Ashes Inn" though he had not yet begun it. Likewise George Otley about twelve years ago had " near 30 " trees for building a barn, and the surplus " he converted to privet youses [private uses] & Chists for his Children." And this year again Mr. Dickson (the bailiff?) has set out for Otley a quantity more wood, eleven trees —three or four " fine Spires " of large timber thickness among them—being already cut down ; though all that is required is for two new doors and a "paint-house [pent-house ?] along the barnside over the doors."

Next John Park of Nab " being Mr. Knots' nephew " induced the same officials to "set him out sixteen trees in Bainrigg, though he had plenty of wood on his own estate ; and last year he had seven more." John Fleming had cut down fourteen or sixteen trees about six years since ; and next year, with Mary Park, nearly twenty trees. John Birket too, had cut down about twenty trees in the last two years. Altogether he reckons that some 200 oaks have been taken by his neighbours from Bainriggs since Sir William's accession to the manor. Finally Scott complains he had lost a beast, which ate the " Oake-Broom " that was cut unknown to him, that the herbage of the wood is destroyed by the trailing of the wood and letting it lie ; that the fences are broken down to bring it out ; and that the croppings are flung into the water.

Two years later, Scott writes to Sir James Lowther, the acting trustee for Rydal manor. He recapitulates his grievances, adding that Mr. Moore has stopped them carting of some " Botch Wood " he had sold, which—though worth over £1—now lay rotting. " As for Botch and Hasel Wood it is an Undisputable right to the Tenant all over Ingland both by Law and Custom " The agent has besides tried to frighten people these last two or three years, so that the writer can scarce hire labour " To Crop Oake according to custom." He puts forward again the old freehold tenure of Bainrigg ; and finally, in face of the many difficulties, offers to sell the estate (which he values at 400 " guines ") to the manor.

But instead of a purchase, we hear of a law-suit, which cost the manor, from 1762 to William Scott's death in 1771, £73 12s. 10d for barristers expenses alone. Scott in his will provided for the continuance of the struggle, but the lord was clearly tired of it, and agrees with the dead man's trustees for the purchase of it for £400.

After this, the lord's officers watched the tenants closely to see that they did not exceed the green-hew rights now allowed to them. The letters of John Gibson, who acted for some years as bailiff to Sir Michael, record for his master's satisfaction his own ceaseless vigilance in this and other matters On June 9, 1781, he writes :—

" Mr. Knott has Let his House here to his Sister, and he is going to make great Alterations and Improvements, for which purpose I have Set out Eight Trees in his own Wood and Two in Wm. Park's wood, the Reason of going to Park's, was by Mr. Knotts' earnest request, Park having gone the last Year into Mr Knott and Thos Fleming's woods, Cut, Peeled, and Carried away either Two or Three Timber Trees and the Bark, without the knowledge, leave or Consent of any one, and said that Mr. Dixon (the late bailiff) had set them out the year before.

I have set out Four small Trees in Geo. Birkett's Wood for Wm. Swainson, being all that were worth taking, and the rest were One from every Neighbour

Have also Set out Two for Geo. Rigge, and Three for Jno Barnes in their own Woods , They are all Peeled and I have taken care of the Bark, but shall not sell or dispose of it without your Directions George Birkett has never Used or taken away any of the Timber which was Set out and Cut for him above Three Years since, altho' he promised you so to do, and it is now not much more than half the value, being so much decayed."

Again in 1782, he reports that George Rigge, who owns a messuage and tenement in Rydal by right of his wife, has instructed the man who rents it to grub up three oak trees avowedly for the improvement of his ground fence, but without any reference to himself as the lord's officer; and that when he had remonstrated with the men at work, they had answered that the lord could not hinder a tenant from grubbing wood for the improvement of his ground. The bark, however, was saved for Sir Michael. Also he informs against William Park, who about three years ago grubbed some wood and sold it to three men whose names are given The name of the family of Parke has occurred several times in these green-hew disputes. Like others of their neighbours, they were perhaps not above the hopeless and irritating game of reprisals, which was so often attempted in the absence of a disinterested court of appeal in disputes. And in their outstanding homestead, with its own patches of woodland, they had always taken up an independent attitude as to rights of timber Simon Parke was fined by Sir Daniel. At a court held on February 7, 1769, John Parke was fined 6d. " for cuting down wood with^t having leave from Bailif." Early next century, John Simpson, son-in-law and successor to William Parke, was indicted for the same offence. He refused to make amends. An action was brought against him in a distant court, in which the lord of the manor pleaded that the Rydal tenant had only right to cut down trees on his own estate " by the Lord's direction," and then for repairs solely It was contended that most of the tenants were at this time conspiring to establish the right to cut down timber for new buildings. From this agreement we may conclude that of the various versions still told of the ruin of the Simpsons, the one is correct which makes the use of timber for the building of a new barn (the one standing at right angles to the road) the cause of offence and of conviction. John Simpson lost his case, the cost of which he could not pay. Various loans—of which the strange history is told in part vi. by the De Quincey letters—put off only for a year or two the evil day; and in 1834 the family left the Nab, which had been their inheritance as far back as record goes, penniless and homeless.

APPENDIX.

G. BROWNE'S MSS VOL. XIV 145 *Green-hew*

"The Five and twenteth daie of Aprill, Anño diñ, 1633 Knowe all men, That whereas some question is or contrau^{er}sye likely to growe amongst some of the Tenannts of Amblesyde tuchinge the grubbing of there Woods as alsoe the use of the Timber and other Woodes groweing claymed or belonging unto eu^{er}y mans Tenem^t in Amblesyde, and likewise tuchinge the P^{r}servacoñ and cherishing of there Woods, according to our Costome, and according to an Agreem^t made by the Consent of the most part of the Tenannts in Ambleside tuchinge there said Woods and there Usage thereof, It was heretofore and nowe is fully concluded and agreed by us whose names and m^{ar}kes are Underwritten, that eu^{er}ye Tenannt in Amblesyde, that shall have anie occasion to use anie Tymber or Timber trees for buildinge or repaireing of his howse or Barne, shall serue himselfe of his owne woode belonging to himselfe, and not to have or take anie Timber or other wood claymed or belonginge to an other mans Tenem^t wthout the likeing and Free consent of such Tenannt as doth clayme or owe the said woods, And if anie Tenan^{n}t or other pson or psons whatsoeu^{er} doe or shall heareafter goe about to infring or breake this our agreem^t tuching the Usage of Timber and other Woods, Wee whose names and m^{ar}kes are underwritten for the better Cherishinge and prserueing of the said Timber and other Woodes, and prformance of this agreem^t doe hereby seu^{er}allie and respectively Couenn^t and prmisse too and wth Samuel Jackson, George Atkinson, John Brathwaite, and Willm̃ Jackson and too and wth eu^erie of them. That wee and eu^ery of us whose names or m^arkes are underwritten shall and will paie or cause to be paid unto the foresaid Samuel Jackson, Georg Atkinson, John Brathwaite and Willm Jackson or some of them, w^thin one Month after demand thereof all such some or somes of money as wee and eu^ery of us shalbe assessed to paie by the foresaid Samuel Jackson, Georg Atkinson, John Forrest, Edward Brathwaite, & Thomas Mackereth, five Tenannts beneath the stock. And the foresaid John Brathwaite, Willm Jackson, Edward Forrest, Edwin Brathwaite, and Dauid Erey, five other Tenannts aboue the stock or the more part of them, wth the umpage and Consent of Gawen Brathwaite, esquire, towards the defence of our title and right herein, the Cherishinge of our Wood and the prformance of this agreem^t according to the Custone if anie Tenannt or other pson shall attempt or goe about to hinder or breake the same, And as witness hereof wee have sette our names or M^rkes the daie and yeare first abouewritten

Gawen Brathwaite	Samuell Jacksonn
	John Brawhat
	Georg Atkinson
Thomas Fleming	Edwin Brathwaite m^rke ‖
Thomas Ellis	Willm Jackson m^rke M
	Dauid Erey m^rke ‖
	John Forreest m^rke ⊢
	Edward Forrest m^rke I
	Thomas Macherth
	Edward Brathwaite m^rke ⊢
	Richard Forrest marke Λ
	John Newton marke IC
	Robart Newton marke D
	Georrge Mackereth marke C
	John ellis marke O
	Robart partridge marke 9
	Thomas ellis marke J
	George Jackson marke Ic̄
	Ather Fishere mark C·
	Georg machrath mark λ
	Willm Borwicke mark ñ
	Edward Brathwait mark V
	Edwine Jackson marke X
	Robert Newton marke u
	sonne of Myles

CHAPTER XII

THE COURTS

For Shire; Hundred or Borough; and Vill; also Court Baron or Hall Moot, Election of Parish Officers; Appendix; Witheburne Court Baron.

THE Anglo-Saxons kept law and order, and administered justice, by means of a graduated system of courts. Beginning with the village moot, which controlled all matters of the *vill*, and punished small offences by fine, it passed upwards to the hundred-moot, controlling a group of *vills* or a district of a certain size; and higher still to the shire-moot, where in the face of a conclave made up of freeholders and representatives from the towns with their reeves, the highest dignitary, [the bishop and Eoldarman, or in their places the shire-reeve or sheriff], gave forth the dooms for the graver offences, and settled all disputes.* A burh-gemot, too, meeting twice a year in the peace and security of the walled town, administered justice for the city or borough, which was independent of the shire. These moots for *vill* and borough and shire, may perhaps be traced in their later forms in our district. Anything like indeed a county court for all Westmorland must have been of late origin, since it never was a shire before the Norman times; and the courts presided over by the king's officer on the creation of the county were for long disliked

In 1275 and 1276 the complaints of the men of the baronies of Westmorland and Kendale were deliberated over in London. They contended that the sheriff of Westmorland ought to have "of fee" no more than two horse and two foot sergeants to attend him, and that now more than three appear as his officials, exacting

---

* *Political History of England*, Hodgkin.

lodging and payment, and compelling men to come to certain assemblies "they call the sheriff turn." Moreover, they cause innocent persons to be molested for larceny, &c., and imprisoned until they extort from them heavy ransoms.* It seems as if crime in those days, as in these, was scarce in Westmorland, and a few cases had to be manufactured by unscrupulous officials of the court. Witness these extracts from the Calendar of Close Rolls, temp Ed. I.

1280 *Statutes made by the king and his council in Westmorland.*

The king has heard complaints when lately in the county of Westmorland, viz. that the *Sheriff* has made his "*tourn*" more often than necessary, requiring *four men and* the *Reeve* of every *town* to repair to *divers places* where he administers justice The King orders that the Sheriff shall only make *one turne* each year and *that in Kendale and elsewheres in Westmorland four* men and the Reeve shall com from each town once a year at a certain day after Easter and at a certain place to wit *at Kirkeby in Kendal* or at *Kirkeby in Lunesdale* before the Sheriff and coroners, to do what pertains to keeping the peace in those parts to wit to indict *outlaws, theives, felons, evildoers, and receivers, in* the same manner as the King does elsewhere in the realm And the *other towns of Westmorland* are to come to certain other places most convenient to them for the same purposes, and there state their complaints and other grievances against the sheriff and his servants as to taking fines for detaining of prisoners, &c

And moreover the King wills that when the men of the county ought to be amerced the amercements shall be made and taxed in full county by good and lawful men as ought to be done and according to the statute and not at the will of the sheriff or his sergeants For the rest the King wills that *women brewers* (braceresses) in that county may not for one amercement brew and sell all the year contrary to the assize and to their profit and to the damage of the people ; but that they shall be punished according to the award of the county (court) as is done elsewhere in the realm

In 1285 a law was passed, appointing justices to hold in every county, three times a year, assizes, juries and

---

* Calendar of Patent Rolls, 2 Ed I.

inquisitions, and two years later William de Stirkeland and Robert le Engleys, on behalf of Westmorland, were bidden to enforce this law, as it was found that the justices were not holding assizes as often as was intended. But these assizes were outside the courts of custom.

The expenses of the king's justices at Kirkeby-in-Kendal are accounted for in 1352 (Min. Acct. Gen. Ser. Bdle. 1118 n. 5), when they seem to have sat three days, only once in the year.

The court of the hundred is supposed in very early times to have administered justice chiefly for the theft of cattle, which was the only valuable asset of the landholders that could be stolen. It was necessary to convene the court frequently, for the thief who had lifted the cattle had to be followed hot foot and caught, and it was the duty of every man of the hundred to join in the pursuit, which was called the " Hue and Cry." It is said, accordingly, to have been held every four weeks. See Hodgkin and Stubbs, who say that both shire-moot and hundred-moot were restored by Hen. I.

Probably the court which is found meeting at Kendal every three weeks, or month, is the representative of the hundred and the borough courts in our district. The Inquisitions of William de Tweng in 1341, stated that he held his lands in the barony by doing suit in the king's county court of Westmorland, every month. But a court is spoken of in the Inquisition held at Kendal on the death of the Duke of Bedford, in 1436, when the courts held for the villages in his lands are enumerated as meeting there every three weeks

In the Ministers Account for 1453 * the proceeds of this court are entered as those of the " court baron of Kendale called county court [Curͫ Patrie] and borough court held at Kirkby in Kendal each third week."

---

* Min Account, Bdle 644, No 10,444.

In Queen Elizabeth's Inquisition of 1574, for both the Richmond and Marquis Fees, the three-weeks court held at Kirkby Kendal is mentioned, with a statement that is dealt with plaints and actions under 40s. This Inquisition speaks also of the Court Leet held twice in the year in the same town; the jurors for the Marquis Fee adding besides two " head Court Barons," also held twice. For these courts the various divisions of the barony provided free-holders in due proportion to serve on the Jury, six from the Richmond lands, three from the Marquis lands, and three from those belonging to Sir Alan Bellingham, sometimes called the Lumley Fee. The profits of the fines levied at these courts, as well as the tolls on Kendal fairs and markets, were divided in the same proportion among the lords of the lands. The time for holding these courts is stated by the jurors to be the Monday and Tuesday after Low Sunday (first after Easter), and those of the week next after Michaelmas Day. A roll of one of these courts remains, but worn so thin as to be in great part illegible * It records what was done in the " Chief court of the Barony of Kendale held there at Kirkby-in-Kendale on Tuesday next after the Feast of St. Wilfrid 20 Henry VI." [A.D. 1441]. Several free-holders (and among them Ralph, late Earl of Westmorland) are fined 4d. " for default of suit of court." The pleas are mostly for debt, trespass, detention, or breach of agreement, and the legible fines extracted from the offenders run no higher than 6d. Fresh agreements are arrived at by means of an " imparlance " held in face of the court, when the disputants state their grievances (and possibly bring forth witnesses) before the jury. A Langdale man, one John de Gr . . , has to appear for an imparlance on the charge of Henry Betham.

The Court Baron, or Hall-Moot, presided over by an

---

* Public Record Office, Court Roll 202/3.

officer of the lord of the manor, carried forward the tradition of the old village moot. Though later degraded into a mere vehicle for the lord's requirements and even his exactions, it was originally a court of justice, and the methods of law-giving remained in force till at least the sixteenth century. It must be noticed that with its law and its judgments neither the lord nor his officer had anything to do. The officer, indeed, presided ; but no indictment would be made against an offender except by two land-holders of the *vill*, who in technical language " presented " him, while judgment was declared by a jury chosen from the land-holders themselves.

The fines, which followed in general a fixed code, were assessed not by the jury, but by two tenants, chosen on the occasion These " assurers " are named in the Windermere roll of 1443 ; and names are given of the assurers of John Parke's fine in 1769.

The payment of the lord's rents appears to have been no part of the proceedings. They were collected and paid in by the grave or reeve, who was likewise bound to be a townsman The office of graveship was a yearly one till the close of the sixteenth century, and was presumably one of election by the court, like those others that concerned the administration of the *vill*, viz. :—the constable, the bierlawmen or house-lookers, the hedge-lookers, the moss-lookers, the frithmen. Later, the grave kept his office for a term of years, or for life. Edwin Green filled it for Rydal from (at least) 1631, till his death in 1668. He was followed by William Walker, and it was not until after the latter's defection that the lord's faithful factotum, John Banks, took it over, having by that time acquired a holding in the village which qualified him for it. The grave was also responsible, in the Richmond and Marquis Fees of the barony, for the payment of fines and heriots.

Parish Officers.

(1). Paper in Sir D. Fleming's handwriting
"How ye Constable is to go by ye Turne every third year (Loughrigg serving two years) in Rydal, beginning A° Dom 1667
Imprimis Keen Tenem^t for ye year 1667
Then Parkes Tenem^t p^r A° (pro Anno) 1670
[and so on through the seventeen holdings of the manor of Rydal, concluding]

"The overseers of ye Poor, & ye surveyors of ye Highwayes, are for ye year 1667 Rich. Nicoldson & Widdow Harrison" [the twelvth and thirteenth on the list] " & so every 3rd year two by course as above written goeing downward to ye bottome, & then beginning at ye topp againe This was agreed to by all ye Tenants May ye 9th A° Doī 1667 before mee

Dan · Fleming."

Such was the method which superseded the old election at moot or court, which after this no longer met with regularity. It will be noticed that each man served by right of his holding.

The payment of the green-hew-penny by each tenant, apparently went with, or represented, his suit of court to the lord, which he was bound to acknowledge on each occasion. The God-penny, paid likewise in the face of the court, was the mark of admission of a new member to the community, and a new tenant to the manor The ceremony, which of old gave the only security a man had for his land (this being *alod,* or held by witness of the community), was long regarded as essential. After the Rydal court had been reduced as regards the administration of justice, and was held intermittently, it was specially convened for the admission of new tenants The presentments of offences and the judgments appear to have followed. These were of a minor character, affecting only the welfare of the *vill.* The roll of 1604, shows that Grasmere and Langdale men were presented and fined for keeping pigs either unringed, or turning the lord's soil, 3d. to 9d.; for driving neighbours' sheep or horses on the common 20d., or for "turnynge on the common," 3s. 4d.; driving cattle unreasonably (in number?) there, 20d to 3s. 4d , for cutting neighbours' oaks, 2d.; for making "levy (?) huble howe" on a neighbour, 5s. 0d.; or for putting a scandal on a neighbour. The word "hubles-how" appears constantly in the rolls of the neighbourhood as a highly reprehensible offence, to be reported and punished; it represented some sort of a row or commotion, often accompanied no doubt by blows (see Holm and Fisher).

The Court roll of 1443, shows that several Ambleside men were indicted and fined 3d. for beasts being taken under "le Garth"; for beasts, horses, and pigs being taken in the forest, 1d. to 12d.; for two fires in one tenement, 6d.; for a gap in the hedge, 2d.; and one for felling an oak—though this was pardoned, because it was used for repairs

Not every township of our valleys, had in Plantagenet and later times, its own court baron; for neighbouring ones, if under the same lord, joined at one Also if two lords possessed lands in one township, they joined at the court, as we are told that the Hothoms and the Coucys did about 1400 in Grasmere.* Windermere like Grasmere, was an old manorial centre, probably because their churches offered a large roofed space for this great and solemn legal concourse. It is expressly stated that the Windermere court of July 9, 21 Henry VI. [1443] was held within the church. As a rule, the Langdale men, and those of Loughrigg that did not belong to the Rydal manor, had their court at Grasmere; while the Windermere one drew the men of Applethwaite, Troutbeck, and Ambleside, as well as the ward of "Ald-park," which was represented by a separate bailiff in the court just mentioned.

---

* Levens Rental

This order did not, however, always prevail Langdale was called to Windermere 7 Henry VII. [1491-92]. And by this time Ambleside town had so much increased in importance and size, that courts were held there. Two are mentioned 9 Henry VII., viz. :—on the Tuesday after the Exaltation of the Holy Cross [Holy Cross Day, September 14, 1493], and on June 11 of 1494 The arrangement would be favoured by the chapel, which was almost certainly built by that time.* In 1603 again, the Grasmere men were for some reason summoned to a court in the Moot Hall of Kendal.

The expenses of these courts are always entered on the roll and deducted from the profits (fines, &c.) which go to the lord.† At the Moot Hall in Kendal, 1603, they were 6s. 6d. ; at Grasmere next year, as the lord's officers had further to go, they naturally stood higher, the township of Grasmere costing 4s. 0d., and Langdale 6s. 0d The roll of July 9, 1443, gives some interesting particulars, under expenses of the steward, viz. :—bread, 3s. 8d. ; ale, 2s. 8d. ; meat, 2s. 10d. ; one kid 4d. ; one capon, 4d. ; salt, 1d. ; oatmeal, 1d. As it would be impossible for the steward himself to consume this bread, ale and meat in one day (the kid and the capon more probably serving for his private meal), it seems that the dinner which in later times was the invariable accompaniment of a court, must have come down from those times. Men, indeed, drawn often from long distances, and engaged in lengthy proceedings would have to be fed.

The Court Baron was held professedly twice a year both for Windermere and Grasmere, at dates which followed Whitsuntide and Martinmas, when the tenants' rents (paid half-yearly) were due. That these times

---

* As the men of Amb and Ald park repaired to Windermere Church for a court on July 9, 21 Hen VI ; I would hazard a conjecture that the Ambleside chapel was built between that date and this, 1443 and 1494

† In anglo-Saxon days the profits went to the lord. (See Hodgkin).

were not adhered to, the existing rolls show. The half-yearly rent is still adhered to in these parts, the 12th of May and 11th of November being the fixtures.

If we look to the Rydal manor, we find no early evidence of its court. That the strong Sir Roger, who exercised manorial jurisdiction over large and scattered lands, would establish one for his isolated *vill* over against his deer-park, is certain, and in this the half of Loughrigg that belonged to him would join, but no records remain. The men would naturally meet at Old Hall, where Sir Roger's "loge" or Peel tower stood, but the lord's steward then, and later, would ride away with rents and rolls, and the latter would be deposited with the muniments of the de Lancasters of Howgill Castle, of which nothing now is known. Squire John Fleming kept his courts in due and proper form, as a paper shows that admits a Loughrigg tenant whose holding had been alienated from the manor for a time, and who then, he states, "did attorne unto me." All sequence of courts must have been lost after his death, when the estates were sequestrated. Sir Daniel held them whenever they were necessary for his purposes, but it is doubtful if they served any purpose connected with the *vill* or the welfare of its people, except so far as their admissions were concerned. We have seen how he wrote out, in a mechanical rotation, the filling of the village offices of constable, of overseers of the poor, and surveyors of the highway. The frithmen too probably took their turn, without open election.

The court-roll of September 23, 1749, is a very meagre sheet, being practically only a rent list. The names of the jury are written on the back, sworn in groups of 4, 4, and 3, with Mr. Michael Knott separate as Foreman. A court was held at Thomas Fleming's Inn, and the court convened in 1835 was probably the last in Rydal.

The inn had become indeed the refuge of the court in these latter days, when it shows but as a feeble relic of

K

the past. No customary lands remain in Rydal, but some few exist in the townships round. For these portions of the barony the family of Lowther provide, holding a court of admission on the death of a lord, when the old skeleton of an archaic instrument of justice is galvanized into life for a day, and the Norman cry of *Oyez! oyez! oyez!* is sounded before the assembled townsmen. Such a court was held for Grasmere, Langdale, and Loughrigg, at the Rothay Hotel, on April 2, 1906, when the Right Hon. James William Lowther, M.P. succeeded as lord of the barony the Right Hon. James Lowther, the last general admitting lord. The two joint holders of Fox Gill, belonging to the Richmond lands, then paid a fine of 1s. 0d. each. The latter novel charge would provide for the expenses of the court, and the dinner of the coachman, who carried the fines.

In the absence of particulars of Grasmere and Rydal courts, a form for keeping the adjacent court of Wythburn, which Sir D. Fleming possessed, is given.

APPENDIX — RYDAL HALL MSS

(Outside in Sir Daniel's Hand, "Witheburne" Court Roll)

" The Ancient order and way of the holding of the Court Baron of Witheburne, the Last Court Roles perused and the new tenants then found, called by the baylife unto some convenient place to the Steward to be Enroleed that they may doe service & 4ᵈ paid for Enroleing of every one ... proclamation made ... freeholders called   A : B C · D :

Tenants at the will of the Lord Acording to the Custome of the mannor Called   A : B : C D · E : F .

| Proclamation made ... If there be any Tenant or ocupyer belonging to this manor that Can Cleare themselves of the payment of a greenehew to the Lord or his oficers let them apeare So to doe now in open Court Acording to Ancyent Costome before the Jury be producted and called or otherwise the greenehew is payable as formerly. | This greenehew is levied upon every Tenant that doth not thus excuse themselves at every Court. |

The Maner of the Excuse.

If any apeare to make excuse they are to be sworne after this maner You shall declare the truth the whole truth and nothing but the truth Concerning such things as you shall heareafter be examined of so holy you, &c.

The Examination . have you neither Cutt nor Cropt Topt Lopt nor feld peeled nor grubd Syelk nor wand ash, Oake nor birch, hollin Crabtree nor white thorne: hassell wyeth nor Elm, Ramtree, ewe nor Ellers within this maner since the last Court holden for this maner nor any other wood that therin groweth

If the person that thus apeareth say they have not it shall serve for an excuse

Notice to be taken in a by Role who excuses themselves

The Jury called
  A B
  C D.

The fforeman Sworne . . . deligently to enquire and true presentment make of all such things as shall be given you in charge So holy you &c . . . .

The Rest of the Jury Sworne by fours together . the same oath that A B your foreman hath taken the same shall you & every of you take So holy you &c.

The Preamble to the Artickles of the Juryes Charge Acording to the Stewards discretion

The Artickles of the Charge . . . you are first to enquire for the lord First you are to enquire and find all new tenants fallen since the last Court holden or before not yet enroleed whether by discent or Alination

Also you Shall Enquire of all the Lord's wood within the manor if there be no wast made therein by Cropping, toping, loping, or felling; neither by peeling nor grubing since the last Court holden or before which hath not beene presented how when and by whom neither by any other way or maner unlawfull or unacustomed : . . .

Also you shall enquire of all forfetures to the Lord be they by Indictments for felony special or they fall by escheats or mortmaines or the non payment of the yearlye Rent by which the land is holden all which are forfeture to the Lord . . .

Also you shall enquire of all goods or Chattels which are or hath been Lost or taken as weafe and Stray and hath Remained within this manor a year and a day never chalenged by the right owner they fall unto the Lord .

You are also to enquire if their be any Concealed Rents or writings whatsoever belonging to the Lord what they are and by whom Concealed.

Also you shall try all Actions of debt or trespas which may by enterance to the Steward be thus presented unto you by the best evidence that shall be exhibited unto you ; one plaint not exceeding thirty-nine Shillings Eleaven pence halfe peny Also you shall enquire of all things Amongst yourselves known to be done Contrary to Custom or that Remaines under penalty in any Court Role or other perscription or that can be made Evidently Aware the Antiquity of it by proofe or that hath formerly beene given you in particular Articles though now in general · that Such ofences may be punished by Amerceing the ofender acording to Custom all which things as by-Lawes and made amongst yourselves it canot be expected that a Steward shall perticuler them, but putt them all in a generall word, that all which you know or that can be made out unto you you shall as well enquire of them present them and punish them as if they were particularised unto you, so be you impanelled

The Jury is to be put in minde by the Steward that they forthwith bring in the names of the new tenants that theire fines may be Asesed as the Steward shall have Authority when the Lord is absent . . .

Then shall the Steward Examine by the last Court Roles or the information of the baylife who was oficers of the last Court as mos-Lookers hedge-Lookers wood Lindrers, pendors and persons of goods distreaned by the baylife of the manor . and examine what they have to present and take these presentments if they have any . and put the Jury to apoint others for the time to come that they may have their charge by the Steward Acording to Custom . .

Then the Jury is to proceed and Come on to the Examination of particular presentments and give in their verdict Acording as them and the Steward shall think Convenient.

CHAPTER XIII

MILITARY SERVICE AND WARFARE

Bannockburn, Border-wars and Taxes; The Clergy and the tithes, Devastated Vills; Appendix; showing calls on the County for Military Service and contributions.

THE chief service of the Westmorland land-holder was originally that of warfare. He had to ride out under his lord's banner whenever called. As the Inquisition of 1574 declares, every tenant between the age of 16 and 60 was to be ready for war, at his own charges, night or day " at ye west borders of England " . . . " Being Warned thereunto by beacon-Fire, post or proclamation " and to continue with the army at the Lord Warden's pleasure. There was a traditional limit, however, to the service, and it came to be the custom, when warfare with the Scots became incessant, to call out the forces in autumn, at a time the men had reaped their harvest.

Land-tenure by military service is of course the oldest existing; as it is a man's first duty to protect against a foe his homestead, his *vill*, his hundred, his shire, and his kingdom. For free-holders all over England the obligation existed, as well as for the men of the old district of Northumbria, but for these the obligation, instead of being relaxed by the general peace of a united England, became confirmed and increased by the quarrel of England with Scotland, and the chronic condition of border warfare that resulted from it; a condition which only ceased with the Union of the two kingdoms. Westmorland, unlike her sister counties to the north, was no border state, but—as in the days of Northumbria—she fought with the men of the north in all their battles. Sometimes, though she did not suffer as frequently as they did, the Scots pushed within her borders, and slew and burnt and wasted. Witness in proof of this the petition of the commons of Westmorland and Cumberland to Parliament in 1390, against the action of the tax collectors of the tenth and fifteenth in seizing their possessions, when, by reason of the frequent burning and destruction of their tenements, goods and chattels by the French and Scots, they were unable to pay their fines and taxes, which was responded to by exemption and even by repayment, when sums of money had been extorted.

In all the Scotch wars our valleys and their little towns were concerned. The dalesmen of the *vills* were tenants of the Barony of Kendal; they drew into Kendal upon call by beacon or proclamation, and marched as Kendal men with the baron or with the succeeding lords who over-ruled their lands. When the prowess of " Kendal men " was honoured in the field, it included that of the dalesmen of Rydal and Loughrigg with the neighbouring townships.

The call to arms must have been infrequent in Norman days, and after the anarchy and bloodshed of Stephen's time, when Westmorland must have suffered sorely from the King of Scotland's raid, the county had a time of peace in which to recuperate and to prosper. The wars of the Barons may have drawn fiery spirits of younger sons and landless men from the district, and a number may have followed William de Lancaster, third baron of Kendal of that name, who fought against John and was taken prisoner; but the call could not have been universal, or frequent.

It was a different matter when the strong Edward Longshanks determined to subdue Scotland; and after the revolt of Baliol (1296) invaded Scotland, and won the battle of Dunbar. The number of Westmorland footmen who accompanied him is not certain.* The success of

---

* For stipulation of men of Cumberland and Westmorland that this should not form a precedent, see Cal Patent Rolls 1300, in appendix to this chapter.

Wallace at Stirling Bridge in 1297, kept the men of the county at their homes, defending them against the raiding Scots. In the next year, 1400 Westmorland footmen followed the Earl of Surrey into Scotland. Except in 1299, when nothing was done, there were yearly musters till 1304. 1000 foot were summoned from Westmorland, though only 732 served, and almost all the men returned.

In the two next years, when Edward remained in the field, and completed the conquest, barely more than 600 Westmorland men followed him.* Edward's revenge for a time was complete, but the work was all to be done over again when he died on the border, a baffled man, with Robert Bruce, the newly crowned king, defying him. His weak son was not the man to accomplish what he had failed in. No time however was lost in attempting it. In the same September the knights of the north were bidden, instead of attending the parliament, to assemble against Robert ; and two lords of the barony, John de Lancastre (of Rydal and Holgill) and Ingelram de Gynes (of Loughrigg and the neighbourhood) were specially commanded to the service.† Preparations for the invasion of Scotland in June of the next year were on a large scale Amongst the provision of carts to be made by every county, Westmorland had to furnish 15 wains drawn by 8 oxen, to be ready at Carlisle. Writs to the northern lords were repeated in the succeeding years, showing at least an attempt at a continuance of the warfare ; John de Lancastre was again specified in 1310 ; and in 1313, Ingelram de Gynes was again enjoined not to leave the north, as well as Marmaduke de Tweng, another lord of our district.

The latter in January of 1314 was excused from parliament, because defending Scotch marches. Probably this

---

* See "Cumberland and Westmorland Military Levies," J E Morris, *Transactions* C. & W A & A Society, vol III, N S
† Calendar of Close Rolls

service, if carried out, was but that of guarding the borders; for it was only in 1310 that Edward II. really invaded Scotland with an army, and then unsuccessfully. Bruce was now becoming strong enough to take the offensive and to raid the border counties Carlisle was garrisoned with a larger force, and placed in 1313, under the care of the doughty Andrew de Harcla. One of Andrew's knights and lieutenants was John de Lancaster of Holgill, soon to possess Rydal, who seems to have fought, not as leader of a feudal host (who took the field but for a short time), but as a regular professed soldier, receiving pay. He remained with Andrew, when the latter held Carlisle after the terrible defeat of Edward II. and his great army, at Bannockburn, in June, 1314.* This defeat left the northern counties for a number of years open to the raids of the Scots, and the decreased inhabitants were little able to repel them without assistance. We now hear an incessant plaint of disaster and impoverishment. In 1315, the men of Westmorland complain that, while suffering from the " burning and oppressions" of the Scots during their invasion, they likewise, when they carry victuals to sell in Carlisle, are robbed of those by the king's officers. The mills, the bakehouses, the prison, at Penrith are wrecked ; mills in other places too, are destroyed, and oaks are granted from Inglewood forest for their repair. The clergy of the whole district (1318) grant 12d in the mark from their revenues, to aid the king in continuing the war and defending the district. This money was doubtless expended in raising the army to recapture the lost Berwick in 1319, when Cumberland and Westmorland supplied one-sixth of the 6,152 footmen. But for this sacrifice by the clergy, they later demanded some allowance in return.

In 1320 the priors of Cartmel and of Furness declare

---

* *Transactions* C. & W. A. & A Society, vol. III, N.S

they cannot pay the general tax of an eighteenth of their goods owing to the burning, destroying and stealing of the same by Scotch rebels. In 1327, the clergy are excused the general tax of a tenth. In 1330 they resist, on the same ground, the pope's usual quadrennial demand for a tenth of their revenues, and they request a new taxation. This would seem to have been granted by parliament, and the tax fixed as a sexennial one. The pope however, by his nuncio and sub-collectors, continues to press for the old taxation, and in 1336, the clergy—the depression and impoverishment still continuing from the waste of the Scotch wars—are said to "have clamourously besought the king to provide a remedy"; whereupon the nuncio is begged to desist from all tax-collection till next parliament.

The men of Westmorland generally demanded consideration on the same ground, and in 1314, they and their neighbours of Cumberland are declared exempt from the general tax of a twentieth and fifteenth. The frequent coming of the "Scotch rebels," is the plea put forward for exemption from taxes or payment of debts, till the end of Edward II's. reign, but the king's invasion of Scotland in 1322,* with a large army, when Andrew de Harcla was ordered to assemble all men between 16 and 60 in Cumberland and Westmorland, only increased the misery. Bruce followed the remnants of it over the border, and in perhaps the most terrible of his raids pushed as far south as Lancashire and Preston, devastating and burning. Possibly it was this raid that particularly affected our district, and produced the impoverishment described in the Inquisition taken on the death of Ingelram de Gynes, lord of Coucy. Part of his possessions lay in the track of the invaders. A "capital messuage" or manor-house, at Little Strikeland is described with all the tene-

---

* Close Rolls which seem to put Edward's invasion at 1323

ments or houses in the same place, as having been "burnt by the Scots and now are waste." The free rents due to the lord from the barony have fallen from 20s. 3d., to 6s. 8d "Burgages" in Kirby Kendal have fallen for the same reason from 40s., to 6s. The court of the borough there, from 26s. 8d., to nothing. The free tenants there and in Westmorland from £14. 11s 4½d., to £11. 4s. 0d. Pleas and perquisites of the (County ?) Court from 13s. 4d., to 6s 8d. The fishing of the Kent, which should bring in £4, is only 40s.

And up the valleys from Kendal there are wasted lands and desolate homesteads Empty tenements are enumerated in Hutton, in Crosthwaite, in Applethwaite; while in the *vill* of Troutbeck are six empty, all of which have fallen into the hands of the lord, and which had formerly paid a rent of 11s. 2½d.

" In the said hamlet of Hamelsate (Ambleside) was one tenement which ought to render 13^s 4^d and now nothing, because in the hand of the lord for default of tenant

Two tenements in the said hamlet of Langeden which ought to render 3^s 6¼^d yearly were in the hands of the lord the day of his death for default of tenants and now lie waste.

The herbage of the forest of Langeden should be worth 40^s yearly, but now worth nothing for default of beasts

In the said hamlet of Loghrig were 10 tenements in the hands of the lord which ought to render 10^s 2¼^d yearly, together with the fishery of Rawthemere and of the water of the Dubbes and a certain (*bracina*) there which ought to render yearly 3^s 6^d now rendering nothing for default of tenants

In the said hamlet if Gressemere are 11 tenements in the hand of the lord which ought to render 20^s 6^d yearly, together with the fishery 1^s 6^d the forest there 20^s and certain *bracina* there 2^s and now rendering nothing for default of tenants "

It appears, therefore, that in these valleys Grasmere and Loughrigg suffered the most. In Ambleside one homestead was abandoned; in Langdale two out of thirteen, eleven being accounted for in the receipts of rent given earlier in the document; in Grasmere eleven out of thirty-two, or one third, and in Loughrigg ten out of nineteen, being a little over one-half. The case of Rydal is unknown.

Though small parties of raiders no doubt penetrated these valleys from time to time by the passes of High Street, Kirkstone Raise, and Dunmail Raise, it is hardly to be supposed that the Scotch main army reached them and ransacked them. The route by Penrith and Kentdale was their usual and open road for conquest and plunder. It seems more likely that the empty holdings hereabouts were due to the loss of men in battle, and the absence of any successors to fill their places; for the drain on the male population of the district, in the incessant engagements and skirmishes, must have been heavy. The absence of cattle, both in Langdale and Grasmere, bespeak the extreme poverty of the remaining townsmen, whose only wealth lay in their beasts. Even if the herds were not forcibly driven off (and a very small body of the light Scotch cavalry could effect this, even by mountain pass), they would have to be parted with, in the general depression that all alike suffered, in this protracted and disastrous time of border warfare. The defeat of the Scots at the battle of Dundalk, 1318, gave some pause to the raids, and with the accession of Edward III., in 1327, and the death of the great Bruce in 1329, a happier period for the northern counties dawned. The new king, in his warfare with Scotland, encouraged a more chivalrous spirit among the northern nobles, and rewarded individual effort. To John de Coupland of Northumberland, who at the battle of Neville's Cross (Oct. 17, 1346) performed great deeds of valour, and captured King David of Scotland, alive, he gave that half of the barony of Kendal which then opportunely fell into his hands by the death of the lord, William de Coucy, without direct heirs. The men of Loughrigg and the valleys must therefore, when called out for warfare, have marched with this brave man. Another lion in battle, John, Duke of Bedford, was lord of the same lands, and created Earl of Kendal, in 1414. He was warder of the marches, and engaged in border warfare until the death of his great brother, Henry V., called him to pursue the wars in France.

APPENDIX.

SHOWING CALLS ON THE COUNTY FOR SERVICE AND CONTRIBUTIONS

Cal. of Patent Rolls.

1297. Rob Lengley of co. West. is "taxor" for ⅛ of movables of lay persons outside borough, & ⅛ of persons of boroughs for co. of Cumb.

" Alan le Norreys of co. Lanc. for co. of Derby

John Wake, Rob. de Clifford & John de Hudleston app. captains of custody of march of Scotland in co s Cumb & West.

1299 Rob. Tyliol to lead 2000 footmen fr. Cumb. to Scotch borders, & Hugh de Milton 1500 fr. West.

1300. Jan 17. Westmorland has to furnish 300 qrs of oats at Carlisle on Midsummer Day

" Ap 30 At the same place & time Hugh de Multon & Tho. de Derwentwater are to lead 1000 footmen fr. West

1300. 28 Ed. I. Sep 20. The men of Cumb. & West. receive at Rose Castle a ratification, fr. the K. that the foray (equitatus) wh they recently made ag. the Scots, in the 25th year under Henry de Percy & Rob. de Clifford sh. not be to their prejudice, or drawn into a precedent, or that bec of it the K. & his heirs sh. claim further service.

Cal. Patent Rolls

1304 Aug. 22. 32. Ed I " John son of Silvanus le Fisshere of Hamelset, for the death of Adam Erewell & for robberies "

Given as *Ambleside* in Index.

Cal. of Patent Rolls.

1303. Ap. 9. 31. Ed I. App of Harseulph (*sic*) de Cleseby, John de Barton & Robert de Furnens to select 1400 footmen in " northbrithing " c. York, & conduct them to Rokesburg, ag the Scots.

MILITARY SERVICE AND WARFARE 141

Wil. de Dacre & 2 others to select 700 " in co Lanc
Robert Langleys & Walter de Stirkeland to select in " Westmoreland & the parts of Kendal " 1000 footmen to be at Appleby May 6, & to conduct them next day to the king : their wages to be paid for 5 days. (Spelt also *Lengleys*).

Same for Cumb. (1000 men) except parts of Coupeland John de Hudeleston to sel in parts of Coupland c Cumb. 3000 footmen, & conduct them to Carlisle Wages to be p for 4 days " Estbrithing " & " West brithing " ot Y. mentioned Marmaduke de Twenge one of the 3 enlisting knights for Yorkshire.

1307. Mar. 19 Five gentlemen (Alan le Noreys one) to select 1000 footmen for Lancashire & lead them to Carlisle, for service in Scotland ag Robert de Brus, who is in hiding in the moors & marshes John de Castre, to take 200 fr. Eskedale & Gilleslande Richard de Cletere, 200 fr parts of Coupland & Cokermuwe Mathew de Redman & the sheriff of Westmerland fr co West & in Kendale, 300 to be at Carlisle at the morrow of Easter.

1307. Feb. 20. Lanercost.—Selection of men fr various parts of Cumb " Robert Lengleys, Henry de Wardecop, Walter de Stirkeland, & Robert de Wessington, to select 500 men in the bailewick of Westmorland " to be in Carlisle next Monday

1302. 30 Ed. I. Adam Pertrick of Patrikedale pardoned for larcenie in co of Westmorland, by reason of his service in Scotland.

Cal Pat Rolls Ed II. [War]

1322 Dec. 10. King sends 2 men to survey the munitions of men at arms, stock of victuals & other things in castles & towns of West & Cumb & in liberty of Tyndale.

,, March 31. Mandate to men of West &c &c. to assemble with horses & arms to repel invasion of Scots , & to obey Andrew de Hartcla Warden of those parts.

,, March 25 3000 men to be raised in Cumb. & West.

1323. Feb. 10. Men of West. & the North to attend no more upon An. de Harcla . . . he having joined the Scots & made a treaty with them.

p. 341. Cal. P Rolls Ed II 1321-1323

A John de Lancastre frequently sits with 2 others on trials

about trespasses. He is called "keeper" of certain of the king's lands in Lancashire.

One case is an attack by a family de Farequeton & their allies on the town of F co Lan " owned by Abbot of Evesham, comm. on an assualt (sic) on the Abbot's Agent, when beginning to hold a court there," Can he be same as the one who leads West levies to the war?

Cal. Pat. Rolls. 1321-24.

3 letters patent dated from Laskill or Lascales, co. York.

Cal Pat. Rolls.

1323 Oct. 1.   King in Yorkshire

Several letters patent dated from Skipton in Craven on that date, In Sep , from Barnard Castle & Richmond.

Cal Patent Rolls   War.

18 Ed II. 1324 Nov 17 Commission to array the knights, sq & other men at arms & all fencible men "to be ready by Candlemas for serv. in Gascony ag k of France, add. to 2 gentlemen of each county For West —John de Lancastre of Holgil & Hugh de Louthre ; Cumb —Peter Tilliol & Rich. de Denton , Lan —Walter de Stirkeland & Ed de Nevill.

1324 Aug 1. 18 Ed II Com. to supervise the array of men of the county, & to report number of men, horse & foot, to be armed with sheet armour, & of the residue of fencible foot to be ready by Mich next for war with Aquitaine . for Lan.—Rich. de Hoghton & John de Haveryngton . for Cumb.—Hugh de Louther & Rich de Denton , for West —Walter de Stirkland & John de Lancastre of Holgill

Aug. 6. Commission to . . . select, to arm, & array of footmen in var counties, Lanc 240, West 80, Cumb 160.

1326. Ap. 13. 19 Ed. 88. Anthony de Lucy, warden of Cumb & West ; directs the arrayers for Cumb.—Peter Tilliol & Walter de Kirkebride to bring their levies wherever he shall require ; also to arrayers for West.—Walter de Stirkeland, Gilbert de Lancastre & Roger de Brendvesheved ; ditto for Lanc.—Rich. de Hoghton, Michael de Haverington, & Thom. de Latham.

The comm to these gentlemen "to make the array" . . . "& see that beacons be erected & watchmen & sentinels placed " is dated Dec. 25. 1325.

1326   Jan 24   The like sent to the "chief arrayers" in Lanc & West viz West.—Rob de Wells, & John de Stirkeland, Lanc —Rich de Hodelston & Thom de Latham

1325   Feb 20   Com. to Hugh de Louthre, in place of Rich de Denton & Rich. de Hodeleston, as leader of the 120 "hobelers" selected by latter in Cumb & West. & power to raise 80 more, to be marched in same manner
      Cal of Patent Rolls.   Strickland & War

1325.   Feb 26   Walter de Stirkeland to join Edmund de Nevill in raising 80 "hobelers" & 100 archers in co. Lanc, in place of Michael de Haveryngton, who is going to Gascony

1325   Sep. 1. Anthony de Lucy app. warden of Cumb. & West while K. goes to Aquitaine.

1326.   Supervisors of array, to proceed from hundred to hundred, punish all persons in default, & act as leaders of array. For Westmorland, Robert de Welle & John de Strikeland, For Cumb. Anthony de Lucy, & Randolf de Dacre.
    Pat Rolls 9 Hen. VI. P. 1.   [Levy]

1431.   Com. to Rich E of Salisbury, Wil. Harynton, Thom Tunstall, Rob Haryngton & Thom Strykland, kn s to John Morley, esq. & to Thom. Wharf & Nicholas & Leyton, to 2 more of them, to array & muster 200 archers of the parts of Kendale, Landedale & the Westriding of York, . . . by feast of St George next.

(1429) July 17   Com to Rich E of Sal Thomas Strykland, chiv John Lancastre, chiv. Rob. Laybourne, chiv. Christopher Moresby, chiv. Thom Bedome, Rob Warkup & Nicholas Laybourn, in view of threatened invasion, to array all the men at arms & other fencible men, whether hobelers or archers, dwelling in co Westmorland & to cause them to be put in oooos, ooos & oos, twenties or otherwise as may be convenient, & lead them to the coast or other places as occurence may arise, & to take & survey their muster. All men of the county capable of labour to go before the com ers at whose discretion they shall be arrayed, armed & equipped "Bekyns" (beacons) to be set up in suitable places to give warning of arrival of the enemy.

	Chris. Culwen, chiv. John Penıyngton, chiv & among com.ers for Cumb.
1429.	Sep. 28. Com. to enquire in to breach stated to have been committed by Chris Moresby, K's sheriff of Cumb. who after Wil. Legh, chiv; & Thom. de la More had been duly chosen knights of the shire on Aug. 30 last in the county court at Carlisle, on writ of summons to Parl.—had yet, though no later county court was held, procured one Thomas Parre & the said Thom de la More, to be declared elected at another time & place.
p. 76. 1430.	Mar. 6. Com. of array for co. West.—Rich. E. of Sal.—Henry E. of North, Thom. Stirkeland, chiv. John Lancastre, ch. Christopher Moresby, ch. Henry Thirlkeld, ch. Nicholas Layburn, Hugh Salkeld & Rob. Warcopp.

CHAPTER XIV.

THE LORDS' DEER-PARKS.

Inglewood; Kendal and Troutbeck Forests; Ambleside, Rydal and Calgarth Parks; the word "Banner"; The Troutbeck Giant; Appendix; Summons for Forest Trespass.

OF great interest in the history of the barony of Kendal, and of our lands which belonged to it is the part played in the life and welfare of the people by the deer-parks, so extensively laid out by the lords of Norman and Plantagenet times. The subject has been already touched upon, in connection with the lords and the forest dues they exacted; but it may be well to give such scant particulars as are forthcoming of the tract of country specially set apart for deer.

The early conditions of the primeval forest, that filled the valleys and reached high on the mountain sides, are but guessed at.

Certain spots within the woods would be reserved by early man for his primitive worship of the forces of nature, and the sun god, or for later duties that belonged to the Anglo-Saxon and the northern races. If the word *grove* may be allowed to lead us to where he and his priests performed their sacrifices, then we shall find that he loved to set them in high places, like the idolatrous Israelites. The word clings (in High, Middle, and Low Grove) to the western slopes of Wansfell, to a cottage in Grasmere, at the foot of a western slope, some distance below the mysterious enclosure called Chapel Green; to a beck that flows down the western slope of Rydal Head, from the height called Greaves or Groves; while Greaves is attached to a stream in a similar position in the vale of Troutbeck. We cannot but note that all these "Groves" are placed on a western slope. Wansfell, if its name be derived from Woden, kept from Celtic to Anglian times, its sacred character as a mountain; and if we might accept Symeon of Durham's Wonwaldermere as being the original form of Windermere, we should arrive at a simple and suggestive meaning for it as the lake of the grove (or wood) of Woden.

When the Norman kings pushed into this north-western corner of England and began to organize it and the alien Cumbria, they at once recognized the capability of its forests for the preservation of the already abundant game, and for the pursuit of their favourite pastime (to which they heedlessly sacrificed the interests of the people) of hunting the deer. To mark out large tracts of it as royal park was an easy matter. It is certain that William Rufus, short as was his stay in the newly conquered Carlisle, and closely as it was followed by his death in the chase, appropriated the great tract of land between Carlisle and Penrith, which became the royal forest of Inglewood. To this Henry II. added pieces east and west, and north, including in it much of the barony of

Allerdale; and all the barony of Brough, so that it extended to the Solway, and measured, roughly, forty miles by twenty-five.* It was in his days that the assize of the forest made legal provisions for the protection of game, and the punishment of transgressors against their stringent laws (see appendix). The early administration of Inglewood Forest has been fully dealt with. It remained a notable place for game and for hunting, and kings and royal dukes, when campaigning in the north, must often have taken their pastime in it.

Its value too, must have been great in supplying the royal larders. In July, 1315, the foresters were ordered to take 12 bucks and 40 harts from the open forest itself, and from the adjacent chases and parks of Mallerstang, Whinfell, Flakebrigg, Burgh-under-Stainmore, 38 bucks and 64 harts; and after salting the carcases well, to carry them to the king's receiver at Carlisle.†

The barons and the lords naturally followed the king's lead, and from the lands granted them, marked out forests and parks where deer were to be cherished and bred. When Gilbert fitz Reinfrid secured from King Richard, in 1190, his charter for the forest of Westmorland, Kendal, and Furness (which had been held by William de Lancaster I.) the grant went back beyond the reign of Stephen, to recapitulate the possession of the forest of Kendal by Nigel de Albini, in the reign of Henry I. The "afforesting" of lands became so general and extensive, that when reform was the order of the day in John's time, an attempt was made to check it. This took, finally, the form of the Charter of Forests, limiting the extent of the royal chaces and mitigating the punishments imposed on offenders, which was passed in Henry III's. reign, in 1217. At the same time, the enclosures made

---

* "Inglewood Forest," F H M. Parker, M A , *Transactions* C & W A & A. Society, vol v , N S
† Calendar of Close Rolls The "Bucks" were fallow the "Harts" were red deer See Manwood *Laws of the Forest*, chapter 4.

THE LORDS' DEER PARKS

by the nobles were supervised ; and William de Lancaster, who followed his father, Gilbert fitz Reinfrid as baron of Kendal, was warned of " grave complaints " that had been made by knights and proved men about the recent afforesting of Westmorland lands which had been before dis-afforested ; and ordered to put the matter right. This was in 1225, the year of the conformation of the Forest Charter with the Great Charter by the young king.*

That William cherished his forests, is certain, for when he allowed to the Abbey of Furness the right to two boats on Lake Windermere and the fishing with nets, he stipulated that the men who worked the boat and nets should do no damage to his forest ; and if they did, that they should be punished by his own court †

Of the acquisitiveness of William's half-brother, Roger, in the matter of forest and park, something has been said A professional forester in the royal demesne of Inglewood, he early secured for himself some of the valleys that descend from the Fairfield and High Street ranges into Ullswater, and on his brother's death he received the rest of what was then known as the Forest of Westmorland. The break-up of the barony lands at that time brought to the heirs of William's sisters the Forest of Kendal, stretching along the shores of the great lake to the heads of the valleys. From one of them Roger got Rydal, for a deer-park ; from the other he appears to have held, though as underlord, the vale of Bannisdale, whose stream flows by the Mint into Kent ‡ Also for his manor of Witherslack, where he had stocked a deer-park, he paid a rent to the same fee of " one niais (nestling) sparrow-hawk." He therefore had an enormous hunting-range, which

---

* Calendar of Patent Rolls, Hen III , vol 1.

† West's *Antiquities of Furness*

‡ The inquisition of William de Lindesay (1283) speaks of Roger holding " the moiety of Barnasdisdale " worth four marks

comprised valleys on three sides of the mountain-masses of Fairfield and High Street, and extended to the tidal waters of Morecambe Bay. Hemmed in between his valleys of Rydal Head and Bannisdale, lay the now attenuated forest of Kendal, the hunting-ground of the Lindeseys and their followers, de Coucys and branches of the royal houses In 1272, it is spoken of as the Forest of Troutbeck, worth, with a certain park there, £40. In 1283, it appears under the name of the Forest of Skamdal, worth £17. 6s. 8d. In 1352, the park of Troutbeck is called the principal park of the manor of Kendal.

The open, unenclosed forest of Kendal, therefore, which had probably once embraced the whole of the Rothay and the Brathay valleys * became the Forest of Troutbeck, and this reached in the fourteenth and fifteenth centuries from Applethwaite to Rydal Within it lay two *vills*, Troutbeck and Ambleside, and it is possible that the lesser fines paid by them on death of lord or tenant, than were paid in the rest of the barony, were a concession made because of the greater restrictions they suffered, from being surrounded by a deer-forest The forest was divided into three wards, Troutbeck, Ambleside, and Aldpark, which were each represented by a bailiff at the court baron of Windermere, 1443.† It is probable that at one time a forester was assigned to each, and the *Maister Forster Place* that appears in the Ambleside rentals, and which (alone of all the statesmen's holdings) is "farmed" or let at a high figure by the lord in 1453, and was subsequently divided into several holdings, was the house of the Master Forester of Ambleside, before that office was abolished. The office of Master Forester had become a sinecure in the days of the weak King Henry VI., and in 1437 we find him

---

* The Penningtons held Little Langdale by a free rent of venison to the chief lord

† Public Record Office, Court Roll $\frac{1}{2}\frac{1}{2}$

conferring the "master forester-ship" of the forest of Troutbeck and Ambleside in the lordship of Kendal, on his groom-of-the-chamber, William Clement, to hold himself or by deputy, with accustomed wages, fees and profits. William, however, preferred a sinecure closer to London, so surrendered this in 1440, with the proviso that another should be found for him of equal worth. Besides the open forest, there were several small enclosed parks, where deer were kept under closer supervision. The park of Ambleside is mentioned in Roger de Lancaster's 1275 Charter of Rydal. It lay in Scandale, and his new park of Rydal touched it, with the Weythesty (or hunter's path) descending from "le Swythene" to it. Its neighbourhood to the Castle Field and problematic castle of Ambleside (see *ante*) may be noted. The park at the head of Troutbeck is often mentioned as "le Dale hede." The park of Calgarth seems to have been a later enclosure, though it became the most important. When in 1347, Edward III. took over the lands of the barony on the death of William de Coucy, and bestowed them for life on John and Joan de Coupland, he reserved for himself the forest of Troutbeck and the park of Calgarth. From the name we may conjecture this garth or close to have originally served the neighbouring *vill* for the herding of the town calves, which were kept apart for some months of the year. The king added to it the land on the shore of Windermere belonging to the Chapel of St. Mary Holm, which was left to decay.* He granted to Adam de Ursewyk the office of forester for life, and Thomas de Stirkeland was keeper of his lands and his woods from 1351 to 1355, in which latter year he gave the "park of Troutbeck" over to John de Coupland.

Several times did these lands and woodlands of the barony fall into the hands of the crown. On the death

---

* See Inquisition of John de Coupland in Nicolson and Burn.

of the Duke of Bedford, they were inherited by his nephew, Henry VI., who continued to hold and administer them. In 1437 Walter Strikeland was appointed receiver of the lordship " for as long as he bear himself well," at a fee of £10 a year, as William Bedford had had, and other profits, as for instance, wages of 2s. 0d. a day when riding to London. This service, performed twice from Kendal and back in the next year, and in 1440, took 94 days, and cost the king £9. 8s. 0d. Walter was also appointed keeper of the king's park of Calffegarth for life, at 6d. a day, as Robert Pylton, late keeper, had had.* As the lordship was saddled likewise with the young French duchess's dowry of one third and annuities, granted by the late Duke, there must have been little profit from it to the king, even when he farmed the park of Troutbeck, as he certainly did for the years 1437 and 1438, to John Frank, one of the servants of his chamber. When he granted it to the Earl of Richmond in 1453 (after a previous grant to the Duke of Somerset in 1442), the proceeds of Aldpark, of the parks at Troutbeck and the Dale Head, and Calfgarth are all mentioned. The last was " occupied " by Walter Strickland and Robert Pilton.† Christopher Birkhede collected the forest silver for Dale Head, and mended its hedges.

Sir William Parr, when receiving the lands in 1472, from Edward VI., took also " the close or park of Calgarth." In 1493-4, when they had reverted to the Countess of Richmond, Richard Dukell was master forester of the forest of Troutbeck, with 43s. for wages, and Sir Reginald Bray was parker of the park of Calgarth, at 3d. a day. Richard Berwyke was " bowderer " at 2d. a day.‡ In 1502, the park of Troutbeck with Dale Head

---

* The Ministers Account and Sizergh Castle documents

† Sir Thomas Strickland and his son Walter had obtained a confirmation of the stewardship of the lordship, and of the latter's office of keeper of Calgarth Park in 1446. See Sizergh Castle MSS.

‡ The bow-bearer was an under officer of the forest, whose duty it was to report trespass

was let for a term of years to Sir Walter Strikeland, for forty marks, £26 13s. 4d , he to maintain all charges, and to keep up the fences [note Ministers Account Hen. VII., 577]. The park of Calgarth was kept in the lady's own hands, Thomas Phillip being parker, at 3d a day.

Now this forest of Kendal or Troutbeck, extensive even after curtailment, must have been a favourite hunting-ground of its lord, or it would not have been preserved with so much care and expense. Its earlier lords were certainly resident in its neighbourhood. Kendal Castle was their seat, till the division of the barony. It is not certain where the Lindeseys and de Coucys lived, though we hear of the decayed manor-house on the great holm of Windermere, of one at Warton, and another at Little Strickland. Christina de Gynes (the Lindesey heiress) signed the Charter of Ulverston after her husband's death, in Windermere, which looks as if some residence were maintained on the island.* Later, a hunting lodge was doubtless built where old Calgarth Hall now stands.

The customs of the chase on these southern mountain slopes are less known than those on the northern slopes, but they were probably much the same. The tenants of the manor of Martindale are stated, in an Inquisition, of a date so late as March 25, 1702, to hold their lands by the boon service of assisting the lord and his officers in the hunt, by keeping the deer from ranging , and that when a hunt is forward, they shall on notice given, take their several stands or stations, for that purpose.† The ancestors of the present owner of the forest of Martindale, J. G Hasell, esquire, frequently called upon the tenants to perform this service in the eighteenth century ; but he himself does not exact it, as the red deer—that still roam

---

* West's *History of Furness.*

† " Local Antiquary" in *Westmorland Gazette*, of April, 1876 (the first to my knowledge to draw attention to the point) says that these stations were called *banner-dales*

at large in the forest—are not now hunted * It seems very possible that this service accounts (as has been suggested) for the occurrence of the word *banner*, on the borders of the forests of Troutbeck and Martindale, which were originally those of Kendal and of Westmorland, and held by different owners from the middle of the thirteenth century. Cleasby and Vigfusson (Icelandic Dictionary) give "banda . . Germ *banner*, to make a sign with the hand, especially to drive back sheep or flocks", and "banna = banda, to stop, drive back." Now we easily find upon the map four apparent survivals of this old Norse word in the district of the deer forests. There is Bannisdale, whose beck flows east into the Mint, and so into the Kent, owned by the doughty Roger the huntsman in 1283, according to the Inquisition, where it is spelt *Barnardisdal;* and taken over into Edward III's hands in 1352, owing to the death of a later Roger, and the minority of the heir—here *Banadesdale;* and in 1375, held by Margaret, Roger's widow We can well understand the lord's tenants being posted at one or more stations on the heights here, to turn back the deer fleeing from the neighbouring forest.

Then there is Banner Rigg, the 871 feet height, rising above Orrest and the modern town of Windermere. Here, when a hunt was up in the forest of Troutbeck, the deer could be stopped from escaping over the boundary of the lordship and away south into the Prior of Cartmel's lands, and so lost to the pursuing lord and his followers.

Again there is Bannerdale, in the Forest of Martindale, next valley to Boardale, whose waters flow into Rampsgill and so to Ullswater. On the heights above it, men of Roger and his successors might jealously guard the borderland where the two forests touched, lest some noble stag

---

* Kindly communicated by Mr Hasell, who confirms the statements as to the contents of the 1702 Inquisition (which I have not seen) and speaks of many earlier improvements of the forest being in existence.

should elude the huntsman and reach the land of the Lindeseys.

And last, there is John Bell's Banner, a name that has already excited comment.* It is attached to a height of 2,474 feet, which—exactly on the boundary between the two forests—commands the head of Candale, whose waters trickle northwards, the springs of Troutbeck, flowing south

Now there is no evidence that there were customary land-holders in the neighbourhood of Troutbeck of the name of Bell, very early. The court-roll of 1442, mentions several for Applethwaite, one being a John Bell, who pays 2d for green-hew, while his neighbour pays 1d More-over his servant, Roland Bell, is presented at the inquest for assaulting another man, and John Bell pays the fine of 2d. for him

The existence of these forests and parks, and the presence of so many deer upon the mountain slopes above the great lake, must have added a keen flavour to the practice of archery, which was necessary for warfare. As a matter of fact, the Kendal men, as they were called, were noted bowmen. We have evidence, from the name, of where the practice went on, both below the villages of Rydal and Ambleside, for the land at the turn of the river was called the Butts.†

The tradition of High Hird, the Troutbeck giant, is an interesting one. It is said by Clarke (*Survey of the Lakes*, 1789) to have been written down in 1786 by Matthew Birket, who had received it from a man who lived to be 104. Hird had become celebrated for his deeds of strength and feats with bow and arm (lifting,

---

* See " Local Antiquary," *West Gazette*, April 18th, 1876, and " Ambleside Bible," *Transactions* C & W A & A Society, vol vii, N S

Mr Collingwood first called my attention to it along with other business in connection with John Bell, curate of Ambleside, in 1905 , but this connection did not appear to work out reasonably

† In this district the word also occurs in ploughed land, "Sandy Butts" in Grasmere, &c.

for instance, a beam-end of timber that 10 men building Kentmere Hall had failed to stir), and he was taken up to London to be shown to the king. A bow was given to him in the king's presence, for the display of his skill, but he objected that it was no weapon for a man, and a second (presumably larger) was fetched, whereupon he laid the two together, and broke them. He is said to have lived at Troutbeck Park, and when the Scots came on their raids along the road still known as *Scot Rake* (part of the Roman road, High Street) which lay about a mile from his house, he would watch their approach, and kill them with his bow and arrows. This confirms the belief that the Scots penetrated even these valleys in their raids, and it is possible that when they rode their little ponies along that straight way through the mountains, that they aimed at killing the lord's deer, as much as driving off the tenants cattle They claimed, indeed, a certain right (leave being asked) to an annual hunt in English forests.* The name of Hird Gill is attached to a portion of the beck at the head of Troutbeck where the Scot Rake is seen descending the opposite slope. There is nothing improbable, since the king's officers were to and fro in the parks and forests, in the story of the gaint being taken to London; though it were hazardous to guess which monarch delighted in his strength of arm and appetite, the latter being unappeased by half a sheep. Edward IV. would be a better spectator than Henry VI.

The forest of Troutbeck was probably disforested in the sixteenth century, when the success of the woollen industry gave the breeding of sheep the first importance. The fashion of hunting the stag too, had declined in Tudor days. Even the park of Calgarth, with its pele or hall, passed into the hands of private holders. Christ-

---

* See Nicolson and Burn, vol. i. cv. and cvi.

opher Philipson, who acted as Receiver for the barony lands under Edward VI., left it by his will in 1566, to his son Rowland, in whoses line it continued till the eighteenth century.

It was in 1552 that a division of the forest was first made between the two now thriving *vills* of Ambleside and Troutbeck. Until then it had lain open and unenclosed. The matter, subject to the approval of the lord and of his officers, was left to be settled by townsmen, who appointed fifteen men of standing and repute—Christopher Philipson among them—to act as arbitrators, and by whose demarcation of boundary they pledged themselves to abide.

The demarcation of the forest of Rydal was made nearly three hundred years before, and it is to the history of the man who made it, and of his descendants who kept it, that we must now turn.

APPENDIX.

Summons for Forest Trespass

Calendar of Patent Rolls. 10 Edward III.—Part I

May 8th Commission of oyer and terminer to Robert de Clifford, Richard de Aldeburgh and Robert Parnyng, on complaint by *William de Coucy* that Thomas son of William de Roos of Kendale William son of William de Roos of Kendale, Robert his brother, Marmaduke de Twenge, Thomas son of Thomas de Levens, Adam de la Celere, Roger Oteway, John son of Thomas de Levenes, Henry son of William son of William de Rispeton, Thomas Roke, Robert son of Adam Walker, Adam son of Thomas Warde, Robert de Caplesheved, William son of John of Benedict, William son of Peter del Mire, Roger, his brother, Nicholas son of Baldwin, son of Gilbert, Robert Dennyson of Capelsheved, Robert Tilleson, Patrick son of Patrick Bronnson, Robert de Greteby, Richard Robertservaunt de Roos', William son of John son of Patrick, Richard son of Richard de Caplesheved, William his brother, Roger de Caplesheved, William son of Henry de Caplesheved,

William son of Patrick son of William Mons, Adam son of Thomas del Holme, Alexander de Middleton, William son of Thomas del Holme, John de Eskebank* and others entered his free chace and broke his park, *at Troutbeck*, hunted there, carried away deir, and killed two Mares of his, worth £20.

By fine of 10/- Westmorland.

1335

June 11, Pickering Commision of oyer and terminer to Robert de Clifford, Ranulph de Dacre, Richard de Aldeburgh and Adam de Bowes, on complaint by *William de Coucy*, that Thomas de Ros of Kendale, William & Robert his brothers, Thomas de Levenes, John de Levenes, Adam de la Solare† of Kyrkeby in Kendale, Roger son of Adam Otteway of Kyrkeby in Kendale, Robert de Capplesheved, Patrick de Shepesheved, William de Aldehargh, and others broke his park at "Hoton in the Haye" hunted there and carried away deer. By fine of 20/- Westmorland.

---

* Repeated with slight changes for June 6, when the following names are added: Roger de Levens, Ralph de Levens, Gregory de Holme, Patrick de Bland, Adam son of Henry Shepherd and others The Judges this time were Robert de Clyfford, William de Shareshull, Richard de Aldeburgh, Robert Parnyng and Edmund de Dacre

† Repeated with slight changes for Nov 11th

SOPHIA ARMITT.

TO FACE P. 157

PART II

CHAPTER I

THE DE LANCASTERS

Roger the Hunter ; His robberies and extortions as seneschal of Inglewood Forest ; Boundaries set up by Roger and Will de Lindesey at Rydal, Dies 1291, His widow Philippa has Witherslack and Rydal as dower, John of Howgill at Rydal 1338 ; a de Lancaster and Le Fleming marriage, Appendix I and II.

IT is with Roger de Lancaster that the actual history of Rydal begins. A man of powerful personality, who came to enjoy wide possessions, his name frequently appears in the records of the time, and yet his parentage on one side at least is doubtful. William de Lancaster, last baron of Kendal, when endowing the Abbey of Furness with lands in 1240, chose " my brother Roger " to be a witness, and this, which is twenty years after the death of Gilbert fitz Reinfrid, William's father, is probably the earliest mention of him that exists. The monks of Furness wrote him down as bastard brother of William ; but they had a quarrel with him (like many others), and he may well have been a half-brother who could not share an inheritance which—if originally brought by Helwise de Lancaster to her husband—was yet granted to the latter by the king as lands held in chief.

But whatever was the bar to inheritance, bar there was, and the lands of the barony went in the main, after William's death, to his sister. Roger however was quite capable of securing lands by other methods than inheritance, though when and where he began is not known.

When William in dying left him Patterdale and the forest of Westmorland, on the northern slopes of the Windermere mountains (including the service of two free tenants of his name) the exception was made of Fensdale and S. Cartefel and the head of Martindale,* which he held before, it is stated, " of ancient feoffment." He had also received from his brother half of the manor of Ulverston, to hold of the Abbot of Furness He held Witherslack and Morland He later secured Rydal from his kinswoman Margaret de Ros. He married (possibly for his second wife) Philippa the eldest of four sisters who were co-heiresses of Hugh de Bolebeck,† and gained with her lands in Essex and Cambridge.

Probably he had acquired Holgill or Howgill, in east Westmorland, which remained with his descendants. It lay conveniently for his business, which for a number of years—from 1256 to 1271 at the least—was that of seneschal of the royal forests north of Trent, including Inglewood, the great open chase that stretched with its subsidiary parks from Penrith to Carlisle.‡ This district, Roger, aided by a band of inferior officers, ruled with an iron hand; as is shown by certain Inquisitions that exist yet in writing at the Record Office.§ The circumstances of the case in dispute were strange and involved. The King of Scotland held six manors at that time within the forest which had been granted in 1242, in satisfaction of the Scottish claims in the northern counties ‖; one of them being the important *vill* of Penrith. Roger seems to have set himself to circumscribe the rights of the men of these manors and to annoy them in every way possible.

---

* Fensdale and Martindale are valleys that open out on the centre of Ullswater; the other name is obscure

† *Victoria History of Lancashire*—Feudal Baronage

‡ See Parker's " Inglewood Forest," note to p 5 of *Transactions*, C & W. A & A Society, vol vi., N S

§ They are given fully in Mr Parker's " Inglewood Forest," *Transactions*, C. & W. A & A Society, vol vi, N S

‖ Cox's *Royal Forests of England.*

First, by writ from the king, he held in company with the Sheriff of Cumberland, two Inquisitions at Maiden Castle near Penrith in 1268, by which he obtained countenance for the extension of the king's park at Plumpton, though this deprived the Penrith men of old rights of common pasture for their beasts. Loud complaints finally secured a counter Inquisition in 1271, when Roger no longer held office, and in this the grievances of the men of Penrith were fully heard. The indictments against the late keeper are, enclosure of Plumpton, imprisonment of the men who tried to protect their pasture there ; imparking land where the men of Scotby had pasture ; fencing the water where the Penrith cattle had been accustomed to drink, stopping the supply of wood which the men had a right to take for the repair of their houses and fences, so that they had been without timber for fifteen years, and further, when the men had obtained a mandate direct from the king for obtaining the same, delaying to take action ; fining the Sowerby men heavily for beasts taken on what had been their common pasture ; enclosing a piece of Penrith common and letting it ; stopping the right to take dead wood, and a cartload of dead alder and birch wood yearly for the repair of their waggons and ploughs ; seizing the swine on the common pastures when near park enclosures during fawning time and taking the best pig of the herd for himself ; stopping the right of the men to free fishing ; permitting the foresters to enter the manor and eat and drink there against the will of the townsmen, and likewise to seize the townsmen in their own houses, and imprison them without any license from superior authority.*

These indictments, though possibly exaggerated, are hardly favourable to the character of Roger. Mr. Parker

---

* An old custom, of quartering the foresters on the tenants within the forest-bounds, called *puture*, was often abused. Edward I called a further Inquest in 1274, to decide upon the rights of King Alexander's men of Penrith and Salkeld in the forest. Cox, *Royal Forests*.

sees in him, indeed, "a man of great, but perhaps indiscreet loyalty, who would guard what he supposed to be his sovereign's interests, even at the cost of neglecting orders and branding himself as a petty tyrant." But another story may be read from them, that of a nature strong and unscrupulous, who, where there is no risk of punishment, is robbing those who are not under the authority of his own master. It was the true Border raiding spirit, that kept the war with Scotland alive for centuries, displayed early by one in royal authority.

And Roger (if later accusations against him be correct) was not guiltless, even towards his master, the king. He was a mighty huntsman, it is certain, and loved the deer, as Norman William did, "like a father." It was an inherited taste perhaps, for Gilbert Fitz-Reinfrid had been appointed keeper of the Lancaster Forests by John in 1206 (Cox). The only public office Roger is known to have held besides that of keeper of the forests was Sheriff of Lancaster in 1265 and 1266. To be seneschal of vast Inglewood was a post after his own heart, but it did not quench his desire for parks of his own.

When at an early date (1255) the king (Henry III.) gave him a warrant for two harts and eight hinds from the forest of Lancaster, it has been conjectured that he was stocking a park at his manor of Witherslack.* Later, he obtained a charter to hunt smaller game in all the king's forests north of the Trent, which runs thus :—

Charter of Roger de Lancastre

Henry, by the grace of God,-etc. to all to whom these present letters shall come Greeting.

Know ye that we have granted for Ourselves and Our heirs to our beloved and faithful Roger de Lancastre that during the whole time of his life he should have this liberty, to wit, that he may hunt with his own hounds the fox, the hare, the badger and

---

* *Victoria History of Lancashire*—Feudal Baronage

the wild cat * throughout all Our forests beyond Trent wherever he shall wish (excepting the fence month),† and take and remove them without let or hindrance from Ourselves, Our heirs, our foresters, verderers or other bailiffs of the forest.

Provided always that he shall not by occasion of this our concession take our larger beasts, nor course in our warrens nor the warrens of others

In witness whereof we have caused these letter's patent to issue

Witness Myself at St Pauls, London, the twenty-first day of June, the fifty-first year of our reign

The temptations of his office, however, would seem to have been too strong for Roger, and he by no means restricted himself to the limits of the charter. For when an Eyre of Inglewood Forest was held at Carlisle in 1285, and the trespasses of twenty-three years were brought before the justice,‡ his name was quoted among the many and various defaulters.

" It is presented and proved by the foresters and verderers that lord Roger de Lancastre, at the time when he was keeper of the Forrest of Inglewood under Roger de Leyburn Justice of the aforesaid forest did in the 51st year of King Henry take six harts and hinds

Furthermore it is presented and proved that in the 52nd year of the same reign, Roger took five harts and hinds in the same forest and that the same Roger in the 53rd year took three bucks in the same forest and that in the 54th year the aforesaid Roger took four hinds and two does "

The indictment appears too likely for it to be false. Roger's own forest, which by his half-brother's bequest had spread from Martindale to Patterdale and " the whole forest of Westmorland," was very handy for transactions of the sort The deer had but to be driven

---

* These were classed as beasts of warren, as opposed to the higher class of preserved animals, called beasts of the forest.

† "The close season, a fortnight before and after St John Baptist's day, June 29 "

‡ " Inglewood Forest," F H. M Parker, M A., *Transactions*, C & W. A. & A Society, vol vii , N s

across the Eamont, and turned at Tirrell up the rising moorland road (made by the Romans), to attain with ease all the mountain recesses at the head of Ullswater that were Roger's ground and which he would be keen to stock. The whole region round about where the masses of High Street, Fairfield, and Helvellyn fall abruptly to the lake level, and where deep-cleft, wooded valleys rise to grassy mountain tops, is favourable to game of all kinds It is dotted over with names reminiscent of wild life, *e.g*, Grisedale, Boardale, Martindale, Buck Crag, Hartsop, Brock Crags, Hart Crag, and others connected with the chase Clarke's Survey (1789) shows how it teemed with wild life even in his time, and to this day the red deer roam at large in Roger's vale of Martindale.

Probably it was the game that caused Roger to covet Rydal, and which brought him over the mountain crests to our valley. Many a time, when he had followed the hart up his wild glens on the far side and reached the windy summits, may he have seen it plunge down the vales to the south, and away, far out of his bounds and reach. Our upland valley of Rydal Head, surrounded by an amphitheatre of mountains, was peculiarly adapted for a sanctuary for deer. It is possible that Roger introduced here the fallow deer, where hitherto the red only had roamed wild, and in contradistinction to the numerous Hart Crags of the heights, we have Buckstones, the haunt of the small race, in the seclusion of the upper park. And moreover—for it is hardly to be supposed that Roger would let the simple matter of a boundary stop him when following a hard-pressed stag—it would be guarded from intrusion by those men of Rydal whose village was clustered on the right bank of the beck, and who would certainly guard the forest rights of their lady from foreign hunters over the mountain. Besides, in connection with his choice of Rydal, Roger might find his kinsman William de Lindesey, who owned all the southern slope of the mountains with vales and forest, from the Rydal bounds over to Bowness by Windermere, unwilling to come to terms. Whereas with Dame Margaret de Ros he prevailed as we have seen, and he secured Rydal, along with half Loughrigg and some uncertain and unknown part of Ambleside. His charter remains in the Record Office and is given in the appendix.

Only two years after Sir Roger de Lancaster had secured it (1277), he was at variance with his neighbour, he met Sir William de Lindesey, lord of the forests of Ambleside and Troutbeck in solemn conclave, and the two " having touched the holy gospels," swore to abide by the agreement made between them and written down on the parchment still existing at Rydal Hall. The two lords were at too close quarters. Roger would not brook the straying of the cattle of the men of Loughrigg and Ambleside (William's men) over the becks (low in summer) into his park, and dealt high-handedly with them, as had been his manner when keeper of the king's forest of Inglewood, William, on the other hand, came forward to defend his men from arbitrary forfeits exacted by his arrogant neighbour in place of the customary small fine An enclosure of Roger's lands, where they touched those of his neighbour's, was decided on; and both Sir William de Lindesey and Lady Margaret de Ros agreed to share with him the cost and labour of rearing what were probably the first boundaries in the district.

It is of some interest to consider of what material these boundaries would be made. Where enclosure was not necessary boundaries were fixed by remarkable natural stones or by upright stones erected for the purpose, or by a cross or well. We hear of the standing-stone in this deed Solid building in stone could not have been lightly entered upon in that age. The rock of the district is hard to cleave or rive, while from the abundant forest, wood could be easily felled and split. Even the outer defences or peles of castles were at this time constructed of wood, oak uprights being solidly set close together for the purpose (see Peel, its meaning and derivation, by George Wilson). It is probable therefore that these boundaries were not stone walls, but a permanent development of the summer hedges in use, young growing trees partly cut through and laid horizontally with smaller stuff interwoven.

The garth and the summer hay, and corn fields of the townsmen were protected by light fences of wood or basket-work of boughs, but these were of a temporary character and easily removed, while the mark-land had hitherto lain open between *vill* and *vill*; so Rydal became cut off, once and for all, from the lands about her.

If we examine the agreement, it seems to work out as follows. The enclosure had only to be made on the two descending mountain ridges north and south of Rydal, because towards the west the river and lake naturally enclose it, while from the summits to the east Roger's own lands fell away into the steep glens of his forest of Westmorland. Firstly, Roger is to start his share of wall or fence from the top of his park—and it should be noted that the park is mentioned as distinct from the forest of Rydal, it being no doubt situated on the sloping ground or hanging valley which is still kept enclosed as park-land, and to run it down for 160 perches along the boundary between Rydal and " Stamdal " (Scandale) towards a place designated as " Rogerlloge " Then William has to begin his part of the fence where Roger started, running it in the other direction, upwards, for 160 perches towards " le Grag in le Grencone," where presumably the top of Scandale is reached, and danger from straying cattle averted. Now " the Crag " is difficult to define, as many Crags score the ridges hereabouts. It may mean a Little Dove Crag which is mentioned in a boundary riding of 1613, as being the next named station to the High Pike, and this may be synonymous with the Dove Crag of Roger's charter-boundary of 1275, which is selected to make a starting point for the descent by Scandale. It is strange that while " le Swythene " is mentioned in the 1275 boundary, it does not come into the 1277 enclosure-deed, while in the latter we have a district or a summit called " le Grencone." In neither does the word Fairfield occur; and the charter, when reciting the circuit of the horse shoe of mountains, passes from Brockstone by the lake upwards, by the Nab, by Laverd or Lord's Crag, by Erne Crag and thence upwards " unto the bounds of Westmorland, and so by the bounds of Westmorland unto the summit of the Dove Crag." This, while evading the name of the mountain, shows that Westmorland was still considered distinct from the barony of Kendal, and that the boundary between the barony of Kendal and the forest of Westmorland stood also for the boundary of Rydal.

On the north or Grasmere side, Roger undertakes again to start his fence from the lake itself, and run it up the slope of the Nab, and on as far as Laverd or Lord's Crag. Thence William will carry it half way on to Arn or Erne Crag, and Lady Margaret de Ros (who jointly with him holds the manor of Grasmere) will complete the portion between the two up to Erne Crag, where the enclosure ceases.

It is interesting to note that this manor boundary still runs up the face of the Nab, till stopped by sheer precipice, and again on, separating yet Grasmere from Rydal. Across the short meadow to the peninsula of Swan Stone which is certainly the Brockstone of the charter—while the latter name has been transferred higher—it has been removed, probably by John Park, of Nab, who secured a piece of Grasmere common land here, and so extended his meadow by the lake. The meadow now stands in two townships. And this is a good place to emphasize the fact that the lake now called by extension of the name Rydal Water, had little part in Rydal; two thirds of its shores being in Loughrigg and in Grasmere, and the lords of the latter manor possessing the fishing of its waters. It was Routha mere, the lake of the river Rothay.

The agreement continues that these fences are to be completed by Michaelmas of that year, and that if cattle should up to that time be found in Roger's forest, he is to charge no more than the customary half-penny for them, until the matter can be carried before the king and his council, who shall decide, once and for all, whether this customary sum, or whether " amercements in another manner " shall become legal. This appeal shall be put off no later than All Souls' Day

Further, there seems to have been some dispute or uncertainty about the true boundary on the lower ground by Scandale Beck, therefore—" that right bounds shall be made between them at Stamdalbeck near the park between Rydal and Stamdal " as well as in other lands in dispute at Witherslack, a jury shall be called in the customary manner, and the matter shall be decided by the " oath of honest sworn men."

This Indenture, which is of great interest in giving us old names for Rydal, is at Rydal Hall. The seal, tied up for protection, is unfortunately shattered, or we might have learned what arms Roger the hunter carried.

Of Roger's keen oversight of his forests and their game, there is evidence in the indictments he brought at various times before the courts, for trespasses on his parks in the county of Essex and in Rydal. In the last year of his life he sued Richard, son of Alan, John Lyam, and others for breaking his park of Rydale, hunting therein and taking his deer to the damage of £20.*

---

* De Banco Rolls, No. 87, n. 28d

But his hunting days were then over. No more would he follow the stag the live-long day up the glens from the north and over the crest, to drop down as evening fell, to rest and sleep at his " loge " or tower by the Rothay.

He died shortly before March 1, 1291, when certain manors in the south were ordered to be delivered to his widow Philippa.* The assignment of his estates occupied the king's officers in the next few months. By April 18, Philippa had done homage to the king for the lands she and Roger had held " in chief of her inheritance " and was granted seisin of them. Moreover, other lands which had not been hers were given her as dower, and an order was issued on May 2, and repeated on June 5 and 8, for the king's escheator

" to deliver to Phillippa, late the wife of Roger de Lancastria, to be held by her in dower, the manor of Wythirslack, co. Westmorland, which is extended at 15li 19s. 10d. yearly, the valley of Ridal, in the same county, which is extended at 20li .... as although the king lately took the homage of John de Lancastria, Rogers son and heir, for the lands that his father held in chief, and caused him to have seisin thereof, it was not his intention to omit assigning dower of the lands to Phillippa, and he has accordingly assigned to her the lands specified above."

A memorandum records the fact that John had been warned to appear in chancery " on the morrow of the Close of Easter," when the assignment of Philippa's dower was to be made, and that as he did not come, it had been conducted in his absence.†

While Philippa, therefore, was to enjoy for her life, along with her own lands, Rydal and Witherslack of the lands of Kendal, John was declared to be heir of all that his father, Roger, had held in chief. An elder brother, Robert, there seems to have been, no doubt by a first wife of Roger, who took apparently lands of less honourable tenure, and with them Holgill or Howgill.

---

* Cal of Close Rolls, Ed I.   † Cal of Close Rolls, Ed I

But though for the moment we hear nothing of him, John of Rydal was the great man, tenant in chief, and baron of the realm. He appears later in various state matters; attended parliament, and in 1301 set his seal, along with the other barons, to the joint letter of expostulation which Edward I. caused them to draw up to the Pope, concerning the latter's claim to Scotland.* He was also active in the Border warfare of the years between 1297 and 1301.† His wife was named Annora, and along with her he made a settlement of his estates during her lifetime—a procedure at that time not unusual.‡ According to this arrangement the manor of Rydal was to pass, after the death of the two, without heirs, to John's brother Roger for his life, and after that it was to revert to a John of Lancaster, described as "of Holgill," and apparently son of Robert (the son of Roger by an earlier marriage?) The manors of Barton and of Witherslack, also to be enjoyed by Roger for his life, then passed by arrangement to strangers.§

John of Rydal died childless in 1334 (he is probably the man referred to in the footnote), and by 1338 his widow Annora was likewise dead; for an order was issued on December 15 for the escheator

"to deliver to John de Lancaster of Holgill the manor of Rydale, co Westmorland, ... as the King has learned by inquisition that Annora, late the wife of John de Lancastre, held the manor with John for life by the grant of John de Lancastre of Holgill, by the late King's license with remainder after their death to Roger de Lancastre for life, and then reversion to John of Holgill and his heirs, . and that Roger died 11 years ago; and John of Holgill is of full age, and that the manor is held in

---

* The Ancestor, vol vi
† Feudal Baronage in *Victoria History of Lancashire*
‡ Cal Pat Rolls, 1317-21 Inq. ad quod damnum, 1 209
§ Cal of Close Rolls, 12 Ed III Ralph de Dacre took up all Barton but one holding, perhaps Sockbridge which was later held by this family and the Harrington family of Witherslack

chief by the service of a fourth part of a knight's fee . , the King has taken the homage of John of Holgill "*

Time went by and another Sir John held Howgill and Rydal.

Now this Sir John had four daughters only, and they were very desirable matches for the young knights and squires of the country side. Sir Thomas Fleming of Coniston, Lancashire, early sought to secure one as bride for one or other of his sons, having in view doubtless the manor of Rydal, held in chief of the king. The race of Flemings can be traced back to a certain Sir Michael " le Fleming," who had obtained lands in Furness and the sea-board of Cumberland in the time of Henry I. The manor of Coniston was acquired by Sir Richard, reckoned fourth in descent from Sir Michael,† through his marriage with the heiress Elizabeth de Urswick. It formed part of the Ulverston fief, to whose lord its holder owed suit and service, and we find that Sir Richard's son, Sir John, who fought with Edward I. in Scotland, procured a grant for a free chase or deer-park at Coniston from his feudal lord, who was Sir John de Lancastre of Rydal, son of the great Sir Roger, to whom half Ulverston had come from his brother: for which grant he was to pay a rose yearly, on St. John the Baptist's Day.‡

This fragile token may have been carried over each year to Rydal, as being nearer than Holgill, and laid down

---

* Cal of Close Rolls *Lancastrie*, 1 Edward III
1327. *John de Lancastria*, confirmed in his office of keeper of the castle and house of Lancaster
1328 John de L , who has custody of certain lands in co Lanc & collected money from them, carrying to the Exr at various times £1,400, has complained that he incurred many charges in carrying same (men at arms, &c) to Westminster & cannot secure an allowance for same charges fr treasurer & barons K. orders his reasonable expenses to be paid

† See Pedigree

‡ Sir D Fleming's MS pedigree The holders of Coniston owed suit and service likewise to the lords of the Lindesey Fee, to whom the other half of Ulverston belonged " John Flemyng holds Conyngston by the said [knights] service, half a carucate of land " Inq p m , No 63, 20 Ed III [1347] " Richard Flemmyng knight, holds the manor of Conyngston by homage and fealty and the service of 2½d as of the manor of Ulverston " Inq p m , No. 29, 49 Ed III.

solemnly in the lord's Hall on the rock, where his courts would be held. It served to keep up a connection between the two families of de Lancaster and Fleming, and also as a reminder that one was a step higher in feudal rank than the other In the failure of male heirs to Sir John de Lancaster, the astute Sir Thomas saw his opportunity, and the bond drawn up between the two for the marriage of their children is in existence.* It was dated thus—

"at Rydale in Kendale on Thursday next after ye feast of ye exaltation of ye holy crosse, in ye tenth yeare of ye reigne of King Henry the fourth after ye conquest,"

which was within a week of September 14, 1409 ; a date not easily understood, in consideration of Sir John's fine of 1425. It is certain, however, that the young people were, at the time of its writing, under age, for Sir Thomas undertakes to keep them " during their nonage." The dower which Sir John is to give with the young Isabel, his second daughter, is eighty marks of silver ; thirty to be paid on the day of the marriage, and the remaining fifty within the next two years, by half-yearly payments. Sir Thomas on his part is to supply an income of ten marks a year [£6. 13s. 4d.] to the young couple. No clause deals with Mistress Isabel's ultimate share of her father's lands, but it is a notable fact that the lord's seat at Rydal is given her as a residence, since a stipulation is made that if her father-in-law fail to produce the promised income within forty days after it is due, she and her husband Thomas may forcibly seize cattle upon the manor of Coniston, drive it to " Rydale in Kendale " and there keep it impounded until full satisfaction be made. A later clause arranges that if young Thomas should die without children by Isabel, then a second match is to be

---

* I have not found the original document, which Sir Daniel Fleming possessed but only the copy made and " translated out of french " by his friend, Dr. Thomas Smith, later Bishop of Carlisle

made between his younger brother John and one of Isabel's sisters, without either of the fathers laying down more money. This clause implies considerable determination on a match between the families, along with extreme youth in the parties contracted in marriage.

Thus the Le Flemings reached Rydal five hundred years ago. They had been in the country already at least three hundred years. Sir Michael "le Fleming" was at Furness in the reign of Henry I. Sir John the fifth in descent was at Coniston, after fighting against the Scots under Edward I. and one of his descendants, having four daughters, gives the second, Isabel, in marriage to Thomas Le Fleming, son of Sir Thomas of Coniston, in 1409.

APPENDIX I

Chart R 3 Ed I, m 4 Roll
1275. [Deed of Lady Margaret de Brus to Sir Roger de Lancastre of Rydal, and so much of Loughrigg and Ambleside as were of her demesne]

The King to Archbishops, Bishops, &c., greeting. We have inspected a charter which Margaret, formerly the wife of Robert de Ros of Werk made to our wel beloved and faithfull Roger de Lancastre, in these words —

Know all men present and to come that I Margaret de Brus, formerly the wife of Sir Robert de Ros of Werk, in my liege widowhood and full power, by the assent and will of my august Prince and Lord, Edward, by the grace of God, King of England, have given, granted and by this my present charter confirmed to Sir Roger de Lancastre, the whole of my forest of Rydale, with all its appurtenances, without any retention, that is, by these bounds. Beginning from the Dovekrag by the ridge of the mountain between Rydal and Scandal as the water deals, following that ridge unto *Standenesstan* (standing stone) in the Swythene, and so descending from the Swythene by a certain path that is called the *Weythesty* unto the park of Amelsate, and so following outside the park unto *Scandalebec*, and so following *Scandalebec* unto Routha, and following Routha in going upwards to Routhemere, and so following Routhemere to opposite the *Brockestan*, and so in a straight line unto the Brockestan, and from the *Brockestan* to the summit of the Nab, and so ascending by the ridge, as the water deals unto Laverd-grak by the heights ascending by the ridge unto the *Erne* grak, and thence ascending by the ridge of that mountain unto the bounds of Westmerland, and so by the bounds of Westmerland unto the summit of the Dove grak

"Incipiendo del Dove cragg per attiora montes inter Rydal et Scandal, sicut aqua si dividit, sequendo altiora montis illius usque ad Scandendestay in le Swythene ; et sic descendendo de Swythene, per quandam semitam quae vocatur le Waythesti, usque ad parcum de Amelsate, et sic sequendo parcum dexterius usque in Scandelbec ; et sic sequendo Scandelbec usque in Routha, et sic sequendo Routha, ascendendo usque in Routhemere ; et sic sequendo Routhemere usque ex opposito del Brokestay ; et sic linealites usque le Brokestay, et de le Brokestay usque ad summitatem de la Nab, et sic ascendendo per altiora, sicut aqua se dividit, usque Laverdkrag, et de Laverdkrag per superiora ascendendo per altiora usque le Ernekrag, et inde ascendendo per altiora illius montis usque ad divisas Westmorlandiæ; et sic per divisas Westmerlandiæ usque ad summitatem del Dove crag predicti"

Moreover, I have given and granted to the said Sir Roger, the whole of my part of Amelsate and Loghrigg, with all the appurtenances, by their right bounds, without any retention, with common pasture within the bounds of Gressemere, for all manner of his beasts Also I have granted, for me and my heirs, that the aforesaid Sir Roger and his heirs, and their men dwelling within the aforesaid bounds of Rydale, shall have common of pasture everywhere with my men of Gressemere, To have and to hold to the said Sir Roger and his heirs or assyns and their heirs, all the aforesaid forest, with free chase of the said forest and all the appurtenances, with nothing retained, as is aforesaid, without gainsay of me or my heirs, as freely, quietly, well wholly, in peace, right and inheritance, as Peter de Brus, formerly my brother, or William de Lancastre, formerly my uncle, in their time held the same, without any diminution or retention, in ways, paths, meadows, marshes, waters, pools, mills, woods, all manner of deer feeding-grounds, pastures, plains, and all other liberties and easements to the said forest and lands belonging, of the said lord the King and his heirs in chief, in the third year of the reign of the said King by the service of the fourth part of one knight's fee, for ever, for all service, customs, exactions, demands, and all manner of suite which at any time by me or my heirs or assigns or their heirs could be demanded For which forest and lands aforesaid, the said King has taken the homage of the aforesaid Roger, by my assent and by my instance, and to the lord the King and his heirs I have remised and quit-claimed, for me and my heirs, all my right and claim to the homage and service of the said Roger or his heirs for the said forest and lands and their appurtenances whatsoever And I Margaret and my heirs will warrant to the aforesaid Roger and his heirs or assigns and their heirs all the aforesaid forest and all that is aforesaid, without any retention against all people for ever. In testimony of which, to this present charter I have placed my seal, these being witnesses Thomas de Musegrave, then sheriff of Westmerland, John de Hyrlawe, John de Morevill, Ranulph de Dacre, Henry de Stavelegh, Michael de Haricla, and Roger de Burton, knights, William de Wyndleson, Roger son of Sir Gilbert de Lancastre, Thomas de Derleye, Ralph de Patton, Roger de Brunuluesheved, Gilbert his son, Thomas de Lancastre, and others

We, moreover, grant and confirm the aforesaid gift and concession to the aforesaid Roger and his heirs, as the charter reasonably witnesseth, so that the said Roger and his heirs shall have and hold the forest aforesaid, and the said part of Amelsate and Loghrigg and all others contained in the charter aforesaid, of us and our heirs in relief, performing therefor the service of the fourth part of one knight's fee for all service, for ever Witness, Robert of Bath and Wells, and Walter of Rochester, Bishops, William de Valencia, Edmund our brother, Earl of Lancastre, John Fitz John, John de Vesey, Pagan de Chaworth, Robert de Typetot, Stephen de Penccastre, William de Helyun and others. Given by our hand at Westminster, 30th May (1274).

(*Charter Rolls*, 3 Edw I, No 68, m 4, No 11).

APPENDIX II.

Agreement between the neighbouring land-owners at Rydal.

May 3, 5 Edw I, 1276 This writing indented witnesseth that since many contentions had arisen between Sir Roger de Lancaster, of the one part, and William de Lyndesey, of the other part, on the day of the Invention of the Holy Cross in the fifth year of the reign of King Edward first to wit, that when the said Roger sought forfeitures of the men of the said William for their cattle taken in the forest of the same Roger in Rydal, and the same William said he and his heirs ought not to be amerced, but to give so much for each ox, cow and mare found in the aforesaid forest by escape, and also for a pig a halfpenny, and also for five sheep a halfpenny, and for five goats a penny, it has thus been settled between the same that the same Roger has granted for himself and his heirs that he will cause to be enclosed 160 perches by a rod of 20 feet, namely, from the upper part of his park of Rydal, where the park was on the day of the making of these presents, towards Rogerlloge following the right bounds between Rydal and Stamdal And the said William has granted for himself and his heirs that where the said Roger fails to enclose by following the right bounds aforesaid that he will cause to be enclosed 160 perches towards le Grag in le Grencone. The same Roger has also granted that if he shall enclose anything of the land of the said William by his park, he shall let so much of his own land outside his park to the said William in exchange, and upon his land there let outside his park (as far as the park of the said Roger extends towards le Grag in le Grencone, and not on the other side of the water of Routhmer outside the close towards le Lauergrag) he shall make no imparkment The same Roger has also granted for himself and his heirs that he will cause to be enclosed on the other side of Rydal from the water of Routhmer as far as le Lauerdgrag by the right bounds between Rydal and Gresmer And the same William has granted for him and his heirs that he will cause to be enclosed the half of le Lauerdgrag as far as le Arngrag by the right bounds between Rydal and Gresmer And Margaret de Ros shall cause to be enclosed the other half between le Lauerdgrag and le Arngrag by the right bounds aforesaid And these enclosures shall be made before the feast of St. Michael in the year abovesaid It is agreed also between the same that if the cattle of the same William or his men be taken within the aforesaid forest of the aforesaid Roger de Rydal by escape, they shall give for each animal as above, until it has been discussed by the consideration of the lord the king or his council whether the said Roger shall take halfpence for cattle taken in form aforesaid or amercements in another manner. And both the parties have granted that the discussion shall be made within the feast of All Souls in the year abovesaid Also that by the giving and taking of the aforesaid halfpence, to neither party (nor to their heirs until the aforesaid discussion be made between them, which shall be made within the aforesaid time) shall any prejudice be done, and both parties shall show for their state, before the lord the king or his council, without plea, what they see to be profitable for them, and upon this they shall take consideration, and with that consideration they shall be content for ever Both the parties have also granted that right bounds shall be made between them at Stamdalbeck near the park between Rydal and Stamdal, and also of the land of the same Roger in Wythirslack according to the tenor of his charter on the oath of honest sworn men Both parties have also granted that according to the extent of the honest men exchange shall be made between the same of the land of the same Roger in Lickeberg and the land of the same William in Crossetwayt, so that the same Roger shall have, by right extent, against the land of Lickeberg, which shall for ever remain to the said William and his heirs by exchange, the land of the same William to the value in Crossetwayt. And that these agreements may be faithfully observed by each party, having touched the holy gospels they have sworn and obliged themselves by mutual faith, and to the present writing indented have mutually affixed their seals These being witnesses, Sirs Henry de Staneley, Roger de Burton, knights, William de Wyndesheuer, Gilbert de Quythy, John de Crashuthyn, Gilbert de Brímolsheuid, Richard de Gilpyn, Richard Fitz Julian, and others These interlinings, namely, " as far as the park of the said Roger extends towards le Grag in le Grencone, and not on the other side of the water of Routhmer outside the close towards le Lauerdgrag," " nor to their heirs until the aforesaid discussion be made between them, which shall be made within the abovesaid time," were made before the signing of these presents.

CHAPTER II

THE FLEMINGS OF RYDAL

Knights, Squires, and Retainers; Wars of the Roses; The Luck of Muncaster; Families of Bellingham and Parr; Warwick the king-maker; Appendix showing agreement for military service.

NO doubt Sir Thomas the father, in forwarding this arrangement for the marriage of his son to the young Isabel de Lancaster, remembered the power that lies in possession. But when Sir John de Lancaster died, and his various lands were divided among his four daughters, the coveted little manor of Rydal did not fall wholly to Isabel. In the strange method of partitioning that then obtained, she was ordained to share it with her sister Margaret, who married Sir Matthew de Whitfield. The Whitfields were a family of long lineage, who took their name from their place of residence in Northumberland. They had no wish apparently to dispute the occupation of the lord's seat at Rydal with the Flemings and almost from the first an arrangement seems to have been made by which they "let to farm" to the latter, their half of the manor at the fixed sum of £10 per annum. This arrangement is expressed in a parchment document of 1475, drawn up by the successors of Thomas and Matthew, in which John Whitfield, for the said rent, lets his share of the manor to John Fleming, reserving only to himself as part lord the right to hunt in the forest, to keep a chamber within the Hall court, and to enjoy the profits of the brewery; with an added receipt of five marks as "gressum" from John Fleming, no doubt as acknowledgment of his use of the other's share in the lord's seat. This John Whitfield died on July 6, 1487; and the inquisition held at his death declared that he owned a "moiety" of the manor of "Ridell," worth £4, with a moiety of the manor of "Lowthryg," held in chief by service of a quarter of a knight's fee, and the rent of a red rose on Mid-summer Day, if demanded. His son and heir, Robert, was 38 years old.* This old compact was carried on by the representatives of the two families for a space of some hundred years, and two documents exist, of the years 1544 and 1547, in which a John Whitfield acknowledges the receipt by the hands of his attorney, William Sandes, of £5 half-yearly rent from Hugh Fleming.

But before following the history of the manor and the lord's seat further, it is necessary to notice the succession and the fortunes (as far as we know them) of the holders.

Thomas and Isabel had at least one son, William. He was alive in 1474, as were they, when a family deed was drawn up, conveying to their "kinsman," John Fleming, the manor of Beckermet, Cumberland, the most northerly of the family possessions. It is easy to suppose that this John was the brother of Thomas, for whom in youth another de Lancaster match had been proposed. He is put down in the usual pedigrees as son to Thomas; but Sir Daniel Fleming, who had examined all the family documents, ventured on no nearer title than the "kinsman" of the Beckermet deed.

But William, when the deed was drawn up, may have been dying. Both he and his father were seemingly dead the following year, when John Fleming made his agreement to farm John Whitfield's half of Rydal. Isabel survived as a widow, to what must have been a great age. For in 1483, she made her will. This proves her still in legal possession of her patrimony of half Rydal and Loughrigg, although she had probably on her husband's death handed over the management of them to the heir. By this will she constituted "her beloved in Christ John Flemyng" son of John Flemyng deceased, to be her attorney and executor, in handing over her Rydal and Loughrigg

---

* Cal. of Inq. p. mort., Hen. VII, vol I, 314

estates to John Fleming of Coniston and John Utlyng, chaplain. There is an ambiguity of "Johns" here hard to follow; but she seems at all events to have left all her inheritance by the Rothay to the heirs of her husband's family in the right line.

In the person of John Fleming, the new lord of Rydal, we are brought into relationship with the great events of the times. The cliques at court, and the parties among the nobles that began to form at once round the young King Richard II., and which were not to die out till the rival descendants of Edward III. and of the old noble families of England were well nigh extinct, either by murder or combat, were in all probability little felt in these parts. The old kingdom of Northumbria that had once fought so fiercely for rival dynasties of its own, had always been indifferent to the cabals of the court in the south; and so long as it was not grossly oppressed, it took the side, as a rule, with the old order. Besides, the north country was still absorbed in the Scotch wars, of which it had to bear the brunt. Richard's ill-advised raid upon the great towns of Scotland brought no real relief and was soon to be revenged in the English defeat at "Chevy Chace"—Otterburn—by Hotspur, 1388, which left the victory with the Scotch. But with the opening of the fifteenth century, and Henry of Bolingbroke's seizure of the crown, the nobles and knights of Westmorland and Kendal began to be caught up in the current of party strife. The increasing power of the nobles, in face of the weakness of the crown, had by this time fostered a new method of warfare. By this method each great nobleman carried a small army of his own into battle with him, which had enlisted under him, and was personally bound to him. Not content with his own officers of the household and personal retainers, he engaged the services of knights and squires, who undertook to bring along with them, in their turn, the men they could command, and to fight with him upon his personal summons. This system was called "livery and maintenance," because the noble supplied to all his following while "out," food as well as wages, and the badge that betokened them as his men for the time. The bond or contract drawn out between noble and knight, contained always a clause that the latter should not be called upon to fight "against the King," or "against his allegiance"; but this was little more than a phase, since a private interpretation was always possible, and there were besides often two crowned heads alive together, who would either of them fit the phrase.

Such bonds are to be found in many of the muniment rooms of these counties; as, for instance one of Richard Otway, esquire, with Ralph, Earl of Westmorland, in 1408,* and the one made out in 1449 between Walter Strickland son of Sir Thomas Strickland of Sizergh, and Richard, Earl of Salisbury. Then in 1478, John Fleming, esquire, indented in like manner to fight with Ralph, Lord Greystoke, as a bond preserved at Rydal Hall shows† (see appendix to this chapter). The stipulations vary little in these documents. In all of them the superior is to be allowed a third share of the plunder taken by the inferior, and of the ransoms of his prisoners; while he gives the latter and his followers "bouche court" or maintenance, and such wages as are at that time customary. The retaining fee in peace varies however. Otway takes four marks yearly, John Fleming four pounds, and Walter Strickland (who could carry a large number of men into the field with him) ten marks.

John Fleming was a free lance, like many another squire of the time, with leisure and energy to spare. The Wars of the Roses offered him excitement and occupation,

---

* Lord Muncaster's MSS. His MS Commission

† I have not seen the original which D F mentions in his List The list in the appendix is taken from that given in Clarke's *Survey of the Lakes.*

as the Crusades had offered in times gone by to men of his race. He would call around him the restless spirits and the younger sons of the dalesmen of Rydal, of Coniston, of Beckermet—manors of which he was soon to be lord ; and with these sturdy archers and billmen, march to answer the call of Ralph of Greystoke, and to fight under his banner. But on which side did he fight, for York or Lancaster, for white or red rose ? That can only be conjectured by endeavouring to follow in the scant records of the period the part taken by his leader in those involved and shifting scenes of warfare

With the House of Lancaster our lordship of Kendal was knit in somewhat close ties. Henry of Bolingbroke's great son, the Duke of Bedford, was its lord ; and in that brief period when he came to fight the Scots, he would surely pause upon his lordship, and hunt the deer in his forest by the lake. On his death, his unhappy nephew, Henry VI. inherited it, and it was administered under the crown. The Stricklands of Sizergh acted as the king's officials, as they had done before *, and Walter, son of the ruling Sir Thomas, held (as already noted) an appointment from 1437 onwards as receiver of the lordship, and keeper of the park of Calgarth. In 1444, two-thirds of it was granted to John, Duke of Somerset , but his death in the same year threw it back to the crown, as his heir, Margaret, was but two years old. The confirmation of father and son in the office of steward of Kendal lands was made out in 1446 (4 Nov , 25 Hen VI , Sizergh MSS.), for [ominous clause !] " so long as they bear themselves well in the office." Discontent, sedition, strife were indeed by this time at large. England's possessions in France were ignominiously lost , the marriage of the king to Margaret of Anjou, which ratified the cession of Maine and Anjou, was not popular , and the Duke of Suffolk,

---

* Under Ed. III —a Strickland acted as collector of taxes and of the king's wool

into whose hands the incapable king had allowed the royal power to slide, was ruling in his own interests alone. The able and the wise Richard, Duke of York, was beginning to be looked to as a possible succourer of England. Perhaps Walter de Strickland, as he rode with the king's monies on the journeys from Kendal to London, the expenses of which appear in the Minister's Account, was caught by the seething spirit of the times and took part in the counsels of the discontented nobles ; perhaps he thought with others, that reform must come with force, and that the enemies of Suffolk need not eventually be the enemies of his master·the king. At all events, he made out his agreement with Neville, Earl of Salisbury, one of the most powerful of the nobles, whose daughter had married York, and whose son was the great Earl of Warwick, the future king-maker. This was in 1449, the year when Normandy was lost, and the Duke of York made lieutenant of Ireland ; and some years before swords were actually drawn. To be sure, York took up arms in 1452, on the ostensible reason of deplacing the Duke of Somerset, who—Suffolk being dead—now took his place with the king, and was only stayed from action by negotiations and compromise : And again in 1453 he marched aggressively to London with an immense following, which included, besides his own son, the future Edward VI., the Earls of Salisbury, Warwick, and Richmond. To this army then, Strickland must have joined himself, with his bowmen and billmen. The die was cast ; he was an open Yorkist. The red rose that it had been his duty to lay down yearly in token of allegiance to the king was no longer paid ; and it is in this year that the grant by which Henry VI. conferred the lordship of Kendal on Edmund, Earl of Richmond, married to Margaret, daughter of the Duke of Somerset, is dated. Strickland's stewardship was over, and he is only named as renting with another man the park of Calgarth.

The king's mind had now entirely given way, and the Duke of York was appointed protector by the parliament. Quiet therefore lasted till the king's recovery, and the restitution of Somerset to power, when the first battle was fought in the long Wars of the Roses, at St. Albans, on the 22nd of May, 1455. Fresh settlements and fresh battles succeeded each other. At Wakefield Green, Yorkshire, on the last day of 1460, where the Red Rose triumphed, York was slain. On this occasion Ralph, Lord of Greystoke, was suspected of treachery towards his party, but succeeded in clearing himself, and swore allegiance to Margaret, and her son.* Salisbury was executed next day. But the tide turned, York's son, Edward, was proclaimed king in London, on March 4, 1461, straight from his victory at Mortimer's Cross. Then, hearing of the immense army of Northmen and Borderers (said to be 60,000 in number) who had gathered to do battle for Henry in Yorkshire, he and Warwick marched north, and, meeting it at Towton near York, defeated it in a fiercely fought battle that is said to have lasted from one snowy afternoon to the next.

From this battle begin the hunted days of the unhappy Henry. His person, long guarded by both parties in the strife, was now not safe from his enemies. He is generally said to have fled after Towton, with Margaret and his son Edward, to Scotland and Edinburgh. But if contemporaneous evidence is examined, it appears rather that he separated himself from his wife and son, perhaps as an expedient for safety, and escaped by a more western route to Scotland. The Paston Letters † tell of his reported escape by a back postern from a besieged castle in Yorkshire, while his followers diverted the attention of the besiegers by a " bicker " in front ; and of the capture of some of his fleeing adherents. Of these, the Earl of

---

* *Victoria History of Cumberland*
† No. 451 of Prof. Gardiner's edition

Wiltshire, and Dr. Morton and Makerell, were taken at Cockermouth. This shows that one pursued party had taken the road over the " Pennine " pass, through Westmorland and Cumberland to the coast, probably to take ship to France or to Scotland. If we could suppose the king to have been of this party, and when the pursuit became hot, to have been dropped for safety in the quaint vale of Eskdale, we should have corroboration of the Muncaster stay, even to the date.* That story tells how the king, wandering in flight after Towton, sought refuge (where perhaps it was expected to be warmly given) at Irton Hall, but he was denied. Some shepherds, finding him on the heights above the Esk, led him down to Muncaster Castle, where Sir John Pennington concealed and cared for him till immediate danger was passed. For this service he presented his host with a cup, which is preserved at the castle to this day as the famous " Luck of Muncaster " ; and in a bedroom of the castle is an old portrait of the king, kneeling with the cup in his hands, bearing the date 1461. The cup, which I saw in 1897, is of antique coloured glass, patterned, and is conjectured to have been a chalice for sacramental wine, and such the pious king may well have carried along with him. We read in a letter dated the close of that summer,

" The King Herry (*sic*) is at Kirkhowbre [Kirkcubright] with iiij men and a childe. Quene Margaret is at Edenburgh and her son "†

It seems likely therefore that he made his way to Scotland from Muncaster by a western route.

The Lancastrian party was for the time utterly broken. The new young king, Edward, who was immensely popular with the people and with London and other towns,

---

*Dr Parker in his *Gosforth District*, places the incident in 1464, after the battle of Hexham.

† No 480

was willing to deal leniently with nobles of the opposite side who came to him. One of these was Ralph of Greystoke, who is immediately heard of as one of the commissioners appointed to array the men of Westmorland and the north against Henry, late king, and the Scots.* From this time his name frequently appears, both as acting in negotiations with the Scots and fighting in the field with Warwick, and Warwick's brother Lord Montacute. A treaty was made with the Scots in 1462, when the queen of the Scots, widow of James II. is said to have met Lord Hastings and other nobles at Carlisle, and agreed that the hunted " King Harry " and his adherents should be given up (Margaret and the prince had succeeded in reaching France). At the same time news spread that Lord Dacre had yielded, and that he, Sir Richard Tunstall, and " one Bellyngham " had been beheaded in Carlisle Castle.† The great Earl of Warwick too, came to Carlisle, in the hope of pacifying the country and border.

But by the end of the year war blazed out again in the north-east, where the whole fighting force of the Lancastrians was concentrated to support Margaret who landed with troops from France; and the three castles of Alnwick, Dunstanburgh, and Bamborough were held for the party. Acting with the besiegers was Ralph of Greystoke. Henry was there; and after the battle of Hexham, fought on May 15, 1464, when the Lancastrians were totally routed, he succeeded in making his escape from the castle of Bamborough. Among those who helped him, on May 31, in this hazardous feat, Sir Henry Bellingham is mentioned, and among the few faithful followers who rallied round him, and " him assisted, succoured, and helped," was Alexander Bellingham of Burneside, in Westmorland, gent."‡ For a whole year Henry wandered,

---

* Rymer's Foedera, under date June 8, 1462, *the Victoria History of Cumberland*, says 1461, also Morris in " Nunburnholme "
† Paston Letters, No. 528
‡ *History of Northumberland*, Ed Bateson, B A

moving from hall to hall as danger threatened or suspicion was excited. In the western wilds of Yorkshire he is said at first to have found shelter, but that he came over on several occasions into Westmorland, is certain. That he should have been hidden for a time in the strong tower of the Bellinghams at Burneside, or even in his old lordship, the forest of Troutbeck by Windermere, would seem likely, but for the dangers of passing Kendal. Besides the powerful Stricklands, who had been his servants, and whose stronghold of Sizergh was hard by the town, there was seated in the Castle of Kendal the family of Parr * Unlike their neighbours, the Parrs had been staunch, from first to last, to the house of York, "Sir Thomas o Parre" being named among those attainted along with the Duke of York in 1459 (see Paston Letters No. 423 †). The citizens of Kendal too, who have half of them owned Henry, not only as king but as manorial lord, were probably by this time, like other townsmen, supporting the rule of Edward, which promised peace,

---

* Cal Pat Rolls, 7 Ed IV p 11

1467 Dec 10   Grant to *Wil Pur*, kn & *John Par*, esq his brother & their heir's of the manor of *Burnaldeshede & the Castle* of same & 40 m   s ? 300 ac of land, 200 ac of mead 100 ac of wood, & 500 ac of pasture in Stirkelondket [tle], co West with kn⁸ fees, adv s' lib s, fran s, and views of frank-pledge, courts leet & all app s, late of *Henry Belyngeham*, k n *rebel*, & in k's hand
York and Lancaster Cal Pat R, 11 Ed IV, p 1, *Wars of the Roses*

1471, July 20   Com to Wil Parre, kn, John Parre, kn, Thom Strykland, kn, & Christopher Moresby, kn . to arrest *Lancelot Thirkeld*,kn, *Joan Musgrave*, widow, Thom Sandeford, esq Wil Musgrave, Nicholas Musgrave, John Musgrave, *Henry Belyngeham*, kn, Roger Belyngeham, Christopher Belyngeham James Belyngeham, Alexander Belyngham, Thomas Skelton son & hr of John Skelton of Branntethwayte, & *Wil Lancastre son & h of Roger Lancastre*, esq who have made forfuture to the king, & bring them before the k, & council & seize their goods & lands to the k's use

1471, July 4   *Lan Thykeld*, kn's name is among some others to be arrested and brought bef k & goods seized, mostly Scarborough men & *Ed Thornburgh & Thomas Danell*

† Cal Pat Rolls, 19 Hen VI, p 111

1441, June 6   The k in his 16th year May 31 comm to *Thom Parre, kn* the reeping of 2 parts of all lands in the hamlets of Crossethwayt & Hoton in the town of Strykelandketyll, & in the towns of Forsethwayt, Strykeland-ketyll & Helsyngton & the keeping of the fishing of Kente, &c West, & all lands & ten s in Whityngton, Co. Lancaster, in the K's hand, by death of John d of Bedford, to hold fr Easter the last fr 10 years, rending yly £25 12 10, the k has granted, to Wil Ayscogh, Jus of the Bench, the said farm fr 10 years, & after that term the whole of the premisis for life

and an increase of trade. John Maychell, of Crakenthorp, after Henry's capture in Lancashire, was expressly pardoned for having several times sheltered and concealed him. One Westmorland gentleman at least sheltered him; and the tradition that lingers still at Crakenthorp Hall, that he was hidden there in guise of a gardener, and the garden shown where he worked, is in essentials true.

It was when at last Edward seemed firmly settled on the throne, in 1468, that our John Fleming made his fighting compact with Ralph of Greystoke. What did it mean? Whether John had previously been in the field—which seems likely—or on which side, we have no means of knowing. It seems probable that the bulk of the statesmen of our valleys would be on the side of their old lord, King Harry. And, although Ralph of Greystoke had for some years been openly fighting for the Yorkists, it is possible that he was at this time secretly arranging for an entire change of flank. If so, he was acting as a pawn in the hands of the king-maker Warwick. For Warwick had now fallen out with Edward, being displeased at his marriage, and he had carried along with him his son-in-law, and Edward's brother, the Duke of Clarence. It is supposed that he intended to raise the latter to the throne instead of Edward. The two certainly instigated the rebellion that broke out in the north in 1469, under the so-called "Robin of Redesdale," which was so far successful that its leader, Sir William Conyers, defeated Edward's forces, and took prisoners the father and brother of his wife, and beheaded them. But perhaps Warwick found that there was little chance of rousing all England for the purpose of setting the worthless Clarence in his brother's place. He arranged to meet his old enemy, Margaret of Anjou, at the French king's court, and there at Amboise was formally reconciled to her; agreed to marry his daughter to her young son, and to set the unfortunate Henry on the throne again. Invading

England with a great army, he actually did this Edward surprised on a march northward, was suddenly deserted by Montacute, Warwick's brother, (who had hitherto continued to fight with him), and 6,000 followers, who at a signal threw the badge of the White Rose from their caps, and cried "God bless King Harry." Edward, finding himself deserted, fled on horseback to the coast and crossed the seas, waiting for the turn of fortune, which in another year saw him again and finally on the throne, Warwick slain, and Henry assassinated.

And where, in these rapidly changing and dramatic scenes, did Ralph of Greystoke and John Fleming with his Rydal men stand? Did they proclaim themselves as Henry VI. and Warwick's partizans by joining the northern rebellion that broke out so soon after their compact? or did they wait, and with Montacute, Ralph's earlier companion in battle, treacherously fling down the White Rose in the moment of Edward's need?

Next year, 1471, when Sir Thomas Strickland was knighted by Edward on the last, bloody battle-field of Tewkesbury,* they and other Lancastrians had to make their peace with him; and apparently he dealt leniently with them. We miss the name of Ralph, Lord of Greystoke, from the commissioners appointed that year to treat with the Scots, and amongst whom was Sir William Parr; but two years later it re-appears. Edward's only confiscation seems to have been that lordship of Kendal which included the Forest of Troutbeck, Ambleside, half Grasmere, Langdale, and Loughrigg; and this he handed over (along with the decoration of the Garter) to his faithful adherent Sir William Parr, of Kendal Castle, with reversion to his brother Sir John Parr.† His son, Sir Thomas, was empowered next year, 1473, to muster in the neighbourhood along with John Sturgeon

---

* Paston Letters
† See Cal of Pat Rolls

thirteen men-at-arms, and 1,000 archers, whom the king wished to send to the assistance of his ally and brother-in-law, the Duke of Burgundy. Such an enrolment was no doubt of advantage. It would draw off the turbulent, fighting spirits who promoted disorder and warfare, and leave the county to that peace which was required, in order to pursue the trade that became its engrossing object for the next hundred and fifty years.

APPENDIX.

From Clarke's *Survey of the Lakes*, 2nd Ed. 1789.
COPY OF INDENTURE, 7 ED. IV.

1468 [Ralph lord of Greystoke sat on all the Commissions for these parts from 1467 to 1477 See Cal of Pat Rolls]

This indenture, made the 9th day of December in the 7th year of the reign of King Edward the IV betwixt Rauf Lord Greystoke and Wemin on the ton party, and John Fleming Esquire on the toder party, witness that the said John is reteined and behest with the said Lord. for terme of his life, as well in were as in peace, against all manner of men, except his legiance. The [said?] John taking of the said Lord four pounds of lawfull money of England , and in the time of were, such wages as the king giffs to such men of such degree, and he go with the said lord. And the said John to take his said fee be the hands of the receiver of Greystoke, that is, or shall be, that is to say at Whitsuntide and Martynmas And if the said John go with the said Lord over the sea, or into Scotland, and then it happen the said John Fleming, or any of his servants, to take any prisoners, that then the said Lord to have the third and the third of thirds. And if it happen that the said Lord send for the said John, to come to him and to ryde with him to London, or for any other matter, that then the said Lord to pay for his costs, and to give him bouche court for him and his feliship. In witness hereof, ayther party to the partyes of these indentures enterchangably hath set to their seales, wretyn the day and yere aforesaid.

Several indentures are extant showing the nature of the agreements. There is one at Muncaster Castle, in which Richard Strong, esquire, agreed to fight with Ralph,

Earl of Westmorland at the rate, in times of peace, of four marks a year. This is as early as 1408.

In 1449, Walter Strickland, esquire, of Sizergh contracted with Neville, Earl of Salisbury to follow him to field with all his tenants, and he was eventually able to provide without horse, 290 bowmen and billmen; again one de Threlkeld, when boasting of the special advantages of his three separate manors, said that Threlkeld furnished a goodly list of tenants who would follow him to the wars.

CHAPTER III

Trade in the Valleys

English wool—Temp Edward III.—to be made up in England; Price of wool; Flemish weavers, no cloth to be imported; remission of duty on Herdwick wool; Walk-mills in the Loughrigg valleys; the Bensons; Kendal Green, &c.; Appendix, Cloths of various kinds and colours.

UNDER the Norman and early Plantagenet rulers, our little townships—Rydal and Loughrigg, with their neighbours higher and lower in the valley—must have passed a quiet existence, quite out of the track of public events, absorbed by their husbandry; and, by the complicated rule of their village lands held in common, each household was self-sustaining. The land and the little flock of sheep with a few cattle supplied food and clothing, which was worked up by the family. In a petition of the customary tenants of the barony of Kendal to Charles, Prince of Wales, A.D. 1619, the tenants thus describe their estates and their own condition :—

"Which Estates are verie small, and the soile thereof for the most part verie barran yet by reason they trade in making course clothes, they are the better enabled to live, and their houses better builded, but not by goodness of their tenements"

The wool was spun and woven into a rough cloth in the house, and then carried to the lord's walk-mill to be fulled, before it was stitched into warm, simple garments worn by the folk. There was little need for the dalesman to leave his *vill* from one year end to another, unless he were called with the "grave" to the higher court at Kendal as representative of his township, or to obtain justice there against a serious wrong.

Then came prolonged warfare, when he was forced to take a wider out-look and to rub shoulders, through the hardships of short campaigns, with county men who were not his neighbours. He must have become, through the fourteenth century, when the bickering warfare with the Scots rarely ceased, except from exhaustion, a man of wider experience and knowledge, as well as a pretty good fighter with pike and bow. But his home and his village suffered; and it is clear that in that age our valleys languished both in population and prosperity

Then came the age of trade. True, it was not yet the age of peace; but civil warfare in England, as has been remarked, rarely interfered with and never ruined trade. After the time of the Conquest, war ceased to be ruthless; the husbandman and his cattle were always respected. England with its moist climate grew wool for all western Europe; and the canny Englishman guarded the fleece that made his gold. So it was that through the Wars of the Roses—the most bloody fought on English soil, and in which Kendal and our John Fleming and his men had large concern—the infant trade in cloth did not diminish, but rather increased. It had its rise in Edward III.'s reign, when it occurred to some wise mind in council or parliament, that it were well to save the money paid to foreign countries for cloth made from English wool. Wool, indeed, had been pouring out of the country for long. It was wool and not gold that paid the ransom of our careless king, Richard I. Edward the III. paid for his

French war with it. Foreign merchants—Spanish or Italian and Flemish—crowded our seaports, buying and exporting it, and ever ready with their superfluous cash, to lend money in place of the Jews, expelled by Edward I. Even the plant that *teased* the wool ready for the spinner (the teasle) was grown in England and exported.

And in this export trade our county, and possibly our valley, had early come to share. When Edward III. procured from parliament the large grants of wool, that served him instead of taxes, Cumberland and Westmorland furnished their contingent along with other counties. In 1335, John Strickland and Roger of Burneside, being then the king's wool-collectors for Westmorland, the amount furnished by the county with Cumberland and Northumberland, was 600 sacks.* In the previous year, when 30,000 sacks had been levied from the whole country for the royal exchequer, the amount fixed as payment for wool from these counties by indenture with the wool merchants was five marks the sack (£3. 6s. 8d.) Now this was the lowest price paid, the next lowest being five and a half for Craven wool; while the range increased, until twelve marks was paid for the wool of Herefordshire.† Indeed, when in 1341, the king's grant numbered 20,000 sacks, three wool-merchants of York were empowered to take 400 sacks from Cumberland and Westmorland, described as "fulle (foul) & of little value" at as low a price as four marks (£2. 13s. 4d.) the sack.‡ Prices had fallen somewhat, as the highest was now for Leicester wool, at eight marks the sack.§ But in 1342, seventy-eight odd sacks of Westmorland were sold for the king at 110s. the sack, with half a mark for "custom."

---

* Calendar of Close Rolls. The sack was very large and was said to contain 26 stone. See Smith, on *Wool*.
† Calendar of Close Rolls
‡ Smith
§ A little over 4/- a stone. In 1195 the general price had been 2s. 6d a stone. Smith

It was about this time that the most strenuous efforts were made to encourage the manufacture of cloth in England, and to stop its importation from foreign countries.

The edicts of Henry III., of 1270 and 1315, which expelled all foreign cloth-weavers, were reversed, and Edward issued letters of protection to foreign workers in cloth whether weavers, fullers or dyers who would settle in England for the pursuit of their "mistery" Such encouragement bore fruit. Some weavers are known to have settled in London, two in York, Thomas Blanket in Bristol; John Kemp indeed, who brought over servants, looms and apprentices, in 1331, is stated by a local tradition to have made his way to Kendal, though there is little likelihood that the early immigrants pushed so far inland, and there is nothing to substantiate a legend that is also cherished elsewhere. The Flemish settlers were certainly most numerous in East Anglia, which traded freely with Flanders and was easily reached from that country.* Again in 1337, the king issued letters of protection to foreigners, including a French dyer, who in response was then "plying his mistery" at Winchester.† That year parliament went so far as to ordain that no person but kings, queens, and their children should wear cloth that was not made in the realm, as well as that no cloth should be imported.‡

Results were speedy, and by 1350, the erection of new, mills and weirs on the navigable streams of the land was so loudly complained of as affecting the passage of boats, that a law was made that permitted the pulling down of all those which had been erected later than Edward I.'s time.§ Complaints continuing of the invasion of this law, it was enacted in 1399, that commissions should be appointed to view the obstructions thus offered to navigation,

---

* Cunningham's Alien Immigrants
† Calendar of Close Rolls
‡ Statute 11 Ed. III , c. 2 and 3
§ 25 Ed. III , Stat. 3. c. 4.

and that the justices were to take action according to their decision, and to see that the condemned mills, weirs and obstructions were actually pulled down.*

Laws, too, were soon promulgated to control and regulate the manufacture of cloth. Certain makes or varieties of cloth—generally confined to certain families, cliques, and eventually places—were to obtain certain prices; the accredited width and length of each piece or "web" of the different makes, as well as its quality, was to be maintained; and a public officer, called an alnager, was appointed to examine every web, roll or pack as it came into the cloth market, and to set a mark of its length upon it. It was also to be sealed by the collector of customs, when the king's tax was paid. It is from a perusal of these laws that we learn how soon our barony of Kendal came to the fore in the newly established manufacture of cloth.

The Westmorland dalesman had in fact a peculiarly valuable asset in his flock of sheep. His small and hardy race of Herdwicks—whose progenitors may have been introduced by the Norse settlers—were admirably fitted to graze in summer on the wide barren fells. There the deer were at first their only rivals; but the deer along with the primeval forest, and the lord's personal presence and his interest in the chase, kept diminishing; being more and more restricted to enclosures and parks. The age of wool in fact succeeded that of sport.

The summer pasture on the mountain tops being almost boundless, the dalesman's flock was only limited to the number which his holding would support in winter. The greatest care was taken to increase natural provision. The leaves of the ash were garnered like the grass, for fodder; holly trees were planted and cherished, as was the ivy, because their foliage furnished a winter food for

---

* Stat. 1 Henry IV., c. 12.

sheep.* The animals of the first year, called "hogs," were kept through the winter in houses, and there fed from racks of hay ranged round the walls, never being taken out but to water.

And now the mountain of Rydal, with its wide grassy top and its range of lessening heights (nameless in Sir Roger de Lancaster's deed), became Fairfield, the sheep-fell.† The fleece, grey as it was, and short compared with the longer whiter fleeces of the south country, and low as was the price it fetched, was yet of commercial value, and was carried to Kendal, thence to be transported across the seas, either by York and Hull (for the Westmorland man long gravitated to his old Deiran capital), or to Newcastle, which later became his invariable seaport

In the Cal. of Close Rolls, 21 Edward III., we read :—

1347 "The colls & rec s of King's wool in co of Lancashire ordered to stop all 'feeble' wool fr. Cumb West & other ports from being fradulently passed into the 20,000 sacks due from Lancashire, instead of the better wool of that county."

Then again, when English cloth became the rule of wear for all classes, the thrifty dalesman saw his opportunity and quickly used it. The simple loom had always been plied for his household needs: why should it not spin webs for sale in Kendal market? From the very disadvantages of his material he made profit. His fleeces fetched a lower price than any other ; his grey home-spun web showed but poorly against the fine alien-spun cloths of the south ; but it was strong and durable, and he could (with his industry, his few outside wants and independence of land-tenure) put it on the market at a price that commanded a speedy and extensive sale. Accordingly,

---

* In the New Forest holly used to be the regular winter food of the deer.

† From the Norse It was De Quincey who first suggested this derivation which has been recently accepted

from the time that Kendal cloth is first named in the statutes, it appears as the wear of the working classes.

In 1363, 37 Edward III It is enacted that no man practice more than one mystery or craft. Women however, are allowed to be brewers, bakers, carders, spinners and workers of wool, linen and silk. Further, the apparel for different ranks is graduated, handcraftsmen and yeomen are to wear cloth the whole price to cost not more than 40s., knights and gentlemen owning £100 a year may go to 4½ marks (60s.), those with £200, to 5 marks the piece, those owning £300, to 6 marks, while all above £400 a year may wear what they please. Craftsmen had to have a larger income than the gentry in order to wear the same. Carters and ploughmen were to wear nothing but " Blanket " and russet wool of 12d.

That time is 1389. Enactments had been made in 1350-1,* 1353, and 1373, concerning two classes of cloth which were described as Coloured Cloth and Cloth of Ray,† and which were originally to be woven, the former 24 yards and the latter 26 elles or yards long in the piece, with a breadth respectively of 6½ and 6 quarters, but were afterwards allowed at 26 and 28 yards long,‡ and 6 and 5 quarters broad. Cloth, however, to be sold to poor folk was excepted, and by 1389 it became necessary to specify that a certain class of goods called " Cogware " and Kendal cloth were exempt from such laws. These goods, it was stated, were made " by common custom " in divers counties, of the breadth of 3 quarters or one ell, and were used to be sold by the piece of five folds for forty pence (a quarter mark), and as such cloth was made of

---

* Statutes of the Realm 25 Ed III, Stat 3. c. 1.

† Striped cloth Strutt.

‡ The Statutes of the Realm give 28 But we also find it put at 27 In all cases the French " aune " is translated " yard " and not " ell " Strutt says that the word aulne or aune (properly ell) is rendered in the Old English translations Yard but it really was equivalent to 1 yard 1 inch, or in London 1 yard and a hand breadth, but the measure 1 yard and an inch was enforced all over England by law in 18 Hen. VI.

the worst wool, that would not serve for superior stuffs, and was moreover sold to " cogmen " for export, or to " poor and needy people " of England, it was ordained that it might still be made of the old width and length, without interference from state officials.*

This shows that Kendal cloth and "cogware" were made not only at a low price, but on a narrower loom than the finer cloths ; and perhaps it may be inferred, especially as use and common custom are spoken of in connection with it, that this manufacture represented the work of native weavers, who followed the methods and used the tools and looms of their forefathers, and were little, if at all, affected by newly introduced methods.

In 17 Richard II. a law further declared that while such cloths could be made of any length or breadth, they were to pay alnage or aulnage duty on each piece, and be officially sealed. That was considered a grievance, and in answer to a petition, 1 Henry IV. (1399), another law was passed concerning it, whereby it is ordained " for the ease and relief of poor common people of the realm" that for a period of three years all " drap (cloth) kersy Kendal cloth frise-de-Coventre Coggeware " or other cloth that is sold by the dozen yards at 13s. 4d (one mark) shall be exempt from the usual subsidy and the sealing which enforces such payment.†

In the Cal. Pat. Rolls, 1 Richard II. (1377) we find the appointment of John de Pathorn, York, draper, as collector of subsidy on cloth for the counties of York, Northumberland, Cumberland and Westmorland, with power to retain all forfeited cloth, and in 1379 Thom. Forster of Drybeck to the same post and to seal the cloth when it has paid subsidy, to make provision against unsealed cloth, with power to search and seize the same in houses, shops, &c.

In 5 James I., an Act was passed allowing all cogwares,

---

* 13 Rich. II Stat. 1. c. 10.
† 1 Hen. IV c xix

kendals, coarse cottons, and carpmeals (Cartmells?) made in the counties of Cumberland and Westmorland, and in the towns and parishes of Carpmeal, Hawkestead, and Broughton, in Lancashire, not exceeding 13s. 4d. the dozen yards, should be unrestricted in length and free from subsidy or alnage.

In accordance with this law, several officials of the counties of Norfolk and Suffolk, including the king's alnager or aulnager, were next year bidden to seize all cloths within those counties, that were not of the prescribed lengths and quality, except "coggeware" and "kendale-cloth" of the value of 6s. 8d. each *

Already, in 1326, it was ordained that all cloth worn in England was to be made in England, and the export of all appliances connected with the trade forbidden, such as fuller's earth, madder, woad, and more especially of "the thistles commonly called tasles," or teasles, which it was said the merchants of Flanders, Brabant, and elsewhere were buying up and even destroying the roots of, in order to stop the home manufacture; and so great was the zeal, that the sheriffs of London had to be made to release 29 barrels of "thistles," which it was ascertained had been bought by three Flemish merchants before the law had gone forth.†

Again in 1407, it was ordained that "no cloth called Kendale," which was offered on the market at 6s. 8d. (half-a-mark) the dozen, should be required to be sealed (for payment of subsidy 4d. the piece, and scartel 6d.) or to pay alnage (the fee of ½d. the piece to the alnager, or official cloth-measurer).‡ From which we may conjecture that Kendal cloth (no other is mentioned) was distancing all other low-priced competitors, and placing a servicable stuff on the market, at a greatly reduced price.

---

* Cal of Patent Rolls, 13 Rich II
† Calendar of Close Rolls
‡ 9 Hen IV, c. 11

The cloth merchants of our barony were by this time becoming well-known on the great trade routes. It is related by Fuller, in his *History of Cambridge*, that the great cloth-fair of Stourbridge owed its origin about 1417, to a Kendal clothier, who had had the misfortune to get his cloth wet on the road to London, and so stopped there and then sold it for what he could get; making so good a bargain that he returned to the spot next year with others of his townsmen. He adds that "Kendal men challenge some privilege on that place, annually choosing one of the town to be chief, before whom an antic sword was carried with mirthful solemnities."

When a rood chantry was founded in Skipton Church, for a priest to say early mass every day (at six a.m. in summer and seven in winter), it was for the express purpose that not only the inhabitants might attend it before the day's work, but that "Kendalmen and strangers" should hear the same, before continuing their journey.*

The part played by our valley in this cloth trade of Kendal has to be considered. For it must again be noted that Kendal still stood for the barony, and not for the town, which was Kirbey in Kendale, or the Church-town of Kendal. And the steady increase of the home-manufacture in these remote parts can be gathered even from the scanty records, inquisitions and rentals, that we possess.

In 1283, one fulling or walk-mill apparently served for Grasmere, Langdale, and Loughrigg, where the cloth made for household wear in the valleys could be "y-walked" or dressed † It was held by the lord, and situated at the parochial centre.

---

* *Mediæval Service in England.* Cha. Wordsworth.

† It is supposed that the cloth was in primitive times fulled by the feet, hence the word *walk* Cunningham (Alien Immigrants) says that the word was directly introduced by the Flemish weaver of the 14th century It was however, apparently in common use at that time in these parts The official papers always use the word *full*, indeed; but we have mention of one William, son of Robert *le walker* in Eskdale in 1338 (Close Rolls); and a John Walker

In 1323-4, the Inquisition of Marmaduke de Twenge shows that, as lord of half Grasmere and Langdale, he had held half of two corn-mills and of one fulling mill (R   MSS.).

The Grasmere mill is mentioned in 1324 and 1335, as bringing in a rent of 6s. 8d. (half a mark). But before long, mills sprang up in each township, worked by the enterprise of one man or by partners. The increase spread, as was natural, from Kirkby Kendal as a centre; for thither the webster had at first to carry his cloth for sale in the market. Through Staveley, Applethwaite, Troutbeck, it advanced to Ambleside and the remote valley-heads. And the first new mill in the parish of Grasmere, of which we have notice, was situated in Loughrigg, worked by John Walker, and paying 3s. 4d. (a quarter mark) to the lord   This was at the close of the fourteenth century, when already three walk-mills were working in Troutbeck, with several men as partners in each.

Loughrigg in fact, the rocky fell rising between the streams of Brathay and Rothay, was destined to play a conspicuous part in the cloth trade The inhabitants of this little division had been accustomed, like those of Ambleside, to pay a tax of Walkyng-silver to the lord.* Perhaps it was a coincidence that both became the seats of prosperous fullers who founded families of freeholders. As our chief concern is with Loughrigg, it need only be

---

of the Loughrigg fulling mill at the end of the 14th century As mentioned in part 1. chapter 10 Wycliffe's translation of St Mark's Gospel ix., 3, gives "a fullere or walkere of cloth" *Walk*-mill remains the traditional phrase The invention of fulling-stocks, worked by a small wheel, caused the discontinuance of the old hand methods, which however caused loud complaints (Strutt's, *Dress and Habits*)

The word *stock* commemorates many a vanished mill in these parts

In Langlands' Piers Plowman, 15, 447, is the following —" Cloth that commeth froe the weaving is not comely to wear, Till it be fulled under fote or in a fullyng stocks , Washen well with water, and with tasels cratched, y-touked and y-teynted, and under talours hand " &c

One MS has y-Walked in the place of y-touked and Langland often uses " touker " for " fuller."—J A Martindale

* See ante part 1 chapter 10.

said of the general increase that by 1453, there were six mills working in the parish of Grasmere; in another forty years there were ten on the Richmond half alone; and in another hundred, as many as eighteen, if our reckoning from the rentals of the two fees be correct.*

It is clear that the Wars of the Roses favoured, indirectly, this increase of the cloth trade in the remoter parts of the barony. The Parrs, seated at the castle by the Kent, had the welfare of the borough and its trade largely at heart. The forest and the deer became less of interest to them than the people and the cloth manufacture, which also brought wealth to themselves. Their policy would seem for some time to have been a liberal one, for the refusal of the Troutbeck tenants to pay gressums in 1453, was ascribed to the king having pardoned these, as shown in the accounts of Sir Thomas Parre, late sheriff of Westmorland. And when Sir William Parr, owner of half the lordship of Kendal, was rewarded in 1472, for his fidelity to the cause of the White Rose, by the other half, or Richmond Fee, he apparently gave every facility to the tenants of the valleys for the establishment of new walk-mills; for the rental of 1493, for that fee, when the Countess of Richmond had again resumed possession of it, expressly mentions that the third mill accounted for in the townships of Grasmere and Ambleside was constructed in the time he had been lord. One of these was fixed on the Rothay, between the lakes of Grasmere and Rydal, in Bainrigg.

We have thus certified, to within twenty years, the date of the foundation of one cloth-mill in our division, the only one on the left bank of the Rothay, though there were two then, or a little later, on the right bank. The next record available † shows that about this time a

---

* "Fullers and Freeholders of Grasmere, *Transactions*, C & W A & A Society, vol viii, N S
† Public Record Office. Ministers Account, Hen. VII., 877.

great deal was being done on the lands between the two rivers in the way of improvement and mill-construction. The Ministers Account for 1505-6, runs under the heading of Loughrigg, and the money produced by John Gerigge, reeve, thus :—

"And (he is charged) with 13s 4d of the rents of all the tenants there yearly, as well for all ap-provements, Intakes, and other waste lands by them newly encroached upon, as for license to enclose the said approvements of waste land, thus demised to them by the Lady's auditor and receiver general, ..." [The Lady = the Countess of Richmond].

No heriots have fallen in, as the accountant takes oath. But he answers for . . . . 2s by him likewise received from (blank) for two fulling mills newly built there"

It is unlucky that the names of the fullers at these two new mills are not given. It is in connection with Langdale that the name of the family that was to occupy so largely these valleys, and particularly Loughrigg, occurs. The entry may, however, concern Loughrigg, the skirts of which slope down to the common lands of Elterwater, at a spot which might be fitly described as "the foot of Langden," since it is here that the first valley chamber (the *long dene*) closes, and where, after issuing from the lake, the river becomes the Brathay. A large intack skirting the common, and rising towards High Close, on the Loughrigg and Langdale border, was later in the hands of the family, but this, being of the Marquis Fee, is not the one meant in the entry, which runs :—

"And (the reeve is charged) with 12d of the rent of John Benson, William Benson, and Robert Benson for one intake newly enclosed lying at the foot of Langden, containing 5½ acres by estimation ; and 1d of the rent of John Benson for one intake containing by estimation (blank) acres, yearly."

There was also a Thomas Gyrryge who had recently enclosed " three intakes in divers places " from the lady's waste, containing three roods, and who paid a rent of 4d.

Now it is tolerably certain that these improvements and enclosures from waste land were made for the milling industry. The very fact that most of the land of Loughrigg, and much of Langdale, was waste, and too rocky and barren for the husbandman to deal with, explains in part what appears the strange spread of a manufacture into the very heart of the mountains. Hummocks of rock that would scarce give grazing to sheep, served for the drying of cloth on the tenters ; and it could be had cheap. The becks and even the small sikes were enough with their swift flow to turn the primitive wheel of the old walk-mill ; there was no question of previous bank and water rights to hamper their use, no risk of weir-disputes.* Everything needful was at hand ; the dalesmen with their fleeces, the scattered homesteads where the wool was spun by the women and woven at the looms by younger sons ; the ground and the water. It needed only a group of men with enterprise and capital to produce commerce from industry ; the walker first, to set up his mill and full the cloth on the spot ; then the clothier or cloth-merchant to buy up the finished article and carry it straightway with his gang of pack-horses to the great cloth markets of the south. And both walkers and clothiers were supplied in the family of Bensons. Though not without rivals at first (for John Hawkrigg ran the Bainrigg mill in 1493, and Robert Wilkinson with partners one of the three in Langdale, and Brathwaites and Jacksons the three in Ambleside, while later Reginald Holm perhaps had another at Skelwith, and the Griggs one in Langdale) they yet became dominant ; and increased in wealth and numbers, till they occupied customary holdings on almost every tributary stream of the valleys, and bought up

---

* Two of the old weirs connected with mills can yet be distinguished on the Rothay, below its exit from the two lakes. It may have been a weir-dispute which brought Reginald Holme, the miller of Skelwith, into trouble, and caused the destruction of his weir and dam by the magistrates. The present weir that holds the Brathay up involved its builder in a law suit. See Fullers and Free-holders.

freeholds whenever attainable. In Loughrigg alone, they were probably in the sixteenth century working six walk-mills; and about 1570, three clothiers of the name, representing different lines of Loughrigg holders, bought up the whole of the freehold in that division that belonged to Rydal Manor.

Rocky Loughrigg was indeed, in late Tudor times, their stronghold, but it is impossible to date their arrival there, or even to trace the descent of the various branches who possessed holdings in that division of our township. It is of interest to note that one, Ralph Benson, is spoken of in association with a William, son of Robert *le Walker*, who—as already mentioned—held lands and apparently mills in Eskdale in 1338.* From Eskdale the way is short by the Roman and mediæval highway into Langdale.

It may be conjectured that the first walk-mill of Loughrigg would be planted on an old agricultural site; and none is more likely by situation to have been so used than the holding called Miller Bridge; for here the wide arc which the river described about alluvial land could be easily segmented by a straight cut, which is probably now absorbed in the present artificial course. The ubiquity of the term Miller applied to the adjacent *field, bridge, brow, hagg*, and extended by the terms *high, low, little*, attest the ancient presence of a mill with its bridge over the dam, of neither of which the slightest tradition remains, though fortunately there is documentary evidence to prove their existence. It may have been here that the fulling-mill, accounted for in the Levens Rental, stood, at the close of the fourteenth century, this plot indeed, known as Low Miller Bridge, with the adjacent one of High Miller Bridge, is the sole one—besides High Cockstones, belonging to the Lindsey or Richmond Fee, that lay along the river bank. The 1453 rental of the fee,†

---

* Calendar of Close Rolls.
† Ministers' Account, Bdle 644, No 10444

speaks of a corn-mill, and says that 3s. 4d. (the old sum) is received for " the moiety of the fulling-mill there." The first corn and fulling mills may indeed have run together, for it was not unusual for two wheels to be turned by one race. In Ambleside a wooden aqueduct across the beck connected corn and bark mills; at Skelwith Bridge the two wheels of corn and bobbin mills sat side by side in the flow, pivoted from either bank. We have the word *kiln* associated with a corn-mill or brewery, as a field-name on High Miller Bridge.*

A corn-mill must have been re-established here, perhaps after the failure of the walk-mill, and right down to the middle of the nineteenth century, High Miller Bridge seems to have been held by the Mackereths.

Now a certain Thomas Benson " of Loghrig " was fined in the court of the Lindesay Fee, on July 9, 1443, for allowing six pigs to unduly forage in the lord's forest of Ambleside †; this proves him to have been a tenant in that fee, and no doubt pitched at Miller Bridge. Again, a John of Loughrigg whose *alias* was Jenkyn,‡ and who served as one of the fifteen arbitrators of the division between the townships of Ambleside and Troutbeck in 1550, was doubtless another of the same line; for we find an old field-name of *Jenkyn* on the Miller Bridge plot. It was a " Loughrig " Benson who was rich enough to marry the daughter of Miles Sawrey, gent., of Graythwaite, in the time of Henry VII.,§ but we have no clue to guide us to his exact date.

It was Barnard the clothier, who was partner in the freehold purchase, thereby securing his capital messuage on Housesteads, a plot below Miller Bridge proper, with

---

* On Mear Ings, close by, the top of a quern was recently turned up. It is of coarse, granular texture, 15 inches in diameter, dome-shaped with a height of some four inches, and with a boring not much larger than a man's finger.

† Court Roll, 21 Henry VI.

‡ Mr G Browne's MSS

§ West's *Annals of Furness*

other lands and tenements higher up the stream ; and it was his son Edward who lost or sold this.

Another old homestead and agricultural settlement, where a mill could be readily planted on the river, and where even now part of the mill-race can be traced, was Cote How, between the old fords of the Rothay. Of this line of Bensons we know nothing till the partition deed, when Michael the clothier appears as a powerful and wealthy man, who sweeps off the freehold, not only of Cote (or Coat) How where he dwells, but of tenements and lands right and left. He was apparently eager for freehold, and when the manor of Baisbrowne and Elterwater, secured from the derelict lands of Conishead Priory by a rich John Benson of Langdale as early as 1546, was being parted with by John's successor to James Brathwaite the fuller of Ambleside, the seller stipulated that it should not be passed over to Michael. Michael, according to Nicolson and Burn, married a rich cousin, one of the heiresses of Barnard Benson, of the Fould.

At the time of the joint purchase of the Loughrigg freehold, Barnard of the Fould, who had married a daughter of Gilpin of Kentmere,* was already dead. His widow, Elizabeth, was seated at the principal house there ; while two other widow Bensons held adjoining houses.

It is difficult not to associate this little community of Bensons, pitched in the central and remote hollow of Loughrigg, with the fulling industry. We may conjecture this rich Barnard with his fellows Robert and Thomas— all dead before 1580—to have been sons of the John, William, and Robert, who were busy enclosing intakes "at the foot of Langden" in 1505-6. No river, indeed, is here ; but the wheel of the primitive walk-stock could be turned by even such a sike as drops down through

---

* The Gilpins of Kentmere probably owed their rise, as did a few other families, to the need for local officials to serve the royal holders of the barony In 1440, William Gilpyn received the post for life of the office of clerk to the king's lordships of Kendale Cal Pat. Rolls

Stock Field (where its course has been manifestly diverted) into Loughrigg Tarn. There is "Tenters Pool" still on the rocky top of little Loughrigg, where springs abound, such as dyers want. There is "Tenters" again by Mill Brow, on the slope, where a little beck runs into the Brathay, and which was a customary holding of the Bensons, not of the Rydal Manor.

It is not easy to see, indeed, where a mill could have stood at High Close, another important seat of the Bensons that lies on the neck or pass between Loughrigg and Silverhow. Yet Edward of that place, the third partner in the freehold purchase, is called a clothier too. Possibly one may have stood on the Mere Syke, near its source; for from a field there called Long Brow, a building is known to have disappeared.

At the foot of Loughrigg, but on the farther bank of the Rothay, there was the Bainrigg mill before spoken of. This freehold—one of the few bits existing from early times in these parts—was bought by a John Benson, in 1480. He probably kept only the low strip of land where the mill stood, which early in the nineteenth century was still in separate hands; for in 1487, he sold Bainrigg itself to the lord of Rydal. In the deeds at Rydal Hall, he figures as John senior.

Of the walk-mills of Langdale and Grasmere, it is not needful to speak fully.* Enough has been told to show that in Elizabethan days there were lines of Bensons who had secured their holdings in freehold from the Rydal Manor at Miller Bridge, at Cote How, at High Close, at the Fould; besides Bainrigg; and that all these as well as other lines of customary holders in our small division of the district had acquired their wealth in the fulling and cloth trades.

And what manner of cloth, it may be asked, was our

---

* See "Fullers and Freeholders," *Transactions*, C. & W. A. & A. Society, vol. vii., N.s.

district busy turning out through the Wars of the Roses and the Tudor rule?

In endeavouring to answer this question from old records, and principally from wills of tradespeople, we are met by a confusing number of names, applied to the cloths of various localities, and of varied manufacture and colour. The "shepeculer"* "grays" and "fell-side-stuff" we may conjecture to be the natural homespun "Kendale cloth" which in such early days was expressly made exempt from the alnager's requirements, lest the poorer classes who bought it should suffer. A "shepe culered gowen," was apprised as worth 30s. at a Kendal man's death in 1578. But the "Kendall" so frequently found in the Kirkby Kendal shops of the sixteenth century, was presumably the "Kendal Green" which by that time had become noted all over England. This most durable dye was produced from *Genista tinctoria*, a plant which grows wild in these parts, and gives a lively yellow colour.† Cloth treated with this, was then immersed in woad (imported),‡ the blue of which, uniting with the yellow, becomes a fast green. A steady demand made this colour the barony's own peculiar possession in dyes; but many others seemed to have been used. There were motleys, fantastic variations and patterns, perhaps applied by hand on a white ground. Nicolson says these spotted with red, blue, or green, were called ermines, or spotted cottons. The stout bowmen of Kendale were distinguished at the battle of Flodden Field by their "milke-white coats and crosses red."

> "The left hand wing with all his route
> The lustly Lord Dacres did lead,
> With him the bows of Kendal stout
> With milke white coats and crosses red."

---

* One of the colours allowed by Act 5 Ed. VI, Strutt (See Appendix)

† *Reseda luteola*, which grows on the lime stone near Kendal, also yields a yellow dye

‡ Some woad was grown near Kendal also, and it is still grown in two places in Lincolnshire Boston and Spalding.—Ed

A "black and grene motlaye"* was in stock at a Kirby Lonsdale shop in 1578. "One cloth of colour called milk-and-water," (see Appendix) was in a Kirby Kendal shop in 1562: a strange colour indeed! but hardly stranger than "sad-new-culler" † or "browne-blew." A "blew-and-blacke bayse" may have been a motley also A colour of which we find no mention is "murray"; ‡ but this esteemed dark-red dye, that fetched for cloth dipped in it a much higher price that the green, § was certainly produced in our district, and must have constantly filled the vats of the Benson firm up at the Fould. It is extracted from a white lichen, common to the mountains, probably either *Lecavora parella* or *L tartarea* ‖; and as late as 1772, the Rev. W. Gilpin¶ found a number of old people and children busy collecting the growth from the rocks, between St. John's Vale and Ullswater. Perhaps it was included in the "russets" so frequently found.

Cal. Pat. Rolls, 18 Henry VI., Part 2.—1440. Ap. 25. A burglary in house of John Lyde, "cooke," of St. Katharine Crichirche in Algate ward, comprises—after many pots and pans, and household utensils and furniture, 2 tunics of russet ... 1 *gown of Kendale*, double, with stains, 1 ancient doublet of fustian, 1 old broidered gown ...

Besides baize, "rugs" and "ketters" are spoken of; also "packe (?)" and "selblacks." Carsay or kersey, a favourite cloth in these parts, was much made in Yorkshire and Lancaster.** We read of it, in the sixteenth century, of a "skye culler," ††

---

* Perhaps the *old medley colour* of Edward's Act, Strutt
† Mentioned in 5 Ed VI
‡ The "mockadow black redd" (See Appendix), mentioned in 5 Ed VI.
§ Murray for Edward IV's wardrobe cost 3s 4d a yard. Strutt.
‖ Mr. J A. Martindale kindly furnishes the probable name.
¶ Observations, &c
** Sir Daniel procured it from Wakefield
†† Mentioned also in inventories of wardrobes, and possibly another name for *azure*, or *watchet* mentioned in Edward VI's Act. Strutt

a "white," a "grene," a "contre russett," and even a "gilloflower" variety, which surely was reaching an æsthetic height ! In the seventeenth century, Sir Daniel Fleming bought it in grey for making long coats for his young sons ; for saddle-cloths it was blue. Tammel was also made into coats, Sir Daniel procured it in white and then had it dyed. Chamlett would be procured of many colours, also mockadows and frescadows.

There were Cartmels as well as Kendals, and later, when the clothiers had failed in Loughrigg and our valleys, an Under-Skiddaw cloth, made presumably at Milbeck, below that mountain, by Sebastian Zenogle, or Senogle, was in demand at Rydal Hall.

Cottons, associated with Manchester, Lancaster and Cheshire in Act of 4 Edward VI., were made in Kendal.

There is reason to believe that the clothiers and wool-merchants of these parts were in direct touch with the London market. An early enactment provided for *Rews and Places* being provided in staple towns where wool and goods could be stored, and which were to be leased on reasonable terms.* And that Kendal men—far travellers as we have seen—had footing in London, besides their commerce at the fairs, is certain. Mr. Henry Fisher "of Kendall" held at his death in 1578, a lease of two boothes in London. A widow of Crook "near Kendal," who presumably had carried on her husband's business, had in 1557, debts in London, and cloth standing in Blackwall Hall, the great cloth market, to the value of £17. 2s. 2d.

A plea in chancery, of some time between 1433 and 1472, shows that a clothman of Kirby-Kendal had been detained in a London prison over Easter-tide, for a debt which he affirmed was not yet due.† As his prosecutor was a London grocer, it looks as if the clothier did a little

---

* Statutes of the Realm. 27 Ed. III , Stat 2, c xvi
† Early Chan Prot , vol. ii. Bun 46, No. 74

carrying trade too, so that his horses should not return unladen. The clothier's little gangs of pack horses were indeed constantly on the road; and there is little doubt that the Kendal cloth was not only spun, woven, milled and dyed in our valleys, but was carried off directly to the south by the richer firms, like the Loughrigg Bensons.

APPENDIX.

Kendal Cloth Trade.

Some particulars from "Wills and Inventories of the Archdeaconry of Richmondshire." Surtees Society.

1542. Will of Edward Pykerynge of Scelmisyer (Skelsmergh ?) parish of Kendal includes, VI Kendals, IIIJ li, VIII ketters XL s.; IJ russetts, XVIs,; IJ tentors XX s.; a payr off stock cards, XVIII d; IJ payr of small cards IIIJd

1553. Will of James Layburne of Bradleyfield, par. of Kendal. Owing to him " for Kendall of ye last yere XX s " Ditto " for Kendall LVIIs" Ditto " for Kendall, XXVII "

1557. Will of Anne, widow of Christopher Nycolson of Crook near Kendal. Debts include London ones " desparate debts and all," £128 13. 4 " clothe in Blackwell halle XVII li. IJs. IJd.

1562. Robert Storeye of Kendal " one cloth of colour called milk and watter", IIJ mellyd russets XIIIs; IJ other selblacks XX; rugs, ketters, and a blakene, a selblacke in the studles; Taysles, IIJs IIJd.; a roppe of hylds VIIId; IIIJ paire of Shearmans shears; shear borde handills with other geare XLs; Flocks, wool and yarn; A paire of studles, wheills, and cards, IIIJs IIIJd tentures with tenture barres, XXXIIJs. IIIJd.

1562. Robert Doddinge of Stramongate, Kendal. Cardstocks, Stock cards and hande cards IIJs. IIIJd.; IJ back-bords XIJd Tenture posts and woodde VJd; IJ tentures XXs In the shoppe, shears, shearborde, and wyrkingere XJs; IIJ peces of clothe XLVIIJs, IIJ wheeills, IJ pare of garne-wyndills, XVIIJd. A pece of clothe in studles XIIIJs.; In nyoyn bords and ellerbarks VIs." Debts owing him for cloth include "a russett XIIJs.; a selblacke XVIIJs."

1578. Edward Kyrkelands of Kendal, 4 tentors, 40s, 6 selblacks and 4 grayes £8; 7 grayes, 28s; "A pair sheares, shere bord, IJ thrumed bords, and all workin geare" 12s.

1578. "Mr. Henri Ficher of Kendall" leaves among his clothes "A shepe culered gowen XXXs." He has "Clothe in gaige"; wool, yarn, and "floks" Among debts owing to him "A lease for twoo bouthes in London. A bill . . . for XIIIJ stone wooll selblack

1578. James Backhouse of Kirkby Lonsdale had a shop in Kirkby Lonsdale that contained a great variety of cloths, of which the retail price per yard is given. Among them: red fresadow, 6s. 6d; Turkye culler, 4s. 0d; browne blew 9s. 0d; skye culler carsaye 1s 7d; black & grene motlaye 2s. 6d; contre russett carsay 2s. 4d; grene carsaye, 1s. 10d; gilloflower carsay 1s. 6d; sad new culler, 3s. 2d; shepes culler, brod a yard & ad (?) 13s. 0d (the piece ?) blew and blacke bayse, 7½ yards, 15s 4d; brode pucke 4s 0d a yard; red frescadow 2s. 0d; mockadow black redd 1s. 6d or 1s. 7d; single mockadow 1s. 1d; mockadow blew & browne; red borato (double mockadow) 2s. 2d; red chameltt 4s. 6d; purpel chamlet 4s. 6d; b. & browne chamlett, 9 yards, 26s. 6d; whit carseye in remblands; checker remblands; fustion 1s. 1d; whit holme fustion, 1s 1d; blacke rashe 2s. 4d.

CHAPTER IV

THE LORDS OF RYDAL

1483, *Fleming and Whitfield joint owners of Rydal Manor; Marriage agreement between Johan daughter of Hugh Fleming and Lancelot Lowther; William Grandson of Hugh becomes Lord of Beckermet, Coniston, and Rydal; Buys the Whitfield share of the manor, 1570; Dies 1600; His widow [Agnes Bindlosse] survives him 33 years, Appendix I.—Settlement between John Fleming and his stepmother, A.D. 1484; Appendix II.—Agreement [Lat. and Eng.] between John Benson and John Fleming for sale of freehold; Appendix III.—Letters from Mrs. Agnes Fleming and W. Tyson to John Fleming, A.D. 1631, Bainrigg, 1485.*

THERE is no reason to suppose that the ruling family at Rydal interested themselves in the walk industry that was growing to such large dimensions in the valleys round them. Barons, knights, and the smaller gentry did not concern themselves with trade. Besides fighting, which often enough was their profession, they served as commissioners of peace for their county, as escheators who watched the king's interest in the affairs of his tenants-in-chief, as receivers if the king had manors in their neighbourhood, as assessors for the subsidies, even as assessors of the wool which the king claimed from each shire. Only with the sale of the wool and with its production into cloth had they nothing to do. They left these branches to freeholders and customary tenants under them, who amassed capital and finally land, and whose daughters they were many of them willing to marry when the riches had been gained.*

It is true that the Flemings were a race of practical

---

* See Paston Letters.

men, and if their home estates did not keep them busy, they looked abroad for other business. An agreement exists, made out in 1482-3, between Dame Mabel Louthre and her son Hugh, and John Fleming, son and heir of John " of Ridale," whereby the latter leases the mill at Newton for 21 years, at six marks a year, with a view certainly of making a profit on the grinding of the corn. But this was work done by deputy, and John would sub-let the mill to a miller.

In 1483 too, John junior renewed the agreement made by his father (John "senior") seven years before, with the Whitfield family. By this, John Whitfield leased for his lifetime his half of the manor of Rydal and Loughrigg to John, junior, who in return was to pay £10 a year for it. The deed was executed at Penrith.*

This John it must have been who in the next year is spoken of by the aged widow of Thomas as " my beloved in Christ," son of John now deceased ; and it was probably the recent death of the latter that caused her to make John of Coniston and John Uttyng, chaplain, her trustees.

But John, son of John of Rydal was doubtless her heir as well as attorney, and probably came into her lands in Rydal and Loughrigg soon after the date of the deed. In 1485, he is found settling his disputes with his stepmother, Anne Broughton, who had succeeded his own mother Joan. Four arbitrators were called in for this purpose, one being the parson of Windermere ; and Anne and John were bound to accept their decision, under a penalty of one hundred marks. This decision gave to Anne the lands and houses in Claughton in Lonsdale which she had held jointly with her husband, and also a certain " tenement with appurtenances " in Coniston, and the pasture of twenty lambs yearly on John's lands there. This tenement, however, was in the occupation

---

* List of Rydall Writings, Sir D. Fleming.

of two men, Henry Benson and Richard Brokbanke, and if they refused to evacuate quietly, Anne was not allowed, for the space of six years and eighteen weeks (perhaps the term of their lease) to turn them out, she was moreover to pay John 8s. 4d. a year for this dower-house. But he was to give her yearly from Coniston Park a buck, or a saure (see Appendix I. to this chapter).

John had now ended his long juniorship. He was clearly a prosperous man, for in 1686 he added to his lands by the purchase of a freehold tenement with appurtenances called Bainrigg, outside the manor of Rydal. At this transaction he came into contact with the rising cloth trade; for the John Benson who sold to him, kept apparently the second tenement at Bainrigg and the walk-mill on the river.*

He married Joan Lowther (her name was spelt also Johan, Jennet, and Jane). In 1508, John Whitfield apparently being dead, John renewed his lease, in conjunction with his son and heir, Hugh, "of Rydale" for the half of Rydal and Loughrigg with Robert Whitfield and Robert's son, John. This time it was made out for a hundred years and a day; and in 1518, John Whitfield acknowledges the receipt of £6, from John Fleming and his heir Hugh, being "halfe their farme of ye Manor of Loghrigg and Rydall." † This was an advance upon the old rent, but we find Hugh paying only £5 half-yearly in 1544 and 1547.

How long John, "the beloved in Christ" to old Dame Isabel of the de Lancasters, lived after 1518 is not known. He was dead in 1538, when his wife was still living. He is so persistently spoken of as being "of Rydal" that we may suppose that he resided on the demesne, following his father there and the relict of Sir Thomas. It may be

---

* See Appendix II.
† Sir D. F.'s List of Rydall Writings

therefore, as the books assert, that he died at Rydal Hall, and was buried at Grasmere.

His son Hugh, who married Joan or Jane, daughter of Sir Richard Huddlesden of Millom, had probably resided at Coniston during his lifetime, and continued there. We find Hugh in 1538 drawing up an agreement of marriage for his daughter Johan to Lancelot Lowther, by which he undertakes to give the bride a dower of 100 marks (£66. 13s. 4d.) to be paid at the parish church of Lowther, presumably at the ceremony. He was also to provide meat and drink for the same, and the license; and for the household of the young couple "Bedding and Inseygte [furniture] as shall stand with his worship to give."* Each party to pay for their own wedding apparel. An obligation to carry out this deed exists at Rydal Hall, signed by Hugh (Hew flemyng) of Coniston, and his son and heir Anthony (an flemyng), dated May 30, 29 Hen. VIII.

His heir, described as "of Ridall" had in 1533 been mated with Elizabeth, daughter of William Hutton, of Hutton in the Forest; the marriage portion of the bride being in this case six score pounds, of which the second and last instalment was assigned to buy furniture for the young couple, who were to live "o'th' fourths."

Hugh, who served the office of escheator for Cumberland and Westmorland in 1541, had more children than Anthony and Joan. There was Thomas, who had business faculties, for he became steward to William Parre, Marquis of Northampton, the favourite of Henry VIII., and the last ruler at Kirby Kendal Castle.† Thomas was styled "of Coniston, gentleman," and his descendants were living at New Field in Sir Daniel's time.

---

* Sir D. F.'s List of Rydall Writings.

† Nicolson and Burn say that his brother David held this position; but Sir D F says that the great nobleman was the "master" of Thomas, as the will of the latter proves

Another of Hugh's children was David. He resided at the Old Hall of Rydal, perhaps after his eldest brother, Anthony's time, and came to have a vested interest in the lands. He had six sons, two of whom will be mentioned later.

Hugh's heir Anthony, though he had time to marry three wives, did not survive his father. His first wife, the daughter of Jeffray Middleton, must have died immediately. Perhaps Elizabeth Hutton did not live long, for by her he had only his heir, William; Thomas and Charles of Wedderar in Lancashire were born of Jane, daughter of John Rigmadon.

William therefore, on the death of old Hugh, became lord of Beckermet, Coniston and Rydal. He was already twenty-two on his grand-father's death, which happened on June 8, 3 and 4 Philip and Mary,* and obtained the livery of the lands he held in chief, in 1557 (June 25, 5, Philip and Mary)

With William record grows clear, and individual touches of character begin to give interest to names. He came early in life to power. Living through the times of change, and unrest, when the shock of the Reformation passed off into that short burst of national energy, of literary and poetic power which characterized the age of Elizabeth, he himself reflected the spirit of change and of unlinking from immemorial custom; and on his death, forty-four years later, his lands and houses were in a widely different state from when he inherited them. He himself passed his life as a country gentleman, living on his estates; but some of his kinsmen were at the heart of the national life, in the times when it throbbed high. His cousin David, son of David of the Old Hall in Rydal, was falconer to Queen Elizabeth, and must therefore have been in close attendance at court. His

---

* Deed at Rydal Hall

own son William, noted for his stature, was a sailor, and is said by Sir Daniel to have been in the ship that first sighted the Spanish Armada.* His elder sons were educated at Jesus College, (Oxford ?), as a letter addressed thence by his second, Thomas, in 1591 attests.

He was a man, according to West, of some magnificence in the style of his living, and he is said to have re-built Coniston Hall, which the heads of the family had, for perhaps two generations, used as their chief residence. The fine old block stands yet, little shorn of the ample proportions he set it to; and, before it was stripped of its garnitures of oak, and its great hall was turned into a barn, and other vandalisms done, it must have shown as a fair lord's seat for the far northern parts of Furness. The only letters of William that exist concern a great entertainment " of worshipful friends and strangers," he held in 1576, for which he craved the loan of silver plate from his cousin William Lowther A chalice sent excites his interest, and he asks for the " patorne " belonging to it It has been suggested that this chalice and patten may have been church plate, sold at the Reformation. It is perhaps idle to conjecture the cause of this concourse of friends and strangers. It comes, though near, yet too long after the birth of his son and heir, which is given by Sir Daniel Fleming as 1575, for it to be a christening party. Was it a house warming? or had William adhered to the now reformed church, and was it a secret mass?

His first wife was Margaret, daughter of Sir J — Lamplugh. By her he had three daughters only The eldest, Jane, married Richard Harrison of Martindale; and her sons came to have much to do with Rydal in its stormy days.

---

* It is difficult to see how this could be, unless boys were placed as midshipmen at a very early age; and according to Macaulay it was a merchant man See Macaulay's Lays, *The Armada*.

His second marriage was productive of far greater results. It made him the father of nine sons and daughters, but more than that, it gave him a wife whose shrewd temper and business faculty were the means of building up the fortunes of the house through years of widowhood. Agnes Bindlosse, indeed, was a great factor in Rydal history; and probably with her began that hedging in of the Rydal statesman's rights, which caused their early downfall. Her genius for management was probably inherited; for she was born of that new class of gentry who had acquired their lands in the cloth trade. Her father, Robert, had amassed wealth enough in the days of Henry VIII. to purchase an estate at Helsington, that passed to his son, Sir Robert. He dowered his daughter Dorothy, who married Thomas Brathwaite, the heir of the rich family of Ambleside fullers, with Asthwaite Hall in Staveley*, and, though we do not know exactly the sum he gave to Agnes, it was described in the Indenture made on January 11, 1571, between father and husband (for Agnes was already William's wife) as a "Competent Joynture ... in recompense of her dowere" [Copy of deed at Rydal Hall]. Agnes was indeed a widow when she was married to the lord of Rydal; and as her first husband's name was Benson—the only fact Sir Daniel Fleming seemed to know about him, when he drew up the family pedigree—he was not improbably connected with the cloth trade, as were all the wealthy members of his clan.

It would be a mistake to ascribe to Agnes Bindlosse's shrewd sense, all the reforms which her husband made in his property. It was before this marriage, which took place apparently in 1574, that he set about that consolidation of the Rydal manor, which no one before him had attempted. The ownership of this manor, as it came

---

* Communicated by Mr. J A Martindale

down to him, was confused and unsatisfactory. Only half belonged to him, and even that half was not clear of claims from his uncle's family. It was in 1569, according to deeds of that year and the following, that he set about the purchase of the half of the manor that had belonged to the Whitfields. It was now in the hands of a certain John Vaughan and his wife, Dame Ann Knewt.

They consented to part with it to William for the sum of £400. This purchase should not be overlooked, as it but balanced that sale of the Loughrigg portion of the manor which later was so much begrudged by his descendants, who tried to prove that he had unlawfully sold entailed property. This sale was effected in 1575, at the time of his agreement with his father-in-law, Robert Bindlosse, and the fact that in that agreement he settled only the lordship of Rydal upon his wife, shows that the Loughrigg was already sold. The lordship of Loughrigg or such portion as had descended from Roger de Lancastre, became by this transaction, as we have seen, the property of Bensons, clothiers, who were resident there.

From this time William's interest seems to have turned to Rydal, which he not only secured completely as a lordship, but proceeded to lay out as a property that would produce substantial returns, both as a manor and a farming centre. There is no need to doubt Sir Daniel's statement that it was William who killed off the deer, and changed the park from a sequestered woodland devoted to game, to plough-land and pasture. Two deeds exist between him and his tenants. One of 1575, lets to John Grigge

" the corn-mill of Rydal with orchards and garden neare adionynge unto ther Capitall messuage of Rydall callid the olde hall and a fishing for the sum of £8 13s. 4d. yearly."

a very respectable rent. In the following year he buys from John Grigge and his son, probably a well-to-do man connected with the cloth trade, who had emigrated from his native village, a messuage and tenement in Rydal, of the exceptionally high rent of 22s. yearly. This deed was only executed a few months before John Grigge died, as Squire William had next to covenant with his kin. His uncle David, who had lived at the Old Hall, and who had assisted him in securing the Whitfield half of the manor in 1570, died in 1571, according to the Grasmere register. His "Relict" Jane was still residing there when William made this settlement on the new wife, and she lived on till April, 1600. But already in 1582, Henry Fleming, the son of David and Jane, called "gentleman, of Kirby," agreed with his cousin William to part with all claims in Rydal lands for the sum of £80. This finally cleared the manor of Rydal, and left it entirely in the hands of William and Agnes. William himself died on the 22nd, of June, 1600, and was buried in Grasmere Church, on the 24th. Among his other gains was the advowson of the ancient church of the valley, which he purchased from Alan Bellingham, of Fawcet Forest, executor of Marion Bellingham of Helsington in 1575,* and there his body was laid, doubtless with all the state that had belonged to his life. His widow survived him thirty-three years, and of her doings as mistress of Rydal Hall there is something to say (see Appendix III.).

APPENDIX I

[January 17, 2 Rich III.]. A.D. 1484.
This endenture made the xvij^{te} daye of Januarie in the 2nd yere of the Regne of kyng Richard the iij^{d} witnesseth that where variannce and discorde hase beyn hade and monet betwix Anne, late the wyfe of John Flemyng, apon the tone parte, and John Flemyng, son and heyre of the foresaide John, opon that other partye, as wele for the ryght, title, and possession of all suche landez and tenementez as the said Anne was Joyntly seaset

---

* See *Grasmere*, p 66, by M L Armitt

in with the forsaid John, hir husband, as of all other landes and
tenementez where-in the saide John, hir husband, was seaset at
any tyme aftre the Espouselse hade and made bytwyx the forsaid
John and hir, wherin the saide Anne claymes to haue hir dower.
Of all whiche variannce and discorde and ryght and title the
partyes aboue-said by mediacion of thaire frendes hase submytt
thayme to be bounden ayther partie to other with sufficiannt
persons with thayme in thaire seuerall obligacions of C markes
to obeye, perfourme and fulfill the ordinannce, deme, and awarde
of vs, Thomas Biggynges, person of Wynnandermere, William
Huddilston, person of Whityngton, Richard Newton, and John
Ambros Whereopon we, takyng opon vs the office, charge and
busynes of Arbitroures in the premisses, has cald before vs bothe
the saide partyes and the right and title of bothe the said parties,
and also the chalangez and answares of thayme by vs wele
conseyuet and vnderstand and of thaire awen propre will and
agrement, ordeynes, demes, and awardes that the saide Anne,
late the wyfe of the forsaid John, the fader, occupye and reioyse* all
suche landes and tenementez, with thaire appurtenannce, in
Claghton in lonnes-dale, wherin she stode Joyntly seaset with the
said John, hir husband, to haue and to holde all the forsaide landez
and tenementez, with thaire appurtenannce, to the said Anne
and to hir assignes for terme of hir life, withoute interrupcion,
lettyng, or distourbance of the forsaid John, the son, or any oyer
person or persons in his name, right, or title, or by his will,
procuryng, or assent, the remandre ouer aftre the decesse of the
saide Anne to the said John, the son, and to his heyres Also we
ordayne, deme, and awarde that the saide Anne shall haue and
reioyse a Tenemente, with the appurtenannce, liyng in Conyngston,
nowe in the holdyng of Henry Benson and Richard Brokbanke,
duryng hir lyfe, with all the comoditez therto belongyng, paiyng
therfore yerely to the said John, the son, iiijs ijd at ij festez of
the yere, that is to saye, at Martynmesse and pentecoste by euyn
porcions, or within xl dayes aftre ayther of the saide festez
Also wee ordeyne, deme, and awarde that the said Anne shall
haue xx^{ti} lambez euery yere grisset apon suche grounde as is
conuenyent for thayme of the said John, the son, duryng the space
of vij yeres, withoute any gyeste paiyng for thayme to the said
John · Providet alway that the said Anne, nor none other person
nor persons in hir name nor by hir title, put oute, interrupt, nor
lett the saide Henrie and Richard nowe beyng Tenanntez of the

---
* = enjoy

tenemente abouesaid in the occupacion of the said Tenemente, with the appurtenannce, duryng the space of vj yeres and xviij wekes next folowyng the date of this endenture, withoute she maye agree with the said Henrie and Richard to avoide from the occupacion of the saide tenemente of thaire awen voluntare will. And if hit happyn the said Anne so to agree with the said Henrie and Richard that thaye will of thaire awen voluntare will avoyde from the occupacion of the saide Tenemente at any tyme within the spacez of vj yeres and xviij wekes next folowing the date of thees presentes, Then we deme, ordeyne, and awarde that the saide Anne shall take and remeve hir said xx^{te} lambez oute of the grisse of the said John, the son, in all gudely haste after the said Henrie and Richard be remevet from the Tenemente afore saide: Also we ordeyne, deme, and award that the said Anne shall make a suffyciannt relesse and quiet clayme unto the said John, the son, and to his heyres, of all hir ryght and title that sho hase in any parcell of the lyfelode of the said John, the fader, by reason of his dower or of any other astate to hir made · Except suche landes and Tenementez as beyn abou[e] specifyet within xl dayes aftre sho be resonably requiret by the said John, the son, so to do · Also we ordeyne, deme, and awarde the said John to giff yerely vnto the said Anne duryng hir lyve a Bukke or a saure oute of Conynston Parke in the (greatest?) hast possible aftre he be requiret so to do. Also we awarde the gressun of the tenemente above saide to rest still opon vs the forsaide Arbitroures to be demeanet hereaftre as vs thynk best In wittenes where-of to theis presente endentures [we] haue set oure seales, giffen the daye and the yere aboue saide.

[Red wax seals gone]
[Late endorsement]

APPENDIX II.

(1486) DEED AT RYDAL HALL *Bainrigg Benson.*
[July 12, Sciant presentes et futuri quod ego, Johannes
1 Hen VII] Benson de Grismar, senior, dedi, concessi, et
A.D. 1485. hac presenti carta mea confirmavi Johanni
Flemyng de Ridale, armigero, virum tenementum, cum pertinencijs, in Grismar predicta vulgariter vocatum Baynryg. Habendum et tenendum predictum tenementum, cum omnibus suis pertinencijs, prefato Johanni Flemyng, heredibus et assignatis suis, de capitalibus dominis feodi illius per seruicia

inde debita et de iure consueta imperpetuum. Et ego, vero, predictum tenementum, cum omnibus suis pertinencijs, prefato Johanni Flemyng, heredibus et assignatis suis, contra omnes gentes warantizabimus et imperpetuum defendemus. In cuius rei testimonium huic presenti carte mee sigillum meum apposui. Hijs testibus, Waltero Flemyng, Jacobo Chamer, capellano, Roberto Girrig, et alijs. Datum duodecimo die Julij anno regni regis Henrici septimi post conquestum Anglic primo

[Broken red wax seal with the letter "R" on it. Late endorsement]

(1486)   [TRANSLATION]

July 12, 1 Hen VII   Know both present and to come that I, John Benson of Grismar, senior, have given, granted, and by this my present charter confirmed to John Flemyng of Ridale, esquire, a tenement, with appurtenances, in Grismar aforesaid commonly called Baynryg To have and to hold the aforesaid tenement, with all its appurtenances, to the aforesaid John Flemyng, his heirs and assigns, of the chief lords of that fee by service therefor due and of right accustomed for ever. And I, the aforesaid John Benson, and my heirs will warrant and for ever defend against all people the aforesaid tenement, with all its appurtenances, to the aforesaid John Flemyng, his heirs and assigns. In witness whereof to this my present charter I have affixed my seal These being witnesses, Walter Flemyng, James Chamer, chaplain, Robert Girrig, and others. Given on the twelfth day of July in the first year of the reign of King Henry VII. after the Conquest of England.

APPENDIX III.

LETTERS FROM MRS AGNES FLEMING AND W TYSON.

To her verie loveing sonne John Fleminge esq. at Speake these.

Sonne Fleminge these are to let you understand that you[r] husbandrie goes not so well forward as I could wish it, for all I can do is but talke to tysonn whom I do daielie as hard as I can but for all my talke I feare we are behind wth the worke & that you will fynd it so when you come, for he hath so manie busines of his owne & other mens, that he cannot both looke to his owne & you[rs], & further for all that I can do I cannot get the grounds set frith (?), but if he will not cause them be done shortlie I will make it be done & cause some other to do it ; we have great want of you heare, & that I doubt you will fynd so when you come, so

as I could wish you if you can by anie means and that it wilbe noe great hinderance & losse unto you & that you could get good securite to get you done in anie indifferent time to make an end before you come, or els Resolve to take some good Course wth all you^r grounds & busines heare, & take you^r barnes wth you if you can have thinges there wth quietness & content otherwise not to trouble you^r selfe as for all you^r barnes praysed be god they are all well & comes forward well; my ladie is well also & takes what cheare as can be gotten & is verie well content therewth : M^{ris} Elsabeth I doubt thought much at you that you writt not 2 wordes unto hir, who is a verie good gentlewooman & loves you^r barnes well; so as I tould hir it was but you^r forgettullnes, & that there was noe such matter as you thought much at hir for anie thinges. I my selfe am verie weake & ill so as I am like to be gone before Easter then otherwise but so longe as my health will serve I shall talke hard to tysonne that thinges maie be plyed & set forward wth all speed possible; tyson is Resolved & doth purpose to buy xx^{tie} bushell of seed otes & doth confesse there is enough of ou^{r}owne that would serve, & neare as good as he can buy anie, but that you wished him to buy some for a change, so as if he buy some there wilbe more to make into malt -you^r shepe good be thanked scay(p?)ed well both heare & at Conistone, & you^r chattell in verie good order & I do talke hard unto him to haue a speciall care that there be not want of fother & that there be noe waist maid nor moe horses kept in the house then is needfull & he saith there wilbe noe want; but I doubt it, for wood gettinge it was never in this order in my time, though it was ill enough before, for the fishinge of brathey unlesse you get a warrant for the mentenance of it wth wood you nor I can make either Pffit by kepeninge or lettinge of it; further I will talke & give my Ladie a little touch (?) to looke a little into thinges as well as I in Regard it concerns hirs, Thus haveinge manie other matters to write of unto you, but I would not trouble you in Regard this bearer can Relaite them unto you wth gods blessinge & myne & my prayers unto almightie god to bless you once more wishinge you to Resolve if you can to (give) your mynd to make an end wth you^r busines in that cuntrie or els to staie heare I rest.
your Loveinge mother, Agnas Fleming.

[William Tyson, agent and bailiff for John Fleming, Esq. at Speke, Lancaster] dated May 3, 1631. After much detail of business with tenants and tithes, &c].

.... " I doe all I can to give yor mother Content & haue

giuen this daie a book of all pticulers rec: & disb & she shall doe or haue [any?] thinge eles to laie quiete, for unquietnes blendes my braine & vexes me more then all yor business " [Weather dry, "chattels" dear, and his own stringency towards Squire John's refractory tithe-payers and tenants commented on, &c]. " I doe earnestlie desire your despatch in Lanc. that you might liue at home, for I neu^{er} quietlie when yo^u are awaie." . . " I pray yo^u (if yo^u goe to London or Yorke) remember you^r neighbo^rs that are proud & willfull & doe not forget it for heare will be nothinge but extremitie & the hornes of an unrulie bull must be Cutt." [His master need take no care, as the writer will look to things] " neither neede you loose 3^s 4^d by Rydall more then if you weare heare "

May 1631   RYDAL HALL MSS.   *Mrs. Agnes Fleming*
               143 of His MS. Com.

Sonne Fleminge I se into this world everie daie more and more that it is nothinge but trouble & in Regard thereof I would advise you to consider well wth your selfe, that if you purpose to staie anie longe time out of this cuntrie, to inquire & cast aboute to provide betwixt now and michaellmas for some honest farmors who would take it & giue a good rente for it for I knowe that who soeu^{er} hath there worke done by servants beinge from them themselfe, unlette is both at great Charges & Losse & there worke & busines neglecked unlesse they had one that would be both up earlie & laite, & follow them to there worke wch I knowe you haue not you^{rs} so done, so as it were you^r onlie way to let all by a Rente, in Regard you^r mynd & desire is to luiue quietlie & hath noe desire to trouble you^r head wth wordlie busines, wch rente would come in easilie wthout anie charge or trouble of mynd unto you for although you Let it to an honest man that would kepe up houses & hedges & woods although you Lost a little by it, & let him have it at that raite that he might Liue of, yet it would be a great ease unto you: you^r worke heare goes forward, but it is of the easieth fashon as this bearer can tell you but this daie there are begun to sowe bige, nothinge is sett downe as you wished tyson to do either for what is, laid out or Receiued not as yet neather can I get it done, but you are like to fynd it as you Left it for he hath so manie thinges in hand what of his owne & you^{rs} that he cannot do everie thinge: when you haue settled you^r barnes at Speake wth you, wch I pray god to send them well unto you, I could wish you to take a time & come over hitther so shortlie after as you can conveanientlie to sette all you^r thinges heare,

Q

for I feele my selfe but weak & ill, so as I could wish to see them setled in my time & further I thinke if you purpose to come backe againe, it were a fitt place for you to luive at Urswicke where you might luive both quietlie & neare market & you^r frinds wch if you should haue a mynd to do then you must cast to mend houses, Will$\tilde{m}$ Ambrose was wth Richard Barwis and toke the writings sealed for me wch he will make you acquainted wth all, but it is agreed so that if the writinges be not to you^r Likeinge he will mend them when I please, so as you maie talke wth him of it as you thinke fittinge : Tho. Fleminge sends you a note of such wronges as you suffer at conistone wch by you^r sufferance both bringes losse unto you^r selfe & you^r goodes . & makes them the tenantes p^{re}sume much upon you now in you^r absence : of wch thinges I would desire you to consider & of all other matters that this bearer can tell you & do not driue you^r thinges but set them in order   Thus & prayinge to almightie god to both blesse you & you^r Children & to send them well unto you & they well to Like, hopeinge to se you as shortlie as conveanentlie as you can I rest

Rydall 3j may 1631.   You^r Loveinge mother,
                                    Agnas Fleminge.

CHAPTER V

The Lord's Seat.

The Logge; The Old Hall at Rydal; Its birth and its passing; Appendix—Sir Daniel's alterations in the Low Park

BEFORE touching on the new state of husbandry it is necessary to consider the position of that "capital messuage" or Hall, which formed the centre of the demesne. Such a messuage existed, undoubtedly, from the time of Roger de Lancastre who so strictly defined the boundaries of his deer park, amongst which "Roger loge" is indeed mentioned, a term probably signifying a hunting lodge such as was usually erected for the lord's convenience in forests or parks devoted to deer.* It would be a small rough structure built of wood, as were the peles and lodges of this period. Sir Roger had larger manors and halls for residence, notably Howgill Castle which remained the chief seat of his race, and Witherslack, where he was in residence with his chaplain at the time of the signing of the foregoing document. Therefore, it would be but a knight's chamber with a larger room called a hall, which Roger would reserve for himself when he pursued the deer over the mountain, or rode more quietly by the Hunter Path from Scandale, Caistone and Patterdale, while accommodation for his men, his foresters, his hounds and his hawks would be wanted.

We know fairly well from contemporary evidence what such a lodge would be like. It would not be so spacious as the king's lodges indeed, one at least of which must have been in Roger's care while he was Keeper of Inglewood, and another of which, built in 1285, in Woolmer Forest consisted of a "camera" or chamber, with chimneys and six windows of glass, a hall of wood, plastered and painted, with wooden shutters, a kitchen, two wardrobes, and a queen's garden. (*Mediæval England*, by Mary Bateson).

But a copy of these on a small scale it would be; built of oaks of the surrounding forest, split into stout logs. Defensible also it would be made, and though in a slighter degree than the peles of the border, constructed by Edward I. to hold his conquest, yet suitable for rough times when marauders and deer-stealers were rife, and when it was often an advantage to be able swiftly to drive the cattle of the demesne and even of the little *vill* into the ringed palisade about the lodge, and bar the entrance. Such palisaded places, the first peles of the

---

* In the Cal. Pat Rolls of Richard II., the king's "keeper of the Laund" is authorized to enclose 10 acres of Inglewood Forest and "to build a Logge thereon"

north built on a mound or rock,* were surrounded by a deep ditch and fosse, which made their defence the easier.

We find the word *loge* in use as late as 1462, when an attack of the Duke of Suffolk's men on Hellesdon—a small manor claimed by the Paston family, on which the lord did not reside—is described in the Paston Letters.† In this account, the pulling down of the *logge* is several times mentioned, with the aggravating circumstance that the tenants of the manor were compelled by the duke's men " to help to brek down the wallys of the place and the logge both " ; showing that this building, which served as a manorial centre and lodging, was defended by a wall.

Where then was Roger's lodge in Rydal ? where he rested after a hard day's hunt, and listened to complaints from his parker, of broken fence or stolen deer ; or heard the report of his bailiff, and received the dues from the sturdy townsmen—now his tenants—whose houses were pitched on the ground outside his new park. There is nothing conclusively to show. His fence, indeed, is stated to have run down from the upper part of the park towards *Roger loge.* It may possibly have stood on the confines of Rydal, within Scandale Beck, where later the close called Sturdy Park was found, and a seventeenth century mention of a mill occurs,‡ and where the modern lodge stands for the new hall-drive.

Or it may have been placed on that rock by the ford which in later times, at all events, carried a building known as the Old Hall. This rock, situated as it is, directly on the line of the Roman road, where this enters

---

* See Pele · its origin and meaning, by Mr George Neilson The work of repair at Liddell, in Cumberland, in 1300, included the strengthening of the pele and palisades, and making " lodges " within the mound, in which to house the men

† Nos 615, 616, and 617 of Prof Gardiner's edition.

‡ Account Book of 163.

the gateway into the mountains, and a natural fortress in the midst of running waters and morasses, may have served as a military post, used in times of warfare and by invading armies, and afterwards abandoned. That some chapel or sacred building once stood upon it seems almost certain, from its early name of St. John How, which happily is found in one document. Such a structure may have been erected by the Northumbrian Church in connection with the perils of the ford, which in times of winter rain must have been great.

The chapel again may have fallen into ruin before the manor-house was placed on the rock. There is in sites an extraordinary continuity; and besides, an easily defended one was probably still needed when the lord of Rydal pitched his seat on this steep and narrow how. The manor-house, with all its accessories that grew upon and round it, as the once wild deer-forest passed into demesne, could hardly, at any time, have been a "*mansio*" in the most extended sense, serving as the administrative centre to a large district, such as the one mentioned as being in decay six centuries ago on the great island of Windermere, or as Mourholm, near Carnforth, the seat of the Lindeseys and de Coucys, who were lords of half of Loughrigg. This last is described as containing, in 1347,[*] one hall with one great chamber, one kitchen, one chamber for knights, one chapel, two granges, one turf-house, one carpenter's house, one house for dogs, one stable, one dove-cote, one smithy, and a garden outside with its fruits. At Dufton, in Westmorland in 1323,[†] there stood within the court of the manor a great chamber or hall, a

---

[*] Inq p m No 63 (2 Nos) 20 Ed. III.

[†] Cal. of Close Rolls. It is interesting to note, in connection with the minute divisions of the age, that the lady Alicia had assigned to her in dower a share of the various chambers. In another place the widow is to enjoy one third of the dove-cote.

chapel, with a little chamber between them, a bake-house and barns, and an orchard without.

Yet most of these accessories can be traced, as well as the usual fish-ponds, about the now deserted rock of Old Hall, or St. John. The little chamber, indeed, where in a stately household the ladies were wont to retire, may not have been represented here; nor is it likely that the customary chapel would be maintained, while the lords were only rarely, and for short times, in residence. But the great hall—the living and eating room for master and servants—the dog-house, the stable, the smithy, the dove-cote, where the tame prolific birds were kept on which to feed the caged hawks and sometimes to be used for the table, were certain fixtures. Also the "knight's chamber," an invariable adjunct, that seems to have served as a guest-house for travellers of rank or distinction: for the manor-house was in a measure a hospice, and no wanderer could be denied shelter who knocked at the court-gate, which was barred by sunset. It is often mentioned.* We have seen that John Whitfield, when making his compact with John Fleming, in 1475, as part owner of Rydal, stipulated that he might have "a knight chamber," doubtless for his own use while he exercised his "freedom to hawke, hunt, fisch, and fowle within the lordeschip."

---

* There was one in the Fawsett manor-court in 1272-3, with an upper chamber or soler [see *A Norfolk Manor*, by Miss Davenport]; while as late as 1639, the "knight Chamber" is mentioned in the inventory, whereas it was apparently only one of the apartments of Skerwith Hall, Westmorland. Rydall MSS. Sometimes the apartment was a source of profit to the lord. The Inquisition of John de Belleme in 1301, concerning his possessions in Kentmere, states (after mention of other assets) "There is a chamber together with a fulling-mill, which renders one mark yearly. *Lancashire Inquests, Extents, &c*, W. Farrer.

The *Ancient State of the Border*, by Nicolson and Burn, p. liv, Feb., 1547, thus describes an attack of a party under Lord Wharton, on the laird Johnston's chief house in Annerdale "It was a fair large tower, ... with a barnekin, hall, kitchen, and stables, all within the barnekin. They get over the barnekin wall in dark, and stole into the "house," where only women were sleeping, 2 men and a woman slept in the tower, wh was secured by both an iron and a wooden door. In the "house" plenty of beef salted, malt, barley, havermeal, butter and cheese"

Not all the manorial buildings could be found room for upon the narrow rock. Solid ground about it was gained by drainage. A deep cutting circling round it to the beck and river achieved that object, and formed a moat, filled not only with ooze from the morass, but also by the sikes that flowed down the steep sides of the upper park into this cup-like hollow. It is difficult, indeed, to realize what must have been the watery state of this catch-ground in ancient times. Besides the morass where beck and river met, with its islands and its " allows," (hollows) dangerous ground till late times, there were also stagnant pools and wet places to the south-east. Indeed we have the names of Great and Little Island in the park where now no water shows. " Midge-mire " still lives in memory, showing now as only a well-marked depression by the side of the drive, where running water may be heard in the paved channels (called cundreths by the people) made below the sod to carry it off. A circular depression between Rydal How and Silver Hill still shows traces of a retaining wall about its reaches, and a fragment of a building is remembered by it. This doubtless was one of the fish-ponds stated by Nicolson and Burn to be still traceable.* And though artificial fish-ponds might be supposed to be superfluous where the river and its chain of " dubs " was teeming with fish, it must be remembered that the de Lancasters had originally no rights in the river or the mere (see Fisheries), and that it was convenient to keep the fish which formed so great an article of diet ready at hand, almost within the defences of the manor-house.

The drainage from these depressions is now conducted underground in a curved line, which circles round Old Hall at a short distance away from the rock. It flows beneath the high-road—where in flood times it may be

---

* Is it possible that one of these pools may have been the one commemorated in Wordsworth's poem, which Professor Knight has sought for in vain?

heard roaring—and enters the river close to its union with the beck. This curve may represent the actual line of the old moat, which was much more evident according to a former woodman before certain alterations were made in the level of the park some years back. The old causeway, re-paved by Sir Daniel in 1686, came down past the rock to the ford at the same point. On the other side of the causeway, the present double line of sunk wall may represent the line of the old moat and the limits of the demesne to the west, being, no doubt, a later improvement of Sir Daniel's double ditch constructed for drainage in 1682. Beyond, a long low mound, possibly artificial, or once carrying palisades, defines the limit of the outer defences as far as the rising ground of Low Park How; and completes the circle of the manor-house's precincts, enclosing the garden with its fruit-trees, now a cricket ground and field, but still known as Old Orchard. The position of the former lord's brewery may be guessed from the name Kiln-How, applied to the knoll rising from the bridge over Rydal Beck. This bridge is locally known as Smithy Bridge, and here a fragment of building is still remembered. The history of the smithy is clear, though the last smith to use it was Adam Fisher, who died in old age in 1660, and was himself connected with the clearing of the Old Hall; it was afterwards used as a little dwelling-house.

Lord's Oak, a tree now in decrepitude, and never seemingly of phenomenal size, stands not far off.

Here then once stood, on St. John How and round about it, the group of buildings that once served as the capital messuage or "mansio" of Rydal. Whenever it was planted, or by how many of the de Lancasters it was used, it must certainly have been under its hall-roof that the youthful couple, Thomas and Isabel, were placed when their "nonage" was past, and they began housekeeping together, it was within its walls that they had

leave to drive the cattle of the father from Coniston, if he should not promptly supply them with the stipulated income. In those turbulent times, when the small gentry of Westmorland (and notably Isabel's family) made petty warfare on each other, unrestrained by a distant and weak government, it no doubt played its part in strife as well as in peace. We know, indeed, that Rydal cattle claimed by Isabel's sister were forcibly driven off by her enemies. Probably by this time the hall on the rock came to be built as a high, strong tower of several stories, like the so-called " peles " that sprang up about this date, newly constructed on old sites, on almost every lord's seat of the border counties, and of the district round the great bay. Isabel, in spite of other claimants, kept, till near the end of the fifteenth century, her hold upon the place ; and from the frequent mention of John " of Ridale," and of John's son, John her beloved, of the same place, we may conclude that they were at least sometimes resident here. Hugh, John's son, who lived a long life at Coniston, allowed a younger son of his, David, to take up his abode in the hall of Rydal, and even granted him, it seems, some possession in its lands. David here brought up a large family of six sons ; and the younger, David, afterwards to have charge of the queen's falcons, must as a lad have scaled the heights round and above the park, seeking the hawk's nests and bringing down the young birds to nourish and train. Earne Crag would still have its brood every year, no doubt. Jane, the elder David's widow, lived on in Rydal as we have seen twenty-five years after the date (1575), when the place is called the Old Hall in a deed of Squire William, who was then engaged in consolidating his interests in Rydal, and eighteen years after her eldest son Henry parted with his rights in lands thereabouts. When she died in 1600, the building and its accessories were probably dilapidated. Agnes, who in the same year became, by the death of her husband, squiress of Rydal, had certainly already with him made their home in the present Rydal Hall, probably then known as Rydal House. The old one was deserted, and the flat ground round the rock was marked out as "closes" to fit into the new scheme of husbandry.

A casual mention here and there tells us the fate of the ancient "lodge" and manor-house. It was probably left, getting more ruinous, its buildings being used for agricultural purposes only, through the era of the Civil Wars and the Commonwealth. Sir Daniel, on wresting the property from his opponents in 1557, clearly found nothing of the Old Hall worth repairing. He began, indeed, to demolish what of it still stood. The demesne corn-barn, built no doubt when the Low Park was "set" as a farm, beyond the line of old defences, and repaired in 1643, was in need of enlargement; so, economical of stone and labour, he set old Adam Fisher, of the Smithy hard by, to "trail" the stones—doubtless on a small sled—from the ancient manor-house and across the flat to the barn, where the wallers were busy. In the autumn of the same year, 1659, he took in a mare of "Thomas Benson's, of Coat How," to graze "in the close call[d] ould hall," at 1s. 4d., and next year he let off entirely to his tenant, David Harrison, the "little close called the ould hall." From that time it became only grazing ground for cattle, regularly let to tenants. But still, apparently, the knoll was crowned with fragments of buildings, for Nicolson and Burn wrote, in 1777:—

"Upon the top of a round hill . . was anciently placed the manor-house or hall near to the said Low-park. But upon the building of the other hall . the said manor-house became ruinous . . . where is now to be seen nothing but the ruins of buildings, walks, and fish ponds; and the place where the orchard was, is now a large inclosure without even a fruit-tree in it, now called the Old Orchard."

Its stones were again to be of use. When it became the fashion to remove the farm buildings of the demesne from their immediate association with the squire's hall, and Sir Michael le Fleming, a lover of London, let the demesne farm, a house for the farmer was erected in the Low Park, hard by the old corn barn. This must have been done between 1847, when the plans of the house were paid for, and 1850, when Edward Fidler, farmer, was in possession. Old inhabitants say that the last stones of the ancient hall were at that time cleared for the farm building, and it was doubtless then that the quern or hand-mill for grinding corn was turned up. This was placed in the rockery of the Vicarage, but has now unfortunately disappeared. The farm, once called Fidlers, and afterwards Crow How, and then Rydal Farm, was greatly enlarged lately, when the ancient barn called Birkets, on the other side the Old Hall, but beyond its precincts, that had become useless as a hoghouse, was completely cleared for its stones This illustrates the mode of the country, which demolishes all old buildings for present use, even in a day when blasting is easy, and leaves no record of the past but, possibly, a name and a bare site.

Superstitious terror, indeed, kept the memory of the Old Hall alive through many generations. Stories sprang up to explain its abandonment ; and the deserted rock, crowned with its pile of ruins, struck awe into the heart of the traveller who after dark passed it on his road to Rydal. Strange sounds, strange sights, pervaded it by night. Wailing voices, as of spirits in distress ; headless ghosts (three in number), that danced upon its summit ; and later, a white dog that followed the terrified passenger across the Old Orchard, even, it is believed, to the middle of last century. No one now living owns to having seen the white dog, but old men and women confess to having often in childhood, laid their ear to the road-wall that leans against the How, and to thinking that they heard, while they listened in breathless expectation, strange muffled sounds issuing from its depths—the " dirge-like note from inmost chambers far remote." Such stories, current once amongst the village folk—who still adhere to the tradition of a buried treasure at the Old Hall, and of an underground passage from it to the New Hall—found echo in verse. " The Shield of Flandrensis " * embodies in rhyme—along with a good deal of pure fiction—the legend of the strange sounds, and of the spirits

> " That pipe as they whirl around lattice and gate.
> With their grey gaunt misty forms "

Wordsworth did better. In a note to one of his Duddon sonnets, he speaks of the haunted character the place had obtained, to which its desertion was ascribed; and the sonnet above expresses the feelings excited by such a site, desolate after many centuries of stirring history.

> " There dwelt the gay, the beautiful, the bold,
> Till nightly lamentations, like the sweep
> Of winds—though winds were silent—struck a deep
> And lasting terror through that ancient hold,
> Its line of warriors fled. . . . . "

It is possible to guess a rational explanation for the " lamentations, like the sweep of winds," and even for the mysterious white forms seen by night about the how. Its situation is directly in the road of the peculiar current of air that, from the very summit of Fairfield, charges down Rydal Head with frequency, and often at a high rate of speed. Blasts strike across the Old Orchard when there is comparative stillness on either side the encircling hollows of the how. Then white close mists

---

* *Lays and Legends of the English Lake Country*, J. P. White.

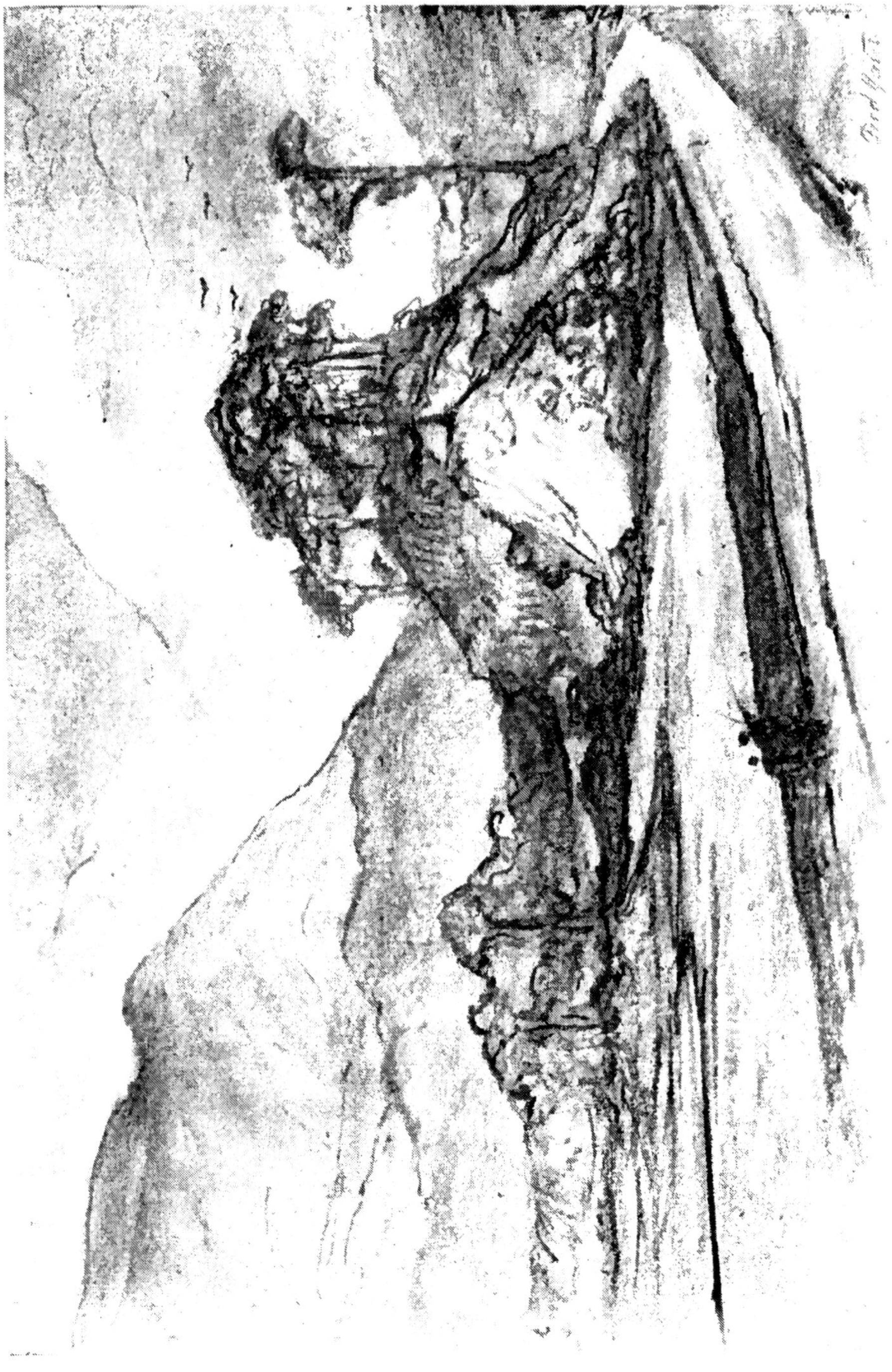

are apt, even yet, after centuries of draining, to rise and cling at night-fall (and in mid-summer too) to the flat fields and hollows round the Old Hall. These, if stirred and broken by a current of air from the Head might assume curious shapes, that would be readily distinguished and described as ghosts by the heated imagination of the rustic.

But all this is past. Almost the name of the how, Old Hall Hill, is forgotten, as the earlier St. John How was, long before. The present Rydal child gives it not a thought in passing. The modern cricketers and tennis players, whose pavilion leans on one side of it, have not a notion of its past ; while the tourists who upon every kind of vehicle—cycle, motor, coach and carriage—roll in hundreds along the highway on the other side, scarcely note its existence as a picturesque mound

Yet there the rock stands, beautiful, wooded, fir-crowned. Few, indeed, who climb its steep slope and view the exquisite scene around—of curving river and mountain gateway—could guess its ancient state. The nettles that grow on the shale of the summit, the few rooks that build in its crowning firs, are the only things about it reminiscent of man. After a thousand years and more, and the centuries through which it played a stirring part in the history of the valley, it has become a thing of nature's solely.

In connection with the alterations at the Hall, a new road was designed up Hall Bank. The tenants, whose estates lay on one side, were clearly alarmed lest their " fronts before door," as the expression went, should be encroached upon. On December 25, 1782, Gibson writes, " Mr Knott and the tenants came here some time since and have Staked out the Hall Bank (he said as you Directed) but neither Mr. Harrison (the steward) nor I tho' it prudent to hold a Court, nor meddle with it, till you be present and see it."

Next April, he reports that he had had "Two Course Ash Trees opposite to James Dawson's & one large one above Ja⁸ Atkinson, which stood where the R^d (up Hall Bank) will be if Shifted, Grubbed up; the last of which I hope may be sold very well."

When Mr. Knott sold High House (Rydal Mount) to Mr. North, the new-comer was prepared to contest his rights of timber with the lady of the manor. Of the sorry "Battle of the Woodlands," as it may be called, we are apprized by a letter of Dorothy Wordsworth, sister of the poet

[From Letters of the Wordsworth Family, ed. by Professor Knight Letter cxcix]

Dorothy Wordsworth to Thomas De Quincey.

Grasmere, Saturday, 6th May, 1804

. . You have walked to Rydale under Nab Scar? Surely you have? If not, it will be forever to be regretted, as there is not anywhere in this country such a scene of ancient trees & rocks as you might have there beheld—trees of centuries growth inrooted among & overhanging the mighty crags These trees you would have thought could have had no enemy to contend with but the mountain winds, for they seemed to set all human avarice at defiance, & indeed if the owners had had no other passion but avarice they might have remained till the last stump was mouldered away, but *malice* has done the work, & the trees are levelled

A hundred labourers—more or less—men, women, & children, have been employed for more than a week in hewing, peeling bark, gathering sticks &c, &c., & the mountain echoes with the riotous sound of their voices You must know that these trees upon Nab Scar grow on unenclosed ground, & Mr North claims the right of *lopping & topping* them, a right which Lady Fleming as Lady of the Manor claims also Now Mr North allows (with everybody else) that she has the right to fell the trees themselves, & he only claims the boughs. Accordingly he sent one or two workmen to top some of the trees on Nab Scar; Lady F.'s steward forbade him to go on; & in consequence he offered £5 per day to any labourers who would go & work for him At the same time Lady F.'s steward procured all the labourers he could also at great wages, & the opposite parties have had a sort of warfare upon the crags, M‍r North's men seizing the finest trees to lop off the branches, & drag them upon M‍r N.'s ground, & Lady Fleming's men being also in an equal hurry to choose the very finest, which *they* felled with the branches on their heads, to prevent M‍r N. from getting them, &, not content with this, they fell those also which M‍r N. has been beforehand with them in lopping, to prevent him from receiving any benefit from them in future. Oh, my dear Friend! is not this an impious strife? Can we call it by a milder name? I cannot express how deeply we have been affected by the loss of the trees (many & many a happy hour we passed under their shade), but we have been more troubled to think that such wicked passions should have been let loose among them. The profits of the wood will not pay the expenses of the workmen on either side! !

A law-suit will no doubt be the consequence, & I hope that both parties will have to pay severely for their folly, malice, & other bad feelings. M‍r North is a native of Liverpool. I daresay you may have often heard us mention him as a man hated by all his neighbours, M‍r N. has taken an active part in the business, ...

APPENDIX.

Sir Daniel's alterations in the Low Park.

1631 12ˢ 0ᵈ paid for " Gutteringe " by Sturdy Park

1658 " Sold unto Will. Holme out of yᵉ wood of yᵉ Low parke barne for yᵉ sum of 00 06 00

,, Rich Nicoldson buys 3 little trees and in Keen Ridding.

1658 Feb 24. " Paid unto Adam Fisher (besides 3ˢ 4ᵈ allowed him in his fine) for 24 days gardening, making hedge in yᵉ Low parke ; & cutting of Briers, being all now due unto him 00. 08. 00

1657 May 21. " Paid unto Adam Fisher for 14 dayes worke in coaling a Pitt " 00 07 02

1658 May 8. Adam is paid for 5 days work " i'th' Round Close Gutters " .. ..

March 28. Adam is paid for 11 days work in the new orchard and garden, and one day carrying lime and rubbish. After another payment for twelve days.

May 2. " Paid unto Adam Fisher for one dayes worke in yᵉ garden, 5 dayes in traleing stones at yᵉ old hall, one dayes worke w‍h hee's yet to doe, & 2ᵈ I owed him since my last paying him being all now due . .. 00. 02. 06

June 22. "Old Adam" paid for 10½ days work "at yᵉ old hall in traleing of stones."

1659 May 7. Two wrights begin to fell wood for "yᵉ Low-parke barne"

,, June 14. Contract made for "walling" same at 18ˢ p. Rood.

June 29. Four pounds is paid for 4½ roods "for walling" of yᵉ Low-parke-barne "besides 16 yards of old wall which was not medled withall."

July 9. The wright is paid £2. 12. 6. for the woodwork of the barn.

July 16. Grigg has "more paid him for a dayes getting of Stones at yᵉ Low-hall," and 12ˢ. 6ᵈ more paid him for 50 Load of Slate getting for yᵉ Low parke barne."

1667 April 2. "Paid to a Dyker in yᵉ round close 15 dayes at 4ᵈ 00. 05. 00

1677 June 18. "yᵉ Birket-barne is repaired for the second time.

1680 March 31. Wil. Wilson is paid 5s. 0d. for "guttering of yᵉ Round Close, viz. for 56 Rodes of old at 0ᵗ (=½d.) and 31 of new at 1ᵈ, at 7 yards yᵉ Rode."

1682 March 4. "Paid unto Will. Harrison of Langdale for Ditching between yᵉ old Orchard & Birket-moss (a Double Ditch at 6 per Rood) being 38 Rood, yᵉ sum of
00. 18. 00

1686 March 9. "Iᵗ to Edward Hird of Gresmere for 5 dayes in paveing yᵉ Cawsey in Birket-moss 1ˢ 8ᵈ, to Robert Hawke-rigg 4 dayes for yᵉ like 1ˢ 4ᵈ, in all" .. 00. 03. 00

PART III

AGRICULTURE AND FISHERIES

CHAPTER I

Husbandry in Rydal

Change from Forest to Farm; Valuation of Demesne, 1655.

IT was at the end of the sixteenth century, when the deer-forest was swept away, that the history of husbandry, as we know it, began in Rydal. And it was under the rule of the widow Agnes, upon whom the demesne was settled, that the woodland solitudes were changed into a busy, well-ordered farm. Here, and doubtless at the new Hall, she lived for 32 years after her husband's death, bringing up a large family of sons and daughters, marrying and dowering the latter, and setting the former on in the world, even to the extent of buying the Manor of Skerwith for her son Daniel. And there can be little doubt that her thrift, her sound sense and business-like habits laid the foundation of that wealth which her eldest son, John, acquired. It is fitting, therefore, that these letters of hers to him—Part II., Chapter IV., Appendix—which are all that remain, and are altogether about the farming of Rydal, should start the account of it. She had now, professedly, given up the reins, having let the demesne to him to farm for £200 a year; but her active spirit was overlooking all, and fretting her old body; and there is no doubt that those

R

urgings with her tongue, which she called "a little touch" when applied to her daughter-in-law, and a "talk" to Tyson—promising even to keep this up as long as her health shall serve—was regarded by them both as scolding. Poor Tyson is forced to complain to his master, that nothing "blends" (or confuses) his brain "more than inquietnes", and it is to his determination to justify himself before her complaints that we apparently owe the earliest account-sheets existing at the Hall. They date from 1631, and close in 1634, showing that Tyson triumphed in a sense, and held his own in the office, and entered his "olde mistress's" funeral expenses in them. They were audited from time to time by Squire John, and show his signature, as well as the trust he placed in his man in a very varied range of business.

It is from these stitched-together sheets of old paper (of which some are torn) that we get our first glimpse of the methods of husbandry pursued on the Rydal demesne, and of which we obtain clear light in Squire Daniel's time, from the "Gist-Book of Rydal," kept by John Banks, from the last page of the great account-book, where a record of the corn sown between 1669 and 1674 is kept, and from the excellent little book (cut and stitched apparently by its writer) entitled "An account of Setting Rydal Demesne Yearly." In its pages, of a few inches in dimension, Richard Fleming, who became steward to his father in 1693, set down in fine script, every detail of the work of the demesne farm and the cost thereof. It closes in 1699. The method of farming as displayed by these books is much the same, though Squire Daniel wrung a larger income from the land than his predecessor.

The value of the demesne must have been largely increased by its change from forest to farm; and the increased income would be started by a lump sum from the felled wood, always wanted for the Furness ironworks.

It may, indeed, have been from the oaks of Rydal that Squire William rebuilt his Hall at Coniston,* where the deer were retained in the small park that continued to give dignity to the estate. That change involved other changes, some of which affected, undoubtedly, the village lands The extent of the demesne before it, and of the High and the Low Parks, is not exactly ascertained. It was rated from the time of Roger de Lancaster as worth one quarter of a knight's fee, or £10 in money. The tax paid by its owners in 1302-3 and in 1353 as succession duty was 35s. (Rawlinson MSS.) The Flemings, as we have seen, rented the half at £10 in 1475, which gave its worth at a nominal £20 a year, and this rent was maintained until at least 1547

A copy of John Banks' Valuation of the Rydal Demesne, at the time that it came into his master's hands (1655), is found in Richard's " Setting " Book. It gives the names of all the " closes " into which the Low and High Parks had been split up, and of their worth as pasture. It should be noticed that no acreage is given, only the number of " grasses " in each close—that is to say, the number of beasts that such a ground space would feed. This ancient mode of reckoning land and its value continued till the eighteenth century, as the account-books of Ambleside Hall estate and of Kelsick of Ambleside show. It will be seen, too, that the demesne had been thrown into three classes of land ; the deeper soil reserved for the plough, a portion much enlarged in Squire Daniel's time ; the flatter stretches of the Low Park for a crop of hay ; and the rough ground—the hows in the valley and

---

* In " A general view of Agriculture in the Co of Westmorland " by M A. Pringle, date 1797, it is stated that it is more profitable to fell oaks of 50 or 60 years' growth than to let them stand for 80 or 100 years for ship-building In the same treatise we hear of a stratum of grey limestone found near Ambleside, with regrets that it is so little used for agriculture. It might be burnt with faggots or " chats " instead of going to the trouble of bringing the limestone from Kendal or up Windermere Lake at great expense He also tells us that women work in the fields and drive harrows and ploughs, and that clogs are worn by both sexes, the soles being made of birch, alder or sycamore

the wild steep mountain slopes of Rydal Head—for the pasture of cattle. The squire's farm buildings around the new Hall were steadily increasing. Besides a swine hall (1659), a calf hall and a brew house, a "Keslop hall" two new stables (1660), and accomodation for oxen under the great new corn barn (1680), he had erected in 1671, a slaughter-house or keslop in the upper park. These extensive outhouses in turn drew rats, of which fact, likewise, we hear in the account-book :—

"Dec. 18. 1686. Paid unto Tho. Lofton of Rufford near York, Ratcatcher besides 2^s 6^d I am to give at Easter next if he kill ye Rates for a year .. .. £ s. d.
00 01. 00.
Dec. 24 Paid Michael & Richard (his son) for
Rats .. .. 00. 00. 06.

It may be interesting to place against this estimate of cattle-gates the modern acreage, taken about 1810,* which, including some parcels in Loughrigg, brought the total demesne to 1594a. 0r. 35p.

"A Perticuler Account of the Names of the Cloyses belonging to the Demasne of Rydal in the County of Westmerl^d April the 16th 1655. By J B S^t"

      Imprimis
1. The Low Parke all Meadow.
2. Birket field and Stonewaite.
3. The Close called the Old Orchard
4. The Tip Close 4 grasses at 6^s 8^d p grass
5. The Close called Round-close and Long-close (7^a. 2^r 28^p)
6. The Close called Lands a p^t of it Sowne (8^a 0^r. 5^p)
7 8 9 The 3 Closes called the Hag's 20 grasses at 8^s 0^d per grass.
10. The Close called Rydal-haw 10 grasses at 6^s 8^d per grass.
11. The Close called Low-parke-haw 6 grasses at 6^s 8^d per grass
12 13 The Close called Old-hall and Birket Moss 3 grasses at 10^s per grass.

---

* Valuation Book of Rydal and Loughrigg

14 15 16   The Close called Adam-haw with Allans—9^s 0^d
17 18 19.   The Closes called Springs 4 grasses at 6^s 8^d p grass
- 20. The Close called On-man haw 4 grasses at 6^s 8^d p grass.
- 21. The Close called Frith in the Nab 6 grasses at 6^s 8^d p grass
- 22. The Close called New-close 6 grasses at 6^s 8^d p grass.
- 23. The High Orchard.
- 24. The Close called Berk-hagg 5 grasses at 6^s 8^d p grass
- 25. The Close called Watley-hagg 8 grasses at 6^s 8^d a grass
- 26. The Close called Parke 60 grasses at 7^s 0^d p grass.
- 27. The Close called Buckstones 60 grasses at 7^s 0^d p grass
- 28. The Close called Low-pike 4 grasses at 7^s 0^d p grass.
- 29. The Close called High-pike 4 grasses at 6^s 8^d p grass.
- 30. The Close called Dale-green 8 grasses at 6^s 8^d p grass
- 31. The Close called Dale-head-close 30 grasses at 3^s 4^d p grass.

The above is the Valuation of Rydal Demesne by John Banks Steward Anº Doi. 1655.

CHAPTER II

Cattle-Grazing and Marketing

Draught Oxen and " Fat beifs."

AGISTMENT, indeed, or the pasturage of cattle, was at first the main source of the lords' agricultural wealth. He not only taxed his tenants for the grazing of their stock, but he bought beasts to fatten and sell, and he took in stranger's cattle to graze on his ground at a fixed rate. Squire John went so far as a cattle dealer, that he set his baliff to buy cattle at fairs to be fattened at Rydal and then driven to Speke in Lancashire, where presumably they fetched a higher price. On May 13, 1631, Tyson writes to him " I thinke heare will come jeaste (strangers' cattle) to sett you^r grounds but neu^{er} the lesse we will buy beastes to send yo^u as you have written." Next he reports that he has bought thirty beasts, most of them oxen and runts, and will buy ten more His master may have what he wants for Speke " for the worst and least price are best for this Cuntrie." It will not do to buy at the Ravenglass fair, as " the sickness " is rife in Walney, and dealings with any man of Cumberland and Furness must be avoided. In another letter, of May 3, he tells how he will send the fat runts to Kendal for sale; but the stotts are not ready, 10s. 0d. or more would be lost on each beast " for want of a little grasse." Next he reports the sale of five fat runts for £21. 10s 0d., which is more by £2 than the next highest bid. The account-book gives the purchase of " 2 read Oxen & one Cowe " at £8. 15s. 0d., while cows varied in price from 22s. to 29s. 6d.

After Squire John's death, Harrison, the steward, records in 1646, the purchase of 14 oxen at Rosly for beef by the shepherd, £43. 1s. 0d.; again, in 1647, the purchase of ten beasts at Carlisle Fair (including charges and toll) £29 10s 9d. Two years before, the shepherd had purchased two draught oxen at Kendal for £9. 13s. 4d. These no doubt would be needed for the plough, which was then and later drawn by these great oxen. The shoeing of the oxen is a regular charge at the smith's. In 1647, is paid " for showeinge oxen 2 tymes 10^s 6^d " From 1656 onwards the regular charge was 5s. 0d. for the team, only once rising to 5s. 10d As in '67 the shoeing of three comes, on March 5, to 2s. 3d., and four on May 25 to 3s. 4d; and the re-shoeing of five came to 4s. 2d. in 1668, we must conclude that the full team was six, and the usual charge, 10d. a beast.

He likewise was a purchaser of cattle, and his dealings in live stock greatly increased as his capital grew. His emissaries, John Banks, or another servant, his brother, and later his third son Daniel, who became his factotum on the farm from about 1688, were present at all the great fairs of the district, buying for him; and beasts were driven by many an ancient road over moor and fell to

Rydal, from Rosly, from Broughton-in-Furness, from Penrith, from Dumesdale, from Egremont, from Beckermet, but most frequently from Ravenglass, which had two fairs in the year.

In 1658, £5. 3s. 4d. was paid for 2 black stotts, at Kendal, £2. 7s. 0d. for a heiffer; £5. 4s. 0d. for a pair of red stears; for a black one £2. 5s. 6d.; another £2. 2s. 0d.; while the toll cost 7d., and expenses of driving 1s. 2d. At Cockermouth, in December, four oxen were secured for £4. 10s. 0d., but the 6 oxen which fetched £19. 10s. 0d. at the Ravenglass fair, July 23, must have been larger beasts. Again, in 1662 beast were brought over the pass of Three Shire Stones; a couple of pairs of oxen being purchased, respectively for £8. 10s. 0d. and £7. 10s. 0d.; they cost 4d. "for a fold to put y^m in," 8d. for toll, and 2s. 6d. for charges all night.

In May, 1682, the seven beasts bought by Daniel needed help to drive them to Dalegarth (4d.), and 4d. was spent at Fell Foot, bringing the amount paid to £23 19s. 10d In 1669, a very large purchase was made, the Squire's three emissaries buying at Cockermouth, 24 oxen and a bull for £95. 4s. 6d., which cost 8s to bring them home. At Rosley "8 oxen for beifc" were purchased in July, 1771, for £20. 12s. 0d, a supply that could hardly be consumed by the family.

Thus buying and selling went on. £34. 1s. 0d. was spent at Ravenglass and Beckermet on May 29, 1676.

But the largest deals were perhaps done in 1684 and 1685, when a certain Mr. Tickle of Rainford, Lancashire, agreed to purchase 40 oxen from the squire For the first 40, a sum of £146 was paid in instalments; for the second I trace but £118. 14s. 6d. To supply this demand as well as his private ones, the squire proceeded to buy largely and in advance. Through the summer of 1683, at the fairs of Hawkshead, May 17; Ravenglass, May 28; and Lancaster, September 28, at least 77 beasts were bought, at prices widely varying. A pair of oxen ranged from £5. 6s. 6d. to, in an exceptional case, £7. 13s. 6d., but for young beasts much less was paid, bringing the average lower; so that upon the price received for the 40 oxen, which amounted to £3. 13s. 0d. each, or £7. 6s. 0d. a pair, the squire no doubt pocketed a substantial profit. In the succeeding May, the average of 20 oxen bought at Ravenglass came to a little under £2. 18s. 0d.; though for "2 large oxen" bought at Hawkshead (which no doubt were not drafted into Mr. Tickle's lot) £8. 12s. 0d. was paid. The largest outlay was probably in 1685, when £94. 3s. 2d. and £39. 16s. 7d were paid at the two Ravenglass fairs, making with other purchases a total of £145. 19s. 2d. At the Kendal fair in 1686, Daniel secured from "Mr Tickle's man" £46. 10s. 0d. for 12 oxen; and for eight others sold at the Hawkshead fair, or privately, £40. 16s. 6d.

Some loss there was in these deals, as is shown in the account-book, which grew more exact as the keeper grew older. For instance, he marks opposite the three oxen bought at Hawkshead in 1686 for £9 5s. 0d., "Beifs," which shows their destiny; while opposite the seven pairs of Ravenglass oxen six are marked sold, three as "beif" and three "Dead." The skins of these oxen that died, probably of the murrain, are sold, respectively at 12s. 0d., 12s. 0d., and 13s. 4d.; but we have note of "a great Oxe Skin y^t was poysoned" fetching 16s. 6d. This was in 1679, and the previous month 8s. 6d. only, had been procured for a cow skin "which dyed of ye murraine." At the same date, October 1, we find an entry:—

"Given to ye Miller of Ambleside for blooding and givin a Drink to my Cowes for ye murrain   ..   ..   ..   00 01. 00.

But the usual price of a cow skin was from 9s. 0d. to 13s. 6d., and nine ox skins fetched in 1666, £8. 10s. 0d., which was £1. 4s. 0d. more than the same number brought in 1658. In 1673, nine ox skins, one bull's skin, five cow skins and two horse skins fetched £18 10s 0d.

Richard's Setting-Book tells when the start was made to "kill fat beifs," which varied from October 1 to 26. The salt for 12 beasts cost £4. 10s. 0d. in 1697. The year before, 12 bushels at 6s 8d. had been bought at Keswick for the same number—10s. less. The custom of giving of "flesh" to poor folk on All Saints Day (November 1) which, obtained at Rydal Hall in Squire John's time, was clearly connected with this slaughter and salting of beef for winter use.

Richard's book tells us too, with particularity, the number of beasts which—after grazing in the "fog" or new-grown grass, till shelter was needed—were kept up through the winter. In 1694, 10 calves were taken or "laid" in the "Low Parke Cow-house" on November 5; 15 cows into the one by the new Hall on the 8th; again, on the 15th, 31, "Geld Beasts" were housed; and six more, with 16 "Whys" at Christmas. By the middle or end of April, or even in May for cows, some 60 to 70 beasts were turned out or "laid" again; and we are not only told the exact status of each beast in age and sex, but also to what member of the squire's family each belonged, whether to the squire, or to himself, Daniel Fletcher, and Alice; for to each of his children who took to it, did the squire allow a share in the cattle breeding. It seems, indeed, as if the pigs belonged to the ladies of the house, and perhaps served, to supply them with pin-money, like the poultry.

Squire Daniel's income from agistment in the Park seems not to have risen, which was a likely result of his own increase of stock. Perhaps this explains the "publishing" of his ground, which occurs later on. In early days at least, cattle came for summer pasture to Rydal Park from a distance; from Sawrey, Cartmel Fell, Crook, Winster, &c.

In 1686 the Agist money is set down as £15. 2s. 0d., but this may not have included all. The sum in 1689 is £48. 8s. 5d.

The "Jeast booke" for 1631 showed payments for grazing amounting to £23. 17s. 2d.; and the next year, "in part," to £36. 7s. 4d., to which £4. 5s. 0d. was later added. Squire Daniel secured a larger though a varying income from the same source, and his "Jist-Book" gives :—

	£	s.	d.
"The totall sum off the grasse bottom in the prke this yeare 1656 is	64.	4	0.
And of those (beasts) taken in the dale heade	5.	15.	3.
	69	19	3

He seems to have advertised (probably by cryer at fairs or markets) his grass, as entries in his account-book show

May 12. 1686 for publishing a Jist-note at H 2^d
Ap 14. 1686 paid for Publishing of 6 Notes for Agist 1^s
Spent Apr. 16. 88 at Hawkshead 1^s, for Publishing a Note there, for Agist at Rydal 4^d. And in 1657 he refunds Edwin Green 1^s 0^d spent in Ambleside when Low Park How was let."

At the end of the reign of his son, Sir William, in 1756, it stood at £62 4s 5d But probably the home cattle breeding was by that time at an end. In 1757, it reached £70. 0s. 2d., and in the next year £99. 10s. 4d.

CHAPTER III

CORN-GROWING

Wheat in Rydal; Women in the fields; The Coniston Limestone.

WHEN Squire Daniel let on lease, in 1681, "Frith i'th' Nab" for five years to his tenant David Harrison, it was "with liberty to plow so much thereof for *Oates* as he shall manure and sow with Bigg (= Barley) the next year."

This was the only rotation of crops observed in these parts, except that on the third year the ground was allowed to fall back into meadow, or ley. Then a portion of ground was "laid" each year, and another portion "broken up." We may trace the start of corn-growing on a considerable scale upon the demesne from Dame Agnes' time, for it was said to be she who made a bargain with her tenants to lead manure for her one day a year as boon service, in return for "a calf-garth" or field conceded to them in the Nab; but of this transaction we only hear (and indistinctly, from notes for counsel) from the one side.

It is from Tyson's account-book again that we first hear of the corn harvest of Rydal. On March 16, 1631, he paid for "12 bushels of seede Otes 56^s, and for Chardge" in all £2. 17s. 10d. It was, not without opposition from the old Dame, as her letter shows, that he bought 20 bushels, when "there is enough of ou^r owne that would serve, and neare as good as he can buy anie," but Squire John upheld his bailiff in the desirability of sowing fresh seed.

Ploughing began when threshing stopped, in the first days of February; and it is clear that Plough Monday that followed anciently the festivities of Twelftide,* was not rigidly adhered to in these parts. Then the slow beasts began the work of breaking up the soil, headed by the ploughman, who, if not in yearly wage, received from 4d. a day (1697); and tailed off by the boy who "held" or "drove" the plough, and whose wages were but half that amount; for in 1645, he received 16s. 6d. for 16 weeks, or 2d. a day, and in 1697 only 1½d. a day; and in 1693, indeed, this labour was secured for 1d a day.

The sowing of oats began in mid-March. In 1656, at the start of Squire Daniel's reign, John Banks could not

---

* Tresser's Husbandry.

"set the plough till March 1," for a boy to drive it could not be heard of. While bigg (or barley) started from the 20th of April, onward to early May. Tyson writes, on May 3, that they had begun yesterday to "plowe bigge," which is early, but "the weather being dry and warm invites to it." On May 13 " we have sowne all ou^r bigge but about two dayes worke wch will rest till the next week."

The seed-oats were almost always bought at the Ulverston market, no doubt because of its being the centre of a good corn-growing district. John Banks, too, early found out its cheapness, for in 1656 only 3s. 0d per bushel was asked there, while at home 3s. 8d. to 4s. 0d. His 32½ bushels were all bought there. It is a question whether the Rydal pack-horses travelled thither with the deputy buyer. Probably not; for on the occasions, 1695-98, we have particulars of 8d. a load having been paid for their carriage as far as "Borrecks" (now Borwick Ground on the road from Coniston), where no doubt they would be met by the demesne horses. Prices varied. In 1645, 40 bushels cost only £4 8s. 0d. But there was soon a rise, probably because of the war, and the soldiers stationed in the country-side. Harrison naively writes, under March 27, 1647 :—

"pd for oats bought at seaverall tymes for scots when they were wth us, and would have better then we had of our owne £2 17s 6d."

Indeed, much of the corn-ground must have fallen into fallow during this disastrous time, or Harrison would hardly have noted that year that 7½ bushels had been sown at Miller Bridge, which then belonged to the demesne. In the previous year £4. 6s. 8d. had been paid for only 20 bushels for sowing.

The price however had dropped by 1656, and in 1674, £7. 13s 9d. was paid for 40 bushels at Ulverston. The lowest was possibly reached in 1687, when the majority of the usual 40 bushels bought for sowing was secured at 2s. 9d., and none of it cost more than 3s. 4d In 1695 it was 4s. 0d., and only 31 bushels were bought. In 1693 it had risen to 4s 4d. and 4s. 6d. costing besides 8d. a load to Borwicks, £3 4s. 8d.

Bigg varied from 4s. 10d., in 1655, to 5s. 8d. and even to 8s. 0d., but this was when a tenant paid his rent in it. The amount sown was never larger, but an increasing quantity of barley was bought for malt ; so that in 1698, while 7 odd bushels (the average being about six) were sown, 52 bushels were got for brewing, making an expenditure of £15. 10s. 4d.

If we look to the total amount of corn-land on the demesne, we find it given not in acreage, but named in *dales*, in measure of seed, and even in *stooks*. For instance, the oats sown altogether in 1675, were 50 bushels, 3 pecks ; and the bigg 3 bushels, 3 pecks, 2 hoops In 1694, 37 bushels 1½ pecks were sown, producing 1,256 stooks ; next year, 47 bushels and one hoop producing 1,511 stooks ; while in 1696 from 51 bushels 3 hoops 1,571 stooks were counted. Next year, only the same yield was obtained from 58 bushels 3 pecks.

The yield from bigg was in 1694, 524 stooks from 4 bushels 1½ pecks of seeds, and next year, only 471 from 5 bushels, 2 hoops.

In the next century, when the lord's watchful eye was not upon the husbandry, it was found expedient to sell the crops as they stood before reaping In 1757, the growing corn was sold for £47. 3s. 0d., and the hay meadow for £81. 10s. 6d. But this was a fine season for the seller ; for the steward, Mr. Michael Knott, wrote on February 3, " At the present 'tis worst times ever known for poor people in this Country. Wheat at 40^s p load, Oats at 7^s & 7^s 6^d, and 11^s & 12^s per Bushel, and we have had a great Storm of Snow for near a Month & Excessive Frost."

Later on, when John Gibson was managing the farm and demesne for Sir Michael, corn as well as potatoes were grown in Bainriggs. The seed cost £1. 8s. 0d in 1782, and it was reported on September 22, that it was not ripe by a fortnight. Next year, manure was to be procured and lime, and one part of Bainriggs to be sown with barley and the other with wheat ; and next year with oats, " and then lay it down for either Hay or Pasture." By this means it is hoped the bracken will be eradicated. Older farm ground, the Old Orchard, near to Crow How, is reported as so poor for hay, that it should be sown with oats, then (adding manure) with two crops of barley and corn, after which hay would be abundant.

This is the only time we hear of wheat growing in Rydal. Formerly a little was bought, for use at the lord's table, where alone it was needed. In 1644, the half bushels cost 4s 6d. and 5s. 10d. ; and it rose later to 8s. 4d.

Hops in 1643, were 2s. 0d. a lb. ; 26 lbs. being bought.

Into the corn fields were turned in June the little band of women " lukers " or weeders, who a month earlier had " dressed " or stoned the meadows. These were almost all of the poorer families of tenants, and their wages varied according to their age. In the beginning of Squire Daniel's time the fixed rate was 4d. a day ; in 1697, Richard was paying for him only 3d. without meat to the dressers, and 4d. to the " lukers." Women, too, came to be largely used as " sheares," 4d. again, being their wages ; while they received 6d. for working in the hay.

The meadows were regularly limed in early spring. The cost of this application was considerable, and the fullest particulars of it are often given. In 1631, Tyson paid 6s. 8d. for 80 loads of lymstone, firing 6d., leading £1 15s. 2d. Again, he paid Edward Benson £1 for 300 loads ; the firing cost 6d. and the " leading " £1. 15s. 2d. Another year he enters :—

"Paid for breaking 318 loads of lymstone 14s. 10d
Paid for worke at Lymekilns in all £1. 5. 0."

In 1647, the breaking of stones for a lime kiln cost £1. 9s. 6d. Now whence came the limestone? In 1656 it was fetched, indeed, from Kendal, and probably by the demesne horses, two loads of lime costing 3s. 6d.; and in 1662, 10 loads, £1, were actually procured at Cockermouth, the carriers receiving a gratuity of 2s. 0d. It is of great interest to note, however, that an attempt to utilize the small vein of limestone at hand was later made. This curious narrow band, known as the "Coniston Limestone," is intruded through the slate rock from a point near the summit of Wansfell, where it shows fossils, and across the head of Windermere, where it shows in Low Wood Nab and the island called Sea Mew Crag; thence tending in the Coniston direction along the summit of Black Fell. Everywhere plants, special in character, follow its line; and old neglected lime kilns are to be found along the route. There is one close to the high road near Low Wood; another stood till about 1820, in the field at the lake head; another, again, in a lane between Brathay and Black Fell; still another exists by Sunny Brow, below Black Fell, and there is a last one in wooded Yewdale, by Coniston.

Sir Daniel, mighty in bargain, seems to have been using, about 1690, this local supply. His son, Michael (then acting as steward) wrote full particulars of the transaction.

"Paid unto Rowland Braithw^t of Brathay yards for Quarry-roome to getting two hundred loads, Such as a horse can carry in Crokes 20 or 30 yards from the Quarry

	£	s	d.
at Six Score to the Hundred	0.	6	9.
Item for getting of them	1.	4.	0.
Item for great Boat 2 days and a halfe	0.	11.	6.
Item for Breaking of ym w^{ee} meat	0.	9.	6.
	2.	11.	9.

Another entry is :—

Ground Limed.

"The lower halfe of the cross dale in Low-parke, which goes down to the Tarn pot and a little in Stonewhaite Sprinkled here & there"

The boat mentioned would be the one for heavy goods, and it would bring the stones across the lake head, and up Birdhouse mouth to the kiln. The Braithwaite family of Brathay were well-to-do states-people.

Next year a better deal was done. We read :—

"Paid unto Matthew Mackereth of Ambleside for Breaking up a Quarry for Lime-Stones, to gett two Hundred Shifting loads or Sixteen Score of such as we can carry Streightaway * for 5^s 0^d the getting of them again cost 14^s 0^d, the breaking 'without meat' 17^s 0^d Total £2. 6. 0 This, counting 5^s 6^d as the value of the 'meat,' makes a clear advantage of 10^s 6^d, besides fourscore more stones given in."

Next Edward Forrest of Ambleside was tried. He gave "Quarryroome" for the getting of an equal quantity of stone for as little as 4s. 0d. ! Perhaps the horse or the man succeeded in staggering away the requisite number of yards from the quarry with larger loads than before, for the breaking of them without meat cost 1s. 0d. more. In 1695, Matthew Mackereth gave quarry-room for 3s. 0d., and the price for breaking fell back to 16s. 0d. Under particulars of "Ground Limed" we hear that "The Kill rendered in Fuller Lime 25 Coops, and were Sett upon the Great Dale in the Birket field."

Thus, under the most careful supervision, the work of the demesne farm went on.

---

* See Note page 267

CHAPTER IV

SHEEP

The Clipping; the Salving; the Wool; Market Prices; the "Setting" book; Age Names of Sheep and Cattle.

BUT perhaps before all, in Rydal husbandry, came the sheep. Not alone the statesman, but the lord, possessed in his flock, with their fleeces, sound capital that yielded a steady income. On the wide grassy tops of the mountains, the *faar-fell*, did the hardy little creatures roam at will through the summer. While the deer-forest existed, indeed, the statesmen must have been the only wool sellers of the valley; and it was not until after the lord married the rich cloth merchant's daughter that a stock of demesne sheep was established. Whatever this stock was in number at its start, it was reckoned as 1,200 by Dame Agnes when she made her will in 1630. It was all her own; and she determined, if her son John's heir did not live to be 21, that William, eldest son of her deceased son Daniel, should inherit it, as well as £40 John had had when he farmed Rydal of her, and all the household furniture she possessed at the Hall. Tyson, whose evidence was taken when the great family law-suit came on in 1653, declared that John had taken them over at her death as 1,200, at a valuation of £400. Upon his death, nine years later, the sheep were not valued with the rest of his property, being entailed. Various witnesses declared them to number then, upwards of 1,200; the shepherds saying that 1,300 and four score (reckoning as usual six score to the 100) had come to the clipping; besides 1,200 lambs that followed the ewes. This great flock which was reckoned as worth £6 a score, or 6s. 0d. apiece, represented then a capital of some £400, which might mean as much as £2,000 of present money.

S

But William, and William's son Daniel, had a hard fight to obtain possession of the Rydal flock, and when they succeeded, it was a much smaller one. Some 600 to 700 sheep from it had been sequestered by the parliament; and Richard Harrison, the steward, Roman Catholic and Royalist though he was, was suspected (in his hatred of the claimants) of conniving at this appropriation and of compounding for them himself quietly.

How many Squire Daniel possessed, when he came to Rydal as the conqueror in a hard-fought fight in 1656, there is nothing to show; but by 1667 he had secured an enormous flock. A memorandum exists of that year which shows the attention given to every detail of the estate. It is written in three hands; first (probably) the shepherd's; next the bailiff's (John Banks) and last the endorsement by the master.

"Sheep shorne at Ridall June ye 21st 1667 old sheep thirty six score and two sheep
Lambs marked nine score & eighteene
of Mr William's tenne sheep clipped, & 4 lambs.

. . . . .

Moore ould sheepe since the cliping two score and six marked And Lambs twelve" A total of 992, besides the 112 skins, as below.

. . . . .

Skins delivered betwixt clipping 1666 & 1667
79 y^t were killed, 33 y^t dyed, in all 112 at 9^d p skin £4. 4^s. 0^d."

The Mr. William referred to is the little heir, whose father endowed him, as he endowed his first-born grandson and godson Wilson later, with lambs at the cost of 11s. 6d.

This enormous flock of over 1,100 could hardly be sustained. Richard writes down in 1694 that all together amount to 1,200; while the numbers clipped during the years of his stewardship varied between 697 and 918.

After Sir Daniel's time, the numbers of sheep kept on the fell, apparently diminished. At his son's death in 1763, they were valued at £170; while nineteen horses were set down as £51. 10s. 0d., forty six beasts (oxen, cows and heifers) as £75, and six fat cattle at £13. 10s 0d.

When in 1741, the heir to the estate, the Rev. Archdeacon Fleming, proposed to let the demesne farm, a flock of 891 was to go with it, consisting of 20 rams, 273 wethers, 416 ewes, and 182 hogs,* which were to be returned at the end of the tenancy

In 1748, Sir William reckoned his flock as 596, 440 of which he had bought from his uncle's widow for £142. 15s. the next year the sheep and lambs amounted to 798.

In 1759, when the sheep were let with the demesne to William Mason, 500 sheep only were accounted for, viz.—40 wethers, 210 ewes, 130 twinters, and 120 hogs; the wethers and ewes being valued at 10s 0d each, the twinters 8s 0d., and the hogs 7s 0d.

The sheep now running on Rydal Fell from the farm let to Mr Fletcher amount to between 800 and 1,000

Clipping.

The shearing of the sheep made one of the great agricultural occasions of the year, and was also a village festival. The lord, indeed, demanded boon service for it of his tenants, and though they were not bound to give more than one day's work, it required sometimes more than their number to cope with the flock in two day's time. Bread, cheese,† and ale were supplied in abundance, and there is evidence to show that Squire Daniel provided also every incentive to industry and competitive joviality among the shearers. The date for clipping varied greatly.

Sep. 21. 1683 Given to Geo. Benson Piper for playing to my Shearers when they got ye Churne this day .. 00£. 00s 06d

June 30. 1684, 6^d is given to "Renny Fidler" for playing "this day to the Clippers"

---

* See end of chapter

† In 1632 Tyson paid 2s 0d "for cheese against clipping" In the extravagant time of Harrison's executorship (1644) both butter and cheese bought at Keswick "against Clipinge" cost 10s 6d.

"Aug 25 1685 Given to Geo. Benson Piper for 2 dayes being with my Shearers, who did shear all this day .. 00£ 01s 00d.

In June 1661 an item stands of 1s. 0d. paid "for a pound of Tobacco to ye clippe{rs}" and one individual on that occasion received a sum of 4d. There are no regular entries, however, for the wages of the shearers, though help came to be needed beyond what was given.

In 1645, " 2 paire of shearers " had been supplied " at Cliping," whose wages with meat came to 2s. 4d. But what paid service was required was afterwards lumped together with hay-making (likewise a boon service) and the leading of corn, making a sum that stood at £2 19s. 9½d. in 1682, and £3. 19s. 11½d in 1685. Richard, indeed, makes no account of the clipping The Rydal sheep-shearing maintained its popularity till the next century. Benjamin Browne, when on June 29, 1709, he went to Ambleside to try to affect a sale of the Ambleside Hall meadow lands, found " the whole Country was gone to Sr Willm Fleming's sheep Clipping." (Mr. G. Browne's MSS).

' Thus were the golden precious fleeces cut from the backs of the sheep for a nominal sum, besides the cost of food produced first-hand on the premises. The piper (not always supplied) and a few hundred rud-balls, at, from 6d. to 8d a hundred, " for smitting of ye Sheep," added a bare couple of shillings to the expense.

Not so the salving, which was a great ceremony yearly performed for the health of the sheep; and the labour for which had to be paid for at a comparatively high rate. Tyson, in 1632, enters " for washinge sheepe " the substantial sum of £5. 12s. 6d. In 1645, Richard Harrison paid through the shepherd £4. 5s. 0d for " greasing ninescore & fifteene days "; which comes to a little over 5d a day, and was " without meat or drinke "; and in 1644, for 252 days £5. He enters in 1646, " eight score and six days for the service " at 5d. the daie, and ye over at all the dales" £3. 11s. 2d. But the service was nothing to the cost of the salve, made up of tar and grease. Harrison's payment for the ingredients stands thus, in 1646.—26 stone of butter, £5. 3s. 0d.; 5 more, £1 7s. 0d.; 8 of tallow, £2. 13s. 4d, and 3½ loads of tar, £4. 10s. 0d.; which reaches a total of £13. 13s 4d

But not lightly did Squire Daniel pay such sums as these. The salt butter in his time was obtained from far and wide, wherever it was cheapest. For instance, in 1682, he obtained it from Greene of " Aisdal," in Grasmere at 3s. 2d. and 3s. 3d a stone, with an additional quantity bought in Kirkby at 3s. 0d His shepherd even succeeded in obtaining it in 0086, at 2s. 5d., when his salve bill stood.—butter, £2. 2s. 11d.; more 12s. 3d.; 41 gallons of tar at 10d, £1 14s 2d.; total, £4. 9s. 4d.—a very different one from Richard's! This, however, was the lowest drop in the butter market. The price varied as a rule from 3s 4d to 4s 4d. a stone; and it is interesting to observe that this price kept steady, as in 1745, only 4s. 0d. a stone was paid for 22 stone 13 lbs. Sometimes, when butter was dear, and a large amount used (from 19 to 24 stone) that item stood as high as £5. 8s. 4d. in the account-book. In 1696, however, at 3s. 4d. and 3s. 5d., it was as low as £1. 3. 6½d.

Squire Daniel was not able to hire salvers under 6d. a day. In 1656, he employed 13 Grasmere men and 5 Rydal ones, at a cost of £2. 16s. 0d. In 1682, £4. 3s. 0d. was paid for 166 days; in 1698, £4. 16s. 6d., at 6d. " without meat." This meant that no provisions were supplied; but in later times, when the second Sir William was beginning in 1748 his rule, 16s. 6d. was paid " In ale, when 466 were salved"; which, at 1d. a quart, from the village inn (it was 3d. a gallon in 1678) must have represented a good deal of drinking. Richard gives minute details as to the greasing. For instance, in 1698, the butter cost at Hawkshead, £3. 14s. 11d.; tar—4 " costrels " at

Ambleside—£2. 13s. 0d.; wages, £4. 16s. 6d.; total, £11 1s. 11d., and he adds that the hogs took 6 gallons of tar, and 5 stone and 3 Featlets (a Featlet = 4 lbs.) of butter; while the old sheep took 25 gallons of tar, 16½ stones of butter, and 3 stones of tallow.

This ceremony was performed at the "back end" while in spring the "hogs" were treated to a special wash with tobacco.

Of the price of sheep we hear incidentally. In 1647, three score of the Rydal lambs were sold for £10. 19s. 0d., about 3s. 8d. each.

Squire Daniel rarely sold his sheep. He bought frequently at his smaller neighbours' sales, where no doubt there were bargains to be got. His purchases on that account may not be a fair test of the market, or of general Westmorland prices. It is interesting to note the gradual rise of these.* The sheep of William Benson, of Kendal, were in 1568, valued at 3s. 2d. each.

In the seventeenth century, as we have seen, they were reckoned as worth 6s 0d. each. Prices perhaps fell during the Commonwealth. The Rydal squire bought Widow Thompson's nineteen sheep in 1671 for £4. 14s. 8d., practically 5s. 0d. each. At Jane Mackereth's sale, however, twenty came to £6. 5s. 8d., over 6s. 3d. each.

In 1671 19 sheep were bought for £5. 1s. 0d. practically 5s. 10d. each.

After 1674, the year of great scarcity (see later) when poor men could not afford to keep their cattle, prices dropped sharply. At William Grigg's sale in 1675, 2 wethers, 3 ewes, and 3 hogs, knocked down to the Squire, actually fetched but an average of 4s. 4d. each, and the same year he got 59 old sheep and 17 hogs at Jane Fleming's sale

---

* A ram, valued in King Athelstan's time at 4d, had risen by 1185 to 8d One shilling of Saxon money was paid in A D. 1000 for a lost sheep; while 40, in Henry I's reign (1100-35) were valued at £1, or 6d each (Smith's Wool)
The "Demies" or Scholars of Magdalen College, Oxford, still receive once a year (on Founders Day?) a threepenny bit. The Statute, dated about 1466, time of Henry VI, saying that each scholar is to receive 3d or half a sheep.—Ed.

for £9—under 2s. 5d. each! Next year prices had somewhat righted themselves. Forty-one "fat wethers" were bought for £16. 11s. 6d., " besides 5s. 2d. given back," practically 5s. 0d. a piece; 50 hogs at 4s. 6d., " besides 1s. given me back"; and 42 lambs from Furness Fell for £6. 6s. 0d., or 3s. 0d. each In 1687, the squire succeeded in getting 6s. 9d. for 26 sheep (£8. 15s. 0d.) sold to the butcher.

We have already seen something of the valuation of the succeeding century. In 1748, ewes were bought at Dame Dorothy's sale by Sir William at 6s. 10d., and twinters at 5s. 9d.; in 1659 wethers and ewes were valued at 10s. 0d., twinters 8s. 0d., and hogs at 7s. 0d.

Squire Daniel frequently sold his rams at fairs. In 1677, he sold one at Ambleside for 15s. 4d. " besides 4d. given back and 4d. given ye Sheepherd," who deserved a tip for the good bargain. As a rule, 8s. 6d. to 11s. 6d. were the prices fetched. In one year, 2 rams cost £1. 4s. 4d. in another 8s. 9d.

The sale of sheep-skins made a considerable sum. The blind skinner of Grasmere at first, on Squire Daniel's coming, agreed to take all for three years at 10^d each, the income varying between £4. 12s. 8d and £5; then he dropped to 9d. At this price the skins of 1667 made £4. 4s. 0d., those of 1669, £9. 12s. 5d., and those of 1673 at 6d., £6. 17s. 6d. By 1684 no more than 5d. a piece could be got. However, two years later a purchaser was found to take 7 score and 11 at 6½d.; but on his complaining of " an ill bargain" the squire gave him back the halfpennies. By 1697 the price rose to 8d.

In 1686 and thereabouts, William Satterthwaite, tanner, of Cott-house, near Hawkshead, was taking the Rydal hides; and as much as £10. 4s. 0d. was paid for them in that one year.

But the wool was of course the prime source of profit alike to statesman and squire. In 1198, the price of wool was reckoned at 2s. 6d. per stone, and 26 stones went to the pack. It was in wool that King Richard's ransom was paid. From Harrison's account-book, begun on the death of Squire John in 1642, we learn many particulars of prices, for as the latter had largely invested in church tithes, the tithe-wool came into the demesne store houses for sale As no balance was ever struck in the old account-books, and part payments were constantly made, it is impossible to gauge profits, or even to compute exactly the year's income from this source. One entry among receipts, stands " for eight & 20 score of wool " £164. 10s. 0d. Many smaller sums occur, which show the price of wool to vary from 6s. 0d. to 8s. 0d. a stone.

Squire Daniel did not deal in tithe-wool. We learn from his account and " rent " books that bargains were made with the wool merchants before ever the demesne sheep were shorn He realized in general from these men 8s. 6d. a stone

We can reckon what the income was from this source in 1668, when 600 stones of wool were taken up at 8s. 6d. by two chap-men—it being usual in a large transaction of the kind, to lessen risks by partnership. The transaction brought some £255 into the Hall coffers. Next year, when three men took up the wool at 8s. 6d., there were only 135 stones, besides 40 stone un-washed which went for 5s 0d ; and 5s. 0d. was given over This would produce about £70. The stone was 8 lbs., making fourteen to the hundredweight.

Prices fell somewhat, however, and Richard enters in his Setting Book for 1695 :—

"*Wooll Sold* S[r] Daniel Fleming Sold all his Wool then Clipped for 8[s] 4[d] p Stone which came to as I remember—In all—185 Packs 13 Stones & a halfe, unto M[r] John Harrison of Kendal, and M[t] Bottomley a Yorkshire man."

The squire recorded in his " rent-book " the splendid total of £610.

Prices must have fallen rapidly in the next century. In 1730, the agent reported to the next heir that he could get no chapman to offer above 3s. 0d. a stone for the Rydal wool, so he had decided to hold it back. Again, in 1752, the report went that there being little demand for wool " of our Sort," the Rydal fleeces will fetch no more than 4s. 0d. or 4s. 6d , even when " laid at Halifax." The agent, therefore, would dispose of the two (sample) packs he had, and return the sheets.

In 1757, the demesne wool realized £33. 6s. 0d., and next year £39.

While it is impossible to compute the total income derived from husbandry in any one year on the Rydal demesne, it is clear that, where the expenses were kept so low, the profits must have been considerable. It may be interesting to print entire, from Richard's "Setting Book," his accounts of the year 1693, when the cost of labour and appliances came to only £15. 12s. 5½d. It is true that the amount rises, to £16. 3s. 3½d. in 1694 ; to £25. 13s. 8½d. in 1695 ; to £17. 17s. 4d. in 1696, and even to £58 16s. 5d. in 1698. But then the young steward was adding each year expenses that were extraneous, as in the last year, when a large purchase of malt (bought at various places—Staveley and Troutbeck being carefully labelled with " their measure " as if it were different from Ambleside and Ulverston) should reduce the total by £15. 10s. 4d. Again, he enters the supply of salted fish (called Killings and evidently a large fish) for the winter, heading a line " *When to bye Killings*, Dec. 24. John Nobb brought 15 Killings—a Horse load—for 1s. 6d., which cost at Ulverstone 10s. 8d " The geese were more relevant, as they probably ate a little Rydal grass before being killed " Oct. 18. *Geese bought*. Bought by Adam Fleming (of Coniston) 19 Geese at 8^d a piece 12^s 8^d." Not so the following " Jan. 4. *Peace for Pottage*. Bought by Adam Fleming 1 Bushel of Gray Pease for 13^s. and

Carriage 1ˢ. in all 00£ 14ˢ. 0ᵈ." Peas, however, were sometimes sown. Again, "March 15. *Herrings for Lent.* Pd. for 400 Herrings at 2ˢ. 6ᵈ. p 100 (which is 3 a penny, with half a score thrown in) and Carriage from Whitehaven, 00£ 11ˢ. 6ᵈ.

Two hundred loads of "Christmas Firing" was got in, in 1694. Richard tells, indeed, all the outdoor proceedings on the farm, how many "bracken Trushes" were got in, or " Crabs got for Vergis " (= Verjuice), 20 bushels, as well as the dates for the start of threshing, ploughing, killing of fat beef, &c.

From the " Setting Book " of Rydal.
RICHARD FLEMING STEWARD ANNO DOMINI 1693.

Ground Laid.

The Stone Waite.

Ground broke up.

Were the Higher halfe of the Crossdale at the Low Parke hᵈ (head ?) and all the Lea upon the Crabtree Side in the Lands "

Ap. 20	Oats Sown	.. ..	32 bushels
M. 15	Bigg Sown	.. ..	06 bushels

	£	s.	d.
the 12 pᵈ for Mending the Fell-Walls at 4ᵈ a day	0.	16.	0.
the 10 pᵈ for Stoneing and dressing the ground for 3ᵈ a day	0.	6.	9.
16. pᵈ for driving the Plow for 1ᵈ a day for 36 days	0.	3.	0.
28. Pᵈ for helping to gett Peats	0.	1.	1.
June 5 Pd. for 3 hundred Rudballs for the Clipping	0.	2.	0.

17 Sir Daniel's Sheep Clipped

Gild Sheep	..	439
Ews	.. ..	224
Lambs	.. ..	144
		807

	£	s.	d.
Au. 8. Pd. to the Gras. Mowers	1.	2.	0.
12 Pd. to the Hayworkers for the Working of as follows	4.	1.	10.

July 3. Orchard 28 trs. (trusses) Round Close 58 trs. Long Close 30 trs Lands Meadow 38 trs. Old Orchard M.

26 trs. Birket Moss M. 20 trs. Birket Field M. 53 trs. Low Parke M. 26 trs. Birket Field L. (ley?) 63 trs. Birket Moss L 10 trs. Tip Close L. 31 trs. Hagg 66 trs. Lands L. 25 trs. Brackenbedd 14 trs. Stone Waste 34 trs.

			£	s.	d.
In all	746 trusses				
Sep. 8. P^d for Shearing and getting in the Corn	.. ..		0.	6.	6.

Bigg in Stooks.

Aug. 15. Lands 91. Low Parke 294. Birket Field 167. In all 552 Stooks.

Oats in Stooks.

Stirdy Parke 48 ½, Lands 167 ½, Low Parke 160 Old Orchard 283. Crabtree waite 84 Stirdy Parke 127. Drye Lands 126 In all 996 Stooks.

	£	s.	d.
June 5. My Bro:(ther) bought 4 pair of New truss Rops for	0.	10.	6.
Oct. 23. P^d for 19 Stones and 4 pound of Salt Butter for Salveing the sheep ..	3.	11	7½

For Hogs.

28 The Sheepherd tooke 3 Stones and a halfe of Salt butter for 9 gallons of Tarr.

For Old Sheep.

31. He tooke to 27 gallons of Tarr, 13 Stones and a halfe of Salt butter and 6 Stones and 3 Featlets of Tallow

For Getting of Lime-Stones.

No. 16. P^d unto Ed^wd Forrest of Ambleside for Quarry-roome to gett two hundred loads Such as a Horse can carry in Crooks, 20 or 30 yards from the Quarry, and Six Score to the hundred, or Sixteen Score of Such loads as can be carried streight away for*

	£	s.	d
	0.	4.	0.
Item for getting of them	1.	4.	0.
Item for Breaking of y^m without meat	0.	15.	0
In all	2.	3.	0.

---

* The loads to be taken "streight away" to the field are less than two-thirds of what can be just brought out from the quarry to the road.

Ground Limed.

Feb 14. The higher halfe of the Cross-dale at Low Parke head, and the date in the Lands betwixt the Crab-tree and the Sike Sprinkled a little.

Salt for Twelve Bags.

Sep. 23 They have twelve Bushels Lancaster measure at 3ˢ 6ᵈ pr Bushel, which comes to in all   2£. 1s. 0d.

Thressing of Corn.

	£.	s.	d.
Pᵈ for Thressing, till the 2ⁿᵈ of February 53 days at 2ᵈ a day	0.	8.	10.
Item for 70 days at 2½ᵈ a day	0.	14.	7.
	1.	3.	5.

Oats Winnowed.

In all One Hundred Eighty One Bˡˢ and a halfe.

Bigg Winnowed.

In all Seventy Seven Bushels and a halfe.

	£.	s.	d.
Disburstments of all In all	15.	12.	5¼.

If to Richard's "In all" is added the wages of the shepherd, £3; the under shepherd, £1. 10s. 0d.; the ploughman, £3; and a couple or so of outdoor men, which is at the highest rate paid (see Wages), the total working expenses of the farm will reach but £23. 2s. 5½d., hardly more than William Satterthwaite paid for the skins.

And when the assets are considered, from pasture, from cattle selling, from corn and hay, and above all from wool, it is clear that the profits of the farm must have been very large.

AGE-NAMES OF BEASTS.

Mr. G. Browne gives the following information about sheep-names :—

The *lamb* after salving or dipping at Michaelmas, becomes a *hog*. It has two narrow centre teeth called lamb teeth, until next year, when they are cast for two broader ones. It then (and formally from its first clipping) becomes a twinter. Next year, having cast two more, it becomes, at dipping, a Thrinter (Westmorland) or Thruntor (Cumberland). These names, now in common use among the shepherds, were clearly once applied, as the Agist Book shows, to cattle as well. There, too, we find the *duntor;* a beast probably in its fourth year. These words remind one in their alliterative sound of the Celtic numerals in use till recently in secluded parts of our country for the counting of sheep, but of which I can find no memory among Rydal shepherds.

There were other varieties of names for beasts according to sex and age. The " key " (with a plural kyne) stepped up from calf to " why " and heiffer, and we find these specified as 2-year or 3-year heiffers.

The " runt " and the " stot " were young oxen, while the steer was a gelded male from 2 to 4 years old (Webster).

The word " stag," seems to have been used hereabouts, for a young stallion.* See "Agriculture in Cumberland," *Transactions*, vol. viii. In Lincolnshire it is used for a cock barn-door fowl or Turkey.

CHAPTER V
THE FISHERIES

Eel and Trout in Rydal Mere, Rothay, Brathay, Elterwater, and Loughrigg Tarn ; Char in Windermere and Coniston Water ; " Case " in the Brathay and Elterwater ; Char-pie, Colossal size in 1673 ; Potted Char, last mention, 1797.

IN ancient times the rocky rivers and meres of our district abounded in fish ; and that the abundance continued down to recent times is shown by the fact

---

* In the account of the Kendal Horse Fair, Nov 3rd, 1915, in the *Westmorland Gazette*, of Nov 6th, we find that "stags and foals were plentiful," and "heavy stags" and "light stags" are spoken of The meaning of the word here being unbroken animals of either sex When broken they all are termed colts, a name which elsewhere signifies a young male.—ED.

that the great bird that follows the fish—the heron—had a nesting colony on the island in Rydal-water up to 1870. Diving birds there were, too, that pursue the fish under water, of several species; and there is reason to suppose as Mr. Macpherson shows, that the mysterious *Gravye*, which Sir Daniel Fleming described as resorting to Windermere, and building in hollow trees, may have been the goosander.

But there was enough fish in the pure streams, fed by the great flows or mosses that lay in the hollows of the hills, as well as in the deep, tranquil tarns and meres, for both bird and man. The fisheries seem to have been actively pursued from the earliest times, and we find, from ancient records, that they had a marketable value, like the land, and that the yield of the waters was reckoned in the rentals along with the yield of the land.

No doubt the Celt pursued his fishing industry here on the lakes of Cumbria, as he did in Cambria, by means of his basket-work corracle. But we have no records of the craft, earlier than the times when the Barons of Kendal ruled under the Norman kings, and were lords of all those waters that poured into Morecambe Bay by the Lune, the Kent, the Winster, and the Leven. And, indeed, it is by inference from later records that we gain knowledge of the descent by inheritance of the ownership of the fisheries.

For instance, we know from subsequent record, when the great estates that made up the Barony of Kendal were divided between the sisters and heiresses, Helwise and Alice de Lancaster, that the rivers and meres were divided between them scrupulously and in various quarters like the land. To Helwise went the waters of the Kent, which passed to her eldest daughter Margaret, and remained in that line, till it came to the Crown (as the Marquis Fee) in Queen Elizabeth's reign. Helwise had possibly some part of Windermere, and certainly a share in the rivers Rothay and Brathay, which share apparently comprised the head-waters of both. For we find these fisheries later in the hands of descendants of hers, by her younger daughter Lucy, who married Marmaduke de Thweng. The de Thweng line again broke its inheritance amongst heiresses in the reign of Edward III. (Nicolson and Burn), and part went to an elder sister Lucy, who married Ralph de Lumley, and part to Margaret, who married John de Hotham. The fisheries that went originally to Helwise and then to her daughter Lucy must have been once more divided between the two. For we find, in a rental of 1375 (now at Levens) of that portion of the barony that belonged to " John de Hothome and Walter Pedwardyn, knight, that they owned the fishery of the waters of " Gresmer." And Alan Bellingham, who succeeded to the Lumley portion, and who likewise secured the Hotham portion (uniting the two again) was found on his death in 1578, to have been possessed of a fishery in Windermere, one in " Skelefwater" (Elterwater ?) and one in " Gresmyre."

But it is with Alice de Lancaster's share of the fisheries of the barony that we are chiefly concerned, for she took, besides the main portion of Windermere and the lower portion of the Brathay, the immediate waters of our parish of Rydal; and these were kept in her line long after the grant, by her sister Helwise's daughter, Margaret, of the isolated manor of Rydal to Roger de Lancaster. In the Inquisition held in 1283, on the death of Alice's grandson, William de Lindesey, which is in the Record Office, it was found that he held a fishery at " Gresmer " that was worth 6d yearly, and a fishery called " Routhemer " (Rydal-water) worth 18d. yearly. To obtain the present equivalent, the sums should be multiplied by forty. Again, in an old deed that gives the boundaries of Alice's inheritance as they were " ffrome the tyme of Sir Walter of lyndesey and Sir Wyllm hys son and hys heyre, and the tyme of dame Cristiane, the doughter of the same Sir Wyllm" many quaint particulars are told of the fishery of Windermere which, however, are not easy to make out. The deed goes on to enumerate, as part of the property "And also holffe loghryge wth the holl Watter to the ou' brygge at Skelgwth."

In a rental of this inheritance, at Levens Hall, of uncertain date, because the heading is mutilated and destroyed by damp, we get full particulars of the fisheries, and to whom they were let. It states that "William Lancaster, knight, holds a fishery in Rothm' (Rydal-water) and renders yearly 3s. 4d." and that "Thos. Harreson Mackerth and Jacke Johnson," who were estatesmen of Loughrigg, "hold the fishery of Rathaw (Rothay), 6d." This MS. is believed to be of the time of Henry VI. or Edward IV. If so, the Sir William Lancaster, who rented the fishery of Rydal-water for 3s. 4d. could not have been the owner of the manor of Rydal, as the last William of that line (of Howgill), died in the eighth year of Henry IV. There was, however, a Sir William in the Sockbridge line, descended from a younger son of Sir Roger, who acted publicly in the fourteenth year of Henry VI. He owned Barton, the adjacent manor to Rydal.

We have, however, certain dates, though fewer particulars, in other Rentals of Alice's inheritance in the Record Office. In one of 1453, when Henry VI. gave over Alice's share (which had come to him from the Duke of Bedford) to the Earl of Richmond, the fisheries are mentioned, though not to whom leased at that time. We are told of "Gresmere" that there is a "defect of farm of the fishery in the several waters there above charged at 2s., because it lies in the King's hand for a lack of a tenant for one year of the period 2s." Of "Loghrigge" (Loughrigg) it is stated that the "farm of fishery in Rawthmere (Rydal-water) comes to 2s. 2¼d., and the "farm of the fishing in Rawthey (Rothay) to 4d.";

mentioning again a " decay of fishery," or some loss of revenue upon it, which brought it below former receipts.

It was but twenty-two years after this time, in 1475, that John Fleming and John Whitfield, having both married daughters of the last de Lancaster of the Howgill line and taken equal shares, through their wives, in the Manor of Rydal and Loughrigg, made the agreement that is yet preserved at Rydal Hall. And in this John Whitfield, while letting his share of the manor to John Fleming, reserves his right " to make a brewere in the sayde lordschip and to hafe a chamer and freedom to hawke, hunt, fisch, and fowle within the lordeschip." Unless the ownership of the fisheries of Rydal-water and the Rothay had been made over by the lord of the Richmond Fee to the lord of the manor of Rydal in those twenty-two years, this freedom to fish that John Whitfield kept for himself could only have extended to the waters of Rydal Beck (see Sizergh MS).

No particulars have, so far, come to light to show when the transfer of ownership was made. Two hundred years later, when the fisheries of our parish come again into evidence, they were not only in possession of the Flemings, lords of Rydal, but those lords claimed also the whole waters of the Brathay, including Elterwater, and also Loughrigg Tarn. And all memory had passed of the time when they had not been theirs, for Sir Daniel expressly says, in his description of Westmorland, that they had belonged to the lords of Rydal " time out of mind "

That the fisheries were worked by his immediate ancestors is proved by papers recently found. His wise old great grandmother, Mrs Agnes Fleming, writing to her son John shortly before her death in 1631, recommending his speedy return to Rydal to look after his " husbandrie " and other matters, says, " for the fishinge of brathey unlesse you get a warrant for the mentenance of it with

T

wood you nor I can make either proffit by kepeing or lettinge of it." As neither the land nor the lordship of the Loughrigg shore of Brathay was in the hands of the Flemings, but only the waters, the "warrant" here needed was probably one from the owner of the land to fish from it, and to erect some kind of wood-work in the nature of a fish-garth in the running stream. And possibly the entry we find in Sir David Fleming's account-book under October 11, 1658 : " Paid unto Robert Shackley, junior (by J B) for yè halfe yeares Rent for ye fishing of Braythay due at Michaelmas last. 00.02.08." represents that warrant to fish from Robert Shackley's land. We shall see later how frequently the Rydal squire let his fisheries on the far Loughrigg side to estatesmen who owned adjacent land, thus obviating the need to pay for their permission. And Squire John, son of Mrs Agnes, had obviously attended to his fisheries, as the following entries in the account-book of his bailiff, William Tyson, show :—

	£	s	d.
1631, Sep 21st, paid Edw. Pegg for 2 newe netts and mending an old one and yarne .	01	6	6
Nov. paid for roups for newe nett	00	2	2
1632, Aug , paid for an Eile net for Brathey .	00	12	0

Later, in the mass of papers left behind by Sir Daniel, there is continual reference, in memoranda, in bills of craftsmen, and in correspondence, to the fishing that went on. We learn that there were fish-garths in the Rothay and Brathay valleys that were regularly in use ; there was a boat for fishing on Rydal-water ; floating boxes on both rivers for keeping fish in, called coups or arks ; and some kind of fish-enclosure called floaks in Rydal beck.

The memory of the fishgarth and of its construction is lost. It was the work of the carpenter, and we may suppose it to have been some kind of fence made of hedging stakes, that enclosed the side of the river at a wide part The bills of Richard Nicholson, the Rydal carpenter, show entries of his work upon the garths almost every year.

	£ s. d
1657, One daye mending the Fishgarth at Brathey	00 00 06
And another daye at the Fishgarth and making the Rouller in the garden	00 00 06
1658, Att the Fishgarth at Brathey 3 dayes ..	00 01 00

Twice over we find entries of the work of Richard and one of his sons at Floakes in the Rydal Head, where a deep pool below a fall still goes by the name of Buckstones Jumb or Jum. This is conjectured by the present beck-watcher to have been a rough boxing-in of the stream at a suitable place, with a shutter or door that could be let down, to keep in the fish that had entered.

	£ s d.
1656, For himselfe and sonne either two dayes ffor makeinge Floakes at Buckstone without meate at 5d a day	00 01 08
1657, One daye and a halfe when we made the floake betwixt the Buckstone and Dale Head Green	00 00 06

The coup or ark was no doubt an open-work or perforated box in which fish were kept in readiness for the table at any time. They are yet used at Baden-Baden and no doubt many other places, where the curious traveller may see the fish he has ordered for dinner drawn out of the box that is anchored in the running stream. Char were kept for the tourist in Coniston-water by this method as lately as 1835, as related by Thompson (Macpherson's Fauna of Lakeland). The coup, when placed in a lake, would doubtless be fixed near the entrance of a rivulet, which ensures a flow of water through it. In 1663, Richard Nicholson gets " for mending the manor coup " and another piece of work 8d. The modest items of his bills cause us, when we come to the following entry in Sir Daniel's own account-book, a start of surprise.

1680, June 28th. Sent for ale to the workmen who
  made and this day set a new ark in Rydal-water   00 02 06

Unfortunately we have not the bill for this coup.

The Rydal blacksmith, George Ottley, charges in a bill of 1665, " for a claspe to the boatte " 0s. 4d.

Sir Daniel Fleming, in his description of Westmorland, speaks of there being " store of fish as pikes, perch, trouts, and eels," in Rydal-water. These fish were taken by net in the summer-time, and we must conclude that the multitude of them made the drawing of the net something of a sight. For on April 12, 1682, Sir Daniel took his visitors down from the Hall to the lake, to see the draught of fishes; which caused him to tip the " fishers " 1s. and enter the amount in his account-book.

This was early in the season, and the haul must chiefly have been trout. It is not till late summer that the eels are worth taking. Then these curious and still (to zoologists) mysterious fish, which in spring-time have sped up the rivers from the sea as short and wire-like creatures, have waxed gross, and lie on the lake-bottom in numbers, and of so large a size as to be " thick as a man's arm," waiting the time when they shall speed back again to the sea. Eel-fishing by net has long gone out of use, but it was the practice, till quite recently, for the men of the estate to take a boat out in early morning-time, and to spear the fish that lay at the bottom from above; which must have been an adroit sport.

The waters of Rydal Beck, of the river and the lake would more than supply the needs of the Hall in trout and eel and odd fish; while from Coniston lake, owned by the same lord, an abundant supply of the much-prized char could be procured. The outlying fisheries were let, therefore, as they had been in early times. We have seen Mrs. Agnes Fleming's anxiety as to the fishery of the Brathay, which was an important one, as it included the char. And when her great-grandson, Squire Daniel, settled on the patrimony he had fought for and wrested from Commonwealth and relatives, he set about letting the fisheries, which had probably run to waste. His account-book shows some entries on the subject, while a careful study of his rent-book and its microscopic writing furnishes a good many more particulars of these lets and leases, which did not always run smoothly. Payments were frequently behindhand; and the lessee was sometimes forced to join with a neighbour in a bill that secured to the lord the rent stipulated.

The account-book shows that in 1663 the eel and char fisheries of the Brathay were let together for the considerable sum of £1. 4s. 0d., in 1666 the fisheries of Elterwater and Loughrigg Tarn were let at 12s 0d. a year, in 1669 James Benson who held the char fishery of the Brathay, paid two years rent for Elterwater; but in 1674 the rent was overdue by three years, and remained so for seven years In 1675 it was divided, and Edward Fisher took Loughrigg Tarn for three years, paying 3s. 4d., and delivering " 20 of ye August eels yearly." In 1681 both tarn and lake were let to Bernard Benson of the Fold, on a lease of seven years, for 16s a year This substantial freeholder was, however, a bad payer likewise, and only continual bills, to which his neighbours put their hands, extorted arrears from him in 1691. In 1690 therefore Sir Daniel let the same fishing to Thomas Roberts (doubtless of Ellers) who the year before had taken the tarn alone at 3s 4d., reducing the rent to 12s 0d. again, with the addition of a " good dish of fish every year " for Rydal Hall.

The " Braythey-Ele Fishing," now separated from the char, was let in 1666 at 20s. 0d a year, which was regularly paid till 1674 In 1676, Sir Daniel let this " Eale fishery " to Regnald Holme, of Skilwith Bridge, and as the draft of the agreement is preserved, we have more particulars of it The lease was fixed at the optimistic terms of 1,000 years Regnald, or Reginald Holme, on the part of himself and his heirs, undertook to fish the Brathay from the foot of Elterwater to the head of Windermere, for all fish but case (char) and to make " no other fish-garths for eles than the present ones," and to furnish 20s. and " such eels and other fish " as Sir Daniel and his heirs might require " before any other are served " at reasonable prices. If the rent should not be paid six days after due, it was arranged that the goods of Regnald Holme could be seized and sold.

Regnald Holme stuck to his bargain apparently as long as he could. But trouble was brewing for him, as we learn from other MS records. For in the very year of this lease one Reginald Holme, a Quaker, of Loughrigg (and that there were not two of the name we know from the registers) is the subject of two resolutions passed by the body of Friends, one at their monthly meeting at Swathmoor, and the other at their quarterly meeting at Lancaster; which ordain that as he has long resisted their counsels to settle peaceably the dispute between himself and another of their body, that other may now have recourse to the law for the recovery of his rights. But Reginald Holme was a man who resisted law, as well as counsel. In 1684 Sir Daniel, as a magistrate, issued a warrant for the appearance at the Kendal court of Reginald Holme, his sons John, Jacob, and George, and daughter Dorothy, who did altogether, when the officers of the law appeared for " the sequestration of Reginald's estate, not only hinder them but did also riotously fall upon them, beat, and abuse them, and did also threaten them and speak very contemptuously concerning their authority."

The end of the matter is not recorded; but in 1695, John Holm (doubtless Regnald's heir) was paying the stipulated 20s od. for the Brathay eel fishery.

The next evidence we have of the eel and trout fisheries

THE FISHERIES

of the Brathay valley occurs in the lifetime of Sir William Fleming, son of Daniel. He drew up an agreement, July 10, 1729, with one Hammond Metley, by which Hammond took over the fishing of Elterwater, of " Loferridge Tarn," and of the river from Elterwater to Windermere, for all fish but case. For this he was to pay £3 yearly, unless he could prove it to be unremunerative at the price, when an abatement of £1 was to be allowed. He also had leave to get " Rushces " (which no doubt had a certain marketable value) ; while on Sir William's side, angling either for himself or " his order " was to be allowed. In 1758 the Rydal fishery was leased to a Mr. Braithwaite at £1 1s 0d. yearly.

Particulars of the nets for eel fishing are often given in the old account-books. Squire John, as we have seen, paid 12s. 0d. in August, 1632, for an eel net for Brathay. Richard Nicholson, the Rydal carpenter, charges for " A frame for ye ele net " with other items, 8d. In 1674, Sir Daniel secured a very cheap net from the fishermen of Windermere to whom he had sold his Brathay fishery.

" Allowed unto Christ. Roberts and his son for 4 doz of case 3s 4d , paid him in full for an eel net 1s. 6d , and given back 2d. in all 00£ 05s 00d "

It was perhaps this one-and-eightpenny net that Sir William was thinking of when he made his bargain for a " New Eele Net " in 1704. He had to pay, however, 2s. 0d. for the yarn and 4s 0d for the making In 1708 yarn had risen by 2d., so 6s. 2d was the total cost of the fresh net. In 1714, however, the net-maker made the net one yard shorter than the old model, whereupon Sir William paid him only 3s. 6d., instead of 4s. 0d.

In 1784, eel nets had gone up to almost their ancient price, for to one Anthony Garnett was paid for " an eal and trout net 10s. 6d."

The following three " notes " in Sir William's handwriting, were found carefully pinned together, with a round-headed pin of the time.

I.

New Eele Net 1704

Note. Wednesday July 12. Lanty Lancaster came to make me a new Eeelnet, and he proposed to take 3d. a day, and meat—6d. a day without meat or 4s. for all; which I agreed to

Note I had 3 hanks of yarne by Will Benson from Ulverstone for Which I pd him, July 14. 0 3 0

of which only 2 hanks was used for the nett.

And I pd. Lanty Lancaster July 19. 1704 4s. for making the net which was just 5 yds. long all.

Soe the net cost me

2 hanks yarne	0 2 0
making	0 4 0

Note he made it in 6 days and was 6 thread all, and 3 of the last Rows double on 12 threads.

II.

Agreed with Henry Jackson July 17, 1708 to make me a new Eel-net of the like Lake Length, widenesse, and thicknesse with that I had July, 1704, and for the like price

Given him 2 hanks of yarne had of Baxter of (*) to the Hank which cost 13d a hank.

and two clues of the yarne that spared of the last Eel net.

Note. he brought me the new Eel net July 27 1708, and I pd. him 0 4 0

to Banks for 2 hanks of yarne 10 (*) in a hank 0 2 2

                                                  0 6 2

Note he brought a mint (?) yarne back of the quantity of the 2 Clues given him for 2 hanks sufficed.

III.

Agreed with Henry Jackson June 27, 1714 to make me another Ele Nett of the Like Length with that of July 12 1704, and that of July 17. 1708.

Note he had 2 hanks of yarne given him what weighed (not filled in)

Note he brought it July 22. 1714 said it was all Long but 4 yds. had 50 meshes at small end and 66 at the wide end.

the old one had 50 or 52 meshes at small end and 67 at wide end

---

* Word not made out

Soe the new one had all the faults of old and one yard shorter. Pd. him July 25 1714 owing of being a yd shorter   6 6 for which he said it was better but my servant said the Contrary. soe if found to short upon his mending it he was to have 6^d more.

Certainly the fish of most repute in olden times was the char, the golden Alpine trout, as it has been called (*Salmo Alpinus*, Linn.) of our mountain lakes. Peculiar as this species is to deep, rocky meres, it very early excited attention, and the "case charr," the "red charr" and the "gilt charr"—all only seasonal phases of colour in the same fish—were spoken of as distinct varieties. Sir Daniel Fleming even explained the supposed difference between the identical case and char. He says, "Up the river Routha go yearly great plenty of large trouts, and up Brathey many *Case* (a fish very like a charr, but of different species, it spawning at another time of the year), and tho' these waters runs a good way in one channel before they fall into Winander-meer-water, and are both very clear and bottomed alike, yet the owners of Rydal Hall (to whom the fishing of both these rivers doth belong, and have a fish-ark or coop in either river), scarce ever get any trouts in Brathey, or *Case* in Routhameer." He invariably spoke of the fish caught in the Brathay as case, and that taken in Coniston-water or Windermere as charr.*

The char-fish still preserves the habit he described, in spite of lake pollution and of great alterations in the bed of the river. As winter approaches, and the swarms leave the deep hollows of the lake-bottom, where they have passed the hot weather, to seek the shallows for a

---

* The Char or Charr (*Salmo Alpinus*, Linn) is believed to be extinct in Ullswater, but is found in Windermere, Coniston, Hawes Water, Crummock, Buttermere, Ennerdale and Wastwater. Mr Macpherson quoting "Jenyns, cited by Day" identifies the case and the charr which D F separates (LXXIII, p 152) "This fish," he says, " in its ordinary state is a *case charr* of Pennant; when exhibiting the bright crimson belly which it assumes before spawning, it is called the *red charr*; when out of season, the spawn having been shed, it is distinguished by the name of gilt charr."

spawning bed, great numbers run up the wide and rocky Brathay. The spawning ground is about a mile up the river from Birdhouse Mouth—which is the name of the short course of the joint streams of Brathay and Rothay. Here a projection of Loughrigg plants a rocky foot athwart the path of the river, forming a natural weir, above which the water moves sluggishly through flat and oft-flooded meadows, and is known as the pool. This natural weir presented (before alteration) a series of short cascades, which made this reach between the Pool and Brathay Bridge one of the most beautiful bits of river scenery imaginable. It had its flat stretches too. Between the highest broken water and the once fine cascade by Brathay Church there was a level stretch, where the river spread over sandy shallows and meandered by side-channels; where tangles of water growths, of bushes and of flowers —specially of the golden globe flower—pressed in upon it and seemed to impede its course. It may be these sandy shallows, peculiar to the river—for there are not any such in the course of the Rothay—that form the attraction to the fish; hereabouts, at any rate, it is that they have been in the habit from time immemorial of spawning; and still do spawn, though the rocks of the cascades have been blasted away, and a narrow canal cut for the river through the gravelly flat, in order to prevent the valley flooding at the Pool. The beck watcher considers that these changes have greatly incommoded the char, but have not caused them wholly to forsake their old haunt.

The land adjacent to this strip of river is still known as Fish-garths, though all memory of systematic fishing has gone; and only the poaching that went on here till quite recently—and even by daylight on Sunday mornings when decent folk were in the church hard by—is remembered.

Here it must have been that the lords of Rydal, from

the time they possessed rights over the river, had their fishery for case, which, as they had abundance of char in their lake of Coniston for their own household use, they generally let. Sir Daniel's Rent-book gives us many particulars of these lets and leases, details of which may be filled up from his account-book, which begins earlier.

In this we find, as early as 1658, an entry he made

"July 14th.—Received of Edwin Greene part of ye case fishing ye last year   00lb 12s. 06"

Now Edwin Greene was an estatesman of Rydal, who collected the lords rents of the manor in the years between 1642 and 1645, as is shown by an account book which exists for those years in the handwriting of Richard Harrison, executor of Squire John and steward for the ill-fated young Squire William. It is possible, therefore, that he did not lease the fishing, but only collected the rent from the lessee.

The next entry shows that two men undertook the responsibility of the fishery, one of whom, Reginald Brathwaite, was an estatesman of Clappersgate, who had no doubt land adjacent to the fishery.

"1663, July 14th—Received of Reginald Brathwait and Geo. Jackson for two yeares rent of ye ele and case fishing of Brathy   02lb 08s. 00d"

In November 18th of the same year we have a confusing entry

"Received of Geo. Braithwait (besides 4d in earnest and 2s. allowed for two dozen of case) for Brathay Fishing now due   00. 10. 02"

In 1666 both books show that Squire Daniel received 14s. 0d. for one year for the case-fishing and from one James Benson. Next year Thomas Roberts had it at the same price; while in 1668 it reverted to James Benson who paid 15s. 0d. When entering this sum into his rent book, March 22nd, he adds, "This fishing is let unto James Benson for 5 yeares longer upon ye same terms as above, and when I have a mind to have ye Holme Dubb drawn, then he's to do it for one halfe of ye fish." * The next account-book entry shows, however, 14s. 0d. received, but also that some bargain had been made as to the supply of so many case (valued at 1s. 0d. a dozen) free to the Hall.

"March 23rd—Received of James Benson for ye fishing of Elterwater, due Aug. 1, 69, 12s., and for ye Case Fishing due Nov. 30th, 69, 14s and for 6 case wanting ye last year 6d,
in all 01lb. 06s. 06d"

In 1670 and 1671, 16s. 0d. was paid, but the additional shillings may have balanced the gift-fish which the squire had not had, or "case wanting," for in 1673, £1. 8s. 0d. is the sum of two years rent.

This fishery had a growing value, perhaps because of the increased appetite for char pie, and the increased export of that dainty to London. For at the end of this lease Squire Daniel was able to secure a rise, and he let it for seven years to two men of Windermere, for 17s. 0d. a year, with the stipulation that fish should be supplied to him, if wanted, at 10d a dozen. We find that he made use of this, for in 1674 he had four dozen of fish, in 1675 three dozen and a half, in 1676 eight dozen, and 1677 as many as ten dozen. In this year there was also a deduction from the rent "for a net and mending, of another 6s." In 1678 he had four dozen of fish, which lessened the rent by 3s. 4d.

In 1679, a better bargain still was made. Two men of Applethwaite took the Brathay Fishing, on a lease of nine years at 18s. 0d. a year, " and to deliver so many dozen of ye best case quick as I shall at any time demand ye same, allowing 8d. ye dozen in ye rent." In this way Squire Daniel secured, in 1687, five dozen fish for 3s. 4d.

---

* A pool in the now diverted course of the Rothay, near Miller Bridge, is remembered by the beck-watcher to have been called Brig Holm Dub That, being nearer to Clappersgate than to Rydal, may have been the one which the squire arranged to have fished by the Brathay fishermen.

And the demand still grew. Five years before this contract expired, the squire arranged the next run for twenty-one years at the same rate, with the same Reginald Holm (coupled with another man) who held the 1,000 year lease of the eel fishing of Brathay.

If we follow the fortunes of the Brathay char-fishing further, we find, after a long gap in the evidence, that Sir William Fleming let it in 1755 to Gawen Braithwaite at £1. 1s. 0d. a year, for a period of eleven years, with a stipulated gift of two dozen fish, and a right for himself and his " company " to fish without a net.

For angling had come into fashion, as the first Sir William's stipulation in 1729 to angle in Loughrigg Tarn and Elterwater shows. And that his successor practised the gentle art we know, for in 1752 his London agent writes to him that he has " found it Difficult to get a few hairs from the King's Horses." He sends therefore, only the two dozen of these desirable articles that he has been able to procure (price 2s. 0d.) along with a fishing line, which he hopes will prove of the right sort, as " it's reckon'd to be the best hear for the fly "

The last we hear of the Brathay fishing is in 1772, when it seems to have been netted for the benefit of the young squire only, and a record left of the " Chare Fish taken in the River Bratha." A lamentable taste had arisen for the fish in their red-coated state, that is, before they spawn, and when they are said to be actually the poorest in flavour; and we find that this draught of 1772 was taken at a time when they must have just run up the river to seek their spawning ground. On October 13, twenty-one dozen were netted, all of which—except four and a half dozen reserved for Sir Michael's use—were despatched as presents for friends, whose names are recorded. On the 19th, twenty-nine dozen more were netted, twenty dozen of which went to Rydal Hall, doubtless for pie making and potting.

Perhaps it was this suicidal policy as regards the fish that brought the prices up so high. In 1781, six dozen of char were bought for the Hall at £2 8s. 0d., being 8s. 0d. a dozen! A different price this from Sir Daniel's 8d a dozen, which was not even the minimum price, for we read in his account-book for 1671, November 16, "12 case 6d" Eightpence a dozen was never, however, the true market value of the fish. We find that in 1661, when Sir Daniel bought outside his domain from the Windermere fisheries; that he had to pay 2s. 6d. a dozen. In 1673, when procuring fish for two pots on behalf of Sir George Fletcher, he paid 14s. 0d. for seven dozen. This seems to have been the current price for some time. When Sir William Fleming let his Coniston fishing in 1703 for £3 a year (through his uncle Roger), it was with the understanding that he could have as many fish as he wanted at 2s. 0d the dozen, which was probably somewhat below the market value

But the value of the char was well established and increasing, as is shown by a curious transaction that Sir William entered into in 1726. The owner of Ambleside Hall had possessed an old right to have two boats on Windermere, as well as to exact a tax from the fishers of the lake of twenty chars yearly, or 5s. 0d in their place. As the Ambleside Hall property was being sold piece-meal, Sir William bought from the owner (along with a pew in Ambleside Chapel that carried with it a charge for the curate's salary) the right of one boat on the lake and the char for £6. 4s. 0d. Mr. Dummer, who sold it, wrote to him from London at the conclusion of the bargain, " I heartily wish you joy with it, for I hear the charrs are worth all the money and more." And though Sir William could proudly reply, that the char were of no moment to him, as he had plenty in Coniston to be had for less, there was no doubt some truth in the remark.

From the char-fish to the char-pie is but a step, and one

almost as inevitable to the minute historian of the twentieth century as it was to the housekeeper of the seventeenth. A dish that figures so largely in the bills, the correspondence, the memoranda of the latter period, that was so mysterious and colossal in size, and that became so famous, can hardly be overlooked by the local antiquary Though originally baked no doubt for household use only, in homes hard by the lake where the fish was caught, it was presently sent as a speciality to friends and relatives in neighbouring Westmorland halls, then, its fame spreading, it was carried into Lancashire, to Leeds, to London—as far as pack horses could carry it—and finally became, in the hands of Sir Daniel Fleming, an instrument of social diplomacy, whereby he sweetened (or savoured) his intercourse with politicians and friends at court.

The antiquity of the char-pie we can hardly guess, but its genesis we may Food in ancient days was simple, coarse, and unpalatable. The bread of the district was made of oats or barley (bigg), the only two cereals grown in Rydal, and in the seventeenth century wheaten bread was procured even for the Hall in small quantities, and generally ready baked, from Kendal or Ambleside Fresh meat was enjoyed only in the summer, even by the wealthier classes. The cattle that could not be sheltered through the winter in byre and hog house were killed in autumn and laid down in salt. The butter of the summer, too, was kept by salting Lent, in fact, fell at an exceedingly appropriate time for the larder, when the stock of winter food was running low, and even becoming putrid

To make a virtue of necessity is well. But religion has never controlled man's appetite, nor prevented him from seeking alleviations to a bare and meagre diet. Fresh eggs, which become plentiful in February, and which even furnished the old pre-Lenten feast of pancakes, were never denied to the accredited faster; nor was fresh fish. And how delicious to the palate, wearied by the coarse briny food of winter, must the taste of fresh fish have been!

Now it was just at the opening of Lent, when winter storms were over, and the lake maybe thawed from its armour of ice, that the boats and netters went forth, and drew the yearly yield of char. For then, as now, a close season for the fish seems to have been kept, which extended, if we may judge from the dates in Sir Daniel's records, to early February, if not as now to the 15th. We know by the tip given to the Coniston man who brought the haul of fish to Rydal Hall, when it was taken; and we find it was February 18, in 1661, February 19, in 1662, March 8, in 1668, and February 20, in 1671. On February 4, 1660, some were brought, but only half-a-dozen. So February 18, 1661, was the date of the Windermere haul, and though another on that lake was January 31, 1673, this but shows that though there was a wise law of custom in the matter, there was none of prohibition, that might not be broken. The dates of the despatch of char-pies, baked almost immediately, confirms the supposition of a close time; they range from February 22 to March 22, and generally occur on the last few days of February, or the first of March.

Now the yield for netting was large, and it was an economical measure, as well as a satisfaction to the palate, to preserve the fish that could not be immediately eaten, and to prolong the season of feasting. This was done by the old expedient of baking in a crust of pastry, with a heavy seasoning of salt, pepper and spices. The phrase " to season," as applied to culinary ingredients, show their ancient use in preserving food beyond its natural time.

The method of keeping food by spices is so old that its beginning is not known. It is surprising to find how early imported delicacies for spicing were present in English kitchens. Our typically English dishes, plum-pudding and mince-pie—dishes created to furnish a feast that fell in the mid-winter scarcity, and which have lost their savour now that a variety of foods, and fresh foods, can be easily procured—are almost wholly made up of foreign ingredients. The dried fruits and spices with which they are loaded, drown the original English ingredients—minced suet and beef (the latter boiled, no doubt to extract salt), which they were intended to make palatable. These dried fruits came from south-eastern Europe, as did no doubt cummin, the dried seed of an umbelliferous plant, which was used for flavouring. Cummin was so treasured in Westmorland homesteads of the better class, and its use (probably to season cakes) so general, that the complimentary payment of a freeholder for land to his lord often took the form of a pound or half a pound of it. An Inquisition of 1283 in the Record Office shows that a certain freehold in Grasmere paid half a pound of cummin yearly to the de Lindeseys. Bainriggs, in Rydal, anciently a freehold, was held by the payment of the same, from time immemorial.

Pepper, cinnamon, nutmegs and cloves came from Eastern Asia and the far Spice Islands. Professor Thorold Rogers tells us something of the ancient overland routes by which men made the immense and hazardous journey to Europe and the west. When these routes were blocked by disturbance in Asia, the trade sought other channels, and came round partly by desert, some of it passing through Egypt. In the fifteenth century prices fell, and pepper dropped to one-half. This may have stimulated the making of char-pies in Westmorland, but pepper had been in use here long before that Like cummin, it served as a fee on freehold land, and some of the lands of Kendal were held in 1301 by payment (besides money) of three pounds of pepper, two pounds of cummin, one pound of wax and twelve arrows (Nicolson and Burn.)

The art of baking with a raised crust was doubtless

also a very ancient one. There is no time when the record of feasts does not include pastry. There were game-pies, veal-pies, eel-pies and venison pasties, as well as char-pies. In the list of dishes suitable for a wedding feast, copied by Sir Daniel in his youth, there appears a strange pie made of sheeps' heads, only the horns of which were to appear (pointedly to the occasion) from out the enclosing crust of pastry. Perhaps this humorous dish was peculiar to East Westmorland, where he was brought up, for there all the sheep are horned; it must certainly have been of large size and involved great skill in the making. But great skill the dames of the old English household undoubtedly possessed; and cooking, like needlework, was practised as a fine art. It was learnt traditionally, but sometimes professional instruction was given in it, as we find by the following entry in Sir Daniel's account-book about his daughter :—

"1671, April, 19th —Delivered to Katy to give unto a cook at Cockermouth for teaching her pastrywork, 00lb 10s 00d"

The art of making the "raised pie" as it is professionally called, though almost extinct,* is still practised by a few old-fashioned housekeepers of the Lake country. Within the memory of the aged, it was usual in every substantial household. An old lady tells me that in her childhood, when a pig was killed, pies were baked in large numbers, and stored in a cupboard, for use in rotation. It was considered a disgrace to the maker if the pies would not keep as long as wanted. Miss Harriet Martineau, who was a practical economist and kept pigs with profit, had a cook who was a notable maker of pork pies, and they were sent round as presents to friends, in the old style. The eel-pie seems to have become extinct early in these parts, as there is a note of July 7, 1781, that no "Eals" had been procured for potting. I am told that it long

---

* It is by no means extinct in Lincolnshire, in Notts. or Yorkshire —Ed

survived at the feast of the Chapter at Ely, where it was an indispensable and immemorial feature, like the boar's head of the Christmas Feast at Queen's College, Oxford. The game-pie, though made with a crust until recently, is now often sealed with lard or butter, or cooked in a special dish with a lid. Nothing, indeed, is left but the pork-pie of Melton Mowbray, made by professional cooks, to show us what the "charr-pye" of old was like.

But whatever its age as a culinary institution, it is significant that in the very first account-books of the Fleming family that have so far turned up, and which represent but two years' expenditure, the char-pie makes an appearance. William Tyson, bailiff of Squire John Fleming, wrote in February, 1632:—

Paid for Chardge with the Charr Pyes .. . 9s. 7d
Itm Gerrard Chardge wth them . . 8s 6d

Now the heaviness of these items should be noted. Tyson was at this time paying 10d. for a quarter of mutton; for nine chickens 1s. 6d.; for eggs for three weeks at the Hall 3d , for butter, eggs and onions on another occasion 8d

The 9s. 7d. probably represented the condiments for the pies alone, the fish costing nothing. The 8s. 6d. was clearly paid for carriage, as Gerrard appears in the next item as furnishing herrings, which would come from Morecambe Bay. And the pies were probably despatched to Speke Hall in Lancashire, where Squire John in these years spent a great part of his time.

It was when the young Squire Daniel had taken unto himself a wife, and was about to begin his long and notable reign at the Hall, that we hear next of the char-pie. His father's and his own faithful bailiff, John Banks, wrote to him, February 11, 1655, from Coniston, where the family had been established in the years when Rydal Hall was still kept from them, and where his widowed mother continued to live: "I hoope wee shall gett the pye backed (baked) and putt fforward on Saturday next." And further, "And ffor the ffether bed tickes the are heare and will be sent" (no doubt to Rydal Hall) "the next week, ffor yo'r mother will send a Horse w'th them and some Chares and some Chares to Yanwath and Hutton John." At Yanwath lived the Dudleys, who were uncle and aunt to Daniel, and at Hutton John the Huddlestons, also relatives.

After this we have abundant information, from Sir Daniel's account-books, from memoranda in his handwriting, and from a bill lately discovered, on the subject of char-pie.

Entries in his account-book show that the first pies despatched to London were sent to his Aunt Dudley, then residing in town, and who no doubt would have missed the annual delicacy to which she had been accustomed at Yanwath. For in 1660, March 12, 7s. 0d. was paid for the carriage of a pie to her, and on February 28th next year another went in company with one for Sir George Fletcher (Squire Daniel's father-in-law), the two weighing 7 stones, 9 pounds, only 6 pounds short of one hundred-weight! and costing 14s. 0d in carriage; while next year again, on February 23rd, another pie was despatched to her that cost 6s. 0d in carriage, at the rate of 2d. a pound. This last pie weighed, therefore, 2 stones 8 pounds, or 36 pounds, and is the lightest recorded. The weights from that time continued to increase, and the pies presumably to get larger, while they were sent with a frequency that makes enumeration wearisome The entries need not be quoted verbatim, as some of them have already been printed in the volume on the Rydal Hall papers published by the Historical MSS. Commission, some in Macpherson's Fauna of Lakeland (Article *Char*), while all of them appear in the excerpts from the great account-book, given in Dr. Magrath's *The Flemings in Oxford* (2 volumes).

Briefly then: In 1663, two pies were despatched on March 8th, to Mr. Joseph Williamson and Mr. Newman, which cost £1 in carriage at the 2d. rate, and which, therefore must have weighed 4 stone 4 pounds each. In 1664 Mr. Williamson again had a pie (sent February 25th) which cost 9s. 6d. In 1665 he received another, which, with the one sent at the same time to Lord Arlington, weighed 7 stones 6 pounds, and cost £1. In 1666, this influential man was the recipient of two pies, weighing 9 stones 1 pound, costing 18s. 0d., which is less than the 2d. rate; while two days later (February 23rd) a pie was despatched to the Earl of Carlisle, weighing 4 stones 5 pounds, and costing 9s. 0d. In 1667—and on the exceptionally early date of February 8th—two pies went to Mr Williamson that cost £1. 0s. 6d., at the 2d. rate, and must have weighed 8 stones 11 pounds. In 1670 the pies were smaller, as the two that went off to Mr Williamson and the Earl of Carlisle weighed together 6 stones 8 pounds, and costing 15s. 0d. It was in 1673 that the maximum was apparently reached, when a couple of pies were despatched to the Earl of Carlisle which weighed " near 12 stone," or 84 pounds each.

The weight of these pieces of pastry has excited comment. And enormous the pies must have been to attain it; even considering the fact that consolidated food of this character weighs heavily. The quantity of fish used in them we know, as eleven dozen in one case served for four pies, in another seven dozen for two; and three to three and-a-half dozen seems to have been the usual allowance for each; while for the two colossal pies of 1673, eight dozen were used. Then the condiments and pastry added to the weight. But besides this, there was the packing of the pie for carriage.

This point has been hitherto overlooked. Yet it is certain that the long, slow journey to London, by indifferent roads, slung on the back of a jolting pack-horse, could not be made by a piece of pastry without protection. And that it was the weight of the package, as made up for the carrier, and not of the pie, as it left the kitchen, that was paid for, is shown by a small piece of paper in the nature of a ticket, written in Sir Daniel's minute hand, which evidently accompanied the two pies, mentioned above as weighing 6 stones 8 pounds, as addresses. On one side is written—

" For the Right Hon'ble the Earl of Carlisle, at his house in ye old Pallace Yard hast (hasten) these with care   London "

And on the other —

" For Joseph Williamson, Esq , hast these with care, at his Lodgings in Whitehall, London "

While scrawled across each, in a rougher hand, is the weight, " 3 stone and a halfe," " 3 stone and 1lb " So evidently the carrier handed this ticket back with the attached weight on his return journey, for payment. The fact is proved by entries found in the bills of Richard Nicholson, the Rydal carpenter.   He notes—

" One day caseing up ye pyes   00£. 00s 04d.
" One day and a halfe for making foure frames, 3 for pyes and one for Mr Bracken   00s. 06d "

Whatever the fourth frame might be (and as Mr. Bracken was a portrait painter, it seems to have been for a picture) the three for pies would no doubt be constructed of the *lats* which Richard was in the habit of *rieving* for partition work in houses, and which would make a good and tolerably light cage for the great cheese-like presents on their journey   Some later ones, as we shall see, went in boxes

It is certain that these earlier pies, cased by Richard, were made in the kitchen of Rydal Hall. But the increasing dignity of the dish, which went to the tables of noblemen and courtiers, as well as its increasing size and fame, lifted it about 1670 out of the hands of the amateur pastry maker; and a class of professional experts sprang up, who undertook to concoct the delicacy for export from the district. The bill for the colossal pies of 1673, which Sir Daniel preserved, has fortunately been found, and shows them to have been made by one Mrs. Ann Potter, of Kendal, whose husband seems to have been a general provider, since he sold wine and candles. In her large handwriting, which appears in two other bills, and in her extraordinary spelling, every item is set forth. The squire docketed it Mrs. Potter's Acq. for 2 charr pies."

"Mrs. Potter's Acq. for 2 charr pies"
A Not what the to pyes comes to

	£	s	d
for one pye in mace	0	4	8
Cloues	0	4	4
numuges	0	1	0
Sinement	0	1	8
peper	0	1	0
buter	0	7	6
wheate	0	5	0
mece	0	4	8
cloues	0	4	4
Nutmuges	0	1	0
Sinement	0	1	8
peper	0	1	0
buter	0	7	6
wheate	0	5	0
peste boude (paste-board?)	0	0	6
for becking them in the Ouen	0	4	6
To boxes and Cords	0	4	4
	£2	19	8

After the settlement of the bill, on 7th March, 1673, comes a note in the squire's hand "There was 8 dozen of charrs in these 2 pies, and they weighted almost 12 stone, the carryage the Earle of Carlisle paid."

The items of this bill are worth noting. They include a special paste-board. Wheaten flour for each pie cost 5s. 0d.; butter 7s. 6d., and this at a time when salted butter was sold in autumn in the Hawkshead market at from 2s. 10d. to 3s. 0d. a stone. Fresh butter, however, may have been used. The charge for baking and fuel seems heavy, but it perhaps included the cook's fee, which makes no appearance in the bill. Altogether each pie cost, without counting its chief ingredient, the char, 29s. 10d. This, if we multiply only by eight (and Bishop Creighton allows a multiple of twelve to translate the money of the previous century into present value) brings the value of the pie, in modern coin, to £11. 18s. 8d. !

But in these two culinary creations of Mrs. Ann Potter the climax of the char-pie seems to have been reached. Perhaps some pie cracked on the journey, and there was a catastrophe · perhaps in the effort to stiffen it, the paste became so hard (like that of the recent game-pie) as to be practically uneatable ; but certainly the inconvenience of making and moving such mountains of meat and paste on horse-back must have been felt. It is clear that about this time, pots and tins (called pans, just as the mince-pie tin was called patty-pan) began to be substituted for the crust of pastry. Some ornamental tins seem to have been invented, that simulated the raised crust, and in this the seasoned fish were baked. In 1674, February 20, John Banks bought in Kendal " Two Tin-charr-pans, 5s. 6d.," and also paid for " carryage of a chair-pan to Mr. Secretary 4s. 8d." which shows the great lightening of the dish without pastry and wrappings. An acknowledgment of this old dish in its altered form has been preserved, written by the frequent recipient of it, Sir Joseph Williamson, Secretary of State.

Whitehall ye 2 Apr. 1675.

Deare Sr

You see how ungratefull a Sort of people Courtiers are I have quite devoured yor Present before I came to acknowledge ye having receiued. But if comending & admireing yor Pye were to deserve it, I have right to another ye next yeare. Indeed nevr better came to ye Table, & it is concluded by those that haue experience in that sort of Regalle, that this way of Tinne Crusts does infinitely better. Sr, I beseech yu accept my humble thankes how late soevr it comes, for ye favor of this & all yor other kindnesse and believe there is nobody values & desires it more heartily than I doe, nor can be wth a more perfect esteeme then I am

   Deare Sr,
    Yor most humble and faithfull
     Servt
Mr Fleming   J. WILLIAMSON.

It will be seen by this that he calls the dish a pie still, though made without paste. In the same way the terms pan and pot were used indifferently for some time. A small note is preserved in Sir Daniel's hand that evidently served as directions to a messenger to Kendal.

"If Mrs Forth hath made ready ye 3 Pans of chars, Get Mr Simpson to send them by ye carrier, and pay for ye Carriage of them; thus directing them

For Sr Christopher Musgrave these, at his house in Newport Street, near Saint Martin's Lane, London.

Send me word by Jo. Banks, by what Carrier ye Charr-Pans are sent by"

Doubtless Tho. Brigg's receipt of February 26th, 1686, refers to these same, for it describes his freight as " 3 *panns* of Charrs directed to Sr Chrr. Musgrave, weight 5 stone and 10lb." And Thomas signs below for " thirteen shillings in full of 3 *potts* Carriage to Lond : "

Mrs Forth who cooked these was the good dame who boarded, or " tabled " the squire's sons while at Kendal school; Mr. Simpson was a general provision merchant of the town, who supplied the Hall with many things.

But the earthenware pot, that served at first perhaps for homely use only, soon ousted the pan or tin. Already in 1672 a " Pott of charrs," costing 8s. 4d. in carriage, had gone to Sir Joseph Williamson Its superior convenience must have been felt, and it cost only 1s. 0d., as against 2s. 9d. for the tin. Another bill of Mrs Ann

Potter has been preserved, for two pots of char, which were procured for Sir George Fletcher, through Sir Daniel.

As usual, her spelling is extraordinary, and almost incomprehensible.

A not Theas to pottes Liseing In
Pade for cloues } Pade for mace }	..	£0 9 0
Pade for nutmuges } Pade for Sinement }	..	0 5 0
Pade for pepei } Pade for buter }	..	0 8 10
Pede for backingen the to pottes in the Ouen	..	0 2 0
Pede for the to pottes	..	0 2 0
Pede for to boxes peper and Leder and Cordes	..	0 2 8
(=paper) Sum In all	..	1 9 6
(In Mr Potter's hand) Carriage to London	..	0 11 6
		£2 1 0

The 7th March, 1673, Rec. in full of this note forty-one shillings by me, S S Potter.

Sir Daniel added to this, " It. 7 dozen of charres 14s." and a later acquittance shows that Lady Mary Fletcher paid him £2. 15s. 0d.

This bill, if compared with one for pies, shows that the *pot* or *pan* cost about two thirds of the *pie* for nearly the same quantity of fish. Also that the spices used were different in quantity, the *pot* having nearly twice as much nutmeg and cinnamon.

The pot clearly came to stay. George Fleming, writing to his father from Queen's College, Oxford, on March 16th, 1696, says :—

" Sr I give you my most hearty thanks for the Charr-Pot you was pleased to send me, and have dispos'd of it as directed ; Mr Principal and Mr Waugh give their serv's to you."

No records of preserved char have been found for some time after this. The following paper perhaps shows that in the second William's time the dish was re-instituted in the Hall kitchen It is docketed, "a Receipt from Mrs. Holme at Ramside, Dec'br the 15th, 1749."

"I generally put 2oz. of black pepper to 1oz of mace and 1oz. of cloves, 1oz. Jamacoe pepper finely bet and mix'd as y'u use it of the finest Seasoning will be gone first Have y'u Seasoning mix'd so when y'u find the Seasoning leave the salt add more and not much more Salt, then Spice If Conistone fish after they are gutted and wip'd sprinkle them w'th Salt for an hour or more. Wipe them clean and Season them well Lay them in the pot y'u intend to bake them in and if they can lay all night, it will be better as they are large Fish Cover them well wth clarified butter, and when you pott them throw a little good spice on the bottom of the Pot and amongst the Fish Let them Drain well, and don't cover them wth butter till Quite cold If Conistone fish, and large, 9 will fill half a Guinea Pot one Layer "

By this time the potting of char had become a trade in the district, and a lucrative one too. It seems to have been in the hands still of innkeepers, who also sold fish and game ; though professed cooks were to be found in several homesteads of the district. In 1745, March 1st, Sir William sent a "Pott of Charrs" from one Singleton, Wine and Provision Merchant, as a present into Yorkshire, which cost 10s. 6d. This was the usual price ; and the next squire, Sir Michael, who was an absentee, had sent to him in London, between January 2nd and March 12th, 1778, twenty "Potts of charr," two every week, besides two to Scarborough at £1. 1s. 0d the pair of pots. He had, indeed, received, in 1761, two pots which had cost 21s. each, and carriage 3s. 7d , while two pots of Woodcock had gone off at the same price.

In 1783, Mr. Thomas Rigge, of Hawkshead, who was agent for the Coniston slate quarries, despatched to Sir Michael a pot of char as a present, doubtless on the occasion of his "nuptuals" which the writer mentions. He sent this off on March 28th by the Kendal waggon, and hoped it would arrive in London about April 2nd. This present seems to have whetted Sir Michael's appetite, for he apparently wrote to his factotum at Rydal Hall,

John Gibson, to see if he could get the delicacy concocted for him upon the estate. The Coniston fishery was, indeed, let this time to Mr. Knott, still fish could be procured from it by arrangement. John Gibson replies that he went to Coniston on the 14th.

"No chars had been taken for some time before, by reason of the calm and bright weather, and the Season is now past that they leave off killing them, nevertheless, Wednesday being a dark Day and some Rain and Wind, they took some Fish, and Mrs Walker (the housekeeper at the Hall) made up two Potts, which I forwarded yesterday by Mr Wikeman's Waggon, and will be at the Castle Inn, in Wood Street, on the 1st May. And I hope to forward two Potts more, to be made up by Mrs. Rigge (who did those which were sent you by Mr. Thos, Rigge) they will leave Kendal on the 27th inst , and be at the Castle Inn on the 8th May. And as these Potts by the Waggon are so long in coming to Town, I purpose (if Possable) to forward a Box with One Dozen fresh Fish on Thursday, the 24th inst , by the Coach which will leave Kendal on that Morning, by way of Preston and Warrington, and arrive at the Swan with two Necks in Lad Lane, London, in three Days"

His next letter, on May 21st, says —

"The fishers at Conistone did with some difficulty take as many fish as made two Pots, which Mrs. Rigge Potted, and forwarded from Kendal by the Waggon on the 8inst , and I hope w'd come safe to hand on the 19th They were Trouts (not being possible to get Chare), which, if good, are at this season preferred before the Chare, and am sorry to say that no more can be had"

It is said that a good deal of the reputed potted char was in reality trout, as this was. In the following winter John Gibson began again his exertions to procure the delicacy. Mrs. Walker, the housekeeper at the Hall, was never tried again ; and the fish were despatched to a certain Mrs. Braithwaite, of Mislett. Gibson thinks her "a very proper person," as she has done a great quantity, and formerly some for Sir Michael. But if the recipient does not like her potting, he will for the next make "tryal of one Mr. Barwick, near Hawkshead, who Potts all Mr Knott's Charr."

It will be seen by these letters how much communication with London had been improved. The turnpike road had lately been laid, and instead of the string of pack-horses, laden with goods of all sorts, that trailed along badly-kept roads, wheeled traffic bore goods and passengers easily to the great city. It will be noted that John Gibson mentions the route through Preston and Warrington. Indeed, these were early days yet both for carrier's cart and coach, for Nicholson, in his *Annals of Kendal*, dates the start of the mail-coach to London as two years later, viz. 1785-6. The carrier's cart (though optimistically given by Thomas Rigge five days for the journey) is clearly stated by Gibson to have occupied eleven, while the new coach did it in three days. It was thus possible, as the alert Gibson saw, to use it for the conveyance of fresh fish to London. It is interesting to know, however, that the early Kendal coach often carried a more serious freight than dishes for the epicure. It was to the Swan with Two Necks, in Lad Lane, that Charles Lamb a little later was in the habit of despatching parcels of books to one or other of the Lake poets—perhaps ancient treasures from second-hand dealers, or presentation copies of his own works; and by the same coach he received as a gift first editions of theirs.

The last we hear of the coach and char is from a letter dated December 5th, 1797, when the Rev. T. Jackson writes to Sir Michael that he sends off from Rydal Hall, two dozen fresh char and four fine trout.

"They were all alive when put into the Box at nine o'clock this evening, and shall send Tom with them in the morning to Kendal to be forwarded by mail."

But even that wonderful improvement, the mail-coach, has vanished into the past, as the pack-horse did; and with the rapid transit of food by railroad there is no longer need for the old delicacies preserved in spices; and the char-pie is now a thing of tradition only.

PART IV

A LAKELAND TOWNSHIP AND ITS FOLK.

CHAPTER I.
A Typical House.

NO early particulars have come down to us of the people of Rydal. In mediæval times they would share the conditions of life with other settlers of the valleys, and those conditions must have been singularly free, until the ordering of the counties and the making of the Barony of Kendal. After that, they would become subject to those feudal laws which obtained over the rest of England; though still, with no intermediary lord between them and the great baron, the laws must have pressed more lightly than where a residential knight was fixed. The Westmorland dalesman was practically a free land-owner in a self-governing village community, and so he long remained. Rydal, however, was cut off from her neighbours under a separate lord as early as 1275; and ultimately she suffered from the creation of a demesne within her township on which a lord was seated, alike in the crippling of her lands and in the enormous increase of dues extracted from her.

But old customs continued to prevail, founded on the tenant-right that was rooted in an immemorial past; so that when we learn details of the life of the people in the seventeenth century, the little *vill* does not differ materially — in outward appearance at least—from those higher and lower in the valley. Her population, however, was stationary, nay, had fallen back, while her neighbours had more than doubled or trebled theirs. Besides being shorn of much of her arable land, she was not able to engage in the lucrative cloth trade. Husbandry was still the hub of her wheel of industry, though most of her "statesmen" had begun to associate some other occupation or craft with the care of their scanty lands.

When Daniel Fleming entered the manor as lord in 1655 there were but thirteen or fourteen of these statesmen from whom he demanded the customary fine ; though one of these possessed more than his ancestral holding The holdings, too, could not have included all the homesteads in the place. A full messuage or tenement often consisted of two dwelling houses, as old rentals show , and there labourers and landless craftsmen lived ; for of these at least half a dozen kinds were at work—tailor, weaver, carpenter, shoemaker, blacksmith and miller, besides a fiddler. The hatmaker and the pedlar lived in Loughrigg.

The houses formed a more compact cluster than any other *vill* about, except Ambleside after its rise ; and they had no apparent connection with the lord's seat on St. John How in the lower park. They started high on the spur of the scar, though well below the possible site of a primitive settlement ; they straggled down irregularly, pitched here and there as the hummocks of rock permitted. The extraordinary nature of the ground for the site of a village, chosen probably because it was dry and lifted above the floods, and also because it left the deeper soil of the valley free for the plough, may be seen in Green's etchings. Yet clearing and blasting have gone on continually from Sir Daniel's time. In 1662, for instance, 2s. 6d. was " Given to ye wallers of Ambleside to drink for breaking of ye great Rock in ye way up to ye gates," which stood at the top of the street. The use of gunpowder made levelling comparatively easy. When the church was built in 1800 extensive blasting was done ; and in fact every improvement in the village has seen a clearance of the rocks, down to that of Coat How in 1905.

The nature of the ground prevented any formal row of houses being built. "Sands" onsett, as we know, stood at the back of "Banks." A house that occupied part of the churchyard was reached by a passage between the house lower down and an abutting barn, as is remembered; and within the courtyard stood an ash tree of remarkable size. "Hobson's" again lay edgewise to the highway, though it may possibly have fronted another route that sloped up from the ford where the footbridge now stands. Still a rough line of houses descended on the right of the street that came to be known as Hall Bank, the last three standing between the church and the bottom of the hill. The left side of it below the Hall had, by the time that we know the village, become almost absorbed by the demesne. At the bottom of the slope, by the river, the houses turned to the south along the valley road, which was known here as the town gate, and finished at the old smithy by Rydal Beck. The houses on the further bank of the Rothay, of which there were four at least immediately opposite to the village, were reached by stepping stones and fords; they no longer belonged, however, to the manor of Rydal, though like the rest of the holdings that straggled under Loughrigg, they joined it as a township.

Each little farmstead stood with its barn and byre grouped round a small enclosure or garth, and often a little field was attached to it called a parrock, where an animal could be turned in to graze. But the door of the house opened in general on to a grassy space bordering the street, which, though unenclosed, actually belonged to the holding. This "front before door" was convenient for the grazing of a beast, or for use during the holding of a fair (and mention is made of one in Rydal in 1718); also pigs were wont to wander over it. These spaces were later enclosed as gardens ; but one cottage opposite the Hall gates (which were only themselves erected to enclose the front after 1770) still remains open to the road.

Barn and byre occupied more space than the statesman's dwelling. The barn was constructed of the loftiest "crucks" (naturally arched timber) that the forest would yield, or the lord would permit to be felled. We can see what a barn might be in the great structure at Grayrigg Hall, near Kendal, or at Esthwaite Hall. The "raising" of a barn anew was the occasion of a village gathering, when each man of the community lent a shoulder to the heaving and the planting of the great rough-hewn principals that formed the arch, and the owner gave a feast to the boon workers. The primitive house, too, in the order of its construction, was begun by the rearing of arched timbers, to which huge cross-beams roughly split were tied ; and on this skeleton the roof was fixed without reliance on the walls, which, when they came to be of stone,* instead of wood or wattle-and-daub, were piled up against the wooden pillars as if by an after-thought. The house was of lower pitch than the barn, and was besides divided into two floors, so that the tall statesman had often to bow his head as he passed his threshold. The lowness of the Westmorland rooms, even in the Halls, may be noted in many remaining examples, and this feature was likely to be exaggerated where the tenant's rights to timber were continually questioned or curtailed. How could those few lopped oaks of Nab Wood do other than furnish as time went on poorer and yet poorer roof-timbers for the homestead ?

On entering from the porch that shielded his door, the statesman not only bowed his head but lifted his foot

---

* For the primitive method of building by fork or crucks, see Addy's *Evolution of the English House*. A couple of crucks are still to be seen in the older house at Orrest, above Windermere, and in *Transactions* of the C. & W. A. & A. Society, vol. xiv, p. 280, N.S., is a photograph of them as now existing in a barn at Raby Cote.

to avoid a piece of wood that crossed the bottom of the door cheeks and stood five or six inches above the ground This was called the threshwood according to old writers, but I have found no other term remembered but sole, or sole-foot. In 1713, Brathay Hall was reported to have " neither Door Cheeks, Leafes, nor Soles about ye house, but wanted repairing." Soles are still to be found; there is one downstairs at the Green, Ambleside. When several were removed from Townend, Troutbeck, an old relative of the family was observed still to lift his foot over the imaginary obstacle.*

Within the door was a passage some four feet wide, where sacks of corn were placed on the night before market, or pigs were hung after killing, and where implements were kept. It passed straight through to a door at the back, recalling those we find in many Westmorland Halls. According to some authorities the passage—now known as the entry—was originally called the hallan,† though others assign this word to the wall that formed the passage.

Passing down the entry, the smoke-house, or house, lay on one side, and the down-house on the other. The down-house was usually shut off from the entry by a light partition of wicker-work or oak staves, in which case it was entered by a door close to the back door. Here the " elding " (either wood or peat) was piled, and here the rough work of the household was done—baking, brewing, washing, etc. In the loft above—supposing there were a second storey—was fixed the malt-mill, used for the crushing of the bigg; and the great arks or kists stood there. Of these there were generally three, made of oak and often carved—one the bread-kist, made long enough

---

* See *The Remains of John Briggs*, who quotes from and comments upon the Rev M. Hodgson's description of a Westmorland house in Lonsdale : also Mr. H S Cowper's *Hawkshead*

† Addy says that hallan or halland was in N of Eng. and Scot. the seat within the outer door

to hold two stacks of oatcake; another the meal-kist in which was stored the haver, or oatmeal; and the malt-kist. The size of the last two varied according to the needs of the household. Very large must have been the "Great Ark in the Storehouse" made for Sir Daniel in 1696, at a cost of £12. 4s. 2d.—a large sum in those days Then there were the vats lying round; the gyls or guil-vat or wort-tub, and the mash-fat, both used in brewing, the flesh-fat, and the souse-tub, for the pickling of meat. The empty cheese-vats and rims would stand here, but the cheese-press was farther to seek It stood under some convenient tree about the garth, which served as a fixing post for its huge pendulous stone weight. Wordsworth in his guide mentions this custom; and two trees in Hall Bank are still remembered to have had presses attached. Other utensils, too, were kept in the down-house, of which the principal was the bakstone Once doubtless a stone slab, this was later made of iron and on it the haver-bread or oat-cake was baked. It was circular, sometimes three or four feet in diameter, and was raised above the embers on tall feet. The girdle was a smaller and lighter plate for the same purpose, two feet in diameter, fitted with a bow handle, and was placed upon a separate iron tripod, called a brandreth. Then there were the racks and the spits, standing, too, on legs and feet, and adjustable to various heights to suit the roast. There were besides, the skellet, a pan with a long handle, whose foot, repaired by the blacksmith, doubtless rested in the embers also. Other cooking utensils were the chafing-dish, a bucket-like metal receptacle, with handles, in which burning charcoal was placed, to heat a dish or to raise the temperature, the cockle-pan, and the scummer, a long-handled spoon for skimming the salt meat as it seethed in the cauldron. The battling-stone was used for beating clothes in the wash, and appears to have had a handle, as it needed "setting" from time to time (at a cost of 4d. in 1660). The cresset must also have been much used in winter about the byre and outhouses, for it held in an open iron frame a torch or light. Not far off, in stable or under pent-house or gallery of the barn, would stand the weigh-balk, and all the trappings for the pack-horse, in saddles, wantys, halts and hames; as well as gavelock, mell, mattock, hack, scythes, and sickles. Then there were the teams, yokes, sucke, coulter, swingle-tree, hott, cowell, sled, trail-barrow, peat-spade and flaying-spade.

The partition on the other side of the entry was of stone Against it, on the inner side, the hearth-stone was placed, slightly raised, and above it rose the vast chimney. This was built out from the wall in a hood shape, its sides in early times being constructed of wicker-work daubed with clay or cow dung, or else of lath-and-plaster, and from the width of six feet at its spring above the hearth it gradually narrowed to the outlet above. In this funnel-like opening, joints of meat were hung to dry; close about it, when dark came on, the women drew to spin or knit, the men to card wool, and the clever boy of the family—so the Rev. Mr. Hodgson says—to con his Latin task (a touch which tells how often there was a scholar in the family), while grandfather regaled the circle with tales of Hob-thrust. In wet weather a sooty moisture dropped down the chimney called the hallan-drop, which may have been the reason why the men kept their hats on as they sat.

But to reach this social centre, it was necessary to turn through a doorway in the stone partition and enter a second passage formed by a partition that jutted out some six feet from the chimney side, and screened those sitting by the hearth from the wind.

About the name of the passage and partition there has been likewise confusion, for while some authorities call the partition a heck, others speak of the passage by that name. The derivation of the word, however, from hedge (Icel. *hagi*, an enclosure, German *hag*, a hedge) as well as its present use, supports the former statement. "The word heck, for hedge, survives in heck-berry," the common name for Prunus Padus (Mr. W. H Hills). The original hedges were made of cut boughs twined in a rough basket fashion, set up to protect the hay and corn as it grew in the common field, and removed at the harvest. This ancient style of fence is still adhered to by Christopher Roberts, the last statesman of Loughrigg The word survives in the water-heck, a light frame placed across a beck to keep cattle from straying ; and in cart-heck, the back of the cart which will take off. Heck was also the name of the low wooden partition of the byre, and an old native remembers her father calling " Shut heck," meaning the little gate through the partition. Mr. Browne says that heck also stands for a small gate, such as is used for a sheep-fold. The Rydal Hall bills (c 1660) illustrate the word both as a rough partition and a swing gate, for the carpenter makes a calf-heck and the blacksmith " gimmers for ye kitchen hecke "

Addy speaks of heck being used for the racks against the wall into which food for cattle was thrown. Atkinson gives, besides water-heck, the heck as a half-door or hatch-door within the old house. For derivation he also goes back to a hedge made of boughs (Dan *haek* or *haekhe*) Perhaps then the heck may be comprehensively described as a light frame partition, hinged or otherwise

The heck is said to have been frequently carved with the date and the owners' name ; and in most ancient houses it stretched as far as the first beam of the upper storey, where it was finished by an octagonal post. In the post an augur-hole was bored, and a cow-hair inserted by a wooden peg to clean the wool combs upon.

The floor of the house—generally lower than the threshold

is said to have been coarsely paved with pebbles.* Pebble pavements, done in patterns, were indeed an art of the country. Later, when smooth slabs of slate came into use as flooring, the pebbles were banished to the yards. This comfortable house-place was lighted by three windows: one large one, of three or four lights set either in stone or (more often) in oaken mullions, broke the face of the front wall, as well as a second one of two lights, the last being close to the porch and chimney-wing, making a recess where the Bible and Prayer Book were placed; while the third window looked to the back, and was close to the end of the heck.

The furniture was as follows :—A long oak table stood under the principal window, and since no aperture would have admitted it, it was built within the house. Forms—pronounced and spelt firms—stood on each side of the table. The long settle stood with its back to the heck, and was often a fine piece of carpentry. From its being but lightly fixed, it was one of the first articles to be carried away by the dealer to richer homes. Under the settle sufficient elding was deposited each evening to keep up the fire, for this was never allowed to go out. Within the stone partition on the settle side of the chimney was a small oven, where it is said yarn and stockings were kept; on the other side of the chimney was the locker, a little cupboard made in the depth of the wall and used for such treasures as the household possessed. Its door was always adorned by carving or initials and date; it is to be found yet in many houses, as in Rydal Mount and Loughrigg Holme. The "Catmallison" was also a cupboard, made over the fire-window and fronted with panelled doors. A chair or two of heavy wainscot and with high arms, stood about, as well as three-legged stools Chairs increased in number, however, when they began to be made with spokes turned on the lathe or "thrown," and this

---

* See *Manners and Customs of Westmorland*, by John Gough, Kendal, 1827.

fashion gave work to several Rydal carpenters. Matthew, son of John Fleming, of Rydal, cooper, was in 1741, apprenticed for 8 years as a thrower. In an inventory of 1697, of goods at Monks Hall, Keswick, only "One Trown Chare" is mentioned (the one wainscot chair being relegated to the parlour), while there were eleven "Throwen Chairs" disposed of at a Grasmere statesman's sale in 1710, at from 5d. to 9d apiece.

A light upright pole, fixed in a log of wood, stood near the hearth. It was called a standart, and was pierced by a row of holes on one side, into which a long peg or a bit of iron was stuck. This made an adjustable socket for a candle, or else it would hold a little pair of pincers into which the rush-light was slipped.* It was the pith of the rush dipped into fat which made the feeble light; and these prepared piths were called seaves, an article in constant demand, whether in hall or cottage. Though on sale at fairs, they were generally prepared by the women at home.

Across the mouth of the chimney, high up, from wall to hood, were fixed two short beams, and on these was placed a long beam, known as the rannel-balk, or the randle-tree or poll. As this was not fixed, it could be rolled back and forth, so that the cauldrons and pans which depended from it by a chain could be adjusted according to their size—the great brewing kettle, for instance, being drawn forward to prevent contact with the wall. "Two iron Randle Trees" are given in the Monks Hall Inventory and these surely would be safer than timber, though, from the scarcity of iron, not generally in use. The racken-crook or ratten-crook, consisted of a chain slung round the rannel-balk, to which two crooks of different sizes were attached. By catching the little crook into a link higher up the chain and so shortening it, the pan (suspended on the longer crook) could be raised.

---
* *Manners and Customs of Westmorland* Kendal, 1827, by John Gough

This simple contrivance has been superseded by the one now in use, a piece of iron pierced with a rack of holes or notches. Clark remarks that the "black-hood and the stoothing," terms not now remembered, enabled the winter provisions to be dried within the chimney.

Most of the women spun, and hand-cards for teasing out the wool ready for the spinner were in constant requisition.

The spinning wheel was a picturesque bit of furniture, though it is said that the women formerly spun with the distaff. When knitting came to engross so many of their quiet hours, the knitting-stock or needle-rest* ornamented in many curious ways, was a common utensil. But another essential article of household industry there must have been, at least in early days. This was the spinning-loom on which was woven (and generally by the women) the cloth for family wear. From references to the narrow width of Kendal cloth, it must have been a small simple machine. Possibly the word studdle, which I have met with occasionally, may refer to it.†

But the finest article of furniture and the largest—for it reached up to the rafters—was the bread-cupboard, which stood opposite to the chimney. It was a fixture, and therefore may still be seen in many old houses. It was always of one design, modified in the hands of the craftsman, the projecting cupboard below being carried up by pilasters to a cornice. It was generally decorated by patterns cut with simple tools, and, somewhere on its front, initials and date gave a clue to its owner. To the right and left of the great cupboard opened narrow oak doorways, let into the wainscot. They led into apartments essential to the family life. One was the aumbry or pantry, which Briggs says was always placed on the northern side, for coolness. The other was the bower,

---

* See *Transactions* of Ant. Soc. for knitting-rests.
† "Studle" obsolete. An implement belonging to a weaver. Wright.

one-third larger in size than the pantry, and raised slightly, according to Gough, above the level of the house floor. In the bower slept the statesman and his wife, and within it must have been enacted the striking scenes of birth and death. Here would gather the wives of the village, flying at sudden call when the babe was born, then, again, the whole "laiting"* would troop in—though now in ceremonious fashion, to bring offerings, when the wiving or upsitting of the mother took place, an occasion when rum-butter was the principal delicacy offered to the company. Here, too, when rest came after toil and pain, the corpse was "straiked," and was waked with lit candles through the long night before its burial.

A flight of stone steps led to the upper floor. Originally, they may have been placed outside under a gallery, but they are said in general to have been situated near the bower. This may have been after a roomier chamber had been built, as at Low House. A few old specimens may yet be found.

The upper floor was no more than a rude loft open to the rafters, and divided by rough oaken partitions some six feet high, such as are still to be seen at Old Orrest. Here slept the children and the servants, under an open roof said to have been thatched with heath or straw, though later it was covered by slate, which was early found to rive sufficiently thin for the purpose. The outside of the homestead was covered with roughcast and white-wash, which tended to warmth and cleanliness. The out buildings, however, had no such dressing, but across the face of the high barn (which well out-topped the house) frameworks of wood were fixed as galleries, with steps and pentroof. These, which are looked upon now as so picturesque in effect, were essential to the life of the times. They gave shelter while men carried on all

---

* Late = to seek or invite. The laiting represented the village circle invited or bidden to all gatherings.

kinds of occupations. skins were hung and dried upon them, and wool could be sorted and heaped up close to the weigh-balk.

A yew tree, good for bows and for shelter, was generally planted over against the homestead; and—though this was probably a later custom, a sycamore tree also for summer shade.

Such in its main features was the dalesman's home as known to the older writers. John Briggs in the "Lonsdale Magazine," vol. iii., 1822, quoted and commented on the Rev. Mr Hodgson's description of a Westmorland house in " Beauties of England and Wales "; and as a man of the people, at home in farm and cot, his account may be relied upon. He says that the type thus jointly described was still, though vanishing, to be met with frequently, and Clarke's succinct account agrees with theirs. He wrote, (*Survey of the Lakes*, 1789,) " I cannot, however, pass over the method of building each particular house, especially as it is somewhat singular, and begins to be disused. From the front door an entry runs close behind the fire-place of the better kitchen, directly across the building, to the back-door, which opens into a yard where the byres and stables generally are. On one side of this entry is the door leading into the down-house or kitchen, where they brew, bake, etc., on the other side of the entry is the passage into the house itself, for so the better kitchen is called, but this passage is close to the back door, so that before you arrive at the fire you have almost gone round it. The various parts and doors of this entrance into the house are known by the names of Hallan, Heck, and Mill doors. Opposite to the fire-place is the door of the chamber, or bower, where the master and mistress of the family sleep." John Gough, too, in *Manners and Customs of Westmorland*, Kendal, 1827, describes such a house.

Even in the time of these writers the primitive method

of building by forks or crucks had passed away; straight timbers and slated roofs had become general. In fact, the ancient way of rearing arched timbers in couples as the framework for a house (like a ship reversed) which the Rev. Mr. Atkinson found in ruined houses of the Dane-settled parish of Danby, was considered by Mr. G. Browne, whose opinion has great weight, not to have been practised in these parts after the close of the sixteenth century or beginning of the seventeenth; though doubtless buildings so constructed were kept in repair. Barns are still to be found with crucks, but only a solitary instance of one pair in situ can be given in an inhabited house, at Orrest.

The characteristic features of the Westmorland house may be summed up, then, as follows.—First, its long shape and internal space contained within four walls and beneath the roof, doubtless resulting from its original cruck-supported frame. Next, its one stone partition within the walls, built no higher than the first floor; this carried the huge chimney. This internal wall without doubt husbanded the warmth from the fire; while the approach round the chimney along two passages would have the same effect, very necessary at the time when the pattern was evolved, for then there was no glass in the windows, which could only be protected from blasts by the closing of wooden shutters. It was no doubt after glazing became common that the dalesman showed an increasing inclination to enter his "house" straight from the porch, with only a wooden screen or heck to keep off the draught. Especially was this the case when he had turned the bower into a parlour or built on another room at right angles to the old block. The window to the back of the house, by the heck, often disappeared, probably because the weaver's loom (which may have stood near it for light) was banished to a special craftsmen's shed. Also an addition to the house was often put out on that side.

It was to additions and improvements that the second staircase may be due, which is so often found in the better class of statesmen's dwellings as well as in the smaller halls. It was circular, its steps being cut in solid blocks of oak. It is found in the ruined wing of Coniston Hall, at Town End, Troutbeck, and How Head, Ambleside.

Other changes, too, came to the old-time home The statesman, having left his bower, had to make better accommodation upstairs. The stone steps were replaced by an oaken stairway, finished with well-turned balusters; while better and higher partitions, though generally of " lat "-and-plaster work, divided the bedrooms. Still, however, they were open to the rafters; and often the moss that stuffed the chinks between the slates failed to perform its office, and—as Robert Hayton, of Easedale Tarn, used to tell—the snow would drift in and lie upon the sleeper. Larger things came through sometimes. Thomas Mandall, of Tarn Foot, awoke one night to find a Jenny Hullet perched upon his bed hooting at him; and forthwith he got his bedroom ceiled

But deterioration as well as improvement tended to alter the old form. The oppressive hearth-tax, which allowed but one fire free, quenched many a down-house smoke, and put that convenient cooking place out of use. Chimneys were stopped up in Rydal by the poorer or more penurious statesmen. Similarly, when the window-tax came in, windows were boarded or walled in, even by the well-to-do Flemings of the Inn, as has been recently found; while the poorer dwellings suffered terribly in an effort to evade the " sess " as the tax was called.

This type of dwelling, even in its rudest and most ancient form, cannot fall, it seems to me, under those censures invoked by old houses in Danby and elsewhere, as miserable, unclean, and indecent. It was at its best, both commodious and compact. The heads of the household in the bower commanded the stair, and in the cubicles of the loft only the children slept. The hinds slept in outhouse or barn, and on large holdings, like Ambleside Hall, provision of bedstead, etc., was made for them there

Variations on this type there must always have been. Briggs says that the cotter's home was simpler still, and had neither down-house nor entry It was these houses that mostly survived the poverty of the late eighteenth and nineteenth centuries, while the larger ones were either swept away or greatly altered. Indeed, they were often inhabited by the smaller statesmen, as is shown at Hart Head (before its rebuilding) and Mill Brow, in Loughrigg, where the barn was carried under the same line of roof as the humble dwelling. It is difficult now-a-days to get old people to furnish instances of the entry or hallan, as so few remain, but there is one at the Nab. But of the altered fashion, when the wealthy statesman turned his down-house into a kitchen, stopped up his hallan, broke a new entrance straight into the " house," and either turned the bower into a parlour or added another room, can be seen several examples. At Mr. Browne's, Troutbeck, the old hallan was used as a pantry, while the mell-door in the chimney-wall has been made up, and another door broken in the wall opposite the new porch. The hallan at the Green, Ambleside, now serves as a dark cupboard. Mr. Browne remembered the disapperance of several entries in his village.

How far the homesteads of Rydal conformed to the special Lakeland type at the middle of the seventeenth century would be hard to say Hardly one remains in anything like its original condition. The ruin of the statesmen as a class, which took some 150 hard years of struggle from that date to effect, found at its completion no more than half-a-dozen of the dwellings in proper habitable repair. The rest were ruinous, and finally, having fallen into the hands of the lord, they were swept away, and most of them rebuilt on a modern plan. It is notable that in 1896 there was not a house in the parish, except Rydal Farm, that did not stand on an ancient site; though since that time quite a number of cottages have been built. The better houses had, by additions gradually made, become homes for the gentry. Such were "Knotts," or the "High House," now Rydal Mount, and "Davids," (Ivy Cottage or Glen Rothay). Both of these possess a central chimney, but the entrance into the house-place or kitchen which it warms, is no longer —whatever it once was—round its back, but straight in by the front.

CHAPTER II

THE ROUND OF HUSBANDRY FOR THE YEAR.

Village Holdings and Rentals.

> Good husbandmen must moile & toile,
>   to laie to liue by laboured feeld:
> Their wiues at home must keepe such coile,
>   as their like actes may profit yeeld.
>   for well they knowe,
>   as shaft from bowe,
>   or chalke from snowe,
> A good round rent their Lords they giue,
>   and must keep touch in all their paie;
> With credit crackt else for to liue
>   or trust to legs and run awaie.
>
>   MAY HUSBANDRIE.
> To gras the calues in some medow plot nere,
>   where neither their mothers may see them or here,
> Where water is plentie and barth to set warme,
>   and look well unto them, for taking of harme.
>
>   DECEMBER HUSBANDRIE.
>   (Ordering of cattel).
> Serue reistraw out first, then wheatstraw and pease,
>   then otestraw and barlie, then hay if ye please:
> But serue them with hay while the straw stouer last,
>   then loue they no straw, they had rather to fast —TUSSER.

SOME thirteen or fourteen farmholds stood, as we have seen, on the left bank of the Rothay. Each of these represented, as a complete messuage with its parrock and garden or orchard, a fixed unit in the joint possessions of a composite village community. It carried with it the rights over a certain amount of plough-land, of hay-meadow, and of pasturage for cattle. Each hereditary holder was therefore by birth-right a free husbandman, and—however frequently he might be driven to add another occupation or craft to this primary one—this title expressed alike his status and his privilege.

Reasons there are for the supposition that the village plough-lands once lay in the bottom of the park. But when light becomes clearer on the subject, the tenants' fields, with the exception of some few strips, are found restricted to the right bank of Rydal Beck and the shores of the lake. They were likewise at that time enclosed, and it is probable that each man had now his fixed portion of land which he might plough or mow in independence. The fact, however, that to the last, two or three holders had rights in one field shows that mixed, and at first interchangeable, land had existed in this as in other village communities. Each holder remained, too, bound up with his fellows in all the great tasks of husbandry brought by the revolving year.

Candlemas, which in Old Style fell in mid-February, saw his new labours begin. Then the sound of the flail, beating out last year's grain from the husk on the barn floor, ceased.* Fresh corn must be sown. Plough-Monday brought its neighbourly discussions, though the strips† that should belong to a man through the season had no longer to be decided in full conclave of townsmen.

---

* Threshing done at Borwick Ground as late as 1886
† Such strips of arable, undivided by fences, are still in use in the Isle of Axholme in Lincolnshire —Ed

The plough was an implement of value when iron was scarce, and in Rydal a common one appears to have been kept for the use of the smaller statesmen at least, who had not one of their own. This had to be brought out, and its turns arranged The oxen that drew it had to be produced or loaned. It seems unlikely that a full team would be required for the small, sloping fields of our *vill*, probably the statesmen might keep one apiece, and loan them by arrangement. John Fleming, miller, statesman and innkeeper, paid for the grazing of two oxen in the demesne in 1699. It was in a barn abutting on the inn-premises that the old reputed village plough lay till 1897 or 1898, when the agent, having attempted to clear the bed of the river with it, broke it up. With it had laid an old winnowing machine, likewise kept for common use. A bull was jointly possessed by the village, and probably a horse. The village pump stood open to the street near the inn ; but this is said to have been a comparatively modern erection.

The cattle made the next care of the husbandman. The lambing season was an anxious time with him, for, from the renewal of his flock and the wool it furnished, he chiefly looked for a profit in ready money.

The season of spring, marked by Lady-Day, saw the few beasts kept on the holding over winter, brought from the byre and the hoghouse to green pasture. Every farmhold or cot had its cow, or perhaps two, though never more were kept, except by the richer cattle-breeders, both because fodder in winter was hard to come by, and because there was (singularly enough) no free common for kine.

This scarcity of fodder caused trees and shrubs to be used. The holly bush was preserved on suitable ground in order that its croppings might be eaten by the sheep, and it appears that even ash leaves were valued as furnishing food for cattle. A few young sheep (called hogs after the salving* of autumn) were kept up in a detached building, where they pulled at the hay in the racks, and were occasionally taken to the beck for water.

And before cattle were brought out, there were fences and hedges to make, alike for the field of corn, the hay-meadow and the common. Every statesman had to share in the labour. The men of Ambleside, as court-laws emanating from the time of Edward IV show, had to have their "Old Field" enclosed by April 1st, and April 24th was to see the fence finished and hinged. It was the duty of the two Frithmen of Rydal, elected each year from the statesmen, not only to overlook the common and the beasts put upon it, but to see that the "Pairable Hedge" was made. The demesne "Setting Book" for 1695 shows that the lord's cattle were turned out from April 27th onwards, beginning with the young ones, the calves ("twinter" and new), then the cows; and lastly the eight draught oxen on May 10th. It was a fineable offence for Ambleside tenants to

"suffer their Kine or Chattell to bee or remaine amongst the Houses or Doors beneath their Fineable yeats from mid-May till Michaelmas."

The calf-garth of Rydal was Little Nab field (up to which one can still mount by broken through-stones from the road, a token of its once common use); and thither the calves of each farmhold were driven when separated from their dams in May.

The driving of the cattle to the fell must have made a great village commotion. The custom in Rydal was different from either Ambleside or Grasmere or Wythburn. In Ambleside, once chained by forest laws, there had apparently been an equalising of the holdings, called a

---

* The salving of sheep has given place to the dipping, but there is still, each November, a Salvers' hunt—a reminiscence of an annual Shepherds' holiday on the fells.—ED

"New Rental." Henceforth these were classed as five or ten cattle messuages; and this marked the number each tenant was permitted to put on the common, driving them thither by a path or "rake" sanctioned for him by custom. For a quarrel over the matter see *Transactions* of C. & W. A. & A. Society, vol. iv., N.S. In Wytheburn the men of the town, since their common was a "stinted" one, assembled at the Steading Stone —a well-known mark, now buried under the extended waters of Thirlmere—and there settled the number that should be allowed to each steading or holding. Grasmere, freest of all, had an unstinted common on the far-reaching heights, and its beasts were driven on to them by one of four ley-gates (pronounced lea), according to the situation of the holding There were quarrels here, however, as in Ambleside, over the "frith," and in 1658 two Grasmere men were presented at the Quarter Sessions for hindering John Dawson from driving his cattle, as " has been done from time immemorial," from a " platt called Thornehow to a platt called Broadraine," and thence to the common of Grasmere Fell.

That common of Grasmere had once been open for "pasture everywhere" to the men of Rydal, as Margaret de Brus' charter of 1275 attests; and in fact the Rydal common must in those early days have been one with it upon the heights of Nab Scar and upwards. When the boundary that shut in the Rydal Manor came to be built soon after, there was left a gap or gateway through it for the passage of the cattle. But by the seventeenth century the Rydal men had lost their privilege, and only the lord claimed a right to put 60 head through the gap to graze; while the village pasture was shut within the narrow limits of the wall upon the height as far upwards as Erne Crag, whence another enclosing wall shot down abruptly to Rydal Beck It had become, by the exigency of size, a "stinted" common, and each messuage-holder, large or small, was permitted no more than 30 sheep and one horse free upon it. For every score of sheep beyond this number 2s. 0d. was paid to the lord, and 1s. 0d. for every cow.

The day fixed for the tenants to put their "goods" on the common was "on or before ye 14th day of May"—old-style May Day in fact. Then in assembly the two tenants whose turn it was, took oath to serve faithfully as Frithmen, and after that began the business of swearing each tenant to put on only the stated number of beasts, while the lord's man entered in the Agist Book the surplus that were not free. The inadequate nature of the common to the needs of the holding is shown by this book, for in 1665, the year it was begun under the new squire, every messuage-holder except Thos. Hobson, paid for surplus cattle, and only two besides, Nicholson the wright and Widow Harrison, failed to put on more sheep than the allowed 30. The wealthier men, who bred cattle, were besides forced to rent closes in the demesne, of which Low Park was let (at first) for £1. 16s. 0d., Frith £1. 16s. 8d., the Allans 12s. 0d.; and New Close was also let. David Harrison, who was butcher as well as breeder, paid £1. 12s. 0d. in 1656 for beasts being grazed in the Dale Head. Thomas Fleming, inn-keeper, paid for the "summerage" of a single cow in the demesne fields 7s. 6d., and Edward Greige for one at "half gest" 3s. 9d., which looks as if even their paid-for tale of cattle on common was also restricted. The total of the extra dues on the common alone this year came to £2. 15s. 6d., and it remained at about this figure for fifteen years.

The clipping of the sheep, which St. John the Baptist's Day ushered in, brought the village into close community again. Nothing is more distinctive of the life of the past than the joint labour that was voluntarily performed by townsmen The lords' "boon-days" had, to be sure, come to be a fixed bargain, which when not wrought had to be paid for ; but the boon-day a man gave to his fellow was a free gift as a rule, though it might be returned to him in like measure. The custom of boon-shearing, when neighbours gather for a hard day's work and good and plentiful food is their only guerdon, has survived to this time, like the boon-plough to a new settler, as a relic of the ancient method of neighbours working together at a stiff task. Yet formerly it was but one of the many instances in the year's round of husbandry ; and I have been told of women no longer than 50 years ago " proffering " to do a day's work in a neighbour's hay-field, when it was a " throng " time with him. The corn cutting must have been a light matter from the small amount grown by each holder ; and women sometimes wielded the scythe, cutting high in the stalk, so that the straw was left for fodder Each stook as it stood in the field was built up of ten sheaves, which made easy reckoning for the tithe-collector.

Into the big barn then went these garnered fruits of the earth, which were to sustain life in man and beast for the year round. The great trusses, composed of as many as seven stooks sometimes, according to Mr. Browne's calculation, were fixed on to horse-back with the truss ropes (four pairs of which cost 10s. 6d in 1675), and carried to the barn. To house them there with a minimum of loss, the barn was often built with its corner rounded off, and with wide low doors. Some richer holdings had a place apart for the corn ; this was called in Troutbeck, within present memory, the " haverlaith," a word for barn which occurs in old deeds. These barns had their uses often accommodated to the inequalities of the site, as in the Black Forest, and an upper floor might be reached on the far side from the rise of the ground or a drop would give opportunity for a winding-loft, such as can be seen at Town End, Troutbeck. To dress or " deet " corn, before the winnowing machine came into use, appears to have been a simple yet ingenious task. The grain, oats or bigg, was tossed from the floor between two open doors, these openings being, where it was possible, at a good height from the ground; and the through draught thus produced separated the chaff from the grain.

When the corn was carried, the few beasts were turned into the stubble, to eat what they could find, and to give natural enrichment to the soil. The meadows, too, furnished by the "fog," or aftergrowth, the last eatage for the cattle. This was the time when fairs were held, and the statesman disposed if he could of his increase for ready money.

And at fairs too, money was expended; for though old Tusser says that buying in is properly done on St. Bartholomew's Day (August 24th), it was in these parts reserved for the back-end, when the housewife replenished her stock of utensils, and young people, if they had the cash, bought "gew-gews."

Then at Martinmas the remaining stock (perhaps a beast or two) was slaughtered and salted for the winter's household use. The pig was killed, and sausages and pork pies made a surfeit of dainties, though these were perhaps delights of later days, since wheaten flour in old times was rarely indulged in except by the gentry

After that, the sheep and a few cattle reserved for the coming year were housed, and winter closed in, when tasks that could be done under cover in barn and house were undertaken, such as threshing, carding, spinning, weaving, knitting, rushlight and soap-making.

Village Holdings.

Such was the round of husbandry for the year, which the messuage-holders of Rydal had followed time out of mind. If we look into the question of the amount of land they had to work out a livelihood from, only an approximate answer can be found. Land, as has been seen, was measured of old not by acres, but by the number of cattle it would feed; and the closes were reckoned in cattle-grasses, not extent, so that the more barren, stony ground was not over-valued. There is a fine estate map, not earlier in date, however, than 1842, which gives a complete acreage for Rydal, and from this can be extracted and summed up the fields which had belonged to the statesman in 1656. The estimates agree fairly with a Valuation Book made for taxation in 1843, though they are higher than another made between the years 1810-13, which is more likely to be correct for the older state of enclosures. We must consider therefore that the total of 119a. 2r. 36p. to which the statesman's fields in the map add up, is, if anything, too high. This total when divided by 12, for there were (excluding the smithy and the shop, which had common rights, but little land) 12 holders in 1656, gives an average of something under 10 acres each. If, however, we divide by 13, since one statesman at that time had absorbed at least another holding (Studarts), we reach an average per holding of 9a. or. 33p.

And this low average very nearly tallies with what can be made out from the township Valuation Book of 1810-13. At that time many of the holdings had fallen into the demesne, while others had been bought up piecemeal by the wealthier of the few statesmen who remained. Thomas Fleming, for instance, held 14a. 1r. 37p besides 13a. 3r. 32p. in Loughrigg; George Birkett 15a. 2r. 5p.; and Mr. North, who held the double messuage of 1656 (High House or Rydal Mount) 33a. 2r. 3p. William Park, again, held in Rydal and Loughrigg from his ancestors 20a. 1r. 31p., but from this must be deducted at least 4a 2r 3p. for the "Back of (Rydal) Water" purchased by John Park. The Nab, however, would remain one of the largest holdings of the manor in land extent.

THE ROUND OF HUSBANDRY FOR THE YEAR

But besides these, there were left, in 1813, two holdings apparently in their original state of 1656. One of these had lately been held by the Barnes family, and had once been Green's, as its old rental was 5s. 4d.—one of the lowest in the village—it may always have been one of the smaller holdings; its average is given in separate fields as 8a. 2r. 34p. The other was the Grigg tenement, paying the fair rent of 7s. 5d. It had passed down to James Backhouse, and its acreage reaches only 8a. 3r. 9p. The table of fields belonging to these two holdings is so similar, that they may be given as examples of the small tenures appertaining to Rydal.

James Backhouse (Griggs)	A	R	P	Late Barnes (Greens)	A	R.	P.
Low Close	1	0	2	Low Close	1	0	13
Nab Close	1	1	24				
Little Nab		2	36	Little Nab		3	8
Rash	1	1	22	Intake	2	2	13
House* Close	2	2	0	Rudding	1	0	25
Burn Mire	1	1	18	Gill Close	1	2	32
Garden			9	Burn Mires		3	32
Parrock		1	18	Parrock and Garden		1	31
	8	3	9		8	2	34

It will be noticed that both had portions or dales in Low Close and Little Nab. Then, in Gill Close and Horse Close Thomas Fleming had shares, and George Birket had one in Gill Close. This shows the intermingled-state of the fields, even after enclosure; and the statesmen's dales therein were doubtless marked by mear-stones, as is the case to this day at the old common field of Boothwaite in Grasmere.

The two holdings quoted come somewhat below the estimate of the 1656 average. It must be remembered, however, that the messuages were of devious size, as is

---

* (or Horse ?)

shown by the rental drawn out by the lord. The rents varied from 13s. 4d. (one mark) to 5s. 3d., or something under half a mark. This irregularity may have accrued through a long course of years by sale or exchange, and we see that "David's" at least had been divided; or the holdings may have been found by the first lord to be unequal. The earliest Grasmere rental shows great variations. But whatever the cause of irregularity, we know that there had been a Rydal holding in the sixteenth century rich enough to carry a 22s. 6d. rent. This had passed to the demesne.

If we look at the stock of cattle kept on these farmholds, we find it by necessity small. Each, beyond its couple of horses and cows, had a small flock of sheep on the common, which in 1656 varied between the minimum of 30—found only in two cases—and the 85 of David Harrison, cattle breeder. Thomas Fleming, Jane Walker, widow, and Edwin Green had 50 each; Symond Parke and John Thompson 45; Charles Wilson 60, and Edward Grigg 75.

Holdings and stocks so small as were some of these of Rydal could hardly keep the family in those thrifty times, and almost all, as we shall see, joined another occupation or craft to their husbandry.

The following rental, made out when Daniel Fleming succeeded as lord, shows the village holdings at that time. The history of each will be given in the same order:—

RYDALL.

The Tenants names.	Tenements. s d.	Generall-fines. £ s. d.
Richard Nicoldson	5 10	4 00 0
Widow Harrison	7 8	
Ed Walker, for Keine tenement	8 0	
more for Studarts	3 8	
more for Thompsons	2 6	33 0 0
more for ye Frith	2 6	
more for halfe of Davids tenemt	2 6	

RYDALL

The Tenants names	Tenements s d	Generall-fines £ s d
Simond Parke	11 6	13 00 0
Eliz Gregg	0 6	0 15 0
Jo Thompson	6 8	5 10 0
Robert Taylor	6 8	10 0 0
Edwin Green	5 4	
Tho Hobson	13 4	6 13 4
David Harrison	3 6	2 3 0
Tho Fleming	7 2	7 0 0
more for a parcel	3 4	Ibid.
Charles Wilson	5 3	4 0 0
Edward Gregg	7 5	4 10 0
Adam Fisher	1 0	0 15 0

RENTALS.

If we come to look more closely into the actual amounts, annual and periodic, paid by the statesmen of these parts to the lord of their manor, we shall find far earlier records for Loughrigg than for Rydal. This is probably due to the fact that while Loughrigg remained parcel of a great landed estate—which sometimes fell into the hands of the crown, whose officers furnished accurate written rentals—Rydal became detached in 1274 as an isolated manor, paying to a minor local lord, who either received the rentals directly through his steward, or let the rents to farm.

It has been shown how Rydal and one portion of Loughrigg, as manors, came to be parted, when the sister heiresses of the house of de Lancaster, Helwise and Alice, shared the wide lands of the Barony of Kendal between them. And the text of the charter has been given, by which Helwise's daughter Margaret granted Rydal to her kinsman Roger Her grant is recapitulated in an Inquest held on her death in 1307 (given in Mr. Farrer's *Lancashire Inquests*), when her affairs were dealt with by a body of responsible men of the district, who gave their witness as jurors, as to her estate at the time of her demise.

There exists also, a very interesting recital of the boundaries of Alice's share (called the Richmond Fee) as they stood in Dame Cristiana's time, in which the passage occurs

"And also halffe Loghrygge wth the holl Watter to the on' brigge at skelgw{th}"

But in the Inquest of 1283 concerning her estates, Loughrigg is not mentioned by name, but seems to be included in Langdale.

There are at Langeden, (it runs) 15 tenants holding 136 acres and 1 rood of land, each worth 6⁰ yearly
Six tenants there holding 28½ acres of waste and rendering nothing
Two cottagers there who ought to render 8 yearly. Now waste and rendering nothing
A certain parcel there whereof the herbage is worth 50{s} yearly
A water mill there rendering yearly 7{s}
A fishery called Routhemer worth 18d yearly
All the aforesaid tenants render yearly for Goldwethers 5{s}
Total .. £6. 11s 7½d

Again, we find in a rental of 1375 that exists at Levens Hall, Loughrigg is included in Langdale. The names are here given of 13 tenants. They furnish jointly, with forest silver and water-mills 12s. 0d., a total of £6. 10s. 0d. The bailiff or receiver is Alexander de Bulderby.

But a far more interesting rent-roll exists in the Record Office, its heading mutilated and destroyed, though apparently of the reign of Henry VI. or Edward IV. For this gives the names of the tenants of Loughrigg, apart from Langdale, as well as of Grasmere and Ambleside. Ambleside's 28 tenants include one named John de Lowerige. He joins with Wy Mylner, jun. at one holding, for which they pay 20s. 8d. yearly. Indeed, several

"HARTSHEAD" IN RYDAL.

From an Etching by W. Green, 1822.

TO FACE P. 331.

pairs of tenants join there at one messuage or holding between them ; a possible example of the old method of making two men responsible for one piece of land, in order that while one went to war, the other might till it. The 28 furnish, altogether, with 20s. 0d. for the corn-mill, and 6s. 8d. for walking-silver, £28. Again, the Grasmere tenant, John Walker de Loghrigg appears as holding one cottage for which he pays 8d. The Loughrigg roll, date about 1460, follows :—

LAUGRIGE.

	s.	d.
Wy. Mylner holds 1 cottage and renders yearly		6
Jhon Wylleson de rydall one cottage called Cokerstone		6
Jhoes Wylleson elletson one cottage		13
Thos. Jhonson terreson 1 toft		8
Adam Jhonson terreson 1 messuage with appurtenances	4	0
M'garett Cockers 1 messuage with appurtenances	2	3
Wy Makerth holds half an acre of land		6
Jhoes Smeth 1 messuage		18
Jhoes Smeth senior 1 messuage	2	6

CHAPTER III

THE FARMHOLDS

1 "*Hart Head*"; 2 "*Sadlers*"; 3 "*Keens,*" *Walker, Knott (High House), W. Wordsworth (Rydal Mount);* 4 "*The Nab,*" *Parke;* 5 "*Littlehouse,*" *see next chapter, 6 "Sandes," Neuton; 7 "Thompsons"; 8 "Banks"; 9 "Greens"; 10 "Hobsons," or "Causeway Foot"; 11 and 12 see Inns, chapter VI; 13 "Wilsons"; 14 "Griggs"; 15 "The Little Houses."*

1. HART HEAD.—This holding stands first on the rental of 1655, and is represented by the top-most house of the village. It carried a lord's rent of 5s. 10d.* and

---

* It is difficult to believe that any statesman's dwelling with land came under a valuation of 20s annually

was one of the humbler of the statesmen's dwellings, as is shown by the fact that it paid no hearth-tax. The family of Nicholsons who owned it were workers in wood, and may have exercised their craft through several generations, living by that rather than by the soil. A certain Richard, who witnessed a deed of Squire William Fleming in 1550, was no doubt the one whose burial is registered in 1627. His successor, "Dick," called himself a dish-turner, and was paid 1s. 0d. for dishes by Squire John in 1631, and £1. 4s. 0d. for work done in 1648 A Thomas of the name was a millwright, and was employed with his men on the Rydal mill from the year 1632 to the closing of the Hall. He, however, was not a village land-holder. The Richard who was in possession of Hart Head in 1655 was about the only statesman in Rydal who could write his name, and the caligraphy shown in his bills suggest the thought that he may have been one of those scholars who helped the Rev. John Bell, curate of Ambleside, to make a causeway across the Old Orchard. He was clearly a quick and clever craftsman, and two at least of his sons worked with him; yet their sad downfall will be traced in the chapter on work and wages. The long struggle of the family to keep by unremitting toil its ancient holding, was closed apparently about the year 1695, when the name of Nicholson disappears from the Agist Book. An absence of rentals for this period leaves the fate of the farmhold in doubt; but it is probable that a Francis Walker, who did boon-mowing for the lord by deputy in 1710 and 1720, was the holder, and the husband of the widow, Jennet Walker, who in the rental of 1724 to 1734 heads the list with the old sum of 5s. 10d., together with 1s. 8d. for a pasture. But in 1735 the well-to-do John Park, of the Nab, bought it, and farmed it with the rest of his growing estate. His death in 1748 severed it again, for while his older lands went to his eldest son John, he willed Hart Head and a piece of Hobsons to George, his son by a second wife. But not until 1759, when the widow Mary died, did George receive his inheritance, paying unto the Rydal court a fine of £5. 16s. 8d. for it. His interests, however, were elsewhere, for he pursued the sadler's trade in Hawkshead, and in 1769 he disposed of his Rydal property, when it was split up; John Bateman, a newcomer, taking the house and part of the land, and George Birkett, —one of the village family who had prospered by woodcraft when the Nicholsons had failed—the rest. John Bateman, of Town Head, Grasmere, was content to forego his half to Birkett in 1783, for the sum of £38. 10s. 0d. Henceforth it remained with the Birketts, who apparently made it their home in preference to Sadlers, the house next below, or to Hobsons (see house No. 10). George died in 1822, at the age of 84, after playing a prominent part in the village life as a shrewd well-to-do statesman His son John, from whom the manor extracted fines to the amount of £25. 5s. 6d., was a city dweller, and let his Rydal property, until he sold it to the Hall in 1840 for the sum of £850. His special mention of a cupboard and chest made by his grandfather, shows that there were some oak fittings of value in the homestead. Ninety sheep were running on the common at this date, which were known as Scar, Hart Head or Birkett sheep, and this old stock remained till the last tenant went out, and he carried them away upon some dispute, as was his right if he paid a certain price The house was rebuilt for an incoming tenant, whose daughter remembers it as a little old place. In this condition, it is figured in "Green's 40 Etchings of Old Buildings," published 1822.

2. SADLERS.—Of the family who gave their name to this holding nothing is known, unless "Sadler," who paid 5s. to Squire John for an ash tree in Hall-bank (1631), and the "Sadler-wife," who bought decayed wood in 1645 to the extent of 14s., and received 3s. 10d. for a

calf in 1657, belonged to them. It is possible, of course, that sadler was the trade, and not the family name. It was Widow Elinor Harrison who held the place when Squire Daniel came, and she paid a rent of 7s. 5d. She was taxed on one hearth not declared, but added on survey in 1665, which looks as if the farmhold were superior in the comfort of its down-house fire, as well as in size, to the one above it. It is difficult to disentangle the Harrisons, of whom there was a flourishing branch lower down the village ; but Elinor was seemingly the relict of the Anthony who figures in the register as a father in 1619, acted as supervisor of his neighbour Walker's will in 1643, and was buried in 1645, at which time she paid to the manor £1 10s 0d. as a heriot. Probably a son William or " Willing " was associated with her on the farm ; he put his mare to graze on the demesne for a fortnight (1s. 6d.) in 1658, and in the search for arms in 1660, he had to give up a rapier, which he may have used on the Parliamentary side. The widow served with her neighbour, Richard Nicoldson, as overseer for the poor of the township in 1667, but two years later death closed the career as stateswoman she had so long enjoyed. An Anthony followed her ; three neighbours being bound over for his fines up to the inexplicably high sum of £16. 19s. 2d., while an Edward signed another bond. Anthony was possibly an absentee, or died soon after, for in 1672, Isabel Harrison, widow, with George Otley, the smith (and one of the guarantors), paid up £1. 10s. 6d ; while the latter shortly after paid 19s. 2d. " for consideration of Anthony Harrison's fines." It is he also who paid a rent in 1678 of 7s. 8d., the amount of " Sadlers."

An Anthony Harrison, who came into prominence as a yeoman about 1690, probably belonged to David's branch lower down the village The " Sadler " branch becomes obscure, but a Widow Harrison paid its 7s. 8d. rent till 1729 ; she being probably the Dorothy who took the oath at a special Quarter Sessions in 1723. But in 1730 a certain Margaret Atkinson's name occupies the second place on the rent-sheet, paying that rent, which Thomas continues in 1749, for " Harrison's Tenement." He was a butcher of Kirkby Lonsdale, and in 1750 he sold the place for £40 to John Birket, of Rydal, when it was described as " Sadlers, once belonging to Edward Harrison." John, who was the second village carpenter of the name, was followed by George the farmer, whose son John sold it along with Hart Head and his other property.

The homestead, let off as a cottage from 1750, clearly sank into a derelict place. It stood just below Hart Head, to which its garden is attached yet ; and, according to tradition, it fronted Nab Lane, a barn or outhouse (later a stick-house) abutting on the lane. It is remembered as a one-storied house , and could it have been left we should probably have found in it an example of the primitive dwelling. John Backhouse, who died at Ambleside in March, 1909, *æt.* 90, remembered old James, elder brother of Fleming Backhouse, the last of the Rydal professional fiddlers, living there about 1830. It was James' habit to make a round of the village houses and Hall at about two or three o'clock of a Christmas morning, to wish the inmates a merry season, and play them a little tune—a forced merriment for himself, certainly, in the cold and darkness of a winter's night. After this foretaste, he would return in the afternoon to play again, when the house-wife would give him 2d. or 3d. Also about Christmas he held " a merry night," when folk would come even from Ambleside to dance. The Christmas Day round was indeed the custom of the vales. A charming description of the Grasmere fiddler's visit to the Dove Cottage kitchen in 1805 is to be found in a letter of Dorothy Wordsworth, though it was only the children who danced there, their wooden shoes pattering on the stone floor with a joyous sound that penetrated to the parlour.*

An old man named Mason followed the fiddler as tenant of "Sadlers," and then the place was pulled down, probably to build the barn at the improved Hart Head.

3. KEEN'S; HIGH HOUSE OF THE KNOTTS, RYDAL MOUNT.—The family that gave its name to this holding had vanished before record began, except that on the first faded page of the church register the death of one child of John Kene, of Rydal, and the baptism of another (Jenet) are inscribed for 1574 and 1575. The rent of the place was no more than 8s., but it was its fate to be held by wealthy and prominent families, and it emerged as one of the most substantial houses of the village, eventually becoming famous as the residence of the poet Wordsworth. A family of Walkers owned it from the seventeenth century, and their first traces are found in the registers, an Edward marrying Mabell Jackson in 1572. Edward was clearly a notable as well as a well-to-do man; he was had up to the Hall to witness deeds in 1613 and 1617; and he lent Jackson, of Baise-browne, £2. 2s. 11d. in 1619. He doubtless had made the position in which his successor was found, renting the village corn-mill from the lord after Grigg's time, and acquiring lands beyond his own, viz., "Studarts," a toftstead rented at 3s 8d. (which may be the little two-storied place that stands below Rydal Mount and is used by it as a tool-house), "Thompsons," rent 2s. 6d., and therefore probably only land bought from Thompson, a statesman whose homestead stood next again below; the Frith, a large field on the slope of the Nab, rent 2s. 6d.; and half of "Davids," rent 2s. 6d, which again must have been land once belonging to the David Harrisons, who lived at the foot of the hill. The second traceable Edward

---

* See Wordsworth's dedication of Excursion for mid-night fiddling at Grasmere.

Walker married Isabell Thompson in 1620, and Alice Richardson in 1630. His position had apparently become unsound by 1629, when—and again two years later—he repaid Squire John £20, described as part of a debt. Edward's payment of interest on a loan, also figures in Tyson's accounts as £2. It is significant that the squire, in signing the acknowledgment of the first, does not express the amount of the " more sum," yet owing to him. Walker's reckoning with his lord is as follows for 1632 : he pays £26 " on his bill " (making a repayment of £66 in three years, besides interest) ; 13s. 4d. for the cow-grass, £5 for mill-rent, £2 for Nab (not explained), and £4 " in part of his mortgage " ; total £38 ! Edward, in spite of growing difficulties, remained on terms with his superior, bought cattle for him at distant markets, furnished the Hall with "bigg malt," and in 1632 collected the tithes of the three Cumberland churches, receiving 3s. for his expenses. The next evidence shows " old Edward Walker " in July, 1642, borrowing £5 from Squire John's executors, upon his and his son's bill, due at Martinmas of the following year. But before that date old Edward had left money-entanglements behind him. He was buried on August 6th, having followed his wife to the grave on the preceding June 18th. His inventory was written on a strip of parchment, as the custom was, at the direction of the three neighbours he had appointed as " supervisors." It ignores his chief difficulties, makes out his assets as £59. 13s. 5d., and his debts, with funeral expenses, £9. The list of his possessions gives insight into the goods and chattels of a Rydal homestead.

As in all probate valuations, the animals are put at a very low figure : sheep only 4s. a head and cattle 30s.

1643   The Inventory of all the goods and chattels of Edward Walker of Ridal prysed by Thomas Richard * for Thomas

---

* Another copy of this inventory gives Richardson

Fleming, Anthony Harrison, and Edward Gregge the first of August, 1643.

	li	s	d
Imprimis his apparrell	2.	0.	0
Item brasse, pewther, and pans	6	18	0
Item 3 kine and a heffer	6.	0	0
Item one old Mare	1.	13.	4
Item 40 Shepe	8.	0.	0
Item ix Stones of Woll	2	5.	0

The moneys oweinge unto him.

	li	s	d
Imprimis, by William Jackson * and his mother	2.	19.	6
Item by John Knotts	4.	0.	0
Item by John Ottley and his son	3.	12.	10
Item by Regnald Wilson	7.	0.	0
Item by Thomas Richardson	2	6.	0
Item by Michaell Watson	0.	14	0
Item by Thomas Benson	15	0	0
Item by Charles Wilson	3.	4.	9

Debts which he ought at the tyme of his decease

	li	s	d
To Thomas Grave	7.	0	0
Funeral Expenses	2	0.	0

The younger Edward took up the burden, marrying Jennett Forrest in November after his succession to the estate, and in December paying £4 interest on a mortgage of his tenement. What fines were fixed for him does not show; but in 1647, the year he served as Constable for the township, he paid £20 on his mortgage. Failing men rarely attain old age. He died in 1652, his inventory showing £57. 1s. 8d. assets, and £34. 7s. 9d. debts. Strangely enough, though buried at Grasmere, his executors paid a mortuary fee to the vicar of Kendal of 5s.

RYDAL HALL MSS   *Rydal Statesmen*

(On a strip of parchment)

1652 The Inventorys of all the goods & chattels of Edward Walker of Rydall, Prysed by Daniel Harrison, John Parke, John Hunter, & William Makereth, the 16th of December, 1652

---

* "of Loughrigg"

	li.	s.	ffe.
Impr His Apparrell	1	10.	0
Itm Horned Chattell	11.	0.	0
Itm 65 Sheepe	14.	0	0
Itm A horse & a mare	2	0	0
Itm Haye & Corne	10	0	0
Itm Brasse, Pewter, & pannes	1	7.	0
Itm Flesh, meal & mallt	0	12.	0
Itm Chests, Arkes & a Cupboarde	1.	0.	0
Itm Bedding & bedstockes	1.	0.	0
Itm Iron implements	1.	5	0
Itm Wooden Vessell, wheeles, Cardes, Chaires & stooles	1.	0	0
Itm 3 stone of wooll	1.	4.	0
Itm Roapes	0.	4.	0
Itm Sackes & Peakes	0	4	0
Itm Plow, plow-geare & other things belonging horse	0.	14.	0
Itm Poultry	0	1.	8
Itm Money oweing to him	10.	0.	0
	li	s	d
Summa totl	57.	1	8

Money wch he did owe at his death.

	li	s	d
To Ellis Walker	30	10	0
To Daniel Harrison	0.	11.	7
To Richard O'senhouse	0.	12.	0
To Mabell Robinson	0.	2.	6
To John Brathwhaite	0.	17.	8
To Elizabeth Knotts	0.	2.	0
To Adam Fisher	0	1.	0
To John Makereth	0	1.	0
Funerall expenses	1.	10.	0
	li	s	d
Summa tot.	34.	7.	9

Widow Walker is in 1654 found paying an aggregate rent on the property of 19s. 2d.; but when Squire Daniel made out the tenant's fines in the following year he set down the name of Edward as tenant, and fixed the fine at £33—an enormous sum, being over 30 times the rental. But it is Widow Jane who continues to pay taxes and puts cattle on common. With more land, the Walkers had more live stock than their smaller neighbours.

Edward's flock of 65 had, however, diminished to 50: while 2 "key," 3 "thurntors," and 1 "duntor" paid on the common.

In 1662 a certain William Walker appears as representative of the family, willing to take up the burden of the encumbered farmhold. An entry in the Account Book runs :

"Feb. 10, 1662. This day, Will. Walker, of Rydall, agreed with mee at Ambleside (for his Generall fine, and fine due upon ye death of his Grandfather, for all his Lands in Rydall of ye yearly Rent of 19s. 02d , and for ye confirmation of a Close called Thompson-frith, paying ye same like other Tenants) to pay unto mee upon ye three next Candlemas-dayes (by equall portions) ye sum of 33li. 00s. 00d. (vid Deed).

But "Willing," flourishing as was his start, soon proved unequal to this call for ready money. Only £23 was paid by 1665, when the prudent Squire bound over his father-in-law for the rest, which was paid by him two years later. Now this father-in-law was John Fleming, " of ye New feild," whom Daniel shows in his pedigree to have been a distant cousin of his own. The marriage therefore must have given "Willing" distinction, though at his wife's " upsitting " the usual 2s. 6d. was sent from the Hall. The Squire made him bailiff, in the place of old Edwin Green, who for so long had been the Rydal rent-collector—an office that by ancient law could be held only by a statesman. He used him for business too, employed him at the cattle fairs, and bought provisions, meat and game and grain from him. But it is a question whether there was much profit in these things, except for a cute man ; and as early as 1666 William went up to the Hall to borrow £5 till Candlemas. The next year finds him only able to renew his bond, and in the following he borrows £7 more. And so the depressing tale goes on. By 1671 he had accumulated a debt of £41. 15s. 9d., for

which he gave the squire a mortgage on "Studarts."
Presently the Rydal rents were not forthcoming, and his
neighbours, Richard Nicoldson, and his son (struggling
themselves with debt) had to stand surety for the deficit.
Other neighbour's aid was invoked, perhaps on the refusal
of the squire to lend more, and the latter exacted a tax
of 15s. for his consent to William borrowing from David
Harrison on a further mortgage. Matters by the next
year had grown acute. John Banks also lent money
on a deed, for which the squire extracted another 15s.
"forthwith" from the unfortunate William, who now
—owing £53 to his superior—handed over to him a deed
of his whole estate. What more hope for William?
In the January of 1679 his wife Jane was buried. No
wonder we hear of arrears "when Walker went away"
a ruined man, leaving neighbours (David Harrison and
Robert Barnes) to pay the 19s 2d. rent on "Walker land"
until a sale or settlement could be made up among the
creditors. Another Walker indeed sprang up, a George,
styled yeoman, who from 1690 to the century end figures
as a Rydal statesman, but in the absence of a rental for
the period it is not certain what lands he had. He paid
a land tax of 6s., and borrowed £2 in two years from the
lord. When next particulars occur, the Knotts are found
in possession of the Walker patrimony.

The Knotts, who followed the Walkers in Rydal,
present the cheerful (and unusual) spectacle of a rural
family who rose by steady steps to wealth. To be sure,
if their record be examined, it will be seen that in this,
as in others, their advance to riches and gentility was
not made by husbandry alone, but by trade, by office,
or by commerce. Thus it was that while statesmen as
a class were gradually sinking by husbandry, the Knotts
rose steadily, till they left that class behind them. The
steps of their progress were slow, but sure ; and the
ability of the race may be guaged by the fact that hardly

a document has survived connected with the township of Grasmere or its welfare but contains their name.

Records begin in a rental of the Hotham (later Marquis) Fee for the year 1375, when Henry " del Knot " stands as possessed of one tenement in Grasmere. It is quite likely, too, that the Michael " de Knot," who in 1347 served as juryman at the Inquisition held at Kirkby Lonsdale upon the lands of the De Couceys, may have represented there his township. This early form of the family name suggests a derivation from the Celtic " Cnoc," probably referring to the hillock or knoll on which their farmhold stood. There is still a farm called Knott-houses in the portion of Grasmere known as Aboon Beck, which —like Knott Place, Broaderaine, and Greenhead—was once theirs. For by the days of Elizabeth the clan had not only increased in numbers, but had multiplied their holdings. An Edward of the name was at that period a prominent townsman. With some others he carried out in 1564 an extensive deal in timber, purchasing from Squire William Fleming the wood of Watley Hagg in Rydal Head, which they undertook to fell and clear under a penalty of £40. As there was practically no export trade in timber at that time, this may mean that Grasmere was then *coaling wood, i.e.,* making charcoal, and smelting iron for its own use, probably by arrangement with the lord. A cinder heap, indicating the site of an old bloom-smithy, can be traced in the wood above Winterseeds, upon the beck. Again in 1584, when the Crown had let off the rents of the Richmond Fee to Squire Thomas Strickland of Sizergh, Edward headed the tenants, who made a covenant with the latter, that he should exact no more than the customary rents and fines. In 1598 also, when the Grasmere men agitated for a market of their own, and guaranteed the expenses connected with the same to the son of the Squire of Rydal, Edward " Knottes " was the first after the parson to inscribe his name on the document.

It is clear then, that Edward was the foremost of the numerous Knotts of the valley, one branch of whom, according to the register, spelt its name Knoth. But he was dead by 1603, when we have interesting evidence of the possessions of the family in a Court Roll preserved at the Record Office. At a court held in that year at the Moot Hall in Kendal, John Knott appears as heir of Edward to lands in the Marquis Fee. The rolls run :—

From John Knott for his fine and entry into a tenement there (Grysmyer) at a yearly rent of 2s 6d and one third of a penny, late in the tenure of Edward Knott his father, at the rate of two annual rents (for this time only) because he paid to the Receiver of the lord the King aforesaid at the general survey the fine for the said father thereupon, at the rate of three yearly rents which he ought to pay, for him only at the rate of two yearly rents, because he was an ancient tenant   5s 0d.

For the same John Knott for his fine and entry into another tenement there of his said father, at the yearly rent of 4s 5d (at the rate aforesaid)   8s. 10d.

From the same John Knott, for another tenement (as above) yearly rent 2d   4d.

At a court held for the Marquis Fee in the following year, John Knott paid the usual green-hew penny (vert in technical language) for each of these his three tenements; while a Roland, a Roger, and the widow of a Michael—all Knotts—paid theirs likewise. Further, at a court held on the same day for the Richmond Fee, three separate pennies were paid under the name of Michael, and another under that of Robert ; which makes in all ten landparcels, if not ten full messuages, held by the clan. Robert of the Richmond Fee would seem to have been a man of violence ; for he was presented before that court for having made an assault " called A hubleshow " * on his kinsman Michael, for which he was fined 10s.—a large sum in those days ; while for the like offence upon

---

* Hubleshow or Hubbeshow from Hubbub—orig Whoop hoop—a confused noise or tumult —Ed

William Hawkrigg, the Marquis Court fined him 5s. Michael was unfortunate, for he had suffered besides from "a scandal" put upon him by one Elizabeth Hirde; but the jury let her off without a fine.

The Marquis Fee branch of the family, now represented by John, was still the principal one. It was earning wealth by shop or store keeping. Each township had one general store, at which the inhabitants could supply those few wants not furnished by the soil and the stock of cattle. As the keeper of the store was taxed upon his stock, we may sometimes discover, from stray subsidy roll, who he was. One such roll for the year 1625, fortunately preserved at Rydal Hall, enters John "Knotts" as paying 10s. 8d. on goods valued at £4; while another roll for 1641 enters the like name (doubtless son of the former) for the same tax on goods, besides another tax of £1 1s. 4d. upon land rated at £13 6s 8d., this being the only subsidy money taken in these years from Grasmere. Such possessions in goods and land meant affluence. The burial of John Knott "of Knott place in Grissmire" is recorded for 1638. The word place signifies something superior to the usual dwelling of the statesman, and in this era of their prosperity the Knotts appear to have built a dignified residence. A tradition of this, and of the "gentleman" who built a dignified residence. A tradition of this, and of the "gentleman" who built it remained, and was used by Wordsworth with poetic licence in his Excursion, Book 7; and he expressly says in a note that "the pillars of the gateway in front of the mansion remained when we first took up our abode at Grasmere." John Knott's name often appears in the register during the early years of the seventeenth century as the father of children baptised or buried; and four years after his own burial comes that of (apparently) his son, dignified by the title Mister. An Edward next followed (one of this name was elder of the reformed church in 1645) at Knott Place, and he had a son Robert baptised in 1652; while another Edward " of Broade Raine " was buried in 1658. A Marquis Fee rental for 1675 records only a John paying 6s. 11d. for what may have been Knott Place. The race was clearly diminishing, and this branch of the family may have died out altogether. When next we come upon traces of Knott Place, it had clearly been sold, and like many other of the larger houses of the district, cleared away. The lands belonging to it were divided, and in 1712 part of them were in the hands of the wealthy Richard Cumpstone of Ambleside.

The Knotts of the Richmond Fee were likewise thinning, and the same rental for 1675 shows only a John paying 1s. 10d. and a Michael 6s 4d. But with Michael (doubtless son of Edward of Broad-Raine) the family entered into a new era of prosperity, and we have evidence that he was able to leave to his sons four tenements situated at Grasmere. These sons were Edward, born 1665, who inherited three tenements, and John, who took the remaining one, born 1667. Michael's children were likewise enriched by his wife, who was Jane, daughter of Thomas Atkinson, of Howe, in Applethwaite. This wealthy statesman dying in 1680, made Michael's second son John his heir to the Howe estate, provided that he paid on inheritance £30 from it to his three sisters. The eldest grandson, Edward (well provided for), got only a bequest of £5, while Mrs. Knott and her sister shared the residuary estate. John, who resided at the Howe, had much intercourse with the Brownes, of Town End, and Benjamin Browne stood godfather in 1728 to his child Dorothy. She was probably the Mrs. Dorothy Knott, who, living to a ripe old age of spinsterhood, paid for the recasting of the third bell of Grasmere Church in 1808, and who left at her death in 1812, £100 to the school.

But it is with the eldest son's line that we have to do.

When next evidence is forthcoming, Edward (his father Michael being dead) is found to have migrated to Rydal, where he was acting, apparently, as agent for the Rydal Manor; for he gave evidence in 1713, when he was 48 years old, in a law-suit, as to what papers he had found in Sir Daniel Fleming's closet at the time of the latter's death in 1701. He had established himself in " Keens " —soon to be called "High House"; and improvements were speedily made in the farmhold of the Walkers, as is shown by a locker still left in the parlour of Rydal Mount which is carved with the date 1710, and the letters E.A.K., while the tax-paper of 1726 shows that there were nine windows in the house. Not only " Keens," but the whole of the Walker property (rent 19s. 2d.), was in the hands of the Knotts, but the odd thing was that it stood in the name of Agnes. Edward, as agent for Sir William, made out the papers of the boon mowers which exist for 1710 and 1720 and in these she is down as working by deputy in the hay four days—which represented the number of her holdings; and she figures as tenant till the rentals cease in 1734.

Edward, the agent, died in 1734, he being styled in the register " yeoman " His son Michael, indeed, was the dominant spirit in Rydal for some thirty years. He acted on behalf of the son of Major Michael Fleming (sixth son of Sir Daniel) as early as 1723, when there could have been no thought that this boy William, with uncles and cousins in plenty between him and the succession, would eventually come into estate and title. The boy was boarded with Mr. Benjamin Browne, of Troutbeck, and he and his sister attended the latter's funeral in 1728. The sister is called Susan in the pedigree, but both the Grasmere tablet and the Hawkshead register give her name as Susannah. Michael, who, we know from another source, had an eye to a lady's fortune as well as face, married Susannah about 1739. The marriage can hardly be said to have been beyond his station. Susannah's mother was a Dorothy Benson, possibly of Coat How, and if so, a freeholder's daughter. On the other hand, Michael's sister married John Park, a yeoman of Rydal, which shows how near the statesman was to the smaller gentry. Michael's settlements were good for a probably penniless girl. He agreed to settle on her his estate of three tenements in Rydal. Should she survive him childless, his trustees (among them Mr. Archdeacon Fleming, and her brother), were to pay her a dower of £200 a year—quite a large sum in those days for a Westmorland widow.

It is clear that Michael was becoming a considerable person, with ventures beyond land and agency; though the Rydal business papers were still written in the fine Knott script. The "coaling" of woodland, or making of charcoal, for use in the iron furnaces of Furness, was becoming a lucrative business, and Michael Knott—though only a customary landholder, obtained permission apparently to fire the woods on his Rydal estate. He was doubtless doing well for the squire by his management of the demesne woods, but it was more likely the connection by marriage (possibly aided by a rent) that gained him this unusual concession When William Scott, owner of Bainrigg, complained so bitterly in 1759 of the unjust stripping of his timber for the uses of other tenants he mentioned that Mr. Knott had a few years previously cut down over 60 trees there for the building of his own house and even of a coaling-house, in order to save his own woods for the actual charcoal. This high-handed proceeding on the steward's part shows that High House, though not entirely rebuilt, received some substantial additions in Michael's time. Doubtless a new front was erected at right angles to the old, which remained practically unaltered to the poet's time, and the ancient toftstead was fitted to the larger fortunes of a man whose brother-in-law had come to the Hall as squire in 1747, and who had safely passed the border line between yeoman and gentleman. In 1770, " Mr. Knott, of Rydal," figured among the gentry who sent Livery Men to the Carlisle Assizes, as did his heir, " George Knott of the same " For Michael's eldest son, Edward, had died in 1766 at the age of 25, and a newly-purchased tenement in Rydal—" Banks," which his father settled upon him, passed then to George. The Mother died next year, and Michael in 1772, at the age of 76. George soon afterwards made application to the lord of the manor that the enfranchisement allowed to his father by Sir William might be confirmed, and " Banks " be added to the tenements enfranchised. But the position was now changed; apparently Mr. Knott had given up acting for the Hall in 1756 when Sir William died · and his younger son Sir Michael, had been brought up under the guardianship of Sir John Lowther, educated at Eton, and nourished upon lordly ideas. To free any of the lands of Rydal was outside the policy of his advisers, of whom Thomas Harrison, the steward, was one.

George Knott never made his home in Rydal Following his father's lead, he appears to have been concerned in the iron works and export trade of iron from Furness. His marriage, too, increased his land, and carried him over the county border into Lake Lancashire. It is, interesting to trace this second migration of the family of an agent and relative of the le Flemings to the estate of Waterhead, Coniston. For we have seen that Richard Harrison, nephew of Squire John Fleming, had become possessed of the property at the close of the Civil Wars; and that Squire Daniel had made peace with his old enemy, or at least with his enemy's son, and had visited there. This second Richard had left a daughter Catherine, who married William Forde, of Ulverston; and it was their daughter Catherine who married young George Knott, and carried to him Waterhead. Perhaps it was George who rebuilt the house, which was figured in all its glory of " modern Gothic " in the *Lonsdale Magazine* of 1822.

George's life was short. He died at the age of 40, in 1784, and his young wife followed him next year. His son Michael was a minor, and trustees managed his estates. Possibly an aunt or aunts kept the house

It was reported in 1781 that Mr. George Knott had let his Rydal house to his sister, and was to make great alterations and improvements in it, which necessitated trees being cut down, eight from his own wood and two from Parke's being allotted by Sir Michael's bailiff. However, the tenant who in two years' time took the house, was a Mr. Doulby, from Ipswich, probably one of the new race of scenery lovers, and he remained there till his death in 1798, when his widow removed. Colonel Thornton in his *Sporting Tour* (edited by Sir Herbert Maxwell), taken probably in 1786, gives us a glimpse into the Waterhead establishment shortly after the death of George Knott. With a party from Rydal Hall, he had ridden over to Ponsonby, and on returning, after the passage of the Duddon Sands, when twilight was falling (October 30th), they paused at Coniston, and " Drank tea at Mrs. Knott's." He goes on to say, " These ladies, who have also a seat in the Highlands, praised Scotland above the Lakes," in which the traveller, who had just returned thence, agreed. Then, after more fashionable and artificial discourse, the gentlemen returned to Rydal by moonlight, mid sounds of waterfalls, leaving Miss Fleming, sister of Sir Michael, to remain for the night. It may be mentioned that the Knotts finally migrated to Scotland. The death of Eliza Alice, last surviving child of Michael, at the age of 77, is announced in the *Westmorland Gazette* as having taken place at Essex Park, Dumfries, on the 14th of March, 1895.

George Knott's son, Michael, apparently came of age in 1797, when his father's executors conveyed to him the Rydal property, consisting of Keen's, rent 8s. 6d., Stoddarts' 3s. 8d., Thompson's 2s. 6d., half of David's 2s. 6d., Frith 2s. 6d., besides Banks' 6s. 8d., garden 6d., old house and orchard 6d.; total £1. 6s. 10d. In 1803, Michael paid an unexplained sum of £25. 16s. 0d. as fine; and he wrote to Sir Michael Fleming from Penny Bridge that, having bought an estate in that neighbourhood, he was wishful to sell his Rydal one, and explained that Mr. Ford-North, of Liverpool, had offered £2,500 for it and for the rough pasture near Clappersgate; the sheep were to be taken at a valuation. He gives Sir Michael the first chance of purchase. But at such a price the lord of the manor had no wish to buy, and the estate passed to the Liverpool man, while the late possessor is reported in 1807 to have left without paying his general fine. From Rydal Mount, John Ford-North had children baptised in 1805, 1807 and 1810, but from the first he found himself entangled in jealous contentions, and in 1812, after a bootless attempt to obtain an enfranchisement of the property and after a fierce fight over green-hew law, he was glad to sell it to the lord of the manor, and departed to the estate of the Oaks, Ambleside, which he had bought. For a time Rydal Mount must have been in the hands of William Moore, as he paid rent in 1819 on all the old items, except the garden and old house, £1. 5s. 10d.

In 1813 the poet Wordsworth entered into a tenancy of the house, and he remained there till his death in 1850. A letter of his concerning repairs, addressed to Lady Fleming, may be given here, as it shows how frequently the old dwellings required renovation.

His. MSS. Com., Rep. 12 (5698).

Knowing your Ladyship to be indisposed, I am sorry to trouble you with this letter, but as your tenant I should not feel myself justified on the present occasion were I to omit stating to your Ladyship the nature of the repairs necessary at Rydal Mount, which have been from time to time delayed, and, as we are now informed, are not to be done at all

The back apartments of the house ever since we entered it, have not been habitable in winter on account of the damp, and in wet seasons not even in summer   Lord Suffolk's agent some years ago, from the state of the timber, gave an opinion that a new roof was necessary, and estimated the expense at £10. Since that time temporary repairs have been made, which were to have been completed at the first convenient season Those repairs never made the house watertight , and to give your Ladyship an idea of its state, I need only say that, during the last heavy rains, an empty trunk standing in the best of the three rooms, was half filled with water.

Last summer, the late Mr. Jackson and the workmen examined with me the premises, and it was our joint opinion that when the rooms were unroofed, if the walls were raised, it would be an advantage to the house very far beyond the additional expense, and one which we had little doubt would be approved of by your Ladyship. Lord Suffolk's agent was consulted , and, as I understood, the plan was not, in the end, opposed by your Ladyship On my part I was to pay interest upon the sum laid out, and on this supposition my family prepared for the workmen. To my surprise it was afterwards required that I should relinquish the barn, and other out-buildings, or the work in the dwelling was not to be done This, not only on account of the comfort and convenience to myself and family, but from respect to your Ladyship's property, I could not consent to, the character of the place would be entirely changed and vulgarized, were these premises turned into a common farmyard This we have proved by experience, for upon our first coming to R(ydal) M(ount) as a temporary accommodation, the farmer had the use of some buildings, and the annoyance of cattle hanging about the gates causing filth and intercepting the way upon the public road to the house may easily be conceived To palliate this (and various other inconveniences) Mr J(ackson) proposed that the yard should be divided by a wall, and a gate broken out below, but this, without removing the evil from us, would only have thrown it nearer the gates of the Hall, and probably have occasioned the felling of trees, and exposed the fold yard to the road Besides, a part of the barn we could not possibly do without, and an apprehension of that very evil—fire—which has already taken place in our neighbour's premises—from the ingress and egress of a large family, many of them children, over whom I should have no control, was of itself sufficient to prevent my acceding to such an arrangement.

I have nothing to add to this long, but necessary statement, except to remind your Ladyship that the rooms under consideration only in one part allow a person to stand upright, and that it remains to be considered whether it may not be better to raise the walls according to the plan proposed, or merely to make them water-tight, which can only be done by means of a new roof. For notwithstanding what I have heard, I cannot conceive that it is your Ladyship's intention that it should remain in its present state, especially after the long inconvenience we have suffered.

The alterations suggested were ultimately carried out, with others. A bedroom was added to the back, over passages and low spaces that may have been dairies, and this was done apparently between the date of Green's sketch of 1821 and Dora Wordsworth's sketch of 1826. The poet's bedroom is said to have been added later.* The old entrance was made up on the south side, and the new one opened. The old "house," happily, remains as a parlour; while the kitchen (once possibly downhouse) has had its floor lowered to procure height. So by gradual stages "Keens" has become the present Rydal Mount. Wordsworth paid for it in 1822, £35, quite a large rent in those times.

4. THE NAB.—With this number on the list of 1655 we come to one of the most interesting as well as picturesque of the Rydal homesteads. It stands apart, at the foot of the steep scar from which it is named, looking across the waters of the mere to the fine, rough slope of Loughrigg. Externally it is but little altered from the time when it was rebuilt by John Parke in 1702, and it is a fair example of the dwelling of the prosperous statesman of that period.

The family of Parke owned the Nab when record begins; and the origin of their name is as clear at that of the Knotts. In an existing Subsidy Roll for 1332 the

---
* In 1829,—ED

possessions of one "Ede de le parke" are valued at 15s. The three townships contained within the parish of Grasmere are not separated in the roll so that we cannot tell where this Edward's holding exactly lay, but it appears likely that he or his forbears were connected with the lords enclosure for deer. In 1583 a Henrie of the name, " of Rydall," was buried, two years earlier a William had a son John baptized, and it was doubtless he who witnessed a document for Squire William in 1589. From 1612 to 1614, three Parkes of Rydal (John, Leonard, and William) all had children baptized; but John, who lost a daughter from smallpox in 1636, must have been the head of the clan, for in 1642 he stood surety for £5, which his neighbour Charles Wilson had borrowed from the executors of Squire John. William died in 1639, and from him or Leonard may have descended the artizan Parkes of the village, amongst whom were a " George Parke sonne " with horse on common in 1665, another George, a flourishing weaver at the end of that century; and a third George, a tailor, in the next. John the landholder appears to have died in 1653, having married for his second wife Jennett Walker. His son Simond or Symond, was much in favour with the race of German or " Dutch " miners, who settled in Keswick and Coniston in Elizabeth's reign, spreading thence over the district, and it suggests an intermarriage with them by one of the Parkes. Simond married at once on succeeding to the estate, and his son John was born in 1656, when the usual offering at the christening was sent down from the Hall.

By this time the new squire had arrived in Rydal, and the tenants were faced by the trying necessity of compounding with him for the General Fine exacted on his entrance to the manor. The young owner of the Nab had moreover to pay an additional fine called an alienation one, which was due from him on the death of his father.

and which had not been collected. Accordingly he set his special mark to an agreement, in which he undertook to pay £13 by equal portions in the February and September of the year following, the amount of his rent being 11s. 6d. But this he was by no means able to do, and it took a little over two years to finish the payment.

Meanwhile, he had other difficulties to face. The sharp pull-up of the reins of manorial rule, followed by that of church rule at the Restoration, produced friction. In 1658 he was formally charged, along with his neighbours, David Harrison and Thomas Fleming, with felling wood unlawfully on the manor, and was fined 10s.; 2s., however, being returned to him by favour. It is clear that money was short with him, for in the following February he was forced to borrow 13s., from the squire, "wh. hee promiseth to repay about 3 weekes hence," and he was as good as his word. His accounts must have been complicated, for this year he took his turn as constable, and the various "sesses" paid to him for the desmesne are all put down. Next came reprisals from monarchy and church. In 1660, the search for arms made on all suspected Parliamentarians deprived him of sword and belt; and—far more serious—he was cited in a Bill of Exchequer, with a goodly number of parishioners, as a defaulter in the payment of church tithes during the Commonwealth. As arrears were demanded, the amount required of him must have summed up to a large total. But to fight this battle there were bigger men than he, amongst them Mr. Robert Braithwaite, of Baisbrowne; and moreover Simond left all disputes behind him in January, 1662, when the register records his burial at the early age of thirty-three. He left behind a widow and three baby sons (a fourth had died), the youngest being only six months old. Margaret Parke had thus suddenly to face calamity and need. There was apparently no money in the house, and the funeral must take place the day following, as was the custom. She hurried up to the Hall, to borrow 16s. " to bury her husband." Then came the sale of the household effects, quite usual on the death of the head of the family; but which left the home empty except of " barnes," since she had no coin with which to buy things back. The sale enabled her, however, to wipe out debts. On February 5th she paid back to the squire—who had purchased a candlestick and chafing dish at the sale—the money she owed him. The stock probably was also sold; for, whereas in 1655 the cattle running on the common were three " key," two " twinters,' one horse and forty-five sheep, there were none to pay for, nor does her name appear again in the Agist Book until 1673 She had also to find £3. 10s. for a heriot, two of her neighbours pledging themselves for her, and this she succeeding in doing in the next year.

Now followed years of bitter struggle. Of her industry through them, while her boys grew up, we obtain a glimpse through the Account Book. She paid the squire 15s. in 1670 for three stone of lockings (the leavings of wool), as well as 5s. and 4s.; and at the end of 1671 her half-yearly account stands thus :—

	£	s	d.
Rec. of Simond Park's widow for her Rent	00	06	00
It. for ye last part for 4 stone of Lockings (besides 1s. given back)	00	08	00

For what purpose was this wool bought? We can only suppose that Margaret spun it into thread ready for the weaver. What hours of toil at her wheel, probably during the long nights of winter while her babies slept, must this weight of wool represent! Besides her indoor labour she worked in the harvest-field for money, where four and a half days of toil brought her in one July, 1s. 6d.

Her fortunes may have touched a low ebb about 1672, as we find her joining with two neighbours in an obligation to the squire, for the payment of 10s. yearly for ever

years; and this was so hard a matter that the bill was not cleared until 1689, when a total of £4. 5s. 3d had been paid. Then 2s. was " Sent unto Simon Parke Wife's Drinking," which shows that she resorted to the expedient of a merry night, when her neighbours gathered under her roof for festivity, bringing money for expenses and to spare in their hands. But she struggled through, even though the famine year wiped her name from the Agist Book; and she started afresh in 1676 with one cow on the common. Her eldest son John was now ready to take up the burden, and next year to formally pay the rent of 11s. 6d. He shortly stood too for the town's office of frithman and of churchwarden. No doubt he was all the sturdier for the misfortunes of his childhood and his mother's bravery, and he prospered from the first. Even when (as in 1681) he had to work off the arrears of the past year's rent by salving the lord's sheep and making hay, it did not mean that he was falling back, but rather forging forward, and spending on cattle; for next year he is found paying 4s for " goods " on the common—a sum which had increased in 1699 to 8s. 6d., for two fillies, three " whies," and thirty sheep, making in all a flock of sixty. In 1690 he rented the Frith from the squire on a life-lease, and four years later New Close also, at £2. 12s. a year. His stock must by this time have been large, and he clearly knew how to make a profit on it. His property was assessed at 5s 4d. annually. By 1702 he was well enough off to rebuild his house, according to the inscribed stone on its front, which in the good old fashion couples the initial of his wife Anne with his own. He died in 1713. The inscription is:—

$$\left.\begin{array}{c} I \\ A \end{array}\right\} P \ 1702$$

This John, son of Simond, undoubtedly laid the foundations of the family prosperity. His own son John increased it by his marriage and by the purchase of land.

NAB COTTAGE.

From a Photograph by Walmsley Bros., Ambleside.

TO FACE P. 356.

His first wife was Dorothy Knott, daughter of Edward the demesne agent; and he paid an equal window-tax with his father-in-law. He was ambitious, as well as prosperous, and so he added field to field, extending his little estate—that touched the bounds of the manor—beyond those bounds, as often as opportunity occurred. He bought from Edwin Green, in 1726, Dunna Beck Close, which is in the Rydal Lake-basin, though belonging manorially to the Marquis Fee, besides pieces of land in Grasmere. Before 1735 he had acquired the messuage of Hart Head in Rydal, to which he added Gill Close from shoemaker Harrison nine years later. Again in 1741 he secured Otley Intack, adjoining the common near Dunna Beck. Several adjacent closes too were his. They filled up the space between his purchases and the higher part of his land within the Rydal manor boundary, which later passed to Lancelot Fleming, the tailor, and subsequently to the Poet Wordsworth. Beyond the lower part of the boundary at Swan Stone, he obtained an enclosure from the Grasmere common. His increased estate thus gained compactness, though it was of so composite a character as to be owned under two, if not three lordships, with some small lots of freehold. It was probably not until his estate fell to the Hall that the actual boundary on Swan Stone was removed, leaving one-half of the undivided field in the township of Grasmere and the other in that of Rydal and Loughrigg, as it is at present.

This second John Parke in 1730 lost his wife Dorothy, who left him an infant son and daughter; but he repaired his loss, and by his second wife Mary had two sons. William, born in 1741, and George in 1744. At his death in 1748 he left the old Nab estate and contiguous lands which he had bought, to his eldest son John, while to the younger George (missing William, who may possibly have received a legacy in money) he left, after the death of his wife, the little estate and homestead of Hart Head. Widow Mary remained in possession of this until 1760, and nine years later it was sold in two portions by George. This was a time of change in the village. The little farmholds, each one, from time immemorial, compact and self-contained, were now, by purchase of the richer holders from the failing ones, either being lumped together or split up and sold in separate fields. The young men were leaving the village, even the eldest inheriting son often thought it better to pursue a trade elsewhere, than stay and tend the fields and flock of his forefathers. George Parke himself preferred to settle in Hawkshead as saddler, and he must have been a man of parts as well as substance, for both his son and his grandson attained to the position of vicar of Hawkshead. When the former was baptized, the registrar thought that George's own extraction was worthy of being written down in full.

John Parke, third of the name, and now the head of the family at the Nab, was wealthy in land and in cattle. In 1751 he had a flock of a hundred and ten sheep on the common. A valuation of the estate in 1810 (when certainly it was no larger), gave its extent as 20 acres 1 rood 31 poles, and it was valued annually at £15. 14s. 4d. On this he paid a land tax of 2s 6d. He too bought land, and in 1768 was fortunate enough to secure for £59. 1s 6d. two fields across the lake that had belonged to the Barrows, of the Oaks, in Loughrigg; for these being part of the Heald were freehold, paying only a complimentary rent of 2d. and a peppercorn

This John's name occurs in green-hew disputes. Scott, owner of Bainrigg, complained of "Mr. Knot's nephew" for felling timber from that wood without his leave But it is possible that his uncle, the agent, favoured him. Indeed, had John held his Rydal land in freehold or without interference from the unwritten law of green-hew, it is probable that he might, by the opportunity of wealth that the thriving iron-trade of Furness offered to those who could coal their own wood, have now passed, like the Knotts, over the border-line of gentility which he almost touched. But the green-hew law held him fast; and when Sir William Fleming the second was dead, and the Knotts—who were mutually connected—no longer in power, John was made to feel its force. In 1769 the agent of the manor proceeded against him, and he was fined 6d. in the Rydal Court for cutting wood without the bailiffs' leave. Then, too, John died young in 1770, leaving no son to follow him. His executors (of whom his cousin George Knott was one) had instructions to sell his property for the benefit of his wife and little daughter —both Janes—with the exception of one small house in Rydal, with stable, orchard, etc , rent 1s. 0d., which was reserved for their use. But young Jane, in possession of a handsome dowry, with " two pair of bedsteads and one wainscott chest " that had remained at the Nab till she was grown up—no doubt fine pieces of furniture— was not long unmarried ; and three years after the little house and premises had been formally conveyed to the two by the executors (in 1786), it was sold to the Rydal manor for £20, the mother Jane being described as " now of London," and therefore having no further use for it.

It was the custom of the country, though daughters inherited, for favour to be shown on sale of an estate to the nearest male relative, if he were disposed to purchase. William, second son to the third John, now stepped in as purchaser of his half-brother's patrimony. The register shows that he was actually resident there, and doubtless farming it as tenant, in the year following John's death, but it was not until 1778 that he was ready with the £300 which he paid for the old Nab estate with house and customary land (rent 11s.), and for the Grasmere portion that went with it (rent 1s. 8d.). He was then solemnly admitted as tenant of the manor, paying fines of £11 and

£1. 13s 4d. A further £100 paid to the executors probably purchased the Heald or some of the small pieces in another fee ; but only in 1802 his final purchase was made from them, and the trust closed.

William Parke remained on the Nab until his death in 1825, at the ripe age of 84, and he played a prominent part amongst the few statesmen left on the manor. His son was an idiot ; and when in 1794 his daughter Mary married John Simpson, described as waller of the parish of Grasmere, the young people made their home with the parents Simpson worked on the Nab almost as a joint owner, often taking the old man's turn in public offices. The tale of the ruin of the house, and the part that De Quincey played in it, will be told in another chapter. It happened after William's death, but he undoubtedly, by his feud with the Rydal lord, sowed the seeds of it while the heavy mortgage on the property which events shortly disclosed, may have had its origin in his time. In action he seems to have been both obstinate and unwise. Then, too, the account given by Mr. Ford North of the attempt he made, along with his son-in-law (doubtless led by him) to close the upper road of the Nab to passengers from Grasmere, does not create a favourable impression of him. But those were difficult times for Rydal folk !

LITTLEHOUSE, number 5 on the lord's list of 1655, will be dealt with among the village centres, as it was apparently the shop or general stores. Next to it comes

6. SANDS. The history of this is disconnected and obscure. It was perhaps one of a close-set group on the descending slope, and has wholly disappeared. From a later description of it being " on the back side of Banks House," (supposing the latter to be the present house opposite the Hall gates) it would appear to have stood off the street, and below the mound. The record of owners is a confusing one The register records a William

Newton, of Rydal, buried in 1640, the year after his wife Jane. In 1641, a second William had a child baptized, while in 1645 a Lancelot began his family with an Edwin. William, however, was the land-holder, and he must have died early, for a jury of the village court declared in 1655 Robert Taylor to be " next heire ot Willing Newton " for one tenement, of a rent of 7s. 6d. Robert, however, though cattle went on to the common in his name in 1657, may have been resident elsewhere, as he paid John Banks at the same time 1od. to clear his " Boone-day shearing and the leading of manour," and his rent was paid by (or probably through) his neighbour, John Thompson. In 1666 it is recorded that " Robert Talor is to pay to John Thompson 5s. for gerdoing ye frithman," which possibly means acting as his representative in that office.

Meanwhile, Lancelot Newton—probably a kinsman, without wealth to purchase—seems to have farmed the holding as tenant under Taylor, for he is found putting cattle on the common and paying for 10 beyond the 30 sheep in 1663* with an extra five for his son Edwin. He also paid a tax on one hearth. This branch of the Newton family removed later to Grasmere—the name Lancelot being repeated in Edwin's son; and the next available evidence concerning the farmhold shows one Myles Sands to be paying (in 1679) a 7s. 0d. rent upon it. Already in 1673 Myles had served as Frithman, and his cattle ran on the common from 1682, while his widow worked the boon-days by deputy in 1710 and 1720, the latter tasks being done by Robert Jackson, who also paid down 7s. 0d. rent in 1724. Myles Sands must have been a man of mark, for the place retained his name, though it had passed to another Taylor (William) in 1725, who lived at Sawrey, and for whom Thomas Jackson did boon-work in 1733. William paid a land tax of 2d. next

---

* A Thomas Newton " Yeoman " puts cattle on the Common between 1692-8.

year, and his rent for " sands Tenem^t " until 1755, when he sold it to Thomas Fleming " Turner," an innkeeper, (see Inns) for £22. 10s. 0d. It is then described as consisting of the closes called Ridding, Gill Close and Horse Close, with one calf's grass in the Nab and one " Onsett or Houstead " on the " back side of Banks House." The word onsett was often used for a derelict dwelling or the

VIEW OF A RYDAL HOMESTEAD ABOUT 1822.

site of such ; and this statement of position (which was unusual) implies that the farmhold, long let, had at the least been neglected. It was certainly never used henceforth by the holder, whether there remained enough of it to let or not, for the Flemings laid its fields to their ancestral ones to farm, and with them it passed on to the Rydal Manor in 1845.

It is possible that " Sands " was a homestead still remembered, though, if so, it would seem to have been placed a little out of order. This was approached along the side of a barn (latterly used for storing of bark) that abutted on the road about where Church Cottage now stands ; and the path led into a neatly-kept court-yard paved with cobble-stones, where grew an ash-tree of great size. Here lived Mrs. Ann Harrison, said to be of a Grasmere family, whose sons were wallers at a time when wallers were itinerant ; her close white cap was a pleasant feature of her appearance. There was a labourer's cottage attached to the house.

Possibly we have a back-view of Sands (if it be not Hobsons) in Green's Buildings in Rydal (1822), a view of a Rydal Homestead, which is highly characteristic of the place and the century.

7. THOMPSONS OR BANKS.*—Of the race of Rydal Thompsons, who were apparently husbandmen only, there is little to be told, except their ruin. Squire William called in one of them to witness a deed in 1589, a Richard Thompson died in 1600 ; a Thomas in 1630, in 1635 a wife of Robert, and in January and February of 1637 (following the year of the smallpox epidemic) a " Jefferay " and a William. Jefferay was certainly the land-holder, and probably the last to hold the full messuage or tenement. At any rate his successor (William) is found in 1645 paying the high sum of 16s. 0d. as half-yearly interest on a mortgage, which, if foreclosed, would account for the statement that the 6s. 8d rent paid by John Thompson in 1656 was for " Jeffrey Thompson half tenement ; " and we have seen that a portion of the Thompson land already had been joined to the Walker property before 1656. So it was with straitened land that John essayed the life-task of his race. There must have been some

---

* If we may identify " Banks " with the house fronting the Hall gates, tradition says that it was occupied later by James (popularly Jimmy) Dawson, overlooker at the Hall, a strange character who decked himself in antique gentlemen's clothes, to the wonder and awe of the village boys
It was afterwards used as a dame's school

doubt of the value of the holding reaching the stipulated value, for it escaped the hearth-tax of 1663, but was added to the survey of 1665. In cattle John was not short, for he had a flock of 45 sheep in 1656, with a cow and a twinter, and 50 next year with three kyne and a heifer. But he had no money in pouch or purse on that day when the new lord called him up to compound for the dreaded fine.

" John Thompson of Rydal is to pay mee for his General-fine 2lb 15s 0d at Candlemas, 1657, and 2lb. 15s. 0d. at Martinmas then next following, in all 5lb. 10s. 0d."

writes the squire in his account-book.

But John's payments did not start till 1658, with £2, and they dribbled on till 1662, before he finished. Then, while putting together all he could for the fine, he got behind with other payments. The Agist-book for 1657 states that he owed three half-years rent, and 5s. 6d. for his cattle; which should total 15s. 6d., though it is given at £1. 10s. 0d. The utmost exertions could not repair such a sliding-back, not John's own labour in greasing sheep at 6d. a day, nor his wife's in the Hall hay-field at the same rate, nor even the sale of two sheep to the squire for 12s. 0d., and a fat calf for 7s. 0d. It is a ruinous policy to part with cattle for debt which hard work cannot clear, and the end was now only a question of time.

John's final release from his fine was secured, indeed, at a great cost, viz, by a loan from the squire himself.

1662-63, Feb 7   Lent unto John Thompson, of Rydal, ye sum of 9lb vid. ye Deed of his tenemt. for security

And John is found paying 10s. for " consideration " in 1667 and again in 1669, which looks as if he were then borrowing elsewhere on mortgage, doubtless from John Banks The failing man loses heart and vitality; and John Thompson,[*] of Rydal, was buried on New Year's

---

[*] John Thompson, of Rydal, had sons buried in 1687 and in 1688

Day, 1670. Two days later the sale of his effects took place, when the squire bought 19 sheep for £4. 14s. 8d.—under 5s. apiece. There remained only the transfer of the property to the (probable) principal mortgagee.

"1669-70, Feb 3. Rec of Jo Bankes wch I had lent John Thompson Feb. 2, 62 upon ye receipt whereof I gave him in a grant of ye whole Tenemt. 09lb. 00s 00d.

The name of John Banks, now for the first time a land-holder in Rydal, has often occurred in the preceding parts. He was indeed a notable man. Born no doubt of the humblest parentage, probably in the neighbourhood of Skirwith (the manor possessed by Dame Agnes Fleming's son Daniel) he remained in the service of the Fleming family during the whole of his life. For a wage that appears merely nominal, he devoted all his superabundant energy, all his abilities (which were of a high order), and above all, the rectitude of a truly religious mind to the direction of their concerns. He was their all-round man, acting as agent, farmer, rent-collector, land-surveyor, nay, almost as attorney. He was despatched on long journeys to push difficult law-suits in strange courts; to take the sickly heir to cures of various sorts, to ride with up-growing sons to town or college; and, while there, to apprentice youths from the country to trade; and he was even deputed once to turn an officiating minister out of pulpit and church in face of the congregation. There was nothing honest John would not do, if he were told to do it by his master, though often the spirit within him quailed at the enterprise. So loyal was he to the family, that he not only worked for them heart and soul, but he lent to them his small savings, in order to push their claim to Rydal (then but doubtful) against bitter adversaries, and to tide young Daniel over a time of great straitness of money.

We first hear of John Banks in an inventory of Skirwith Hall, where the meagre contents of his chamber are set down. He threw in his lot with William, son of Daniel, who preferred to farm his uncle John's property to settling with an angry mother on his own small patrimony. It is at Coniston, when William's health was failing, and the great struggle for Rydal had started, that we find John Banks to the fore, and absolutely sole actor for the family. When William died, leaving his eldest son little more than a lad, John accepted him loyally as his master, followed him to Rydal, and served him all the remaining days of his life.

That he was valued by the family was but natural, and marks of esteem are shown by higher tips than was usual in the account-book. For instance, when his wife, Elizabeth enjoys an "upsitting," 6s. is given by her lady instead of the 2s. 6d. usual for tenants' wives. And when a son is born to him, William, the young heir, is allowed to stand sponsor, and to present 10s. for the occasion It is cheerful to know that John, who lost several children, had at least one son who grew up and went forth to prosper in the world as a scholar. For in 1683 we read that 10s. is presented to William Bankes "he goeing to-morrow againe for Cambridge."

On coming to Rydal, John Bankes must have been accommodated in some cottage belonging to the demesne. It was not until John Thompson's failure and death that he had the opportunity to invest his savings in property, and to become one of the village land-holders. Poor Thompson's steading had doubtless got out of repair, but the purchaser (or forecloser) had good money in hand, and as soon as summer came procceded to set it in order. We read

"1670, July 11 Sent by Katy for ale last Thursday to John Bankes his House-raising   oolb. o1s. ood.

So there was the usual boon labour among the neighbours, ending with a feast, when John took the proud position of statesman. That he made a good sound house of Thompson's is certain, for in 1727 the holder of it paid a tax on nine windows, an unusual number for a simple farmhold. While some of the adjacent houses went to ruin, and were cleared away, this one was saved by Bankes' money, and—if we may accept traditional evidence as to its position—stands to this day as a comfortable roomy cottage opposite the Hall gates. In it he settled with a rank equal to his neighbours, and with them was entitled for the first time, as the Agist Book of 1671 shows, to put his cattle on the village common. He was also now able to act as bailiff, and to collect the lord's rents, which he proceeded to do, on the failure of William Walker. He likewise served as Frithman; and up to 1688 he stood for his township as one of the "Eighteen" (or Questmen) who controlled the finances of the church of Grasmere. John's own monetary transactions with his master are not easy to fathom. Apparently he let his wages lie, and applied for a lump sum when he wanted it. The account-book gives under February 23rd, 1673-74.—

"Allowed unto Jo Bankes 20lb. which I had lent him Jan 21, 67, and 20lb 14s 00d which I had lent Edward Benson o' th' High close, due Feb 2, 73; being in part of his Wages, and in all 50lb. 14s. 00d.

More singular is the following, entered for April 30th, 1685:—

"Paid unto Jo Bankes of Rydal my servant (in full of all Wages, Debts, Accompts, Claimes and Demands whatsoever from either my late Father or myselfe on his release) ye sum of 100lb. 00s. 00d
Memorandum   I then promised him (in consideration of his being an ancient Servant to my Father and me, ever since I was 2 years old) to give him meat and Drink, when he would come to it, and to pay him 40s per an during his Life and mine; but not to have any Land or Goods but what he shall pay for, saveing a little he hath plowed onely for this year.   00lb. 00s 00d.

No doubt this settlement of outstanding moneys between master and man meant practical retirement from service on John's part. He had become, with the opportunity that land gave to him, a prosperous husbandman. He rented the New Close in 1681 at £2. 10s. 0d. In the year of settlement he paid strictly for the grazing of three cows in the demesne, and in 1688 he arranged for "two Cowes to go amongst our owne Cowes at 10s. a Cow." From the wording of these passages, it is probable that he had been allowed, while restricted to a cottage, to turn a cow free into the Hall meadows; just as it was the privilege of the shepherd that besides his wages he should have a few sheep of his own in the flock.

John's death soon followed the settlement. He was buried at Kendal, November 24th, 1688 (Grasmere Register), and the name of his widow, Elizabeth, replaces his in the Agist Book for 1689, her cattle continuing to run on the common until 1696, in which year "her son's horse" is also paid for on the demesne. Elizabeth "relict" of John, was buried at Grasmere, Mar. 29th, 1697. Banks left no son who cared to succeed him in Rydal. The farmhold was bought by John Fleming, the miller, and he passed it on (along with the trade) to his son William When William died, his brother Thomas, living in Yorkshire, did not care to keep it, and sold it to his connection, John, the cooper (see Inns), and he re-sold it to Richard Shacklock. The new owner's occupation lasted twenty-five years, and then it passed into the possession of the Knotts. "Mr Edward Knott, minor," who figures in the Rental, was probably the heir of Michael. He died young, leaving it to his brother George. Thus, united to the well-cared-for Knott estate, it shared the same fortunes, and finally passed to the manor.

---

* For other passages about the Banks family, see *Flemings in Oxford*.

9. GREENS.—We find the burial of one "William Grene, of Rydall," on the 27th of January, 1579—a month and year of great mortality from the plague. Five years later another William had his infant daughter carried to baptism, followed by a son David. Still another William (we must suppose) had in 1620 a girl baptized. An Edwyn also had children baptized and buried from 1600 onward, and was buried himself on the last day of 1623. His wife, "Hellen," was buried the day before, so it seems as if plague or other infectious disease may have carried them off. The next Edwin was a land-holder of a little estate paying 5s. 4d. rent. For many years he served the office of village "grave" or bailiff, first under Squire John Fleming (as the accounts of 1631 show), then under his executors and heirs; next presumably, under the sequestrators of the county, and last under the strong young squire, Daniel. He must have been somewhat of a favourite with the latter, as besides the rent collecting, he was much employed about the estate, paying often the wages of the out-door men, more especially of the shepherds; and a leather cap was specially bought for him in London by John Banks. That "Evan Green," of Rydal, was charged at the Kendal Quarter Sessions in 1657 with carrying off horse and arms belonging to George Parke, of Windermere, value £3, does not necessarily mean that he had stolen the same, for quarrels led to strange charges. His name sometimes crops up in its colloquial form as Evan a Green, which suggests that the surname may have arisen from some open space about the farmhold that was used for village purposes. His hearth-tax proves the house to have been a fairly good one; and his cattle were perhaps above the average in number. In 1655 he had 50 sheep on the common, three cows and one "turntor," and next year he had 60 sheep. Later his name appears irregularly, but in 1660 he rented New Close from the squire for £2. 12s. 6d. In 1667 he paid in the village

rents for the last time, and his death occurred in the February of the next year.

Possibly a nephew succeeded him, as 2s. 6d. was sent to John Green's wife's upsitting in 1676, but Evan's holding soon passed to Robert Barnes, whose name, though appearing in the registers from 1671, only shows in the Agist Book from 1681. John Barnes followed Robert, and his rent-arrears increased from 10s. 8d. in 1724 to £1. 6s. 8d. in 1735. The family, however, held on, Bridgett (perhaps his widow) came next; and a Thomas paid the land-tax of 1s. 2¼d. in 1751 on "Greens," while Bridgett continued the rent till 1769, besides paying another rent on " Wilsons " (No. 14), another farmhold that meantime had been acquired by the family of Barnes. Perhaps it was for the renovation of the latter dwelling, that her successor, John Barnes, who lived in Cumberland, had in 1781 three trees " set out," for him by the lord's man in his own wood; he was not admitted to " Greens " until 1783, paying £5. 6s. 8d. as " Gressom." His fine on the two properties in 1788, when Lady Dorothy Fleming died, was £15. 15s. 0d., on a joint rental of 10s. 7d. His son John, of West Crosthwaite, on succeeding by will in 1796, paid a fine of £10. 11s. 5d.; and at the same time—not having apparently any use for them—he sold " Greens " and " Wilsons " to the Rydal Hall estate for £200. The rateable value of the two in 1810 stood at £6. 3s. 6d., with an extent of 8 acres 2 roods, 34 poles.

It seems likely that " Greens " was soundly repaired by the Hall authorities, and remains to this day as Undermount. If so, it is undoubtedly represented by Green's " Cottage in Rydal," 1822. Tradition assigns it at a period between that date and 1845 to two occupants. One was Isaac Pattinson, who lived to over ninety years of age. Adjoining, and behind Pattinson's—which was the present backdoor of Undermount—lived Mr. Carter with old Jonathan Udall.* John Carter, described as Land Agent, came to Rydal as Clerk to the poet Wordsworth, in his office of Stamp Distributor in the County of Westmorland. But Carter was soon able to acquire a place of his own under Loughrigg (see Low Cockstone, now Loughrigg Holme), and there, after the removal of his tenant, John Clarke, mason, he resided, lodging with his new tenants named Walker.

Green's etching of this farm-hold shows an abutment over the spot (now under the present dining-room) where a well—deep and dark—is remembered. The gateway served for both houses. The tree on the left was an ancient eller (alder), beneath which a cheese-press stood.

10. Hobsons or Causeway Foot.—At number 10 we reach what was once an important village holding. It might, indeed, have been classed among the village centres, insomuch as it was at one time the abode of a general provision dealer and carrier. It stood at the back of the two pretty, new cottages on the high-road, but endwise and askew. It seems (according to the account received from two grandsons of James Backhouse, who owned two of the three dwellings into which it was eventually broken up, as well as the Rash Field above it) to have fronted the grassy way that leads through the Rash. Should this path present an ancient route from the adjacent river-ford up through Nab wood to the higher road, its name, Causeway Foot, would be explained, since if it were only a way used by Hobson, he would doubtless pave bits of it, past the several springs to give footing to his pack-horses.

The name of Hobson appears in the earliest page of the parish register, when "Myles Obson" marries Margaret Ellwood, and starts a large family. There were also

---

* In an estate-book of 1822, I find an entry, "To Isaac Pattinson ½ years rent for Heald Field and Round Close £6 2s 6d." From this it would seem as if he were a land-holder. This *Healdfield* could hardly have been the one across the lake. Was it the present Church Field?

Nicholas and Michael, heads of families; but it was the latter who succeeded Myles (buried 1618). He is in evidence from 1617, when he witnesses a deed for Squire John; and in 1631 borrows £2 from the same for six months. He died in 1638. Thomas, his successor, had been married in the previous year to Annas Parke, doubtless of the Nab; for we find that in old times intermarriages among members of one small village community were very common. Thomas was a well-to-do man; he had not only his large holding in Rydal, rent 13s. 4d. (one mark), but he had apparently some sort of footing at Keswick, whence he brought the cheap cloths and the meal so frequently sold to the Hall. Probably it was at Monk Hall, Keswick, which belonged to the Rydal Squire, that he met William Fleming, at the time when the latter farmed it for his uncle John; for he assisted William's claim to the Rydal estate in 1651 by the loan of £40. The bill for this amount was renewed year by year at 8 per cent. (the customary interest), till it was cleared by Squire Daniel in 1657. It may have assisted Thomas in procuring easy terms when "compounding," for he paid a fine of only £6. 13s. 4d. on a rent of 13s. 4d. His reckoning stands in 1657:—

	lb.	s.	d.
Allowed unto Thomas Hobson (in his Sheep rent) for ye Consideration of 40lb. for ye last year	03	04	00
more for three Load of Meal	02	14	00
more for two cheeses	00	02	08
Given him back	10	00	04

The final reckoning is made out apparently by John Banks (who loved a double f) and is dated

January the 27th, 1657-58.

A particular of the account made with Thomas Hobson off the 40lb due to him by bond as alsoe ffor some other disbursed by him.

THE FARMHOLDS

	lb. s. d.
Imprimis.	
due to him the 29th of September last by bill	40 00 00
And ffor the consideracion ffor it ffor one yeare at 8lb per cent	03 04 00
ffore sixe load off lime at 9d. ye load	00 04 06
seaven yards off cloth at 1s. 4d ye yard ffor Suite	00 09 04
more ffor 2 yards and a halffe off cloth ffor the boy at 1s 2d ye yard	00 03 00
One pecke of meale	00 01 08
One pecke off groats	00 02 08
	44 05 02

This payed to Thomas Hobson.	lb. s. d.
August the ffirst payd	20 00 00
The rent off the Sheepe at Munck hall allowed in his hand due at martinmas	14 12 04
Payd to him by willing Atkinson w ch. was the ffrst parte off his ffin	04 02 06
Payd to him by Thomas Lancaster being Tyth ells ffne (?)	02 03 04
And payd to him this present daye in money	03 07 00
	44 05 02

Thomas bought a foal of the squire's breed next year, but died seemingly in 1663, as his wife is found promising to pay £2. 10s. 0d. for her heriot between April and Martinmas. She paid it in October; likewise in 1665 a tax on one hearth not declared. But the prosperity of the house departed with Thomas. The widow, as was customary in the fee, nominally kept on the holding, while her son Michael (who must have been young, as he only married Margaret Benson, of Grasmere, in 1669) worked upon it, took his turn as constable, churchwarden and frithman, and put cattle on the common. He apparently continued his father's carrying trade, as we find him occasionally supplying the Hall with meat (at 6d. per load for carriage) as well as with other things from Keswick. Perhaps the trade diminished, and he himself was not sharp at business; or else the famine year overwhelmed him. At all events, the estate books tell the sorrowful tale—which has to be told of so many Rydal holdings of lessening weal, arrears of rent and debt. The details need not be given here; they are much the same as in the case of other men cited in *Work and Wages*. It is sufficient to indicate the steps of the slow downfall. In 1676 he joins his mother in a bill for £2. 13s. 2d. from the squire; and his wife (who is having a considerable family) turns into the Hall hay-field, and earns 10s. 0d. to help to pay it off. In the winter he begins to thresh for the squire, at 2d a day, and next has that festivity called a " drinking," towards which his superior furnishes 2s. 0d. He also salves the sheep—a better paid job. His wife adds to the well-paid hay work, the cutting of corn in autumn; and then, in 1682, " dresses " the meadows, a back-breaking labour, generally left for young girls and poorest women, and paid only at 3d. a day. The 2d. " given unto Michael Hobson for bringing mee some money, 1683," helps little, and Michael only manages with it all to pay 8s. 0d. of his rent, which now (probably reduced by some small sale of land) stands at 12s. 4d. In 1683 he pays the squire £1. 3s. 4d. for Edward Harrison's bill (doubtless a mortgage on his property), and his wife earns 6s. 0d. in the hay-field to be placed to his credit. He dies in his prime, like so many other failing men, and widow Margaret and her son Michael are left to face disaster. Money is so scant, that they need to borrow 5s. 0d. from the squire for their hearth-tax. The reckoning placed now before the young man is a terrible and a complicated one. Arrears of grass money reach back to 1679, and of rent to 1681. Then a mysterious 10s. 0d. is popped on " for a fine due An. 1675 for 6d. rent," while the new fine " upon the Death of his Father " is set down at the hard figure of £12. 16s. 3d.—being nearly double what his well-to-do grandfather paid in 1655. Against this there stands only his father's labour for sheep-salving for 1697, and for threshing from 1681 and guttering—reaching altogether a paltry total of £2. 15s. 9d. With what consternation must the simple young statesman have seen the long intricate sheet of credit and debit made out for him by the ruler at the Hall, in which the balance dropped so fearfully low on the debit side. There was nothing for it but to sign the mortgage deed of half his tenement prepared for him, in order that the sum total of his debt, £22. 12s. 9d., should be secured. This sum he manfully strove to pay, bringing £1 or £1. 10s. 0d. up to the Hall at a time; but by 1697 he had only made £9. 10s. 0d. way with it, and had besides to be supported by the bills of neighbours and by borrowing. He was then at the end of his tether, and he mortgaged another part of his property to a wealthy townswoman, Agnes, mother of Antony Harrison, who had become Mrs Dixon. With this deed the unfortunate Michael passes out of record,* though his mother must still have lingered on in a part of the old homestead, as in 1710 her boon-mowing was done by deputy.

Henceforth "Hobsons" was two dwellings, of half tenements. In one, Edward Harrison plied his trade as shoemaker, uniting this with a little husbandry; for his cattle, including two cows, ran on the common. But even he gets behind with his half rent of 6s. 3d., and in 1744 sells a piece of land, called Gill Close, to prospering John Park, of the Nab, for £10, so that the rent falls to 3s. 9d. This bit was sold off in 1763 by one Isabel Harrison, spinster, of Rusland, for £39. 0s. 6d. to Matthew Fleming (whose story will follow), and henceforth it passed on with the Grigg property.

The other half of Hobsons likewise went to a craftsman. For in 1714 Fletcher Fleming, the youngest son of Sir

---

* Michael Hobson, of Rydal, buried Oct. 11, 1691. John Hobson, of Rydal, buried Oct 27, 1691. Michael Hobson, of Rydal, bur. June 13, 1693

Daniel (who probably had received the mortgaged property from his father) is found selling it for £24, to John Birkett, one of a family of wrights or carpenters who had made their way upwards. John removed to it from the little house (rent 6d.) that his father John had first purchased; and after the death of his elder son and his grandson, it passed by his will to his younger son George. George, styled "of Stott-park, Colton," had already been picking up property in Rydal, and presently was in possession of three houses and some scattered land. He removed to Hart Head some time after his purchase of its two halves, (1769 and 1783) and became one of the most prominent and characteristic statesmen of the village at the close of the eighteenth century. In 1788, for some reason, he was willing to part with Hobson's, which had been let to a tenant for £3. 15s. 0d.; and the Hall agent, anxious to secure it, reports much "discussion and grog" at the parley over it. The canny townsman asked £50 for what was then described as a cottage with barn, cowhouse, orchard, etc., while he reserved two fields and the "layes" belonging to the half tenement, to be divided; and, after a year of haggling, he got his price (1789). The woodmeres called Nab and Dickey Spring passed with the rest of his Rydal property to his son, and shared the fate of Hart Head.

Old John Backhouse, born 1819, told me that he lived as a boy with his parents at Harrison's, one of the "Hobson" half-tenements, owned by his grandfather (see number 14). He describes it as being the upper of three houses, that faced on to "the Ragh." The lower house, he said belonged to John Fleming of the Inn. Only the middle house—which may have been the Birkett half—was then in decent repair: the other, chuckled the old man, "must have been old when Adam was young."

Perhaps these fragments of "Hobsons," soon after

swept away, are represented as "Buildings in Rydal," in Green's etchings of 1822. Mention should be made of the sale of the "Rash," which was part of "Hobsons"; for after its sale, "Hobsons" was reduced to a rent of 1s. 3½d

WILSONS.—Numbers 11 and 12 of the village houses will appear under the Inns, so we can pass on to number 13. This was held by the Wilson family, of whom the registers give a John and a Charles, in the first quarter of the seventeenth century. Charles, supported by his neighbours' bond, borrowed £3 from Squire John in 1642. He was apparently a carrier and provision merchant, like so many Rydal men, supplying to the Hall corn-seed from Carlisle, bigg, meal, apples for Christmas, and even, in 1665, after the death of Thomas Hobson, the cheaper cloth required for the clothes of the house-boy. His herd of cattle was at least up to the average number; he had in 1665 upon the common 60 sheep, two horses, and four "twinters." By 1673, when his working days were probably over, he was paying only on two kine and one heifer, beyond the allotted number. He died in 1674, having survived his wife six years, and left his daughter Jane to inherit. She had married in 1649 John Udall (sometimes spelt and pronounced, Yowdale), and had continued to reside at the old homestead. On the death of her husband in 1659 she paid a heriot, and the fine on her father's death was fixed at £5. 5s. 0d. upon a rental of 5s. 3d. His fine in 1654 had been only £4.

Jane Udall's son Charles now stepped into his grandfather's place, and picked up the old business of carrier, the beat being apparently between Kendal and Keswick or Workington. It was a fortunate moment for his start, for the deaths of the younger David Harrisons in 1679 and 1681 left a vacancy, and the squire was free to transfer his custom to the new man. He used him frequently, and recommended him to Sir John Lowther, when the latter proposed to establish a regular service of pack-horses between Kendal and Whitehaven.

There would seem to have been more than the usual improvements done at Wilsons on change of tenant; for 2s. 6d. was given in 1680 for "Jane Yowdall's House-Raysing," and 2s. 0d. next year for Charles Udall's barn-raising; with again a 2s. 6d. for his house-raising four years later. Charles increased his live-stock, and paid 11s for the grazing of "2 stags two years old" in the demesne from September to April. In 1681 he rented New Close at £2. 12s. 0d. on a seven years' lease, and next year took for three years a portion of the Park near the junction of beck and river. This was charged 15s. 0d., the squire bargaining that his own sucking calves should continue to be put in "Old Hall." Next, Charles made the bold stroke of renting a second village holding. This belonged to William Grigg; and Charles took it upon a six years lease, at a rent of £2. 10s. 0d. His reason for this move may have been the superior situation of Grigg's (placed at the southern entrance of the village) as an inn, for we find Charles' name in the list of licensed alehouse keepers for the next year, 1691. His agist money, with as many as 80 sheep on the common, ran up to 8s. 0d. in 1689, and to 10s. 0d. next year: the flock of Grigg's holding being doubtless added to his own.

But in spite of these signs of prosperity, Udall's position was not sound. He was behind-hand in payments, and in 1688 his arrears of rent, of agistment and pasture were added up to £2. 0s. 2d., for which he gave his lord a bill. Five years later he borrowed as much as £21. 16s. 8d., it being necessary to cover the sum by a deed of his ancestral estate. After that the end soon came, and Charles Udall, his pack-horses, and his inn, ceased to be in Rydal. By 1699 one John Nicolson, or Nicholsen, was in possession of "Wilsons," paying the rent of 5s. 3d. and grass-money until 1739. Then the property passed to the Barnes family, who already held "Greens," and with it was sold to the Hall in 1796. The position of Wilsons is not certain. If the order of the 1655 Rent-list be followed, it stood on the highway between Flemings and Griggs; in which case it has been etched more than once by the engraver Green, being best portrayed in his "South Entrance into Rydal," one of the set of Forty Old Buildings, 1522. This shows its round chimney, its tablet for owner's initials, its single glassed window, its rocky approach; along with the "Little House" next to it, and the weaver's shed and outbuildings beyond. The two last were converted into a house that was for some years placed at the disposal of the parson of Rydal, a tenancy which came to an end when the new vicarage was built. These stood in one block, including the neat cottage and garden on the south, which may have been Wilsons.

14. GRIGGS, with Jobsons and Lowhouse in Loughrigg.—Of the great clan Grigg—or Grige, Greig, or Gregg, as the name was variously spelt—something will be said in connection with the Rydal Mill (Village Centres). The family began to wane in numbers and in wealth by the close of Elizabeth's reign. A William, of Rydal, had children baptized from 1612 to 1619. He died in 1639. It was probably his son Edward who married Isabell Flemyne in 1640, when he succeeded to the estate, as was the prudent fashion of the time. He must have been well-to-do, for he purchased the freehold of two bits of property at the other side of the river from Thomas Benson, of Coat How. This consisted of a tenement called "Jobsons," rent 1s. 2d., and another called Lowhouse, rent 9d.; along with Jopson Island in Rydal; for all of which he paid £7. 7s. 0d. These were parcels of the Loughrigg freehold which Squire William Fleming had sold to the clothier Bensons in 1575, and they had probably in the interval become ruinous and deserted by their

holders. The one called Lowhouse may have stood on the wide meadow beyond the bridge still known as Grigg Field; for the site of a minute house can be made out to the right of the path, scarcely lifted above the flood level; while plough ridges show on the neighbouring knoll It was very likely the tenement mentioned in the sale-deed of 1575, as held by Robert Griegge, being then rented at 11d. The other was doubtless the tenement that the same document states to be held by John Jopson at a rent of 2s. 10½d. This house-stead may have stood across the river in the field called Steps End (from the stepping stones that once touched it), where another site was discovered by the late woodman of the demesne. It was perhaps the house called Steps End, Rydal, in the register, as late as 1792, when a child was baptized. But the Jopsons had died out or left, long before this. There is scant record of them. In 1505 Richard Jopson's wife paid 6d. of his " gressum " to John Grigge, he being then grave or bailiff of Loughrigg. In 1586 John Jopson buried his wife, while a Robert " of Rydal " had a son William baptized in 1632. The name still lingers in Jopson Close, where the quarry beck tumbles down Loughrigg-side into the lake.

Edward Grigg's deed of purchase of what were either derelict buildings or fit only to be let as cottages, is undated. Other indications show him to have been a prosperous man, and a provision merchant and even possibly another carrier! He supplied the Hall in Squire John's time with bigg, and in 1646 was paid 8s. od. for a " veale calf had long since." His rent was entered by Squire Daniel at first as 7s. 7d., and then 7s. 5d. ; and with that astute lord he managed to compound for his fine at the low rate of £4. 10s. od.

His flocks were large ; he had in 1655, 75 sheep on the common and two horses, and he paid for cattle in the demesne as well. Three years later, besides 85 sheep, two horses and two kine on the common, he rented Low How from the squire for £1. 16s. 0d., the latter writing on the bargain " And they are to cut the Brakes in it in midsomer month." In 1666 he paid as much as 11s. 2d. for extra cattle on the common. His wife was seemingly not only a hard worker, but a powerful woman She could join the men at the sheep-clipping, for in 1667 she did this for the Hall, earning 5d. thereby for the day. (The men had 6d.) She had 4d. per day in the hay meadows and her daughters 3d. Then Elizabeth and Isabel Grigg, her daughters also may-be, dressed the meadows at 3d., and they even bore sods at 2d. Thus it will be seen that the women of prominent statesmen's families often engaged in field labour. The Griggs, however, had a genius for work.

Edward's career was now at its close, he was buried on February 26th, 1668 His widow, Isabell, survived him only four years. It was her name that first appeared in the Agist Book, and was later followed by the son " Willing " or William. It is clear that ready money at this time was scarce, for the fine levied on the father's death (£7. 8s. 4d.) was secured by bond. Money no doubt had to be paid out to the brothers and sisters, as was the custom when the eldest son took the farmhold. Willing must have added a carrier's business to his husbandry, for he was paid for the carriage of meal to the Hall. But business must have been slack, and certainly the times were bad. By 1674 Willing owed his lord £11. 9s. 4d., and was obliged to mortgage his tenement. This was, besides, the year of famine, when the villagers had to sell their stock for whatever it would fetch. Grigg tried the expedient of a public sale, held on March 2nd, 1675, at which the squire bought eight sheep, paying £1. 15s 0d. for them " into his sister Margaret's hand,"

Now began, on the statesman's part, a stupendous struggle to keep his holding, by which he became truly a bondman to his lord. A few extracts from the account-book will tell the tale. The squire had in 1677 further secured himself on William's bond by taking the assurances of Mr Thomas Benson of Coat How, and the rich David Harrison, that they would pay £2 if his mortgage was forfeited. William saw no other way to meet his difficulties than by manual labour performed at the Hall; and next year when he was straight with his rent, and even got a cow and an extra horse on the common, he performed the heaviest and worst paid task of the hireling, and threshed corn at 2d. a day. To be sure, it was but for a few days. Yet when his next account was made up in the new year of 1681 he had threshed 35 days, led manure for 12 (also at 2d.), done 19 days' mowing and 12 salving; earning thereby £1. 3s. 4d. This threshing must have represented the work of the previous winter, for on April 13th another account was made up.

"Paid & Allowed unto William Grigg for 72 dayes thrashing at 2d. the day 12s, three dayes makeing the Hedge in ye Low grounds with meat at 3d. ye day 9d, one day filling of manure 3d, five dayes holding ye plow, 1s. 3d. one day makeing hedge about ye clothgarth & grubing 3d, one day Salveing with Tobacco 6d in all.

	lb	s	d
It four days at ye Outwalls without meat ..	..	00	15	00
Paid him in money 7s, & allowed 10s ..	..	00	03	00

His account next January, made up of various kinds of labour, mowing, salving, threshing, helping "to Inn ye Corne" in all 55 days, comes to £1. 8s. 11d. Of this, £1. 2s. 1d. is "allowed," 2s. 6d. is

"kept in my hand for a Syth had of Geo. Wilson of Ambleside,"

so that William receives "in silver" (noble sum!) 4s. 4d. In the next account, May 21st, his wages amounted to £1. 1s. 2d. This finishes the season's threshing (making a long winter of 91 days at 2d. a day); and includes hedging, ditching and walling. From the total 6s. 0d.

is "allowed," which William's wife had been obliged to ask for at the Hall in order to buy the "Seed-Oates" requisite for sowing the home-patch of corn, and which is described as "borrowed." There is also a deduction of 12s. 0d.

"for consideration due June 24, 80,"

and our statesman goes away with 3s. 2d. in his hand.

His next account waits for a whole year—till May 25th, 1683, and shows that he has achieved the maximum of threshing in 106 days, with mowing and walling, in all 143 days, making a total of £1. 16s 2d. earned, which is an average of barely more than 3d. a day. From this he is "allowed" £1. 10s. 6d., and receives 5s 8d. in cash. He is clearly just keeping his head above water, in paying lord's rent, agist money (with special item for a mare), interest on mortgage, only that there is the mortgage itself! His wife, who, along with the daughter, had been taking the spring task of "dressing" the lord's meadows, earning her 3d. a day, dies this year, 1684. He repaired this loss, by marriage with Grace Harrison, and we read in the account-book for January 30th, 1686-87.—

	li	s	d.
"Sent by my Son Roger to give at Will Grigg's Offering at Amb.	00	02	06

In February the Account Book gives particulars of his earnings, which were £1. 8s. 8d

A way out of the labyrinth was to open in front of William Grigg, which saved him from becoming a landless man, as did so large a proportion of his towns-fellows. With that rash young neighbour, Charles Udall, he, "William Greige," drew in 1690 an agreement to "sett and to farm let" his whole messuage and tenement for six years at a rent of £2. 10s. 0d., he paying the lord's rent, assessments, and half the charge of putting the house in repair; with a proviso that Charles might break his lease in three years. William was now free; his chain to his lord was unloosed ; he could seek a better market for his labour. And we may infer that he did so, for his mortgage, written down in 1690 as £17. 2s 4d, was paid off gradually through Udall and John Birkett, as the " Hall Rent-Book " shows.

And so (after a gap in evidences, such as occur from this time onward), we find the Griggs still upon the little holding to which they had returned. From 1710 the Boon-work papers give the name of William Grigg, perhaps a son of our worker, who does the work by deputy. He served in all public offices—was Frithman, Constable, Surveyor, Churchwarden in the good old style, had a sufficiency of cattle on the common, and died in 1745 or 1746 His son and heir, John, was then admitted to the ancestral messuage and tenement " at Rydall Town " before the Customary Court, paying a fine of £7. 8s 4d. But the ancestral landholder, if he had no trade but husbandry, was by this time recognised as a person who had little or no chance of success. John was resident at Whitehaven, a town to which the folk of Rothay valley often migrated, and is described in the deed of sale as " labourer " ; for he was willing in 1760 to part with the immemorial " Grigg Tenement," the last of all the holdings once possessed by the clan, to Matthew Fleming for £57

The purchaser was a craftsman, to whom the traditional feeling for " property " still appealed. By birth he belonged to the village, being one of the enormous and most astute clan of Fleming, who had always united a craft (or two), with the pursuit of husbandry. (See Inns). A son of the wealthy John, " cooper " and innkeeper, he was apprenticed when a youth at Keswick as a " Thrower " for eight years ; and must have been a cunning man at his trade (which he pursued elsewhere), for he saved enough to buy part of " Hobsons," as well as " Griggs." He had no children, and after his death (his will was dated 1771) and the death of his widow Jane, some 17 years later, the holdings passed to his brother John. John's daughter, Mally, was married to James Backhouse, and she inherited in 1803. Her husband, a butcher by trade, took up the more dignified position of statesman with its various social offices But it was in a hollow state. Even by the exercise of frugality James was unable to sustain the position to the close of his long life. In 1842 he and his wife entered into an agreement with General le Fleming to sell both Hobsons (except a piece that must have been the Rashfield) and Griggs, provided they were allowed to live at the latter for £6. 6s. 0d. rent, until the last of them died.

By this time the little homestead was so ruinously out of repair that something needed to be done. It was described by an old man, since dead, as being so low-pitched of door and roof that one could just about get into it, and that was all. John Backhouse, a grandson, remembered it as some six feet below the road ; but this would be in part due to the levelling and raising of the great highway in front of it. For it seems to have been situated in a slight hollow, which stretched down its own parrock ; and the field was finally made flat by the casting of the rubble of the ruined cottages at the other side of the road into it. A low shed abutted on to the road, joining at a right angle to the little homestead, which was entered across a cobbled yard The low gable-end and chimney are seen well in Green's etching of Pelter Bridge in 1808, as well as in Mr. W. Collingwood's sketch done in 1841 ; but the latter pictures a barn that answers to John's description. The barn stood close by the river, and was reached by a gate from the parrock. It was fitted up for three horses, two cows, a calf-stall, with storage for some 100 carts of hay. Possibly the bigger barn was a new building.

All this was cleared, and a new, tight and neat little

homestead rose in its place about 1844.* Within it the last statesman of the village passed away at over 90. He is remembered as a tall, fine old man. His daughters let the rooms as lodgings; and one lodger remembers him with a knife constantly in his hand, whittling wooden skewers, the last token of his trade.

15 LITTLE HOUSES.—Besides the farmholds which were full "messuages or tenements," there were a few smaller houses distinct from these, as well as from the cottages that were so often attached to the larger dwellings, and were reckoned as one with them. These "little houses" had rights upon the common and the woodland, with other communal privileges; and they appear to have been so far part of the original village community as to have shared in the allotment of land for the homestead, within the village, though not in the open lands outside.

Such was the Shop and the old Smithy, as well as another small house used for a short time as a smithy (see Village Centres), and which was probably the one which became the dower house of Mrs. Parke, of the Nab. There was also a fourth, which in late times went by the name of Shacklock's Toftstead, and was possibly connected with the Robert Shacklock "of Rydal," who paid for a horse grazing in the demesne in 1663, and who yet makes no appearance in the rental. Certain it is that when a Richard Shacklock subsequently took over "Banks," he paid, besides the 6s. 8d. rent, an "Item for the House Stead," 6d. Now the word toft was applied to a piece of ground where a tenement had once stood. In 1600 there were four tofts mentioned as belonging to the Rydal village, a fact which proves the decay of the place, and reduction of the population. So when Shacklock's small holding re-appears several times in the rental as a toft-shed we may conclude it to have become ruinous. It was lumped with Bank's holding through the time

---

* Subsequently "Rydal Cottage" the home of the author.—Ed.

PELTER BRIDGE. RYDAL.

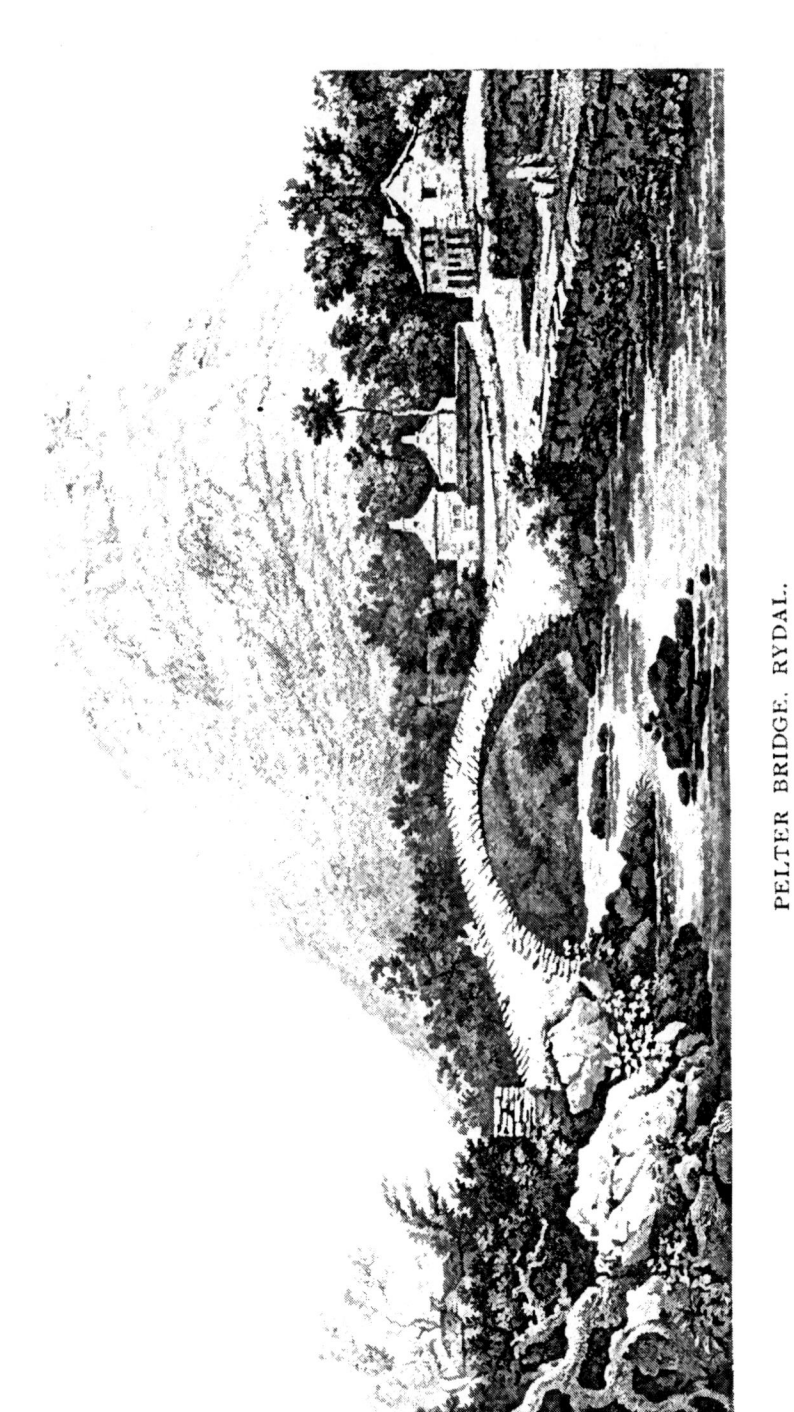

From an Engraving of a Drawing by Farrington.

TO FACE P. 387.

of the Knot tenancy, though in 1749 the names of Elizabeth Hutchinson and William Hodgson are connected with it, as if it might have been let as a shop. In 1769 it is described as "a Toftstead not paid for many years." It figured in George Knott's will as "An old dwelling house and orchard, rent 6d." Along with the Knott property, it eventually passed to the Hall. When it disappeared, or where it stood, is hard to say. It seems unlikely to have been the small stable now attached to Rydal Mount, though this is a two-storied place. Was it the "rude hut" described by T Q.M, who made a tour of the lakes in 1827, which apparently stood on Hall Bank?

One or two cottages are known to have stood where the coach-house of "Rydal Cottage" is placed, but nothing of their history is known. Possibly they represent a former village holding, which belonged to those lands (also upon the park-side) which went by the name of "Birketts," and that subsequently belonged in part to Mr. Ball. They are not represented in the rental of 1654.

The cottages are well shown in Green's 1808 view of Pelter Bridge. They had fallen out of repair, and were used for storage of bark, when extensive wood-cutting went on in the Park. Old John Backhouse remembered a privet hedge ran down to the roadway, enclosing their little garden and fruit trees from the park, and this orchard bit is still marked by a few daffodils that spring year by year. They were finally cleared when Backhouse's farmhold was rebuilt; and a stable and byre were erected for him upon the site.

With the Birkett lands a certain Thomas Hudson, described as yeoman of Rydal, seems to have been connected, for in 1658 and 1662 he was paid 6s. 8d. for hay in "Birkett feild-head." The "Birkett-barne," which was mended in 1659, was included in the demesne;

it was no doubt the hog-house which stood until 1907, when its stones were cleared for alterations at Rydal Farm. Thomas Hudson, who is not represented in the rental either, died in 1666, making the simple will of the statesman. It is given below—

WILL OF THOMAS HUDSON.

December ye 6, Ano. Dom. 1666.

In ye name of god Amen I Thomas Hudson of Ridall, sick in body, but of good and perfect remembrance, thanks be to god doe make this my last will and first of all I bequeath my soul to ye maker of it and my body to be buried in ye Parish Church yard of Gresmere : Secondly I give unto my Daughter Margarett 2s. 6d.

All the rest of my goods and chattels moveable and immoveable I give unto my wife Chatherine & my Daughter Alice to be equally divided betwixt y'm paying ye debts and legacies herein mentioned :

	s	d
to Robert Walker of Ambleside	5 06	00
Thomas Mackereth, of Ambleside	00 00 06	00
George Otley	00 04 00	00
Thomas Fleming wife elder	00 00 06	00
John Mackereth, fiedler	00 03 00	00
David Harrison, wife, elder	00 04 00	00
David Harrison, elder	00 04 03	00

In witnesse hereof I have hereunto set my hand and seale

THOMAS HUDSON.

Witnesses
Lancelot Newton
Edward Grigge
William Grigge
George Ottley
William Baxter.

VILLAGE CENTRES

CHAPTER IV.

THE SMITHY

Adam Fisher; David Harrison; Some Old Bills; The Shop or Littlehouse.

THE last Rydal holding of the rental of 1654 (number 14) was the first house of the village (as approached from Ambleside) and one of the chief village centres from primitive times. This was the smithy, which stood at the foot of Kiln How, at the point where the highway crosses Rydal Beck. From its position it was clearly one of the manorial buildings that once clustered about the Old Hall, and was the only one performing its office when our record begins. One Adam Fisher was then the smith. The register tells that he (Adam Fysher) married Mabell Partrige in 1614, and thereafter had children; and if the 12s. 0d. set down in Squire John's book as his rent for 1631 was paid for the smithy, that sum must have been charged for the business, which was once the lord's monopoly; the rent of the little holding being 1s. 0d. only. For Adam had not only smith's work for the demesne to do (which often came to a good sum), but what he could get from his neighbours, and from horsemen on the "broad-gate" who might have slipped a shoe. In November, 1632, Adam was paid upon "accompt" £1. 6s. 10d. It is true that the shoeing of the "Light Horse" for Rydal was done during the Civil Wars by Anthony Skelton, who rode the stallion, and there is entered (1643)—

"pd. for Gunpowder ned pedler had at seuerall tymes for Anthony when he showed light horse olb. 2s. 6d."

Adam's bills for general smith's work were fairly large, being £1. 14s od. for six months of 1643, £1. 0s. 6d., from June to November, 1644, with another bill of £1. 14s. 6d. for the same year; and £1. 5s. 0d. in 1645, as well as an extra £1. 2s. 2d. Adam assisted to get in the Grasmere tithes at a time when tithe-collecting was no sinecure, and it was as well to have a big strong man to demand them. Then he had another and very different occupation · for he was skilful as a gardener. His own garden is always mentioned with his holding, and he was employed in the Hall gardens.

1642, " pd. for worke done in Garden by Adam Fisher at Seurall tymes before this 8th of Aprill olb 2s. 6d.", and in 1645 he is paid 3s. 3d. for six and a half days in the garden, making 6d. a day.

But harder days and sorrow were in store for Adam. In the previous year William Fisher, presumably his son, who would have followed him, had died, and in 1653 and 1657 William's sons, Adam and John died[1] also: Old Adam, as he now began to be called, had to face his fine at the new squire's coming, and on October 9th, 1655 he set his mark (very like a horse shoe) against an agreement to pay 15s. 0d. on or before the 26th of the next April. The proportionate amount of fine to rent shews that business, or a money turnover, was reckoned on. But business had become slacker. The smithy at the exit from Ambleside up on the Brow which it named; (and there was another at the entrance), was barely over a mile distant; and the new lord gave his work to a Grasmere man. Adam was glad to work off his fine by mixed labour, and subsequently at a drop in wages of one-third the old rate. At first, indeed, he was paid the same, as Banks' account of his fine-debt proves, alike for guttering the Round Close, graving peats, manuring the bigg; though it dropped to 5d. for eight days work

" beffore Candlemas." Then he is paid 2s. 0d. for four days in the garden, with " one att Brackens in Rydall-how " thrown in. An entry for February 24th, 1656, shows the squire's method of keeping his labour-accounts.

"Paid unto Adam Fisher (besides 3s 4d. allowed him
in his fine) for 24 days gardening, making hedge in ye
Low Parke, and cutting of Briers, being all now due   lb. s. d/
unto him 00 05 00

His fine was not finally worked off until May 21st, 1657, when he was paid " for Coallinge off the pitt at Lowe Parke Barne."

Now this entry proves that Adam was a clever, all-round craftsman, for the burning of charcoal is a special and highly-trained occupation; and the squire, when he paid the smith 7s 2d. for " 14 dayes worke in coaling a Pitt " no doubt saved money, as well as the trouble of procuring a couple of experts from a distance Adam likewise collected moss (doubtless for the roofs), helped in the hay, and finally was set to the task of clearing the site of Old Hall, and trailing stones thence for the use of the builders of the adjacent new barn. He was paid in October, 1659, for

" 4 days getting and setting of Crabb-tree Stockes " ;

and such work in the orchard must have been nearer the old man's heart than dragging stones on a sled like a beast of burden. But Adam's strength was failing; he was buried on March 27th, 1660; and henceforward his cot was known as Fisher House, and the knoll behind it as Adam How—a late instance of place-names arising from a strong individuality.

The house and garden now fell into the hands of the lord, probably for want of heirs; and he disposed of it to David Harrison, junior, son of the inn-keeper, who was himself trading as a carrier like his father, and who being newly married, needed a house. The agreement furnishes an instance of land-tenure in Squire Daniel's time ; it is given below.

Young David appears to have flourished, marching with baggage of all kinds—char-pies, money, &c., to Kendal, and there transferring his burdens to the string of pack-horses bound for Oxford and London ; bringing back wheatbread, salt, wainscot from the joiners, etc. His alternate march took him to Keswick, whence he brought back meal, etc , wanted at the Hall. Like his father, he dealt in cattle, renting the " little close called the ould hall" and later on Adam How and the Allans, as well as New Close He tired of the bargain that the squire's calves should go free in the close, and for 1670 we read :—

"Given back unto young David Harrison of ye new
close 6d , and because calves were in ye old hall, 1s , lb s   d.
in all   .   ..   . oo o1 o6

In 1674 old David of the Inn died, and young David moved to the ancestral farm-hold. (See Inns).

The old smithy remained long in the Harrison family. An Anthony is represented in the Agist Book from 1694 to 1700, and in 1710 he did two days boon work in the lords fields, one doubtless for Fisher House. A widow Harrison did the same in 1720 and 1733; and in 1746, William, second son of Anthony, was admitted tenant to Fisher House. He was a cooper living at Sawrey ; and in 1768 it was sold by him for £11 to William Richardson, of Clappersgate, with all privileges belonging thereto. A fine of £1 was paid. John Richardson " of Grasmere " followed William, and in 1801 he parted with all rights in " Kiln-howe " to Sir Michael Fleming for the sum of £24.

In 1755 the Rev. Isaac Knipe reported the robbery of a shoe-shop in Ambleside, adding that Rydal smithy was also "broke open, but nothing I believe taken from thence."

A fragment of building stood, until recently, by what is still known as Smithy Bridge.

The Smithy
(Deed of Purchase)

This indenture made the twenty eight day of May in the year of our Lord God 1660, Between Daniel Fleming of Rydal in the County of Westmorland Esquire of one Part and David Harrison younger of the same Town and County aforesaid Yeoman of the other Part Wittnesseth, that the said Daniel Fleming for divers good causes and valuable Consideration Hath granted aliened and confirmed and by these Presents doth grant alien and confirm unto the said David Harrison, All that house and little Parcel of Ground here before used for a little Garden to the North End of the said House adjoyning Both situate at the Kilne-howe at the head of the Long Close in Rydall aforesaid, and parcel of the Demesne there, and Both lately in the Tenure and occupation of Adam Fisher of the said Rydal Blacksmith, and also one Calf Grass in the Nab in Rydall aforesaid, And thirty sheep Grass, and one Horse Grass upon the Pasture and Commons of Rydall aforesaid, And Liberty to Grave and Digg one days work of Turves or Peats in and upon the Pasture and Commons of Rydall aforementioned as other the Tenants within the Manor of Rydall usually have. And one Cow Gate or Grass upon the Pasture and Commons of Rydall, aforesaid, Paying yearly for the Same As other the Tenants of the said Manor do usually pay. To have and To Hold the said House Parcel of Ground, and other Premisses unto him the said David Harrison his Heirs and Assignes for Ever So As the said David Harrison his Heirs and Assignes and every of them shall for ever hereafter well and truly Yield and Pay unto the said Daniel Fleming his Heirs and Assignes the yearly Rent of Twelve pence And yearly do one Boon-day Mowing, One Boon-day shearing, And one Boon-day Leading of Manure at the several usual Days and Times according to the Custom of the said Manor of Rydal As Also all Fines, Heriots, Dues, Duties, and Services which shall be hereafter due for the Premisses according to the Custom of the Manor of Rydall aforementioned there called Tenant Right And in such Manner and Sort As other the Tenants do hold their Tenements within the said Manor In Wittness whereof Both the said Parties to these Presents have Interchangably put their Hands and Seals the Day and Year first abovementioned,

Signed Sealed and Delivered in presence of us.   Daniel Fleming
    John Ellis his Mark T
    Edward Greige his Mark ⊓   O
    John Bankes   *(Seal)*

After Adam's time a small house in the village, now vanished, served as a smithy. It stood in the present park, almost opposite to the vicarage, upon the town-gate, and within a field called Round Close. It may possibly be the subject of a deed dated 1567, described as "Tho. Fleming of Rydall Waller his grant unto Rich. Philipson of an House in Rydall of 12d. Rent per annum. Dated Aug. 6, Ao. 9, Eliz.*" Of the Rydal Philipsons little is known; an Agnes was buried in 1573.†

THE SMITHY AND WHITE LION INN, AMBLESIDE.
Sketch by Mr. J. Harden, 1825.

When Squire Daniel came to Rydal old Adam may have been unequal to work at the anvil. At any rate he patronised at first the Grasmere smith, one William Mackereth, as the bills show. The whereabouts of this "smiddy" is uncertain. It was usual in old days to place the blacksmith's shed—unless it was an adjunct

---

* D. Fleming's "List of Rydall Writings."
† A marriage is recorded for 1621, which is difficult to assign to the correct family branches, between Dorothie Flemyng of the parish of Grasmere and John Phillipson of Windermere parish.

of the manor-house—at the entrance of the little town, handy to the traveller whose horse had lost a shoe. In Ambleside one stood on the right of the road from the south, before the White Lion (Kiln Sike) was reached; and here one Holm worked within the memory of Edward Wilson. Another was situated at the exit of the town. At Grasmere one stood conveniently at Town End, as we shall see. Yet another, and doubtless a far more ancient one, since it apparently lay on the line of the Roman road, existed and is still to be seen at Winterseeds, and here John Watson worked the existing hinges of the outer church doors. After the turnpike road took the bottom of the valley, this position—accessible only up a steep rise—became inconvenient for custom. Accordingly, another smithy was opened below, where William Simpson, son of John, the Rydal statesman, worked until his early death through fever.* Besides these, a smith's shed, long unused, still stands at the cross-ways, near the Hollins.

But "Gresmer Smith" did not work long for Squire Daniel, who procured a special "Rydall Smith," in the person of George Otley. The little Philipson house was apparently bought by George, who began work in 1659, and married Agnes Harrison in 1663; for he is found paying a 1s. rent for a little place variously described as "ye little house by ye Highway side," or "joyning to ye Round Close." Here George stayed until about 1672, when he acquired the substantial farmhold of How Head, rented at 6s. 8d. This holding, though within the boundary of the Grasmere township, was reckoned as an asset of the Rydal Manor; and may have been acquired (like Pavement End) by Squire John, to whom the Hawkriggs—long in possession of it, had mortgaged at least one portion. Here Otley worked as Rydal smith, catching custom as we must suppose from wayfarers

---

* Also remembered by Ed. Wilson, who died in 1910

over White Moss; and here his descendants remained till a late date.

A few extracts from Otley's beautifully written but strangely spelt bills will instance the range of a smith's work. It will be seen that the squire sometimes produced the iron from his own foundry; and that the smith demanded drink-money when young horses were shod.

The Round Close house was perhaps used again as a forge, for the death of a blacksmith of Rydal, one John Holme, is recorded in 1725. The fate of the house is uncertain. Well-to-do John Parke, of the Nab, died (1770) in possession of a tenement in Rydal, with stable, orchard, rights, easements, etc., of a customary rent of 1s. 0d., which may have been it. As this alone of his property was to be reserved for his wife and daughter, it must have been a snug place. The widow sold it, however, to Sir Michael in 1786, and he probably razed it to the ground when he improved the Hall and Park.

Rydall Smith's Note, concerning ye Mill, and for all due till Nov. 27, '59.

	s.	d.
first of all		
there is a mill sprinte	6	0
for the gugan lying[1]	4	0
for the mill hoopes	2	0
for the spikinge[2]	4	10
for half a hundred little spiking	0	5
for tow plates	0	10
for loapes and stapels	1	6
for the mell[3]	2	6
for thre punchaws tow of my iron and one of youres and lying of them	2	0
for punchaws and pickes sharpinge	1	0
for the mill chisell lying	1	0
for the fire shoule	1	0
for the hay crouke	0	5
for the dune horse tew showes of mine and tow of youres	1	0
for the worke horses 4 new showes of mine and tow of youres and tow remoues	1	8

THE SMITHY

	s.	d.
for the bey mare tow new showes	0	6

November the 27 : 1659 receuied in ffull off this note ffor all the worke that did belonge to Daniell Fleminge the sum off
lb 01 06 06.

By me Georg Ottley.

The following items are picked from later bills :—

for famors to a bed	00	00	8
for the grindstone axeltree	00	02	4
for a croping axe lying	00	0	9
for cakers and nailes	00	0	8
for the oxen showinge	00	5	0
for a new sucke and the coulter lyinge of your iron ..	00	5	0
for the coulter and sucke lyinge of my iron[4]	00	2	0
Two pair of gimmers for ye new garden doore[5] ..		1	4
for mending two wedges for ye stone getters		00	15
Two hackes lying for ye stone getters ye one your own ye other John Holmes[6]		01	00
ffor a laddle shanke		00	04
for makeing a broyleing iron		02	04
A loup and and a crooke for a wichett[7]		00	04
two sithes crammeing[19]		00	04
two hakers for Robin[8]		00	02
a staple for a pair of swingle-trees Aprill ye 5[9] ..		00	02
A scrath ye same day[10]		00	09
spikeings for ye nursey floor Aprille ye 20 (1667) ..		00	02
A Kettle banding May ye 29		06	06
four pair of gimmers and eight clasps for ye new chamber window June ye 26		02	08
a new jocke[11]		04	00
for lying a jocke		00	08
swine rings		00	03
a split		02	06
For tow heatens (heaters ?) one of youre iron ..		0	1
For tow bands one for the hekon sadle and the other for the male pilyon.		0	10
for frosting of all the horses		1	8
for 2 andirons of youre iron		2	6
for lying of 22 harrow Teeath		3	10
for a yoke mending and a shackel mending		0	4
for a forcke show[12]		1	0
for the yonge hors and yonge mare in drink		1	0

	s	d
for the Mestris mare the elder 10 new showes three of youres and 7 of mine and 5 remoues	03	3
for a snek and a famor[13]	00	3
for 2 skelats[14]	01	0
for a new skrat[10]	00	9
for mending of the broyling yron	00	4
for drinke when wee did show the yonge horses	01	0
for laynes for the plowe[15]	00	09
for 3 new haera-teth and other sharpinge one shillinge		
Gimmers for a chest	1	6
for mending a ratton crooke[7]	1	8
four reekes for ye brewhouse chimney[16]	0	8
for the siev mending	1	0
for the chafing dish	0	1
for a pare of swinaltres and a teame mending[9]	00	8
for a new brandiron	02	6
for 4 pikes to the yeats	02	6
for 4 paare of famers and cronkes	10	0
for a peare of tonges makeing and a pare binding	01	0
for 2 boltes for a cheese pres	00	5
for Ironing 2 whele barrowes	01	7
for a Fleshe axe lyinge	0	9
for a pott startt[17]	00	5
for a plugh clouts[18]	00	7
for a cronke (?)	00	10
for a new goike (?)	4	0
for a pere of famers to a bed (?)	1	0
for curting rods and heukes	0	8
for a claspe to the boatte	0	4
four pair of Gimmers for ye slaughter house doore	05	00
for makeing a cockle panne	03	04
for craming a sith[19]	00	02
Gimmers for ye beef fatt[5]	01	02
for lying ye flour axe and striking knife[1]	01	09
Gimmers for ye Kitchin hecke	01	00
spikeings fetcht by ye Coupers for ye mash-fatt[2]	00	01
A seatt for ye Low parks cowhouse	00	00
a byer crooke	00	04
for two keders (?) one your iron and the other mine[20]	0	9

NOTES FOR BILLS.

[1] To "lay" an implement was to set it in its handle or into position.
[2] Spikings were small nails.
[3] Mell, a hammer or Mallet.

[4] The *suche* or *sock* was the nose of the plough, and the coulter the blade of the same. Entries for the shoeing of the plough oxen occur from time to time.

[5] Gimmers, hinges.

[6] Hack, a pick.

[7] Wicket, a little yeat or gate. The *heck* that follows is a short light gate also. The loup slipped over the upright of the gate. The *crook* (a piece of bent iron) was of many kinds ; ratton-crook, an iron bar on which the kettle was held above the fire.

There was a crook by which the plough leader guided the plough, which could pull or push.

[8] Robin was the scullion, whom the squire dressed. Kaker = calker, the iron rim or plate on a wooden clog or shoe heel (Wright).

[9] Swinaltree or Swingle-tree, the cross bar of wood, bound with iron, between horse and plough to which plough traces and plough are both attached.

[10] Scrath, or skrat, a rake.

[11] Jock, the northern form of *Jack*; but which of the several implements called by this name is referred to, cannot be determined. The best known is a machine for supporting the axletree of a cart.

[12] Forcke-show = the shoe (into which to insert the handle) of a fork.

[13] A snek and a famor = a latch and (?) See also a pair of famers to a bed, 4 paare of famers and cronkes.

[14] Skellet, a pan with a long handle.

[15] Laynes for the plough = plough-lines or reins made of cord.

[16] Reekes or rookes, bellows.

[17] A pott start = a handle to a saucepan.

[18] Plugh clouts or clates = the shoe or foot of the plough.

[19] Cramming a sith, to *cram* a scythe seems to be synonymous with the modern *laying*, which means the fixing by the smith of the " heel " of the blade in the handle. The "grass-rail" is then secured across diagonally, which prevents the grass getting into the space between blade and handle.

[20] Keders, implements of butchery.

The Shop.

Number 5 of the 1654 Rental closes the list of Little Houses in Rydal. If it be identical with the shop of later days, it was joined on to a small farmhold (probably Wilson's and now Ivy Cottage) and consisted of but one room upstairs and down, with outhouse behind. Subsequently it was used as a school, and finally, after a modern house had grown on its further side out of cot and weaving shed, it degenerated into a coal-hole. From this degradation it has been lately rescued ; and we step down now on to its ancient paved floor (two feet below the present level of the road) with a respectful sense of the part it played in the past life of the village.

It was Anthony " Greige " who compounded in 1655 for the lord's fine on Littlehouse, on behalf of his daughter

Elizabeth. The rent was but 6d., and the fine being fixed at 30 times that amount, suggests a tax on a monopoly of the lord—for such the village shop was in early times. The turnover on the business could not have been large, for in 1665, Elizabeth had not only leisure for carding wool for the Hall (10d.) but for "looking (weeding) in ye garden" (2d.). Certainly it did not keep Anthony. He was a man of education, writing his name to a contract, and apparently a favourite, for in 1656 John Banks brings back from London "a sun dyeall ffor Anthony Grigge." He was a mighty worker, whose labour yet (as with some of his neighbours) did not keep him straight with the world. Settlements always with him meant further borrowing. He had been in the habit of working for the estate—walling gaps, or breaking stones for the lime-kiln, as the account books of 1645 show; and the new squire at once took him on, generally using him as a hewer of wood, though sometimes as a waller. Entries of his labour in the Account-book are endless, this early one being ominous and characteristic.

	lb. s. d.
Jan 24, 1656-57, Lent unto Grigg	00 06 00
Paid more unto him in full of all wood cutt (excepting onely 28 load)	00 03 00

On June 20th a grand result is attained, for Anthony not only pays back 5s. 0d. borrowed in March, but 6s. 0d. besides, the last sum owing of his daughter Elizabeth's fine. However, the other side runs:—

Paid unto Grigg for ye cutting of 12 score & 8 load of wood beeing all now due unto him	00 12 00
Given him backe of his fine	00 01 00
Lent unto him	00 06 00

Of the 8s. 0d., therefore, that Anthony carries away, 6s. 0d. have yet to be worked for, in 120 loads (probably as big as he could carry) of wood cut up for fires. When paid " for three dayes workeing in getting stones for ye Oven and mending thereof " his wages are 4d. per day. He also lays " ye Lime in ye Garner," and " plasters of ye hal-loft doore," at the same rate. Anthony's last debt invariably wiped out his earnings, so that even for 1s. 0d. " to lay his Axe with," he had to make a journey to the Hall. However, for " 12 days working at ye hal-banck " in 1658 he receives 8d. per day, and 1s. 0d. for " a wood Bottle," and seems to be straight. Work next year at walling the boundaries (called the Outwalls) and " walling of ye new gate at ye Garden-corner " at the same rate and 2d. given over, helps him too towards solvency. But the terrible " Lent unto Griggs " of some amount or other soon recurs, with credit on his side of numerous wood-loads. Work at the "swine-hull," at the " lead " help hardly at all; and mending the kitchen chimney (1659) he too, like old Adam, gets stones at " ye Low-hall " and 50 loads of slate " for ye Low-parke barne." This last job brings him in 12s. 6d. He walls " up ye closett " mends Birkett-barn at 4d, helps at " payveing of ye highway in Rydall Towne-gate," and so forth; but his labour becomes ever more restricted to wood-cutting. In December, 1671, he has 90 loads to his credit, but alas! this still leaves him with a debt of 4s. 0d.; and 1s. 6d. more is lent him. In April, fourscore more loads leaves his debt at 1s. 6d., but 3s. 0d. is lent him. He is evidently living from hand to mouth. But his toils and his debts are soon to be over.

Sep. 10. Given towards ye burying of Anthony Grigg, who was yesterday in ye evening found dead in Rydal-Park, near a Tree wch he had newly felled for ye Fire, ye sum of 00 05 06

A certain Gawen Greige was about this time resident in Rydal, paying the hearth-tax, and running cattle on the common; but he had no permanent hold over Little House, for after Anthony's death it appears to have been

2 D

purchased by a Richard Dixon. Richard probably left the tendance of the shop to his wife, for he interested himself in husbandry, renting two meadows from the squire at 11s. 0d. on a life-lease. In two more years he was dead (1681), and his widow Jane continued the rent and the cattle on the common.

In 1707, however, a prospering mill-wright of the village, John Birkett, is found buying the place from William Tyson, and paying, besides a fine of 10s. 0d., and another " Income " one of £2. This was the first footing the Birketts obtained upon Rydal land ; but John's son John (who paid 6d. rent for Little House) had other holdings, and left the place " in which Thomas Jackson lives " to a second or younger son Thomas. But Thomas had sought, like many another, to better his fortunes elsewhere, and being settled in Ulverston, preferred in 1777 to sell to William Swainston of Kendal for £15. 7s. 0d. a " messuage or house with shop and garden commonly called Little House, formerly Dixon's," with all right of common, etc. In 1781 Swainston renovated his house, four small trees from George Birkett's wood, and one from every other neighbour's being set out for him by the bailiff. Another William followed, who paid in 1788 the enormous general fine on Lady Dorothy Fleming's death of £15. 15s. 0d., and then came a John, currier by trade, who sold messuage shop and garden to John Fleming of the Inn for £45. John's will was proved in 1834, and in it he left Little House, with right of herbage in Nab wood and ground by the lake, also of cutting underwood and cropping the same, to Lancelot and Thomas Fleming. They parted with it in 1840 to Lady Fleming, John Scales, schoolmaster, being then the occupant (see School).

CHAPTER V.

THE CORN MILL

Applethwaite; Grasmere; Langdale; Loughrigg; Ambleside; Troutbeck; Brathay; Skelwith; Calgarth and Rydal; The Millers.

TEMPORA MUTANTUR.

Troutbeck's turned upside down,
    And wise men wane in skill,
Wives are leaving off to frown,
    And Browne has sold his mill.

And if a new mill be erect,
    This question pray explaine :
Is it for public respect?
    Or is it private gaine?

Shall Israel ever be opprest,
    And plagued by Pharoah still?
For thus cry out some fickle heads,
    Let's have another mill!

For me, I am not of this mind,
    For this is my belief—
You may as soon the Phœnix find,
    As a mill without a thief.

A head off Hydra cut,
    For one there springeth twain;
More mills more thieves in them are put,
    Which the country must maintain.

Written by Thomas Hoggart, native of Troutbeck, who died in 1709. He was uncle of Hogarth the painter.

NO institution of the tûn or the manor was of greater importance than the water corn-mill. It began to supersede the hand-mill or quern in Saxon times.* though these primitive stones continued to be used in out-of-the-way spots till a recent period; and two of them have turned up from the soil of the Rydal and Loughrigg township, one (now missing) on the likely ground of Old Hall Hill, the other near Miller Bridge, this being a mere "crusher" or hollowed stone, in which a few handfuls of grain could be pounded by a pestle-like stone held in the hand. The improved contrivance, by which a wheel set in running water turned stones of a comparatively large size, was the property of the lord, who no doubt originally introduced it; and in return for his outlay of capital, and upkeep of gear, in stones and wheel and shed, he enacted that his tenants should desist from the use of querns, and bring their corn to his mill and no other to be ground; and in payment thereof the miller, who was appointed by himself, was empowered to take a certain measure of the corn before it was poured into the hopper for grinding.

Originally, this toll may have been taken by the handful[†]; but a measure came into use, called a toll-fat, or dish, which the miller dipped into the sack and brought out full as his portion. Now the law exercised no supervision over the miller's dish, the size of which became a matter of local custom, and the tenant had no redress against extortionate or over-full measure, but by appeal to the lord or the village court.[‡] And, to read poets and rhymesters from *Piers the Ploughman* (where "Maunde the Miller" personifies the thief) down even to Hoggart, of Troutbeck, one would suppose there had hardly been an honest miller in the land. The lines at the foot of this chapter suggest a few of the ways by which a deft man might increase his gains, most of them causing

---

* It is mentioned in a charter dated 664 See *History of Corn-Milling*, Bennet and Elton, vol, 11, p 76
† The same, vol 111, p 148
‡ Not a single presentment of a miller for extortion occurs in the few local court-rolls extant

a scattering of the flour over the floor, to be swept up later.

Yet the miller was often hated without cause, from the nature of his bond with his lord. While he took his pay in kind, he in turn paid his lord a rent in kind (besides grinding all the manor corn free)—occasionally and in part in the eels that fattened in his dam, but generally in grain. Now the amount of both was fixed; so when corn was dear, and was therefore also scarce; he had to indemnify himself by taking larger toll from the people, at the very time that the pinch of scarcity was upon them.

But of ancient squabbles between miller and folk, local record says nothing. In these valleys, indeed, where the land mostly belonged to those two great fragments of the old Barony of Kendal, called the Richmond and the Marquis Fees, and no resident lord (except of Rydal) was seated, the tenure of corn-mills and their customs was peculiarly free, like all the other manorial institutions; and it will be seen that not only restrictions of soke disappeared, but that the township at large might even exercise an entire control over the mill. Possibly, however, the mills were early leased at a low figure by the lord to some private individual, and after being held in one family for several generations, were bartered for a good price to a new holder, who continued to pay the original small "free rent" to the superior.

Local Mills. The table on page 406 shows the rents of the town mills belonging to the lord at a few scattered periods, according as record has been found available. In some cases the mill-rent, not specified, is being included in the general rental-receipts.

The table shows quickly the relative importance of the mills, which depended upon the size of the particular township, and the amount of corn ground at it.

WATER CORN MILLS.

Date.	Applethwaite.	Ambleside.	Grasmere.	Langdale.	Loughrigg.
1283	..	..	..	7s.	..
1324	Reputed worth £6 6s. 8d. but now let at 60s.	8s.	20s.	10s.	..
1334	60s.	8s.	20s.	10s.	..
1379 | 1403	Leased to Roger de Byrkett at 40s.	Leased to "all the tenants" at 20s.	..	..	..
1436	..	..	..	..	..
1453	"Farm of 2 parts" at 31/1¾d. 46s. 8d.	"Two parts," 13s. 4d.	"Two parts," 13s. 4d.	"Two parts," 6s. 8d.	"Two parts," 3s. 4d.
1493	..	..	"Farmed," 13s. 4d.	"Farmed," 6s. 8d.	"No Corn Mill."
1505-6	..	..	..	..	Tenants pay 6s. for "Multer Ferme."

Applethwaite.—At the head of the list stands the mill that was undoubtedly the adjunct of the ancient, and possibly Anglian, manor of Windermere. The Hall on the Holme Island, the church by the shore, the mill turned by the fall of Winlas Beck to the lake, all belonged to one manorial group, and after the manor with an increasing population had been broken up into the townships of Troutbeck (with Ambleside below Stock), Applethwaite and Undermillbeck,* and others had been established, it retained its pre-eminence as the " common mill " for the whole parish. When Margaret of Richmond leased in 1472 her greater half of the barony to the Parrs and others, this " corn-mill of Appulthwayte " is, while all the other mills are lumped together, mentioned specially as one of the larger assets.† Its early rent seems to have been 10 marks, but with the depreciation of property that took place during Edward II.'s lamentable

---

* In 1436 " le milnebek " is spoken of. 1443 " Suthermylnbek " ... as being on south side of Milnebeck.
† Cal. Pat. Rolls, 12 Edward IV., p. 1.

wars with the Scots, it fell to £3. A rent once dropped, practically dropped for ever. We see, in the rental of 1453, that one-third was deducted from all the mills because that was part of the dower assigned to the Duke of Bedford's young widow, Jacquetta; yet, after her death in 1473 such mills as are mentioned remain at their " 2 parts " figure.

The Grasmere Mill ranks next, as is likely, this being the seat of an ancient parish church, and of some sort of a manorial establishment, though neither ancient nor complete. The rent here also may have been originally higher. Also after the one half of the town not represented in the above rentals had become sub-divided, it is stated that the joint owners joined at a water corn-mill*; there may, therefore, have early been a second lord's mill in the valley.

Langdale comes next. Mentioned as early as 1283, it even shows a rise in rent, no doubt as the early settlers' families multiplied and the forest got cleared. Little is known of the mill. It was probably the one that stood until recent times on Mill Beck, under the Pikes, and was long owned by a branch of the Benson family. The Skelwith Bridge Mill was at a late period a corn-mill.

Loughrigg was so small and rocky a division, that there would be few tenants there to grind at a lord's mill, especially after Roger de Lancaster had drawn off half of them into his manor; and the quarter mark rent of the 1453 document seems an appropriate one. A very ancient mill, however, was probably seated at Miller Bridge, where the old curve of the river would suggest the earliest dam; but the paucity of custom on this fine flow of water may have caused its conversion into a fulling-mill, now becoming lucrative. Some arrangement between lord and tenants was certainly made, and doubtless at the time of its abolition; as the emphatic statement of

---
* Rental.

1473 that there was then no corn-mill in Loughrigg, is superseded in 1505-6 by one that the tenants pay yearly a rent of 6s. 0d. called Multer ferme. They doubtless had by this arrangement freedom from soke. In the next Century there were Mackereths here, and the family of Mackereth held High Miller Bridge (of which one close was called Kiln How) until recent times.

The Ambleside Corn-mill shows, by a considerable rise in rent, an inversion of the usual process. But the place had sprung rapidly from a mere clearing in the forest to a compact little town, whose men were eager to take advantage of their position on a rushing beck, and to join in the fast-developing fulling trade. A new rental had to be made out for them ; and with that solidarity they later displayed over church affairs they easily clubbed together and leased from the lord the corn-mill, over which they thus obtained entire control. This must have been the " Old milne . standing upon Sleddall becke.* " which—as well as the " new " one in Stock Gill became absorbed by the Jacksons, who are found in 1639 disposing of their rights in both to the owner of a third corn-mill at Stock Bridge, Gawen Braithwaite. The minute " milne " rent of 4½d then paid to the lord for the first could barely have represented one lease-holder's share of the original 20s. 0d.

A tendency towards monopoly of a mill by a family, long after the lord had yielded up his own monopoly, is further exemplified in Windermere and Troutbeck ; and along with the tendency went a multiplication of mills. The original manorial mill for this division at *Applethwaite* had been leased as early as the close of the fourteenth century to one Roger de Byrkett. In 1445 we find a Katharine Berkehed suing two members of the Addison family of Milnebekstok, Westmorland (who doubtless

---

* See deed of sale of this and a newer mill "Ambleside Town and Chapel," *Transactions* C. & W. A. & A Society, vol vi , N S

had the fulling-mill upon that beck) "touching a trespass.*" The mill remained with the Birketts, for in an award concerning it, dated 1535† the arbitrators declare it to have formerly been in the occupation of "Walt{er} byrkhed, Thomas byrkhed, John byrkhed, milners to the said parishe, yerly paying the Rent." It had, however, passed to one Hugh Bateman, whose children were now in dispute with the present miller, John Dixon, as well about the mill as a right of way to it. The decree of the twelve arbitrators allowed the hereditary claim, for it was settled that Dixon or any other "mylner for the parishe" should pay the Batemans 2s. 0d. yearly. At the same time the occupant was confirmed in his post as "one able honest and lafful mylner ffor the holl parishe;" the right being reserved, however, by the folk as a body to "pute furthe" him or any other miller who should "doe wrong or apos theym Selse to the parishe." This is an interesting example of the lord's jurisdiction passing to the people. The later history of the place is one of decay, like most other mills. "Milne House" as it was called through the seventeenth century, then Milners, and Milnes Ground through the eighteenth, retains now nothing but the name. In 1712 it was sold by one Rowland Cookson of Troutbeck Park to Dr. Miles Atkinson of Troutbeck Bridge, being

"All that his Water Corn Miln and Kiln and one Housestead, and one parcel of arable and waste Ground of the yearly rent of 2ˢ or thereabouts situate Lying & being at Milner Ground in Applethwaite."

Even the house-stead has vanished. It lay on the north side of the present building, and since the time

---

* Cal. Pat. Rolls, 23 Henry VI., p. 1. One Addison is described in the printed Calendar as "of Adylthwayt," but this surely, in connection with the other names, stands for *Apylthwayt*.

† This interesting document was in the possession of the late Mr. G. Browne of Troutbeck. It is printed

(still remembered) when the last stones were carted away for adjacent walls; its site has been alone marked by the "Lent Lilies" that bloom there in spring.*

The original Applethwaite mill had its rival—no doubt by arrangement with the lord—fairly early. Situated at Limefit, on the Troutbeck, it was within easy reach of those thriving homesteads that became closely grouped along the brow of the valley. It was owned by the Browne family: George, a wealthy yeoman of that ilk, bequeathing it to his eldest son Thomas in 1558, while another George, who sold it in 1699 to one James Longmire (which was the cause of Hoggart's rhymes) asserted that his ancestors had possessed it for hundreds of years, though it is extremely improbable that it existed before the Countess of Richmond leased her lordship in 1472,† while it may have been granted shortly after. A monopoly was in this case, which illustrates a statesman's hereditary holding of a mill, clearly intended also, though perhaps limited to the hamlet or township; for George, writing in the year of sale to the then lord of the manor, Viscount Lonsdale, complains that the latter has granted a licence for another (and apparently pre-existing) mill to be removed from Rowlandson's Gill to the main beck, naturally with prejudice to the Limefit custom. Mr G. Browne considered that the rhymester's new mill, with which the people were threatened, was realized in part only, as a Malt Kiln was built on the Ambleside road; which as "Kilne Cottage" still bears the date 1700.

George Browne may have the more readily disposed of the Limefit mill from the fact that his father (also George) had in 1649 purchased the half share possessed by Henry Birkett, M.A., of Oxford, in the *Water Corn Mill at Troutbeck Bridge*—the other half remaining,

---

* For all the later particulars of this mill I am indebted to the late Mr. G. Browne, who had traced it exhaustively by means of his numerous papers
† Cal Pat. Rolls, 12 Edward IV, p 1

apparently, to other members of the Birkett family, who sold to Mr. Robert Philipson of Calgarth in 1668. This additional mill probably originated in the fulling-mill which was still running at the time ; and it affords an excellent example of the way in which fluctuating trade controlled the water-wheels of the district. Many an old fulling-mill survived almost to our times as a saw-mill ; but the Troutbeck Bridge mill-stream beats all record for the number of industries to which it has successively lent a motive power. Cloth and corn kept it busy till 1673, when George Cumpstone* of Ambleside—whose father had run a paper-mill upon Scandale Beck—rented it on lease for paper making. This was continued by Thomas Jones and Robert Tubman, both wheels under them working paper ; till in 1720 it was let again (and to a Birkett) as a water corn-mill, the working miller (another Birkett) paying a rent of £3 10s 0d, which under a new man rose to £4 4s. 0d. The paper-mill expired before 1788, and in 1801 the wheel saw a flax-mill. This was superseded, before 1829, by a more usual bobbin-mill, and this again by the present electrical works. This corn-mill was ruined by fire in 1653.†

Another mill that had several changes of trade was the one on the Brathay at Skelwith Bridge in Loughrigg. Doubtless constructed as a walk-mill, it became (when monopolies had ceased) both a corn and a bark-mill, with twin wheels, and it still works as a saw-mill.‡

The following letter speaks of a mill which was at Calgarth —

---

* The Cumpstons seem to have had footing first in Rydal, where a Richard died in 1600

† All these particulars were furnished by the late Mr. G Browne

‡ "Fullers and Freeholders," *Transactions*, C. & W A & A Society, vol viii, N S.

Troutbeck,
Windermere,
Feb 1st, 1911.

Dear Miss Armitt,

Philipsons of Calgarth

I have just been looking over an old deed dated Dec. 18th xxth Chas. 2nd confirming a marriage settlement made on the marriage of Robert Philipson of Calgarth & Barbara daughter of William Pennington of Seaton co. of Cumberland. There are very full particulars of R Philipson's Estates, but there is no mention of any Island or Chapel on Windermere There are some mention of Milnes that may interest you, some of them are not exactly in the Lake District. ' And a Milne & one close or p̃cell of ground called Briery close lyeinge and beinge in Crocke And also all that water corne Milne situate and beinge at Ulthwaite (Ulthwaite is near Staveley, between Stavely & Kentmere) And also all that messuage and Tenement at Gate Mill how near Calgarth aforesaid And also that his Water Corne Milne wth the appurtance called *Calgarth Milne,* And the moity of the Milne situate at Troutbeck-Bridge (The other moiety of Troutbeck Bridge Milne belonged my ancestor Geo Browne at that time) This shows that there was a corne Milne at Calgarth and also one at Troutbeck Bridge '

Yours faithfully,
GEO BROWNE

P S.—Robert Philipson's and Barbara Pennington's marriage settlement was made April 22nd 1665, and the marriage would be solemnized not long after —G B "

Of the Rydal mill, there is no early record When first heard of, it was—as it remained—a strictly manorial institution, and had no doubt been maintained by the lord from the days of Roger de Lancaster. He and his descendants of Holgill were men of keen business minds. Some of them had, in the beginning of the fourteenth century, shares in a distant fulling-mill. One of the Fleming branch leased in the fifteenth century an alien corn-mill, certainly for profit, and probably this branch, which inherited but the half-share of Rydal, ran the village corn-mill, since the Whitfield branch had the manorial brewery, as part of their share.

THE CORN MILL

But it is not until Squire William Fleming consolidated his interest in the manor, by buying out the joint holders, that we hear of the mill, for a deed exists, dated 1575, by which he leases it to John Grigge. The deed is here given :—

"This indenture maide the twentie daye of Marche in the Eighten-the Yeare of the Reigne of our Soureigne Ladie Elizabethe, by the grace of God of Englande, Frannce, and Irelande, Quene defender of the faithe, etc. Between Willm̄ Flemynge, of Rydall, in the Countye of Westmerlande, Esquire, and Agnes his wief, on the one partie and John Grigge, of Rydall Aforesaide, yeoman, on the other partie. Witnessith. That the said Willm̄ Flemynge and Agnes his wief, for the causes and consideracions hereafter in theise presentes conteyned have graunted demised and to Farme letten and by the same, do graunte, demise and to Farme lett unto the saide John Grigge, all that ther kylne and corne mylne in Rydall Aforesaide, together wth all watter courses and Raises, soken, suyte, and toole, belonging to the saide mylne, and all those ther two Orcherds, & one garden or lookegarthe, neare adionynge unto ther Capitall messuage of Rydall callid the olde hall, and the whole fishinge in all that ther meere and standinge watter called Rydall watter, togetter wth that ther fishgarthe and Eell arcke at the foote of the saide standing watter, one boate maide for the fishinge of the said watter, and all ther Free and seuerall fishinge wthin the River of Rothey and the River discendinge from the saide standinge watter of Rydall. To Haue, Hold, and Enioye the saide kilne, corne mylne, Orcherdes, Garden, and Fishinge and other the Premesses aboue specified unto the saide John Grigge his Executors and Assignes from the makinge hereof for and duringe the spaice and tearme of ten yeares nexte Ensewinge, yeldinge and payinge for the same yearlye duringe all the said tearme of ten yeares unto the saide Willm̄ Flemynge and Agnes, and the heires of the saide Willm̄ at his now dwelling howse in Conyston in the Countie of Lancastre the Annuall and yearlie rente of Eighte pounds thirteene shillinges fowrepence, of lawfull Englishe monye at the feastes daies of Saynte Mychaell tharchanngell and St Mathew thappostle by Even porcons, And the saide Willm̄ Flemynge and Agnes his wief for them, and the heires of the saide Willm̄ do Couenannte and graunte to and withe the saide John Grigge his Executors and Assignes by theise presentes, that it shall and may be lawfull for the saide John, his Executors and assignes frome tyme to tyme duringe the saide tearme of ten yeares to Croope, and loope all the Okes, Asshes, and thornes growinge w^thin the saide two Orchardes, for the vpholdinge, Repayringe, and maynteyning of the hedges, and Fences Abowte the saide Orchardes. And also to gett, tacke, and haue yearlye during the saide terme of ten yeares, one hundretht horse loades of fyrewoode to be spended in the said kylne, and also so often as neide shall require duringe the saide tearme sufficiente tymber woode for the necessarie Repayringe and Amending of the said Kylne and mylne, & of the saide Boate, - fishgarthe, & Eell Arcke the said fyrewoode and tymberwoode to be takyn alwaies of the woodes of the saide Willm̄ and Agnes in Rydal Aforesaide, by the appoyntment and Assignment of the said Willm̄ and Agnes and the heires of the saide Willm̄, or of the Assignes of them or some of them, and not in other maner And the saide John grigge for him his Executors and administrators, dothe couenant and graunte to and wth the saide Willm̄ Flemynge and Agnes his wief and the heires of the saide Willm̄, that he the saide John his Executors, administrators or assignes shall and will yearlie duringe the saide tearme of ten yeares not onlie well and trulie content and paye the saide yearlie rente of VIII*l*. XIII*s* IIIJ*d* unto the saide Willm̄ Flemynge and Agnes, and the heires of the saide Willm̄ at the saide daies and place and Accordinge to the tenor and effecte aboue specified, but also at all tymes duringe the saide tearme of ten yeares, well and sufficienthe repaire vpholde and mayntayne the saide kylne and mylne and all thinges apperteynynge to either of them and the said fishgarthe, Eell arcke, and Boate in such sufficiencte and good repairācons and plite as the same now be, and at the end, expirācon and determinācon of the saide tearme to leave the same and eu^erie of them so repaired vpholden and mayntened, And also that neither he the saide John grigge his Executors ad'strators nor assignes, nor any other P'sone or P'sons by his or ther P'curement or assent shall at anye tyme duringe the saide tearme of ten years putt or cause to be putt, into the saide Orcherdes of either of them, any sheepe, horsses or other beastes or Cattell for the depasture, grasse, baitte, or food ther, *Provided Alwaies* and uppon Condicion, that if it happen the saide yearlie rent of VIII*l*. XIIJ*s* IIIJ*d*. to be behynde and vnpaide in parte or in whole at any of the saide feaste daies when the same oughte to be paied as Aforesaide, That then frome thensfurthe, this present grannte, demise and lease and all Couenentes and granntes

Abouemencionede maide on the P'tie of the saide Willm̃ and Agnes shall cease and be voide and of none effecte, Any thinge abouemencioned to the contrarie in any wyse notw^thstandinge *In Witnes Whereof* the P'tyes Aforesaide to the singular parte of thiese Indenturs Interchanngablie haue sett ther seales the day and yeare abouewritten 1575 [Seals all gone only slits in the parchment remain On the back is the endorsement]—

Seallid and deliuerid the daie and yeare w^thin written in the P'sence of us Jacobi dugdall Cleri.

       oswold thomson
       Henrye myers
       Anthony Siluerwoode.

The Grigg family are found more than once to have been associated with mills in these parts. The name occurs in a rental of 1505-6 when a John Grigg was acting as bailiff of Loughrigg, and again in 1506-7, when Thomas Grygge is found enclosing three intakes containing three roods from the lord's waste in Langdale, probably for a fulling-mill; while in the last decade of the century George Grigge was paying a " milne " rent in the same valley, but in the Marquis Fee The clan was clearly numerous in the sixteenth century in Loughrigg, judging from the registers of their deaths; the burials being, Robert in 1575, Anthony in 1598, Arthur in 1612, Henrie and Edward in 1613. There were also, living contemporaneously, a little later, William, Anthony, Gawen and John, all of Loughrigg. A John held Browhead in 1657, while another branch had a small holding in Grigg field.

John Grigge, the miller of Rydal, was a man of considerable property. His house in the town carried the high lords rent of 22s. 0d., and he had a close in Loughrigg by the lake.* He did not long, however, work the land he undertook to farm on lease, for his death occurred in the following year; and his son Arthur—doubtless a prosperous man on his own account, since he was a

---

* See Text *Rydal House.*

Shearman of Derby—straightway disposed of all the Rydal lands to the lord.

The mill-deed reveals an interesting state of things. Squire William Fleming and his wife, Agnes, living at the ancestral seat at Coniston, let to Grigge not only the corn-mill with the whole of the water courses, and the lake with its fish, the fishgarth, the boat and the eel-ark, but the more private part of the demesne, with the two orchards and the garden adjoining their capital messuage of Rydal. At this Old Hall, it may be noted, a younger branch of the Fleming family was then living. And for these, with liberty to take 100 horse-loads of fire-wood from the forest for the kiln, and as much timber as would be necessary for the upkeep of the premises, Grigge undertook to pay a rent of 13 marks, or £8. 13s. 4d.

For those times it was a goodly sum. Fisheries and land then carried what now appears to us a low rent, and the chief asset in the bargain was clearly the mill, which half a century later was let alone for £5. A good deal of corn must have been ground there to make such a rent profitable.

Whether the corn-mill stood originally on the precincts of the Old Hall is not known. Several " cundreths " cover a flow of water past that spot that would easily have turned a primitive wheel. Then there are evidences of a mill having once stood on Scandale Beck, close to the possible site of Roger de Lancaster's lodge ; though this is more likely to have been a manorial fulling-mill, which went to decay during the Civil Wars. But the site in Grigg's times was probably the same as in later times, where the magnificent rush of Rydal Beck, before it leaps to the last of its many falls, would ensure a body of water at all times, alike in drought or frost, capable of turning stones of a large size.* According to tradition,

---

* Speedy grinding was desirable, as at some soke-mills the tenant had a right, if the corn were not ground within twenty-four hours, to carry it elsewhere. His. C. M , vol iii , p 146.

the mill stood a little below the present Hall, and in front of it; and record bears this out. A plan of 1770 shows that the mill race left the beck above the Hall bridge (as may still be seen), ran thence across the backyard beneath a footbridge, and onward against the side of the house and the garden (planted by Sir Daniel), and so into an enclosure called the Mill Orchard (likewise planted by him), round which several small buildings are seen in the plan to stand—one being doubtless the mill itself. When Sir Michael shortly after this date improved and refronted the house, the defunct little mill would no doubt be an eye-sore, and so it was swept completely away.

There is evidence that in 1632, Edward Walker of the High House was renting a mill on the demesne, yet in the same account-book a payment stands for the previous year to " the milner of his waige " 7s. 0d. From this we must suppose that the alternative method of hiring a miller and taking the profits direct, had been resorted to during Mrs. Agnes Fleming's period of management, and that upon her death the mill was leased.

Old Edward Walker who had got into money difficulties, died in 1643. The account sheets for that year show that a " milner " was now hired at a rate of two marks, or 26s. 8d. the year, and this continued until the sheets close; also that a new in-wheel was provided for the mill at a cost of 11s. 8d. The whole plant and gear of the little structure must have gone down during the years of neglect and dispute that followed, and no doubt the townsmen carried their grain whither they listed, but that it continued to grind is certain, for in 1652 " Edmond Fleming of Ridell, Miller," was buried.

When Squire Daniel caught up with such firmness the manorial reins, the jog-trot of customary law began again inexorably. A miller was at hand, willing to take over the mill by yearly contract. This was another member of the Fleming family (see Inns), by name John;

and upon his milling prospects he felt able to marry, the squire sending down (November 17th, 1656) 5s. 0d. towards the festivity John's agreement was for a £5 rent for the mill—the old high figure ; but he was not content with his bargain, for 2s 6d, was returned to him the first year, and 1s. 0d. the next. It is evident, too, that the need for repairs was pressing, though the squire —where all was dilapidated and money scarce—had postponed them. However, they were undertaken in 1659 The great outlay was in new stones, and these since the district furnishes no free-stone, had to be brought from a distance. But millstone grit, as it is termed geologically, abounds in Lancashire, and the place-name Quernmore is said to have had its origin in the ancient quarries, where the hand mill-stones were cut. Kellet and Capernwray, however, being nearer, usually supplied our district, and these particular Rydal stones came apparently from a quarry north of Carnforth, £10. 10s. 0d. being paid for them to a Mr. West, of Borwick. The note of their cost for carriage, written by John Banks, is interesting enough to quote in full. Their journey across country, drawn by oxen to the foot of Windermere, was apparently not without mishap. Payment for boat does not appear.

"The 20th aboutte the millstones	s. d.
ffor unloading them	00 02 04
ffor drinke and bread and cheise to the men that came with theire oxen to carrie them to water ffoote	00 13 04
ffor mending teames were broke	00 00 05
ffor makeing the drags to straile the stones on .	00 01 00
to the wright that went wth us to ffetch them ..	00 00 06
to the man that brought the l[ett]re to Conyston that the stones were come	00 00 02
	00 17 09

A mill-wright and his two assistants were busy on the

mill for eighteen days ; and another man thirty days. A new spindle cost 10s. 0d

Under these improved conditions a fresh agreement was made between squire and miller. By a legal indenture, the former let to the latter the mill and kiln with their profits for a term of six years at £5. 10s. 0d ; the usual stipulations being added, that the lord's grain and malt should pay no toll, and that the miller should have sufficient timber from the forest to maintain the gear in the order in which he found it. An unusual one was added that the Hall poultry should be kept at the mill, where no doubt they would obtain a good living on spilt grain. A clause provided that either party might, upon a quarter's notice, break the lease in three years time. And this was done, for by the second year John's rent was in arrears, and it actually stood over till 1667, when the account book runs :—

" Received of Margaret Fleming, beeing in full of Jo Fleming her husband's grass money and mill-rent .. . 01 00 00

From this it seems as if John had sought employment elsewhere, where milling paid better, and left his wife to guard the little cottage home and the cow

A fresh miller, one George Cookson, was now found to take up the venture He made a new bargain with the squire almost every year, paying first £6, then £5, and later £5. 5s 0d. ; while in 1674 the squire again secured the highest rent with the sop of board thrown in, letting him the mill " for a year for £6 and his dyet." But the miller soon grew restive. In February, 1676, it was agreed that both food and mill should be thrown in for nothing till May-day, provided he took the premises over for three years at the old rental of £5 Cookson, however, appears to have done few repairs ; and items are set down from time to time for new out-wheel, in-wheel and axle-tree, with some repairs to kiln and mill-race. The payment in 1676 for walling "ye Low-mill and water-well" suggests that Sturdy Park mill still ran, perhaps for fulling purposes. But by 1677 Cookson was likewise in arrears with mill-rent, and it was necessary to look round for another miller. Oddly enough, John Fleming, who now re-appears on the village scene as a statesman, took up his old post, but upon greatly reduced terms. The squire wrote in his rent book that the bargain was for a year, "he paying me 20s. at either halfe yeares end, makeing all my mault and grinding all my Corne gratis, and without takeing of any Mulcture and so for 7 yeares if I and He do both approve thereof." It may be noticed that the squire's grain had enormously increased of late years (see Husbandry); also that neither here, nor in the preceding deed, is the soke of the mill mentioned, John being apparently left to enforce his rights over the village milling as best he might. The bargain continued to work smoothly, though on a renewal of the yearly lease in 1693, John was screwed up to the rent of £2. 10s. But he was a fairly good match for the squire, and usually succeeded (no doubt by systematic grumbling) in getting 2s 6d. returned on payment of his half-yearly rent. "Old Miller," as he began to be called, was a canny member of a canny race. The death of Thomas of the Inn, and the marriage of Jane (see Inns) left the family property vacant, and John slipped into it—no doubt by purchase—in 1677, and added to his milling the occupations of selling ale and of husbandry. He had so much cattle in 1684, that he had to pay 6s. 0d extra for beasts on the common; and from 1688 till 1699, when he had two oxen grazing in the park and two cows and two heifers on the common, he rented Adam How, the Allans, and Old Hall. He had a "barn-raising" in 1686, and in 1689 he appears to have bought that excellent farmhold called Thompson's or Banks's, with which he endowed his second son William. William became miller after him;

and as a holder served as churchwarden for the Rydal township in 1699, his father filling the same office three years later. In 1704 the death of "the Old Miller" was registered, and Margaret, "the old miller wife of Rydall," followed him in 1711. So firmly was his character and profession stamped on his belongings, that when the old family property was sold by his eldest son Thomas (who lived at distant Browham, in Yorkshire) it was described as "Millers." Banks', late in the possession of William, was also sold; so that it is clear that by 1723 the younger miller was either dead or had left the place.

Squire Daniel attended to the upkeep of the mill through John's favourable lease. By 1683 new mill-stones were again needed,* and of this event the account-book gives full and interesting particulars. On June 19th, "when J[ohn] B[anks] and Rydal-Miller did go to buy Mill-stones at Kellet-moor" 3s. 6d was spent, the wright meanwhile being busy with "sowing of the mill-planks," and on July 20th the following payments are entered £9 19s. 0d. To John Ostley "ye mill-ston-getter at Kellet-moor (besides 1s. bef. paid) for a pair of mill-stones deliver'd at Windermeer water-foot". then

" It[em] given his men 3s. Paid to Rich. Robinson
at ye Water-foot for ye stones going over his
ground 5s.
Paid Tho. Braithwait† for Boating of them up Win
dermere-water 16s., and given them in ale 1s.,
in all 01 05 00

Once landed at Waterhead, the carriage of the stones became the squire's care, and so impressed was he by its difficulty that he wrote the following account of it

---

* The old ones had lasted twenty-four years, these only twenty-one, but the work was heavier.—ED.

† The Ambleside Hall family had a great boat on the lake for conveyance of heavy goods

"Memorandu that ye mill-stones paid for July 20 23 was brought to ye Head of Windermere-water soon after, and was landed at (blank) And one of them was (with great difficulty) brought upon a Dragg by ye Tan-pit and so up by ye side of Rowthey into ye Low-park, and through it and Stonewhait into ye Low-How, and breaking through ye wall (below ye gate) in to ye old Orchard, and through it, and ye old Hall into ye Lane, and so into ye Lands ye 19th of October, 1683, But finding this way very inconvenient the other stone was brought Oct. 22 ye way aforesaid (upon a Trail with a pair of Wheels) unto Rydal-bridge end and through ye water directly into ye long-close and through ye Round Close unto ye Mill-Door, breaking a Gap there out of ye said Close into ye Lane And then ye other Stone was trailed over ye Gill unto ye Longclose, and conveyed to ye Mill as ye other was The men had Dinners and Tobacco

No items of expense accompany this entry, therefore it is probable that the work was done as boon service It was obligatory on some manors for the tenants to carry the stones.

Then follow entries of 39 days of mill-work and wheel-work, besides 23 more spent in making "52 Speakes, 3 Draught-trees, 14 Fellows, 4 Naphs," etc., finishing up with the slating of the mill, so that both building and plant were thoroughly renovated.

Little more is known of the Rydal mill. After the Fleming millers had passed away, a new occupant for it was hard to find. In 1725, when Sir William Fleming was seeking to let it, a correspondent writes that if the lord be free to sell the mill outright, he will give £80 "for her," and would rather advance £10 on his price than give so great a "fee rent" yearly. The rent asked is not quoted

When leasing the demesne in 1741, Archdeacon Fleming reserved, among other things, the miln and kiln, with the right of the miller to take peat from the moss. It probably was little used after that time.

The following are the last verses of a song against Millers :—

From a rat, a mouse a rogue, a thiefe,
  (Mill haunters night and day),
From a rent hair cloth and wide dusting sieve,
  Libera nos Domine !

From a Westmorland measure, a Lancashire heap,
  Rines* layed from stones great way,
A large toll dish, dipt twice in deep,
  Libera nos Domine !

From an honest miller with a gilt thumb,†
  That ffans and winnows per se
From a pack of knaves, till the day of doom,
  Libera nos Domine !

The decreasing value of water corn-mills at the opening of the eighteenth century was a matter which all owners had to face, whether the mills were manorial or otherwise. The correspondence of Benjamin Browne of Troutbeck, who in the early years of 1700 acted as agent for the Ambleside Hall property—then possessed by Lady Otway, daughter of John Braithwaite—gives a lively picture of the trials of the mill proprietor.‡ The mill in question was the one by Stock Bridge already mentioned, for which the Braithwaites had acquired a monopoly, and where they reckoned the flour of the whole township should be ground. It was therefore adapted for a large business, conducted under the eye of the owner, whose house stood adjacent, separated but by the width of a

---

* The meaning here is uncertain The rynd is a wooden piece, crossing the hole of the upper mill-stone, into which the spindle is fitted. The space about it permits the grain to pass from the hopper *History of Corn-Milling*, vol 1, p 175 There is a local word " rinning," which is used for the wedge stuck between the stones, to regulate the quality of the flour ground

† The miller's thumb was a proverbial expression for any wide, ugly, or big-headed object. There is a fish of the name ; and the willow-warbler is in these parts called a miller-thumb—for what reason is not apparent Chaucer jeered at the miller for his " thumb of gold." But as the peculiarity grew from the man's necessary care in the exercise of his trade—for by pressing the flour between his thumb and fingers while it poured from the spout, he ascertained whether his stones ground true and of the necessary fineness—the gibe was an unjust one · though it is possible that some nefarious scattering of the valuable powder might occasionly accompany the action. See same, vol iii, p 143-5

‡ Browne, MSS

court-yard from the humming wheels and the roaring beck. The miller might be an honest man, for he took multure not for himself but his master, whose wages he received; he slept in the mill-house, which was fitted up with bedstead, &c., and no doubt took his meals in the open hall with the big household. But when that household had vanished, along with its head, and the so-called "Hall"* of the Braithwaites stood empty, and its shattered windows faced the town, matters were different. Grist came in to the mill more slowly, and a horse-mill at Clappersgate drew custom. The year 1704 spelt actual loss. The miller in charge, besides £2. 10s. 0d. for wages, claimed £3 2s 6d. for his "table", total, £5. 12s 6d.; and he declared that, far from having gains beyond this sum to hand over, he was 18s. 5d. short! Then, to induce a lease-holder to take charge of the mill, it had to be overhauled and set in order. Browne rides to the quarry-masters of Capernwray and Kellett about stones; then on—since they are exorbitant in demand—to Lazonby; finally beating a Kellet man down from £6 to £5. 5s. 0d. The miln-wrights charge 12d a day—double what the squire of Rydal paid in 1659 —with their meat. A new-fangled "Cynder-Kiln" has to be constructed, as folk will bring their corn to no other. Next, when a Coniston miller takes the mill on lease for £7. 10s. 0d., he is not content, but clamours for a drop to £6. Again, a married miller demands more house-room for his bride. After repeated renewals and improvements the mill-rent was in 1715 screwed up to a maximum of £9, the bargain requiring two rides into Cumberland. And this miller was seemingly the man "which broke," causing the agent "ffateague, sorrow, and expense" in distraining for rent two years later.

Browne, who belonged to a milling family, inherited

---

* It was in no true sense a hall, for its owners were but customary tenants or statesmen under the lord.

a half-share in the mill at Troutbeck Bridge. He set about with his partner in 1719 to rehabilitate this as a corn-mill.* The miln-wright contracted to set it in order for £8, but the ultimate cost ran up to little short of five times that amount. The head men worked at 10d. per day and their subordinates—who never outnumbered the masters—at 8d. The mill-stones cost £9 When finished, the partners secured each a rent from the mill of £1. 8s. 6d , though it was sub-let higher

Mr Browne considers that depreciation of mill-property is shown in the fact that his ancestors sold the Limefit mill in 1699 for £100, though twenty-two years earlier it was producing a rent of £12, and grinding, besides, all the corn grown by the owner and his father.

This depreciation, which became so marked later on, when water corn-mills fell into decay one after another for want of custom, is hard to explain It is true that the people resented more and more the *soke* system which compelled them to carry their grain to a certain mill, and claimed freedom to go elsewhere But the corn—of which a far greater quantity was grown there than now—had to be ground somewhere ; and although the prosperity of the country had diminished with the failure of the fulling trade, yet the population, which had grown rapidly then, had hardly diminished, though it might be almost stationary. It is possible that the use of hand-mills worked at home robbed the miller of his earnings ? †

In the *History of Corn-milling* the invention of a hand mill in the eighteenth century is mentioned, which was intended for use by those " distressed by the roguery of the millers " ; and the new practice excited comment in the London Magazine of 1758. But the learned authors

---

* Browne, MSS
† The law-suit which the Earl of Derby, owner of the manorial corn-mill of Bury in Lancashire, won over the townsfolk in 1599, was caused by their use of hand mills *History of Corn-Milling*, vol III , 224-5 These hand-mills could hardly have been querns

of that fascinating history conclude, that "though numbers of hand-mills were put before the public at this period, there was never manifested any popular desire to use them."[*]

Yet a malt-mill, turned by hand, existed in every substantial farm-hold of our district till recent days. One is still in its old position, fixed against the roof-timber, in Low House, Troutbeck, and grinds the corn for the hens of Mr. Birket-Forrest Such handy implements saved the frugal folk many a journey to the corn-mill.

Of all the corn-mills around—lords' mills, town mills, proprietary mills, horse mills—the Braithwaites' mill at Ambleside has alone survived. In spite of all its distresses and ups-and-downs, the great wheel has never ceased to revolve, or the stones to grind. It was to this mill that a sharp little girl (of nine or ten[†]) once drove the sacks of corn to be ground, from Hart Head, Rydal, with injunctions from her father to stay by it while it was ground. So she took up her post on the ground floor, mid the throb and din of the mill; old Towlson, bustling uneasily up and down his ladder, calling out from time to time, "·Little girl, hast nought to do in town? No need to stay here" But Agnes excused herself, saying she must mind the black horse that stood in the yard, and stuck; seeing the measure dipped in the sacks for "moulter," (=mulcture) and watching the flour come down the spout from the stones. And her father praised her on return for the fullness of the sacks.

But sometimes the grain was carried from Rydal the other way, to be ground at Tongue Gill where still the ruined shed stands, and the wheel did stand till 1907. Here Miles Coward worked[‡] and afterwards old Andrew

---

[*] Vol 1, pp 223-4

[†] This was Mrs. Tyson who was born June 8th, 1827, and died in Rydal, April 26th, 1915, at the cottage which was once The Hare and Hounds Inn —ED

[‡] Edward Wilson.

Moor. The latter not only ground the parish corn, but sold meal which he procured from Keswick—for long the great mart for "haver." Aged memory can give no definite account of the mulcture taken by these recent millers*; but no money was paid, unless the grain was damp and had to be dried in the kiln. The weights and measures in the country-side were various and irregular.†

The Westmorland measure referred to in the song is said by Mr Browne to have contained 16 quarts, a peck being 24 quarts. It may have been on this basis that a Kendal miller in 1693 ground eight measures of wheat at 2s. 8d. per measure (= 2d. a quart) for the squire of Rydal, when he was supplying his table with white bread at a more wholesale rate. From this it appears that the Rydal mill-stones would not grind wheat, which is said to require, in local parlance "French Burrs," the *Buhrstone* being a form of silica obtained from the neighbourhood of Paris.‡ The stones now grinding wheat in Ambleside are of this material, while the neighbour stones, busy on oat-meal, are from the Peak, Derbyshire.

CHAPTER VI.

THE INNS

"Davids'", Farmhold number 11; David Harrison; The Bursar of Peterhouse, Farmhold number 12; "The Hare and Hounds"; Thos Fleming, Rydal Lodge; "Udalls'"; The third Inn in Rydal; Chas. Udall, carrier, Sir John Lowther's scheme.

---

* A half-bushel in the quarter is said to have been the usual toll, and the ordinary dish or fat held this amount. When, however, a small-holder brought but a half-bushel of oats to be ground, a smaller dish must have been the measure. *History of Corn-Milling*, vol iii, p 148-154

† See Pringle's *Agriculture of Westmorland*, 1797

‡ Chamber's *Encyclopædia*.

THE sketch already made of the Rydal farmholds reveals the following fact, that every holder, if he were a well-to-do man, had another occupation besides that of husbandry. If he were not a craftsman, he was a carrier ; and it is difficult, where every man was apparently willing to slip a second pack on his horse to oblige a neighbour, and so turn a modest coin, to determine who were the accredited draughtsmen, working upon regular and established beats There were several of these in the village. The Walkers and the Hobsons are the first we know of. Hobson's beat took him over the Raise, and, indeed, he had some footing in Keswick, probably Monk's Hall. Then there was Green, while Grigg probably did business with Ulverston. Later the Harrisons swept all before them, and were not only carriers of reputation, but cattle merchants, butchers, and provision dealers, as Hobson had been They also kept one of the accredited village inns.

To account for the number of carriers found in Rydal during the seventeenth century, we must look to the geographical position of the place, which lies on the north road between Kendal and Keswick, and is almost equally distant from both, thus conveniently dividing the march of the packhorses. It is certain that at least one Rydal man extended his journeys to Cockermouth, and when Sir John Lowther sought to establish a regular service between Whitehaven and Kendal, it was a Rydal man who was proposed for the job. From Rydal, too, a road branched off to Hawkshead and Furness. On the other hand, the carrier for Penrith was at this time located at How Head, Ambleside, which was handy for Kirkstone Pass.

Now every carrier was practically an innkeeper as well. His house was a place of call, where not only packs and parcels, but letters were left. The yard and its shed, the customers who loitered, the bustle when the laden palfreys made their start, the watched-for return, all conduced to thirst, and a good pull at a tankard of that home-brewed ale which every household had store of, and which for long it needed no licence to sell

Number 11 of our Rydal farmholds then, being possessed by the Harrisons, was an inn It was generally called David's, because David (interspersed with Anthony) was a frequent fore-name in the family It stood conveniently for its business upon the town-gate; and it exists still, transformed into the picturesque residence of Glen Rothay The first David we know of had a son christened by the same name in 1625. He must have been a large dealer in cattle, for in 1631 he paid £9. 5s 0d. for sheep bought from Squire John Fleming Next year he rented for the summer Rydal How (the wide knoll that turns the river westward) at £4 a year Besides supplying flesh (specially veal), chandlery, woodcock, etc., to the Hall, he regularly brought salt from Hawkshead, and whether his beat extended to Cartmel, or he made a special journey, he was in 1643 entrusted with the conveyance of money thither, receiving 1s. 0d. "for his paynes." He likewise served the manor in connection with the tithes, apparently collecting them for a small fee (see *Church of Grasmere*). He was a well-to-do man, and stood surety at this time for Charles Wilson's debt. When the new squire wrote down the compacts he had made with his tenants for their general fines, on October 9th, 1655, he entered "David Harrison's rent 3s 6d., Genrall ffine £2. 03s. 0d, which is already payde," showing that—unlike most of his neighbours—he had money in hand, and could moreover for that reason make a better bargain.

The small rent paid may be accounted for by the fact that "halfe of Davids" (probably a portion of land), rent 2s 6d, had at some earlier time been added to Keen's, and remained with it. David meanwhile paid largely for extra pasturage. Besides an additional horse on the common, and 55 sheep—making a flock of 85—he had beasts in the Dale Head, and paid £1 12s. 0d. for them. He also rented Frith, the Allans, and Adam How for £2. 8s. 8d., which he continued till 1664. In the next few years he did, along with his son, much porterage for the Hall. He also supplied meat, game, partridges, many woodcocks, tongues, etc. The squire likewise patronised his inn, frequent entries appearing in the account book, such as

	lb.	s.	d.
" Spent at David Harrison's in ale	00	00	03
Spent yesterday at David Harrison's with Mr R Bowes	00	00	06
A runlet of ale, supplied from the inn, cost 3s 0d "			

Among unusual occurrences in the village was the indictment of David in 1658 for felling and carrying away wood unlawfully " by his children and servants from the demesne "; and the extraction of a fine therefore of 5s 0d. In the 1660 search for arms he was deprived of one steel cap, which looks as if he might have been out during the Troubles, and on the side against the king. His wife in an emergency acted as midwife to the squire's lady, and received 5s. 0d. For attending a meeting at Chester with three horses on behalf of the squire, in 1662, he was paid 10s 0d. In 1668 he held some sort of a sale at which " a brass pott " fetched 9s. 0d. The hearth-tax of 1665 reveals three Davids in the little township; one of whom declares three hearths (a most unusual number), this doubtless being old David at the inn; another declares one,—to which on survey a second is added,—this would be young David, who in 1660 purchased the old smithy, as we have seen, while to a third David, called junior of Loughrigg, two hearths are actually added to his one declared. This Loughrigg branch of Harrisons, possibly holding Fieldfoot, will be dealt with later. " Old " David is now frequently specified in the accounts, where he figures in money-matters and in mortgages. The mortgages, however, are on other folks' property; as when he joins Thomas Fleming, his fellow innkeeper, in lending to Hawkrigg of Rydal Water-head and Grasmere Town End; and pays 10s. 0d to the lord for giving consent to the same. Indeed the Harrisons' wealth was often placed at the disposal of their failing neighbours, as in the case of the Walkers. Old David, wealthy to the end, died in 1674, the year of scarcity; and young David seems to have moved to the ancestral home and inn. He paid a fine of £3. 10s. 0d to the lord, who sent down 2s. 6d to the "House Raising" which he held next year, and who often looked in about this time for the good of the house. The year of scarcity affected his flocks, like those of his neighbours, and no extra sheep were put on the common, where 70 had run the previous year; and it took several years for the stock to mount up again. Still this may not have meant entire loss, for he may have sold advantageously in a dear market. He rented New Close, Adam How, the Allans and "ould hall" for his cattle in the next years, took up a mortgage on William Walker's estate, paying 15s. 0d. for the lord's consent thereto, and made himself responsible for the rent of this large property; while in 1679 he added the Frith and Nab to the other closes he rented. But while they prospered among failing townsmen, death struck repeatedly at the line of Harrisons, carriers and innkeepers. On October 21st, 1679, this David was buried and immediately his widow Agnes took up all the threads of his business. Soon after Martinmas she is found paying up the Agist account, with 4d given back; but she must have made some complaint, as at the close of the year comes the entry :—

	lb	s.	d
"Given back to David Harrison's widdow because he had no Horses in ye Pasture save 2 Foals wch we set down 6d a piece ..	00	01	00

She likewise joined with her son David in a bill for William Walker's debt to the squire, paid this defaulter's half-year's rent, as well as their own, and then faced the payment of "five Herriots," set down at £10. It was no wonder that we find her needing to borrow about this time £5. from the banker at the Hall, but it was only for a fortnight, and we presently find her in her own name renting closes for the cattle, as her husband had done. Her son must have been very young. Still, he (or another of his name) acted as Frithman in the next year (1680), and was zealous in the carrying business. He continued the old beat between Keswick and Kendal, and amongst his loads for the Hall were wheat, butter, pewter, plate, books (an Atlas among them), and wheat-bread. In March he receives the guerdon of 6d "for often troubleing of him," but that was an extra. The rate appears to have been 1s. 0d. per load, since a payment of 5s 6d is explained as "being 5½ loads brought by young David." He took up "Frith ith' Nab" in his own name at £1. 16s 8d. "with liberty to plow for oats as much as he shall manure, and sow with bigg next year." This he did on a lease of five years, but before that year (1681) was out, the burial of "David, son of David Harrison, of Rydal, deceased," is recorded on October 9th. Thus three David Harrisons died within seven years, and there remained another, perhaps a cousin, a sickly boy, who in 1684 was carried up to London to be touched for the king's evil; but he may have been the son of Robert of Grasmere. The Grasmere Harrisons likewise kept an inn at Church Stile, now the house of Robert Hayes, the nurseryman. They were wealthy too; and when Lady Crossland (daughter of Squire John Fleming) sold in 1686 her patrimony of Bainrigg, Robert "of Churchsted" bought it, and passed it on to his son Robert. It is a confusing fact that he also appears to have left a widow Agnes, who died 1707, in Rydal.

To complete the list of deaths among the Rydal Harrisons in this decade, a William, son of David (probably the second) was buried two months before his brother, the third David, and their sister Elizabeth in 1684, three years after, finally a Matthew, who filled the office of Frithman in 1684, and must therefore have been another brother, to whom the property had passed, was buried as " son of Agnes," in 1687.

It was no wonder then that, in the failure of her men-folk, widow Agnes is found continuing herself the business of farming and renting. Of the carrying trade and of the inn nothing is heard, except that it was in the house of widow Harrison that many Quakers assembled on September 14th, 1681, to make that Declaration or Test which was now allowed to them in place of the Oath of Allegiance. There were near a hundred of these poor folk, mostly of the lowlier sort, shoemakers and husbandmen; and as they tramped or rode in from far-away quiet Westmorland nooks, and passed along the town-gate to file into the ale-house, where sat two magistrates, Sir Daniel Fleming and his son, the scene must have been a striking one.

Anthony Harrison next became the representative of his family, serving as Frithman in 1694, churchwarden in 1697, and doing two days boon-mowing (by deputy) in 1710. But again it is the man who drops off early, and a widow is responsible for boon-mowing in 1720, while three years later there are two women Harrisons, Agnes and widow Dorothy, who take the oath at a special Quarter Sessions held in Rydal. Dorothy died in 1728. The eldest son of Anthony was the last David of the race. He inherited the principal village property; the second son, William, took Fisher House; David paid the customary rent, 3s. 6d. in 1749 and 1765; his land tax in 1751 was 1s. 1½d., and next year for bridges 4d.; and at the same time an Agnes paid 6¾d. and 2d.

Failure of males carried "Davids" into the Wilkinson family; for, by will of the last David, Jane Wilkinson inherited in 1769, and she was presumably daughter of John Wilkinson and Agnes Harrison, who married in 1729 and who were described by the register as both of Loughrigg, John's patrimony being apparently at Clappersgate. Jane paid an entrance fine of £4. 16s. 8d. She married George Rigge, who let the premises, and who was brought to book in 1728 by the Hall bailiff for ordering his tenant to grub up three oaks without leave. The arbitrary proceedings of seizing goods for a heriot on his death is recounted elsewhere

Though a John Rigge is mentioned as being in possession of "Davids" in 1806, it was the executors of George who in 1810 disposed by auction of all the Harrison property in Rydal. Rich John Fleming of the other inn bought it, and then split it, keeping the land and selling the house, which now bore a reduced lord's rent of 2s 6d. The next purchaser was one of the new race of scenery-lovers, and the first to take an old farm-hold for a holiday resort. He was the Rev. Samuel Tilbrook,* B.D., bursar of Peterhouse, Cambridge, and of his ways and doings we hear in the correspondence of the time. "Davids" as he found it was, according to Green, a good specimen of a Westmorland farm-house, but Green's own drawing of it, made in 1809, shows a place which, if solid and capacious, had clearly ceased to be the home of its owners. The Cambridge don proceeded to "completely renovate it" to the admiration of all tourists It became Ivy House or Ivy Cottage, and is spoken of by the writers of the text of *Westmorland and Cumberland, etc., illustrated*, as a "beautiful and romantic residence"

---

* Samuel was the son of John Tilbrook, of Bury St. Edmunds, and was educated at that school. He became Pensioner of Peterhouse in 1801, and admitted as a scholar in 1802 He graduated in 1806, became M A in 1809, and was selected fellow in the same year In 1816 he became B.D. He accepted the college living of Freckenham in 1827, when he married, and he died in 1835, at the age of 52. These particulars are kindly supplied by the Rev T. A Walker, author of the *College History*

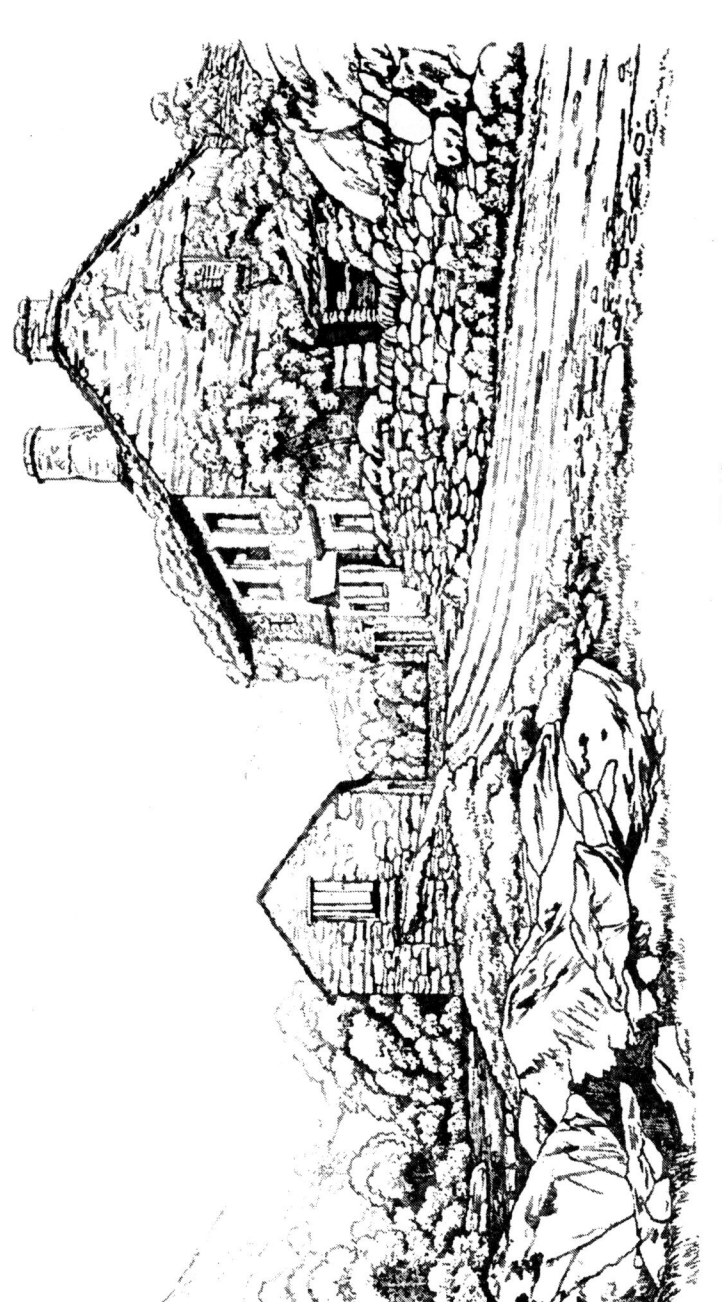

OLD INN CALLED "DAVIDS," RYDAL.
From an Etching by Green, 1809.

TO FACE P. 435.

Allom drew it for this work, and no greater contrast to Green's drawing than his, in technique and spirit, can well be imagined. In Green's picture all is realism and truth on its sordid side ; alike in the bare road (engineered some twenty years before) in the deserted looking house, with its hollow windows, some stopped or latticed ; in the trees, lopped closely ; in all the scenic points—the river, the stepping-stones, the mountains beyond, which are reduced to a photographic scale before photography was known ; the whole conveying not only an impression of remoteness from the world, but of bare meaness, if not of penury

Allom, on the other hand, gives the romanticist's view of the same scene ; for here are craggy mountains piled high against the sky, a full river flowing to the lake, and trees growing to a graceful height. " Davids " too, is transformed by an ample porch, and palings that denote a garden by the river side. Then the whole scene wears an air of animation and joy Smoke rises from the increased chimneys ; a fisherman is seen on the bank ; women cross the foot-bridge that now replaces the stones ; a number of passengers enliven the bit of road , while a horseman denotes cheerful intercourse with the far-off world ; and to crown all, that vehicle newly imported for the firm turnpike road, by which the Mrs Ratcliffes of the period came to shudder at the mountains, the chaise itself, is here !

Perhaps these two little pictures of one homestead may be taken to denote the turning point in the fortunes of the village ; one suggesting the decay and disappearance of the old native class of statesman, along with the industry, the trade, and the ancient customs of a self-dependent village community , the other the advent of the stranger, the enthusiast and the poet, with foreign ways and extraneous money, that was eventually to transform the place.

The don of Cambridge was not long a dweller in these parts, enthusiastic strangers rarely are, but his marks are still left on "Davids." His crest, with initials and date, 1817, in a lozenge (certainly carved in his university town) still adorns the door, shaded by his hospitable porch; and some of the thirteen windows for which he was taxed in 1828 no doubt remain. The panelled house-place, a feature that has just come into fashion again, was doubtless arranged by him too, the initials above the fire-place can hardly be wrested into Harrison names, nor would 1679 (the year of David's death) be a likely time for them to be renovated. The Rev. Samuel had leave from Lady Fleming to fish and boat. He and his friends practised archery by the river, and a small village boy, who told me this in old age, was employed to find and bring the arrows. He knew Wordsworth of course, whose brother was a fellow don, and Dorothy's letters often chat about him. An excursion to Hackett in the summer of 1812 was enlivened by his musical talent. "We had a very pleasant afternoon. Tillbrook stationed himself on a rock, and sounded his flute to the great delight of our own party."

The Fellow of Peterhouse (a bachelor with a slight lameness) was in fact both learned and amusing, and was noted for his social gifts. He must have been, during the vacations that he spent here, an acquisition to the society of the place. All was not smooth, however. The expense of keeping up the country cottage was considerable; and Mr. Tilbrook in 1821 expressed himself as highly incensed against one Mr. Gee, who " kept " the house, and who had spent money unwarrantably in out-houses for animals, etc. There are accounts extant which show that Edward Wilson, carpenter, of Grasmere, did work on the stables in 1817, and "raised a small House," items which may be probably referred to the Gees' expenditure. This couple, also known to the

Wordsworths, seem to have occupied the premises on easy terms; but they were gone by 1822, when the house was sub-let by the bursar to Mr. Edward Quillinan; and it was here that the melancholy death of his wife by burning took place on May 25th. Dr. Christopher Wordsworth afterwards took the place for seven weeks of the late summer. The Bishop of Chester occupied "Ivy Cot" in 1827 in the same manner. Mr. Tilbrook is reported to have been, as was Wordsworth, much excited by the election of 1822.

Then alas! the serpent crept into our Rydal Eden. The Rev. Samuel in 1829 gave up his life in college to marry Miss Frances Ayling, and with her advent as a bride began an increased intimacy with Rydal Mount. This "fascinating woman of the world" threw her spell, we are told, over the guileless heart of young Dora Wordsworth. There was also a relative (probably a brother), a certain Mr. Ayrton, whose offer of marriage Dora refused. The circumstance was awkward; and it is to be hoped that Mrs. Tilbrook's behaviour, in noising abroad a highly erroneous version of the affair, was not so black as it appeared to her neighbours. But the lamentable point was reached when the whilom friends sat in the little village chapel together, and left it without "halting outside to exchange a word." No wonder that the Tilbrooks tired of their cot, and that the poet reported shortly after (September 13th, 1831) "Tilbrook has offered his house and furniture for sale by private treaty, the price two thousand guineas; entre nous eight hundred more than its worth, except for fancy." A different sum this must have been from its sale price as "Davids," a few years before! The place was bought by a Quaker, Mr. William Ball, who is still remembered. It was ultimately sold to the Hall.

Of the inns of Rydal, the most important from first to last was that of the Flemings, which stood at Bank Foot, on the left of the town gate as the traveller came from Ambleside. There is nothing, indeed, to show, on the 1655 rental, that number 11 of the village houses was anything beyond a farm-hold. But there is immediate evidence of its being an ale-house, and this position it maintained, appearing in the list of licensed houses in 1791 under the name of " Hare and Hounds," and continuing as a house of refreshment until recent times. It was used much oftener than " Davids " for official business and for meetings, public and private, as well as for jollity, and in the sad days of the township's decline, its low roof resounded to the voice of the facetious James Backhouse, as he put up to auction the maintenance of the wretched paupers, and to the answering bids and coarse laughter of the overseers of the poor, as they sat round the board with well-filled glasses, drinking ale at the public expense A few of these many and varied occasions may be mentioned ; and it will be seen that Squire Daniel, while patronising "Davids" now and then, took much public custom to Fleming's.

	lb s d
1658. July 24 —Paid Tho Fleming for a Pitcher of ale fetch'd when my Cosen Ambrose was here	00 00 03
1659 Dec 6 —Spent at Tho. Fleming's with my Uncle Kirkby and Brother Roger	00 01 00
Paid unto Tho Fleming wch ye Miller and Smith spent there when they were arrested	00 01 00

A village excitement this, of which nothing is known.

1660. July 12.—Spent at Tho Fleming's 1s. 6d, and in ye Blay-berry Isle 1s, with Sr George, his Lady, &c, in all	00 02 06
1662. Sept 6 —Spent at Tho. Fleming's with my Cosen Ambrose	00 00 06

which is repeated in the following year. Probably the cousin was John Ambrose, squire of Lowick, and not his brother the parson.

THE INNS

1667 May 2 It given my brothers, and ye rest of
my woodmen at Tho Fleming's in ale   ..   00 02 00

Roger and William must have come over from Coniston Hall for some special business connected with the woodlands of Rydal, possibly to survey and fell for the Furness bloomeries, or for the private manorial forge at Coniston

In 1668 the Justice of the Peace summoned a meeting of Constables, Churchwardens, and Overseers at the house of Thomas Fleming.

1669. March 19 Spent at Tho Fleming's with my
Cosin Braithwhait of W and my Cosin P about
ye excise 00 00 06

This must have been the poet and accomplished gentleman, Richard Brathwhait, who—both before and after the Commonwealth—was zealous in public service, and possibly Mr. Philipson, of Galgarth. The cousinship, though always acknowledged, is not yet traced.

The splendid occasion of the squire having received knighthood from Charles II. was commemorated in Rydal's chief inn.

1681 June 10 Sir George Fletcher and my Cosin
Henry Browham comeing to Rydal June 8 a few
hours before coming home from London that
night, this day spent with him, my 2 Brothers,
and my Cosin Jack Browham at J Fleming's in
Rydal 00 01 00
June 11 Given Robert Benson ye Piper 00 01 00

The ale house must have been a throng place that day, when the village folk could pass in and out (partaking, no doubt, of the ale) and take part in the informal levee, held by the new-made knight, surrounded by his relatives and friends.

A General Quarter Sessions was held at Rydal on October 15th, 1723, for the convenience of those required to take the oath, but at what house it was held is not mentioned. It was probably at Fleming's, as "Davids" was now given up as an inn. Later, however, there was apparently another ale-house (perhaps unlicensed); for the Ambleside constable's account shows, for October 4th, 1749,

Att Mrs Phylipson's at Rydal ye 4th of Octr for
    Drink for five men a woman and the Constable   0 0 8

The Diary of Benjamin Browne, of Troutbeck, gives another kind of gathering.

"1726, May 11th, at John Fleming's shooting crows."

Much greater extravagance in ale is shown in the eighteenth century accounts.

                                                                                         lb. s d.
1748   Oct. 26   To the Salvers in Ale when Salved
      466 Sheep 16 6
      Nov. 26   To John Fleming for 22 Mens Dinners
      at 3d. a piece 5 6
      For Ale 15s 6d when salv'd remainder of Sheep.
                                                                            1 1 0

More still was spent in the February following, when John Cookson was paid at the salving £2. 4s. 3d. in "victuils and ale."

But this seems to have been done out of Rydal, as Cookson's inn, (unlicensed in 1698, and then kept by a James), was in Loughrigg.

It was easier to give a village feast at the inn on little Sir Michael's birthday than to open the Hall specially for it, as we hear from the accounts.

1757. Nov. 19. Spent on Sir Michael's birthday at
    Jno. Fleming's 21s., Fidler 1s £1 2 0

Ale flowed abundantly when the crops of corn and hay standing on the demesne were sold, the payments in 1757 being respectively £1. 12s. 4d. and £2. 10s. 8d.

The public meetings at the Inn increased apparently in number towards the end of the century, and so did

COTTAGE IN RYDAL, "HARE AND HOUNDS."

the draughts of ale drunk at the public expense. In 1782 Thomas Fleming was paid 2s. 0d. for ale at two Constable's meetings. In 1804-5 the "Cash for Ale" varied from 3s. 0d. to 6s. 0d., and even touched once the phenomenal sum of 10s. 4d. at one meeting.

Besides these payments, paupers and vagrants were boarded for short periods at the inn The item "Two Lodgers at Fleming's" figures in the Constable's Account for 1784 at 1s. 9d., which appears a reasonable charge. "Jane Horner and son victuals" cost the overseers 2s. 6d. in 1807. But an item of 19s. 6d. in 1797 for boarding three men, while waiting for the day of swearing them for the army, was surely an imposition on the tax-payers of the township, who were bound to furnish one soldier.

There is evidence indeed that the "Hare and Hounds," while furnishing Christmas parties to the towns-folk, and convivial evenings to the officials who gathered round its board, had become a source of unjustifiable expense to the community. Tradition whispers too of slyness and craftiness in the inn-keeper, which eventually wrought his downfall. For the tale is told, in the old house itself, that about one hundred years ago "mine host" learnt that some horse-soldiers marching through the district from Wythburn, would be quartered upon his inn at the rate of 9d. a head by the day. Such a sum was not worth his while to receive, so he considered; and he bethought him of a cunning way of evading the impost. He lifted down his sign-board, and for the nonce ceased to be an inn-keeper. The company had to ride by and seek another hostelry. But it was a case of biter bit. The power that then ruled at the Hall, (and Lady Diana Fleming is spoken of), now stepped in, and declared that the sign-board, once lifted down, should not be reinstated; and the last hostelry of Rydal ceased to be.

The date of this striking village occurrence, if rightly

connected with Lady Diana, is limited to the space between the death of Sir Michael, in 1800, and the marriage of the heiress to Sir Daniel in 1806. This seems probable enough in point of time, especially as the young baronet would be little likely to do the deed; but to the authority from whom the edict went forth, the resident in Rydal has reason to be grateful to this day.

But behind the Fleming's inn we must look to the farmhold and the sturdy race of statesmen who held it, and who from first to last—when prudence and thrift had become meanness and craft—were men of keen spirit and of intellect that carried them successfully through times that ruined almost all their neighbours. Without commerce, manufacture, or agency, they maintained a position of steady weal by husbandry and by wood-craft. For while the side branches of the Fleming clan were corn-millers and tailors, the men of the main stock on the farm-hold were, through a number of generations, workers in wood.

The origin of the statesmen Flemings is not known. If there was any connection between them and the family of David Fleming of the Old Hall, who was cousin of Squire William, the careful pedigree of Sir Daniel does not show it. In 1567 Thomas Fleming, who was a waller, parted with a house in Rydal, rent 1s. 0d. It was he, perhaps who had a child baptized in 1574; and there was also a "Henrie" who had children. A David Fleming figures in the register from 1603, when his son Thomas was baptized, and he was buried in 1630. Thomas had a son David baptized in 1630. No doubt it is he who stands out in the strong light of the squire's accounts, which display him as a man of business, as well as a tenant. With money in his hand, he was able to compound for his fine on favourable terms, and we read on the paper written October 9th, 1655, " Thomas Fleming ffor his tenemt. rent 10s. 06d. Generall ffine

"Seaven pounds wherecoff ffive pounds is payd in hand and two pounds the 29th off September next witness his hand," to which is appended the circle that is Thomas' peculiar mark. Particulars give the rent of the tenement as 7s 2d., with 3s. 4d. " more for a parcel."

Thomas had a fair stock of cattle. Three cows, two " thurntors," and 50 sheep ran on the common, with doubtless a horse which went free. Two years later he had, besides what fed there, a heifer, mare and foal, and two colts in the demesne, at a charge of £1. 3s. 4d. He was one of the statesmen charged with felling wood unlawfully on the manor in 1658, and fined 10s. 0d., though 1s. 0d. was returned. He and his neighbour Nicholson met the funeral of Mistress Isabel Fleming on its way from Coniston, and helped as bearers.

But Thomas had dealings with the squire on another footing than that of tenancy. Craftman though he was, neither he nor his descendants worked for their superior. Yet he bought wood rather largely, which shows that a good deal of business was passing through his hands. For instance, in 1653 he purchased four ash trees from the park for £1. 3s. 4d., in partnership with Thomas Barrow, both were termed " throwers," (= wood-turners) and therefore probably chair and furniture makers in the new style. Among later purchases were six ellers (alders), and a piece of ash (18s. 0d. with 6d. given back); ellers and ashes (£3), two ashes and three ellers (£1. 1s. 0d.). The ellers, a wood impervious to moisture, may have been wrought into churns.

That the son was a worker in wood also is shown by Thomas " junior " paying £2 for ashes and ellers in 1662. Thomas " elder " is specified as paying 7s. 6d. and 8s. 8d. for extra cattle on common in 1666 and 1667. Two shillings were " given to ye rasceing of Tho. Fleming's barnes " in 1660. Ten years later (1671) Thomas the elder's prosperous career came to an end. The younger

Thomas had little time for carrying the family fortunes higher. He had to pay £2. 2s. 4d. for a "Heriot-sow of his Father's," showing that his mother's interest as a widow in the property had to be paid for, although he inherited, also that the Fleming breed of pigs must have been a good one, when the "best animal" it was customary for the lord to claim from a widow cost so much to redeem. Thomas had 60 sheep on the common and four kine in 1673; and on July 7th that year he was buried, only two years after the elder Thomas.

There can have been no direct male heir. For now (October 31st, 1674) we come to the marriage of Jane Fleming with Thomas Benson, of Coat-how, freeholder—a good marriage for her, and one to which she carried possessions, these being as usual turned into money by a sale

Feb 22, 1764-75 Paid unto Tho. Benson, of Coathow   l. s   d.
    (wh was bought at his wife's Sale), for 59 old
    Sheep and 17 Hogs 9li., for Hay 34s, and for
    Oates and Stray 1li, 9s 7½d, in all, vid Acp   . 12 03. 7½.

Who now was to take the family holding?

Two brothers Fleming were about this time becoming prominent men in Rydal—Lancelot the tailor, and John, formerly the miller. That they were kinsmen of Thomas of the inn seems certain, but their claim on the ancestral farmhold had to be established by purchase. John was possibly absent from the village at this juncture (see *Mills*), and from the fact that the thriving tailor put two "kyne" on the common in 1674, and acted as Frithman in 1676, it looked as if he were to secure the property. However, it was eventually taken up by John. For John not only appears from 1677 as a tenant with cattle on common, (Lanty now having to pay for grass in the demesne at the high rate of 6d. a week per cow), but in that year he made a bargain with the squire for the mill. He throve mightily in his various occupations. Of his ale-house we hear little, except for its license in 1691; but in land (see *Banks*) and in flocks he increased. His success as a husbandman is shown by the rise of his common dues, which amounted to 6s. 0d. in 1684, and shortly after this he rented Adam How, the Allans and Old Hall. He had besides a couple of oxen in the park in 1699. In 1686, 2s 6d. was "Sent to Jo Fleming's raiseing of his Barne in Rydal." The "Old Miller" (as he came to be called), after some 30 years at the Inn, died in 1704, leaving his younger son William at the Mill and at "Banks," and the elder, Thomas, in possession of the family farmhold, after the death of his widow. But Thomas, of Browham, Yorks, preferred to sell his Rydal property; and a kinsman and second cousin was at once ready as purchaser. This was a grandson of Lancelot the tailor. Lancelot had gained no footing of land in Rydal, and settled at Cockstone, in Loughrigg, which he may have inherited. He survived the miller by seven years, leaving his land to his son Thomas, also a tailor. (See *Work and Wages*). Thomas' son John deserted the needle for the more strenuous wood-craft. He was able to buy the Rydal holding and village inn in his father's lifetime, being described in 1722 as cooper, of Rydal. He paid a tax on nine windows in 1727. In his triple occupations he also seems to have thriven, and his brood of sons were noted for their height and longevity. He apparently resided towards the end of his life at the High Cockstone, which was his by inheritance, and he died in 1781. After the death of his widow, Mary, four years later, his will was administered by his sons Thomas and Lancelot, who had numerous legacies to pay out from the Rydal and Loughrigg estates before they could themselves enter into them.

Thomas, the eldest, took the Rydal holding and inn, with its goods and furniture and flock of sheep, and pursued the trade of turner; while Lancelot, brought up as a tailor, took Cockstone. A third son of John, Matthew, who had been apprenticed to a " thrower " for seven years, made money somewhere out of Rydal, and returned to purchase land in his native place (see Grigg's). Thomas, now head of the family, had been well enough off to buy Gill Close in his father's lifetime. His own son Thomas (called junior) bought Kittsgill and Little Close in Loughrigg, at an auction held in the inn premises in 1796. He was apparently a wood-monger,* and joined with John Benson, of Tail End (also the younger), in 1793, in a large transaction in timber, buying from the demesne the wood in Birkhagg for £650, doubtless to supply the iron foundries of Furness. It was not, however, he who inherited the Rydal property when old Thomas died (1814), at the age of 95, but John, an eccentric character, who never married. The Fleming family was by that time in possession of a great deal of land on both sides of the Rothay. A valuation book of 1810-1813 gives the Rydal estate of Thomas as worth annually £7. 1s. 7¼d., being 14 acres, 3 roods, 32 poles, while Thomas senior had also a Loughrigg portion, worth £5. 13s. 2¾d., being 7 acres, 2 roods, 14 poles. Lancelot the tailor's estate of Cockstone appears as £11. 2s. 0½d. in annual value, being 16 acres, 1 rood, 32 poles. The lord's rent on the Rydal property included the old homestead (now called " Millers ") " Sands " and parcels, which amounted to 18s. 6d. John, besides his inheritance, acquired Little-house, and half of " Davids," selling the house portion of the latter, as we have seen, to a newcomer, and probably making a good bargain thereby ; while he kept the land portion himself The other house which he (more probably than his father) created in Rydal will be given separately. John had joined in the statesmen's rebellion, and in 1820 had to pay up 14 years arrears of rent, which amounted to £14. 11s. 0d. He was a strange

---

* The local name for one who buys timber uncut.

character, living alone (for all his wealth) in the old homestead, that had once been the centre of the village, with its bustle and stir of inn and wood-yard and farm-work. He was alike the sport and terror of a gang of village boys, who followed his stout figure clad in tight stockings and knee-breeches, at a safe distance to jeer, and whom he followed into John Sproat's schoolroom, throwing apples among them to create confusion, and calling " Give 'em a good thrashing "—an anecdote which, in spite of dark hints as to his character, bespeaks some humour and kindliness of disposition. Dorothy Wordsworth mentions him in her letters occasionally.

He died in 1832, at the age of 76, leaving his property to his brother Lancelot and his nephew Thomas. A rate book of Rydal describes the property as House and land (35a.), a good house and two cottages. The two heirs agreed to sell all the village property to Lady Fleming in 1845 for £3,000, a sum which—comparing it with preceding village sales—shows its extent and value. It was the last village holding to fall to the manor, for John Birkett had sold in 1840, and James Backhouse in 1841. And so the race of statesmen Flemings came to an end in Rydal.

Rydal Lodge.

The creation of a new house in Rydal, where the farm-holds stood upon sites of immemorial age, was decidedly an achievement worth recording in the annals of the statesmen Flemings. Rydal Lodge, now a many-roomed house, fitted with modern comforts, grew insensibly, as it were, as an adjunct of the inn, and apparently without notice of the lord of the manor. The old inn had an unenclosed plot in front, as was customary before the village farm-holds. It was paved, and a pump stood upon it, which was resorted to by some of the neighbours. On one side the ancient homestead was flanked by great barns ; one, abutting on the road, being called " Lanty's," after one of the numerous Lancelots of the Fleming family. On the other side lay the workshop and the wood-yard used by the carpenter Flemings. These occupied the upper portion of the strip of ground between road and river, which narrowed to the stepping-stones or foot-bridge; and this piece also was unenclosed, as can be seen in Allom's sketch.

But when the Flemings ceased from wood-craft, a weaving shed was put up, probably on the site of the work-shop, for it stood close against the house, though advanced to the very edge of the turnpike road. The shed was apparently let by the Flemings to one of those weavers who were resident in Rydal from the close of the eighteenth century and onward, and it may have had a living room attached.

But hand-weaving came to yield too poor a return for livelihood, and it ceased, like the Flemings' trade of carpentry. The shed was next converted into a few rooms, and these appear to have served as an annexe to the inn. They were entered either from the *hallen* or lobby of the old house, or else from the pent-house which is said to have covered the end of the block towards the inn-yard. No doubt the rooms would be useful as extra accommodation for the inn at a busy time, and might serve to lodge those vagrants and soldiers who were boarded there at the expense of the township. But the time came when the business of keeping an inn likewise ceased; and after the eccentric and solitary bachelor John Fleming succeeded his aged father in 1814, the premises must have been far too large for his wants. It is clear that he adapted and altered the new set of rooms, and arranged a separate entrance towards the road, so that it became an individual dwelling-house. Green in his Guide (published 1819) speaks of there being in Rydal " a very neat house built by Mr. John Fleming, inhabited by Mr. George Gee, who has improved it."

And according to the Rydal Hall estate accounts, Mr. Gee dabbled in farming while he occupied this land-less house, renting in 1818 the field called Little Nab for 15s. od , and Birkett's Orchard for £1. 1s. od. besides buying the hay off Barnes' Orchard for 10s. 6d. Mr. Gee, as we know, " kept " Ivy Cot across the way during the absences of the Rev. Samuel Tilbrook, and greatly annoyed that gentleman by erecting outhouses for live stock at his expense. Mr. Gee had vacated the new house before 1822, when Dorothy Wordsworth (always amiable to unsettled friends) was looking out for another abode in the neighbourhood for him and his wife She reports to a correspondent, " John Fleming is no doubt again in his glory, for both his houses are empty, he himself flourishing, for he looks well, and always smiles graciously upon me at least."

The new house must later have been further improved, if it be the " good house " rated in the Valuation Book of 1843 at £22, then held by Lancelot Fleming, one of the heirs of John. Another house assessed at £8, also in his possession, was probably the old farm-hold itself out of which the new house grew ; that being a usual valuation for a village holding which had been kept in good repair. Shortly after, as stated above, the whole of the land and houses belonging to the statesmen Flemings were sold in a block to the le Flemings of the Hall.

At what point of its evolution the house acquired the fine title of Rydal Lodge cannot be told, nor when the range of rooms was built that faces the strip of ground between road and river, now enclosed as a garden. Perhaps it was appropriate that a house which never paid a lord's rent, and began its career as a tramps' lodging, should be subsequently used for sub-letting to transitory occupants. It became, indeed, the one select lodging-house of Rydal, and remained a lodging-house until 1909. Through the long period of its popularity, it has harboured many distinguished visitors. Thither came Dr. Arnold with his little flock in holiday times, while Fox How was being built Sir Thomas Pasley occupied it for a time, and Crabb Robinson resorted to it when he wished to enjoy a little intercourse with the Wordsworths. William Hull, the artist, died in it

UDALL'S INN.

A third inn in Rydal was kept for a time by Charles Udall, the carrier. He succeeded to the farm-hold of his grandfather, Charles Wilson, in 1679, as we have seen; and probably took over the carrying trade from him (see "Wilsons"). Squire Daniel Fleming patronised the young man, and procured Keswick goods through him, and when Sir John Lowther in 1686 attempted to establish a carrying service between Whitehaven and Kendal, the Rydal squire recommended him for the job. It was at Udall's inn that the gayest scene to which Sir Daniel Fleming contributed took place.

1678, May 27. Spent at Charles Udals with my Sons, Daughters, neices, and other weddingers   ooli o5s o6d.

This was the day after Barbara, his youngest daughter, had been married in the parlour of Rydal Hall to John Tatham, Esq., before a large assembly of relatives "& many good friends." It was the custom in those days for festivities to be kept up after the wedding to a late hour, and for guests to remain not only through the night, but often through several succeeding days. Indeed, it was more than a month before gay doings ceased at Rydal Hall, upon the departure of the married couple. The interval was spent in merriment and in visits abroad, one day being devoted to a trip to Sir Christopher Philipson's new house upon Belle Island. The descent of the party into the village on May 27th was clearly meant for the enjoyment of the folk; and no doubt the gay crowds at

Udall's made up of gentry in their fine clothes and dalesfolk in their home-spun, and even of labourers, would disport themselves with songs and with dancing, to the merry tunes of Renny the fiddler, who received 2s. 6d. for his services at the wedding. Ale to the amount of 5s. 6d. would go a good way towards assisting at the conviviality of the occasion. When finally young Barbara and her husband set out for their Yorkshire home on June 28th, they were escorted, says the proud father, by a company of nearly 100 persons on horseback, who were entertained by Mr. Tatham during the halt at Kendal, and for four days after their arrival at his manor of Over Hall

Charles Udall extended his premises in 1690, by leasing his neighbour Grigg's farm-hold (see "Griggs"). But whether he moved his inn business there, is not known. He did not prosper; and in 1693, being in debt to the squire, made over a deed of his own estate to his superior (see "Wilsons").

The following letters (printed with the kind permission of Mr. le Fleming), may be read with interest, as they are connected with the carrying trade of the district, and incidentally with the inns. They throw valuable sidelights on the condition of the roads, the postal service, and communication generally between Kendal and other parts in the seventeenth century. Sir John Lowther, cousin of the Sir John of Lowther, was practically the founder of Whitehaven as a sea-port.

London, feb 16, 1685-86.
Sir,
    Having had a design of setting up a correspondence betwixt Kendal and Whitehaven, I have discours'd ye Carriers about it, and I find they constantly return from London to Kendal upon a Tuesday, and set forward for London again ye Munday following, wherby I find they stay four whole dayes in ye Country besides Sunday; now if two of these four dayes were alloted to goe to Whitehaven and two to return, our correspondence with London

would be ye same as yours, and much better accommodate any Irish passengers, than coming round by Penrith, some advantage likewise we might have in drawing down ye Kendal Cottons at our own leizure to Whitehaven, when we ship them off for Virginea; my desire is to know what sort of Manufacture you have at Kendal besides Cottons Some dealings you have in ye Pewther Trade, but in what manner I doe not wel know, neither what quantity of Cottons are made ther, nor wher vended.
      Sir,
      Yr. Most humble Servant,
          J. Lowther.

For Sir Daniel Fleming,
  at Rydal, near
    Kendal, Westmorland
Sir,
 I writ two posts agoe in answer to yours, and should not have given you a trouble again so early, but yt Mr Benson now here, tells me, ye Carlisle Toll taken upon Meal at Rayes betwixt Ambleside and Keswick is much complain'd off, a Commission wil be sitt at Whithaven upon ye Affair by Jeff Wyker about ye begining of April I pray enquire into it, and let me know how long such Toll has been pretended at Rayes, and when Sir John Lowther and you meet let examination be made into ye pretence of Carlisle, for however I may seem more concerned in Trade than either of you are, you are both too good Countrymen to suffer your Neighbours to be oppress'd, and ye Country for ever disabled of Improvement when they are not in a Condition of going to Market upon ye same termes as others are.
     I am, Sir,
      Yr. most humble sevt.,
London, Mar 13, 1685-86.   J. Lowther.

A letter follows from Mr. Simpson, the prominent mercer of Kendal. He expresses, in involved language, the opinion of his fellow townsmen (which he was been requested to obtain) upon Sir John's scheme. They cannot think that the scheme is workable. The London carriers cannot be true to time. Certainly a carrier living half-way—say at Fell Foot—would have the best chance of carrying it through. He has sounded some of the dealers in cottons (woollen goods) and "Shifts," and finds "they wil not venter any by sea that way" (meaning Whitehaven), "Newcastle (tho' further off) Beeing not so hazardous by much."

Next April comes the following, with its answer in May.

Sir,

I received yours, with your approbation of my setting up a Carrier betwixt Kendal and Whitehaven, which is a great confirmation to me I doe not expect to Perfect your design at first, and concur with you it wil be better done by others than by your Kendal Carrier I hear of One Tyson near you a Sufficient Man, but ye place wher it wil be best done is at Keswick, for ther is but four dayes time to goe and return, so ye middle way is ye best, and I hear of one Hobson there, I have writ Dr Grey about it, and pray doe you advise me

   Sir,
    Yr Most affect Kinsman and servant,
London, Ap 24, 1686   J Lowther

With the letter he sends D. F. a Barometer, by Greenwood, the Carrier, to be in Kendal on Wednesday next, price 30/–. Also six vols. of *Philosophical Transactions*.

         Rydal, May 5, 1686

Sir,

I have received ye Favour of Yours, and ye Barometer is safely come into my hand, for both which I am much your Debter As concerning your Whithaven Carrier, if you resolve ye Carriage shall be brought from Kendal every Wednesday, and returned thither ye next Saturday following, I think no Keswick man can conveniently do it For he must go from home every Tuesday, and he can bring his Packs every Wednesday but to Ambleside or hither, and then it will be too hard for him to go from hence unto Whithaven upon every Thursday and to return hither ye next day, and upon ye Saturdays he cannot go unto Kendal and venture home ye same day, Besides ye Carrier at Keswick is deaf and not fit for such a performance the Kendal carriers bring their Packs into Kendal about noon every Wednesday ; so that no other Carrier can carry them forth from thence that day which makes it too difficult to perform in that week what you desire The way over Hard-Knot and Wryness is often not passable, either by Snow, or by much Raine; there being a great want of good Bridges that way. I cannot see, yt any of our Country Carriers can constantly perform what you desire; and whether ye Kendal Carriers will do it, you know best. for I am clearly of opinion yt no one else can perform it (with any due profit to themselves) in four dayes. The way, I think, for you to fix this correspondence with ease and certainty is to agree with some of our Country Carriers to convey ye Whithaven Goods that shall come unto Kendal every Wednesday from thence unto their own Houses some day that week to go from thence every Munday unto Cockermouth (or near thereunto) and to go to Whithaven every Tuesday, from whence all goods may be carryed so as to be at Kendal every Saturday next following. This may be preferred with some conveniency to ye carriers; and when as anything shall happen to require more speed, it may be performed If you approve of this project, I shall then recommend a Carrier unto you, one Charles Udal, of this town, who hath a good set of Horses (with Bells, etc), and who will perform it as honestly and punchually, I think, as any other you can imploy But he'l expect an allowance for a while, until he will know how he will be weekly fitted with Carriages.

Your most obliged Kinsman and Servant,

D. F.

London, June 5th, 1686.

Sir,

I have yours of the 7th, 12th and 28th of May, consequently ye Money for ye Barometer wch you needed not have been so expeditious in, but tis your method; I thank you for your opinion about ye Carrier and am satisfied none but a Kendal Carrier can perform it in four dayes, ye Country does not co-operate with me in it, answerable to my good Intentions. [He goes on to the question of appointing a schoolmaster for St. Bees].

Yours,

J L.

In a P. S. to a further letter on this last subject, he asks D. F. when he goes to the Assizes at Carlisle, to enquire " upon what pretence ye Citty claimes a Toll in Cumberland when they have nothing to doe, it disturbes all our Trade in ye West of Cumberland, & seems a very foolish pretence."

CHAPTER VII.

The School

Started by Sir Daniel, 1663; "Barring out" and "Cockpennies" at the boys' schools; William Baxter and the Butler, Schoolmasters at Rydal; Dancing and Music Masters for Sir Daniel's Daughters.

UNLIKE the mill, the smithy and the shop, the school was no ancient centre for the life of the village. It is improbable that there was a school before Sir Daniel's time. No doubt in early days the priest or curate of Grasmere, and later the parish clerk, would instruct the cleverer and more ambitious boys of the parish; and we know that from the time of James I. onward Ambleside possessed a well-organized school where Latin and even Greek were taught by the curate. Such advantages as these would be more than enough for the valleys The better educated boys would then, as later, seek a vocation in life beyond them, and evidence points to the fact that those who remained on the farmholds of their fathers had little learning to show. Of the eleven leading men of Grasmere (two Knotts and one Benson among them), who in 1598 guaranteed the expenses for attempting to gain a market for Grasmere, not one was able to sign his name, but all made crosses and scribbles after the name of Parson John Wilson, who wrote the deed.

When in 1655 the Rydal statesmen compounded for their fines, seven of them signed by hieroglyphs that look like individual and chosen marks such as a circle, half-circle, musical sharp sign, etc. One, Robert Taylor, contrived his initials. Two only, Anthony Griggs and Richard Nicholson, wrote their names in full. The latter may have acquired the fine hand which he wrote under the Rev. John Bell, of Ambleside. He used it very little and left the making out of his bills for carpentry to the squire's agent, John Banks. It was naturally a great advantage to the craftsman if he could write himself his demands. The Grasmere smith managed it (though indifferently), but George Otley, who became the Rydal smith, could write a fair hand.

The influence of the Rydal school began to show towards the close of the century, in the increased number of the workmen who could write, for, whereas the accounts were made out generally by John Banks at the new squire's coming, they were later done by the men themselves. Shoemaker Grigg and Thomas Fleming, tailor, made out their reckonings in strange fashion, it is true, but still they did it; while the latter's father, Lanty, so clever in work and in that mental arithmetic that makes a fortune, probably never set pen to paper for a word of writing in his life.

Squire Daniel's account-book tells us much about the start of his village school. It was when the elder of his children were beginning to need instruction, and delicate Wil, the heir, was being caught up by the stronger and cleverer Harry, that he set about making it.

First in 1663, when the new stable was being built behind the Hall, and a good deal of rock levelled, do we meet with the odd entry (June 27th) of a payment "in breaking ye School-house-dower at ye Quarrey." And Richard Nicholson's bill gives :—

	s. d
And about making the gaties (?) and seting seats in the Scolehouse 19 dayes and a half .. .	06 08

The room, indeed, was the simplest contrivance. It had an earthen floor, such as existed at Hawkshead till long after. Perhaps this got moist from the drippings of the adjacent rock, for in 1669, November 13th, was .—

	£ s. d.
Paid ye Gresmer wrights for Laying ye floors of ye Schoolhouse and ye next room to it, etc, being 3 at 6d, 4d., and 2d apiece p diem, in all	00 09 06

And in 1675, Green, the Grasmere slater, receives payment for "mending over ye school-house."

The inference that this room was one of the group of buildings that grew up at the back of the present Hall is verified by a paper of Sir William's time.

Privacy and quietude were not thought of in that age. The park, indeed, was not closed. An open road crossed it, as well as a footpath from the ancient smithy to the new Hall. The mill in front of the Hall was reached by ways constantly trodden by the village folk So that the shouts of the youngsters or the clatter of their clogs on the cobble pavement would mingle unnoticed with all the other sounds of cattle and of labour, and servants going to and fro, all being part of the life of the old manor-house, itself (in its original form) the chief centre of village life. Squire Daniel had already, in 1663, looked out for his schoolmaster :—

	£ s d.
February 19, Given yesterday at Ambleside unto Willia Baxter to drink (having ye hired him to be schoolmaster for a year from ye 3rd of May next p 40s and his Diet, and to suffer others to come unto him) ye sum	00 01 00

"A Hornbook and Wire" had already been procured for 3d., being the first equipment of a scholar, who grasped the handle of its frame and read through the thin covering of horn the printed alphabet. Two Primers were brought on June 14th, p 6d at Ambleside—probably from that universal provider of the day, Kelsick—and Wil and Harry were fitted out. For the first year no expenses are entered for school festivals, but on December 9th, 1664, the item occurs :—

	£ s d.
Given ye other day to ye children at their baring-out	00 01 00

followed by—

Jan. 7 It to ye school-master for bread on New
         Year's eve 00 01 06

which sounds as if this might be a perquisite. And on February 6th, when his third boy had joined the others.—

Given unto Will, Harry and Daniel for their cock-   £ s. d.
   pennys 00 01 06
Paid unto William Baxter, School-master, his whol
   wages, due at May day next to come, ye sum of 02 10 00

Two more primers, and " A Grammar 10d." suggest that little Catherine had joined her brothers on the Rydal benches. The school was now at all events in full swing with work and play. Of the ancient riot of barring-out the schoolmaster, done generally before Christmas holidays, something must be said. It was a custom so universal, that sometimes the charter of a school made rules for it. The founder of Witton school, in Cheshire, prescribed that his " schollars should bar and keep forth the school and the schoolmaster in such sort as other Schollars do in great Schools." The idea seems to have been a mock rebellion, the scholars seizing the school, barring the doors, and refusing to open them until the schoolmaster outside had been brought to terms in the matter of holidays or hours of study. Perhaps capitulation ended in a feast; or else the money invariably given by the parent was spent in " tuck " eaten during the siege. The school was occasionally held through several days and nights, therefore the St. Bees festivity was restricted in the charter to " a day and a night, and the next day till one a clock in ye afternoon." It may be imagined what a pandemonium might be created by a few evil spirits; and the custom was said to have been abolished at one large Westmorland school only when the schoolmaster had had his eye put out. A poem on this outrageous game exists in Daniel Fleming's hand-writing which likens the besieged scholars to Grecian heroes, and gives a high-flown version of their coming to terms with the enemy outside.

Baxter would have no severe struggle with his little school. The barring-out there was clearly in anticipation of Christmas, for though it took place once on November 9th, its date was usually between December 7th and 15th. The children's tip seems to have been at the rate of 6d. each, though occasionally it rose to 1s. 0d. In 1674 the squire gave " ye children 1s., and to a Calgarth boy 6d.," which looks as if a scholar were boarded in the village (unless he walked every day from Calgarth and back). The tip was the same when the boys went to higher grade schools; it was entered at 1s. 6d. when three of them were at Kendal in 1674.

The schoolmaster apparently gained nothing by the riot of the barring-out, except an excuse for granting long holidays. But the authorized cock-fight, which was held in every school at Shrovetide, brought him in a substantial sum, for it was the custom for each pupil to pay him the tribute of a cock-penny. This expression, like the " God-penny " of the ancient village court, may have once meant the old English silver penny, worth a groat, but it came to be variable in value. It differed according to the rank of the pupil and the status of the school. The Rydal account book makes this fact clear.

At the village school cock-fight the squire habitually sent 6d. for each child; to the Ambleside master 1s. 0d.; Hawkshead was higher still, 2s. 6d., and Kendal 5s. 0d.; while at the last great school Wil, being heir, presented 10s. 0d. as his cock-penny. What this fee had paid for originally seems uncertain, or what the schoolmaster exactly provided as its equivalent. One authority says that he furnished cocks for the boys' sport; another that he was obliged to give the boys a premium to fight cocks for. Some entries in the Rydal account book raise a surmise that the scholars in the person of their captain supplied one belligerent bird, while the schoolmasters were bound to supply the other, whence his fee. In that case there would be reproduced the old typical strife between master and pupil. Mr. F. Nicholson,* says:—

"About three weeks previous to the eventful day, the boys assembled and selected as their captains two of their schoolfellows, whose parents were willing to bear the expenses incurred in the forthcoming contests. After an early dinner on Shrove Tuesday the two captains, attended by their friends and schoolfellows, who were distinguished by blue and red ribbons, marched in procession from their respective homes to the village green, where each produced their cocks."

He adds that this appears to have been the practice at Wreay, near Carlisle.

Customs certainly differed, however, according to period and place. The sport was held in Hawkshead, according to tradition, on the floor of the spacious grammar-school itself, and this is borne out by one of the entries to follow, which shows that a pit was dug afresh every year at the expense of the captain, this floor being doubtless kept rush-strewn like the church. The fee may in this case have acknowledged the schoolmaster's permission and protection, even if he did not provide a bird. But many a small village school would be too small to contain a gathering for the sport, and it may then have been held on the green, or in Rydal, in some suitable spot of the undulating ground near the Hall. Again, in the entries concerning the various schools attended by the young Flemings, which it may be well to draw together, no more than one captain is mentioned; and from the character of those who stood for the honour, Henry, George, Roger, James and Fletcher, of whom the first two were decidedly clever and bookish boys, I have conjectured that it was the master who nominated the

---

* See *Victoria History of Cumberland* Game of Cock-fighting

boy for the office as a reward for progress. Of course the father's rank would cause the young Flemings to be more frequently put in office, and that he himself entered with zest into their sport, even adding something for the betting, is clear.

The 1s. 6d.—or 6d. each—first entered as cock-pennies given to Baxter, rose to 2s. 0d. Then on Feburary 26th, 1666 :—

	£ s. d.
Given to 3 ye Boyes for Cock-Pennys 2s, and to bett 6d.	00 02 06

This item constantly recurs, the amount varying only with the number of children at school. In May, 1671, Will and Harry were despatched to the grammar-school at Kendal, Will now being fourteen and Harry twelve, and growing beyond Baxter's tuition. Harry, indeed, was clever, and seems to have been insatiable with his pen, for in 1669 " A Gramer and Inch-hornes for Harry " had cost 1s. 3d, and ink-horns were bought for him again in 1675 and 1677. Besides the usual cock-penny, a boy always carried an " entering-penny "—variable likewise —to a new schoolmaster. The Kendal pedagogue was Richard Stewardson, with whom the squire had had a conference at Fords in October.

	£ s. d.
Given unto Will 3s., and unto Harry 2s., and for ye school-master 10s, when they went first to Kendal School,* in all	00 15 00

But at every return after holidays each boy carried to the master 5s. 0d., while the usher had an occasional 2s. 6d.

Then on the following February 2nd comes the entry.—

	£ s. d.
Sent by Jo. Bankes for Cock-pennies to Will 10s., and to Harry 5s, in all	00 15 00

---

* One of the regulations at Kendal School was that it should be free to all boys resident in the parish of Kendal for Classics alone, excepting a voluntary payment of a Cock-Penny as aforetime at Shrovetide (*Flemings in Oxford*, pp. 424 and 472).

These sums were repeated, but in 1675 Harry, being captain of the sports, presented the master with " a broad 20s. 0d. piece in gold," reckoned at £1. 1s. 6d., and his additional expenses for the occasion came to 18s. 6d.

Little Barbara meanwhile had joined her brother Daniel (good and slow) at the Rydal school. We fancy her a bright little person. Her horn-book (2d.) had already been purchased, so she may have learnt her alphabet at home. And in 1674 an item runs :—

	£ s. d.
Paid to a Scotch Pedler for a bible for Barbara	00 02 06

After no doubt a joyous holiday for the five eldest children at Flookburgh in May, 1672, where the waters of the Holy Well were drunk, Daniel went to school with his elder brothers. George now entered Rydal school. Coming after a girl, he always led the second batch of the squire's sons. Bright, handsome and ambitious, his talents and position raised him eventually to the Bishopric of Carlisle.

The item January 1st, 1763 :—

	£ s. d.
Paid Katy wh she had disbursed at George's baring-out	00 01 00

shows that a bare 6d. would not suffice him. By 1678 his four little brothers—Michael, Richard, Roger and James, were all at Rydal school, 2s. 6d. covering their cock-pennies; and in February, 1679-80, is noted, " Given by Captain James to Edward Sawrey for his Cock, 6d."

In the summer of 1678, however, William completed his education at Kendal with a farewell gift to the master of 10s. 0d., and Harry left for Oxford under the care of trusty John Banks, with £1 to " keep his purse," and a token of gold (value £1. 4s. 0d.). Later, George joined Daniel at the higher school, each carrying 5s. 0d. to the master and 1s. 0d. for their purses. George's entrance fee must have been small, for it is included with other expenses paid the carrier at 2s. 0d. The 10s. 0d. taken by the boys in January, 1679, are put down as 5s. 0d. and 2s. 6d. for the schoolmaster, and 2s. 6d. for the usher, and this is repeated each half-year. Daniel left in 1680, at the age of 20, to become the right-hand of his father at home; and George, after six months at Kendal, was withdrawn and sent with his next three brothers to an Ambleside schoolmaster. The " entering Pennies " to Mr. Thwaite amounted for the four to 5s. 0d., and there was 4d. " to buy Candles for their schoolmaster." George must have been chosen captain at Shrovetide, for besides 1s. 0d. for his cock-penny, a 6d. is recorded. Little Fletcher, who had, after George's departure, joined his brothers at Rydal (again making five), enjoyed the same honour, for besides cock-pennies for James and himself, there was :—

	£	s.	d.
Given by Fletcher to Edw Sawrey for bringing him a a Cock to fight for him, being a Captaine	00	00	06

also is given him " to bett upon his cock." All the boys, except the Oxford scholar, could now live at home, and only dinners (£1. 15s. 0d. for six months) had to be paid for in Ambleside for the three. But whether Squire Daniel was becoming critical of tuition or not it is certain that he now made frequent changes in his boys' education. After only half a year at Ambleside (for which the master got £1. 10s. 0d.) they were all four despatched to the Hawkshead Grammar School, and boarded with a Mrs. Edmondson at a cost of £5. Probably tuition was free, as no fees for it are specified.

Only Mr. Sadler, the master, had a gratuity conveyed to him by the boys after holiday-times, as at Kendal, while the usher received also an occasional 2s. 6d.

	£	s.	d.
Aug. 17th, '81 Delivered George to give Mr Sadler for himselfe, Michael, Rich. and Roger	00	10	00
It. given them to keep their purses	00	04	00

is an entry that recurs on the following January 9th and April 26th. Paper and candles for the term amount to 7s. 0d.

It is interesting to note, however, that in this, as in neighbouring schools, the curriculum did not include writing and arithmetic, which were taught by masters who appear to have visited at stated periods. This instruction had to be paid for.

	£ s. d.
Aug 23rd, 1684. Paid unto Mr Ralph Wilson, Scrivener, at Hawkshead, for teaching of my Sons Geo and Michael to write and Arithmetick 6 weeks 12s., and for teaching of Rich and Roger to write onely, 6 weeks 6s., in all	00 18 00

The festivities of Hawkshead school were seemingly conducted on a noble scale. The "barring-out" was attended by a "professional" fiddler, to whom the boys had before their return at Christmas given 2d. each, a sum which their father refunded. When Shrovetide came round, and George was chosen captain, there was quite a bustle in the family. A cock, doubtless a gamebird of known prowess, was procured from the squire's cousin of Kirby Hall in Furness; another "cousin," John Browham, much at Rydal about this time, was busy over arrangements, and attended the contest with the squire's son Daniel, when they spent a lavish sum of money.

	£ s d.
Feb 5, 1682-3. Given to my Cosin Jo. Browham's messenger about George's Cocks	00 00 06
Feb. 13. Sent to my Son. Dan to give unto Mr. Sadler for cock-pennies, for Captain Geo. 10s. for Mich Rich. and Roger, 7s 6d in all	00 17 6
Given by Dan. to Captain Kirkbyes man who brought a Cock 2s. 6d., to ye Pitmaker 1s, spent by Dan and Cosin Browham 11s 6d. Given by Geo to ye Fidler 1s.	00 16 00

It is necessary, however, to return to our small village school, where changes had been taking place. Squire Daniel, if his transactions are followed closely, is found to improve upon his bargains; and it was a clever thought of his to combine the office of schoolmaster and butler. Accordingly his account book gives, from the year 1673, on a separate page :—

"The Schoolmaster Accompt when every Brewing was at Rydal whilst he was butler there."

No added wages are set down for this additional duty—which may have meant superintendence of the wine and beer drunk in the household rather than waiting at the table; and William Baxter continued to be paid £2 yearly until 1681, though the payment due each May and November, often stood over till £3 or £4 were owing. Baxter's life must have been a penurious one, for the fees of his village scholars would be small indeed, and sometimes he borrowed from his employer a small sum. He paid for a cow on the common. Often he did errands, helping to collect the rents at Coniston, selling skins (generally of animals that died), making purchases at Kendal; and it is possible that he received a small percentage on the receipts he secured, though these are not apparent. Eighteen years after his coming to Rydal his payments as schoolmaster cease, but he cannot have left the neighbourhood altogether, for an entry of January 19th, 1685-6, runs :—

Delivered Alice to pay Wil Baxter for 2 Reams of Paper, marked with a Flower de liz crowned at 6s. 6d. p. Ream ye sum of .. .. . £ s d
00 13 00

There is a tragic touch in this simple particular, for it shows the solitary, ageing man to be doing what he could, and using his penmanship for the ornamentation of note-paper.

Quite a succession of masters followed Baxter, as the account book shows.

"Rowland Noble hired Oct. 25, 82, for 40s per annum to be Schoolmaster and Butler in ye place of William Baxter"

"For an Accidence for my son Fletcher" 4d. is paid in 1683, James had ink-horns, and 1s. is refunded next year to the schoolmaster for two books bought for James and Fletcher.

But Noble made no long stay. He was paid off on July 28th, 1685, with an extra 2s. 6d. given him.

"Richard Powley (my Schoolmaster and Butler) came Ap 8, 85, and is to have 40s per annum."

At the end of 1685, the older boys were withdrawn from Hawkshead, and George, with Richard, was placed at Sedbergh school, in Yorkshire.

Michael (older than Richard, though probably slow) as well as Roger, was apparently set again on the Rydal benches under Powley, and joined the village cock-fight.

	£ s d.
1686, Feb 15 Given unto my Sons Michael, Roger, & James 1s. 6d., & to Captaine Fletcher 1s	.. 00 02 06

And 6d. each was paid for their cock-pennies next year. They had merry times with a football bought them (6d.), and the like sum for apples, and were tipped for catching rats and mice, which were becoming troublesome about the Hall. "My little Boyes" even received 2s. to play cards with Mr. Strickland, on December 31st, 1685. They had 2s. 6d. for their barring-out on December 9th, 1687.

We hear of one famous "cocking" at Rydal, to be mentioned later. This was under Thomas Hobson, who superseded George Yates, "My Schoolmaster and Butler," in July, the latter having served only from April to June. Hobson remained till 1690, when Fletcher was fifteen. After that date butlers were engaged who were not schoolmasters, but at the same sum.

The Rydal school probably lapsed altogether, and the squire had in future to deal only with more distant masters. That he took an active interest in tuition is shown in his correspondence in 1674 with Mr. Mark Lewis, author of an " Accidence and Middle Grammar," which he liked so well that he bought and presented copies to several of the neighbouring schoolmasters. He expressed his opinion that the same author's " Critical Grammar " would " justle Lilly out of most schooles."

The career of another educational dependant of Rydal Hall can be traced to a melancholy decline, in the pages of the account book. He was William Hutchinson, music-master to the squire's daughters. Their mother had received excellent tuition in Oxford from Edward Lowe on the keyed instrument of the period, and no doubt their position required that they too should perform. It was a period when little was spent on the education of young ladies. The money was saved for their dower; and even the pin-money they required when grown-up had to be squeezed by them out of poultry and pigs (generally the latter) which were granted to them as perquisites. Visits to a grandmother, or to relatives, who inculcated manners, took the place of the later fashionable boarding-schools; and occasionally money was paid for a lesson or two in pastry-making or artificial flower-making, if an expert came in the way.

Music, however, and dancing were necessary accomplishments for a young gentlewoman, and we hear of " Kettys Manycords " being procured at the small cost of £1. 6s through her grandmother, Lady Fletcher, when Catherine —the eldest daughter—was but eleven years old. Perhaps the mother, whose harpsichord was the reigning instrument at the Hall, as the cithern had been in Squire John's time, at first instructed the child. But professional instruction was easy to procure, as musicians were at that time to be found who were itinerant. The Civil Wars had thrown all the court musicians on the world, and they had to seek a livelihood where they could.

Even the Restoration brought them little relief, for Charles loved French fiddlers as well as French morals, and the true English school of instrumental music which had reached so high a level, died out as these men died off. John Jenkins, whose concerted music delighted the age, wandered from one country-house to another, where the gentle or noble inmates cherished him for as long as he would stay, and where he directed the " consorts " of viols held among the neighbours and composed special music for the amateur band.

At the other end of the scale no doubt was William Hutchinson, who appeared at Rydal as a teacher, and who had—to judge from his frequent re-appearance—a beat limited to the north or even the county. Under date 1670, September 5th, the account-book runs —

	£ s. d.
Given by my wife to Will. Hutchison for a moneths teaching of Katy & Alice on y Harpiscalls & manicords	01 00 00

The name monochord, originally a single string stretched across a box with a movable bridge, came to be applied to a keyed instrument of the clavichord type, if it was not the clavichord itself, which was of tenderer tone than the harpsichord, the strings being struck from below by a tangent instead of being plucked by a jack. Will Fleming's daughters used the cythern (see *Rydal Household*).

The eldest now applied herself to the latter, and in December £1 was again paid for a month's tuition on " ye Harpsicalls " This was repeated the following February, and in August there were three weeks at a charge of 15s. In December of 1672 " for a fourthnights teaching of Katy of ye vio." (probably violin) Hutchinson was paid 10s. He was even willing to give a week's tuition, and, in October, 1673, the two girls shared this for 5s. ; and next January they had another fortnight.

But dancing now begins to absorb the attention of the young pupils, and the master for this accomplishment not only charged twice as high as his music rival, but demanded an entrance fee as well. Perhaps in consequence he is termed " Mr."

	£	s	d
Jan 12, 1673-74 Given unto Mr Leak ye Dancing-Master as an entrance for teaching of Katy & Alice to dance (besides 20s apiece ye moneth) y sum of	01	00	00
Feb 6, Paid Mr Leak ye Dancing-Master for a moneths Teaching of Katy & Alice	02	00	00

The master, or a relative, cunningly dealt in shoes, and next comes an item of 2s. 6d. " to Harry Leak for dancing shoes." The same articles for Alice only cost 2s procured at Hutton.

In October, 1674, Leak is paid £3, for a month's tuition of both girls at home, and one of Katy " abroad," probably given at the house of a relative, where she was visiting, and he halting on his rounds. He had an attendant for this entry is followed by —

	£	s.	d
Given his boy	00	02	00

The music-master re-appears in July of 1675, after the death of Mr. Fleming, when he is called " ye Virginal-Master," and paid 5s. for two weeks. His next round is made in June of next year, when the squire improves upon his bargains, and gets little Barbara instructed along with her sisters for the same sum, 10s. a month.

In 1677 he gets in a month and a fortnight, and in February, 1678, six weeks. Then in September comes an entry of 15s. " for teaching, Alice, Barbara and Mary six weeks upon ye Virginals." This instrument was a precursor of the piano, and had metal strings struck by a plectrum The name " spinet," which was the same as the virginal, is derived from the spines or quills by which the sound was evoked Katy was now married, and little Mary had passed from the nursery, being provided the year before with "canvis" for her sampler. In 1679 two visits are paid for. In 1680 a dancing-master appears again on the scene :—

Paid unto Mr Tinkler in full for teaching (and entrance) of Barbara and Mary to Dance 02 10 00

William Hutchinson was perhaps getting old and out of fashion. He re-appears in the account book after an interval in a new style of entry, which seems to imply that he had accepted a position as humble retainer at Rydal Hall, and was content with small gratuities of 2s. 6d.—or even 1s.—from time to time, and his clothes, which were often procured with the page-boy's.

July 29, 1684 Given to William Hutchinson besides   £ s d
    a new suit 00 02 06
Aug 5 Sheep Skins for Will Hutchinson & Jacks
    Packets (jackets?) 9d

And on September 17th, 6¼ yards of "brown frezed cloth" are procured in Ambleside for 10s 6d ,

"for Will. Hutchinson, my daughter's Master, 10s 6d"

A New Year's gift of 1s. seems to suffice him till August 13th, 1685 —

Given to Will Hutchinson for Teaching and Tuneing   £ s d
    ye Virginals 00 02 06

And next February he has the same sum for tuning

These dribbling sums continue, and in October, 1686, the village tailors are paid 2s. for making poor Will "a coat, &c." But he was probably kept in decent attire, for he seems to have accompanied the squire and knight as retainer for visits or festive occasions, and a donation of 1s shows that he was present on October 1st, 1687, in a day's expedition to Bowness and to Sir Christopher Philipson's house on Belle Island.

May 1688, finds the entry :—

"Disbursed for four yards of woollen-cloth for Will. Hutchinson's coat 6s 8d , for halfe a yr. of black Shalloon to face his Cuffs 10s "

And with the closing of the account book the decayed musician passes out of sight.

Of Rydal school there is little more to be said. It ceased to be a manorial adjunct after Sir Daniel Fleming's time, and the premises were used as a lumber place. Indeed, it is doubtful if there was any regular school after the seventeenth century. Itinerant schoolmasters there were in plenty about the countryside, and many a poor youth of talent, like Dr. John Dalton, opened and taught school in his neighbourhood for such small fees as the folk would give him. Hartley Coleridge began a school in Ambleside, and at first did well. It was probably on their own initiative that the later schoolmasters of Rydal taught. We have a glimpse of one in the Township's Directory for 1829, which gives the name of John Sproat as schoolmaster. He was the son of the head husbandman on the demesne, and as his father lived at the present Ivy Cottage (probably "Wilsons") it was convenient to him to take the old shop adjoining, and teach there. On the benches sat little John Backhouse (born 1819, died 1909), who has told me stories of his school-days, and who had as fellow-pupils for a time De Quincey's younger boys, Horace and Francis. "Willie and Margot" were considered too old for the tuition. Sproat removed to Ambleside, there to enlarge his sphere. Lady Fleming, who was deeply interested in religion and education, had her own dame's school at Banks' old house, opposite the Hall gates.

As late as 1863 there was a resident schoolmaster in Rydal, one John Butler, whose child was baptized at the Chapel.

NOTE.

The word "stover," in Tusser's time, at the head of chapter II. of this part, seems to mean stubble used as fodder. In the days of reaping-hooks, stubble was longer than it is now. The following note has been kindly supplied to me by Mr. Herbert Bell, the facts being gleaned from books in the Armitt Trust Library, at Ambleside :—

From the *Dict. of Nat. Biography, etc*, I find that Thomas Tusser, agricultural writer and poet was born at Rivenhall near Witham in Essex, about 1524, and died in London in 1580. His first work was the *Hundred Good Pointes on Husbandrie,* imprinted by Richard Tottel, the third day of February, An 1557." In 1573 they were increased to *Five Hundred Pointes of Good Husbandry united to as many of Good Huswifery* An edition (selection) was printed at Oxford in 1848 and the English Dialect Society's edition appeared in 1878. Tusser's works also appear in Southey's *Select Works of the British Poets, from Chaucer to Johnson* (1831).

The *Century Dictionary* gives the meaning of Stover " Fodder and provision of all sorts for cattle " [obsolete or prov. English].

> " Where live nibbling sheep,
> And flat meads thatch'd with *stover*, them to keep."
>
> Shakespeare's *Tempest* iv., 1., 63.

The *Dialect Dictionary* gives " Stover " as used in several counties and the meaning is " Haulm, stubble ; winter fodder or litter for cattle, hay made from the second mowing of clover or from artificial grasses."—ED.

PART V.

UPHEAVALS IN MANOR AND KINGDOM.

CHAPTER I.

Squire John Fleming

WHEN William Fleming, armiger, was buried with the customary state in the choir of Grasmere Church, on June 24th, 1600, his eldest son John was a man of twenty-five, and therefore was entitled immediately to obtain livery of the ancestral manors of Beckermet, Coniston and Rydal. "Although this John Fleming" said Sir Daniel when writing notes of his family, "was in his younger years a kind of Hector, somewhat wilde, yet after his said Father's death, he became a Sober and a very prudent Gentleman, an Hospitable person (killing Thirty Fat Beeves yearlie in his House aforesaid, with Fat Muttons &c. proportionable) and a great Improver of his Estate both Real and Personal."

John remains somewhat of a mystery, in spite of the records left of him A man of apparently great power of mind, as well as of command over others, he threw himself on to the losing side in religion, and thus cut himself off from all those roads in public life by which he might have achieved distinction; and remained content to spend his talents in the amassing of wealth. Yet whatever he was, he was not a simple country-loving squire. Educated probably at the university* he took up residence in London, where he may have studied law, as was the very useful fashion of young men of good family in Queen Elizabeth's reign. Here probably he acquired the new-fangled habit of smoking, to which he remained addicted; and after his death a little bill stood at 6s., for "½ Tobacco for my master." The earliest records of him occur at this time. The Grasmere statesmen were just then striving to obtain a weekly market and two fairs in the year, which would not only save them from the long travel with wool and produce to luckier centres, but would draw the country-side into them. They were in 1598 sending a deputy up to London to forward the matter; and they arranged with Squire William of Rydal that his son John "Now at london" should if necessary supply this deputy with money, which twelve of the most prominent among them undertook to re-fund to him. The following is the bond which they entered into, which still exists.

1598

"Memorndm that whereas Mr Willm Fleminge Esquire hathe by his lett^r under his hands unto his sonne Jhone Fleminge nows at london promised that yf thomas crossewyn comethe there he shall stande proxy of such monie as shall Be nedfule aboute the purchesse of a market and the procuringe of towe Faires and more that he the saide Jhone Fleminge shall make shifte and procure the said thomas all suche monie as shall be nedfule for the same so that iff yt hapen or Fall out & that the said Jhone Fleminge do procure any sum of monye aboute the purchesse of the saide Faires that then we whosse names ar hereunder wrytten dothe by this bill of o^r handes covenant promisse and binde hus and everie one of hus o^r heires executors and assignes to discharge and harmles save (= indemnify) the saide Willm Fleming his heires executors or assignes in witnes whereof we hereunder

---

* His brother Thomas wrote from "Jesus" in 1591, but neither the students register for Jesus, Oxford or Cambridge, began so early as this year. It is therefore impossible to ascertain to which university he was attached. For help in this matter, I have to thank Mr Abbott, librarian of Jesus, Cambridge, as well as Dr Magrath, Provost of Queen's College, Oxford.

CONISTON OLD HALL.

Brantwood, Home of John Ruskin, across the Lake.

From a Drawing by Sophia Armitt.

TO FACE P. 475.

have sett to oʳ markes the seconde of maye in the Fortiethe yere of her ma^{ties} reinge

    John Willson

(Then follows a row of about 10 scrawls, and under)

    Edwarde knottes   John benson   ottlaye
    Robert herd   Willm hede   Christoppere mayson
    Rogere kottes   Jane Walker   anthonie grigg
    Jhone hunther   Jhone thompson

John's own postscript, characteristically concerns money, and shows that he was not only amusing himself by playing cards, but winning at it. In a most polite letter, addressed from Goldsmiths Hall in Foster Lane, he requests Mr. Darley of Greys Inn to pay him the sum owed. Mr. Darley replies, with equally polite assurances, that the money shall be paid, while reminding him that the debt was not incurred by himself, but by a friend for whom he stood surety.

From the life of a gay young man about town, who may have listened to the plays of Shakespeare when first acted, he was recalled by his father's death to the care of his northern estates. His mother Agnes took over Rydal, as hers by settlement; and he must have fixed himself at Coniston, the seat so greatly embellished if not re-built by his father. He married at once, (for the marriage settlements were signed June 6th, 1601,) for his first wife Alice, daughter of Sir Francis Ducket of Grayrigg Hall, near Kendal. He was High Sheriff for the county of Lancashire in 1611. On the death of Alice, he married Bridget, the daughter of Sir William Norris, of Speke Hall near Liverpool. She was already the widow of Sir Thomas Bold, and it was under the name of Lady Bold that she was buried at Coniston, " about Feb. 1625."* John next repaired his loss by marrying Dorothy, daughter of Sir Thomas Strickland, of Sizergh Hall, and by her he had born to him in 1629, after two

---

* See copy of the monumental tablet in Coniston Church, *Flemings in Oxford*, p 538

daughters, an heir. The marriage with her therefore must have taken place no later than 1626, if so late. The two deeds catalogued by Daniel Fleming by which in 1629 Agnes Fleming released Rydal to her son after he had leased it to her in 1625 for seven years may have been connected with this third marriage

" Sir D F's List of Rydal Writings

Le Fleming
Rydal Demesne.

1625 *John Fleming*, esq his Lease of *all his estate* unto Agnes his mother 7 years dat May 6 1 Jas 1625

1629 *Agnes Fleming* her Release of Rydale unto John her son Dat Dec 6. 1629

It is to this marriage with Dorothy that his becoming a Catholic is ascribed, because the Strickland family were firm then, as they always remained, in the old faith. But so equally were the Norrises of Speke, with whom John kept up a close connection, though their daughter had given him no son Sir William Speke was indeed credited with having dealings with the king's enemies abroad,* besides being an open Catholic. Again, John's step-sister, Jane, daughter of William Fleming by his first marriage, had wedded a Mr. Richard Harrison of Martindale, and both sons, whom John eventually made his agents, were Catholic. Their neighbours, the Lancasters of Glencune, were likewise Catholics.

Indeed, the influence of the old faith must have been strong about John. The northern counties, Westmorland included, had not been eager for change or reform in religion ; and though they disliked the arbitrary sweeping away of what was beneficial in the monasteries and beautiful and ornate in the service of the church, they yet accepted the Anglicized rubric as a continuation of the old worship. The Pope's mandate (1566) that no Catholic might attend a Protestant service awoke them

---

* *Victoria History of Lancashire.*

from this position, and close upon the mandate came the missionizing efforts of the colleges of Douay and Rome to recall the county to its old allegiance to the Pope. Many of the priests sent on secret missions from these seminaries were north-countrymen, who returned to their old haunts, and there sowed the seeds of that Catholic re-action that gave Elizabeth's government so much trouble. These men wandered in the lonely vales of Lancashire, of Yorkshire and of Westmorland, and were hidden in Halls and homesteads as was Henry VI. in his last days. And the fate of some of them was no happier: one priest, a native of Westmorland, who for thirteen years had roamed in secret the valleys and climbed the passes, nourishing the old beliefs, and celebrating mass for the faithful, was at last caught, and was executed in 1593.* In this matter, as so often before, the old Northumbrian spirit of insubordination awoke, to help the losing cause.

But these things had happened before Squire John became a prominent figure in the country, and it was not for some time apparent in which direction his sympathies lay. In 1621 he is still addressed as living at Coniston, but in 1624, 1626 and 1629, he was at Rydal, and it was from here that he was "presented" for non-attendance at his parish church of Grasmere. Having submitted himself with his wife on this plea, he and she were admonished by the Lord Bishop of Chester at a court held at Wigan.—

" to repayre dutifully to there parishe Church and other places of Oratorie there to heare Divine service and sermons and to participate of the Sacramentes used in the same and to certifye such there Conformitie in the premisses under the minister and Churchward(ens) there handes in or about the Feast of the Purification next." †

---

* *Victoria History of Cumberland*
† Rydal Hall MSS

But from this position there was a money escape. On September 13th, 1629, Squire John " of Conyston" appeared at the old monastic centre that had so long tyranized over the church of Grasmere, viz.: "att the Manno^r of St. Marye neare the walls of the Citty of York," and there agreed by an annual rent to be paid to his majesty to compound for all his lands and his chattels in the counties of Lancaster, Cumberland and Westmorland. Therefore the sheriffs of those counties are by writing admonished that so long as he pays the rent, he is no further "to bee disquieted or trobled" in matters of recusancy.* On October 29th, 1630 he likewise arranged to pay money instead of receiving knighthood at the coronation of Charles I. Under date, July 1st, 1631, the heavy restriction that was imposed on influential Catholics was removed, and the Council of the north gave him licence to travel beyond the limited five miles from Rydal for half a year, from the next August 1st. He travelled to Speke Hall, to administer the estates of the Norris family, which had been left in trust for the heir during his minority, by the spendthrift and recusant Sir William, who died 1626.

We find from *The Norris Papers*, edited by Tho. Heywood, Esq., F.S.A., printed for the Cheetham Society, that a Sir Wil. Norris, was killed at Musselburgh, in 1547. His half-brother, Edward Speke, died 1596. William his son and successor was a spendthrift, and his father directs that the Cheshire estate should be placed in trust for ten years, and then delivered to his son. However, Sir William pawned everything, down to two suits of clothes. He died 1626, and his son William in 1651. This William had two sons, Edward and Thomas, who fought for the king. Thomas, stated to have been born in 1681 (?) took the estates.

Again in a document of 1625, Sir William Norris is

---

* Rydal Hall MSS

accused of having some years before sent over money and arms to the late king's enemies abroad He paid £60 per annum for recusancy.

From 1626 till at least 1634 Squire John remained in Lancashire, being spoken of as resident there in that year, though he appears to have paid a visit to Rydal in the late summer of 1634. This period furnishes us with a correspondence (the earliest preserved at Rydal) which affords stray glimpses into his exceedingly complicated affairs But it is difficult to understand, in view of those affairs, why he stayed away. The entreaties of his old mother that he should finish his business at Speke, and return, were of no avail. His children, the "sweet bairnes," were sent to him, and the grandmother hungers for news of them. The last months of her life must have been lonely and sad, with only William Tyson to scold, and the husbandry that had been her care for so long, going to rack and ruin (see *Letters*). The death of their mother, presumably "my Ladye," is not yet found. In *Coniston Register*, under February 3rd, 1633, we have the burial of " Margaret w. of Le : Fleminge " See *Coniston Registers*.

Then, too, the proposals she makes to facilitate his return are so mysterious. With his manors of Beckermet, Coniston and Rydal waiting for him, she suggests that he should take up his residence at Keswick, where he would be among his friends. It is true that there was at this time, in all probability, no lord's seat at Beckermet, where the ancient site had become a grassy mound ; that Coniston with its commodious hall was let to farm to John's nephew William,* who was heir to Skirwith : yet even if Rydal were likewise let to farm and so disposed of, as she proposed, why should John—rich and powerful—settle at quiet Keswick, remotely situated between

---

* William's two eldest sons, Daniel and Roger, were born there in 1633 and 1634

estuaries, where he held tithes, indeed, but not an acre of land?

John's career, indeed, offers several queries, the answer to which may lie, in part at least, in the religion to which he was so stubbornly attached. He may have insisted on remaining where he could hear mass, and conveniently harbour a priest. His associates were Catholics; and who knows whether the small clique of recusants—though dwindled and less courageous than in the queen's days—did not harbour hopes that may sometimes have brought them very near to plotting? Then, too, John, a "Hector" in youth, suffered in health from what were apparently attacks of gout. He is congratulated on recovery from his "last sickness" in 1621; a legal correspondent in 1632 speaks of his presence being needed to forward certain proceedings in court, yet would not have him endanger his health by coming to London. Again, when in March, 1634, he was sued by his second wife's nephew, Mr. William Norris, now come to man's estate, for maladministration of his patrimony at Speke, and he induced Lord Wentworth to write from Dublin to the Council of the north on his behalf, the latter remarks that the journey necessary to answer the summons before the Council Table in Easter Term :—

"wilbe something troublesome unto him, consideynge his ould age, and other infirmities incident there unto, yet not wthstanding he is fully determined then to give his attendance upon yo^{ur} Lo^{ds} accordingly"

The letter goes on to say that part of the heir's complaint rests on the fact that John Fleming had continued to pay the £60 a year for which Sir William Norris had compounded, as a recusant "about" four years since,* on the contention that, the heir being also a recusant, it was legally due to the commissioners. He bespoke their favour "in behalf of ye ould Gentleman." †

---

* Sir William died eight years before; see *Norris Papers*.
† Rydal Hall MSS.

Squire John, who had travelled from Speke to London in May, 1633, and thence in July or August to Rydal, may have felt it due to his honour to appear likewise on this occasion ; but most of his legal matters were conducted by deputy. The papers of instructions that remain to his deputies—some of them unlettered men—show how clear a brain·he possessed to control and work these tangled skeins. Besides the control of the demesne farm or farms—with which he intermingled that of Speke as we have seen, by the driving of cattle there—there was all the difficult work of " tithinge " to be performed by his men, in those parishes where he had bought up the church tenths as an investment. There was the salary to be paid to the clergymen of these robbed churches, of Sherburn, of Addingham, of Ulverston, of Grasmere, and of the " 3 churches " in Cumberland, viz. · St. John's and St. Bride's at Beckermet, and the church at Cleator ; and there was besides the repair of their chancels to see to. Vexed questions cropped up here as elsewhere ; and John Fleming is found at variance even to the point of law with his relative John Ambrose, and advising with counsel as to how he may best make a legal demand for the tithes of Lowick. Even his mother's will, though it was evidently sent when written for his approval, was held in dispute. It was proved at York ; but the administrators appointed to see its provisions carried out, amongst whom was his cousin Lamplough, did not please Squire John, and he appealed against them. Tyson had to travel to York, in company with Gerrard, a Rydal man in order to swear to his knowledge of his old mistress' will ; but they failed to obtain a revocation. Sir John Lowther, his brother-in-law, whose wife was also an executor, writes in June 1633 to urge him to " suffer some end be made," so that legacies of the will may be paid, and offers to arbitrate between him and his cousin Lamplough. He has " loved his cousin Lamplough's wife from her cradle "

The business about reprisals and compounding which occupied counsel in London during the years 1631 and 1632 is not easy to understand. Squire John at his death was paying as a recusant £25 every half year. This strange lord of Rydal never in fact shunned the law-courts, with which he was familiar from his youth. Legal business, too, must have occasionally cropped up concerning the private bonds he held. For he was a great money-lender.

In an age when banks did not exist, the country gentleman who had ready money which he would advance upon security must have been a resource for the whole neighbourhood. The nation, in spite of the laws against usury, had never done without credit After the expulsion of the Jews, loans were taken up by the Lombards and the Flemings, whose merchants waxed rich upon the wool which they carried from the country in place of money brought in. But it came to be seen that if English commerce were to thrive, English capital must be forthcoming with which to support it, and the law that forbade lending money on interest, was repealed.

But not alone for forwarding trade were loans wanted. They served to tide a man over a temporary difficulty or shortness of cash, though much more often they assisted, while prolonging, his downfall. All sorts and conditions came to the well-filled coffers of Rydal Hall, which at least for three generations were unlocked to the needy who had sound guarantees to offer. Dame Agnes lent upon mortgage to the people around, to a failing statesman perhaps who had lost his cattle, or more often to a fuller whose trade had declined but who had property at his back. Her largest monetary transactions, that appear in Tyson's accounts, were with three Dutchmen, who were speculative miners at Coniston. They would seem not to have been successful * John, following her,

---

* For Dutch miners see *Transactions* C & W A & A Society, vol v , p. 344 ; and p. 14 of *Squire John Fleming*.

had apparently an extensive connection as a banker; leaving at his death over £10,000 in Bonds and Bills.* His successor Daniel, too, as soon as he had paid off the loans he had himself needed in the struggle for possession, or even before, began to lend, and his "Rent-book" furnishes us with a curious insight into the financial condition of the country at that time. When all classes, from Deans to petty tradesmen and cobblers, came to borrow; and credit was given alike on deeds of mortgage, or more frequently—since deeds were scarce—on the bonds of sound neighbours, or even on a poor man's "word and his cow." The usual rate of interest was, as we shall see in the war-loans, eight per cent in large transactions. In small ones, borrowed for a specified time, the interest was often deducted from the sum lent before it was handed over.

It seems probable that his mother's death left Squire John not only with a freer hand in the management of the Rydal demesne, but in matters of religion. It is in 1633 that we first hear of "your servant Harrison"; certainly from that time he employed his Catholic nephews Richard and Edward Harrison, sons of his half sister Jane (who married a Martindale gentleman) as his agents and clerks. His own return to Rydal, which we cannot date, drew a little circle of co-religionists to the place. A list of them, dated 1640,† makes them ten in number besides himself: Richard Harrison, with his wife and son Lancelot; Edward Harrison, Robert Gardiner, Richard Wilson, Jane Crosbie, Dorothea Barbon, Alice Borwicke and Salomon Benson. With the exception of Jane Crosbie and Alice Borwick, we find all these entered as "convicted Recusants" in the Subsidy Roll of 1641, with fines of 1s. 4d. each to pay. None of these were Rydal folk: where then did they live? The Richard

---
* Evidence of Lancelot Harrison in the lawsuit of 1653.
† Rydal Hall MSS.

Harrisons were probably lodged at the Hall, if not close to it, where Mrs. Harrison would be useful as directress and chaperone for the squire's two girls, now growing to womanhood. "Doll Barbon" was a servant, who had a 30s -a-year wage, while Gardiner and Wilson may have been engaged about the demesne. Edward Harrison occupied the old dwelling-place of the Bensons at Miller Bridge,* the freehold of which with its adjoining colony (once in the lordship of Rydal) Squire John had been able to buy back in 1638, and for which he held a solemn Court Baron, for the re-entry of the holders into his demesne. This little group of Catholics would hardly be unprovided with their own worship. Salomon Benson, whose pension of £3. 10s. 0d. appears in the books, may have been the priest who celebrated mass, and the names of "Chappel Chamber" and "Priest Chamber" were in use for two upper rooms of Rydal Hall until 1750, as an inventory of that date shows. A fall of burning soot in the great hall chimney, in 1905, caused its ascent by a waller; when he found a space some seven to ten feet square opening on to it, on a level with the upper floor, in a twelve foot thickness of wall. This possibly may have served as a hiding-place, such as few Catholic houses were without, for a priest when danger threatened.

Squire John Fleming, though he lived to 68,† had to leave his young children and estates to the care of others, on the eve of a troublous time, when there was most need of his own astuteness. Richard Harrison writes sadly of his condition on February 15th, 1643, in answer to enquiries from his niece, Mrs. Agnes Dudley. Ever since December "one or other waked wth him night by night, for still as he gott but one or tow daies ease of the goute it allwaies took him againe." The writer speaks

---

* Church Registers, where he is styled "gentleman" on the christening of his son Robert, in 1643

† His age was greatly exaggerated by his contemporaries. Even his children declared him to be nearly 80 at his death

of his natural strength of body that could withstand this last " fitt " ten days ago that is the worst he ever had ; nevertheless " I feare gettinge past this springe wilbe a Longe Jurney." John's life-journey closed in fact on the 27th. His riches, may-be, were his greatest achievement. They so much impressed the circle around him, that his nephew, Mr. John Fleming, a lawyer, repeated in court (1653) the statement Edward Harrison had made on his death-bed, that he had never known nobleman, knight, or gentleman to die so rich as the squire of Rydal, in that he left, besides his manors and his flocks and herds, something like £18,000 in goods, money, plate and bonds. Counsel afterwards stated this amount as £20,000—a sum not imposing in these days of American multi-millionaires, but which then—when money was eight times the value of what it is to-day—was an astounding one for a country gentleman to amass.

CHAPTER II

The Rydal Household.

THE death of John Fleming fell out at a most unhappy time for the young orphans he left behind him.
A household marked out already by government for its papistry, Rydal Hall was now to incur the enmity of the winning side by its adherence to the king's cause in the Civil war.

No sooner was the master dead, than there hasted " divine messengers " to his next of kin or of friendship, to the Lamploughs mentioned above, to Meaburn Hall, (Sir Christopher Lowther), to Kentmere and Sizergh (the Stricklands), to carry the news far and wide through Cumberland and Westmorland. But none—if the dates of church register and Richard Harrison's account book are correct—could gather to his burial; for his body was laid to earth in Grasmere choir the day of his death, in quietude and without any state. Only the coffin and bier and grave had to be paid for, besides which 10s. was "given to those that went to Church with him to drinke,"—meaning the bearers; also a gratuity to the clerk and a special one to the parson Wilson (a great Royalist and High Churchman) "for oversight of his buriall" The largest item of the few funeral expenses was 30s. given "to poore folkes the next morning," who had apparently assembled too late for the dole usually distributed at the burial of gentle-folk. Next came the legal business and the will. An accountant came to "drawe the office," for a fee of £2. The will had to be engrossed and proved, and a journey made to York, whither Harrison rode with "Cousin Kirkby and his men," doubtless for protection in these unsettled times. Another journey was taken again in considerable fear, by

"Mr Phillipson, Mr Gilpin, myself, James Tarleton and my brother next and Lanclott's (his son's) Charges, and our horses, amounting to 11s. 8d."

Two Rydal statesmen, David Harrison and Michael Holme, were entrusted with money to carry to Mr Robert Rawlinson of Cartmell, and Mr. Curwen (the amount being £60. 6s. 6d.) and received 1s. for their "paynes." A meeting shortly after was held at Windermere, to obtain powers of administration, at which Messrs. Philipson, Gilpin, Rawlinson, "Jervis" Benson, and Wakefield were present. Finally, at a meeting apparently for the appointment of acting trustees, many expenses were incurred, including those of "Messrs. Curwen, Rawlinson, Kirkby, Ambrose and self all night," with dinners and wine at the high figure of £3. 2s.

Of these gentlemen, some were crown officials, and some "supervisors" as they were called, of John Fleming's will. At the head of them, uniting both capacities, was Mr. Christopher Philipson of Calgarth, a man of great influence in the country-side. He appears to have been a barrister-at-law, and a receiver for the king's lordship of Kendal. It was not surprising therefore that he was a staunch supporter of the king's authority and cause ; and it may well be that he actually served as major in the royal army as is said, when the struggle intensified. Of the fighting prowess of his family, which came to be told in story, more will appear. Jervace Benson was a law officer of Kendal, and served as major in 1644. Mr. Robert Rawlinson was also a barrister-at-law, and seems to have been a trusted friend and adviser to the family. The Mr. Curwen mentioned was probably a relative of his, for he had (in addition to his Cotton patrimony) inherited from his uncle Robert Curwen the estate of Cark Hall in Cartmel where he resided.* The Mr. Kirkby was Roger of Kirkby Hall (whose sister had married William, John Fleming's cousin) who had already been displaced, and was soon to go under in the wars, and leave his great family to the care of his able wife, who had been a Lowther. Mr. Ambrose, too, was a Furness man and a relative, John of that ilk having married John Fleming's sister, and this being doubtless John's son William.

But when the first legal business connected with the transfer of a large estate was got through, the affairs of Rydal Hall were left almost wholly in the hands of Richard Harrison, as his account-book shows He had control over the household and estate finance, referring only in extraordinary matters to the " supervisors," with Mr. Philipson of Calgarth at the head. His wife is never mentioned, except in the matter of a hat which Mr. Dudley had procured for her ; but her presence, whether in the house itself or hard by, may have served as chaperonage to the two young girls left with their younger

---
* West's *Antiquities of Furness*

brother, as orphans, at the Hall. The house now fell back into something like its accustomed ways, from which it was presently to be so rudely shaken

In the forefront of the servants stood Katharine, who paid out small sums for the housekeeping, until such time as the young ladies took this office on themselves. She may have been the " Keatie Benson " who appears in Tyson's short-kept accounts of 1631-33, as paying for butter ; and at that time the butter, eggs, and howleeks(?) consumed in the house from Easter to Whit Sunday cost only 1s. 7d., and eggs and cheeses for three weeks 3d. Her wages were now £3 yearly. Thomas Bussell was cook at £2. He may have been only scullion-boy in Tyson's time, when 1s. is accounted for, for making his clothes and a coat. He now is entrusted with money ; 18s. 6d. being paid for a brass ladle and other things, and has a scullion boy under him at 16s. ; a payment that may be commuted in clothes. " A paire of britches for sculion boy " was bought at Hawkshead for 2s. Again the kitchen boy's " showes " cost 1s. 6d.

Doll Barbon the Catholic had 30s. yearly. She had doubtless been nurse to the children, and she took up that office again in sickness as well as serving as personal attendant to the young ladies. Three " servant wenches " received £1 or something less a year, and completed the in-door workers. Out of doors there were the farm hands : first Wilson the shepherd, at £2. 10s. ; who paid out expenses of husbandry ; then the under shepherd ; the plough-boy ; Anthony Dawson, perhaps the cow-herd, £2 ; two other men at 36s. 8d. each. Then there were irregular workers : Anthony Skelton, who rode armed to all the musters of the county's cavalry, which was called the Light Horse, and furnished by the landed gentry ; he received £2. " Old Jarrot," a servant of Dame Agnes's time had 30s. ; he superintended and paid out for job work, such as walling. Adam Fisher the smith was paid for piecework, like Thomas Nicolson the wright, but he excelled in a garden; and besides tending his own at the smithy by the beck and at the foot of the rise that became known after his time as " Adam How," he worked at the hall garden, where he would sow the cabbage and mustard seed brought from Carlisle by Charles Wilson. The " milner " received 26s. 8d., or two marks yearly

Harrison in a later year (1646) lumps the half-yearly wages, which in general were due at " Penticost " and " Martinmas,"—except the shepherd, who had a " Candlemas" engagement—at £12. 4s. 8d. This makes £24 9s. 4d. for the year; an immense difference from Tyson's total entry of £9. 19s. 6d., paid out at Martinmas 1631, and Whit Sunday 1632 Tyson, however, entered separately " the milner of his waige 7s. 0d.," and " Garrard 3s. 0d.," while " my owne waige due att Midsomer 1632," and apparently for the year, is £2, a moderate sum surely for the hard-working factotum of the estate.

The provisions for the household were furnished from the estate. The oats grown were ground at the mill and made up into the cakes that were the staple food of the people. The bigg, prepared at the kiln, made malt that was brewed into beer. Cattle were killed and salted for winter use, as we have seen.

Even the small requisites of life were manufactured at home. Fat was used for the rush-lights, for which an occasional outlay (of 4d. in Tyson's time) for " candle-seaves," the prepared or peeled rush, was necessary, and for the home-made candles, the wicks of which Tyson bought at 6d.

The powerful light of the candle was only used for the parlour, however, and sometimes had to be purchased on sudden need. David Harrison, the Rydal purveyor, furnished 4 lbs. of candles for 1s. 7d. towards Christmas of 1631. On another occasion 2 lbs. cost 9d. Harrison enters for 1643 :—

"p^d to olliv^r platt for white candles had before cressemas before we had gotten ow^r owne candles made o^l 5^s 8^d;"

and to the same Olliver (doubtless a chandler of Kendal) as much as 4s. is paid about the same time for

"weeke for makinge of white candles"

Soap was made in the house, bracken being used in its preparation, and Tyson's accounts show 8d. "for a makinge of soape, for Speake," actually sent into Lancashire, when the squire was resident there.

Occasional purchases, when the home supply gave out, show the prices of the period. From Tyson —

	s.	d.
paid for a q^rter of meale at Easter	1	2
David H for a q^ter of meale against Whitsundaie	1	3
for a q^ter of fleshe at Shrouetyde	1	0

This would represent the feast before the fast; and is perhaps the one referred to by Harrison in 1645: "p^d for 2 veale Had of Dauid Harrison before Fatnes even. £0. 3s. 6d." For the long Lent fast, as well as for the feasts, special provision was made. The fish was brought from long distances; Morecambe Bay supplying through its fishing towns the shell-fish and flat-fish known as flooks, the Cumberland coast the herrings, and the market of Penrith—into which it was doubtless brought from the Eden fisheries—the salmon.

The supply of fresh-water fish from the estate waters was also large (see Fisheries, p. 269).

The herrings in Tyson's book are 2s. the 100; some 300 being paid for in the season. The cockles, obtained through David, figure at 6d. and 1s.

The price of herrings was the same in 1644, when "6 hunderth," bought at Whitehaven, cost 12s. Two dozen "salt killings," at apparently 5s. the dozen, cost with carriage from St. Bees, 11s. 6d. For

" Fresh Flookes from Cartmell and a bushell of Cokels and to one brought fish from paterdale "

is entered 8s. 6d. ; and the tale of fish goes on from all quarters—a salmon from Penrith, eels from Holker, also char, etc., till we finish with, on April 13th :—

" p^d more for 100 hearings flookes cokels thornebacks and some other fish came from cartmell this weeke 5s. 2d ,"

making a total of 1000 herrings alone consumed by the fasting household.

The fish season of 1645 began with a purchase of 100 herrings on February 16th, when 5 pecks of salt at 4s. was also got. Another 200 followed, after which a more drastic purchase was made of a barrel (no doubt already salted) from Kendal, which cost with the carriage £1 2s. The dear way of buying through a middle-man was resorted to again ; and a further item appears of " salt fish in lent and A Cople of ling fish had at kendall of Josie Ematson " 14s. 4d.—Josie being no doubt the Josephus Edm'dson who figures in the list of Kendal burgesses for that year,* and supplied a good deal to the Hall. Cockles poured in ; towards the end, 3 pecks cost 2s., and another 3 pecks followed in a week.

The next season began with " pease got against lent," with fish and mussels and carriage from Ulverston, 7s. 1d.

On February 7th, 150 herrings and two couple of ling-fish (a fish said to be like the cod, but longer in form) are accounted for. Cockles were 1s. 6d., salt " eles " came again from Holker, and two dozen and two couple of " salt killing " were " bought at St. bees for lent " 13s. 6d., which seems reasonable compared with the price 50 years later. A salmon is 3s 6d. One salmon seems indeed the allowance each Lent, being reserved no doubt for the upper table It was brought by John Brathwaite

---

* *Boke off Recorde of Kirkbie-Kendall.*

of Howhead, the Ambleside carrier to " Penrith." One brought by him on July 27th, cost only 2s. 2d. The Kendal barrel of herrings cost again £1 2s., and cockles " at several times " 10s. 6d. Another 200 herrings come in as a finale, and " red Herrings."

Spices in Lent, used no doubt for the preparation of the rarer kinds of fish, like char, are entered as (including " figgs,") 12s 6d. For the prized Rydal char-pie (see Fisheries).

But the great outlay in spices was of course for Christmas, a feast for which much preparation was made. Tyson's moderate account enters indeed but 10d. for them, but this was perhaps in the absence of the family; his peck of " Aples " cost 2s. 8d. Harrison's are 3s. Pears are mentioned one year, but as with apples they are only 1s., they may have been a present like the " peares and wardens " that came in 1644 from Christopher Fells, and for which 1s. was given to the messenger who brought them from Ulverston.

Very busy must the kitchen have been at these times, when under Katharine's superintendence the young ladies left their parlour avocations with glee to help to concoct the Christmas fare of mince-pies and puddings, whose ingredients cost so high a figure relatively each year. Sugar indeed was never bought but for this and other special occasions.

"p^d for spices 16 dec. at Kendall against Cressemas £ s d.
vigl 6 pound raisings VI^s 4 pound Currans 2^s 8
four ounces sinomond 4 ounces nutmegs 4^s 8^d a
pound pepper 2^s tow Loves suger 9^s 9^d half a
pound ginger 9^d and 6 pound prones 2^s came in
all to 1 7 10

The spices come to £1. 1s. 6d. and £1. 9s. 6d. in other years; while in 1647 " Eamontson " is paid a total of £2. 10s. 10d. for them; and two bushel of wheat " against Gressemas from Archer wife " with carriage cost £1. 8s.

This price for wheat is 2s. higher than that paid immediately after the squire's death, when several bills are cleared off.

	£	s	d.
p^d to P. Brathwaite of Howhead for Salmon he bought at penreth at seuerall tymes	0	10	0
p^d more unto him for two couple of dryed fishe	0	3	4
p^d more unto him for a load and a half of wheate had of him and A bushell of Jo. Archers wife in kendall had at seuerall tymes against Christmas and since and for carriage of it after the rate of 12s the bushell	2	10	4

A half-bushel of wheat had of Braithwaite " against Whitsuntide " is again 6s., and another bushel 12s., while 20 bushels of oats to make into meal for the house is £4, and 30 more for meal and groats £7. 10s. Veal for Whitsuntide, with a head of veal is 4s. Extra wheat-bread from Kendal " on whitson even " is 2s Indeed, in 1644 a half bushel of wheat was 2s. 6d, but rose in August to 5s. 10d. It dropped after harvest to 4s. 2d., when the weekly loaves went down to 1s. 6d. and 1s. " Biskets " are down.

Wheat bread for the upper table was a constant charge and figures very highly in comparison with the consumption of this delicacy under the next squire's frugal rule, when it was not baked in the house, but bought regularly at Kendal at the rate of about 2s. a week. It is rarely in Harrison's account below 2s, and more on occasions, e.g., 2s. 6d. when got for New Year's Eve. Rye bread too was bought costing 6d.

Some special provision was made against Easter too, and when visitors were entertained at the Hall. Tyson accounted for 6s. 6d. spent on butter, eggs, and chicken during his master's stay at Rydal in 1632, with 6s. 9d. for five quarters of flesh. After his death the outlay on chickens between April 14th and May 1st (Lady Blaxton being at the Hall), was 3s. ; butter, eggs, and starch 5s., and half a veal 3s. For the meeting of the supervisors on May 27th, wheat-bread cost 3s., a quarter of lamb 1s., chicken 3s., ¼-lb. of cinnamon, and ¼-lb. of mace and cloves (doubtless for char pies) 3s. 6d. Special dainties were procured sometimes.

Harrison enters " 6 couple of Connies " had from Penrith in his master's lifetime 5s. Generally one couple of rabbits are got. " Doukers " figure occasionally.

Woodcocks are brought in by the Rydal purveyor—David Harrison, caught no doubt by the old method on the fells; on December 4th, he is paid 4s. for birds brought at " severall tymes." Another year they are had from Kendall on October 29th and November 10th, at 2s. 4d. and 4s. 4d.

The amount of sack consumed was large, and was procured from one John or Josie Ellerey, a wine merchant of Kendal, who likewise supplied the Easter wine for the Grasmere and Ulverston churches; the holder of the tithes being responsible for this charge in place of the parson The latter church figures in 1643 at £1. 6s.; the former at £1. 1s. 8d.,..being respectively six and five gallons at 4s. 4d. a gallon. Next :—

	£	s	d.
p^d more for sake had of him in Christmas and since at 3 seuerall tymes being in all 8 Gallons	1	16	0

[4s. 6d. a gal.]

	£	s.	d
for sacke had of him at seuerall tymes before this 30 Sep 1644 and some other things sent for by gentlewomen	3	0	0

Drinking vessels of glass were used, being got from special hawkers.

	£	s	d.
p^d for white drinking glasses and other bottles and glasses to A glasse carrier by Katheran	0	3	0

In 1646, when special provision has been made for Mr. Biddulph's visit, mentioned on March 7th and 14th, and again when " Old Jarrat " procures veal and mutton for the high feast on " Easter even " for 8s. 10d., an entry follows of 2s. 2d. for " Greene glasses and white glasses " and " two little Candlesticks at Hawkshead " 10d., which suggests a festive board. Mr. Biddulph was connected with the family, having married then the young people's cousin Frances, daughter of the late Mr. George Preston of Holker, by his second wife Marjorie Strickland, though it is difficult to explain his presence for so long at the Hall.

There seems indeed to have been a good deal of " company " kept of one sort or another, and intercourse was frequent with the neighbouring halls of Westmorland, Furness, and even Cumberland, where relatives and friends resided. Presents came from time to time: fish from Mr. Philipson of Calgarth, the special eels from Holker ; a doe from Greystoke ; a " whole buck " from Mr. Preston's manor (this was doubtless John of Furness Abbey), a great salmon from him ; venison from " Mr. Laborne " ; venison and pigeons from Sizergh.

With Sizergh, the old home of their mother, the young orphans doubtless had most to do. Their uncle, Sir Robert, the present head of the family, was indeed residing at Thornton Bridge, in Yorkshire ; but two of their uncle Stricklands, Walter and Thomas, were up to this date * in occupation of the old Westmorland stronghold. Their aunt, Lady Blaxton, who more than anyone else supervised the doings of the girls, was probably a Strickland.

These girls, Anne and Bridget, who figure as the " gentlewomen " in the account book, were on the verge of womanhood when their father died, being older than William the heir, who was but a lad of fourteen. They had probably learnt all that was considered necessary in those days, to teach young ladies, who appeared to pick up during long visits to wise and often strict grand-

---
* Father West, in *Sizergh MSS.*

mothers and aunts all the manners and accomplishments required for the "female" mind of the period (See later; for the education of Daniel Fleming's daughters). We hear at least of no actual tuition, though there is mention in Tyson's book for 1633 of a "Citarine," which suggests that they were taught music.* They could while away therefore the tedium of quiet hours by plucking the wire strings of their table instrument with the quill plectrum, and fetching from it tunes and pieces that tickled the ear; or perhaps it served to accompany their sweeter voices. They doubtless embroidered. They certainly, when at home, busied themselves in household affairs, Harrison giving over to them instead of to Katharine money for kitchen expenses; and they occupied themselves in the higher branches of cookery. We find in August, 1645, "A sugar loafe for Gentlewomen for P'serueing things with," cost 5s; and:—

p^d to nedd pedler for 4 bottels full of Rasisolis sent for by gentlewomen at seaverall tymes since 25 nov. till 17 may 0 6 8

Irrespective of any imminent feast too, we find raisins, currants, nutmegs, and loaf-sugar "sent for gentlewomen" from "Josie Eamontsons" and brought by the shepherd.

These young girls indeed, though wafted off into Yorkshire for visits to relatives from time to time, seem to have taken up a singularly independent position, which was strange when viewed with the commotions of the time, and the dangers of war, that thickened round this homestead of the mountain, and threatened its entire extinction. They were of course recognized as heiresses from the first, to whom—though their young brother would naturally take the largest share of riches as well

---

* "Given Tho. lavick for bringing Citarne 4d" This antique instrument remained in favour after the keyed virginal had come into general use. "New Citharen Lessons" were published in 1609, and John Playford's "Musick's Delight, containing new and pleasant lessons on the Cithern" in 1666. (Grove's *Dictionary of Music*) The Rydal instrument may have come from Speke.

as of land—would be meted out very highly-desirable marriage portions. The days were over when they were content with the home-spun and woven stuffs considered meet for their childhood. For instance, in 1632 the spinning and weaving of 14 yards of cloth for the children had cost but 6s., the wool no doubt being from Rydal clippings; and next year their father wrote from Speke "Then tell him (Tyson) to cause such a pice of Cotton be made for barnes as he did last year."

On the father's death the orphans were well rigged out with mourning.

	£	s.	d.
Pd. to Jo. Archer* at seuerall tymes for two suits for M^s Willm a cloke and a smocke cote, A gowne and Peticote for Mrs Bridget, A gowne for Mrs Anne and for two gownes for katherin and doll, and for all other things for makeing and trimming them up as appears by A note of P'ticulars under Jo Archers hand	21	2	0
pd. for makeing all the s^d seuerall things to willm Browne Taylor	0	18	2

The etceteras were numerous, especially for the heir, and some of them procured when the journey to York was made.

	s	d.
an elne of Holland for bands and for little brush	5	3
A bridle leathers bitts & stirrop Irons at Yorke	4	0
A hat for him at Yorke	16	0
at Yorke for him for bands & ruffles & A paire of boote hose tops	15	0
A pair of blake stockings for Mr Willm & 2 p^r for Mrs Bridget and Mrs Anne	12	4
2 pairs of Gloves for Mr Willm	2	0

The other two pairs, set down at 1s. 4d. were doubtless for the girls Their "two pairs of shooes" cost 4s. 8d,

---

* John Archer is entered as "Maren Freeman" in 1635; he is in the list of Aldermen for 1644 In 1648, with mercer after his name, he is recorded as senior Alderman and Justice

and " A blacke phan for Annas " (perhaps Bridget possessed one already) 5s.

The boy seems to have been allowed (unhappily) to take a lordly tone from the first. A horse was got for him, from Andrew Hudleston, for £12; and £10 given to him " by the appoyntmt of the supervisors when he should have gone to Award." Then —

pd for 6 yeards of broad cloth for A cloke and A suite for Lancelot bought by Willm Browne Taylor and sent for by Mr Willm the 22nd of May £4 2 0

Young William had in fact constituted Lancelot Harrison, son of his step-cousin, as a kind of squire or henchman, to ride forth with him, as we shall see later; Lancelot receiving a salary of £3. 10s. After this, and the entry of 15s. for ten yards of " lin-cloth for shirts " for Mr. William, the next sounds rather flat, " giuen him againe when he went to schoole the 28th of May £1. 0s. 0d."

It was time indeed to set some control over this young spark, and to limit the expenditure of the young people. The girls were carried off to Yorkshire with their " Ant Blaxton," as Harrison notes, in the 3s. expenditure for chickens from April 14th to May 1st; and he adds naively:

"pd more unto my lady Blaxtone the first of may when she went away for 16 yeards of welch flannall at 22d the yeard had in my mr (master's) life time for curtaines for A bed wch I thought she had bestowed of him £1 9 4

Anne was despatched for this Yorkshire visit with £20, and £10 was paid to Mr. John Strickland for a horse bought for her there besides £1. 3s. 4d. which she had already borrowed for this purpose while more money was sent to her by Mr. Walter Strickland. The Strickland uncles seem indeed to have encouraged the orphans in a free use of the trust money. It was no wonder that—though Bridget was content with a nag from Robert Benson of Skelwith at £3. 3s.—the supervisors (who " mett " at the end of May, with special extra provision for their use of wheat-bread 3s.; quarter of lamb 1s.; chickens 3s.; spices and dried fruit 6s. 6d) decided to fix an allowance for the young ladies, which reached the liberal sum of £60.* We hear therefore no more of their clothes in the account book

Master William however continues to figure largely there. The school chained him but a month, for on June 23rd he receives £5 on going to Corbie, the seat of Sir Francis Howard,† and Penrith, and while at the latter town seizes the opportunity to buy pairs of "boates and pantofles" at 14s. 6d., also pairs of stockings and shoes, 7s 6d. Then "Britches" of black searge and making come to 15s.; while four yards of "brodecloth black for suite, A Smocke Cote at 13s. a yard and things for making" come to £2 19s 6d. William Browne the tailor is at least reasonable in price, for making one suit 2s. is charged; for another with two pairs of breeches and a coat 3s. 6d. The sombreness of the costume is broken by grey stockings, another pair, at 2s. 6d. The young blade is now fitted out (besides "A spanner stringe(?) for him at Yorke 2s. 6d.") with a "pare of patranals and case" ‡ bought for him specially in the northern capital by Mr. John Fleming at a cost of £3 12s. 6d. And he would seem to have used these weapons during the summer, for early in October John Washington, the Kendal mechanician and clockmaker § is paid 5s. for the repair of them, and for making a new fitting for Anthony Skelton's. After all these dashing equipments, the entry of "A booke called Terence," 1s., comes in strangely, nor do we hear that it ever needed re-binding.

---

* The amount is afterwards stated as £40.
† *The Flemings in Oxford* Dr. Magrath.
‡ Petronel: a kind of carbine or large horseman's pistol. Webster.
§ He appears among the "Armerers Fremen and Hardwaremen," being elected October 6th, 1625, as Burgess in 1645; as mayor in 1657, when he is styled "whitsmith" an interesting bill of his for a clock is given later—*Boke off Recorde of Kirkbie-Kendall.*

The ill-fated lad appears again to take to his studies for a while. We read, under October 3rd :—

	£ s. d.
giuen Mr William when he was affrayed of Lancashire forces should have come when he went away ..	5 0 0

and shortly after 10s was given to Mrs. Kirkby, which her husband had paid " in pt for his wage for his teaching." The schoolmaster with whom Mr. Kirkby was in communication, was probably, since the " school " later mentioned was at quiet Irton-in Eskdale, the Scotchman Mr. Bartle, whom Daniel Fleming mentions as having been his own instructor for a short time in July, 1644.* We trace young William's presence in Cumberland by his purchases of a new suit bought at Cockermouth, which with the making of it there, cost £4. 9s. 2d. A pair of stockings came to 5s. 6d., and a hat at Kendal to 14s. Probably he rode home round by Kendal for Christmas, for Harrison notes that he gave him £2 " to keepe his purse with " for that season. Then comes the ominous entry :—

	£ s. d.
Giuen more to him the 5 Jan^r when he went ouer fell and durst not stay at Home to put in his purse	2 10 0

and a note is added that this makes £30 that he has received since his father's death, including £1 which had been sent him by " Lantie " to Hutton John.

This suggests that the boy had been fighting and feared capture. He had indeed started the roving life that ceased only with his death. Another effort was made to settle him and to withdraw him from the existing fatal attraction of warfare.

	£ s. d.
Giuen to Mr Willm when I got him to goe to Schole Againe to Irton the 4th feb	2 0 0

---

* D F's autobiographical sketch. The notes to this, p 2 of *The Flemings in Oxford*, show the number of private schools existing in the country at this time, some of them taught by Oxford men whom the war had displaced.

THE RYDAL HOUSEHOLD

But it was in vain. The heir to so much wealth had already begun to secure the notice of big people, and the die was soon to be cast that bound his lot irrevocably to the king's cause.

	£	s	d.
Giuen to Mr Willm when he went to Naward (Naworth) to se the young lord that sent for him 2 May ..	5	0	0

to which is added the sum of £1. 15s. which he had borrowed from his henchman " Lantie "

His intimacy about this time with the Howard family is attested by Sir Daniel Fleming, in the family " Notes," * who says that he " paid court " to a sister of Charles Howard, Esq. (afterwards Earl of Carlisle), but the young people not " agreeing betwixt themselves " he went along with Mr. Howard to Bristol, Skipton Castle, and other places where the king's forces were. The succeeding entries in the account book, apparently for the year 1644, corroborate this tradition :—

	£	s	d.
giuen to Mr Willm at seuerall tymes 22 July and 8th of August when he went to Whitehall with his sisters	4	0	0

The next entry chronicles a departure and the casting of the die :—

	£	s	d.
August 10 giuen to Mr Willm by and with consent of Mr Phillipson when he went away with Sr Francis Howard	100	0	0
More to my sonne who went with him for his wages for A yeare ended at penticost 1644 . ..	3	0	0

Further particulars, which show that a large company marched south, and that the actual start was made from Kendal on August 14th, appear in an entry under money lent .—

" Lent to Mr Nicolas strickland 14 August 1644 at at Mr Willm Fleming Desire and his sisters when he went with him from Kendale in Kings armis, to Bristowe by the consent of Mr

---
* Rydal Hall MSS

Phillipson upon his writing 20¹ and more lent him by Sr Geo: Midleton to be allowed in Sr Geo: bond of 100¹ lent him more 30¹ so that Mr Nicolas strickland is oweing due by his bond 50¹ 0 0"

The tradition that matrimony had been engaging his thoughts is corroborated by the account book, which about this time, shows a considerable expenditure in horse-trappings and dress—" grey made cloth and buttons and loupes and other things " for a suit £1. 16s., and later 4½ yards of grey cloth for " A long Cote," with trimmings and making £2 5s. The next entries of money given him announce his entire emancipation; and it is pleasant to know that his sister rode to London with him.

CHAPTER III.

THE TROUBLES.

THE step was no doubt inevitable. The waves of civil war had been rising and falling for two summers in our valleys of Westmorland. The first skirmish indeed took place at Manchester on July 3rd, 1642,[*] and as the winter turned, and the rich Rydal squire lay dying, Preston was being stormed and taken for a Parliamentary force, and Lancaster Castle occupied, only to be presently re-taken by the Earl of Derby. Westmorland was astir. The Light Horse of the Barony of Kendal rode out in the fortnight before his death, with Anthony Skelton his man amongst them; and a general-muster was called soon after, which included the servants of the Hall and the statesmen of the valleys. There is not a doubt as to which side he would have taken in this upheaval and cleavage of society, for every gentleman of Furness (where his mother had said his friends were), as well as of Westmorland, and every house allied with his own (except that of Barwise), declared

---
[*] *Victoria History of Lancashire.*

themselves of the king's side, which was to them simply the side of law and order ; but it would have been interesting to know what course his wise, crafty spirit would have taken amidst the confusion of parties and the marshalling of forces ; and to what extent he would have put his money-coffers at the disposal of his party. Harrison's account book, which starts nineteen days before his death, shows immediate loans that were clearly intended to be used for the raising of Royalist forces. First comes £50 to Mr. William Ambrose, squire of Lowick, who was nephew to John Fleming, through his mother Dorothy Fleming. Then £300 to Mr. Thomas Preston, of Holker, to be lent with a " rent-charge " of £24 a year for three years, and the writings to be kept by the chief executor, Mr. Philipson. £100 also went to Mr. George Preston of Furness Abbey.

These gentlemen of Furness were clearly gathering a body of horse, that, unlike the militia, could be put into action at any time. So were the Westmorland gentlemen.

Lent to Sr Henry Bellingham, Mr Brathwaite and others the first of march 1642-3 upon there bond for good of Cuntry till first of M^{rch} 1643-4   £250 0. 0.

Sir Henry [*] was the magnate of Levens. Mr. Richard Brathwaite of Burnside Hall and New Hall in Nether Staveley was first cousin to John Fleming, through his mother, Dorothy Bindlosse. He will be heard of later. A man of great intellectual gifts, and author of several poems, other than the one he wrote under the name of "Dapper Dick," he threw himself heartily into public affairs, and impoverished himself, as we shall see, for the king's cause. To Sir Ralph Blaxton and Mr. Walter Strickland, the brothers-in-law of John Fleming, £60 was lent.

Besides the forces raised thus, and under the direct-

---

[*] Later Col. James Bellingham was active for the Parliament.

control of their leader, there were the companies of Light Horse, furnished by the county gentlemen in all times of war, and for which the Rydal estate equipped one rider. These in Westmorland were certainly placed on the king's side, and should under efficient generals have done good service The general muster of the militia or foot-soldiers from the valleys could be, and was also resorted to, but apparently with little effect. It could only be kept in the field for short periods ; and, called as the men were from their steadings by the county authorities, they would, many of them, be indifferent to the Royalist cause ; some, and a growing number, even hostile to it. It was always difficult too, to arm these irregular troops satisfactorily. In a search for weapons, which it was thought expedient to make in 1660, the statesmen of our township of Rydal and Loughrigg turned up one a sword and belt, another a steel cap, another a "Little Birding-piece," another a musket without lock, still another a sword, which may have done service in these wars. For the men of the estate three muskets were borrowed at Millom, and repaired

The account book shows too that the troops were in movement during this spring of 1643. What is meant by the grim entry in the church register for April 29th :—

"The buriall of James Tarlton de Rydall
The buriall of Robert Gardiner de Rydall"

cannot be said. James Tarlton's name does not appear among the Rydal Hall servants, but he is twice mentioned as settling accounts, while Robert Gardiner is entered in the list of recusants in 1640 and 1641. That those two men met their death in one day indicates violence, either in a party brawl or in actual warfare ; and if the latter, it could not have been far distant, as their burial place was Grasmere. Nothing in the account book throws light on the circumstance, but there are frequent entries of the expenses of the men called out on military service.

THE TROUBLES

Anthony Skelton's charges " when he went with light horse to Kendale " as early as the 9th of February, and stayed there, were 10s. Again he was at Kendal for a fortnight at a cost of £1. 10s. and there was

"giuen to our seruants . . .   when they went to General muster 5s od."

Then too the taxes for payment of the militia had begun.

	£	s.	d.
p^d the Cunstable of loughrigge for A cast for souldiers the first of march	0	2	0
A cast . for souldiers . . to Charles Wilson Cunstable of Rydall	0	4	6
for a cast of ten subsidies for his maiestie to high Cunstable	12	0	0

and rates and minor " casts " continued through the summer.

Anthony Skelton was out three days in Kendal with the Light Horse from May 10th (at a cost of 7s. 6d.) and again seven days from June 12th. This shows that the Royalist army under prominent leaders, that marched across the Conishead Sands on May 21st, and after three nights' billet in Furness, with plunder and £500 exacted from the enemy, retreated again, were not accompanied by the Westmorland horse.* But Anthony was out again at Carlisle for nine days in August, no doubt with the Cumberland forces.

Some of the officers of these forces, if not a whole company, were entertained at the Hall, possibly on a march through the valley, or for a party consultation as to ways and means.

Pd for wheat bread at kendall 23 sept when Colonell Huddlestone (of Millom) and other company was at Rydall " .. . . £0 2 6.

But feasting was soon to be followed by actual conflict

---

* Park's narrative in West's *Antiquities,* quoted in *North Lonsdale Magazine,* vol 1, p 241.

and disaster, for some at least of the party. The foremost excitement of the summer was the siege of Thurland, that magnificent moated castle on the Lancashire side of the Lune, which Sir Thomas crenelated by license of Henry IV. in 1402 (see Cal. Pat. Rolls). Its owner, Sir John Girlington, had indeed surrendered it in June, but regaining it, he maintained a brave defence against the besieging party through September.* Our Rydal men were out with the county forces on this latter occasion, and Anthony's expenses for six days at Kendal " when Sir Jo: Girlington was besieged 6 Sept." were 15s. He was later out nineteen days with his company of horse at Kirkby Lonsdale (expenses 2s. 6d. a day), and there was

"giuen to our seruants for there Charges when the (sic) went to Kirkby Lonsdall to be mustered and stayed two days and one night 5ˢ 0ᵈ"

The men of our village in fact were part of the troops that lay supinely on the right bank of the river, watching the siege of the castle on the opposite bank without an effort of assistance. The able Parliamentary general, Colonel Rigby, who now conducted the siege, reported to the Parliament *

"During most part of the siege the greatest part of the Forces of Westmorland lay within our view, and daily threatened us, but God confined them to their own County, and every day more and more inclined the hearts of the Commons of Westmorland to decline any attempt upon us,"†

although, he goes on to say, his own position, cut off in an angle of Lancashire and far from supplies, might have tempted them by its fair prospect of victory. It was to hearten and assist these reluctant troops led by Sir Philip Musgrave, and to raise the siege, as well as to combine in a great scheme for the regaining of Lancaster and

---

* Civil War Tracts, xxxvii   *Victoria History of Lancashire*, p. 238.
† Civil War Tracts, xxxvii.

Hornby Castle, that forces were collected in Cartmel and Furness under Mr. Roger Kirby and Alexander Rigby, joined by Colonel Huddleston of Millom and his men. But Colonel Rigby, quick to act, did not wait for their coming; but turning aside, he crossed the sands and easily routed an army numbering 1500 to 1600 men on Lindale Moor (Sunday, October 1st), after which he returned to his siege. "This worke in Fournes" he goes on to report

"had that influence upon all the Castles and all the Gentry of Westmorland and Cumberland who then lay within our sight at Kirby Loynsdale, that within two days after, the Castle was by the negotiation of Sir Philip Musgrave, then commanding in chief in Westmorland and Cumberland, agreed to be rendered unto me to be demolished."

It is clear then, that our Rydal foot-men "commoners," statesmen, and Hall servants, who had lain idly within sight of the siege for two days and a night, had long returned to their home before its close; and it was only the gentlemen or "castlers" with their mounted troops who awaited its lame termination. How badly, indeed, was the Royalist side in need of a good general in these parts! It must not be forgotten that the history of the times is largely made up from Parliamentary Reports, and it is well to set Mr Thomas Park's report of the Furness rout against Colonel Rigby's, still there seems to have been little or no attempt made at a stand on this occasion; and Colonel Huddleston with many others was taken prisoner ' Rigby was concerned how he should keep in security "the most considerable Man in Cumberland," who commanded not only the forces of his county, but had a regiment also in Yorkshire.

Nothing is said of Mr Roger Kirby, who is expressly mentioned in Rigby's report as present, and who must therefore presumably have escaped. If indeed his reported flight to Ireland may be placed after this defeat, instead of after his earlier escape on the relinquishment of Lancaster Castle (thus supposing an error in Dugdale's date), all discrepancy would vanish; and it may be noted that his name of " Mr. Kirby " disappears after this date from the account book, while " Mr. Richard Kirby," his eldest son, at this time 15 years old, is mentioned. This disaster seems to have broken the spirit of the Furness Royalists, and their troops melted away, while their leaders were imprisoned or fled. It seems possible that the boy William Fleming had followed Colonel Huddleston or Colonel Kirby into this fight, which would account for the fear of the " Lancashire Forces " that drove him from home two days later. The men of his manor of Coniston might also many of them be there.*

But the North Westmorland Royalists continued active, at any rate in putting men in the field. Among items of money lent at this time, after November 29th, is

"£100 to my Cozen Willm Fleming, my Cozen Jo Fleming, and my Cozen Tho Fleming in their bond, to pay £8 if kept till Feb. 12, 1644-5; or they to keep it longer"

These would all be sons of Daniel of Skirwith, and therefore first cousins to the young Rydal heir The eldest had left his wife and babies at Skirwith, to lead a company as Major, drawn from his own and neighbouring manors The well-thumbed parchment roll of some 98 men, dated March 8th, 1643-4, exists at Rydal Hall. John was a bachelor and a lawyer; his name occurs frequently in the correspondence, and he died at Skirwith. Meanwhile fresh schemes were concocted and our account book gives signs of considerable activity among the Westmorland troops through the winter, and early months of 1643-4.

The " casts " for soldiers (levied by the constable of Rydal for the Royalist forces) were frequent. From the

---

* See Dugdale's *Visitation*; West's *Antiquities*; and " Kirkby Portraits," in *Transactions* C & W A & A Society, vol. vi , N s

preceding October 10th to February 27th for outlying pieces of demesne they amounted to £1. 2s., from February 27th to April 22nd to 5s.; and from April 22nd to June 22nd, to 17s. 5d. On July 1st, for a cast at the rate of 5d. in the pound, £1. 5s. was paid, with another on the 28th for the same amount to the High Constable. There was a general muster at Kendal on January 11th, when "our mens charges" for the night came to 6s; and

"Anthony, rode out with the light horse, 7s 6d"

Whatever his fate, this is the last time he is mentioned; and Hugh Foord * of Kendal, who proved a true friend to the cause and to the family, furnished a man and horse for duty from March 10th to May 10th for a sum of 13s. 6d. There was likewise a general muster for four days, which four of the servants attended. These movements may have been connected with the large scheme of the party concocted about this time for coalition with the king's army; (see Municipal "Order," May 3rd, 1693, *Boke off Recorde of Kirkbie Kendall*), by which the forces of Cumberland and Westmorland under the command of Sir Philip Musgrave were to be divided, the one to support the Marquis of Newcastle in his advance against the Scots (now threatening invasion for the relief of Parliament), and the other to join Prince Rupert in his march to the relief of beleagured York. Undoubtedly the loan of £100, made from the Hall coffers on May 30th to Sir Philip Musgrave, Mr Philipson and others, was directly connected with this effort; as well as the message which summoned the young Rydal heir to Naworth and gave him an assured position as Royalist.

---

* He is the Hugh Forth commemorated among the burgesses in 1645 and 1654, and again among the "Pewterers" who had been admitted to the Guild in 1629. *Boke off Recorde of Kirkbie Kendall*

Hugh Forth was an ardent royalist. In 1644 he had to give with some others a bond in £20 that he would convey no intelligence to the enemy nor depart from Kendal town without licence from the Mayor

His. MSS Com 10th Rep. Kend. MSS. C. 3.

There would seem however, from some entries of about this time, to have been skirmishes and reprisals going on close over the Lancashire border, if not actually in the Rothay Valley

	£	s.	d.
giuen to A messenger Hugh foord sent from kendall all night to giue us notice to looke to ourselves when grayrigge Hall was plundered	0	1	6

and there are suggestive entries of repairs for broken windows at Grasmere Church, as well as at the Hall.

However that may be, the brilliant successes of Prince Rupert, as he advanced through Lancashire at the end of May and early June raised the hopes of Westmorland Royalists high If indeed he crossed the sands from Lancaster, and quartered himself on Cartmel,* the young bloods of the counties would be at his heels, to pay him court, if not to fight. The entry made after June 2nd, of payment to Edmond Dobson for " riding light horse at Kirkby 14 days" £1. 15s., and then five more 12s. 6d., almost certainly refers to this episode, for Kirkby means to this day Ireleth in Furness, where the Hall of the Kirkbys stands.

With the general movement of co-operation the following has certainly to do :—

"p^d for Irons for 4 halfe pikes to A Smith in Keswicke for our seruants to furnish them with when they are called 3^s 4^d."

But the Westmorland forces were destined to play no decisive part in the war. Arming, mustering, lagging, falling back, dissolving, they ever failed, either for want of true heart, or of a sound general. How many of the gentry followed Rupert over the pass into Yorkshire cannot be said, but their terrible defeat at the battle fought on Marston Moor on July 2nd, 1644, crushed all present hopes for the cause, not only in the county, but through

---

* See *Life of Master John Shaw* Surtees Society, vol. lxv., quoted in *North Lonsdale Magazine*, vol. 1, p 51.

the north. With the Scots army advancing to the aid of their enemies, there was nothing for it but dispersal, either by private flight, or in following the remnants of the king's army to the south; and we have seen how a large party, including young William Fleming and his friends, marched from Kendal under the wing of Sir Francis Howard on the 10th of August. Sums were lent at this time to the leader, Sir Francis Howard, to Mr. Anthony Dushett of Grayrigg, and Sir Ralph Blaxton, as well as Mr. Nicolas Strickland. And not only for them was money lifted from the Rydal chests. Mr. Philipson acting for the party received various small sums; Mr. Philipson of Calgarth borrowed £30 on a bill. Parson Wilson of Grasmere too, that "notorious malignant," came for one of his frequent loans. He was doubtless fleeing, or speeding south to be of use to his party, in the most dangerous of services—that of bearing messages and letters in cipher.*

But there were others, who either could not, or would not, get away. Efforts at a rally are apparent, especially about Kendal, where no doubt the castle was still held for the king; while daily the opposite faction grew stronger, and the Scots' army, under the Earl of Leven, entering England on September 1st,† marched to their assistance.

	£	s.	d.
p^d for our men Charges 2 tymes when they were warned to be there and stayed at one tyme 4 days and at other tyme two dayes and light Horse and Rider's Charges at same tymes 7 Sept to 14 Septem	1	1	6
P^d for A cast of forty shillings in the pound for Rydall to Colonell doding‡ and others to fre them out of kendall after the had entered and taken the towne	10	0	0

---

* Some of these which still exist are stained with blood.
† S. P. Dom Chas I, 20.
‡ Was he Myles Dodding son and heir of George of Conishead (who died 1650) who married Margaret daughter of Roger Kirkby?

p^d more for Gresmire for the same assessm^t ..	.	5	0	0
p^d more for baneriggs for the same assessm^t ..	.	0	10	0
p^d more for milner bridge assessm^t ..	..	..	1	2	0
p^d more for ground in gresmire to same sessi .	..	0	8	6

The " caste " paid to the constable on the outlying portions from June 22nd to October 4th amounted to 19s ; and these may have been the last levied for the royal cause. The opposite side had now the whip-hand ; and heavily and unceasingly was the lash to fall.

No sooner was the king's party under Colonel Dodding ousted from Kendal, than the Parliament began that orderly rule by committees and commissioners sitting in every town, that had its centre in London, and was backed by the powerful system of finance through which the City of London supported the Parliament. There were plenty of rich burgesses of Kirkby Kendal town, who had espoused the Roundhead side, to be entrusted later with this clever system of control ; but at first the governing body seems to have been chiefly military. It was already controlling and issuing orders in November, 1644, for on the 16th of that month the refractory parson of Grasmere entered into a bond in £20 to Colonel James Bellingham to appear before the " Provost Marshall " of Kendal in twenty days time, and was forbidden to travel from Westmorland or communicate with the enemy, or seduce the affections of his parishioners from the Parliament. He was moreover deprived of his office.[*] Thomas Brathwaite, no doubt of Ambleside Hall, attested the bond.

To this body and others sitting in neighbouring towns, Rydal Hall had now to sue, drawing together all the personal influence possible, through relatives not deeply implicated in Royalist plots, to gain favour and some mitigation of threatened burdens. We find the following in (A. 20) MSS. of Cor. of Kendal, His. MS. Com. 10th Report.—

---

[*] *Church of Grasmere.*

"£82 3 5 claimed as due to the inhab. of Kir-Ken. for billitting Col. Bellingham's soldiers ' fr the 3rd of March, 1644, to the 28th of same'; and some of Col Brigg's men, one night or 2, after the rate of 6d per day every foot-soldier, and 13d p d horse and man, ' according to the lord Generall's order ' "

Does this date—which is a quotation—mean 3rd March, 1644 or 1645 ? the year would close on March 25th.

But first there was an effort made to secure again what had been rifled, in some soldiers' visitation of the Hall shadowed in the earlier entry, but of which we have no particulars.

" pd for to redeeme some horses and other goods was taken away, and plundered from Rydall and my Cozen Jo. Fleming's charges in goeing to kendall and diuers other places about them and giuen to Soldiers £2 7 6.

Mr John Fleming also went with the writer and " others " to Penrith and Kendal " about procuring a protection from Scotts," hence the entry :—

" Colonell bellingham and briges and giuen to get our desires affected, (being absent five days) £1 8 ˙6."

This was before October 12th, when there was " giuen to one brought letters from Mr. Willm from bristowe 2s. 6d." But such attempts, even with a gift to ease them, availed little ; for the heavy heel of the Parliament was soon grinding the Royalists into the fine powder of penury, by means of taxes, fines, composition and sequestration. The taxation for the Scotch army now planted on the country, which had bargained for £21,000 a month pay besides provisions, as the price of their help, began at once and continued, as the following entries extracted from the next six months show —

	£	s.	d.
pd to Mr nicolas Tunstall (High Constable) for A cast for the scotts for Rydall for month sessment 25 Nov 1644	5	10	0

p^d more unto him for purveyance money to lay upon
Rydall 1 6 3

Caste to the local constable from July 11th to December 1st come also to £3. 4s. 2d Then:—

	£ s. d.
p^d for the Psonall assessm^t for Rydall to the Scotts in dec 1644	20 0 0
p^d for A month sessm^t for Scotts after rate of XXV^d in the pound for Rydall milner bridge and other places 4 Jan *	7 15 0

And this sum was repeated on February 20th, and on March 15th.

There were besides various taxes paid through the village constable " for soldiers and fynding of Horses and riders "—now for the Parliament !—which for the Rydal demesne from October 1644 to May 1st, 1645, amounted to £11. 11s. 6d. Once again —

	£ s. d.
p^d for A cast for Scotts Pvision the 28th May	0 17 2

The bargain with the Scots was before this time embarrassing the Parliament. Of the various committees sitting in the halls of the rich London guilds, the one at the Goldsmiths was responsible for this business, and the treasurer thus found that the required £21,000 monthly could by no means be squeezed out of the king's adherents, as cash could not be raised immediately upon their impoverished estates. Therefore Parliament decreed that a monthly tax should for four months be levied from the 1st of March on the whole people of the northern counties, for the support of their allies. The discontent that ensued is not surprising. The counties had their hereditary foes from whom they had suffered for hundreds of years forced upon them in the name of the country's allies. They had to give them quarter, with food and lodging, and pay unprecedented taxes for their wage, the while little of

---

* S.P.Dom. Chas. I, 20.

fighting was done. It was a comfortable, nay—remembering old times—an ironically jocose situation for the Scots, who, spending their time for the most part comfortably in garrison, or quartered in county towns, with plenty to eat and good English money to put in their pockets, were in no haste to move. Nor do they seem to have been gentle with the unfortunate folk they were quartered on. On March 13th their Lord General issued an order to all officers and soldiers quartered in Westmorland and Cumberland, requiring that all " cesses " on the people should cease, save those commanded by Parliament, from March 1st.

" They are therefore required not to impose or exact any cess from the inhabitants, nor offer to plunder, impound, or drive their goods or imprison their persons, but content themselves with such entertainment of victuals and provisions as their quarters can afford them, paying or giving ticket for the same conformably to the rates . . . agreed on by the Committee of both kingdoms " *

By April 16th it became necessary to warn the Head Parliamentary Committee for the north sitting at Newcastle of the report sent to Parliament by the generals—

" of some distempers lately grown in Westmorland amongst the people there against some of the Scots' soldiers, which, if it should continue or increase, might prove of very ill consequence. We therefore desire that all endeavours may be used to pacify and quiet them We hope the Scots' army will very speedily be ready to march southward . also sorry that any affronts or discontent should be given to the (parliamentary) soldiers." †

Tension was indeed growing between the Parliamentary forces and their Scotch allies, as may be seen in the letter addressed by the chiefs to Colonels Lawson, Cholmeley, Bellingham, Briggs, and the members of the Committees of Cumberland and Westmorland, on April 21st, in which

---

* S P Dom Chas. I 20, p. 342-3.
† *Ibid* p 413

"the humours of the discontented people in Westmorland" are referred to,* and the need for drawing off, if possible, the Scottish horse from those counties. And in truth "A late tumultuous assembly in Westmorland" had declared its grievances against the Scots, which had been written and delivered to the heads on paper, through the agency of Gervase Benson, Mayor of Kendal, Mr. Henry Massie and others; whereupon promise of retribution, if injustice or ill-usage from the soldiers could be proved, was promised; and cessation of all but the Parliaments tax, in order that "the inhabitants of Westmorland may have no colourable pretence to keep in a body as they have done for some days past." (April 21st).†

Four days later the Parliamentary Committees of Cumberland and Westmorland declare on behalf of "these two poor exhausted counties" that they had far rather undertake the siege of Carlisle (still held for the king) than pay the Scots. They are determined it can be successfully done, and of the 3000 foot and 600 horse required, Westmorland will furnish 1000 foot and 200 horse. They desire only that the Scots may be kept before Carlisle until the country forces are all gathered there. And they are urgent that the Scots horse when withdrawn, should not march through Westmorland

"lest it occasion new commotions there and endanger the deserting of the siege by the Westmorland men, and so expose all to ruin (a measure which prevented the obnoxious strangers from passing over Dunmail Raise and through our valley) Moreover, it would be expedient to set the Scots about Skipton and Bolton, to prevent the enemy there infesting and disturbing Westmorland" ‡

This would indeed have been a time for the Royalists, had they been less broken and dispersed, to have gained

---

* *Ibid* p 423
† S P Dom Chas I, 20, p 422
‡ S. P. Dom Chas I, 20, p 432

the people to their side of the struggle. On May 28th, the Scots were mostly stationed about Kendal or in Lancashire, and their leaders discussing a move south by the pass of Stainmore.* On June 8th, the inhabitants of Westmorland were still in a body, clamouring for the redress of their grievances, and the Committee, with Lieut.-Col. Bellingham at the head, were forced to promise a speedy removal of them " if they return to their own houses in a peaceful manner." The remonstrance and petition presented to Parliament by the inhabitants of the counties recite in detail the burdens they have suffered, both from the Scots and from the furnishing of men to Parliament for the blocking up of Carlisle all the previous winter, so that, being unable to pay any more,

" necessity forced the distressed people in some parts to stand upon their defence against the taxings and drivings of the soldiers " †

The Westmorland forces, it seemed, had been hindered from joining the siege of Carlisle, owing to dissensions among the officers It was time indeed to draw the Scots south , and the embarrassed Parliament, afraid to offend their martial guests, yet equally afraid of driving the people to desperation, or displeasing their own officers, who were themselves squabbling with the Scots, toiled by letters and instructions to their committee. Then came (June 26th) parleys as to the surrender of Carlisle ; and Sir Thomas Glenham, from within the Castle, complained of the detention of his envoy Captain Philipson— though he had obtained a Parliamentary pass , as well as of the fact that Royalist prisoners, whose ransoms had been paid to Colonel Briggs, had not yet been released.‡

The Royalists were in fact completely broken, and in the power of the Parliamentary committees. The squeez-

---

* *Ibid.* p 531
† *Ibid* p. 576.
‡ S P. Dom. Chas I , p 614-5

ing process, by which the financial committees in London schemed to make the Royalists pay the expenses of the war, and which was finally to reduce most of them to penury, was set in motion. It was a dark winter for Rydal, that of 1644-5, while the siege of Carlisle was going on, dark for the tax-ridden people, darker yet for the Hall. In November, Lady Lowther was over. She was aunt to the young people, being sister to John and executor under their father's will; and she was willing to bring her personal influence to bear on the dreaded committee-men, carrying (in the absence of the young heir) her nieces in her train. The account book of the time has the following items :—

	£	s.	d.
Giuen to them that did Inventory the goods the 29 nov· with consent of my lady	1	10	0
p^d for my lady Lowther Mr Phillipson and Gentle-women and all our Charges and horses when we went to Comittis to kendall 3 dec.	1	9	0
p^d more our Charges when Mr Phillipson and Gentle-women went to Ulverstone 4 dec.	0	11	6
p^d for sending A letter to Mr Robert Rawlinson and getting A Commission drawne to Committee att kendal to get some of the forty pounds Abated of the personall Assessm^t	0	3	6
giuen to Mr Rawlinson Lawy^r 9 dec for A fee & drawing of A case sent to Comission^{rs} to newcastle and Charges Aboute it	0	19	0
p^d for m^r Phillipson m^{rs} bridget m^{rs} Agnes my owne and our men and horses Charges when we went into Lanc. to Garstang to speake with the Colonels and Comittee	2	2	0
giuen to willm Tysons man for comeing two seuerall tymes from Ulverstone to giue us notice when the Collonels met at Garstang and to let us know when we should goe	0	2	0

After the turn of the year —

giuen to Mr Tho Brathw^t for his paines to yorke and newcastle and his disbursm^{ts} as appeares by his letter	10	0	0

p^d Gentlewomen Charges and ours when we went 2
    seuerall tymes in to journas to se if we could agree
    with sequestrators for Lanc lands   .   . 0 8 0

Thus it will be seen that the young ladies shared the long journeys on horseback, to interview the committees and plead for lenient terms; but whether the sight of such spirited maiden youth (and possibly beauty) appearing in the counsel-room, even if it stirred the hearts of the stern soldiers, caused them to abate the cash compositions fixed for delinquents and recusants, is very much to be doubted. Mr. Thomas Brathwaite, eldest son of Gawen, Ambleside Hall, who was a relative of the family, was doubtless chosen as an intermediatory at York and Newcastle, because he had a decided leaning towards, if he were not already an adherent to the Parliament, and might have influence

We come now to an event which made a deep impression on the neighbourhood, but of which there is no printed record. When in the year 1713, Reginald Brathwaite of Brathay Bridge, at the age of 78, gave evidence concerning a point disputed in the law-courts, he declared that he well knew—

"that in the times of the late Civill warrs the family of the Flemings were Loyall persons, and for their adhering thereto, one Sir Wilfrede Lawson being then in great power and of the Contrary party came to Rydall hall, with some Soldiers, and plundered the same, and there being at that time two young Ladyes at the hall, daughters of John Fleming Esq they were forced to fly for refuge, and the said Sir W. L: and his company ransacked the house and tooke what pillage they mett (might) away with them " *

The date of this occurrence can be made out from Richard Harrison's account book, in which it is explicitly mentioned in four entries; and it is to be concluded that it was distinct from that occasion, when Hugh Foord's

---

* Rydal Hall MSS

courier rode all night to warn them of the attack on Grayrigg, and when Rydal itself seems to have been visited. That would appear to have been in the early autumn of the previous year, and may have been effected by a marching band of soldiers (possibly Scots), who, emboldened by Rupert's great defeat, stopped to smash windows and to carry off horses and outside things easily reached, which (as we have seen), Harrison thought it possible to recover, as well as to obtain protection against the Scots.

But the raids upon loyalists' houses now became frequent, being officially sanctioned. The Parliamentary committees were gaining a firm grip on the country, and the Church even had to submit to the *classis* established at Kendal. It was Cromwell's stern policy to destroy those gentlemen's houses that could withstand a siege. The moated Thurland Castle, which, like Latham House, was surrendered not taken, was practically destroyed by Rigby, or rendered at all events incapable of defence. Many of the smaller houses, the strong towers (or so-called peles) of the Westmorland gentry, were capable of holding out against a temporary siege. And the siege of the Philipson's house on the island of Windermere, told only by tradition, must have occurred about this time, because Robin the Devil is said to have held it successfully against Colonel Briggs until such time as his brother Colonel Huddleston Philipson (who may have been the Captain Philipson of the despatch) was released from the siege of Carlisle, and could come to his assistance. The proud castellers, as the Roundheads called them, were now to be humiliated by the rifling of their halls, and where possible, they themselves were captured and imprisoned; when their ransoms (of which Colonel Briggs was hauling in so many) came in excellently for the current expenses of the year. Indeed as early as 1644 at the turn of the tide, the account book enters money lent " to John Kirby and others to get cousin Lamplough out of prison." As to those who had fled, their houses were ransacked, special search being made for incriminating papers and for money. It was the preliminary to cash compounding with the owner, or even to sales. It is possible that no Royalist house in Westmorland escaped.

Mr. John Philipson, whose estates are said to have been confiscated in 1652 complained to Squire Daniel Fleming on returning to his ancestral hall at Calgarth at the Restoration, that the house had been searched and that not only public papers had disappeared from it, but those of his own property.* Rydal Hall and its inmates would be held in peculiar odium. Not only was the household Royalist, but "notoriously" Roman Catholic, and its money-bags, once so full, had been much at the disposal of the king's party. It was not likely to be spared The forcible entry and search was made however from the Cumberland side, by a party of soldiers under Colonel (after, Sir Wilfrid) Lawson and Captain Orfeur,† both of them gentlemen of Cumberland families ; and at a time when the desultory siege of Carlisle was going on.

After an entry accounting for 10s. paid to Mr Walter Strickland "for A protection from my lord fayrfax" we read :—

" plundered and taken away out of my trunke by Captaine Orfer, and Collonell Lawson Soldirs out of trunke in gold and money besides plate and all other things to best of my knowledg at least wch I dare take my oath upon wth that wch was taken out of katherans box and other things taken from us to the valew
$£35$ 0s 0d

Such sums did not satisfy the rapacity of the men, if the tradition that they tore up floor and wainscot in the

---

* Rydal Hall MSS. His. Com.

† Orfeurs of High Close, otherwise Plumbland Hall, Wil Jackson, Esq., *Transactions* C. & W A & A Society, vol. III , N s. William, Sheriff of Cumb. 1635, d 1660, had at least four brothers. His sons were : Wil Sheriff of Cumb. 1676-77, Richard, John, Cuthbert, Francis. Charles sold Plumbland in 1692. Charles had many brothers Philip═Mary, d of Rich Kirkby.

search be true. Poor Harrison, who may have effectually hidden a larger treasure, was himself carried off.

> " my Charges when I was prisoner and stayed eight weekes and aboue being from Easter till Trinity cost me aboue .. .. £ s. d. 4 0 0

If this was the occasion on which the young ladies fled, they evidently returned, and with the housekeeper and outdoor man conducted the affairs of the place as well as they could. Amongst the receipts comes —

> " Rec for thre hundreds and thre-score and thirteene stones of wooll sould by Go Wilson (the Shepherd) and gentleweomen betwixt Easter and pentecost 1645 to seaverall men and seaverall periods, when I was prisoner and upon the account made to me £ s. d. 122 2 6

That the raid was made in the week previous to Easter is proved by Harrison's entry of the second payment for the Easter sacramental wine for Grasmere Church, the first lot having been drunk by the raiders.

Then we have the exact day of his release :—

> p^d for wheat bread and mutton and veale chickings Eggs and other things layd out by katheran and Jo Wilson from Easter euen till whitsun tuesday that I got liberty to come Home layd out by them there account made to me .. .. .. £ s. d. 1 9 6
> p^d for Hards (= Coarse flax) for sheetes after we were plundered 1 0 0

A further entry seems to imply that a good deal was carried off.

But a worse blow was to fall on the household. The spoilt heir had spent his winter in the south with the king's army, twice sending letters from " Bristowe " at a cost of 2s. 6d. for the messenger, but early in the year he seems to have ridden north again. We can trace him by the following entry at Skipton, where the Castle was still held for the king, not being surrendered till the following December 23rd.*

	£	s	d
sent to scipton to Mr Willm by Mrs Bridget 10 may 1645 30{l}, and giuen more when he came to Rydall 16 may 20{l} in all	50	0	0

It was a bold step to take and foolish enough to come to Rydal, if he meant to hide. Keen watch was kept on the Hall after Harrison's return, as an entry shows —

	£	s	d
" p{d} for P'uison for house when Captaine Johnson and his company was at Rydall and stayed A weeke 10 June	0	3	10

And this was about the date of young William's capture. A strange entry occurs for about this time :—

	£	s	d
p{d} to Mr walter strickland for clothes for Mr Willm that was Mr Geo Prestons vizt A blacke taffety suite and cloke and A paire of bootes	15	10	0

Whether this second-hand and expensive suit was intended for a disguise or not is only conjecture. At the same time £1 was paid for cloth for a suit for one Regnald Harrison, by Mr. William's order. Next, there comes the entry that discloses that episode of anger, violence and humiliation, and the devotion of the sisters, who lodged with the good pewterer of Kendal, to be near their brother :—

	£	s	d
p{d} at kendall the 23 June and 22 July to Colonel Bellingham mr maior mr walter strickland at two tymes for mr willm Flemings releasm{t}	100	0	0
p{d} more for mr willm dyet drinke and wine and his sisters charges at Hugh foordes for neare six weekes when he was in prison	7	10	0

A sum of ten shillings moreover was paid for fees.

	£	s	d
p{d} for Gentlewomen Charges and mine when they went to Islekirk at Keswicke	0	7	6

* S. P Dom Chas I, 21, p. 533-4

This expenditure might possibly represent the flight before the plundering earlier in the year, or, simply a refuge after this calamity of imprisonment. Islekirk would be safe, as the home of one of the very few among their relatives who were on the Parliament side. Barwise, (either Anthony who married Grace Fleming, sister of John, in 1610, or his son), fought indeed well for that side, and a brave deed of his is told, of leading the forces when on the march to the siege of Carlisle through the ford at Salkeld, when they and their commander hung back at sight of Sir Philip Musgrave, Sir Henry Bellingham, and Sir Henry Fletcher with their local levies awaiting them at the other side.*

The young heir, with ransom paid, now renewed his restless wandering. He had naturally to be at once (July 25th) provided with a new suit on his exit from prison (£1. 15s.), and cash

giuen more unto him the first of August 1645 when   £   s.   d.
he would needs goe into Yorkshire with his Ant
M^{rs} strickland m^r walter striclands wife   ..   20   0   0

Mr Walter himself borrowed £10 on July 12th, and later £40

giuen to m^r willm Fleming the 30 of octo: 1645 w^{ch}   £   s.   d.
he had borrowed when he was in Yorkshire wth
consent of supervisors   20   0   0

The easy system of borrowing and leaving the executors to pay was one which Master William resorted to more and more. His retainer "Lantie" Harrison now received his wages. The intercourse with the Howards continued, for when he rode to Naworth on the 9th of December, £5 had to be produced, and then another £5 "in Christmas to himselfe." On January, 1645-6, he

"received £20 when he went into Yorkshire with his uncle walter strickland with m^r phillipsons aduise"

---

* Ferguson's *History of Westmorland*, p. 213.

The broadcloth for "a long cloke" with its trimmings and making for this occasion cost £2. 7s., and two new riding saddles for himself and his man 16s.

Meanwhile the work of payment and intercession went on. On June 23rd, 1645, while he was still in prison, the Kendal Committee, with Captain Archer at its head, had demanded £50 "to be allowed for in sequestracōns," or else repaid. Later:—

"Sent to the Committee and Captaine Jo· Archer   £   s   d.
now due upon demand or w^{th}in 2 month   ..   100   0   0

Again the nearest executors sued for leniency —

"p^d for our Charges at kendall when m^r phillipson and my Lady Lowther was there about m^r willm delinquency the 31 of octo   0   13   6

In February next year (1646) the bargaining with the committee about his "delinquency" still went on, and £2 was paid to a Mr Fell, a lawyer "for his aduise and Counsell" in the matter.

Many of the crushed Westmorland Royalists of the sober sort, who could neither fight nor flee, were endeavouring about this time by means of money payments to make their peace with Parliament. A list of those who compounded for their estates in 1655 * includes Mr. Gawen Brathwaite of Ambleside Hall, Sir Henry Bellingham of Levens; Sir John Lowther of Lowther; and Mr. Christopher Philipson of Calgarth. On April 3rd, 1646, Mr. Thomas Preston of Holker petitioned the committee for compounding, and on the ground that (though he had acted as a Commissioner of Array) he had never taken active service in the field for the king, but had even on one occasion set 40 of the Parliament's soldiers at liberty; that moreover he was a good Protestant; that he had been at once "sequestered" and charged a

---

* Printed in "A Catalogue" of those who compounded, quoted by Ferguson, *History of Westmorland*

yearly rent, which had already consumed £1,250 out of an estate in Lancashire not worth more than £450 and another in Westmorland of £123 in annual value, and that in November last he had conformed to all Ordinances of Parliament ; he prayed therefore to be admitted to a composition. The only other crime the commissioners could charge him with was that of having

"sent a light horse to the enemy." *

William Fleming of Skirwith who had served as Major, submitted to the Parliament in September, 1646, when he took the National Covenant He compounded for delinquency on the following March 25th, and cleared his score by a fine of £110.†

Even the Earl of Derby, as the gloomy winter of 1645 drew in, made some overtures of peace from his dominion of Man, whither he had withdrawn, and the Parliament answered (November 29th) that they should require those who had fled with him there, " the greatest causers of these troubles "—among whom were Sir Marmaduke Longdale and Sir William Huddleston—to be given up.‡

Meanwhile, with the expenses of the young heir, and the taxes levied by Parliament, the wealth of Rydal was suffering diminution. An abstract of taxes entered in the account book may be given in brief, following those monthly levies of £7. 15s. for the Scots that ended March 15th, 1645, doubtless in accordance with the order of March 13th, that all taxation should be left for Parliament.

" May 28 : ' for Scotts P'vision ' 17s 2d. June 7 : for a cast for a horse to Captain Jo: (Johnson) for month pay, 12s 6d."

---

* They also state that the enemy had advanced into these parts of Furness twice, once staying ten weeks, and it was then Mr. Preston procured the prisoner's release S. P. Dom Chas. I, 21, p 397-8

† Col of Com for Compounding, part III., pp 1695-9. Quoted in *Flemings in Oxford*, p 367.

‡ S P. Dom Chas. I., 21, pp 242-3.

THE TROUBLES

This was the force raised from the county, now in the hands of the Parliament.

"3 months to scotts, 4½^d in the £, 5s 8^d, and a tax to the constable, 7s 8^d

	£	s	d
July 9, for personal assessment " for Scotts out of Grasmere (estate) to High Constable	2	0	0
July 12, to Captain Archer, at 10s in £	2	10	0

Small casts of 9s. 6d. and 4s. 10d. (the last 5s. in the pound) recur; in November followed the one for J. Archer's at 10s in the pound.

The next entries imply that some alteration had been made in the adjustment of the county towns, and that representative men of the township of Rydal and Loughrigg had taken on the business.

	£	s.	d.
p^d to Edward Grigg Cunstable of Rydall for 2 casts for Milner Bridge and baneriggs 11th dec wch was behind for our part of A Horse to Captaine Johnson and for Scotts Carrigs and other dis made the 28 July by the castors for the Cunstable wicke		9	6
p^d more unto him for the 1st two casts for the demayne being A 4th p^t of what was casten in the 3^d Cunstable-wicke for the 1st horse and Carriags	1	17	0
p^d more unto the 3^d Cunstable for Another cast made the 25 nov : for A fourth p^t of the 3^d for the demayne for setting Scotts out of the Cuntrye	0	19	0

A joyful entry surely, if illusory!

	£	s.	d.
pd more unto him for A 4th p^t of another cast made the 25 nov. last for the demayne for two men was raised for maior boufferld and arms	1	3	0

Another company!

The year 1645 concludes with a half year's assessment on the tithes of Grasmere and compound of £5; with a township "cast" for 5s. in the pound for outlying land, Archer's of 10s. in the pound for the demesne £2. 10s.; and still another " to Robt stuenson " of 20s. in the pound, £5, is paid on January 10th.

The year 1646 proceeds—

p^d for A cast upon an order from the Committee 21st £ s. d
    feab for 4 purveys being 3s 9d a peece and XV^d
    to soldiers for there panies y^t came out long since   0 16 3

The township's caste of 5s in the pound, and the committee's of 10s., continue, but are entered too erratically (or were "cast" so) to give evidence of their regularity.

p^d servants wages when they went to be trayned £ s. d
    before captaine birkett 0 1 6

which shows that the Parliament was keeping the county militia in fighting trim.

In fact the "new model" for the army instituted by Parliament now begins.

On August, 1646, we get an entry, of £2. 13s. 6d. paid to Rob Stephenson, receiver, August 30th, for a cast of 10s. in the pound "for newe moddell for Cap. Johnson being for a month paie"

Only the day before the high sum of £5. 7s. had been paid to High Constable Nicholas Tunstall at the rate of 20s in the pound "for a month's pay to Scotts," a tax which is repeated (apparently) in September, when it is collected by Edward Walker, Constable of Rydal, and on October 1st.

These terrible people even re-appeared in person, for we learn that on September 26th, £2. 10s. "more" was given to Mr. William

"when scots came to Rydal to be quartered,"

and when no doubt the young man made off.

It is cheerful to find that in the summer the young man had tried to make himself a little useful to his family and the estate. A debt of his to his attendant "Lantie" has indeed to be cleared off, before he carries £10 (June 26th) to his sister Bridget, who is staying in Yorkshire, on which occasion the broad cloth for his own saddle cloth (1½ yards) costs 13s. 6d. Next he goes off (July 28th) to Sizergh with his aunt Blaxton ; then he is off to into Cumberland, to help to get in the Cleator tithes—for the tithes which were possessed by the estate were proving (now that presbyterianism was established) very difficult to collect, and he gives, as tips at Calder Abbey, where he and his companion stay for the night, 5s. This business again engages him at the close of the year, when he stays with Mr. Thomas Lamplough at Ribton. But in the meantime he had been enjoying himself He goes off to Naworth on November 17th, and takes £10 with him. His friend there " Sir Charles Haward " it may be mentioned, had recently borrowed £20 from the estate , also a Mistress Sayer and others on their bond £40. Then we have

" geaven to Mr Wm 18 dec when he played at cards £1 0s. 0d.",

while the high price of £1 is paid for his pair of boots " by his man Roger." This is the first time we hear of Roger Borwick. Finally, he goes off to London on February 15th, 1647, with £50 in his pocket, by " consent of Feoffes."

Meanwhile the Rydal estate pursues its depressing course of tax-paying. The usual committee's cast (this time at 15s. in the pound) and the one " for captaine Johnson troupe " are paid on November 4th, 1646 , and there follows.—

	£ s. d
p^d to Cap. Elliott men for there pay at sundrie tymes till 2 dec that there cap came out of scotland	1 0 6

On the 17th of December a cast is paid " for Sr. Jo. browne " and on the 27th several casts " to scots " for outlying lands, which are lumped together as £1. 4s. 6d. Then comes—

	£ s. d.
for cap Elliott souldiers when they marched out of yorkshire, till they come to there quarters .	0 16 6

On January 7th the town constable receives 3s.

" for a fortnights pay to scots ended Last mundaie "

For the number and variety of taxes paid in two month's time this record surely would be hard to beat! The tax for Captain Johnson's " troupe " paid now to his quarter-master Myles Dawson, reappears April 9th, 13s. for two month's pay; on May 10th, 7s.; and on August 31st, £2, for " the last part of 6 monthes pay at 6s. in £." This was apparently the rate levied on the whole people, collected by the Parliamentary soldiers themselves. For the sins of Rydal Hall it paid again separately, as under August 20th we read:—

" a cast for Ry. dem. of 15s in £ for Johnson troop paid to James Benson constable £3 15s od "

For May, 17s 8d. had been paid for Rydal demesne " to Moddell men . . . for a weeke pay."

This terrible burden of monthly taxation the Westmorland folk were determined once again to resist. The account book gives no evidence of that tumultuous assembly of 1645, when the people refused to disperse without promise of the redress of the tax-grievance suffered from the Scots; but it tells of an outburst of popular wrath that we do not learn of elsewhere. Under August 31st, 1647, comes the entry:—

	£	s.	d.
p^d on mens charges at kendall when all cuntrie rose when they stayed there allmost a weeke 14 Aug	0	10	6

Matters meanwhile were assuming a very serious aspect, for the estate, witness the following entry:—

	£	s	d
p^d to the cometties in kendall 9 Ap 1647 to be allowed in the sequestration of goods at Rydall accordinge to there order or else a saile had bene made of the goods	60	0	0

It appears also, that while money was thus flowing out fast, it was being checked in its in-flow; for many men were not only, under presbyterian rule, taking the opportunity to renounce the payment of tithes, but doubtless they were afraid of paying their manorial dues, lest the Parliamentary Committee—now threatening to confiscate the entire estate—should make them pay a second time. Mr. Fell, the lawyer, was resorted to, for counsel and intervention with the Committees, and received £1 on April 21st.

"for to get of M^r willms delinquencie and a note that came from comitties to charge all men that was oweinge anythinge to the gentlewoomen to bringe it in and pay it unto them and they should have a discharge"

The executors of John Fleming were probably growing uneasy at the heir's prolonged stay in London. On May 31st, 2s. is paid to a messenger who bears a letter to James Neveson's

"to be carried to London from the sup^{r}visors to M^r willm Fleminge."

The date of his return is not given, but it seems not to have been immediate, for only on August 31st, 1647, was paid—

	£ s. d
"for carrage of 2 trunkes of mr Willm's from London to kendall . . . and carrage of a box in all .	1 19 6

The trail of the young man's debts, contracted mostly during this idle time in London, pass down the page of the account book, as they were demanded; but may be gathered together here. To Mr. Robert Brathwaite, of Ambleside Hall, £15 borrowed from his brother Mr. Thomas in London was repaid in October. In the succeeding February Roger Borwick rides off to London to pay debts to the amount of £80, for which no doubt lenders were clamouring. £20 to himself comes next, which he said he had borrowed "from some one." To Mr. John Fleming £16, borrowed "long since." The heir was even debtor to the estate shepherd, John Wilson, to the extent of £10.

The annuities of the young ladies, paid from time to time, show that Mistress Bridget was the more extravagant of the two, for she often needed her money beforehand. It was in this winter, apparently, that she was being courted by Sir Jordan Crossland, a gentleman of her own Catholic faith, who had probably been introduced to her by the Stricklands. But while her outlook on life was brightening under the glamour that marriage brings, and the hopes of a speedy release from the dangers and alarms of Rydal, her sister Ann was falling ill, and was carried away to York, perhaps to be under a skilled doctor's care Master William who had been enjoying the humours of Kendal fair, as we gather from the following entry:—

	£	s.	d.
p^d m^r willm Charges and ou^{rs} at kendall faire 25 octo and beast grasse when we stayed 2 nights	1	7	6

played now the careful brother, and the account book shows that he reaped some advantage from the service.

	£	s	d.
"geaven to M^r w^m by doll barban (the old servant no doubt in charge of the sick girl) at seaverall tymes when Mrs Ann was not well and in cressenmas	9	1	0

On January 21st, 1647-8, they set out for York, when £10 more is given to the heir, and £3 to his man Roger, for whom "2 frize coats and thinges for makeinge them up" were procured from "Captaine Archer" for £1. 14s 6d. For John of the draper's shop could hardly be dispensed with, though he had become a man rampant for the Parliament, a member of the committee, and collector of taxes imposed by the body. The fees of the York doctors engaged for Mistress Anne are entered —

	£	s	d
phiseeke stuffe for her to m^r prisoe	3	18	6
geaven to doctor stoole for his paynes wth her	5	0	0
geaven more to his man for his paynes	1	10	0
more to m^r Sunt for his paynes	1	0	0

But poor Anne only got worse, and William, who had returned meanwhile to Rydal, was despatched again into Yorkshire on March 19th with £30 " when she was verie ill and had noe money," and the youth himself had £10 " to put in his purse "

Mistress Bridget meanwhile was left in charge of the house, and £3 was given to her on January 28th for current expenses " when we went to Lancashire " Her ordering too was lordly; for besides the fish for Lent, the cockles, mussels and barrel-and-a-half of herrings, and the " Linge fish &c. sent for by Mrs. Bridget " £1 2s 7d. we have the high charge for Lent spices and garden seeds. £1. 15s. 6d. " Nedd makereth pedler of brathey " also furnished her with " things " to the total of 16s. 6d. " Ned " was indeed a favourite with the ladies at the Hall, and earlier is entered —

" p^d to nedd pedler for 4 bottels full of Rosis-oles (?) sent for by gentlewomen at seauverall tymes since 25 nov till 17 may 6s 8d "

He also supplied vinegar, wormwood, groceries, " strong water," and even gunpowder.

But some extravagance in the making of char-pies and other delicacies might be excused, for this must have been the eve of Bridget's wedding, and the following entry of disbursement for Anne was probably connected with it :—

" p^d more for m^rs Ann to Sir Jordan Crosland wch he   £ s d
had layd out for her for a gowne at London   .. 14 9 0

But whether she figured at the wedding in the gown so thoughtfully provided by the bridegroom, and which must from its price (equivalent to goodness knows how much of our money) have been of some magnificence, cannot be told; nor where the ceremony took place. An entry makes it certain it was in Westmorland, and probably, if not at Sizergh, in some quiet upstairs room of Rydal Hall, used as a chapel, where a priest in disguise from a distance (for Solomon Benson's "pension" has by this time disappeared from the books) might be quietly introduced. The heir was again his sister's escort, riding with her apparently in the old-fashioned style to her new home.

"more geaven him when he went into yorkshire 17th £ s d.
    of Ap, 1648 wth his sister my Ladie crosland   5 0 0

The usual correlation follows, and his man Roger posts off in May "by m^r Willms earnest desire" to repay Sir Jordan Crossland £50 he had borrowed. The latter gentleman was now being paid his bride's dower.

"p^d to Sr Jordan Xrosland at 4 seaverall tymes at   £ s d.
    and before 12 Aug 1648 in p^t of his wive's portion 700 0 0

This summer there was another—and the last—rising of the Royalists. The action of the army, which had overpowered the parliament; the triumph of the Independents over the Presbyterians; but more than all, the imprisonment of the king, had stirred the hearts of the nation strangely. Commissioned by the Prince of Wales, Sir Marmaduke Langdale, who had never sheathed his sword, came north to organize the rising. While Sir Philip Musgrave surprised in April the Parliamentary garrison in Carlisle, and took the city * for the king, Langdale himself gathered together a force said to number on May 1st, 5,000 foot well armed and 800 horse. The former must have been the folk of the shires, who had borne such a grievous burden of taxation and were willing again to fight for the king; while among the horse, and at the head of the companies, rode many a gentleman who had compounded for his estates with the Parliament and settled into a grudging acquiescence with the existing order. William Fleming of Skirwith was not there, for he had not yet raised his troop of horse as Lieutenant-Colonel under the newly-made Colonel John Lamplough

---

* Ferguson's *History of Westmorland*

of Lancaster, but his young cousin from Rydal was, and this time not under the wing of the Howards, but of the Stricklands. The general muster took place, according to our account book, on the Penrith fells, where the little army awaited apparently the Highland Scotch, who were coming south to back up this gallant enterprise that was to rescue the king. That a considerable meeting of the leaders was held at Rydal Hall is shown by an entry in the household account :—

"p^d at kendall 6 May when m^r W^m was at Rydall and Sr Robt Strickland and many more gentlemen for mutton wheat-bread and vinegar . . 0 9 6

On May 23rd, Mr. William has £2 on riding to Kendal to buy new saddles, and then come the entries :—

Sent to M^r w^m by his man Roger to kendall in gould when he was there wth scots Amry (*sic*) wch he said I must needs send 80 0 0
more geaven his man Roger sent unto him 29 may when he went wth his unckle Sir Robt. Strickland to a randivow o' to peareth Fell . .. 18 0 0

The considerable delay in the march of this force south must have been prejudicial to the success of the movement; and the folk of the militia in especial, would be inclined during it to slink back to their homesteads and not to re-gather. The force too was lessened by the need to garrison well the castles of Cockermouth, Carlisle, and Appleby, all now in possession of the Royalists. In the middle or close of July, when (on the 19th) Mr. William sends to Rydal for £30 to pay for a horse, a start must have been made. The little army had marched as far as Preston, when it was met by Cromwell himself, on the 17th of August; and in a few hours his mighty arm, wielding his "Ironside" soldiers like a blade, wiped it out. The Royalist cause was now lost irrevocably, so long as his life lasted.

Of the northern leaders none lost their lives as Sir Henry Fletcher had done at Rowton, and some must have escaped south and abroad, following the Prince of Wales. But many of them are found some six weeks later to be holding out in the strong castles of Cumberland and Westmorland. However, after an attempt to concentrate themselves in Appleby, they were forced on the 7th of October, to relinquish their last strong-holds. The surrender seems to have been complete and general.* The terms permitted the common soldiers and inferior officers, after giving up of arms, to return to their homes; while the leaders were to " go beyond seas," with six months' grace allowed for the ordering of their affairs. The list of the officers includes names of some of the leading Westmorland gentry, with many cadets. Besides Sir Philip Musgrave, Sir William Hudleston, and Master William's uncle, Sir Robert Strickland, there were Lieut.-Colonels Philipson, Bellingham, Strickland, and other well-known names.

Master William himself after the disaster of Preston had flown straight back to Rydal and its money-bags.

geaven to Mr Willm wch he said he must and would have the 24 Aug 1648 when the king's partie was routed at preston when he said he would shift for himselfe and goe over sea in gould 200l and in silu^r 50l in toto   ..   .. 250 0 0 £ s d

Unhappy heir of Rydal! To be banished from home, and drift on a sea of trouble. He would seem not to have taken Roger Borwick with him on this flight, but Harrison's son Lantie, a more responsible companion for the guarding of the heavy money, and who received as wages by consent of the executors £4 " before he went to London with him." Roger, who was still kept on as his man, had now to be repaid £60 " which he (the heir)

---

* Civil War Tracts, Cheetham Society, No xlix

had borrowed from him long since on his bill." He had charge of his master's horses, and particularly of a mare, which was kept at Coniston all winter at a cost of £4. 17s. 6d. " which he meant to have ridden when he came "

With the flight of the heir, the home was closed. Mistress Anne was probably in Yorkshire, as her annuity was sent her through Lady Blaxton. An arrangement was now made for the young folks' uncle, Mr Walter Strickland, to take over the Hall, and to live there. Harrison continued the house accounts " till penticost after that Mr walter Strickland entered of Rydall " ; and the servants wages were paid up to May 22nd, 1648, the day " that house was broken up." Perhaps it was considered that Mr. Strickland's presence protected the Hall. He was at this time without a home, and quite short of funds.

	£	s	d
Lent to Mr Walter Strickland the 20 June wch he promised to pay againe at yeares end when he paid his rent wch he borrowed for payinge of sesm^{ts} when he could get noe money out of goods ..	10	0	0

Richard Harrison, with the money-chests and the bonds of John Fleming's trust, would seem to have moved to Coniston, though the house at Miller Bridge, where his brother had lived, and where many papers had been placed, was still in the possession of the trustees. Left to contend with the officers of the Commonwealth as best he might, he had a hard time of it, according to the confidences we find in the account book.

On November 4th two soldiers rode from Carlisle " by order of Committee," and carried him off, with a threat that if he resisted " a partie of horse was to come for me." So Richard sadly went with them, to face the Carlisle committee men " about Cumberland lands," and paid £51. 2s. 6d. before he came away. Worse was to follow.

> pᵈ to mʳ pollard man by John harrison and Tho walker 4 dec 1648, when they did driue and take all the goods at Coniston for pᵗ of the arreare of rents for Ulu'ston and Urswicke some pᵗ thereof beinge due when the sequestrators had all and pᵈ nothinge, and I was arreasted for the same and Imprisoned at kendall and had a keper afterward wᵗʰ me at Coniston 5 weekes, beinge by coɱand from general Lambert, and for there charges and fees and charges I was put unto £37 15s 0d

The Rydal estate was dealt with yet more severely than the lands of Furness. An entry after January, 1648-9, runs :—

> pᵈ at kendall at 3 seaverall tymes for the sequestration of the goods at Rydall accordinge to the priszment to captaine Garnett, for mʳ Wᵐ Flemings delinquence passed over by order from the comittie to be pᵈ unto him or els he to enter to all the goods at Rydall boᵗʰ wᵗʰin house and wᵗʰout, and for charges aboute the same upon his acquittance £310 0s 0d
> pᵈ for my charges aboute goeing aboute that busines to kendall seaverall tymes to get it prvented wᶜʰ I could not prevaile in yet did my best therein £0 17s 6d

Many calls for money were being made too by the absent heir, who seems to have been doing no good in London, where he remained, though he sent once for copies of the charge made out against him as a delinquent.

He wrote a letter in January, asking that Mr. Fell should be repaid £30 he had borrowed. He also wanted £80 for himself; and his man Roger carried the sum to Kendal, to be despatched on January 7th by Richard Robinson, carrier. On March 3rd Roger rode again to Kendal, with £100 for the heir " wch he writt for, and said he was broke and could get nothinge done wᵗʰout it." In April £110 was paid to " Mr. Richard kirkebie " of Kirkby which he had borrowed from his mother-in-law.

But the end of the drifting and the spending was near.

The youth, now 20 years of age, took the smallpox (it is said), and died on the 12th of May, 1649. He was buried at St. Giles in the Fields. It is to be hoped that Lancelot Harrison, though alone of his people, was with him at the end; but of this tragic event the pages of the account book tell nothing. The book also comes to an end soon after. There was an immediate gathering of the trustees; and Lady Lowther, vigorous and kind in emergency, made her appearance, though she had to put up at the Ambleside inn, kept by Brathwaite the carrier.

	£	s.	d.
p^d for our charges at ambleside when my Ladie Lowther and we mett Sr Jordan at Rydall 26 may and stayed 2 nights at how head at ambleside	0	15	0

She went later too, with Harrison to the Appleby assizes, and then to Penrith, where they met Sir Jordan Crosland, Mr. Moore and others.

With the death of the young heir, there was no further need to continue the trust, or at least as much of it as remained in the hands of the supervisors of John Fleming's will. It was closed shortly after, and the money divided between the sisters. Richard Rawlings, clerk, was employed to—

"summe and cast up all the Bonds and Bills . . . delivered to Jordan Crossfield and Mr. A. Fleming. They amounted to £11,000 or thereabouts." *

With the demesne of Rydal, supervisors and owners were alike powerless to deal. It lay in the hands of the sequestrators, nominally let to Mr. Walter Strickland, and with fate wholly uncertain.

---

* Depositions in Chancery suit of 1653

CHAPTER IV.

THE STRUGGLE FOR RYDAL DEMESNE.

NOT Rydal alone, but many another hall and tower of Westmorland lay at this time with lands untilled, desolate and forsaken of its owners—nay, even in some cases ruined. The lord may have been beyond the sea; or gone, if he were young and reckless, to other wars; or he might be only skulking in London. The few who remained, were settling as broken men on their estate, seeking, by any means they might, to release their lands from the sequestrators' hands, and reduce the payments demanded by the Commonwealth.

The most pitiable plight was that of the ladies, who were in many cases left alone in the homestead, to fight with poverty as best they might after their husbands had gone. The pages of Richard's account book give us a glimpse of the straits to which they were put. In the terrible spring and summer of 1645, Mr. Brathwaite's children were at Rydal for a time, which probably means that Burnside was sacked about then, as were the halls of Sir Philip Musgrave, then shut up in Carlisle.* The erudite Richard had married a second time in 1639, and is said to have gone to reside on his wife's estate at Appleton near Richmond † These children may therefore have been the younger ones of his first wife; but it seems more likely that they were the " barnes " of his eldest son Thomas, who had married early and was now 27, and to whom Burnside would fall by inheritance. He was almost certainly out with the king's forces, and indeed is conjectured to have been the Captain Brathwaite who

---

* Ferguson's *History of Westmorland*

† She was Mary, daughter of Roger Crofts of Kirklington. For all particulars of the Brathwaite family, I am indebted to Mr. J. A Martindale

was in exile in Breda.* It is very likely he would leave his wife and little ones (of whom he was eventually to have 15 !) at the family home, and it was doubtless for their succour that on July 26th, 1648 (after the defeat at Preston) Mrs. Strickland conveyed from the Rydal chest £18, to " mrs Brathwaite of burneshead " " at mr Will$\overline{m}$ expresse comand."

While Harrison was in prison between Easter and Pentecost, 1645, young Mistress Bridget went to the estate shepherd, and from the money he had in hand by the sale of wool took £20, " wch she lent to Mrs Hudlestone of Millom upon pawne of goods "

To Lady Middleton, who was first cousin to the young people, through her mother Margaret Strickland, £60 was lent on December 28th, 1648, by the heir's " earnest desire ", which recalls Sir Daniel's statement that after the young man had given up courting Mistress Howard of Naworth, he had " made his Address unto ye Daughter and Heir of Sir Geo. Middleton of Leighton in Lanc " †

A letter from one of these distressed ladies is preserved ‡ Thomas Strickland, heir of Sir Robert (and himself carrying a knighthood which Father West considered to have been bestowed by the king for his conduct at the battle of Marston Moor) married a rich young widow Jane Mosley, Lady Dawney. All the male Stricklands concerned (including his father, Sir Richard, of Thornton Briggs, and his uncles Thomas and Walter, at that time residing at Sizergh) § made a deed settling the lordship of Sizergh upon the bridegroom, on November 21st, 1646. He would seem to have left his bride immediately, if we may suppose her letter of January 13th, 1646, addressed to him in London, to have been written the

---

* See *Dic. of Nat. Biography*.
† D F's Writings.
‡ Sizergh Castle MSS.
§ Sizergh Castle MSS

following January (1646-7). It is a witty and loving epistle :—

" I doe beleve " she tells him " thou hast as poor a wife and stuard as ever man had, for we by (buy) most of our fodher, and he calls of me and I of him for money and I think we neither of us have any . . . the post stays, for God sake writ as often as thou canst for I take noe comfort but in thy letters Thearfor let me not want one as often as thou canst my Deare I am till Death thy poor wife Jane Strickland."

Her postscript shows that our young wife Bridget and other relatives were in London at the time.

" my love to all frends the lady medlton Lady Crosland cozens boyntons and all I should be glad to heare of my lady crosland safe delevry "

In her next letter she regrets the pains and money laid out (on Sizergh ?) since it is of no avail wanting him, and begs he may find some place where they may live together. All her women relatives are in trouble, especially her cousin Waters for her husband; and there is :—

" poor nany who thay say now is extreame ill, and tears all hir hare and flesh of hir, my cozen mary hase beene with hir and is ; and can doe nothing, thay are in great sorrow now . . "

And so went the sad world to the women of Westmorland; which was not soon to mend. Father West says that Jane's husband ultimately (and perhaps after the last rising of 1648) fled to France with Prince Charles, and remained there nine or ten years. He did in the interval, however, contrive that she should join him in London, as is shown by this letter of Mr. Walter Strickland.

From the Abstract of the Sizergh MSS.
made by Thomas West in 1778, and copied by Mr. Forres.
Letter from Walter Strickland, brother of Sir Robert.
" These for Sʳ Tho Strickland Knᵗ at his lodging in Duke street

over against veare streete end at one Mr Porphery's house a dancing Master in London   9^d Bot "

Ould Mr Walter Stricklànds Letter

Leavens 7^{ber} 22

S^r

I have beene this day with my nephew Biddulph at Lighton, who intends to serve my bond which I gave him to secure him from that bond of Sr Jor Croslands, which was to be delivered to me in the payment for newbey and this I have under Sr Jordans oune hand, now S^r thar is 100^{ld} and sixtie od pounds dew to me In Sr Jordans hand for newbey. my desire is that Sr Jordan would diliver Mr Tho. prestons bond in to your hand with an Ingagement from you, by bond or otherwise that I will allowe of that 100^{lb} at such time as Sr Jordan shall thinke him selfe perfectly secured of that estaite   This I desire in regard of Tho: prestons Clamour, which is a daly vexation to me   This I hope you will dou for me, nothing will satisfie but the bond, delivered to him tis so Just and honest a request as cannot be denide by a friend   now for your owne consernes   I have moved my Cosin Bellingham acording to your directions in Tho Shipards lettere, his ansur is he will not take 400^{lb}—except he have it all, neathur can he forbere it till midsumer next   Then I said what if it dou not cume till that time, his ansuer was it would breede a scabe amongst us. All I could dou was to get time till martin-mase next which I would have you observe and faile not. I hope in your next we shall heare of my Ladye safe deliverie which we all pray for, thare are divers came to me this yeare saing they had warrants from you for buckes, as Ja: Dacket and his sonne girlington John lowther and outhere (= others?) now at last thar cumes a warrant under your hand dated the 13 August last past, for a bucke to one Dan. Rawlinson the best of this season which war past 6 dayes before the warrant came to which I would not consent though your man ned has undertaken to serve that warrant tomorrow your hake (hawk) kilde 7 partrige fridy last in 2 houre, my sonn Robin flewe him, who is desirus to carrie him Into Cumberland tomorrow I hope he will be carefull of the hauke, with my man Dikee asistance and my directions I doubt not but thay will bring him safe home   All well at sisergh and heare noe newse but I must leave Leavens which is sume truble to your sarvant

wa Strickland.

Then follows a letter, sent from Levens, April 14th,

from Mr. W. Strickland to Mr. Thomas Walton, saying he will meet latter at " neatby " (Newbey ?) ; that from the interest he has in that land, his cousin Biddulph could not part with it without his consent. His cousin presses him and his wife to desist. He declares he can make good his proceedings against all who oppose him, and seems to defy his correspondent to do his worst.

This letter, addressed to his nephew, the same Sir Thomas, is a striking evidence of the financial confusion of the time, when bonds were capping bonds, and passing from hand to hand ; and may have been written before he took over Rydal Hall, for he must have left Sizergh in 1646, and had now, as it seems, reluctantly to leave Levens, vacated by Sir Henry Bellingham. The traits that gleam from this and from his transactions with Rydal suggest a busybody, always short of cash, and leaning on others' means Sir Jordan Crosland was likewise apparently a homeless man, and mixed up along with Mr. Francis Biddulph with the lands of Newby, on which Mr. Walter asserts, in a further letter, he had incontestible claim, and which he would appear to be then selling to Sir Jordan. The latter is described in Dugdale's *Visitation of Yorkshire in* 1665, as of Newby, so that he must finally have secured this estate. He had undoubtedly been both Royalist and Catholic. He had received knighthood at Lincoln, July 14th, 1642, and at the Restoration was made Constable of Scarborough.* At this time (1649) he is stated to have been of Harmes, near Helmsley, Yorkshire.† With his wife's money, he was now going to push his wife's and sister-in-law's claims to Rydal desperately, and his opponent was William Fleming, nephew of John Fleming. But the first concern of both was to make their peace with the Commonwealth, the arbiter of the destinies of the little manor. Jordan Cros-

---

* *The Flemings in Oxford*, p 10
† Cal of Committee for Compounding, part iii , pp 1695-9

land compounded for delinquency " in being in arms in the first and second wars " on April 20th, 1649, his fine (at one sixth) being computed at £25 or £30. William Fleming had already by a fine of £110 cleared his own estates from sequestration in April, 1647, before the outbreak of 1648 Of this the receipt shows that he paid a second £55 on May 5th, 1649.

Of William's life and the claim he was about to make upon the Fleming manors something more must be said. His own patrimony of Skirwith seems to have had little hold on his affections. Born in 1609, on the death of his father Daniel in 1621, he was but twelve years of age, and his mother Isobel, daughter of James Brathwaite of Ambleside Hall, no doubt ruled the estate, and he seems not to have cared, when she died in 1639, to take over the management of it himself. Instead he let it to his younger brother Thomas " for 3 score pounds," * taking care to draw up a deed and inventory whereby the " household stuffe and implements," granted by " his well-beloved grandmother Agnes Fleminge of Riddell " to his father Daniel should be secured to his own little son Daniel for an heirloom, in accordance with her settlement on heirs male. For he had already taken to wife Alice, daughter of Mr. Roger Kirkby, of Kirkby in Furness, and had, by some agreement with his uncle John, settled for a time at Coniston Hall. There in 1633 and 1634 his sons Daniel and Roger were born. But by 1636 he had moved to another estate of his uncle's, at Monkhall by Keswick, as the christening of his son William shows; and between the birth of one baby John in 1637, and another John in 1641, he had moved again to his own Skirwith, where Isobel was born in 1642, and Alexander in 1644. By this time, as we have seen, he had raised a regiment for the king, and was engaged in war. In February of 1647, his estate of Skirwith and his goods were taken over by

---
* Rydal Hall MSS.

the sequestrators, as the inventory at Rydal Hall shows. The untimely death of his young cousin, William of Rydal, in 1649, aroused his interests, and opened the door to such claims as he possessed as next heir male.

It is difficult to judge of the amount of justice that lay in those claims; John's two daughters were alive, and the ancient customs of inheritance in Cumberland and Westmorland (and all over the ancient kingdom of Northumbria in all probability) had never overlooked the women. The four daughters of Sir John de Lancaster in the fifteenth century had shared his lands, though there were numbers of collateral males eager for any spoil they could by any loop-hole of law lay hands upon. Mr. George Preston of Holker had left his estates to be shared amongst his three daughters, irrespective of relatives of the name. And Sir Jordan Crosland, in the lawsuit of 1654 stated that his wife and sister Agnes claimed Rydal demesne " as co-heirs with William dec. and all other lands which William died seized of."

William of Skirwith's opportunity on the death of the heir male was not neglected. We find a letter, written by his wife Alice, who was perhaps an ambitious woman, to Baron Rigby from Skirwith, as early as November, 1649, begging his " countenance " towards her husband's securing " Cosine Fleeminge's " lands, to which he had a right " by force of an Estate Taile made by his Grandfather and father " It was however thought well to take the opinion of Matthew Hale before fighting the matter. The claim to Rydal is there shown to have rested on William Fleming's settlement on his marriage with Agnes Bindloss (a document not to be found, but sustained, it was stated by his will) The claim to Coniston and Beckermet went no further back than John Fleming's settlement on his marriage with Alice Ducket in 1601, by whom he had no children, but which mentioned heirs male John's will also, in so far as it corroborated the grandmother

Agnes's will, as to the sheep and household goods at Rydal, was brought forward as evidence. The claim on these last, which were expressly left to Daniel's male heirs if John's failed, was indeed indisputable; though it may be questioned whether it in any way furthered the larger claim. At any rate, it was decided to push for all Hale's opinion was not however thought favourable enough for quotation, for we find that the opinion of Mr. Steele, recorder of London, is brought forward before the committee for compounding on William's side, and he is named as referee.* He must have been retained as counsel, as he later receives a fee.†

No time was lost in presenting the claim, and even before this was done, William took the strong step, (and strange one, if without the consent of his cousin John's heiresses,) of moving his family to Coniston Hall; where, if he did not oust Richard Harrison, John's agent, his adversary in the claim, he became his close neighbour, for Richard was later located at Waterhead, Coniston. William's health may by this time have broken, for he made no personal exertion, and the important measure of presenting his claim before the London committee was left to John Banks, his faithful henchman, whom he had brought with him from Skirwith. But with John, a simple if shrewd countryman, there journeyed on May 29th, 1650, William's heir Daniel, a lad of seventeen,‡ who was immediately after entered as a student at Grays Inn, and then proceeded to Oxford to take up his residence at Queen's College. Daniel, therefore, keen-witted by nature, saw the start of the contest when he laid down his father's petition on the table before the committee; and he never ceased to follow it till the fight was won. The

---

* Calendar of Com for Compounding

† *Flemings in Oxford*, p 51.

‡ See his Autobiographical Sketch (3422 of Rydal Hall MSS. as arranged by the His MSS. Com)

committee seem to have accepted the entail claim without much question, and in December decided, of the three manors for which William prayed to be allowed to compound, " that the Manor of Conyston shall be freed, but not Rydal and Beckermot." * Sir Jordan Crosland meanwhile had been busy, and a counter petition on behalf of the daughters of John Fleming had been presented, and the case had to be heard. In February, 1650-1, good John Banks was again in London, doing what he could with the help of Mr. Fell (afterwards Judge), who was William Fleming's neighbour at Swarthmoor in Furness, and who, as a staunch Parliamentarian throughout the wars, might have influence with the authorities. But the moidered state of poor John's mind is shown in his letters to his young master at college :—

" I am sorry that I cannot come to Oxford to see yo^u, But truely *I am soe tryed heare that puts me by* all civilities. I had one heareing yesterday of yor fatheres bussiness and shall have another this daye, god send that I get any thin done. Mr Fell goes out of towne tomorrow and I would gladly goe wth him iff it weare possible "

Then, on March 1st :—

" I have done nothing in yor fathers business but continued it as it was till the laste weeke in next tearme And there is to be a refference to frends in the Contry by consent of Counsell on both sids Sir I desire yo^u to excuse me for I have bene so perplexed I scarce did know what I did Mr Fell is gone yesterday and yor Cousen Richard, (Kirkby) I intend to go on Munday."

John reached Coniston on the 8th, as he writes to young Daniel, telling now all the news of the family, and the courtships of his cousins the Mistress Kirkbys. The parents' letters to the youth breathe a more anxious spirit.† The mother Agnes had written in January, after some parental exhortation

---

* Rydal Hall MSS.
† They are given in full in *Flemings in Oxford*

" dear sonne soe longe ever as I heare yor well doeing tis my dayly comfort and y^u may assure yo^{r}self, there shall be noething wanting in me to prform the p^t of a loueing mother, and thirdly thejse tymes are soe troublesome with ous; and wee are soe prplexed with this troublesome fellow Sr Jordan, that wee are not able to get monye by all the meanes we can make to mayntayne the sute and there for a fregale way must be obserued by us all if it be possible to gayne our right, for the shrist (shirts) y^u wrot for, I will get y^u them as soune as I can and I will send y^u them abut Whutsonday, about then they are the whitest and chipest."

Daniel therefore had to wait for his linen; country-spun, woven, bleached, and sewn, for some four months.

"p^s Your father beds y^u plye your booke and y^u shall want noething."

The cry of the parents is urgent, that he shall be frugal, and that they will do all they can for him, in fitting him for his future station. The father's letter of May 4th (which perhaps went with the shirts as well as with £10 for the youth's tutor) is yet more solemn in its advice as to conduct :—

" Truely Sonn though the tymes goe harde wth me, and that my troubles dayly rather Encrease then otherwise yett so longe as you deserue well in applyeinge yor selfe to yor studyes ..
I shall bee loath to see you want anythinge fitt ffor you : but wth my uttmost powers assiste you in the pursuance of yor accomphplishm^t to make you a Man, and indeed a Gentleman, in hopes you will bee noe less obedient to my desires; and Good to all mine "

The suit dragged on. In February, 1652, the London Committee for Compounding referred the matter back to the County Committees of Cumberland and Westmorland, for examination by witnesses of the conflicting claims.[*] Young Daniel, who left Oxford in company with his uncle John Kirkby, on July 13th, attended a meeting at Skipton, which probably dealt with the enquiry as to John

---

[*] Cal of Com for Com, part iii

Fleming's possessions in Yorkshire, from July 19th to the 22nd, and thence went home to Coniston. His autobiographical notes mention that a "meeting" was held at Ambleside, on November 5th and 6th, no doubt for examination as to the Rydal estates, and another at Cartmel on the 17th and 18th, for the Lancashire portion of John Fleming's estates. Whatever the official reports might be, the Coniston family thought it necessary to follow them up to London; and thither young Daniel journeyed on the 18th of December with John Banks. The heir was now to watch the case himself. The sale of his horse on arrival for £3 10s. is entered in the accounts along with the £40 they carried with them; and he went into residence at Gray's Inn for his course of law on January 22nd. The paying out of "ffees in the case," to Mr. Pennington £1, to Mr. Laton £1; also 1s "ffor a Coach ffor Mr. Pennington to woster house" (where some of the Parliamentary Committees sat),* for a dinner with Mr. Wharton on the 5th, 2s, and on "the 12th ffor our dinere wth Mr Wharton and his Brother and others" 4s., now show how busy the two men were in pushing their claim. Mr Thomas Wharton, in the difficult business of compounding to free estates, was now their chief adviser. He wrote to William Fleming, to tell him that the report of the Lancashire enquiry was

"very full for yᵘ, the other from Yorke very imprtinent and obnoxious, but if Westmʳland and Cumbʳland doe Certifie fully for yᵘ as Lan hath done we shall not much feare that of Yorkshire"

He advises the Coniston squire to furnish certain particulars likely to be of use in the case. He finishes—

"Sir I believe if your Adversaryes doe oppose yᵘ they will Leaue noe stone vnturned yᵗ may annoye yᵘ I doe not yet find them active but yet it is my Caution yᵗ yᵘ doe not trust them in this particulʳ ffor the dangʳ is greatʳ than yᵘ are aware of"

---

* *The Flemings in Oxford*, p 32

The letter of young Daniel, who had been left in London by John with £24 in hand, written on March 29th, shows how keen and independent was his pursuit of this disputed inheritance, as well as how hopeful his spirit He rejects Mr Wharton's advice, reports to his father and goes to Mr. Pennington, who joins him in intercession with the auditor of the Committee for Compounding. He hopes the case, pressed out yesterday, will be heard to-morrow, and that he may by the next post send " glad tidings . . . "

" . . S\u1d63 Jordan and my cosen Collingwood are both here, they doe faythfully promis, that they will not oppose us tomorrow. There hath beene lately a cruell breach betwixt my cosen Collingwood and his father, about the purchaseing of his estate, my cosen would purchas his father's estate but the old man will neither permitt him, nor will he purchase it him selfe ; they doe soe wrangle that its thought y\u1d49 estate will bee lost betwixt them "

This was the gentleman of Northumberland who had lately wedded Anne Fleming, and now acted on her behalf.

Young Daniel's pertinacity and vigour commanded at least a partial success and perhaps deserved it. First however came sorrowful news, no doubt expected, from Coniston —

" My Father dyed May 24 53, which sad news I heard not (being at London) before June 3 53 "

He waited only for the favourable decision, dated September 7th, of the committee :—

" that the sequestration of Coniston and Beckermet manors should be discharged, and the rents to be paid to William Fleming with arrears, from 25 June, 1650," *

to take horse on the 28th and ride home. He had life to face now as the head of the family, to meet a newly widowed mother in a home straitened for means ; but

---

* See *Flemings in Oxford*, p 370

with youth and success at his back, and happily in love, he doubtless cantered northward by the narrow roads in happy buoyant mood.

But the battle was not yet wholly won. Rydal, small, but esteemed the pearl always of the Fleming manors, was yet held by the officials of the Commonwealth. The decision of September, 1653, that was favourable to the Skirwith branch, as regarded the Cumberland and Lancashire lands, concluded with —

"The Committee for Compounding cannot, on the proof before them, discharge Rydal Manor, but leave him (William Fleming) to make further proof."

The house and demesne indeed, which as the residence of a family of papists and delinquents—always ready too to supply the sinews of war from its coffers—had become peculiarly obnoxious to the Commonwealth, was placed on another footing from the other manors. Its case was referred to the Army Committee, and taken over subsequently by the Trustees for the sale of lands forfeited for Treason. The Westmorland Commissioners for Compounding as reported on March 23rd, 1649-50, had at first thought it best to let the premises, pending a decision as to its fate from the centre. They had been already let by the late Commissioners (they report) to one William Beck at £202. 10s. He may have been the agent of Mr. Walter Strickland, of whom we hear no more, and who had clearly vacated them. Now two would-be tenants present themselves, a certain George Mawson, who offers a rental of £220, and John Harland £240. The officials decided to settle between the two by setting up a light, and granting the lease to the one who bid the highest before the light went out. This odd expedient failed totally. Mawson, punctual to the tryst, was the sole bidder, and got it at £180, Harland, coming in too late, bid £200. Apparently he got it *vide infra*. "We think," says the report —

"they were employed, one by Sir Jordan Crosland, who married (young William) Fleming's sister, the other, by Wm Fleming, of Skirwith, Cumberland, who holds an entail. The estate is not worth more than £120 We want instructions"

The struggle had begun in earnest, and the combatants, keenly alert, were acting by silent agents. Both were anxious to obtain the tenancy, since possession is nine-points of the law; yet the County Commissioners, in forwarding rents from sequestrated Westmorland estates to the Committee for Compounding at Goldsmith's Hall in October, reiterate their desire for—

"directions touching an estate at Rydal sequestered from Mr Fleming, for which 2,000 l was offered for one year, though at the utmost value it was never reputed worth more than 120 l ; but it being contest, this was done to gain possession The estate lies waste, so that the profit thereof this year will scarcely amount to 50 l "

In February next year the report runs .—

"The demesne of Rydal in this county being in contest, and the title in dispute, was farmed out for the last year for £200 to John Harland, merely to keep possession, to corroborate the title of the present occupier, but we could never get any security for the payment of the money."

The "present occupier" may have been Sir Jordan Crosland, who backing that extravagant offer of Harland's that had tempted the commissioners, had slipped into possession behind it But he was not to be left in without a fierce fight. As early as July, 1650, two other applicants for the lease had appeared, viz. Thomas Garth, a Penrith solicitor and agent for what may be described as the gamble of sequestrations,* and Anthony Hale. In the following year another aspirant is reported, one Ed. Winter, of whose collusion with William Fleming we have certain evidence in a letter remaining at Rydal Hall.

---
* See *Flemings in Oxford*, p. 337.

"Mr Willm ffleminge

Yor health wisher & : I make no doubt but yᵘ have heard of the objections that is made which hinders yᵘ and me in going on in our bargine, as concerning Rydall, for when you and I agreed at 20ˡᵇ p Ann I supposed that possession should have been giuen me without any query or circumstance at all so that in all probility if yᵘ and I doe any good herein, I must be necessitated to wryte up to London about the same wʰ will be no small charge. therefore I desire to know yor mind by this same bearer or whom yᵘ will els, what yᵘ will giue more than our agrement if the thing be accomplished compleatly   so not doubting but to hear from yᵘ that I may be the more incoureged to goe on therein so with my service prsented to yᵘ I Rest

Penrith this
    4ᵗʰ of febr 1650.
Yor affectionat servant
Edward Winter

Winter was apparently " incoureged " by a rise from the £20 offered—a contrast indeed to the £200 and £2000 of other bidders—to proceed, and proved a most valiant coadjutor. A battered paper of this date, 1650, sets forth the wrong-doings of Sir Jordan, calling him " a Grand Mallignant " and Papist, who is furnishing arms for the king of Scotland to fight the Commonwealth. His possession of the Rydal sheep is dwelt upon, and he is said to declare that he will keep " the house at Rydal though it be sequestered." Through Winter, application was now made for the lease directly to the London Committee. His petition, which seems to have been drawn up by Mr. Wharton, and which was probably the one referred to in William Fleming's letter to John Banks * as sent down to him at Coniston for perusal, was presented on July 9th, 1651. In it, Winter, described as " of Penrith " desired to become tenant at £200, but had much to say besides, even against the County Committee. Rydal manor, he says, was posted up for letting in the previous November, but was not let till May, and then privately for £100 to one Walter Cowper, though he himself had

---

* No 236 of Rydal MSS as arranged by His MSS. Com

offered £200 on good security Cowper had passed his lease over to Roger Borwick, a recusant delinquent (here we stumble on young William Fleming's old servant !) who held it for his master, Sir Jordan Crosland, a dangerous delinquent,

" who keeps possession, to the terror of the well-affected, it being a strong place, and a noted rendezvous for malignants "

The late County Committee he says had previously leased it to Sir Jordan in 1650, for £2,000, but the money had never been paid. Winter, " being faithful and a sufferer for the Commonwealth, is troubled by this abuse," and begs the matter may be examined by the Cumberland Commissioners, since the Westmorland ones have connived at it ; also, that the £2,000 shall be forced from Sir Jordan, and the place handed over to himself for £200. This being handed over to them, along with an order to survey the estate, and report how many acres it contained, how much wood had been felled and to stop any more felling without order, naturally made the Westmorland Commissioners very angry ; they denied the truth of the petition, and stated that Winter himself denies having written it, whereupon the central Committee for Compounding produce Mr. Wharton, who affirms that, though he drew up and presented the petition, he had done it by Winter's instructions. In this unguarded attack on their adversary and inculpation of officials, the Skirwith claimants had probably over-reached themselves ; and this wrangle was no doubt the cause of the estate being turned over to the Treason Trustees, sitting at Drury House, who had power to sell it outright for the Commonwealth. Before the attack had been made, William Fleming had written of consultation between his " Brother " Mr. John Kirkby and Mr. Fell in London—

" at his lodgings, where they had a longe discourse about my business, and wee founde him to bee of very good hope that Ridall would yet be kept from sale "

Whereas on the following January (1651-52) John Banks writes despairingly to his young master, declaring he cannot recount the many bewildering points in the contest

" for all proceedings in theise tymes goes contrary expectacon for now it is not knowne what will be done concerning Rydale for the appeale will not be brought to any prfection and now the presse is to be brought upon the sale, but yet we hope to prevent them and to get it reported in the house wth some other estats in the like condicon."

Moreover, there are fresh troubles to report, for the Coniston squire is summoned to appear at Haberdashers Hall, with £50 to pay, which was an assessment for a forced loan, which Parliament had decided to levy on all who had not supported its side during the war.* This calamity was happily averted by a general Act of Pardon.

William Fleming was in fact in straits for money to support his claim and pay the many law expenses. His servant, John Banks, lent him money, which was not repaid, as we shall see, until much later. Michael Hobson, too, a substantial Rydal statesman lent to further a claim to which he was no doubt sympathetic, and this his son Daniel paid off eventually. He had reason therefore to dread a sale which would carry for ever out of his reach a property he still hoped he could secure on the plea of inheritance. Meanwhile, he joined with his adversaries in endeavouring, by a direct appeal to Parliament, to disassociate the manor he had already obtained possession of, from the estates still in contest,† which was the measure referred to by John Banks. Sir Jordan, meanwhile, had his hands full. He was not only claiming in a petition of February, 1652, all that John Fleming had possessed, on behalf of his wife and sister-in-law, and fighting the Skirwith family for it, but facing an engage-

---

* See *The Flemings in Oxford*, p 22 and 23
† Cal. of Com. of Compounding, quoted on p 368 of *The Flemings in Oxford*.

ment of affairs with two inheritors of estates which John Fleming had held in trust, Edward Norris and Francis Bindloss. The latter, who was son of Sir Francis, and whose grandfather Sir Robert had entrusted his various possessions to the squire of Rydal until he should be of age, filed a Chancery suit against the executors, and had been awarded £4,000, along with the rectory of Sherburn, which had been bought for him by John Fleming for £1,500, and unduly sequestrated. The parishioners of Ulverston again complained in August, 1653, that for two years their minister had been deprived of his salary of £10, which was wont to be paid by John Fleming and later by his executors out of the tithes " of great value " leased to him at £42 rent by king James*; but now, owing to the rectory being sequestrated, " for the Popery and delinquency " of Sir Jordan in 1651, the agent had for two years refused payment of the salary It is interesting to note that Sir Jordan rebutted the charge of Popery, which had been inserted in the sequestration of John Fleming's Lancashire possessions in tithe (extending over the district of Urswick), and boldly declared himself a Protestant.

He was better able, with the portions of John Fleming's daughters to help him, to fight the Rydal matter than was the family settled at Coniston. The demesne was surveyed on January 11th, 1652, with a view to its sale, the very day after, a meeting of the disputants had been held at Kendal concerning it, while another meeting followed in Ambleside on the 19th. It may have been at this last that the depositions were taken of people in the neighbourhood, of which a copy exists at Rydal Hall, under the heading of a law-suit between William Fleming Esq, on the one part, and Dame Lowther and Richard Harrison, executors of John Fleming on the other. This

---

* Dr. Magrath conjectures rightly (p. 34) that the Yorkshire property of John Fleming consisted of the tithes of Sherburn.

suit was a direct attack on a vulnerable point in the action of the executors. It was founded on the will of Dame Agnes Fleming, which had expressly stated that such household goods as were possessed by her at Rydal, along with 1,200 sheep there and a certain £40 in money, were in case of failure of her son John's male heirs, to pass to her son Daniel and his male heirs. Now no attempt had been made to carry out this provision of her will. Rather the sequestration of some 700 Rydal sheep as part of John Fleming's estate had been acquiesced in, and were compounded for by Richard Harrison, John Fleming's representative, who, nevertheless, when the sheep were demanded from him, answered they were not in his possession It was stated moreover that he and Sir Jordan, with his wife and sister-in-law, had combined against the complainant and drawn up articles of agreement as long ago as November, 1649.

This relevant charge, founded on no uncertain deeds, like the larger claim, may have been instigated by young Daniel. He now, on his father's death, 1653, claimed by inheritance, and took the front of the fight himself. He travelled to London again in February, took administration of his father's goods in May, and notes that "Rydal Differences were referd to" on July 5th. It was in this July indeed that there came the tug of war. On the previous September 6th, Daniel had, before riding north, "Given unto Mr Morgan" £1, and in the following March, when back in London, a deed was made out by which Isaac Morgan, acting indubitably for Daniel Fleming, agreed to buy Rydal manor, except the capital messuage from the trustees for the sale of forfeited lands (*see* Appendix), with other sequestered portions of land at Miller Bridge and Grayrigg by Kendal, that had belonged to John Fleming; and this sale by the Treason Trustees is confirmed in the Calendar of the Committee for Compounding, under date March 23rd, discharging the said lands from sequestration. Meanwhile, Sir Jordan was securing his hold on the hall and demesne. A voucher dated April, declares that Sir Jordan has paid to the committee at Goldsmith's Hall a part of the sum of £383 6s. "for the Capitall Mansion House called the Hall of Rydall" with a water-mill and divers plots of lands; and a document of July 31st states that he, having married Bridget, a sister and heir of William Fleming, deceased, one of the persons comprised in the act of sale dated November 15th, 1652, has made his composition for the estate of Rydal; which is accordingly freed by the Commissioners from sequestration, and he is entitled to enter into it.

The valuation of Rydal was made out as follows :—

	£	s.	d.
Hall and demesne per annum	66	4	4
The Manor with its royalties; profits of Court, fines and assessments	2	0	0
(In another statement, the value of this is set down as £24. 11s. 6d).			
Pasture in the forest	30	0	0
The whole purchase money for Rydal	937	18	4

The outlying portions, bought with the manor by Morgan, are valued —Miller Bridge, £10 15s; Hyning tenement by Kendal, £15; with hall and manor severed, how was the matter to rest? The combatants could not sit down together in peace; nor would Daniel's determined spirit brook the loss of the favourite home of the family He preferred, if all else failed, to make monetary sacrifices for it, and as a final resort, to submit to arbitration. Accordingly, his pen notes, after his arrival at Coniston from town on August 11th, 1654, a meeting held at Ambleside, on September 19th, with his adversary, another at Windermere on the 26th, with an award pronounced next day by the five arbitrators who sat in judgment. By this award the two sons-in-law of John Fleming were to resign for ever the claim of their wives on the ancestral manors to Daniel, for the sum of £1,500 paid down by him; while all lands bought by John, including Miller Bridge, Barnrigg, and Hyning, were to remain indisputably theirs. The writings were executed on the following 2nd of February, when probably Daniel paid by bond the first sum of £540 in settlement of the suit.* It was long before he could pay off this undertaking; and an acquittance exists dated 1661 signed by George Collingwood for " the sum of £570 being the one fixed by the arbitrators in 1654." The family feud must still have run high; for in the following year we find Mr. John Kirby, who lived all his mature life with his sister Alice, William Fleming's widow, at Coniston Hall, petitioning the County Committee for Lancashire for indemnity for a certain sum of £40, which he had paid the committee, but which was part of a debt of £100, due to the late John Fleming—

" for which, and the rest of the debt, the executors, Jordan Crosland and George Collingwood, have arrested and imprisoned him "

They were clearly now, having freed in January the Lancashire estates from sequestration, with a grant of arrears from December, 1649, gathering in tithes and other debts with stringency, not sparing even the gentle, scholarly bachelor of Coniston Hall.†

For the same year also (1655) there exists a summons to Richard Harrison, of " Conyston waterhead " to appear at the Court of Chancery, to answer charges against him.‡

---

* See p 10, *Flemings in Oxford*
† Cal. of Com for Compounding.
‡ Rydal Hall Papers.

DANIEL FLEMING

Anno Domini 1665
Aetatis Suae 33

PART VI.

THE GREAT SQUIRE OF RYDAL

CHAPTER I

RYDAL HOUSE

DANIEL Fleming obtained his triumph at the early age of twenty-one. It is true that he was poor, as far as ready money was concerned, that the portion of the indemnity which he at once paid was chiefly, if not all, money borrowed from his family and friends, and that the rest was a debt left for future clearance. But he had gained possession of the manors and lands of his forefathers after a struggle prolonged and almost hopeless; he had ability, determination, and self-confidence with which to carve out his life, that lay all in front of him in glowing hues of hope. For he had other causes of happiness besides his triumph, and in love as in law he was destined to win.

Already as an Oxford student he had fixed his affections. " In June 1651 " say the brief notes he made of memorable dates of his life * " in St. Maryes Church I did first see Mrs B. F. afterwards my wife." It was easy enough for him to obtain an introduction. The fair Barbara was of northern birth like himself; her father, Sir Henry Fletcher, like his, had commanded forces for the king, and had died on the battle-field of Rowton Heath six years before, September 24th, 1645. The widow had also

---

* No (342a) of the MSS, sorted by the Hist. MS Commission, and fully printed in *Flemings in Oxford*.

suffered, being imprisoned in 1645 with her children at Carlisle. She was now sojourning in Oxford, finding there many friends among the loyalists, and obtaining for her daughters what educational advantages were open to them. Young Barbara had instruction in voice and harpsicord from Edward Lowe, an organist and choirmaster deprived of his post by the Commonwealth, who fitted her out with a MS. song book and admonitions, which still has its place in the library of Rydal Hall,* where the following delightful letter is set down from the teacher to his young pupil —

Most virtuous M[ris] Barbara

I humbly beseech you to play thes Lessons in the Order sett downe Constantly once a day, if you haue health and leasure, Play not without turninge the Lesson in your Booke before you and keepe your eye (as much as you can) in your booke. If you Chance to miss, goe not from the Lesson, till you have perfected it. Aboue all, Play not too fast. Thes few rules observed you will gaine your selfe much Honnour and some Creditt to your Master, whose better title is

      Your most humble servant
25 March, 1652   Ed Lowe

Daniel was not one to let the grass grow under his feet. He squired the ladies in a journey westward in the autumn, and another northward next year, and appears not to have parted from his lady-love on this latter occasion, without presenting her with a gold ring. On leaving Oxford for home, in the summer of 1652, he found occasion to meet her brother, Sir George, at a mutual fireside, and was invited to Hutton, her ancestral home in the forest of Cumberland. Thither he naturally rode when the settlement of the estates was effected, and probably now an engagement between the young people was allowed, for he records, in his next absence in London, under December 5th, "A letter from B.F." Marriage

---

* See *Flemings in Oxford*, additional notes, p. 541.

was foremost in his resolute mind, though neither purse nor estate warranted speed. Coniston Hall was in his widowed mother's hands and rule, and she—whose spirit was as keen as his own—had three younger sons and a delicate girl to think for, with her bachelor brother, Roger Kirkby, to swell the household. Rydal, vacated now by John's daughters, whose husbands divided the furniture between them, was not only empty and dismantled, but out of repair, and its lands lying waste. Nevertheless, the young man proceeded to furnish a jointure for his bride, bought his wedding clothes in London, where he had legal business to transact in the summer of 1655, then rode northward and was married at Hutton on the 27th of August.

But before entering upon Daniel's reign as squire in Rydal, the antecedents of the house to which he brought his bride must be considered. It was the present hall, incomparably situated on rising ground by the lower fall of Rydal beck; backed by woods and facing the south, with a far outlook on the shining expanse of the great lake, while " Old Hall," the ancient lords' seat, shows from it as a solitary wooded rock in the valley below. The structure shows in its back portions signs of considerable age, and the walls are on places built of great thickness. Is it possible that two halls existed from early times, or at least from the days when two (if not more) of Sir John Lancaster's daughters shared the manor between them? * Sir John Whitfield, as has been seen, stipulated that he should have a knight's chamber in Rydal; but this seems rather to mean that he was to have lodging within the precincts of the manor court, on his hunting excursions, than that he should erect an independent seat of his own. The present hall was undoubtedly the one raided by the Parliamentary soldiers,

---

* Vinagrodoff says that two brothers sharing a manor might live each in his own Hall

and occupied by John Fleming's family; there is little doubt that it served as the dower-house, in which John's mother, Dame Agnes, lived and ruled, after the " relict " Jane had died in the crumbling pile below. Evidence goes no further back than this time; but between the date of Agnes's marriage with Squire William, and William's death, there are deeds (or records of them) that may possibly throw light on the subject. By a deed of 1575, of which unfortunately only a corrupt copy exists, William made a marriage settlement of the manor on Agnes; and the buildings of the manor are therein described as lying on and about St. John How,* with meadows and closes adjacent to the Rothay. A beautifully executed deed of the same year leases to one John Grigg the corn-mill of Rydal, and all " the orchards and meadows adjoining the Old Hall," and all the fishing of the waters, for the sum of £6. 13s. 4d. (or ten marks) the year, to be paid to Squire William " at his now dwellinge howse in Conyston."

Now this John Grigg must have been the most substantial man in Rydal. He executed another deed with Squire William on March 10th the following year, 1576, of which we have only Sir Daniel's epitome, in his " List of Rydall Writings."

" John Grigg of Rydall his Grant unto William Fleming of Rydall esq of his Tenement in Rydall of 22s Rent per ann; upon condition to performe Covenants."

The church register records, however, the burial of "John Grige of Rydall" on July 25th of this year, and of his wife Agnes five days later, which suggests the presence of contagious disease. Another deed, dated 1592, is described by Sir Daniel thus :—

---

* It further describes the mansion-house, both as being now in the occupation of Mrs Fleming, and as being called the New Hall; but this can only be a mistake of the copyist (to whom the old English capitals were strange) for Low Hall, it being situated in the Low Park, adjacent to Low Park How.

"Arthur Grigg of Darby Shearman his Grant unto William Fleming of Rydall esq. (in consideration of 5^{lb} 10^s) of his Tenem^t in Rydall of ye yearly Rent of 22^s, late in ye possession of John Grigg deceased, and of his close in Loughrigg adjoyning to ye watterhead of Rydall late in ye holding of Richard Hanckrigg deceased and now in the possession of Jo Hanckrigg his son, being of ye inheritance of Edward Benson son of Michael Benson deceased and of ye yearly Rent of 2^s"

The squire of Rydal therefore obtained possession from a relative of John Grigg's who was in the woollen trade (probably a son who had migrated to wider fields of commerce) of a large dalesman's holding in his manor. That it was of unusual size is shown by its lord's rent of 22s., for no other rent in the village was nearly so high; and this tenement was procured by the lord who killed off the deer in Rydal, and turned it from park-land to farm, and who would therefore want good quarters for his farm bailiff. Where indeed did John Grigg's house stand? Could it have been the nucleus of the present hall, altered and added to, until it was sufficient to serve Dame Agnes as a dower-house, when she retired to Rydal in 1600? It is impossible to know what it was in 1592, but if it stood where the hall stands, its connection with the village would be much more apparent then than now, for its position was at the top of the village and open to the street, and so it remained to Sir Michael's time, the plan of 1770 shows this. And that there were other village houses below it, within the present park wall between the street and the beck, as well as the corn-mill, is known. But whether Grigg's large tenement was used as a starting point for a new Hall or not, we can follow by the pages of the great account book the improvements that Daniel made to the present hall, which was, by the way, called Rydal House in the seventeenth century, and from these we may judge something of its status in John's time. The position is not a defensible one, nor was there ever here a pile such as the Westmorland border and the shores of Morecambe bristled with. The style of the wooden pile with an outer fosse and stockade of Edward I's time had been succeeded on most demesnes by the strong stone tower, and we find, in the reign of Edward II. onwards, many licences for the lords to "crenellate" their dwellings

It was from these dwellings that the Roundheads called the Westmorland gentry "Castellans."

These towers with their four floors, the vault, the living room above, reached often by an outside stair, the chamber yet above, and then the battlements, whence arrows could fly far against the approaching enemy, were designed for residence as well as defence. They were compact and self-contained. The cattle could, in case the outer defences of the court were scaled, be driven into the vault, while the lord, with his family and servants, kept the upper rooms, whose narrow lights pierced walls of immense thickness. How great was the need for these defensible dwellings may be gathered from the national Rolls, which show the Westmorland gentry not only to have been engaged for centuries with Border warfare, during the weak government of Richard II and Henry IV., but with the most savage feuds among themselves. The site of many an unsuspected tower may be found by poking about the low homestead or outhouses of a quiet farm, as at Selside, once the seat of the turbulent Thornburghs, or Hugill Hall.

The best example left of the earlier tower proper is perhaps Dacre Castle, whose lords played so important a part in early county history.

The towers that remained seats of the gentry through the Tudor period were gradually modified. A great living room, or "house" was built alongside the tower, as at Yanwath, with oak timbered roof; chambers spread around the court. Later still, ambitious builders and renovators aimed at symmetry, and added stories to the house, till it became a solid block with wings (the tower being often truncated and disguised, as at Howgill), or it assumed an E or H shape. Happily, drastic measures were not always taken, and the gradual growth of Sizergh Castle, and the beauty of Levens Hall yet remain to us as examples of the changes in style that the centuries brought Some halls of later times there were, that seem never to have been defensible. Such was pastoral Calgarth, the home of the Philipsons, men, till the Civil war, of peace and legality, who built for homely uses and for comfort The bit of stained glass that remains in the house place bears the same date that is said to have shown in the new erected hall of William Fleming at Coniston. The Elizabethan era of peace indeed saw the northern gentry expanding into comfort and a certain amount of splendour, while greater exclusiveness attended the luxury they affected. The house-place with its long table and benches no longer served as the eating-place of the whole household, and general living room. An upper chamber, wainscoted and ornamented with plasterwork, was built for the entertainment of guests and used on occasions of state. In the smaller " parlour " downstairs the meals of the family were often taken, since we find small linen tablecloths were bought for it at Rydal. It would serve as the resort of the ladies of the family, while a lord's study became indispensable, even for non-reading squires.

These rooms are all mentioned in the account book, which shows that they were renovated if not actually added by Daniel. But that there was valuable wainscotting in the house before his time is shown by the dispute over it. And an entry of March 4th, 1657, before any radical improvements were begun, proves that this special room was in use.

	£	s	d.
Paid for ye mending of an Andiron which was melted in ye wanscott chamber	00	00.	02

Wainscoting was highly esteemed as decoration by the northern gentry, who seem to have hung very little tapestry over their walls; and that it reached a high artistic level in Westmorland can be seen from the specimen removed from Sizergh to the South Kensington Museum. It figures as an exceedingly heavy item in the costs of building. Stone and wood for essentials were found on the demesne, as well as masons and carpenters, but the wainscot was made by skilled craftsmen, called joiners (an unusual word then) who were not to be found in villages. The Rydal new wainscot came from Kendal, as did that probably of all the Westmorland Halls, and its cost soon apprizes us of the additions the young squire began to make as soon as purse would permit.* Briefly, he seems to have thrown up a room over " ye Hall," called the Hall loft, which was wainscoted; (1657); then to have made a parlour (1658); next to have raised a room above the kitchen, called the kitchen loft, and to have excavated another under " Mr Ambrose's Chamber," which apparently looked to the rising ground behind (1659), to have " flowered " the stair head (1660); to have made a study or closet, and lastly to have dignified the approach by levelling, paving, and enclosing.

It is clear then, though there is no description of it, that rich John Fleming had been content with a simple house at Rydal. Perhaps the stately and symmetrical hall, built by his father at Coniston, with projecting ends and a fine upper guest-chamber stretching between the two, sufficed his pride, and he retired to homely Rydal to die, showing therein the strong predilection of his race. And that his successor in adding rooms above the old

---

* A prudent rector of Buckinghamshire, re-furnishing in 1659, thinks that " 6 pieces of hangings, if met with accidentally at the second hand, might all things considered be easyest had to furnish up the roome," but later he declares " I would gladly bestow a matter of 8^{lb} in Wainscot for my parlour rather than go to a much higher price for Hangings, and then I should like very well this painted lether for a suit of chaires and stooles, and Carpet too for it "—*Verney Memoirs*, vol III, p 401.

ones, aimed at copying, if not equalling, the more imposing frontage of the Lancashire Hall he had left to his mother, may be guessed by comparison of the two as limned by Crosthwaite in his maps of 1788, where indeed Rydal tops the other by a set of dormer windows in the roof. It is unfortunate that the pictures of the hall and surroundings that Daniel caused to be made in 1652 are not, as far as is known, extant. His account book has —

"Given unto Mr Samuel Moore (Mr Adams his
    Artist) who did take the Prospect of Rydal Hall
    and Garden (out of ye Round Close) of ye Grotto
    (out of ye Little House) and of ye Vale from
    Rydal Hall to Windermere-water out of ye best
    Chamber window (Nov 20, 21, & 22) the sum of £01 00 00.

Possibly Mr. Moore was exploiting a subscription work on the seats of the gentry, which may never have appeared, and the only print that pictures the place before Sir Michael put yet another frontage on it, is Crosthwaite's. But the estate map drawn in 1770 gives us a very good notion of the curious back-premises, and explains what would have been otherwise inexplicable in Daniel's improvements. The house consisted of two parallel blocks of building, the back one devoted to domestic offices (and possibly the original homestead), and the front to the more stately rooms, which may have been built in Dame Agnes's time. The two were united by a short cross block, which gave to the whole the form of the letter H. This was the form of Bleaze Hall, and, in a measure, of Middleton Hall,* neither of which places show remains of the old tower-structure, usually found on early defensible sites. The entrance lay in this cross-piece, and may originally have been an open paved passage or *hallan* between the fore and back courts, such as exists at Kentmere; or it may have entered directly into a house-place or hall. Its height necessitated from the village a

---

* See Taylor's *Old Manorial Halls*

flight of steps. Certainly it was this approach that was improved by blasting and paving, and across which a curtain wall was thrown to enclose the court, pierced by gates that were reached by an outer flight of steps. The present front door probably stands where these old entrance gates stood, the intermediate court-space having been built over, and it is difficult now, in the trim seclusion of the enclosed and gradually rising drive, bordered by shrubberies, to reconstruct the former open wild approach, beset by those hummocks of rock that once surrounded all the homesteads of Rydal, and may still be seen at Undermount.* The approach to the other court-yard across the wide park was more level, and crossed the beck as now by Causey bridge, amid a group of clustering houses.

The mill-race left the beck not far above the bridge and ran along the edge of a little garden that abutted on the front block of buildings to the east, and pursued its course through the orchard planted by Daniel, till it reached the mill, that stood in front but considerably below the Hall.† Along this south front there stretched after his time, if not before, a walled garden for flowers and herbs, with a stately, stepped approach as at Calgarth, while another garden lay across the low road (walled at this epoch) in 1770 which gave the villagers access to the mill, and led round the house to the bridge and the park road.

Such was the form of Rydal Hall as Sir Daniel left it. When he entered it with his bride it must have been not only a homely place, but, after its varied fortunes of pillage, temporary occupation and desertion, absolutely dilapidated. Daniel did indeed at first attempt little more than to keep out wind and weather. He notes :—

---

* Rock was blasted for the new stables and the school house.

† An oak that, according to tradition, marked its site has been cut down, March, 1904.

" Left Coniston Apr. 27 1656, when wee began to keep house at Rydal. May 6 Rydal glazed July 28, Rydal plastered "

The young couple visited among their friends between April and August, till house and furniture should be ready for them The Countess of Pembroke put them up for a night, and gave them " a silver salt wch is not used." They took turns, between other visits, at the Coniston home, whence on October 2nd, the bride was taken to see her future home at Rydal, but longer ones at Hutton, where indeed they spent the mid-winter Perhaps it was to make presents on these bridal journeys that the following supplementary dress order was given, in the accustomed manner, through a relative Hugh Anderton wrote from Ewelton that his brother (in-law) Kirkby (probably John, who seems to have been often there) had left London before Daniel's request reached him He therefore has himself done the best he could, and forwarded the articles desired in a box with the bill. This last runs :—

	£	s	d
" A paire of perfumed trimmed gloves	00	18	00
Two paire of lesser trimmed gloves	00	10	00.
A paire of Cordevant gloves with a black fringe	00	08	00
Two suits of knotts	00	15	00.
A laced scarfe &c	01	16	00.

It was usual at this period to give gloves to superior servants as a present. Sir Ralph Verney rewards a certain good " Bette " with a pair of trimmed gloves at £1 5s. and Lady Verney gives to another maid " a pare of gloves trimed." *

There were many things to be thought of and arranged for this winter, besides smart trappings. The young squire, mindful no doubt of interest, was already in October preparing to pay the £600 to John's sons-in-law, which was not due till Candlemas. He was engaged in

---

* See *Verney Memoirs*.

a petty squabble with them about the wainscot of certain rooms at Rydal, and the brewing lead, which he judged to be fixtures and they furniture; and the matter had to be settled by arbitration. Mr. George Collingwood, the husband of Anne Fleming, and the writer of a calm letter, complains that his man has been refused a view of the wainscot, or to take away the press with drawers, which had fallen to his share in the division with Sir Jordan Crosland. Moreover, Daniel's mother refused to let his man meddle with the things at Coniston which are theirs. To this Daniel answers that Richard Harrison had said that the press was to be a gift from Collingwood to his mother; adding that Bowes is so far (over Stainmoor) to send the money, that for the next payment he would wish another place appointed Collingwood obligingly sends over a man to receive this pre-dated payment, but denies that the press was a gift.

Meanwhile honest John Banks, who in feudal fashion had passed from the service of Daniel's father to his own, was busy making things ready in frugal country style for the young couple at the empty house of Rydal. He writes :—

" the parloure table is in all 4 yards and 7 Inches but three qu'tors off it drawes out at one end wch is but seldome drawne unlesse there be much Companie And it wants but two Inches off a yard broad "

Roger, Daniel's brother next in age to himself, was empowered to buy the most necessary article, viz.. a bed, in London. The Coniston parents, who had made the most strenuous efforts for their eldest son, had nothing to spare for the education of their younger children after they had gone through the customary course at Kendal school. Roger, therefore, had been apprenticed by the time he was eighteen to the woollen trade, with a Mr. Lancashire, Manchester, and later he had proceeded to London. William remained at home, probably farming the estate under his mother John, next in age, after apprenticeship in London, took to the sea and was lost. Alexander, the youngest, was also apprenticed in London, and eventually settled as a merchant in Newcastle.

Roger's early letters show him to have been a most loyal admirer of his elder brother, and he was now delighted to do his behests, with the aid of mature female relatives ; and his account of the purchase of the bed, and his own embarrassments when his " Ant " drove up in a " choch " to bear him off from the wool market is too good not to be given in full.

Rydal Hall MSS His MS Com 289   1655-6
(To D F. at Hutton)
In London this 12th March 1655
Kind Brother

I rec^d yours of the 5th Instant, I wrott by my last whatt a good Companie wee wear that went to help to buy your bed, your Ant would ath^{er} have Cosen Lamplue and I to goe with her or else she would not goe ; the first bed thatt wee lookt att did please the best wee went all up and downe untill night but could find non that pleast soe well as the first, I went backe to Queen st ; whear the bed was that all peacht upon to have given him ernest ffor it, but he was gon fforth ; your Ant promised to goe her Selfe in the morninge that was wednesday and agree with him for it ; and then See it taken doune and Boxt up and Soe Sent to mee and then I should pay him for it, on wednesday I was from home all day or else I would have waited on her ; When I came home I rec^{ed} a letter from your Ant which desired thatt I should goe to her on Thursday. I sent her word I could not goe y^t day because I could not leave my Markett, it was all the markett y^t wee have in a weeke, but if she please I would wait on her in the morninge this did not please her butt in the afternoune she came in a choch to Blackwell hall about ffoure acloke the market was all most over, She then would have mee wth her, all Excuses Sett asid to joumar her I went wth her ; I was never So ashamed in my life, She came into the hall, I was very Durtie wth opening Packes and very hott wth showing sume cloth to Marc (cut off) yett for all this to please her I went wth her ; and gott the bed Boxt up and Stules brought a Longe wth mee to the In, whear Kendall carrier Lies   I paid for the bed and gave your Ant whatt she deminded for what Charges she had been abut the buying of The bed

          Your loveinge brother to Command

                    Roger Fleminge."

Details of carriers, &c., follow. Then writer regrets that the bed-ticks he was commissioned to buy were not of the width stated by the seller. Wishes D. F. had not had them cut, or they should have been returned, as his correspondent in Manchester advises. Is very sorry to have been so " Cosened " over the first business his brother entrusted him with, will take any trouble he can.

The writer had already bought bed-ticking for his brother, which had proved to be not the width stated, and expresses his annoyance that he had been so " Cosened." John Banks gives news of the same, from Coniston, where they were doubtless made up.

" And ffor the ffether bed tickes the are heare and will be sent the next week ffor yor mother will send a horse wth them "

But this letter of John's shows that he is dealing with momentous matters on behalf of his master. It is dated February 11th, a time when ploughing ought to commence on the neglected demesne.

" Honoured Sir, I praise god I got saffe to Rydale wth the oxen on Saturday at night where I was fforced to staye all night it was soe late,"

and he then proceeds to tell of the extraordinary scene enacted in Grasmere Church next day.* Oats he finds are to be bought cheap in the Ulverston market, and the plough (for driving of which a boy is still wanted) can not be put out till March 1st.† He is also selling wool, and extracting fines from such tenants as are not refractory ; but Beckermet men are declaring they will not pay without a Court, and the Coniston men demand one too.

---

* See *Church of Grasmere*, p 87
† 283 His MS Com.

Money was of the first import to Daniel, who, like his father, had borrowed money to support his claim and obtain possession of the family manors, and perhaps it was the stress for it he endured earlier and at this time that turned the bent of his mind to a frugality that increased with time painfully. A chiding letter from his mother betrays her annoyance with him once ; and though he took care to pay his adversaries regularly, he held other moneys back ; thus, this February Roger writes deprecatingly to him on the subject of the portion due to him from his father's will. He has already asked for it, and Daniel had retorted, with angry reproaches, that he wonders Roger could ask for it before it is due, when he knows he has so much occasion for it, in his payments to Sir Jordan Crosland   but Roger now mildly protests that it was due in December last, when he was of age, and that though he has good use for it now, he will nevertheless leave it with his brother. Only, will Daniel pay him interest ?   £200 of the portion was paid in February, 1660, " besides £20 paid Jan. 58," £50 more on March 27th, and the remaining £30 of the £300 on April 10th. No entry of interest occurs.

In April, 1661, Roger writes desiring to know what his brother Daniel and their mother intend to do about Alexander, the youngest. He has now been with himself a long time on trial, and naturally cannot be bound apprentice without money. Mr. Smith will not consent to wait for the money ; nor indeed is it to Alexander's credit to ask for time

" It is very strange y^t he should be sent up wth mee, and you in y^r Countrie takes noe more care of him , I sent by Mr Hen . Lowther my sisters petticoat and her silver Boxe."

The apprenticeship to a silk merchant would seem to have been accomplished shortly after for £80, and in 1665 we find Alexander executing a good many comm-missions for his brother, though his "master" he says cuts no stuffs or silks. He is evidently shaping well to the business, which carries him into Yorkshire, and is thinking of independent trade. So in July, after telling of the books he had purchased (having previously been unable to find the desired ones in red turkey leather " in all Paul Curch Yeard ") he proceeds :—

" now Kinde Brother I hope you are nott Ignorant that I am now come to age and that upon the firste of Aprill last past, Therefore my Desire is that what My Father was pleased to Leaue mee, you would gett ready For me against December next,"

or even before, he goes on if it be convenient, as he has an opportunity of "advancing himself by it, not to be missed." In April of next year Alexander reiterates a request for £50 by May 8th, and begs earnestly for it, as he and a partner have bought a bail of silk, price £200. The next letter is yet more urgent. The £200 was by agreement to be paid in four instalments, and his friend had put down his initial £50 at once, which makes Alexander very sore over his own excuses at non-payment. By June 5th, he frantically begs a letter " by next post , " and only on the 11th writes more calmly, having received the money; which, his brother noted in the letter, he had sent " at the end of May." Roger, in spite of his passage of arms, proceeded to do law business and furnishing for the bridegroom. A " fringe " goes with the bed ; and after the young couple are installed in Rydal House, he writes :—

" I have bought a boxe of glasses I fear I have Exceeded order but I hope they will please my sister when she ses them they will compleatly furnish a cubbarts head, I could not accordinge to your order have wared (= spent) twentie shillings in glasses thatt you could give mee better thankes for my pains ; I hope they will (be) of use and credett your ladie beinge as I heare very great "

"An acct of moneys Laid out ffor my Brother Fleminge, R F.

	£	s	d
payd ffor post letters and diurnalls (journals) ..	00.	07.	00
payd ffor a boxe of glasses . ..	01	19	04.
payd ffor a Booke . .	00	07	00.
payd ffor Fringe	00	02	09.
payd ffor 3 q{ers} of Silke .	00	07	06.
payd ffor thinges Bought by yor Ant as apeares by the notes	12	10.	00
payd ffor Chochinge (coaching) and spent yt day	00	03	00
payd ffor a dozen silver spounes	06.	11	02.
payd ffor two dozen and halfe of Glase bottles and caringe from ye Glase house . ..	00	13.	06.
payd ffor cuttinge a stampe for the bottles ..	00	03.	00.
payd ffor winne and a hamper to put the bottles In and Potterarge	02.	15.	10.
	26	00	01.

To which bill Daniel adds :—

Disbursed since for my wives Coat and p{d} ye Taylor as appears by his letter . . 07. 10 00.

The "Morninges Cote" Roger explains by letter, has exceeded the order, being 7s. 6d a yard, and taking 12 yards. His sister Isobel's coat cost £3, which was covered by £4 given by the mother to Daniel. Roger is delighted to hear of the birth of an heir and that the box came in such good time · and is only sorry that the wine "comes short."

Among the first necessities for housekeeping then, after table, bed and spoons had been provided, was clearly a brave display of glass, and wine to drink out of it. With a christening imminent, the laws of hospitality had to be observed, even though the young wife waited for her looking-glass till the following year, when one was procured from Penrith, at a cost of 9s. 6d , with 6d. carriage Local carpenters, on day wages, were soon set to work on needful repairs and structural alterations The bills of Richard Nicholson of Rydal show how busy he was through the summer of 1656, not only in quickly knocking up accommodation for cattle and horses, but in "helping to make the great new bed," (was this the London purchase?) in constructing one for the nurse, (at a total wage-cost of 1s. 6d.!) making new windows, mending the stairs and the parlour table, (clearly a second-hand one), making tables for Mrs Fleming's chamber and the larder and much else; while in succeeding years, as the family increases, he makes beds, "trukel" and others, tables, chairs, picture frames, presses, and the endless implements needed in house and farm, as well as the bier for poor young mistress Isabel, at almost a nominal expense.

In the first year too, he fells trees for the planks for the floors, and in December, one William Benson is paid £1. 12s. for sawing boards and planks, (at the rate of 15s. the rood in wages). This was probably put down in the new state apartment, the wainscots of which form the first heavy items in the expenses of the following year.

	£.	s	d.
June 20, '57. Paid unto Jackson (yᵉ Joyner) in part for yᵉ wainscotting of yᵉ Roome over yᵉ Hall	01.	00.	00.

and the remaining payments (amounting to £1. 2s. 6d. are finished in November.

The freestone mantel of the parlour (next in construction) was also costly.

	£.	s	d.
Jan. 23, '58 more paid by my wife for bringing yᵉ stones for yᵉ Parler chimney up Windermeer-water	00.	04	00.
more paid by her unto yᵉ man upon whose ground they lay upon at yᵉ water-foot .. .	00	01.	06.
July 14. Paid unto Robert ( ) mason in Cartmel for yᵉ free-stone chimney i' th' Parlour, and for setting it up	01.	00	00.

Both Nicholson and Benson (with his man) are thirteen days at work on the parlour woodwork.

Meanwhile two rugs are dyed at Kendal, one yellow,

at a cost of 4s. 6d., another red, 10s , being 34lb. weight, and five yards of "greene stuffe" is dyed. "Six red skins for cushions" are procured for 5s. 9d., with three dozen of leather buttons 3d , and thread 2s. 6d. These doubtless lined the seats in the state room. Chafing dishes were bought at Cockermouth for 4s. 6d.

The webster is busy at work, as payments show, and much "harden" (coarse linen) is bleached

Daniel by this time was launching into more wholesale ways of buying wine. Content at first to send his manservant in to Mackereth of Ambleside for a small quantity of sack (1s. 8d. a quart) and claret, he later tried London. Now he impressed a relative, George Crowle, a merchant with Holland, who had married his cousin Eleanor Kirkby, into his commission service Crowle was clearly a substantial man, and had received £1000 portion in 1651 with his wife. He resided at Kingston-upon-Hull, and in 1657 Daniel, on a journey he made into Yorkshire, was entertained by him, and (though not staying in the house) gave 10s. in gratuities to his servant In 1658 Crowle writes that he is willing to " fitt " his Rydal relative with wines and Holland cheeses, which can be sent by Elizabeth Williamson, the Kendal carrier. In this and following years therefore his bills are extant for " dainty malligo " (malaga) or runlets of sack varying from six to twelve gallons, at a cost of 5s. 6d. per gallon in 1658, and next year at 4s. 6d. In 1663 a runlet of sack is purchased at 4s. 4d., and " white " at Christmas at 1s. 8d., but this comes from Newcastle. The carriage of a large runlet is 10s. 4d. Spanish wines, being prohibited, keep high, we hear in 1659. Two cheeses at 5d. per lb come to 5s. 4d. Crowle appears to have been in partnership for large ventures with two of his Kirkby brothers-in-law. In 1659 Christopher Kirkby wrote on a receipt Crowle sent :—

" Our shipps are this Day Returned from Hamburgh Bringing Welcome Newes of Brother Williams Welfare "

It seems to have been the fashion to procure cabinets from abroad. Sir Ralph Verney, who in exile does any number of commissions for his friends at home, writes from Brussels in 1652:—

"My Lady Lisle desires an Ebony Cabanet, and for Dores or none, she leaves it to me . . . . I cannot meete with an Ebony Cabanet thats good, I can have choice of Tortus Shell, garnished out with very thin silver or guilt Brasse which I like much better ; . . . . the best choyce is at Antwerp." [*]

In a similar manner Brother William at the Hamburg end is utilized. He buys there a cabinet for Rydal Hall which Christopher, on acknowledging the receipt of £4. 4s. 6d. paid for it, remarks had cost £4 in Hamburgh, while the remaining 4s. 6d. is for carriage across country. The brothers then must have shipped it free, besides giving their trouble. It was usual indeed for friends to execute commissions, but the profit made in transactions with Daniel, even by tradesmen, as in the case of the clockmaker (p. 588), is often difficult to make out. Roger too is still busy over London commissions, sending even such small things as needles (1s. 3d. a hundred) and garden seeds 7s. Two "leather table Carpetts" from there cost £1. 10s. Next year (1660) 72 yards of matting is procured, through Mrs Fleming's mother. Lady Fletcher by this time had left Hutton to her son, she herself having married Dr. Thomas Smith, her son's and Daniel's Oxford tutor, and had set up house at Cockermouth ; and it is curious to find him writing to Rydal on trivial and domestic subjects with polish and wit. 1661. June 27th :—

"Next, my most humble thanks to yor good Lady for the cheese, though I must say it againe (and stande to it) that the Newes I sent her was richly worth it. Pray tell her from mee, that before this be eaten I doubt not but to have some further intelligence got from Portugall, and therefore shee may do well to have the other cheese in a readinesse."

---

[*] *Verney Memoirs*, vol III., p. 50.

This refers to the exciting matter of the king's marriage.

Subsequently Smith became Dean and afterwards Bishop of Carlisle. It is this reverend gentleman, therefore, who announces that the matting has arrived from Newcastle, where it was chosen by two persons, and is now forwarded; it has cost £1. 4s., with carriage 5s. Half a pound of anchovies, the best to be had at Newcastle, go with it. To Rydal from Newcastle, via Cockermouth! But Cockermouth begins to figure as a trading place for the Rothay and Brathay valleys about this time, the route being probably over the Wrynose Pass.

At Cockermouth Mr Henry Lowther, son of Richard of Ingleton, of a younger branch of the Lowthers of Lowther,* appears to have settled as merchant. The account book shows that on July, 1658, when staying there, Daniel lent him £5, to be repaid on demand. This must have been a trading venture, for in August, 1661, Henry writes to Rydal that his " cousin " Daniel's " butts and silke be come " and that he has about 200 yards of cloth standing there at Cockermouth. Besides this, his servant has arrived from Yorkshire, and says the rest of the cloth will be in Kendal on Wednesday next: therefore David Harrison (the Rydal carrier) and John Banks had better be at Kendal then with two horses. This Yorkshire cloth was probably imported to Cockermouth; while the butts of wine and silk, which Henry proposes to bring to Rydal himself, were doubtless landed at that place and intended either for private use or trade in Kendal. As this is the last we hear of it, Daniel may have found trading by deputy not a success.

Daniel probably felt by this time he could well afford to put on a good appearance. His building operations had never ceased, and he was getting well forward with the essentials that make for prosperity. He had been busy through the summer of 1659 and on into 1660 with

---

* See *Flemings in Oxford*, p. 395.

the great barn in the Low Park * as well as with extensive repairs at the mill, which required not only new woodwork, but new stones. The "glasner" had been working in larder, kitchen and best chamber, and Greene of Grasmere had been up in the roof "mossing," or plugging with moss as the custom was, all the chinks and crannies of the small, rough slates then in use. A Rydal man had been paid in 1659, 1s. for three days' "paveing and guttering of ye Roome under Mr Ambroses Chamber." It was a thrifty measure indeed to make the parson of Grasmere comfortable, for he no doubt paid for his quarters at the Hall.

There was, naturally, a good deal of intercourse between the Ambroses and the Flemings. William, the bachelor squire of Lowick, writes to Daniel on law business in January of 1662, saying he can keep the papers

"till I shall have the happiness to see you wth y^r sweet Lady, wch will not be before the Gowk (cuckoo) crye"

By 1662 Daniel was well enough off to indulge with his wife in a jaunt to London. There was indeed the sad excuse of little Will's health, the heir, who was now six years old, and who had, at two years old, met with some accident that left him lame for life. Local aid of all sorts, as well as county surgeons had been tried without real benefit; and now the skill of a London doctor was invoked But poor Will's crutches remain a recurring item in the account book till his manhood, and it is possible that amputation was finally resorted to.

Mrs Fleming too required a doctor in this stay which lasted from Easter to June, but she had the satisfaction of having with her her two sisters Mistresses Bridget and Anne Fletcher, who must have made the party much more lively, as well as less costly for the Rydal section of it Bridget chooses for her married sister 12 yards of

---

* See Fisheries and Agriculture

"Flowered Tabby," which figures in the careful husband's accounts at £10, as well as 2½ yards of white satteen for her "wastcoat" £1. 13s, 6d. Two "bands" for himself, then coming into fashion cost 7s 6d., a "Tortose-Toothpicker" 6d., a velvet cap 13s. He changes the silver buckles of his old belt for the price of "Hughes Grand Abridgmt," 25s., and for a new sword belt 12s. He buys besides a number of books, a case of pistols 10s., and shoes 5s. A velvet cap cost him 13s., while a velvet "Mountero" for Dr Smith—perhaps a present—was £1. 7s. He procures two chimney-pieces for his house, which with "boxing up" for the pack-horse came to £2. A "Limner" takes his and his wife's portraits for £5. Many sundries show the jaunts that were taken, both by coach and by boat; to "Tradascenti," the Tradescant collection of curiosities that were the nucleus of the Ashmolean Museum at Oxford, to the Houses of Parliament, to the cock-pit (for the Rydal squire enjoyed this sport) and to Hampton Court, where cherries are bought, and 12s spent. Coaching was a necessary expense, for the streets of London were at that time so deep in mud that no genteel person thought of walking in them. The two coaches, however, for which 3s. 2d. was paid on June 20th, no doubt conveyed the Rydal party to the great inn in Aldersgate Street, whence the northern coaches ran. The return journey, after four weeks in London at an expense of £14. 6s. for lodgings in the Strand, was made by Chester, whither (as well as to York) a coach now regularly ran. Four pounds were paid for four full seats, and 10s. for little Will. The booking-clerk had 1s., and the coachman at the end of the long drive (solaced by "blackberries") was tipped at Chester 2s.

Mr. Harper (C. G.) states that a regular stage coach from London to Chester was established in 1657. Coaches both public and private were largely on the increase.

"If you have not better Conveniency, here are choice of Coaches now, for the South hampton Coachman hath sett up another one wth 6 horses, by Hoburn bridge, at the Rose or King's Armes . . . . there is another sett up lately in Winchester " *

On his return, Daniel proceeded with the improvements at Rydal, and arranged for the wainscoting of a new upper room.

                £ s d.

" July 25. Paid unto Christopher Robinson, being in p^t for wainscotting of ye Kitchen Loft (after ye rate of 3^s p^r yard for all ye wainscott and doores mitred and sifered, and 4^d per yard for ye crest, wee to fetch itt from Kendall, and hee to sett itt up betwixt this and Michaelmas next ye sum of .. .. 00. 05. 00.

The contract is completed on September 26th, when Christopher receives £10. 5s.; and 4 pairs of "asses" 3s. 4d., nails 6d., and snecks, etc. 3s. for " ye Kitchen loft " are accounted for. In the autumn the paving of the Court— no doubt with the rounded stones of the beck, as was usual—occupied 27 days, at 6d. the day. Then on October 7th :—

                £. s. d.

" Given to ye Wallers of Ambleside to drink for breaking of ye great Rock in ye way up to ye gates .. .. 00. 02 6.

Twenty-five days labour at " Plaistering of ye Kitchin and walling ye wall without ye court-gate " cost 12s. 6d., and the " glasener " is paid 4s. 6d. for " ye window in ye Court." The " colouring of ye Gates " two years later actually cost 10s.

In 1663 the new stables occupied Daniel's energy. Stones were got for it by Ambleside men at 4d. per day; and the builders received £1. 5s. For " paveing and breaking ye cragg in ye best Stable " 4d. a day was paid, 2s. 8d.

---

* *Verney Memoirs*, Feb 26th, 1655. An " old chariot " appears in an inventory of Goods at Skipton Castle in 1572 —Whitaker's *Hist of Craven*

Besides this, Daniel indulged in a "wainscott seat" in the church from Christopher Robinson, at the cost of £3 6s. 6d.

"Ye Joyner there" (at Kendal) had supplied a "new Cradle," doubtless a panelled one, in 1657. A chair was procured from the joiner; a wainscot chest in 1667 for 10s., the lock and gimmers costing 2s. 3d., while next year Christopher supplied a table with drawers and four chairs for 24s.

A screen of apparently very large size was brought in 1665 from Yanwath, the home of Daniel's Aunt Dudley, who now as a widow was struggling with the confusion of affairs and poverty left behind by her husband Christopher, the last of his race. It was probably placed in the hall. The carpenter brought it for 6d., and put it up in two days 1s.; ten "leaves" for it cost at Kendal 11s., and "27 pair of Dove-tayle Gimers" or hinges 3s. 6d.

In 1665 Daniel likewise began to adorn his rooms with the only pictures then thought necessary, family portaits. His and his wife's portraits had already been painted in London at £2. 10s. They are at Rydal now.

"October 30 Paid unto Mr Braken for drawing of my Cosin Ambrose, my Mother's, and my owne Pictures, 6^{lb}, and for Sr George's 1^{lb} 10^s, in all .. .. £07. 10. 00.

On April 20th, 1667, six picture frames were bought at Kendal for 13s., and on the 27th Daniel enters.—

"Paid unto Mr Braken for drawing of my Lady Fletchers Picture 1^{lb} 10^s, my wife's 2^{lb} 10^s, Dr Smiths 1^{lb} 15^s, for Bosses and carryage hither, 5^s, for Gold to ye Frames 17^s 6^d, and for Gilding of them 17^s 6^d in all, (ye rest of ye Pictures being paid for Oct. 30, '65) ye sum of (vid his Acquittance) .. .. £07 10 00.

This does not include the "bosses and carryage hither 5s" mentioned above.

But it appears that then the work of gilding the picture frames was left to the artist.

The approach to the house was finished in the autumn of 1665, when two men were paid 3s. 4d. " for getting and setting of Ashes in ye hall banck, & for guttering thereof," at 4d. per day.

Next year, 1665, " houses of office " are built ; and it was said that the Rydal squire was the first in the countryside who provided for the cleanliness of the surroundings of the house. The walling of gardens proceeds, " ye Garding-Side o' th' House " is rough-cast (" ye back side of Rydall house " waits for its plaster three years longer). The mill-orchard is walled, and beyond the beck a high orchard wall is built. In 1668 the little house that still stands by the side of the Lower Fall was begun. It cost Daniel, who speaks of it variously as " ye Sumer house at ye Cawweel," " ye Grothouse," and " ye Grot in ye Mill-Orchard," a considerable sum for walling and odd work, about 16s. slating, to Green of Grasmere, who charged 3s. for twelve loads of slate, and took four days over it, 5s., for " glassing of ye Grott to Christopher Parker " 15s.; for " Slatts " 2s.; and finally to " ye Kendall Joyner for wainscotting of my Grott-House " £3. Next, five men were employed for sixteen days in " walling and makeing of walkes, and ye water-Race, &c. in ye Mill-orchard, and ye walk before ye gates " at an expense of £1. 10s., and three Grasmere " wrights were at work " making and mending the gates seven days. " Setting of Plane and Quince trees in ye Grot orchard (October 1669) cost 3s. 10d., and next March is noted " Given ye 16th instant unto ye grooms at Holker (Mr Thomas Preston's house) for getting some slips of Mulberrie trees 00. 01. 00." while his cousin Wilson's man likewise received 1s. 6d. for " bringing trees " to Rydal.

Altogether the house at Rydal was getting trim within and without. Two leather carpets, procured from London for " ye Parler " cost £1. 13s. Trimmed hangings had already been got for Mrs. Fleming's bed, as in 1659 she had paid the Coniston pedlar 12s. for " 24 yards of Ribband for her stayned Callico-bed," as well as 10s. 6d. for lace, but now £9 was sent by Kendal carrier for Mrs. Ann Sandford (cousin of Mrs Fleming) to procure in London " p^t of a white bed and crules for one, a mantle, and Head Linnen for my wife." It was three years later (1667) that £3 was sent to the Newmans " to buy a Fringe for my wife's white-wrought bed : " so that we may suppose that the work was very elaborate, and the finishings handsome.* The designer and drawer of the embroidery seems indeed not to have been paid till February, 1669.

" It given by her (his wife) to Ro Carr for drawing
of her white bedd 00 05 00

The essentials of the adornments of the house were concluded when in 1670 the Kendal joiner was paid £4 10s. " for wainscotting of ye Balcony-chamber." It had been carried apparently to the height of Crosthwaite's picture, for in 1665 Richard Nicholson had spent a good deal of time in " riving lats," and in " latting the hye rooms " and passages. He probably did the interior plaster-work too, as no separate accounts show for it, and the squire would seem to have been content without the elaborately worked plaster ceilings, friezes, and overmantles, that are to be found yet in so many of even the smaller Westmorland Halls. Nicholson, amongst other furniture, such as a couch-chair, " draw boxes," &c., " ye Hall-presses," " a pair of standards, a hanging shelfe and a pair of standard feet for ye matted chamber," made fittings for the squire's study and the closet. The "standard" was a plain wooden post, on the top of which was a simple mechanism for the raising or lowering of the candle-socket In 1668 the squire used the legacy left

---

* It is probable that the embroidered hangings would completely cover the wood-work of the bed, as is the case with the yellow satin embroideries of Madame de Sevigne's bed of the same period, still to be seen in her chateau at Vitre. If so, the bedstead may have been one made about this time by Nicholson with chairs at an astoundingly low price

him by his uncle, John Fleming, for "a hand Bason of silver," which Dr. Smith chose for him in London, at a cost of £11. 2s. 6d. In 1672 Daniel "paid Lancelot Forth for 2 pair of longe pewther candlesticks 16s . . . 2 Hand Candlesticks 1s 6d." We hear of a hand-screen bought by Mrs. Fleming, "Two Silver-Inck-hornes" were procured by Uncle Newman in 1682 at a cost of £1. 14s. 6d.; and he also got a house-clock in 1679,* while in January, 1696, nearly nine years after the account book has ceased, a bill is extant for a clock, which is curious enough to be given in full. The paper is docketed in the squire's hand as being Mr. Dawson's "Acquittanc for my Pendulum Clock in ye Hall" and runs :—

"For Mr Joseph Dawson in Kendall, Westmorland"

Mr Dawson,

I sent yesterday ye large Clocke for ye Gentlemans Hall. Itt is A pendulum and goes 30 houres If I had itt A ballance Clocke It would have gone but 16 houres and ye prise would have been but 5^s less yⁿ this It cost me 03^{lb} 10^s ood and ye box 1^s and I have charged no more for itt, ye other you writt for shall bee sent next fryday by

Y^r Lo Freind

Sep 26th 1696   Jaspar Harmar.

Dawson's receipt for £3. 15s from the Rydal squire follows, while on the back the latter gives an explanatory column —

		3. 10. 0.
Box	..	0. 1. 0.
Carriage	..	0 4. 0.
		3. 15 0.
Old one	..	1. 0 0
		2. 15. 0

Where then lies the profit to Harmar, the maker, or to Dawson, whom we may suppose to be a dealer in clocks

---

* The entry for this and various other articles amounts only to 4s. 0d, which could only have covered the carriage.

and watches? Possibly in reselling the old one.

Four "Trencher Salts" cost in 1685 £1. 6s. 9d. But, except the making of "ye Hall Door," and "ye new Balcony," which we hear of in 1675 and 1678, the Hall received no further additions after 1670. Premises for agriculture were next proceeded with. The great corn-barn was built; a slaughter-house, a kesslop* hall, a stone chimney for the brew-house (the former having been wood) with two closets over the house, a calf-hull (a word still in use in Westmorland), an ox-house, a hen cawell, made under the corn-barn; a hog-house, and the wooden "Cawbrigge" re-built of stone, with much paving of back premises, and farm buildings. A school-house too was built; for the children, born so rapidly to the squire, had to be taught, and a village master sufficed for the conning of the horn-book.

Under date June 20th, 1688, we have the entry:—

"This day foundations laid of Great Barn at Coniston Hall."

And on October 19th, 1681:—

"Memorandum. This morning the greater arch of Braythay Bridge did fall into the river, a little after Reginald Braithwait's son had gone over it with some cattel."

This bridge, which was originally a pack-horse bridge, has been twice widened, as can clearly be seen.

---

* Cheselop, old English for calves stomach, used to coagulate milk for cheese. See Skinner. *Keselyp* also means the curd milk itself when coagulated, and the *Tela de Keselyp* was the linen cloth, used to collect and receive it before it was put into the vat to be pressed.
See Whitaker's *History of Craven*.

CHAPTER II

Dress and Fashion in the Barony

THE pedigree shows that fifteen " barnes " were born to Daniel Fleming in twenty years of marriage, and of these only two sons died in infancy, leaving nine sons and four daughters to carry on his posterity. Often the babies followed year after year, being handed over to the care of a wet nurse; and one wonders that Mrs Fleming found opportunity to wear those dresses of state, which figure, though less frequently as time goes on, in her husband's account book.

She must have been accustomed all her life to such dressing as had been fashionable at court, though in the troubled years of the war there was little money in Royalist households for extravagance in attire, which was besides discountenanced, at least in the early days of the Commonwealth, in high quarters. Her husband too was accustomed to the style of a gentleman about town, from the days when he was left there by John Banks as a youth of 19, with a bag of money for his expenses. If his sheets of accounts for this time are glanced down * it will be seen that while his bookish and heraldic tastes (as well as a youthful one for carefully restrained pleasure) are already apparent, he took care to make a good appearance in the streets of London. He procured a hat at once for 16s. The cloth for his cloak, 3¾ yards for £2. 12s. 6d., must have been of excellent texture, and certainly the tailor, who charged 5s. for the making, cut it in fashion. His shoes cost 4s., and their ties 6d.; while gloves 1s. 4d.; socks 6d. a pair. He has both " suit " and " gowne " altered, at an expense of 4s. and 3s. By May he was investing in 2 yards of cloth £1. 6s.; in 4 dozen of

---

* See *Flemings in Oxford*, where they are most of them printed.

silver buttons, and in 40 yards of ribbon £1. 2s. These may have been for the "Gray suite," for which his tailors bill came in next month for £1. 10s.; and would with its 40 yards of ribbons make a stylish outfit. The ribbons and knots of the Restoration were indeed pressing in from France already, as is seen from the demand of young Verney from Flanders in 1655, that his father should procure him 150 yards of black ribbon to trim a grey and black cloth doublet (to be worn with scarlet stockings), a demand that is considered excessive.*

Young Daniel procured at the same time 18 yards of ribbon for his relative John Kirby, while for his young sister Isabel, he got, as his mother instructed him, a "rayle" or loose gown of linen 8s., a necklace, and 3 yards of ribbon 2s., with which to make her "a sett of modish knotts," sufficient at least for country wear. But news had already come of his father's death, and 7 yards of black cloth £4. 18s., with 4 dozen of satin ribbon 18s., 6 dozen of hair buttons 5s., and a pair of black stockings 5s., were bought on one day. A pair of gloves was dyed for 6d. The young man's smartness increases. He buys silver lace 7s. His next hat costs £1. 5s., and he procures a case for it. A riding hat and band later is 15s., with "an oyle-coat." He changes his hat-bands often, and finally possesses a silver one. His laundress's bill appears for 15s.: no doubt for the washing and starching of the "4 Holland bands," 3s 4d., and "2 paire of single Holland cuffs"; and the other set of "2 lawnebands, and 2 paire of cuffs single and doub." 5s. 6d. Then 4 dozen of white thread buttons accounted for 10d. Two "holland halfe-shirts" cost later £1. 4s. 6d., a pair of "lane" (lawn) stockings 5s. These fine linen articles were clearly bought made-up; the price per yard in the north will be

---

* Nicety in ribbons became so great, that when the same youth was courting, a few years later, a special suit was got for him by an uncle, with the remark "there are other fasshioned Ribands worn besides these, but fitt for none but footmen or a Morrice dauncer"—*Verney Memoirs*

seen later on. The shirt was only coming in, along with the waistcoat, coat and tight knee-breeches, which at the Restoration finally ousted the cloak, doublet and hose.*

Daniel continued to shop for his mother. Eight yards for his sister's gown cost £1. 5s., and for its making 5s. was paid. A " paire of Boddyes " for the elder lady cost 12s. A " silver Cawl and Rowl " for Isabel figures as 3s. 3d., and a black one for a girl friend the same " All a mode," a thin glossy black silk,† on one occasion 6s. 3d., and later (1 yard)·5s. Two " taffaty-capps "—taffeta being a fine silk—cost 9s. 6d. For " a Gowne to my mother," 14½ yards of black Mohair is got at 5s. 7d. the yard. The dutiful son also bought " a pair of Farthingalls " for 1s. 9d., doubtless too for the ladies at Coniston.

From these items we can picture the Coniston ladies as conservative in name, if not in style of dress. Young Isabel, with her netted cap or caul and the roll or pad for the erection of her hair, was following the fashion that obtained in the court of Elizabeth.‡ The hideous distention of petticoat produced by the farthingale § hoops of whalebone was also at its worst in England in that queen's time. The greater grace of Henrietta Maria had introduced a simpler style both of *coiffure*‖ and skirt; and though Charles II's bride appeared in one from the conservative peninsula of its origin (see portraits by Velasquez) she was quickly laughed out of it by the Frenchified court. Mistress Fleming's mohair too would prove most

---

* *Social England*, vol iv, p 485.

† *Flemings in Oxford*, p 62.

‡ See *Flemings in Oxford*, p 81, quoting Murray and Halliwell

§ In many English dictionaries you will not find farthingale ; but in Skeat's Etymological Dictionary you have " Farthingale *see* Verdant " and on turning to this you find verdant, flourishing, o F verd green .
  Farthingale or fardingale a hooped petticoat ; o F verdugalle " a vardingall," Span , verdugado, a farthingale (lit provided with hoops) Span , verdugo, young shoot of a tree, rod, hoop, from Span verdi, Lat Viridis, green, so that the word has reference to the green withies which were used as hoops to expand the petticoat —ED.

‖ A coif = a close hood for the head, a cap, a cowl Low Latin Cofia = a cap Coif de fer = a hood of mail worn by knights in the twelfth century.

servicable wear; and doubtless for her sober caps or hoods were the short lengths of "Al-a-mode" and taffetas, as well as the " 2 Taff. and 1 love-hood. 2 paire cap" which stand at 18s.

While knocking about town with his future brother-in-law, Sir George Fletcher, in November, 1654, our youth shows greater rashness in purchase. He bought three yards of "blew Tabbie" (a watered silk) to the tune of 9s. a yard, also "a paire of blew-silke-slopps" (loose trousers) at 8s., with a pair of "white wosted-hose" at 7s. 6d , and a pair of "white wosted-stirreps" at 2s 6d.

"A paire of Perfum'd cordovant gloves," 2s 6d., a "bodie-belt" 23s , a "peice of silver and gold Ribband" £1. 3s (for the blue tabby coat or cloak?) a silver Hatband weighing 2 oz. 15s., would complete a costume that would show gaily in the streets of Commonwealth London The "graine of sevit" or perfume, in the "civett boxe" would complete the dandified effect; and it is not surprising to find sums "spent" with various gentlemen thick on the page at this time. He was frequenting play-houses too, and the Sir W. D. is doubtless Sir William D'avenant, the play-wright, who after vicissitudes that included two imprisonments, succeeded in establishing a theatre during this period.

	£	s	d
" spent in goeing unto a Play	00	01.	04
Given unto Revellers	00.	02	06.
Spent with Sr W. D & S^r G F at ye Play-house	00	15	00
Given unto the Musicke at S^r W D.	00	06	00.

This is interesting as showing that D'avenant had concerts (no doubt of viol-music) at his house, as did Coleman and probably other, now office-less, musicians.* But such licence, as well as such extraordinary expenditure as the two last items, was unusual to our Westmorland youth,

---

* See *Memoirs of Col Hutchison*, also *A Richmond Idyll* by M L A and *Viol-Music*

who knew when to pull up, though he occasionally lost money at cards with gentlemen, and at " tables " (backgammon) with ladies. His 2 pound of Spanish tobacco 16s., is a most unusual item, as he certainly had no habit of smoking in later years.

We see him in milder mood when taking his Aunt Dudley and " Mrs Loe " " to see ye Turke at Durham House," where that famous rope-dancer performed,* 7s., when " goeing upon ye water to swim " 1s., or frequenting the cock-pit at Westminster, or Hyde Park (where the entrance was 1s.)*

And all the time he was working at law, advancing his suits, obtaining counsel on various knotty points, and preparing not only to take up the control of his Rydal manor as soon as he had secured it, but to marry. He gravely mentions the dates when he bought his wedding clothes ; but he, besides, fitted himself out with 4 yards of Drap-de-Berry (woollen cloth from Berry in France †) for a cloak, £2 11s., 2 yards of broad cloth for a coat £1. 16s., and 13 yards of black " Italiana " (probably a lining stuff †) ; and afterwards with 12 yards of " Searge de Rohan " (serge of Rouen †) for a suit and coat, £2. 2s. He was clearly well fitted out in clothes for the life he was to begin, as would certainly be his bride. His first expenditure for her was in 1656, as we have seen, for a " coat " which cost " with making " £7. 10s in London. The coat appears to have been an upper dress or loose robe, worn over a gown or petticoat, and its comfort in comparison with the whaleboned bodice must have kept it long in vogue.‡

Next year a Carlisle tailor made her a gown § for £1,

---

* See *Flemings in Oxford* and *Evelyn's Diary*.
† See *Flemings in Oxford*
‡ See Planché's *British Costume*.
§ The " gown " remained the essential over-dress of women from early times (A S *gunna*), while for men it ceased with, or soon after, the Norman period, remaining crystalized only in the prescribed collegiate attire Origin-

and an entry follows —

" more for silver lace 10ˢ, more for whaile-bone 6ᵈ "

She also had a " black silk gown petticoat," procured through Roger, which cost £10, and a cap-lace, 3s. 6d.

" Shagg " was apparently the wear about this time, and in 1660 some " Double red " is bought at 4s. a yard ; while Daniel pays " more for a shagg-hatt for myselfe " 10s.

At a later date (1662) 2¼ yards of " redd London-shagg for my wive's petticoat " bought in Kendal, cost 9s. But stuff got at hand would be only for every-day wear.

Next a " feather'd tabby gowne " is procured by the aid of " Cosen Bouch," which cost £6. 12s., being 12s. a yard. This is made up by the Hutton tailor for 5s., with 2s. for whalebone, and 1s. 6d odds. A " Stuff suite," with a " caster " (*i.e.*, beaver hat : *Lat.* castor = a beaver) bought for the Rydal squire by Sir George Fletcher in London, who no doubt could pick the fashionable thing in hats, cost with the making, £10. 4s. 6d. The Rydal pair must have made a good appearance about this time ; but next year (1661) mourning had to be worn.* On June 13th, the carriage of " a Box full of murnings " was accounted for at the rate of 2d. a pound from London

---

ally a loose, flowing garment, with open sleeves that showed under sleeves and a kirtle or petticoat, it passed through many forms, becoming in Tudor times a composite garment of bodice, skirt and sleeves, all highly stiffened and boned. In the Stuart period it flowed into softer lines, with low bodice and sleeves, either short to show lawn under-sleeves, or loose detachable ones. It was sometimes made in one piece opening over a petticoat, or with bodice and skirt. The bodice was sometimes called the waistcoat (See Strutt, Planché, Georgiana Hill, *History of English Dress*)

It may have been the increasing negligence of the attire of Charles II's dissolute court that caused the return of the *coat* (originally the A S cloak), and which had fallen back more and more to show the splendours of the gown —but it now appears under the name of the *manto* This became more and more used as a " night-gown," for evening wear, and was much favoured by the more modest women, as we read in the *Verney Memoirs*, where, the court being at Newmarket in 1683, the Duchess of York " gave yᵉ Country Ladyes leave to come to her in mantos "

* Dr Magrath has been unable to trace the death that necessitated this. The death of Mr John Fleming, the bachelor uncle who lived at Skirwith, occurred in the following summer

(4s. 6d.) with 4d. on to Rydal This may have been a presentation mourning, such as was received from Sir John Lowther in January, 1676 (carriage 2s. 4d.) on the death of his grandfather, for whom Daniel was executor, with a legacy of £10.

It was the custom for the nobility and higher gentry to supply complimentary mourning to the outside members of the family and even to friends. Sir Ralph Vernon, in 1677, was piqued because the heir of his friend, Sir Roger Burgoyne, when asking him to accept of cloth for a mourning suit, added a request that he will order it himself at a certain shop in town, as it was the custom to deliver the mourning gift at the house.

A Penrith tailor (perhaps the same who had served John's family) was resorted to also in this emergency; a " black Bumbazeen Gowne " was 7s., with 12s for things required for its construction, bringing it up almost to the Carlisle man's charge. However, for a " mourning gowne and Petticoat made here at Rydall," whither he was fetched, only 5s. was paid him Further :—

	£	s.	d.
" It for yᵉ makeing a mourning suite yᵉ cloak here at Rydall for myselfe, beeing all now yᵗ is due unto him for anything whatsoever	00	06	00.
It given him for his comeing and goeing ..	00.	02	06.

Mrs. Fleming's beautiful feathered Tabby Gown and white satin waistcoat, bought during the London visit of 1662, at a cost (without making) of something like £50 of present money, must have stood over; for in the October of her return the sixth child, John (only to live three years) was born. Aunt Frances Newman received in 1664, £4 " to buy a laced-band, a shell, and Ribbands for Sleeves for my wife."

Alexander, apprenticed to the silk trade in London, now did business for this brother, doubtless on wholesale lines. For two pieces of " fine mixt Tamerine " £6. 13s. was paid him in 1665, as well as £3. 17s. for 14 yards of " black narrow silk Florantine." But Mrs. Frances Newman, the "ant," was still called upon to choose the fashionable accessories of the costume. She wrote to Rydal that she had been to many shops, but had been obliged to exceed the order for Mrs Fleming's "hancasiker" (handkercher) by £1. 5s., as one at £3, the specified sum, was too old-fashioned to send. The "shell and knotts" chosen, she declares to be of the newest fashion, and of the "Couler" now worn in winter. This adornment is not much used now round the arms, she adds. The handkercher cost £4. 5s., the "ribbons" 18s. 7d., "a bow" 1s., and porterage 1s., showing that London tradesmen did not then deliver goods. Next year, 1666, Alexander is again useful, and procures one piece of "new wrought Tamerine" for £6; he besides gets two "Taby Pettycoats" dyed, the one "pinke Citt" (Citron?) 8s., and the other a "French yellow" at 6s. Great stringency in the orders was evidently exercised, for when Alexander shortly after sends books to his brother that cost 17s. 6d., he says he went to ten or eleven shops, but could not get them cheaper. In 1666 too the carrier conveyed £5 to Mrs. Newman for the purchase of a "Laced Handkercher and a pair of sleeves" for Mrs. Fleming. It seems, therefore, that a best gown and rig-out was a yearly necessity in the ordinary course, while older gowns were dyed and done up.

But as the years go on, items for children's attire thicken in the account book, especially for shoes, gloves and muffs, which could not be made at home, and were sometimes procured by the dozen.

For "Tamell for children's coates" £1. 4s. was paid to Cousin Lowther of Cockermouth in 1665, being 1s. 6d. a yard, while Cousin Bouch supplied from London 5½ yards of "vermilion," possibly for trimmings, for 10s. 6d. Earlier, white Tammel was "put to dyeing." It must have been one of the cheaper cloths of the country, and best had, seemingly, at Cockermouth, for in 1665 an entry of £1. 5s. occurs. "Paid unto Dr Smith wch my Lady (Fletcher) had disbursed for Tammell for my wife."

Shoes had cost Daniel 3s. 8d. and 4s in London, after he had discarded the 2s. ones bought for him by John Banks, and he got them then for himself, his wife and eldest boy, while in 1665 a dozen of children's boots came also from there, 17s. But he was trying by this time a Coniston shoemaker, who charged only 2s. 2d. for fitting himself, with 1s for pumps, and 2s. 6d for his wife. A Cockermouth workman, however, charged 4s. and 3s. respectively for the same articles, with an additional 6d. for bringing them to the mountains. He also makes a little later " a pair of pinck coloured laced shoes with flaps 8s. 6d, a pair of winter shoes with box golo-shoes 6s. 1d., a pair of shoes for myselfe 4s," in all 18s. 6d Later, Penrith and Bowness men are employed, and in 1686, a Lowther shoemaker supplies the Hall, charging 4s. for fitting the squire and his son, and 2s. 6d. for Mary. Daniel's ultimate patronage of a Rydal man we shall come to Stockings vary in price also. A pair bought at Kendal for Mr. Fleming cost 6s., while six pairs are procured from one Jane, a Quaker, of Ingmeer, for 3s How industrious must Jane have been, to live on 6d. a pair, knitting and wool ! The squire's black stockings are 4s. 2d., and the same later for his wife 3s. 4d "My stirop-stockings " cost 3s 4d. These were probably made of cloth, as knitted stockings were at this time mostly worn by the common folk. The account book shows that the Scotch pedlar furnished in 1688 " 4 yds of Scotch cloth for my Socks " 3s. This would seem to be the linen (always called cloth) which the Scotch were at that time trying to find a market for, for it served in 1682 for " Cravats for the boys 3 yds." 4s., and " necks for them " 3 yards 3s. 3d., in all 7s. 6d. Mary also had a cravat of it, and it was used for aprons and coifs. At the same time wool is spun for children's stockings.

Little Catharine, now aged nine, had to begin to dress in silk as the daughter of a gentleman, and the sarsenet for her "Gowne" cost 19s. 6d.; while lawn and odds figure at £2. 1s. In the winter plainer clothes were bought, and "3 quarters of Watchel Tabby for my wives bodyes" cost but 6s. 6d. at Kendal, Galleon was 3s., and silk 2s. Home-spun, or "Fellside stuff" was good enough for the second and third boys, aged seven and six, and 7 yards for their clothes cost only 7s. 7d. "A semmar,"* however, is bought in London for the wife for £1 10s. Next year £10 is despatched to procure her "a black Gowne and coulloured Petticoat and a pair of Laced Shoes." Nine dozen of silver coat buttons for the squire seem cheap at 19s 2d. The state in the household increases, and "2 Liveries" are had from Cockermouth in 1667, costing £4. 4s. But James Simpson of Kendal, mercer, and mayor (in 1671) begins to figure in the accounts. He furnishes a cloth suit for the squire, for £2. 4s., and a black one later at £4. 12s.; also kersey "for ye children's coates." Three yards and a quarter of "Boddy Tammy" from him cost 5s. 6d., and a yard of "blew Kersey" 2s. "My hatt" at Kendal costs 12s. 6d., and is clearly meant for common wear, as, besides £2 to buy a "wastcoat," £1. 10s. is despatched presently to London "to buy mee a good velvet mounterow," a style of cap that, at this time, no gentleman could be without. "3 Children's hatts" cost 8s. 6d. "A French hat to ride in," cost later but 10s. Four yards of taffety was bought at 9s. 7d. the yard, and "my wife's scarlet Pettycoat & Lace" from London at £1 10s. In the year 1670 brother Alexander is recouped £1. 2s. 6d. "for my silver vest buckels," as well as £10 "for ye buying of my wife a Gowne & a Petticoat." Likewise Aunt Newman buys "a Vest & Fring

---

* *Chammer*, or *shamew*, called by Hall, 10 Hen VIII, "a new fashion garment, which is in effect a goune, cut in the middle" called also a *cote* or *shamewe* Much used by Hen. VIII See also note later.

for my wife" at £3. In comparison with these the following item seems cheap :—

	£	s	d
"Paid to Jo. Little for a pair of pendants for my wife	00	02	00

Then comes :—

"Paid unto John Little's wife for Ribin & a neck-lace 00. 13 00.

John Little may have been a pedlar, for mention becomes frequent of these wandering chapmen, who seem to have carried the lighter and more flashy articles of attire, and we have later " paid to Car's wife ye Pedlor for 2 pair of Pendants " 4s. ; while an Ingleton pedlar is paid 8s " for a laced & nother black hood ", 4s. 6d. for three yards of " Hemp-lawn," 1s. 9d. for 7 yards of black Ferreting, 6d. for a Pomander " Neck-Lace," and 3d for needles, the Cockermouth pedlar supplies " white silk crape " at 2s. the yard.

Instances of the enterprize and wealth of members of this class of tradesmen will be given further on.

£3 was despatched to Aunt Newman " to buy my wife a morning Gowne withall." Meanwhile the carriage of Mrs. Fleming's " nightgowne " March, 1671, from London cost 8d. " A Laced Scarfe, Hood, Peake &c " from the same quarter was £1. 7s., and a black " Farrantine Gowne &c " £6 13s. This is followed next year (1672) by £2 10s. " to buy a suit of night-clothes * for my wife " Young Catharine, now aged 15, begins to flit frequently and independently across the pages of the account book, and when she goes to her grandmother at Cockermouth, has 5s for her expenses ! and 4s for " makeing up her Petticoat." London attire is next year necessary for her budding womanhood, and the squire sends up £7. 7s. for a suit for himself and " Katy's Gowne." " Given Katy to buy a Looking-glass 10s.", is suggestive, and two years later

---

* A term in use for evening attire cf. Macbeth II, 2, " get on your night gown "

"12 yards of Kendal stuff for a Travers Curtaine in Katy's chamber cost 10s" She has an "Indian Petticoat" next at 12s, and then a London costume, viz.: "a black Gowne, coloured Pettycoat, & Ribbons" at the cost of £6, bought by Aunt Newman. Ribbons are increasingly in use, and in 1672 the squire has "black Ribin for my shoulder at 4d p^r yard 8s.," which makes 24 yards in the bow or knot.

"A Suit of Knots for ye Head," which the young heir of Rydal gave later as a valentine to his cousin, cost 10s., and a pair of "Ear-Knots" bought by his sister Alice 1s. Alice's head in 1677 was adorned with two dozen of "Satten Ribbin" (7s.) while two yards for her "Aurm (arm?) Knotts" cost 1s. 2d. Ribin for ear knots, three dozen for 2s 3d, were got from Katie Little in 1679, along with two yards of muslin for "Will's cravate" 6s. 4d. This fashion, which we see in Valasquez's portrait, perhaps followed Charles's Portugese queen into England Black ribbon was also used for cravat strings, the squire having six yards for the purpose, 5s We hear too of "Ribbin for Head Knots" Indeed all the children's requirements in dress are seen growing In 1674 3s. is "paid by my wife to ye Taylors for makeing Geo. & Mich. (his sixth and seventh sons) their first Breaches", while "Hatts for Geo. Mich. Rich. Roger, James & Thomas at 14d. a piece" cost 7s

But the motherly supervision of clothes and household was soon over. After recording the fee of 10s given to the mid-wife on April 15th, 1675, the sorrowful husband continues :—

"Memorand My dearly beloved wife was delivered of a Boy ye 3^d day of Apr 75, being Easter-Eve about 3 of ye clock in ye afternoon, who was christened Apr. 11 following, being Low-Sunday, and hee being not y^n (then) well in health It pleased God to call to his mercy my Dear wife upon Tuesday Apr. 13. 75, between 9 & 10 of ye clock in ye forenoon at Rydal-hall, who was buried at Gresmere church ye next daye in ye evening, to yᵉ great loss of mee her afflicted Husband, & of fourteen children all liveing, whom God perserve " *

In this crisis, James Simpson supplies the mourning wanted immediately for the family. A bill of £22. 3s is followed by another of £7. The eldest daughter, however, is specially provided for.

" Paid to 3 Taylors for 3 dayes in makeing Katys
    mourning Gown ..   .. 00. 02. 09.

while at the end of the year there are supplementary items. " paid yᵉ Taylors for makeing Katy a black Semar," † and " new clothes," for seven children (we must suppose the smallest) 9s. 6d

A Papcastle pedlar supplied 5 yards of broad black ribbon at 3s. 4d ; and two black neck-laces at 2d. In January, from a Lancashire pedlar is got 21 yards of black ribbon 10s. 6d., 15 yards of black ferretting at 3½d., two dozen white at 3d , a " thin black hood for Katy 2s , another for Madam Murrey 2s."

There is one other appearance of this lady in the account book, and four days later, January 12th, 1675-76 :—

" Given unto Madam Murrey, Katy and Alice for   £ s. d.
    goeing to yᵉ Nab-top ..   .   ..   . 00 00 09.

If she were a chaperon, introduced to the bereaved household, her stay would seem to have been short. Catharine assumed command of the women's department at the house, till her marriage in 1677, when Alice, her father's own daughter for frugality, took up the reins which she was never to drop in his life-time. From this time there is certainly less sending to London and other

---

  * As Dr Magrath remarks, John is not mentioned in this reckoning, as he had died

  † Extract from Fairholt's *Costume in England* *Semeare* :—Randal Holme says that this was " a kind of loose garment without stiff bodies under them, and was a great fashion for women about 1676 " Also called mantuas They had short sleeves, and some wore the sleeves gathered up to the top of the shoulders and then fastened with a loop and button or a jewel

cities for clothes, and more buying from pedlars at the door, and fairs of the country-side, as well as using the stuffs and the artizans of the immediate neighbourhood. Dress shows less picturesquely in the account book, but valuable lights are gained as to the state of the woollen trade and the wages of the district. We finally obtain, as the precision of the accountant grows, an accurate knowledge of the cost of living at Rydal Hall in every particular.

The squire did not give his daughters an allowance for dress when they grew up, as was in some houses the custom *; nor is any pin-money entered in the accounts. This, however, was supplied through the pigs, which seem to have been a perquisite of the ladies, and which they frequently sold, among other customers, to their father. The following heterogeneous entry follows on a visiting round of Katy's when she was sixteen —

	£. s. d.
" Paid Katy w^h she had disbursed for learning to make Flowers 6^d, given her uncle Fletcher's man 2^s 6^d, for thred 6^d, paper 2^d, to Bar. Harrison 2^s 6^d, Parson Wilson's maid 6^d, wheatbread 1^s, to Alan 6^d, Taylor's maid, 6^d, Marg Fleming 9^d, to Barnes his maid 6^d, for making a Petticoat 6^d, & for 5 Piggs, 5^s in all	01. 00. 11.
March 74 Paid Alice for Pork 5^s 6^d, for 5 Piggs 5^s in all	00. 10. 06.
Aug 4 Paid Katy for Piggs 5^s	

In 1678 Barbara would seem to have been peculiarly fortunate in the increase of her stock, for she is paid 8s. for " 8 Piggs killed in ye house "

Besides " semmars," we hear frequently of hoods for the girls.† Katy indeed ventured on " a Straw-hatt 2s."

---

* Dr Denton of London was willing to give his only daughter £30 a year (*Verney Memoirs*, vol iii, p 327). The Rydal heiresses had received in 1644 at least £20 a piece See p. 499.

† The hood was apparently worn in the house as well as outside, and completely covered the hair See *Verney Memoirs*, where a young girl receives the relatives of her suitor, who are unable to report on the colour of her hair, owing to her hood It became less fashionable in Charles II's reign

in the spring following her mother's death, (an article only allowed to ladies in the country), and there is shortly after :—

	£.	s	d.
"Paid for a Yellow-hood for Katy 1ˢ 4ᵈ, a black-hood for Alice 1ˢ 4ᵈ, for Ribin & needles 1ˢ 8ᵈ, in all	00.	04.	04.

A black hood and scarf for her are later got from the woman-pedlar for 2s. 10d., and a pair of pendants 1s. Then follows "a vizard for Katy 1s. 4d." Little black masks were still worn by ladies out of doors, though becoming questionable in London where they were as a rule used only in public places and the play, by women of pleasure. But these were the days of her courtship, when a black mask must have been far more fascinating to toy with, in the presence of a suitor, than a fan, and much less disfiguring than the puritanical hood. The making of a "Sarcenet Petticoat" for Katy cost 6d.; and a muslin gown was procured for Alice from the Lancashire pedlar, being "3 yards of Callico" (only), at 1s. 8d. per yard. The same man was paid "for 2 Amber Necklaces for Katy & Alice 10s. 6d.," as well as "for 3 papers of middle Size pins at 11d. yᵉ 1000, 1s. 4d, for 6000 of Little Pins at 9d yᵉ 1000, 4s 6d." Twelve papers of pins cost 2s. 8d. in 1678. These were not all required for garments; a few round-headed ones are to be found still sticking in papers at Rydal Hall, where the careful squire placed them 200 and odd years ago.*

Payments for the boys are quite wholesale, and carefully graduated according to age. Will, when going off to school in 1671, had been fitted out with a satchell 6d., and three skins were procured in 1675 for pockets for himself, Harry, and Daniel. An entry of June 6th, gives hats for Harry and Daniel 7s. 6d., for the next two boys

---

* Prices seem stationary; in 1525, at Exeter 1,000 pins were sold for 8d. The London pin-makers were incorporated in James I's reign. *History of English Dress*, Georgiana Hill.

4s. 8d., the next three 4s 6d., while a hat for Fletcher, the baby, is likewise 1s. 6d. The " bands that go with these," 2 for 6d , and Will's 3d., may have been specially got for little Thomas's funeral It would be a sad procession indeed, if all the motherless bairns followed the small coffin with their father.

But a happier event followed quickly. Katy's marriage with Edward Wilson, son and heir of Edward of Dallam Tower, Westmorland, was already arranged.

" Apr. 16, Given unto my daughter Catharine to give to my Cosin Wilson's man who brought her a Letter and Token," 5s. But as usual at that time the alliance was entirely a business arrangement between the parents of the young couple. The highest figure for the dower of a Westmorland maiden of good birth who was not an heiress, was in this age from 1000 marks * to £1000.

Later, in 1663, Mr James Ducket of Grayrigg complained that the payment of his daughter Girlington's portion of 1000 marks, with other charges, has so impoverished his estate, that the assessment of it which ruled in his father's time, can no longer be borne by it † But the squire of Rydal was now rich enough to afford the largest sum, £900 of which was paid to Mr. Wilson, senior, and the rest to his son. Gratuities flowed on the occasion of the marriage. When on June 23rd, 2s. 6d. was " Given by Katy unto my Cosin Wilson's man," a love-letter must have been in question ; for now the day was apparently fixed. A week later comes the entry —

	£	s.	d.
" Returned by Edward Briggs yᵉ Kendal Carrier unto my Uncle Newman to buy wedding clothes for my daughter Catharine (no longer Katy) yᵉ sum of ‡	30	0	0.

---

* A mark = 13s 4d

† Rydal Hall MSS

‡ £100 for the trousseau was considered barely sufficient for Dr Denton's daughter, but she was a London girl and an only child —*Verney Memoirs*

Mr. Braithwaite, curate of Grasmere, receives 2s. 6d. publishing the banns, and on August 12th, Will is despatched to Coniston with 5s. to kill a buck.

	£.	s.	d
Aug. 15. Given unto Mr Moor (beside 5^{lb} given by my brother Wilson) for his Drawing of my Daughter Catherine's Joynture, who was this day (being Wednesday) married unto Edw Wilson jun. Esq, in Gold	02	10	00
It to his man	00.	10	00

Renny the fiddler played at the wedding, and received 2s. 6d., and the father's heart was so warm, on this proud and happy occasion, that he gave Will 5s. "to keep his purse," and 2s. 6d. between Harry and Daniel, home from Kendal school for the occasion.

Linen-cloth had recently been supplied for Katy's " shifts " at 1s. 11d. a yard (along with the same material for Will and Alice at 1s. 6d, and for the children at 1s. 2d.), but a superior garment was wanted for the marriage.—

	£.	s	d.
It for 3 yards of Holland for Katy's wedding shift	00.	09.	00

For his own shirts at this time it may be noted, the squire procured linen at 2s. a yard, and for the children's (which served likewise for aprons for the housewifely Alice) at 1s. 1d.

The fine linen of Holland came into use in the days of Elizabeth, who received a gift of it at 3s. 10d. the ell. Cambric, lawn, and calico were in demand, for ruffs, bands, cravats, cuffs, shirts, &c The Scotch tried to introduce their linen into the English market, at the close of Charles II's reign, but met with such opposition, that the vendors are said to have been whipped through the streets of London.* It is undoubtedly this " linen-cloth," or often called only " cloth," which the Rydal squire bought increasingly from the Scotch pedlar.

---

* See *History of English Dress*, Georgiana Hill.

Shoes must have been a feature at the wedding. A kind called "Turky" was supplied from Penrith. Daniel's own pair costing 4s., the bride's (who had two pair) 3s. 3d., and Alice's 2s 6d. Alice, with two dozen yards of ribbon on her head, and arm knots, must have been a gay spectacle, but of the more substantial portions of her dress we hear nothing. The occasion made its mark, no doubt, on the young people. Will, the heir, had bidden farewell to his Kendal schoolmaster the year before, and began (lame as he was) to ride with his father to the Sessions, and to the Appleby Assizes, as well as for pleasant jaunts to race-meetings, visits, and hunting the buck. He was in fact of age, with a "Raysor," which the Lancashire pedlar charged 2s for; and the "Riding-coat Lined with Red," which the tailors made up for him, (along with a black-cloth suit for his father for 6s. 6d.) was necessary, as well as the "Castor-hat" at 12s. 6d., and "Fring for his Pistols" 12s. 6d ; while still more necessary were frequent donations of 5s. from the parental purse "to keep his purse with." Calico for his sleeves was had from the "Little Pedlar," who supplied Alice with a "Bodking of Steel" 2d., and a "yellow Skarf" 1s. 6d.

Alice too was coming forward. Her riding-coat this year cost £1 ; and her "Rideing Garter" 4s. She buys a pair of "Ear-Knots" at Hutton for 2s. ; and the tailors are paid 4s. 4d. for making her stays and Barbara's gown. Gloves for the two cost 1s., for Michael and Richard 8d., while muffs for the three little ones are 6d. We hear also of a "Box with muffs 1s. 4d." The muff indeed might be a smart article of attire, made of velvet, and fur-trimmed or embroidered. It was often worn with a fan, and in-doors. Lady Vere Gandy is said to have worn hers constantly, when not in bed.* Fletcher is paid £2. 2s. for two pieces of "Indian Stuffe," "being for

---
* See *Verney Memoirs*

my Daughters." "A Visard" cost 1s. 4d., a necklace 3d.; a yard of "flowered silk Damask for 2 pair of Sleeves" 3s. 6d., which seem cheap. An "Imbrodered Stomager" is 5s., and scarfs, girdles and mantos appear. Neighbour Benson's daughter, when in London in 1679, is commissioned to buy for Alice a "Manta Gowne, 1 lb. 14s, a Head-dress 9s, an ounce of gray silk 1s. 4d," which with box and porter 1s., comes to £1. 5s. 4d. Mabel Benson's letter to Alice Fleming, sending "a manta and a head-dress which is as fashionable as any is worne." (2196) *. Gowns for Barbara and Alice are had (apparently) in the country for £1 14s. 6d. Kate Little supplies, besides silk ferreting and gloves, "9 Knotts & 2 dozen of Farding Ribbin" for Alice, Barbara, and Mary, and "stamagers & a Coif" for 9s. 8d. Five yards of "white silk crape" cost 10s. from the Cockermouth pedlar.

The girls' stays, made by a tailor, appear frequently in the accounts, and a Mr. Gibson seems in 1680 to have been procured specially for the purpose. He makes three pairs, for Katy (now the bride of Mr. Wilson of Dallam Tower), Alice and Barbara, and is paid with other work, 10s. Afterwards 12s. 6d. more is given him " for compleating of the Stayes " The canny father, however, finds that the Troutbeck tailors, George Fisher and his man, who are much employed in the Rydal household at this time, can manage stays likewise; and in 1683, besides concocting stays, a black manto and a petticoat for the little Mary for 2s. 6d., they make two pairs for Alice and Barbara, as well as a riding suit for Alice for only 4s.! Later still a Penrith tailor and his man (no doubt travellers) makes two pairs of stays for the three girls, and alters their mantos, working three weeks and three days at a cost of 17s. 6d., while whalebone comes to 1s. 4d., and silk and tape and ferreting 7d. When Alice takes a journey to

* We hear much of the glories of the manto from the *Belvoir Castle Calendar*, quoted in Geo Hill's *History of English Dress*, but the ladies here pay from 20s. 0d to 35s. 0d a yard for their stuffs. £3 a yard is even mentioned.

York with her married sister, and thence on to "Cosin Crowles" in Hull (where she gives 5s. to the servants) she buys a fan at 4s. 3d., a top-knot and a girdle at 5s. 9d , and a pinner at 3s. 3d. London is still resorted to for the best clothes, though much less often ; and prices in stuffs and dress seem lower, though whether from an actual drop, or from economy on the squire's part, cannot be said In 1681 Mr. Newman gets Alice a " Silk Petticoat, showes and Knots " for £1 13s 4d ; and in 1682 she has " a morning-Gown and muff " from the same agent for £2 Later Barbara and Mary are promoted to " Mantos " and furbishings from London, at a cost of £6. Alice, who became his true daughter in frugality and industry, and never married, outdid them all in cost of a gown.

	£	s	d
"June 13 82. Paid to Troutbeck Taylor for making a black crepe Gowne for my Daughter Alice of her own Spinning & a Petticoat	00	01	00

Fringes too were made at home, doubtless on those wooden frames, of which an example exists in Town End, Troutbeck, and " thred for a Petticoat Fringe " cost 2s * Thread indeed becomes a recurring item for the girls, intent probably upon fringes for trimming, and Mary has given to her in 1687, 5s. 4d. for " 4 ounce of Silk for Fring for her Pettycoat at 1s. 4d ye Ounce " " 2 ounces of Naples Silk for Alice 4s. 0d." was doubtless applied to the same purpose, while the " 3 Knots of holed Footing-Tape for Alice " 2s., which went with " 1 ounce of thred for her 1s," would be the edge of the fringe. Fashion was dear to the hearts of the Rydal maidens, as to all others ; Gales for Barbara are 5d. in 1653, and July 9th, 1656, gives an entry of " Black Gales for Alice 6d," followed by " Temple wyres for her & Barbara 4d. Two

---

* Fringes were at this time so fashionable, as to be set in rows or in " waves " round the petticoat Nine rows are mentioned as adorning one garment ! *History of English Dress*

Steel Bodkins for ym 2d." And this style of coiffure was apparently demanded by the youngest, for a week later is entered " for Temple wyres for Mary " 2d.* Three " cornets "† were procured for the girls in 1680 at an outlay of 5s 3d., and " Black Gales " † were had at 1s. 2d. a yard. Lady milliners existed before the nineteenth century, and indeed with all these furbelows and ribbons, and hair stretched on wire and decorated with ornaments and knots, there seemed room for them. The proud Kirbys of Kirby contributed, in an unmarried daughter of Roger the cavalier, a member to the profession.

	£. s. d.
" July 6 '85 Paid to my Cosin Agnes Kirkby Millener for things for my 3 Daughters	.. 02 17 00.

We now have a new entry in which we find that two yards of " musling " for a *combing-cloth* cost 4s. 9d., and Alice later had the like for 4s. 4d.

Daniel Fleming began the use of powder in London, and bought it later in Kendal, where he regularly paid for the " trimming " of himself and his growing sons.

For three at school in 1676 he paid one George Holme 2s. 6d for the year.

His hair in his portrait is worn long and wavy, a style favoured in youth by both Louis XIV. and Charles II., who both possessed abundant locks.

Of the squire's clothing we hear less and less in the account book, and his suit when made a knight in May, 1681, is not entered

Imported muslin generally bought from pedlars was used for cravats, which had now (1681) come into fashion,

---

* For a distension of the side-curls by wires, see portrait of Catharine de Braganza

† Cornets and gales were both parts of the head-dress, gale, from galea, Lat = helmet or head-piece. Cornets, Lat cornu = horn, were in the 15th century upright spikes from which a lace scarf or veil depended, but in the 17th century they were lace lappets hanging from either side of the headdress —ED

as well as for hoods, and aprons, which needed 1½ yards in construction. Three yards were needed for five cravats, and the price varied for Kendal from 3s. a yard to 3s. 2d. Will, however, had to be content with "Scotch-cloth" for his "Cravat-neckes" at 1s. 6d. a yard, six yards of black ribbon for the "strings" (5s.) being added to the expense. A little later he is allowed muslin, four yards of which at 2s. make him two cravats and two pairs of ruffles. Daniel the third son, though 21 in this year, 1681, had to be content with four cravats at 2s. 4d. He is still classed apparently among the juveniles, and his shoes cost 3s. 6d., Barbara's 2s 6d., Will's were 3s. 6d., with three pairs of gloves 1s. 6d. It is a relief to hear that next year his hat cost as much as 8s. 6d. "from Mr Redman," and that " sleeves " are had for him from Kate Little's 2s. 3d. calico. His sister Alice's sleeves are nicely graded to 3d. a yard dearer. In 1688 Mr Christopher Redman supplied hats for the squire and six boys, with hat-bands for £1. 19s. Michael, Richard, and Roger, were fitted by George Dixon, hatter, at another time, at 3s. 5d each. Harry, the second son, who had been fitted out for Oxford in 1675, and of whose clothing, books, &c., a careful list had been made by his father, ceases to be supplied with the troop. Kate Little, however, supplies "Holland for six bands for Harry" 4s. 6d., and at the same time, " 2½ yds of Callico for 2 Dressing cloths for myselfe 5s 10d." Hemp-lawn too is got for Harry's handkerchiefs, 4½ yards at 19d. (earlier years it was 2s. 2d. and 2s. 8d.) with one yard of holland for four caps, and calico for Mary's aprons, at 13d. Calico is 2s. 8d. a yard in 1678, though three yards make four handkerchiefs and two pairs of sleeves for Will for 6s. 4d. next year.

"Hummum" is also used for handkerchiefs. Muslin is had at 2s. 2d., and dimity at 9d. "A la mode" is 3s. a yard; and "Pludding" had from a Scotch pedlar 8d. Imported fine stuffs appear to drop in price, unless the pedlar began to bring round inferior articles. However, holland appears to keep its price. The squire procures eight yards of it " for halfe shirtes for myselfe " through his cousin Bouch at a cost of £2 6s.

" For my owne little Cuffs " in 1683 Kate Little charged 5s. a yard, and Will's " caps " and sleeves were 4s. 6d. and 3s. 9d.

When " a Surplice for Harry " is required in 1684, it is supplied by Mr. James Cock, Alderman of Kendal, who had succeeded to the old-established mercer's shop of his father ;[*] and $15\frac{3}{4}$ yards of holland at 2s. 10d. are put in it, for a total of £2. 4s. 6d. For Harry's bands the highest price of holland is reached, 6s. ; for Will's caps at the same time 3s. is paid, and for Daniel's 2s. 6d.

Linen of English manufacture remains moderate , and Cock furnishes it for the squire's shirts at 1s. 11d. (it was earlier 2s) for the children's at 1s 3d , for napkins and table cloths at 10d (" abateing 6d " in the $31\frac{1}{2}$ yards), and for children's shirts at 9d. Another time the squire contents himself with Cock's " Lin cloth for shirt at 1s. 5d. ; for Will's 1s. 4d. , for Harry 1s. 2d. ; and the children 11d. ; with 9d. for table napkins. Later " 3 great Table-cloths & one Little one for y^e Parlor " are 1s a yard.

The squire occasionally superintends the making of the Oxford son's clothes in Rydal, though he is a B A. of his University and 25 years of age.

" Nov 8. 84. Paid by Barbara to ye Taylors for makeing my Son Henry's first Black Suit & trouser .. .. 00 04 09.

More and more indeed does he narrow his circle of chafering, and resort to home manufacture and native stuffs, till he can finally in the matter of dress for every day wear, dispense entirely with a middle-man.

---

[*] *The Boke off Recorde of Kirkbie-Kendall*

From the first, indeed, the coarser stuffs for household use were produced at hand. We can judge of the industry within doors by the appliances bought. Hand-cards, for teasing the wool in readiness for the wheel, were bought three for 5s. 6d. in 1665; afterwards for 1s. 3d., 1s., and even 11d each A hopper cost 5d.; spindles 1d, or with whorls 3d. to 4d.; while a spinner and cards were 7s. But maids, busy of evenings, could not keep pace with growing wants. Many are the payments to spinners, at first without note of time, but the usual rate of wage was 1d. a day. The webster too is often paid for weaving cloth blanketting or " happings " from the wool of the home sheep The " Huggabeck-Websters " are constantly at work, no doubt on the linen thread spun in the house from flax grown in the garden.

Then there is " wolking of Blancketting," bleaching, freizing,* and dyeing paid for In November, 1676, the squire sends cloth to his Cousin Browham's miller at Staveley and pays for " milling and Freesing* 17 yds at 2½d. the yard," 3s. 6½d His cousin gets this dyed at 4d a yard, 5s. 8d., and it serves for his younger boys' clothes. Lancelot Fleming " ye Taylor " of Rydal—more frequently called " Lanty Taylor "—had been had in to work for the Hall as early as 1659, and this year, 1676, he " and his two men for helping to make ye children's clothes " are paid 3s. In fact he is yearly at work on the job, and next year his bill is 7s. 1d.; and that of the Troutbeck tailors, also employed, 7s. 6d. It was not yet usual, however, to clothe the children in veritable home-spun, though cloth of the country had been early used; 7 yards of Fell-side stuff at a cost of 7s. 7d. being procured for Henry and Daniel in 1666, while as much as 39 yards for other purposes had been got at 13d. a yard. Kersey, a Yorkshire

---

* To freeze or freize,—connected with frizz and frizzle—was to raise the nap on one side of woollen cloth which was then called frieze or frize —ED

cloth, was had for many uses, and could be had from Wakefield as low as 1s. 2d a yard, though of a blue colour for saddle-cloths it ran to 2s. and 2s. 4d. James Simpson, junior, shearman or mercer of Kendal, and mayor in 1670,* supplied it in 1668 for children's coats (10 yards?) for £1. 0s. 10d. and it remained the wear for the long warm coats that were the boys' outer garments. George, Michael, Richard, and Roger, going to Hawkshead school, were fitted out with it in 1681, 10 yards (15s.) sufficing for the four coats, and the making by Lanty and his boy three days being 2s., total 4s. 3d. a coat, and next year William Benson of Skelwith supplies the same four boys with grey kersey coats at a cost of £1. 1s. 9d., being 11¾ yards at 1s. 11d. But when the four are fitted out for Sedbergh school in 1688, the squire succeeds in getting the same stuff at 1s. 8d. from Ambleside, 14¾ yards making coats and gamashoes;† and the Rydal tailors making the long coats and gamashoes for 3s 6d., and the eight dozen of buttons costing 1s., with galloon, &c., 2s. 6d., the cost is brought up to £1. 11s. 7d "Under-Skiddaw" gray, or broad-cloth, made no doubt in the mills of Skiddaw becks, was cheaper than Kersey, and was used for the clothing of the scullion-boy or for "Nancy" Grigg, and occasionally for the coats of the little boys at home. It varied from 1s. to 1s. 5d; and was bought from Sebastian Senogle, or Zenogle, a descendant probably of the Dutchmen who came to exploit the mines of the Lake District in Elizabeth's reign.‡

While kersey served for coats, the boys' suits, generally had for Christmas, came to be made of real home-spun. In 1685 we have full particulars of the clothes made for the six youngest boys. The squire now leaves the Rydal spinners, at their 1d. a day, and, in October pays one

---

* *The Boke off Recorde of Kirkbie-Kendall*

† Gamashoes, gamashes or gamaches, from It gamba; Fr. jamb, were leggings or overshoes like long "spats"—ED

‡ Mrs Agnes Fleming lent money on Bond to four Dutchmen.

DRESS AND FASHION IN THE BARONY

Elizabeth Robinson for spinning 1½ stone of wool for " my sons clothes at Hawkshead " 5s. 3d. Next month the webster is paid " for weaving of 30 Ells of cloath (for Suits for my Sons) at 2d yᵉ ell " 5s. In December for dyeing 30 yards at 4d., and milling it at 1d., and " freezing " it at 1s. the piece, 13s. 6d. is paid; which gives a total of the cost of the cloth (if we allow 7s. 6d. for the worth of the wool if sold) as £1 11s 3d, or a fraction over 1s. the yard. As Lanty is paid this year (besides much else) for " new Clothes for 6 boys " 9s. 6d, this amount may be added, making the rig-out for the six come to £2. 0s. 9d. Next year the squire has double the wool spun for Christmas clothes, Elizabeth being now paid at a higher rate, 12s. for three stone. George Park, the Rydal weaver, weaves the same at 2d. an ell, 5s. (=37½ yards), and next month is paid 2s 6d for weaving 20 yards of woollen cloth for pettycoats. Jos. Adlington next receives 14s. for dyeing, dressing and freezing 32 yards of cloth for the boys clothes, with four pairs of stockings also; and finally, on December 24th, for making the new clothes for the six boys Lanty is paid 13s 2d. This brings the total outside cost, again allowing 5s. for the price of the wool, to £2. 9s. 2d for clothes for six youths; the eldest, George (the future bishop) being nineteen and Fletcher, the youngest, eleven. Even Dan, the third son, and the young ladies did not disdain to wear home stuffs.

Home-spun for the young ladies is accounted for at this time, Mistress Alice paying to George Otley's wife 5s. 6d. for spinning 1½ stone (at the rate of 3s. 8d.) for white woollen pettycoats for self and sisters," and George Park receives 2s. 6d. for weaving 20 yards for petticoats. The latter also weaves 27 yards of " Happings & Horse-cloths for 2s. 6d., and a webster of Ambleside mills the same for two shillings. An entry of December gives the inclusive cost of spinning half a stone for him, and weaving, milling, and freezing it, at 1s., while for dyeing the cloth of his coat 1s. 8d. is paid. The tailor makes his clothes and alters Will's, which, with " makeing me a Camelot Rydeing Coat" come to 7s. 4d ; while the squire, Will, and Dan have each a winter coat made, besides, at a cost of 6s. Lanty indeed has long been entrusted with other than the children's clothes. He works at suits for Will, long coats, riding coats (even for Harry in Oxford), and livery for the page, with red and black waistcoats, makes even suits (the every day ones we may presume) for the squire as well as ·" a Camelot Rydeing Coat " ; " Barbara's Rydeing Coat & Hood ", " Mary's Manto & Pettycoat & for Jack a pair of Drawers." He generally works with two assistants (see Wages) and in 1679, when the whole family are fitted out, two other tailors, Wil Benson and Richard Forrest are also requisitioned. How busy must the work-room of the hall have been, with cross-legged stitchers! No wonder the buttons were bought two gross at a time! Gimp ones were 2s. 3d. a gross. " Alchimy buttons are 3d a dozen," or 6d. a " knot " " 13 doz. of Plate-Buttons for my six youngest Boyes at 3d ye dozen, 3s 3d " come from Keswick in 1681. Gold and silk buttons are 12s. for six dozen (1685). Taylor's thread was bought by the pound (1s. 2d.).

The account book closes in 1688. But we know that the Rydal tailors continued their labours at the Hall, from two bills that exist of Thomas Fleming, who succeeded his father Lancelot. One for 1697 is most curious and minute, entering even the number of days the three workers—master, man, and boy at 4d, 3d, and 2d. per day—devoted to each person's clothes ; and there are the six sons then at home represented, the squire, the page, and the under-shepherd. The work of 111* days amounts to £1 8s. 1d., and Thomas receipts the bill fully for £1. 7s. 6d. ; that is to say, he throws in above 1½ days of his own or 3½ days of his boys' work gratis. His bill for

---

* They did not all work each day apparently

101* days work in 1695 amounts to £1 5s. 11d. The pay of a Penrith tailor in 1686 presents a very different figure.

The faithful " Uncle Newman " in London is still sent to occasionally. In 1682 he has £2 " to buy a morning Gown & muff for Alice," while the Troutbeck tailors make " a pair bodies " for her, and " a Gown and Petticoat for Barbara," 3s. When Barbara is married in May, 1687, in Rydal parlour to Mr. Tathom, of Overhill, Yorkshire, £12 is despatched, this time to " Aunt " Newman, to buy her wedding-clothes. For her handkerchiefs and " Night-Coifs " 5 yards of hemp-lawn are bought 7s 6d. ; 12 yards of linen for " shifts " at 1s. 10d., £1 1s 6d. This was cheap, for ten years before this " 3 yards of Holland for Katy's wedding shift " had cost 9s. Two ounce of thread for her 1s 6d., and " A Comb-brush for her 3d " The tailors make her, for 2s., a riding-coat and hood, with petticoat, stays, &c Barbara also came off less well than her elder sister in dower, the bargain with her bridegroom being £600 ; £500 on her marriage, £100 to be added on the birth of a son, who was born an eight months child, " little and weak," January, 1688. Mary got less still, her dower with her first husband, Henry Bouch of Ingleton, being £500. Her wedding came too late to be entered in the account book, which tells us that in 1687 the tailors made black crape mantos and petticoats for herself and eldest sister Alice for 3s. 4d., that stuff for their " Gawse Hoods " at 16d. came to 5s. 4d. ; and that in 1688 Simpson of Kendal furnished 9½ yards of " Silk & Worsted Stuff at 2s 4d yᵉ yard (22s 2d) for her petticoat." A white " Sarcenet Hood " goes down at 4s.

Finally, the account book gives us particulars of the amount spent on dress between August, 1666 and February, 1667, upon Mary Dodgson, niece to Mr. John Ambrose, who appears to have been entrusted to Daniel Fleming's care, and whose clothes were, probably, those

---
* They did not all work each day apparently.

of a Westmorland maiden who perhaps could not afford to shop in London. They comprise shoes, 2s. 6d.; "a great black Scarfe" 6s 6d.; 4 yards of silver lace got at Cockermouth 4s. 6d.; Scotch cloth (this was used for stockings for the squire's boys and his own socks), and shoes 2s. 8d.; 10 yards of "laced Tamerine at 2s. p^r yard for a Gowne" £1, and got at Kendal; tape, galloon and thread 1s.; 3½ yards of "Tammey-Bodye for a Pettycoat" 9s. 7d.; red silk 3d; canvas 10d.; buckram 1s. 3d.; whalebone 1s. 6d.; and quarter of "Sempeternum" 1s. 8d.

Sir Daniel Fleming left a suit of clothes, doubtless the one in which he was knighted in 1681, which was entered among the heirlooms to be preserved in perpetuity at the Hall. It has, however, disappeared, and was perhaps carried off by his son William's widow.

Such was the dressing of the family of a northern squire, who became ever more thrifty in his ways. At this same time, extravagance in dress was generally on the increase, certainly about the court; and the highest prices paid in London by Daniel are but a fraction of those accounted for in the *Verney Memoirs*, in the *Belvoir Castle Calendar*, or *The History of Dunster*, by Sir H. Maxwell Lyte.

CHAPTER III.

Sir Daniel's Public Life.

IT would be a mistake to suppose that Daniel Fleming's private affairs occupied him exclusively. All his duties indeed of husband, father, lord of the manor, builder, farmer, and banker were carried out efficiently and even strenuously. But full as these duties were, he had a mind whose scope stretched beyond them. His interest was keen in his country and his county; and his capacity, his quick judgment, his indomitable will, backed by the legal knowledge he had early acquired at

Gray's Inn, as well as in the law-suits connected with his patrimony, made him at once a power in those public offices which he assumed. It is significant that in the portrait existing at Rydal Hall, where the wide brow, the long nose, the firm mouth express the strong and stubborn temper of the man, the dress is the armour of a commander of a company of the trained bands; while his pointed finger rests on what is probably the roll of his office as Deputy Lieutenant of the counties of Cumberland and Westmorland. It seems probable, from one or two indications of his foresight and discipline, that he might have made a great leader in war; certainly he would, under favourable circumstances, have proved an administrator of mark in the affairs of the nation. And it is a question whether his early want of wealth and court influence, or the indifferent action of the greater magnates of the countryside, or his own subsequent tendency to parsimony, most impeded him in that road to national distinction which he undoubtedly missed, and which as undoubtedly at one time his ambition was fired to follow.

To be sure, there was no opportunity at first for use of his powers. A lord of manors in three counties (though straitened for money) at 21, a husband at 22, and a father at 23, his working hands were full. It was besides his policy, as son of a cavalier officer and as successor to hardly-won, sequestered estates, to sit on them tight and quiet in the time of the Commonwealth. And yet his bold spirit, his determination to rule within his demesne as lord and as owner of church advowsons, is shown in his prompt ejection of the unauthorized minister at Grasmere (see *Church of Grasmere*, pp. 86-9;) though he was wise enough not to attempt to place there his cousin Ambrose, who was a known Royalist and Church of England divine.

But when in four short years Charles II. came to England as king, amidst rejoicings that seemed for the moment all but universal, there was no need longer to hide monarchial proclivities or adherence to an established Church. It was difficult indeed not to triumph too rampantly over those who had assumed power and office during the Commonwealth, and who had so grievously taxed and ruined the Royalist gentry in whose seats of office they sat. Who were the tradesmen of Kendal, the mayors, the aldermen and freemen, that they should not be made to rue the part they had played upon better men than themselves?

It was an impoverished and diminished set of gentlemen who throughout Westmorland and its sister-counties raised glad shouts for the king. Some of those who had fought valiantly for his father were dead, some were dispersed, and those who had already crept back to estates for which they had compounded, were broken men in purse and even in spirit and health.

But hopes were high. The king would remember his father's friends and their sufferings; and if he could not find a snug place for each about his court, he would at least see that just debts incurred by the Crown were paid, and that money lent of old to advance the royal cause would be re-funded to men crippled by mortgages for want of it. How fallacious most of these hopes were, and how long it took to realize any of them, is shown in the case of Richard Brathwaite of Barnside, poet, author and squire, who had fought and toiled and spent officially, and was forced as late as 1667 to appeal for payment of his country's debt to him, for which he had stood bond to John Fleming's executors. While he and others were being pressed cruelly, even to imprisonment, for fulfilment of obligations accepted in the war-time, the assessments raised by Charles' government in the county were all passing out of the county, and Sir Philip Musgrave could only hand on his appeal to the Justices of the Peace (see Appendix). Sir Philip Musgrave, doughty fighter as he had been, and Commander in Chief of the King's Forces in the two counties, as well as Governor of Carlisle, who had passed some years in exile, could not be overlooked at the Restoration. On the king's state entry into London, he rode in one of the sixteen state coaches with six horses apiece, having previously met the king at Greenwich with Lord Wharton, Sir George Fletcher (Daniel Fleming's brother-in-law) and Sir Edward Musgrave, splendid doings were reported to the Rydal squire by his correspondents, some of them coming second-hand through Dr. Smith at Cockermouth. His son Kit Musgrave, the able Sir Christopher of later years, was made one of the king's life-guards,[*] and another son was attached to the Duke of Gloucester. In September, Dr. Smith further reported that Sir Philip had left town with great satisfaction of the king's affection, but without the looked for appointment of the Governorship of Carlisle, which was expected for him. There was another man struggling for this, Charles Howard, of Naworth, once the friend of the young William Fleming of Rydal. One of a Royalist family, son of Sir William Howard, and great grandson of Lord William, he had known how to trim his sails to the political wind, had been made Captain of Cromwell's Body Guard,[†] and Lord Lieutenant of the two counties. He served as M.P. for Westmorland, and was called to Cromwell's Upper House as Viscount Howard. But having neatly veered round once more, and helped the king to his own again, he could not be affronted, nor the Ld. Lieutenancy taken from him. He was shortly

---

[*] (a21) MSS of Cor of Kendal, His MS Com 10th Report
1690 The Corporation of Kendal incurs the fol bills for wines —
" 1 bottle of sack to the Commissioners, 2s 6d
To Sir Daniel (Fleming) 1 bottle of sack by Mr Simpson, 2s 6d
Fr the Judges treat, 2l 5s
Spent upon Sir Daniel in sack and ale, 1s 6d
For a treat to Sir Christopher Musgrave, 7s 6d "

[†] See C & W. A & A *Transactions* vol iv

made however, Earl of Carlisle, perhaps as a compensation for the Governorship, which Sir Philip did justly procure by the end of the year.

Another man of these parts who was about the new court, was Joseph Williamson, son of the vicar of Bridekirk, in Cumberland, who had probably made himself known to Charles when acting as tutor in Paris,* and who rose from the post of Under-Secretary to that of Secretary of State in 1674. The message to Queen's College about him shows that he had already the king's confidence at the Restoration,* and to him many Westmorland and Furness aspirants to honour addressed themselves.

In the disposition of honorary county offices, Daniel Fleming was not overlooked He was appointed High Sheriff of Cumberland, and was succeeded in the office next year by Sir John Lowther. He acted as lieutenant of the Trained Bands that were immediately raised in place of a standing army, under Sir Richard Sandford, giving 5s. to the man who brought his commission from Naworth, and spending 4s. 2d. when he was " proclaimed " at Penrith. That he entered upon his military duties with ardour is certain On February 1st, 1660-61, he convened and armed his company of foot, and then marched them to Kendal, where they stayed all night He dismissed them according to his account at noon next day " seeing no occasion for keeping them longer together," but ordering them to rendezvous again on the 14th at Staveley. He proceeds to explain the totally inadequate arrangements for financing this body of troops His cousin Lowther had succeeded in raising ten days pay for his own company (a sum already spent), and four days for Daniel's, two of which he paid to his men on the Friday and Saturday. Some of his men had received

---

* See *Flemings in Oxford*, p 139, note 3. " He matriculated at Queen's College, Oxford, on the same day as Daniel Fleming "

new muskets and pikes, the cost of the first being 8s., and the last 6s. a piece; and how these were to be paid for, and money got for the colours, and further pay for the men, he does not know. The account book shows that his own night's expenses at Kendal amounted to 5s. 6d.

It was perhaps in answer to a letter on this subject, of which only a draft exists, that Sir George Fletcher wrote on March 20th, from London. He had just been in conference with "my Ld Howard" (not yet earl) who is off to the north to settle the affairs of the militia; and he strongly recommends his brother-in-law to interest himself in the movement, as it will probably prove to his advantage. He ends:—

"But you are soe much awake to yor own concerns, & soe Discerning therein, as I shall not be soe confident as to advise you any more"

The "settlement" could hardly have taken place, for on September 21st, Sir John Lowther writes to Daniel that he has summoned his whole Company of Foot to train and exercise on Hayfell (above Kendal) on Friday next, and hopes he will join, as other counties exercise their Trained Bands

"Feb 16 1655 Warrant for Daniel Fleming to the Constables of Kendal town, to summon the trained band of foot to appear before him at Kendal, on March 3 & to furnish every man with three days' pay at 12^d a day, providing each musquetar with ¼ lb of powder, 1 lb of bullets, & 3 yards of match The constables are also to be there, & to bring with them 18^d for each man in their several divisions who is in arrears for 3 years to the musters."*

According to this, Daniel Fleming was in command of a Trained Band before the Restoration.

Administration business occupied Daniel even more

---

* B 36. His. MS. Com. Westmorland, MSS. of the Corporation of Kendal.

fully than military. Named Justice of the Peace immediately, and sworn at Appleby and Carlisle on September 6th and 11th, 1660 (the fees paid by him being 5s. on each occasion) he at once became the leading spirit on the Bench sitting at Kendal for the Barony. These were stirring and combative times for the new-made magistrate Of the gentlemen who had returned to their impoverished and mortgaged estates and dilapidated Halls not all were available for the office. Sir Thomas Strickland, who had followed the Prince of Wales into an exile of nine or ten years, was a Roman Catholic. So was Sir Thomas Brathwaite, eldest son of Richard, to whom his father relinquished Barnside for residence on his second wife's Yorkshire estate.

These men, his intimates, must have been cognizant of the true faith of Charles, which he was so long and successfully to hide, and they doubtless had hopes, if not of his open declaration of it (which the outbreak of fanatical fear as displayed in the Titus Oates Plot was to render impossible), yet at least of toleration and recognition. Sir Robert Strickland did indeed receive the appointment of Deputy Lieutenant of the North Riding of Yorkshire, and was M.P. and Knight of the Shire for Westmorland But it was the fate of the Romanist gentry to fall back into the shade until the excitement over, " The Popish plot in 1678 dispersed them even more signally than the Revolution."

Daniel Fleming's fellow J.P.'s at the Restoration were Alan Bellingham of Levens, John Lowther, James Ducket of Graythwaite, John Otway of Middleton and Ingmire, and Thomas Brathwaite, described as " armiger," being doubtless him of Ambleside

These new magistrates appear in the indictment books of Kendal, in succession to John and George Archer and Thomas Brathwaite, who had served in Midsummer Term. 1659. The change was a violent one Thomas Brathwaite, if the same as the one who continued to serve, and of Ambleside, was indeed of a strangely mild, non-political temper, to whom all governments were alike; but the Archers were strong partisans of the old Parliamentary party, and probably republican in feeling John, mercer, alderman of the borough since 1644 and mayor in 1648, had served as elder of the Presbyterian classes in Kendal, and had been most active against the Royalists, as commissioner under Parliament for Cumberland and Westmorland, until 1654, when, apparently not agreeing with the trend of affairs in London, he resigned. He had sat on the Bench, with two others, who changed, since 1655, when the earliest book opens. He was not one who would lightly brook the robbery of power, nor was he alone in his feelings of despite against the proud " castelers " whom the Commonwealth had crushed, but who now had the upper hand once more The townsmen of Kendal, like the mercantile classes all over England, had early taken the Parliamentary side in the combat, and under the rule of the Commonwealth had settled down very comfortably to the local government of their town and the barony generally. They naturally did not welcome the restitution of a monarchy that brought the gentry again into the seats of rule; and it is evident that in the representative persons of the mayor and corporation they offered resistance to the measures of the new justices. The opportunity rose in the assessments levied on the town by the latter; and though there had been no difficulty in the collection of taxes levied by themselves, they now opposed those fixed under the new regime. The struggle was imminent in March, 1661-62, when Sir James Ducket wrote to Daniel (No. 480) begging him to fix a day for a meeting with himself, Mr. Bellingham, and Mr. Walter Strickland, in order to consult what could be done to meet the objections to the assessment made by the " mayor and his Brethren "; and if possible before Saturday, which, being "the Market Day, is always trublesome," the town of course being then full of folk who might be disaffected. Drastic measures were recommended always by the squire of Rydal, and his position was strengthened by his appointment on April 3rd, as Deputy Lieutenant of Cumberland and Westmorland under the Earl of Carlisle.

He was in London from Easter to June, where no doubt he procured a commission for future action ; but he was soon after his return full of public business. It must have been thought well to make an emphatic military demonstration in front of the refractory townsmen, as on August 1st the account book shows :—

	£.	s	d.
" Given the soldiers to drink at Kendall	00.	05.	00.

which was an unusual amount for the squire to spend.

Then comes, on September 25th :—

	£.	s	d.
" Spent at Kendall when wee were purging that corporation	00	06.	00

The leading spirits of the opposition must have been deposed from their civic seats, an operation no more palatable to them from the fact that they themselves had begun the game, and had previously " purged " their body from Royalists.*

But even so, opposition was not broken. Squire Daniel passed on from this scene northward into Cumberland, spending at Penrith 6s. 6d. at a meeting of the Deputy Lieutenants, and 3s to the soldiers at Carlisle, and 5s. to Lord Carlisle's servant who " delivered a deputation from Westmorland unto me." But trouble remained behind him. James Ducket wrote to him on October 11th at " ye Goose," regretting his absence from a meeting. The sheriff's officers of Kendal had acted badly, he

---

* See *Boke off Recorde of Kirkbie-Kendall*, pp 18, 19, and 20

thought a " further purge " might be necessary, and urges an appointment, as in Mr. Otway's and Mr Strickland's absence, only Mr. Bellingham and himself remained of the Commissioners. It was clear that an angry and obstinate body of Kendalians were not easy to meet or to manage, and that the humiliation of the few had not rendered the rest more conformable to outside authority. Indeed the affront to the town by the public removal of some of its elected officers was no doubt keenly felt, even beyond the section that had been active in the service of the Commonwealth; and disaffection grew. A spirit of rebellion, partly political and partly religious, showed itself up and down, like a flame leaping from a hidden smoulder. Some ministers defied the Act that ordered the restitution of the Book of Common Prayer in the churches; other men, when it was read (as in Langdale Chapel) rose up and denounced the minister (see *Church of Grasmere*, p. 89); while the warrant for the month's assessment of the two counties, signed December 17th, 1602 (No. 510) undoubtedly fanned the flames of discontent Sinister rumours were abroad, and it was thought necessary to procure an instrument giving the Deputy Lieutenants the power to search for and seize all arms found in the possession of persons suspected of disaffection. Accordingly Daniel Fleming and his fellow issued a warrant on November 16th, 1662 (No. 508), commanding the new mayor of Kendal, William Grey (who had succeeded Thomas Jackson, mercer) to carry out this search in the town, including among the suspected, " quakers and other seditious persons." At the same time he directed that new watches were to be set in the highways, and all persons travelling with unusual arms and at unseasonable hours were to be disarmed, and those who failed to give a satisfactory account of themselves were to be apprehended; while vagrants were to be punished. Furthermore, the mayor was to cause to appear on November 25th, at the muster of the Trained Bands, at "Tarney-bankes," six able-bodied soldiers, completely armed, to represent the town of Kendal. The equipment was to be as follows :—

"Every Musquetier is to have a sufficient musquet, a roller of Bandeleers and a sword, and every pikeman an Ash-pike of due length, with a back, breast, head-piece, and sword"

The musketeers are to carry half a pound of powder each, and every soldier to have a day's pay at the rate of 1s. per day The charges are to be taxed on the inhabitants of the town

Nor did the Deputy-Lieutenant's vigilance pause here ; he proceeded to a vigorous attack on those persons suspected of favouring seditious plans, of which dark and sinister rumours were leaking out under the name of the "Plot." This is shown by Lord Carlisle's letter (No 528) to Daniel Fleming of the following February. He is clearly alarmed lest his representatives are going too far in official zeal. He hears that George Archer and James Cock have been committed to prison by them : are these two really dangerous persons ? for if not, it were well to release them. This remonstrance from his superior produced a long explanatory letter from Daniel (No. 534). When he and his colleagues had inspected the "Trained Foot-band,"* they had, as Deputy Lieutenants, met in consultation with the remaining Justices of the Peace, and discussed the question of seizing, and either imprisoning or binding over on securities for good conduct, the most dangerous of the known recalcitrants.

---

* In the order of warfare in the seventeenth century the pikesmen and the musketeers fought together, the former being placed in a clump in the centre of the company, with the flag (which every company carried) in their midst. They were supposed to be equal in number with the musketeers, but these almost always outbalanced them From the weight of his clumsy weapon the musketeer had ceased to wear armour, which the pikemen continued. For these and particulars of the use of the musket, &c, see Oman's *Art of War. Social England*, vol iv, p 228-30 The pay of the soldiers during the first Wars was 9d, and a sword was not part of the equipment.

They had picked out for example four of the most noted, who were George Archer, James Cock, one Captain French, and one Bland, and had apprehended, and examined them as to their correspondence with disaffected persons. They then required from the four (instead of imprisoning them) sureties for good behaviour, and it was only when they haughtily refused to give these, and even disputed the authority of the Justices to commit them, that they were imprisoned.

" If we should not have thus proceeded ag^t them " (Daniel proceeds) " I am confident (especially at this time) ye whole Fanatick party would have beene so Rampant, as our authority amongst them would have signified little or nothing "

Then he goes on to speak of the disaffected in Kendal, who would head a party if there were any opportunity. The town had paid its assessments willingly in the time of the Commonwealth, but will not now. He believes that the measures they had taken were justified by Lord Carlisle's own instructions. (He here probably refers to the communication of the previous August, when his superior had spoken of the new Act of Uniformity, conceiving it to be his own and his Deputy-Lieutenant's duty to guard the peace of the county " by preventing or suppressing mutinous or tumultous Insurrections.") Further, on petition of the prisoners, two had been released on their bond, and the others were kept till three weeks back; when, the " Plot " having been discovered, it was thought no longer necessary to detain them.

The two prisoners longest detained therefore were the two well-known town tradesmen whose pride would not brook submission to the new Justices. George Archer had occupied the position of Justice himself in 1659, as well as the post of mayor. He was described as gentleman, but may have been the one of his name elected " Cordyner freman " in 1648. He must have been thorough in his convictions, for he was averse apparently to ceremonial robes in the civic chamber as well as in the churches ; unlike his Puritan brethren, who objected only to the latter ; and his intrusion amongst them without a robe was resented, as is shown by the amusing " order " made in council, September 23rd, 1655, and entitled " For a gown."

" It is ordered that Mr George Archer shall provide a gown like the rest of the Aldermen's gowns against Saturday come sennight if there be materials for the same within the town upon pain to forfeit 40^s " (*Boke off Recorde of Kirkbie-Kendall*)

Mr. James Cock was the highly respectable mercer who had succeeded to the business long ago established by his father. He had served as mayor in 1653.

The other two prisoners were of another character, men probably who would take the field in insurrection, while others plotted in secret.

It is significant that the king and the greater officials in London awoke to the dangerous state of the country (that had been the ancient Deira and always liable to rebellion) long after Daniel had been dealing with it, and that he and his fellow were instructed to take measures against it even more stringent than those that had drawn the remonstrance of Lord Carlisle upon them. He had spoken of the " Plot " having been discovered three weeks before February 18th ; and on August 10th, Sir Philip Musgrave wrote to the Deputy Lieutenants :—

" the King hath knowledge of a Phanattick desine in hand and that the seance wil first appeare in the Northerne parts. He desires we would have a spetial care to prevent & punish unlawful meetings "

He writes to instruct them to secure dangerous persons, and to exercise the foot companies. The two Archers and others suspected are to be, if not imprisoned, at least confined to their houses. Private intelligence confirms the rumour that there will be on the part of the malcontents a " break out " at York, whither troops are already ordered.

A general account of this obscure plot is to be found in Ferguson's *History of Westmorland*. The local leader was Robert Atkinson of Mallerstang, a doubtful character who had served as captain of horse under Cromwell. While whipping up all kinds of malcontents—Presbyterians, Independents, Republicans, and offended ex-officials, for the projected rebellion—he tried to disarm suspicion and keep in favour with the present powers till plans of a combined rising in the north were ripe, by giving information against the Quakers. This probably is the secret of the undue alarm excited by these quiet people, whose weekly meetings are often spoken of by the leading officials as dangerous to the peace; and that their tenets were totally misunderstood is shown by the fact that they were specially included in the order for a search for arms in the houses of suspected persons.

The alarm amongst the loyal, when the plot leaked out through the treachery, it is said, of a Major Greathead, was great. Sir George Fletcher did the work of examining suspects at Penrith, and notes of the examination of such at Kendal on November 11th by Alan Bellingham and Daniel Fleming exist in No. 573 of the Rydal papers. Amongst them figures again Captain John French, who was afterwards forwarded to Penrith, three ministers, of whom two (George Benson and James Greenod) were released on bond, and the troublesome Wallis sent for three months to Appleby gaol, the two, George Archer and James Cock, also released on bond, and Gaven Taylor, who owned that he had met George Fox at Underbarrow with some fifty others, and who was released on " his own engagement," a fact which should be noted in connection with the later and more prominent persecution of the Quakers. Sir Philip Musgrave, issuing instructions to Daniel Fleming on November 10th, says the

Trained Band which had been called out in this emergency, may now be dismissed, excepting the few men necessary to guard the prisoners ; and that Captain French is to be sent with a couple of troopers to Sir William Carleton at Penrith. He gives the important news that Captain Atkinson " their principal man," who had been caught on October 26th, has escaped from Appleby gaol (since guarded by 20 foot and 10 horse, all volunteers), and is lurking about. Also from Whitehall he is desired to enquire whether there had been meetings of the " Separate Churches " about October 27th, when they had been held in other parts, and were supposed to be the " prologue of some sudden intended tragedy."

Atkinson then, the arch-conspirator, was at large ; and until he was caught the country side could not be easy. Nor was the scheme of the rising with the accomplices at all fathomed. On March 2nd, 1663-64, Sir Philip Musgrave ordered that three persons, (of whom George Walker " described later as a surgeon," and Thomas Wharton, were Kendal men,) were to appear at the Appleby Assizes, to be questioned about " the late plott," which it is supposed they can make disclosure about.

This examination was clearly a failure. And now appears a new figure in the tangle, one who, as a Roman Catholic, stood proudly outside the magistracy, whom he mostly disliked, and yet who was able silently to cut the knot for them. This was Sir Thomas Brathwaite of Barnside, possibly the plotters had tried to engage his sympathy and his help, as being excluded from the privileges of his class ; at all events, he was aware of their secret councils, though probably after the event rather than before it ; but being disinclined to put his information at the disposal of those whom he disliked, (amongst whom it is said Sir Philip Musgrave was chief), he acted for himself, and completely mystified them, as he wished to do. He seized the escaped Atkinson, under the nose of all the officials and gentry, who were searching wildly and ineffectually for him, and rode off with him under a small escort, to London, there to deliver him to the chief authorities, and to prove in person his own devotion to a king who had utterly neglected him and his father and family. The journey was successfully performed, and he had a long private conference with his sovereign, whose companion he had been in adversity.

It had meanwhile become known in the county that Brathwaite had secured Atkinson, and had ridden off with him; but a rumour spread that Atkinson had succeeded in escaping his new captor, and was once more at large, in Westmorland. "It is a mystery" wrote the baffled Sir Philip, whose lawful prey kept thus slipping from him, "and some think Atkinson is still at command."

The odd thing is that the story of the second (and fictitious) escape, thrown off no doubt by the captors to keep Brathwaite's party from being followed, has been repeated seriously in every history since, down to Ferguson's, re-issued in 1905, and with it the subsequent mysterious emergency of Atkinson, totally unexplained, in the State prison of the Tower of London. There is a letter however, amongst the Rydal papers (No. 594 of His. MS. Com), that explains the whole transaction. It is sealed with the arms of the Brathwaites of Barniside and of Warcop, and dated London; and in it Sir Thomas Brathwaite unburdens himself of what information he has to the only magistrate in Westmorland whom he can like or trust, and this is the squire of Rydal. The plot being yet in agitation, he advises Daniel to take Wharton and Walker out on bail, and examine them privately, as, by promises of their life, he may induce them to reveal particulars of it, since they, as well as Atkinson, were implicated in it. He considers that the plot broke down, as far as the Barony of Kendal was concerned, through the vigilance of Daniel's company of foot, which guarded the town, and in face of which the rebels durst not move ; not more than one horseman appearing at the rendezvous on Kettell Ridge at the hour appointed for action. Then in a postcript he gives the news —

" On Fryday last I delivered Capt Robert Atkinson to the Tower of London, where he is secure but younge Musgrave nor his (party) knowe not anything of itt, and dayly they sollicitt that I may be question^d for not bringing him to light, beleueing and underneath informinge that hee hath made an Escape "

The finale too may be read from a Rydal letter, written August 5th, 1664, by Dr. Smith to the squire, after Atkinson had stood an examination in London before the Lord Chancellor and the Lord Chief Justice, and had been handed over to Sir Philip Musgrave for condign punishment :—

" Atkinson (you heare) is removed fro Tinmouth (Tynemouth, the port from London) to Carlisle, by 2 files of Musqueteers, fro whence he is to be brought to Appleby, but not till ye time y^t ye Judges come hither ; but w^t part, he is to act there, I cannot yet learne : most are of opinion he will be hanged, at least they hope & wish he may "

Appleby was the most likely place for his execution, though Ferguson mentions Durham.

Daniel Fleming followed up the suggestion of Sir Thomas, and telling nothing to his " Brethren " of the Bench, as his correspondent wished, examined in private Wharton and Walker, but in vain, as even on a second questioning after a committal to gaol, they persisted in " stiffly " denying all. When reported to him, Sir Thomas " marvels at their obstinacy," but thinks they may not have known of the arrests of Jobbin the grand messenger, and Waller, nephew to Atkinson. Strangely enough, Walker was again under suspicion two years later ; and Daniel in a reply to an order from London for his arrest, which he immediately carried out (No. 5716), says :—

"I commanded also those that tooke him to make strikt search for all fanatick letters and papers, but they met with none of any remark This Walker is a kind of a Quaker, yet much imployed by most sorts of recusants. He is a person as likely for an intelligencer as most wee have in this country, and one whom wee had a long time in custody upon the score of Captaine Atkinson's plott, but wanted then so much evidence against him, as to bee sufficient to try him at Appleby with the rest that were there found guilty."

This letter shows the misapprehension from which the Quakers at first suffered, which was promulgated probably by political plotters for their own convenience, and aggravated by the Quakers' own action in flouting both Clergymen and Justices while officiating, and by refusing to take the customary oath in a court of justice. It became necessary indeed for George Fox to declare their tenets, which in reality repudiated both war and politics. (580 d. of Rydal Hall Papers).*

This should be remembered, as well as the fact that orders were repeatedly sent from London to watch the separatists and, if necessary, to secure them; for a severe stigma has been stamped on the Justices, and especially on Daniel Fleming, for the harsh treatment and long imprisonments meted out to these people of strange mystical beliefs. It was upon the Lancaster bench, on which Daniel also sat, that the hardest measures were taken; for it was in Furness that they had their head-quarters, where George Fox often found a resting-place at Swarthmoor with his devoted adherent Mrs. Fell. Richard Kirby was a fellow-justice with Daniel there, and his violent, unscrupulous temper undoubtedly instigated the judgments there declared; while Mrs. Fell's own son appears to have treacherously acted with him. The Westmorland Quakers fared better, perhaps because they trimmed their

---

* It is this confusion of parties that stood outside church and state which probably caused Ferguson's reflection (mistaken I think) on the Society. Nor were those Brathwaites who had risen to the class of gentry, connected with the Society to my knowledge See *History of Westmorland*, pp 223-4.

sails to contrary winds . though they were now and then called up at the Quarter Sessions, under penalties of heavy fines, on information given of their having met at a house or conventicle. John Whitfield, who long lay in Appleby gaol, was suspected of joining with the king's enemies; and his appeals to Daniel Fleming seem to express a greater confidence in his justice than in that of the magistrates of Appleby who had committed him.

But the turn for other dissentients was to come, and specially for the Roman Catholics in fear of whom, through the machination of Titus Oates, the nation absolutely shook in foolish and fanatical terror. The cool head of Daniel Fleming saw less danger to be apprehended from them than from the Nonconformists, and he probably steadied the action of his fellows towards them. Through all these years the alarms were incessant; and any event, such as the Lord Lieutenant's visit to the county with the imposing welcome given to him (5708), or the news of the Fire of London, caused fresh arrests of Catholics or the ordering out of the militia. The small rising in Scotland in 1666 was regarded as the possible beginning of a new civil war; and the squire of Rydal's care of the public safety was flatteringly acknowledged from high quarters. About this time a letter of Joseph Williamson's to Dr. Thomas Smith, dated December, 1666, says:—

"Mr Fleming's discreet and active care, expressed in his letters, is very well liked of here, yᵉ King having had the reading of them, Indeed we want everywhere such stedy sober heads, those generally in all our business being capricious, humourous, affected, or something worse, God almighty make us all better."

Daniel Fleming managed to secure, by means of the king's popular Declaration against the French (5713), March 3rd, 1666, a loyal demonstration in the city of Kendal; and the scene, where the civic body appeared in their robes and the Squire's company of foot fired a volley with shouts following, must have been picturesque and stirring. But though the Town Council was by this time grown tractable, the mayor even serving as ensign in his Company, there was still an undercurrent of disaffection in the town and barony. Walker was again arrested (see *ante*) and Daniel thought fit to communicate to London his suspicions against the Presbyterians, on May 10th, 1669 ; (5729) ; while in the following February he informs Williamson (now advanced to Clerk of the Council) of the doings of the Independents, who have lately held a great conventicle—

" to the number—as I am informed—(5732) of two hundred, in the night-time and at the house of George Archer, one very active in the late rebellion and still a stiff non-conformist "

He has got a warrant out against them (in spite of the refusal of some of his fellow-justices to act) and is to examine them on Saturday next , and he adds :—

" that severall ministers do ride to and againe and make a bustle, as if they were designeing some more mischeif "

The subsequent trial of the suspected at the Assizes is reported August 17th, 1670 (5734*a*) :—

" Wee have convicted many Quakers and are levying of their fines which make some of them come to church . Our Independents keep close and cunning . . . after wee have routed all conventicles, the levying of 12^d for every Sunday will I hope bring them to church It is as clear as the day that nothing will convince them of their errors so soon as the drawing of money from them , for a great part of their religion—notwithstanding their great Zeal and fair pretences—is tyed to their purs-strings."

Daniel Fleming's proceedings against the Roman Catholics were not of so hearty a character, for he understood them, and knew that the restored monarchy had had no more loyal supporters ; but the warrant that came down to the Lord Lieutenant from the king for their disarmament (November 24th, 1666) he proceeded to obey. His personal friend, Sir Thomas Brathwaite, had never stooped to conceal his faith, as had so many Royalist gentlemen who had returned with Charles, and had hoped for freedom, if not restitution, of their religion. Mr. Nicholas Fisher, of Stainebank Green, had written to the squire of Rydal on the preceding May 13th (1666) :—

"Being this day at the burieing of Mr Brownesword's child, Mr Mayor openlie spoke it, that the masse was familiarlie heard at Mr Braithwaite of Barneyside, upon which another said, that without dispute this morning a great companie from seurall quarters would be there to heare Masse; you may (if you think fitt) acquaint your Cosen Brathwait to signifie this to his cosen at Barneyside; howeuer the mayor told me he would see Ambleside shortlie and acquaint y^{ur} Cosen herewith."

But such open doings could no longer be overlooked with the warrant in hand. Daniel addressed a letter (January 25th, 1667) to Sir Thomas, as well as to Mr. Thomas Leyburne and Mr. Nathaniel West of Nether Levens, apprizing them of the order that he had received for the disarmament of all Popish recusants who refused to take the oath of Supremacy and Allegiance; and saying that as their names had been brought forward at the Quarter Sessions, he was obliged to ask them, should they refuse the oath (which the "Supreme Head of the Church" clause placed beyond the swearing power of good Catholics), to send an account of their arms (825) and to be prepared to deliver them. To this Mr. West replied that he was not so well furnished with arms as he had been against Sir George Boothe's business, a reminder no doubt of an occasion when he had (as Sir Thomas Braithwaite had done in Atkinson's plot), proved his loyalty; and that he had but two fowling-pieces and two swords, and three swords among his servants. He added, feelingly, that the king had no subject who would swear a higher allegiance than the Papist. Sir Thomas' answer is not extant, but the matter seems to have dropped.

That the Romish priest was popularly detested in Westmorland and regarded as a plotter, as many a Jesuit no doubt was, may be gathered from this letter of Mr. Robert Philipson, who had recently succeeded his father at Calgarth. Mine host of the Troutbeck inn listening at the door, while the two Catholics within tried apparently to fix on some house where mass could be said in secret, makes an amusing picture.

1120 Ry. H P His MS Com

Calgarth Feb 8th · (69)

Cozen Fleming,

Being late yesternight at Troutbeck Bridge, about 6 a clock, there alighted 3 men, & a boy, 2 of them were as I perceive fanatick preists, the name of the one is Benson (who I understand, is Tho Sandes of Kendall his brother in Law) The other is the famous Cumberland Larkham, I thought at first, that Benson had Come with him out of Cumberland, but by their discourse, I perceived (though I said not 12 words (I think) to them for I was about my own businesse) that the said Benson met Larkham at Ambleside, all in hast, & soe return'd back with him & perceiving that my presence, made more silence then would have been, I left them, but charged mine host, to take notice not only of their words, but actions, & hee tells mee this morning, that as soon as I was gone Benson pulled a letter out of his pocket & s^d Now I think wee may safely read (but he read it to himself) looking at Larkham, who answered, haue you not a room where none can trouble us ? (speaking to the house) Mine host directed them to a Chamber, & as he tells mee did hearken what he could, at the door, but heard nothing but Mr Cock, named severall times, &, tomorrow at my sister Gosling's, this was he sayes all he could hear S^r these men are not unknowne to the world to be mischievous, & the country is now terrifyed with rumours, and such fellows riding to & fro, & meeting, fright them more I believe a Conventicle wil be this night about Kendall, James Cock's or Plumgarth's, this Sir I thought fit to tell you ; you know, Cure the head & the body may better be dealt with. Your thoughts I beg of you to expresse in answer, none, I am certaine will stirr, except you or I, and my ignorance in the Lawes, will not Let mee, unlesse at your Elbow Good S^r what you think Convenient to be done, be pleased to informe me, and (I wish this pen & I may not part) If it be to the Honour of God, the security of the King,

the preservation of the Comon peace of the Kingdome and your service, if it be not (to the utmost of my power) done I shall trouble you noe Longer but Praying for your welfare as alsoe for a blessing on my Godson I rest
    Sr your most faithfull kinseman & servant
          Robert Philipson
God willing He wait on you on thursday with you know what
   This
To my hon'd Cozen Daniel
   Fleming Esq.

 1130 Rob Brath fr. Calgarth on March 8 sends D. F. the name of Quakers who had met on Sunday fortnight

There was clearly a difference among the magistrates of Westmorland as to the Papist recusants (1508) dictated no doubt in part by personal feeling. The king's proclamation of November 20th, 1673, for the suppression of Popery, gave the handle to those against them, yet nothing seems to have been done till Sir Philip Musgrave and Sir John Lowther decided together to push the matter. The latter wrote to Daniel Fleming, the natural leader among the Kendal justices, (1507) pointing out the action already taken by other counties, and discussing what should be done in theirs. He did not venture to suggest directly, what Sir Philip suggested to Mr. James Bellingham (1508-9), successor to his father Alan, and James to the squire of Rydal, that some of the magistrates of the Barony of Kendal should attend at Appleby to discuss with them a common cause. This measure Daniel could, and did, flatly yet politely refuse to take (1510). For Kendal to ride to Appleby was beneath the dignity of the Barony, even if the discussion to be held there was acceptable. But he was now pushed into action; and at once he explained the legal procedure based on certain Acts, that the Kendal justices were prepared to take, in summoning the recusants who had been " presented " by constable or churchwarden, and fining them 12d. a Sunday for non-attendance at church. It is an instance of his dominance, even over the jealous brethren of Appleby, that they at once accepted his mode of attacking the Catholics, which also touched all Nonconformists.

But the coolness between the Appleby and Kendal benches waxed into contention Sir Philip Musgrave, speaking for the former now, proposed that the General Sessions should be held at Appleby (1574), and the Quarter Sessions alternately at the two towns, thus merging the benches; and he even proceeded to give official orders (1594), for the same. Sir Philip, big man as he was, was no match for the squire of Rydal.* The latter, after he and his fellows had unsuccessfully met the overbearing command by a counter writ, appealed to the Council of State through Sir Joseph Williamson. The case was carried before the Lord Chief Justice; and was decided practically for Kendal, for, while a General Assize was ordered to be held in Midsummer alternately at the two centres, each centre was left to govern its own affairs by its own bench. Thus an effort to piece effectually the two composite counties of Westmorland failed

Daniel Fleming thought it wise, at this juncture, to strengthen the bench of Kendal, and his letter to Sir Joseph in February, 1675-76 (1704), gives us a good deal of valuable information as to the state of the Westmorland gentry The old order was indeed changing. Those Royalists who had returned hopefully to their seats, were falling away by death, disability or poverty, and it was difficult to find men to succeed them in public affairs. The heirs of Sir George Middleton, Mr Ducket, and Mr. Brathwaite of Barnside were out of count, being Papists; Sir John Otway of Ingmire, and Mr. Robert Philipson of Calgarth were too often away, while " Sr Tho. Strickland acts nothing amongst us " cautiously says Daniel.

Sir Thomas, a man universally respected, and made

---

* See sketch of the struggle on p 204 of *Flemings in Oxford*

M.P. for Westmorland at the Restoration, had indeed been able to be overlooked by the magistrates in their disagreeable duties against recusants, because of his residence on his Yorkshire manor of Thornton-Brigg. But now action was to be taken in higher quarters, and it is hard not to escape the inference that the man who had the promise of the next vacancy in the House (1794), Sir John Lowther of Lowther, had something to do with it. Sir John Lowther of Sockbridge, wrote on December 19th, 1676, to apprise Daniel Fleming of the intention of some " more zealous Parliament men " to demand Sir Thomas's removal from the House, on the ground of his recusancy.* He recommends Daniel to let Sir Thomas know this and advises the latter to be beforehand with his opponents, by directing his friends to make the motion in the House for his withdrawal on his own behalf This suggestion, when passed on, Sir Thomas repudiated with great dignity. In an immediate reply he promises to support his successor, Sir John Lowther of Lowther, in standing for his seat (1777), and proceeds :—

" if in my opinion (i e religion) hath rendered mee incapable to serve my country that is my misfortune, for I do not find that I have lost either my understanding or integrity or will to serve that country in particular, or the King and kingdome in generall ; so that your request of makeing it my owne request I think not proper or reasonable, for I will not be guilty of *felo de se*, but if he do it by his friends, and the House adjudge it fit, I shall give it no opposition or take the thing unkindly from himselfe. This I think is as much as can be expected from mee "

The following extract is from a memoir of James II. by Sir J. L. published 1808 :—

" Sir John Lowther, b at Hackthorp Hall, par. of Lowther 1655. Gr. son of Sir John Lowther of Lowther went to Kendal School, 1 year Went then to Sedbergh Queens Col —Gr father d. 1675, when he was elected K for c. of West & remained

---

* The Test Act, excluding all Catholics from Parliament, was not passed till 1678

His own ac. says he was again elected K. for c of West with Bellingham on acc of James II "

The exact words of the Preface to the *Memoirs* are :—

" On the demise of his grandfather, in 1675, Mr Lowther was elected one of the knights for the county of Westmorland, and continued its representative in parliament as long as he remained a commoner The distinguished loyalty of his ancestors, & their constant affection towards the Protestant religion, operated on his virtuous mind as powerful incentives to emulate their examples. He uniformly declared himself an advocate for the test & corporation acts "

This creates a different impression from Sir T. Strickland's letters.

The measure of ejection, though opposed by " some considerable men," and taken so reluctantly by the House, that the Speaker was ordered to write in person to Sir Thomas (1821) and (1822) and (1827) and ask him to clear himself of the conviction of recusancy (when proceedings would at once be stopped), was ultimately carried out.

The current of popular feeling against the Catholics ran stronger as hatred of the French increased ; and on September 30th, 1676, Lord Carlisle in his office of Lieutenant receives an order from the Lords of the Council that the houses of reported Papists in Cumberland and Westmorland are to be searched for arms (2055). This was perforce carried out , and the constables delivered at Rydal one rapier and one carbine seized from Sir Thomas Brathwaite ; a back, breast and head piece (2116), one case of pistols and holsters, and one silver hilted rapier from Sir Thomas Strickland ; a back, breast and head piece, two fowling pieces, one musket with a firelock, one great sword from Mr. Anthony Duckett, being doubtless the armour used in the Civil Wars for the king's father , along with inferior trophies from lesser folk down to one old gun from a certain widow Platt The Papists moreover, numbering by return 143 in the Barony of Kendal (2105), were summoned to the Sessions to take their oath. All who appeared refused the Oath of Supremacy (2113 and 2121), but willingly entered into recognisances to keep the peace. Sir Thomas Strickland, now at Sizergh, was too ill to appear. He wrote therefore to the Justices (2118), and his letter is worth reading, as an explanation of the position of the loyal and moderate Catholics, who were willing to fight for the King against the Pope if it was necessary, but whose consciences forbade them to declare the king their spiritual governor. And Sir Thomas persisted in a personal loyalty to the House of Stuart that eventually brought him as reward exile and a foreign grave. This was not yet to be however. When the Bill for banishing all " considerable " Papists came before the House (1680) (2325), Mr. Christopher Philipson reported to Daniel Fleming :—

"We are troubled about the return of our considerable Papists but we could find none save Sir Thomas Strickland, and that he was soe old and soe weake of body that he was incapable of carrying armes, but that if they thought fit to have him returned we would return him There was little said to it. I think it will die "

Even a fanatical House stopped short at Sir Thomas.

The chief victim of the " Popish Plot " of Titus Oates was William Howard, first Viscount Stafford, who was executed on Tower Hill, December 29th, 1680. Concerning this event we have in a letter from Christopher Philipson to Daniel Fleming, dated December 28th, 1680 :

" Great preparations are being made to secure the quiet of the city tomorrow being the day of Ld Stafford's execution All the Guard and all the train-bands are to be out Many conjectures as to the meaning of the comet but all agree that " ' tis for our sinnes. "

Daniel Fleming was holding a Manorial Court at the

time at Coniston, and in his great account book he has this entry :—

"Dec 14, 1680 Given to ye Jury at Coningston .. 00 02. 06

Memorandu. That my tenants there and I did see a Blazeing Starr with a very long tail (reaching almost to ye middle of ye sky from ye place of ye sun setting) a little after ye sun setting, near ye place where ye sun did set Lord have mercy upon us, and pardon all our sins and bless the king of these kingdomes"

Notices of this comet as seen at Falmouth and Lyme Regis were printed in the *London Gazette*, and Evelyn in his diary notes :—

"1680 12 Dec This evening looking out of my chamber window towards the West, I saw a meteor of an obscure bright colour, very much in shape like the blade of a sword, the rest of the skie very serene and cleare. What this may portend God onely knows; but such another phenomenon I remember to have seen in 1640, aboute the Triall of the greate Earle of Strafford, preceding our bloudy Rebellion I pray God avert his judgements We have had of late severall comets, which tho' I believe appeare from naturall causes, and of themselves operate not, yet I cannot despise them. They may be warnings from God, as they commonly are forerunners of his animadversions"

Flemings in Oxford 507 Note

Lawrence Lee of Godalming in his diary speaks of 1678 as "the year in which Dr. Titus Oates made a discovery of ye popish plot for which in ye next kings reign he was severely whipt" and of 1680 as the year when "that great Comett was seen almost all ye winter ; when we first saw it it seemed to be like a long sword, . . . ye next winter there was another not altogether so large."

Surrey Archæological Collections xxvii , 9

Excitement in London about the so-called Papist Plot (2272), brought down repeated orders to the county magistrates for measures to be taken against the Catholics. Sir Daniel was fain to recommend Lady Middleton, as he had done his widowed cousin Curwen, to marry a Protestant who could protect and convert her (2265) The lady takes it that he speaks " out of drollery " ; and when her correspondent proceeds to try her conversion himself by means of books he sends, she reads them indeed but finds nothing in them to cause her to change. She finally cries out for patience, reminding him that :—

" Rydal was once a good Catholic family, and I am not in despair but it may come to be so againe, (2358) though it is almost treason to say soe " .·

Daniel tried to protect her from the enormous exactions at that time threatened against the Lancashire Catholics (2284), by sitting on the Lancaster Bench when her case came on (2334), a fact remarked against him ; but all was in vain, and she was called to appear at Preston (2339). His advice to her, if she will stick to her faith (which he regards evidently as unreasonable) is to sell her personal estate and live privately in some good town.

It was the general fate indeed of the Westmorland Catholics to disperse themselves. When the plot of 1695-6 to bring James II. back again was discovered and a landing by the French expected, the most stringent orders came down from Lord Carlisle to seize their horses and arms and finally to arrest them. Daniel Fleming and his fellows continually asserted their harmlessness. What there were left, were few, helpless, and detested by the people. A particular report (4935-6) told that Sir Thomas Strickland had gone with wife and children about 1688 to France, and is reported to have died there. Sir Thomas Brathwaite was dead ; and Mr. Thomas had some five years back removed to the city of York. Mr. Anthony Ducket, infirm and aged, had neither horse nor arms over the value of £5 ; and the same could be said for Mr. George Leyburne (4965). Yet in spite of this the latter was threatened with imprisonment, and Mr. Brathwaite summoned to London.

APPENDIX

No 855   Rydal Hall MS.
(Docketed by D F. " Letters concerning   *Brathwaite*
    Rich Brathwait of Bar. esqe ")

Deare S^r/

To inlarge my endearement to yor deserveing selfe wch shall ever really accompany you I am to present a suit unto you . a request just and conscientious wch Armes mee wth an assured confidence of prevaileing in the equity of my addresse and procurement of my speedy redresse, you know well S^r being of Concernment to your selfe, how I stood ingaged for a greate sum of money to Mr Flemings Exec^{rs} for the advancement of his Matie Service, and our loyall desires of promoteing it ; now appeares the opportunity of our releise after our long and heavy Sufferings upon the overplus of this assesment by the benefitt where of wth Sundry other occuring wages, others equally ingaged as wee were, have received plenary satisfaction I tooke occasion to make intimation hereof to some of our Com^{rs} here who had such resentm^t of it, as they held it very conscientious to bee confident of your Influence by an effectual letter to the Com^{ers}, may wth much facility perfitt the worke . aut nunc aut nunquam : no time more oportunite to accomplish it Your concurrence, assistance and advancement whereof (being an act soe Just as it is beyond all exception) shall Infinitely oblige

       Your most constantly affectionate serv^t .

Barneshead April 1667   Ri · Brathwait

Postecript

Att this very present I am under the lash, being highly pressed by the Executors to whome I stand ingaged : and though modesty bids mee silence my necessity, I must pay or suffer by rendering a continued use, and wch burden I have hitherto suffered

      These For Sr Phillip Musgraue K^t and
          Barronett at Edenhall
               Cumberland

Gentlemen/

I request you will please to peruse the inclosed The business I presume you have beene acquainted withall and have a kind sense of it, it is much truble to mee that Mr Brathwaite or any person that suffered soe much in other waies for the King and Country, should bee put into a Sharpe remembrance of it by haveing monies now charged upon their account which weare Borrowed for the Countries Use, In other Pts as well as the Barony of Kendall I have and must Suffer in this kinde and am loath to move in my owne particular, If you please to Consider of any Way to releeve us in this straite, it will be acknowledged as an Act of your great Justice and Kyndnesse, and your comands in what may bee for your Service alwayes Oblidge the Indeavoures of

        Yo^r humble servant
          Philip Musgrave

To my honoured Freinds Allan
Bellingham Daniel Fleming
James Duckett and Thomas Brathwaite
Esq^{ers} his Maties Justices of Peece in
the Barony of Kendall:

875   Rydal Hall Papers

S^r/

 Honest Leonard Smith, hath beene a longe tyme prisoner (for debts) in the Gaolers house at Appleby; and is likely, still to continue soe, excepte wee take course to gett him satisfaction, for what his mother and He disbursed (upon the publiq^{ue} faith) for the Supply of the Garrison in Appleby Castle Anno 48. Wee crave yor assistance to this charitable woorke, and doe desyre that you would rather exceed, then equall us; in yor p^{r}portion of this supply. not that wee conceive yor Concerns to be greater then ours · but that we hope, and thinke, you have a larger stocke ouer, not beinge able to afford aboue 40^{ls}; wch summe is raised out of the pensiones moneys, and ordered to be speedily paid into a friende who is, priuately, to dispose of it, to his use) S^r his necessities will pleade for him, with more moveing Oratory: then can fall from our pen and therefore we shall not enlarge, But (haveinge presented our best respects to yor good Ladye, and yor selfe) wee take leave and remaine

      Yo^r most affectionate
      Couzens and Servants
        (signed) Rich Brathwait
June the 8th   John Lowther, Ju^r
 67.   John Dalston
These/
   For the righte worth. Daniell
   Fleming Esqr att Ridall
     present

Sizergh MSS.   Letter to Sir Thomas Strickland, London.
from " Lady Middleton "

Sir,
   this Last wekes newise putts us all in the Cuntrie in a fright; after all our hopes of good times for Catholicts the pennall stataats to be putt in excuistion I cannott beleve that your Longe sitting could hatch soe much ill: pray doe me the favor to lett me knowe what will be the Isewe of itt

   mʳ middleton presents his sarvice to you & desires to knowe what way you woulld adice him; about the monys hee is to paie for the King, he is Life (sic) to paie itt now in easter tearme; and if his coming upp doe any good he woulld make a Jorny, he desiers to knowe what hopes you have that any Course will be taken by this parlement for paiment of the Kings debbts; or that the King will doe anything of himself if he make his application to him he thinks your assistance in this might doe much to the King; and my Lord Chanclor, whch I desier you will satisfie him in feu Linns as soun as you cann and alsoe my request Conserning catholcts   my services I pray to my Lady
I am
                        Your afectionat Cosen
                           and sarvant
                              Ann Middleton

Leighton this
15ᵗʰ of March
   1662

Another letter (2852) of the Rydal letters published by the Hist. MSS. Com. from Sir Christopher Philipson to Sir Daniel Fleming is dated February 14th, 1684. In it he says :—" This night the late king was interred in Henry VIIᵗʰˢ tomb."

He must have meant Henry VIIᵗʰˢ *Chapel*; for in the actual tomb, as Dean Stanley proved, after three weeks search, in 1869, the only bodies are those of Henry VII d 1509, and his wife Elizabeth of York (d 1503) and James I. (d 1625)   His Queen, " Anne of Denmark," lies by herself; her lead coffin 6 feet 7 inches in length, bearing the date 1618, corroborates the account of her remarkable stature

Really Charles II. lies in a vault under the monument of General Monk, accidentally discovered when the warming apparatus for the Chapel was put in, 1867, and with him lie William and Mary, remarkable for the simplicity and brevity of their coffin inscriptions, also Queen Anne and her husband " George of Denmark " Queen Anne's eighteen small children and eleven of James II are all in the big vault selected by James I. for the body of his mother, Mary Queen of Scots, when he removed it from Peterborough Cathedral where it had lain from 1587 to 1612 Besides the Queen this vault holds the lead coffins of Henry Frederick, Prince of Wales, elder brother of Charles I " in whose grave were buried the hopes of the Puritan party " (d 1612) and of Arabella Stuart, cousin of James I (d 1615) and of two children of Charles I, viz.: Henry of Oatlands, Duke of Gloucester, who declared that he would be torn to pieces rather than be made king in his elder brother's place, and Mary of Orange, mother of William III Here too are Elizabeth of Bohemia, d 1661, eldest daughter of James I and mother of the Electress Sophia, and with her, her distinguished son Prince Rupert (1682).

Anne Hyde, Duchess of York, the first wife of James II. and mother of our two Stuart Queens (d 1671), is the last, but heaped up on those larger coffins are those of the twenty-nine children above mentioned, only one of whom, William, Duke of Gloucester, attained to more than a child's stature, which tell the mournful history of the hopeless fading away of the Stuart race.—ED

CHAPTER IV.

Later Days.

DANIEL Fleming played no part worth comment in Parliament. In early life, he never responded to the suggestions made from time to time that he should stand. He could hardly have given up his pressing private affairs for a life in London, and he was too good a financier to cripple his resources by the lavish expenditure it required. He had once indeed hopes of reward for his public services in Westmorland by some lucrative post, hopes that were not without foundation; for the long Parliament that sat from 1661 to 1679 was dubbed Pensionary from the number of unearned salaries it dispensed,* and his friend Joseph Williamson was high in Court favour. If the char-pies † that about this time were speeded from Rydal to high county dignitaries (even reaching once the palate of the Duke of York!) were sent in the nature of a bribe, they were at least a delicate one; and Joseph's honeyed epistles did sometimes create pleasant expectations. For instance he wrote, on March 26th, 1670.—

"I have ye fauor of y^r excell^t charpye & so I had of a discreet & prudent long letter some time before, for all wch I humbly thank y^u, I am pleased till wee find some other wayes of telling y^u ye esteeme wee have for yor discreet & loyal cares in ye County-affaires. If Requests had or doe goe on, or anything of that kind I pray y^u comand me most freely, who am wth much affection & esteeme

     Deare S^r
      Yo^r most humble Servt
       Joseph Williamson

So when this courtly gentleman became Secretary of State, 1674 (5757), Daniel wrote him a frank appeal, recounting the various honorary offices he had filled in the three counties—Sheriff, Commissioner for Assessments, Deputy Lieutenant, Justice of the Peace, and commander (in various grades up to Lieutenant Colonel) of the Trained Bands in Westmorland and Cumberland. He wishes for neither knighthood nor the honour of being made Baronet, adding characteristically:—

"few enjoyeing it but by purchase which makes it to mee ye less desirable,"

but he would like some lucrative employment, in which he would:—

"truely serve ye King and you according to my utmost ability, and shall be (from time to time) accomptable for what part of ye profits thereof & to whom you shall be pleased to appoint."

---
* For pensions to Westmorland big-wigs see Ferguson's *Westmorland*, p. 227.
† See Fisheries

Williamson's reply is evasive (1581). He is eager to serve the squire of Rydal, either in the interest of others or (much more) for himself :—

" The only thing I have to wish is some occasion such as would be to yo' likeing, by wch I might in some measure make it good. That's what I have long wished for, and I beg y^u will thinke w^t it would be," &c.

And when Daniel lost his wife, he wrote :—

" I am infinitely sorry for ye great losse yor Family has suffered, and if I had not ye hono^r to be somewhat neare in yor Friendshipp, ye part I find all ye Country takes in it, would entitle me to a share too   I doe assure y^u, Sir, I take a very sensible one in all that touches y^u, & I wish wth all my heart I had some good occasion to show y^u I doe so "

But fine phrases remained all he had to offer. He fell under the suspicion of the Parliament in 1678, raging then against Catholics (2078), for an action performed for the king; and in Royal Stuart fashion the king threw him over as a sop to popular faction. An instance of the rotten state of court affairs is afforded by his dismissal. The king told him :—

" one Sunday morninge he was noe longer fitt for y^t employm^t as the Kinges afferes att this time was, and ye secretarie's plaice given to my Ld Sunderland   He is promised to have ye 6000^ls given him he payed for it, together wth 2000^ls Sr Floyde is to pay for his plaice " *

The honour that came to the squire of Rydal appears to have been unsolicited. In March, 1681, the king, being sick of his refractory Parliament (2411), suddenly appeared in person and dissolved it, as Sir John Lowther of Whitehaven wrote to Daniel; while the next Parliament meeting at Oxford, on March 21st, 1681, proving as obstreperous, was also dissolved in eight days. Perhaps

---

* Sir Philip Lloyd, one of the Clerks of the Council   See Hulton Correspondence.

LATER DAYS

he was seeking to make friends with men who would enter a new one. Daniel had already received notice from high quarters. In the preceding August a present of half a buck had arrived from Witherslack, another from Lord Thanet, and half "a syde of Redd-Deer" from Lord Sussex. In September he was invited to dine at Penrith with the latter, once Lord Dacre, a bankrupt roué who had been created Earl of Sussex when he took (along with £20,000) the king's bastard daughter of 12 years of age to wife.* He then passed on, as his account book shows, to Graystoke Castle, to dine with the Duke of Norfolk, who was setting out for London. He also met the Earl of Carlisle in the following February, and visited the Earl of Arundel again. On the 14th of April he set out for London, and his proceedings there are entered also in his account book.

The fees for his knighthood cost him £78. 13s. 4d This honour certainly made him a king's man, as his subsequent actions showed In 1684 the king, who had called no Parliament since the Oxford one, and was probably preparing the way for a more subservient one, made a bold stroke to get the boroughs into his power, because they had come to completely control the local elections. This he did by issuing to them new charters on surrender of their old ones; the new skilfully introducing a clause by which he could remove at pleasure all the town officials.† The squire of Rydal helped the measure on. His account book, from August 3rd onward, boastfully chronicles his doings, as he and the High Sheriff of Cumberland rode to meet and accompany the Duke of Norfolk to Carlisle; then with Sir Christopher Musgrave and other gentlemen to meet the Lord Chief Justice, Sir George Jeffreys. His own little cortege consisted of seven; himself, his sons William and Daniel, his cousin Jack Browham with three

---

* See *Flemings in Oxford*, p 504, note 14.
† See Ferguson, p 178

men to ride behind ; and his expenses in Carlisle for men and horses came to £3 11s. 2d. From Carlisle the great train of riders made a progress to the chief towns,* skilfully extracting from them their old free charters. He writes for August 13th :—

"This day I prevailed with the Corporation of Kendal to surrender their charter, and they appointed Sir Christopher Musgrave to be their attorney."

He repeats this phrase in connection with the resigned charter of Lancaster.

Sir John Lowther of Lowther, who was now in opposition to the Court party, imputes in his Memoir of James II., the blame of this illegal surrender of Carlisle and Appleby to Sir Christopher Musgrave and Sir George Fletcher.

Memoir of James II

". . . S^r C M & S^r G Ff. took possession of the corporations of Carlisle & Applebie, entering into the ffirst in a kind of cavalcade, & ostentation of meritt, when in realitie they had so ffar complied with those times as to deliver up the charters of Carlisle, Kendall, &c. which was the illegall action now redressed" (by James II).

But Sir Daniel's assertion that he "prevailed" at Kendal and Lancaster may be allowed to stand. Strangely docile indeed had the once refractory corporation of the Barony become in his hands.! The new charter, in which the names of various chief tradesmen figure as aldermen is given in *The Boke off Recorde of Kirbie-Kendall*. Ferguson considers that the town hoped for some privileges in return ; but they were disappointed. Nor did Charles even use this acquired command over city elections ; he called no further Parliament, and died next year.

Sir Daniel now felt himself in the full current of success.

---

* These entries are given in full in the His MSS. volume

His August progress with judges and gentlemen, renewing charters and settling differences between friends, was closed by a grand finale, which the Earl of Thanet's marriage at this time opportunely afforded. This nobleman, then Lord Lieutenant of the County, and his bride (the Duke of Newcastle's daughter) were met on their journey to Appleby at the Cross on Stainmoor that marks the county boundary, by (so the account book says) about fifteen hundred horse, who accompanied the wedded pair to Appleby, and "my Lord Thanet haveing entertained us Barony men there two nights," the squire of Rydal gave to the Castle servants 10s. Also Sir Christopher Musgrave, now the risen man, was paid "court" to at Soulby by Sir Daniel, who took with him Sir Christopher Philipson and his cousins Mr. Thomas Brathwaite and Mr. John Browham. Even Sir Christopher's servant was placated, a sword and belt for himself being purchased from this man for £3. 16s. and a fee of £4 paid him, for his son-in-law Wilson being made a J.P. for Westmorland. Money was flowing freely. Lord Thanet, who on his progress to Appleby had given his own tenants "thirty guinnies" to drink the king's health, included all Westmorland in his bounties. In the following February Sir Daniel received, by the hands of Mr. Lancelot Forth, the mayor of Kendal, under the new charter, £10

"to give in y⁶ Parishes of Gresmere & Windermere to y⁶ poor Householders there that go to Church"

But before this, on the 11th of February, 1685, news had arrived of the king's death on the 6th, and on the 12th the Rydal squire writes :—

"haveing early this morning given notice to the Barony gentleman, I and my three sons did go to Kendal, where King James the 2nd was proclaimed with loud huzzas and health drinking; the day being concluded, after Mr Forth had entertained the gentlemen at his house, with bell-ringing and bonfires"

Addresses and rival petitions to the new monarch now engrossed the attention of Sir Daniel. Sir John Lowther seems to have been beforehand with the Tories by getting an address sent up in the names of the king's tenants in the Barony (account book), and on February 16th Sir Daniel met Sir Thomas Strickland, Sir John Otway, with Sir Christopher Philipson and other " Barony men " to discuss a counter-petition along with a letter to Sir Christopher Musgrave. Possibly it was this address which was signed on the 21st, when Sir Daniel actually paid 12s. 5d. in gratuities at Kendal. On April 25th we read that " ye Justices & Jurors joyned in an Address to his Majesty ; " while the entry of May 6th of 1s 6d. " Spent at Kendal, when we Justices sent away our Address which S^r Jo. Lowther had kept from us " seems to intimate that Sir John Lowther had detained a document which he was not favourable to.

Sir Daniel was clearly marked out as a man of James II's first Parliament. On March 11th he notes in his account book :—

" Memorandum   This day the principal burgesses desired me very earnestly to represent the town of Cockermouth in the next parliament which is to meet the 19th day of May next   £   s   d
00. 00 00.

Accordingly he rode to Carlisle in the train of Sir Christopher Musgrave, now made Governor of Carlisle, and proceeded there to do his electioneering business with great ease and cheapness.* To two men who went to Lorton and other places to secure the votes of some doubtful burgesses of Cockermouth, on behalf of himself and his fellow candidate, Sir Orlando Gee, he paid 5s., and on the day after the election he gave the bailiff of Cockermouth " for my part of his entertaining of the burgesses " £10, adding :—

---

* See Account Book entries in His MSS Com

"Memorandum Mr Morrison and I promised to pay him either of us 5^lbs more, in case he should not get 10^lb from my Lord Wharton, or some of his agents for entertaining of his son William Wharton's voters against us two"

There was a further bill of £3. 3s. 6d. produced four months later by a servant of Sir G. Fletcher and another man, for expenses at the election. From the tone of the entry, Sir Daniel shows annoyance at what he considers may be an imposition.* But all told this would bring his expenses up to something short of £20; a very different matter from the sums paid even in those days, as is shown by the contested election for Knight-of-the-Shire for Westmorland on the death of Sir Philip Musgrave in 1678. Sir Daniel had been pressed to stand himself at this time, but had prudently decided instead to assist Mr. Richard Lowther as candidate against Mr. Alan Bellingham; meeting the freeholders at Tebay (1994) on Mr. Lowther's behalf, at seven in the morning on the day of the election. Mr. Richard, who had travelled from London by the "four days" coach for the election was much disgusted at his failure. He had no intention of hazarding a second election, he wrote to his aider —

"as the Barony men have failed you so badly and the charges, already nearly 600^lbs, have much exceeded my present ability &c" (2013)

Sir Daniel therefore, under a Court influence so strongly exercised as to form afterwards the subject of a protest by the Whigs in the House, headed by Sir John Lowther of Lowther, slipped easily into Parliament. Tips to great men's servants he could not neglect; and besides a fee of £1. 1s. 6d. to Lord Thanet's servant for a fresh appointment as Deputy Lieutenant and Lieutenant Colonel of a foot regiment, he gave to my Lady Thanet's page and a

---
* This could hardly have been the cause of a rupture with his brother-in-law; but on September 16th, 1686, he and Sir George Fletcher went to Rose Castle, "where the Bishop & Sr Christo. Musgrave made him & me Friends"

black boy whom, in the fashion of the time, she had brought to Skipton Castle, the sum of 18s. On May 5th the three Westmorland companies met at the earthwork by the Eamont called the Round Table, where Sir Daniel gave 6d to the poor assembled to see the spectacle, and thence they marched into Penrith, where the officers were entertained at dinner by Lord Thanet. The Lord Lieutenant likewise gave £5 to the troop of horse, and £2 to every foot company. From Penrith the squire of Rydal journeyed to London to take his seat in Parliament for the first time His stay was not long, and his expenses from May 8th to July 16th (exclusive of purchases) are set down briefly as £29. 8s. 5d.

That this occasion was a proud one to him is shown by the entry in his account book for July 17th. It represents indeed but a 6d., but this was given to a fiddler who graced a great merry-making at Rydal when most of the squire's relatives came to congratulate him on his return.

Another gala-day, for the village more especially, was arranged on the 26th, as a Thanksgiving Day for the king's victory over " ye late D. of M. & Earl of Argile." Then those local favourites, Renny and Robert Benson, were busy with their fiddles, and had 1s. for their music, while the expenses of a " Bone-Fire " came to 2s. These jovialities were no doubt greatly enjoyed by the village folk, without their feeling any keen sensations of loyalty for the king, or relief at the tragic ending of the Duke of Monmouth's rebellion.

In October the squire again journeyed to London, and most comfortably and cheaply. His old friend and tutor, Dr. Thomas Smith, who had remained perhaps the most interesting of his many correspondents, had married Lady Fletcher, his wife's mother, and had successively been made Dean of Carlisle and Bishop.

To such high dignity, a coach was indispensible, and going up to Parliament in October (2952), he wrote to the new M P. that he could easily spare him a seat therein. In easeful glory therefore the squire travelled, taking with him only a boy and horse. He had, to be sure, to tip the Bishop's coachman £1 ; and the expenses of the journey, which took twelve days going and fourteen returning (the roads no doubt getting more mirey in the short December days), amounted to £5. 7s. 9d one way and £5. 16s. 8d. the other. He seems to have stayed in London only a fortnight (this was in November, 1685), putting his horse up at the Swan-with-two-necks, in Tuttle Street, at the rate per day of 1s. 8d. for oats and hay, amounting (with 2s. 6d to ostler) to £1. 9s. 2d. , while his own " chamber " with a glazier in the same street came only to 14s , or 1s. a night Besides, his general expenses amounted only to £2. 15s. 7d ; and his only purchase was a leather hat-case, 3s. 6d.

This seems to have been his last effort to sit in the House. Perhaps, like the Scotchman with his " Bang went saxpence ! " he felt London was too dear a place for him ; perhaps he found, as did so many other of the king's friends, that the royal policy was too high-handed for him to follow. At any rate, when the king in 1687 dissolved a Parliament which had already come into opposition with him, the Rydal squire had had enough of it.

Lord Thanet pressed him at once to stand for the next Parliament, promising that if his Cockermouth seat were unsafe, he would support him for Appleby , and adding that " Great interests are already making."

But Sir Daniel was making up his differences with the Whigs, in the persons of Sir John Lowther of Lowther and his relative of Whitehaven. He answered cautiously (3134) that he found absence from home in London very prejudicial to his large family of children, and therefore declined to stand for Appleby. It was now that the king took the extraordinary measure, in order to pack the next House with men already pledged to his side, of sending the Lord Lieutenants down to their counties, to personally examine the views of all the gentlemen and electors as to the Acts he had failed to pass, and to extract from them promises of support. Such arbitrary dealings were even beyond Lord Thanet's sense of compliance. He resigned his office, which was promptly filled by Lord Preston. The greatest excitement prevailed in the county over the matter, and all the examinations by the Lord Lieutenants of Lancashire and the East Riding of Yorkshire, which took place before these for Westmorland, were fully retailed to Sir Daniel by his correspondents.* The categorical set of questions which the officials and gentry were to negative or affirm were known beforehand, and there was time for consultation and preparation of answers. Sir Daniel had one ready, which the Bishop of Carlisle had read and approved on January 20th, 1688, at the same time advising the writer to follow the courteous custom of meeting Lord Preston a stage on his journey, and to accompany him to Penrith. It was at the George Inn at Penrith that the Deputy Lieutenants and J.P.'s of Cumberland and Westmorland were bidden to meet the king's inquisitor.† On the questions being put—whether as either Members of Parliament or burgesses, they would assist at taking off the Penal Laws and Tests, or would give their support at the elections only to such as would—Sir John Lowther of Lowther proposed that the answers should be written, and Sir Daniel seconded the motion.

We find this extract in Sir John Lowther's Memoir of James II..—

"These questions were brought into this countrie by my Ld Preston, Lord Lieutenant for these two counties. And the gentle-

---

* See Rydal Hall Papers His MSS Com

† Ferguson says on December 27th, 1687, but the meeting was arranged for January 24th, 1688 as the letters and account-book show, as well as the summons. See 3164.

men were summoned to meet him at Penrith A day or two before the time appointed, Sr Daniell Ffleming came thither, & desired to know my opinion about an answer to them I showed him my thoughts, wch he pleased to approve, & my answer was so universallie liked, that, excepting by two or three att most, it was given verbatim by all the gentlemen that did comply with the questions, wch were about 17 or 18."

The answers given in by all but five of the Protestant gentlemen were to one effect · a refusal to bind themselves in any way, clothed in courteous and loyal terms * James II. had practically failed, and the loss of his kingdom soon followed With this revolution Sir Daniel had nothing to do, as Sir John Lowther of Stockbridge, had, and (more secretly †) Sir John of Lowther; but it appears to be clear that he went along with the general feeling of the country in his rejection of the last ruling Stuart. The close of his account book shuts the door upon the details of his private life, and there remains only his correspondence.

That he loved the pomp of life, when it could be had at a reasonable cost, is certain. His little cortege, when he rode to the Quarter Sessions or the Assizes with two or three of his sons at his side and a couple of men at his back, is clearly sketched in his account book with a note of pride. One such riding to Carlisle in 1686, that included a pause at Rose Castle, where his old friend lived in state, cost for six men and horses, and wine, etc. " in parting with Sir Christopher Musgrave," the sum of £5. 0s. 3d.

William III. was now king and Daniel's sons were now growing up about him, and had their places to find in the world. He kept a firm hand over them and over his household affairs, as his correspondence shows , and none

---

* Perhaps it was his action on this occasion that caused him, the Earl of Derby and four others to be left out of the Commissioners of Peace for Lancaster.

† See Ferguson, p. 235.

felt this more sorely than William the eldest. Besides the usual discontent felt by an heir who is not allowed much money, he added the fretfulness of feeble health and lameness; and the home was without a mother who would have sympathized with him and smoothed the friction that was natural to the circumstances. Nothing had been spared certainly, in the effort to cure Will's leg. When bone-setters and specialists had been given up in despair (see Health), and the boys "staffs" were a constantly recurring item of charge, visits to the Holy Well at Humphrey Head were made almost annually, and we hear finally of a long visit to Bath in 1692-3, where he bathed and drank the waters in a fashionable crowd, and his father scathingly writes in hope that he will not only perfect the cure of his leg, but—

"the cure of your itch of rambling, talking and scribbling imprudently and undutifully." (5825)

But that was after Will's emancipation from home life. He had been kept at Kendal school till close upon the age of 20, and there seems to have been no thought of college life for him. Then began his ridings with his father to county functions (for his lameness seemed not to stop his horsemanship) in the riding coat smartly lined with red or blue with a liveried boy of his own, to follow, with visits to cousins and friends and mild junketings to race-courses or stag-hunts and fairs with 5s. or 10s. given him "to keep his purse." He was Justice of the Peace when 22, the fees for which in London cost £6 16s. But of all these things he grew weary, as also of clothes made at home, even if they were carefully graded to cost more than his brothers and to look smarter. He wanted to marry, but his desire had been constantly frustrated, owing, as he thought, to his father's niggardliness in settlements proposed, though—poor youth!—it was quite as likely to have been caused by his own lameness and want of favour in the young ladies' eyes. He grew bitter; wanted freedom, and an allowance, complained he could not even visit his friends, not having enough money for the usual tips to servants; and it must have been a relief on both sides when his father at last agreed to an allowance and he removed himself from Rydal Hall, and the wrangles with his maiden sister Alice, (who became a housewife after her father's heart, but was not perhaps sympathetic or sweet-tempered,) could cease. On setting up for himself he took quarters in Kendal, where, to the reproach from home that he kept company beneath him in station, he replied that he could afford to keep no higher

But Will was neither a spendthrift nor wild; and though not very wise, he had some not ignoble ambitions, as well as some friends in high quarters. When Sir John Lowther of Lowther was created Viscount Lonsdale in 1696, Sir Daniel wrote his congratulations (4982), and added, " I am surprised and annoyed to hear that my son wishes to succeed you as member for the County." It was not till after the Viscount had replied, approving of William's candidature, that the latter ventured to write to his father, stating his intention And in November accordingly he was elected as Knight of the Shire, without opposition. His father still protested (6047), writing to Sir Christopher Musgrave that it was " much against my will," feeling that it will not be for his real advantage; for when young men's heads (Will was forty years old !) are filled too full of public politics, it often prejudices their own private concerns.

So William proceeded to London, and in December, " after a most extraordinary ill journey," was introduced to the House of Commons. There he was a conspicuous figure by his lameness, and no doubt engaged some sympathy He wrote home on the 12th of January, 1697, of his introduction to the king (5075) —

" Last Wednesday night a Lord, who is extraordinary kind to me, went with me to Kensington, and carried me into the King's chamber, and (gave) his Majesty such a character of me as that he called me to him, and when I was going to kneel down " (no mention of the crutches !) " the King bid me not give myself that trouble, and gave me his hand to kiss without my kneeling, a favour not usual After I had kissed his hand, he asked me how long I had been in town, and when I had given him an account he said he was very glad to see me. I stayed with him till he went to supper, attended him there, and returned with him to his chamber, till he was undressed to go to bed Then my kind friend & I came away "

His uncle, Sir George Fletcher, wrote that he attended with great diligence, " and will make as good use of his time as any can."

William could have made no figure in debate, but he settled down to write dutifully a full report of the proceedings of the House to his father, the autocrat of Rydal, who had always claimed from his friends such public news as they had to transmit. These letters continued till his father's death; and one or two personal touches show the gratification caused in William's mind by notice from high quarters.

Henry, the second son, accepted his father's surveillance better. But he was more fortunate in never living at home. Of good parts, his father sent him from Kendal school to Oxford, in 1678, where he spent over six years, till he moved in January, 1685, to the family living of Grasmere, vacant by the death of his relative, the Rev. John Ambrose.*

Daniel, the next boy, remained at home and became his father's right hand in the work of the estate. The silence of the correspondence and the account book regarding him, except when his goings and comings are recorded, or the cost of his home-spun clothes is set down, bespeaks a silent yet steadfast and hard-working dispo-

---

* See *Church of Grasmere*, p. 162-3. Also *Flemings in Oxford;* where all extant particulars of his college career are given.

sition. At twelve he left the village school to join his big brothers at Kendal, where on Harry's departure in 1678 he was left to keep the accounts always required by the father for himself and his little brother George, now sent to join him. He was now nineteen, and an entry—

"To ye Groum & Chamermade at Dalegarth   .. 00. 01. 00.

shows that he had a Christmas visit to the seat of Edward Stanley in Eskdale, whose boys John and Thomas * were apparently his school companions at Kendal. Indeed he had visited them the previous June with Harry,† and in July, 1680, when he left school he went again, and his father set down 6s. he spent there and at Kendal.

Well must Daniel have come to know the passes from Westmorland to Cumberland, though this is his last trip of pleasure recorded, except when he went to Cartmel well with Will. His father immediately put the farm and estate into his hands, and we find him buying and selling cattle, paying the field-workers, and attending the distant manor-courts at Beckermet and Skirwith. At first he had the trusty John Banks as supporter, or the relative John Browham, who seems to have been much at Rydal about this time; and always on his attendance at Ravenglass Fairs he had of necessity several men with him. He would drive over, by Three Shire Stone, as many as eighteen great beasts or twenty-seven from Kendal, or again eleven from Lancaster Fair

On these occasions his expenses are so small as to arouse a wonder as to where he slept. It is a satisfaction to find an entry showing a halt at hospitable Dalegarth, where for help to drive the beasts he paid 4d. (1652), while his spending at Fell-foot, when the drove made another halt,

---

* See *Flemings in Oxford*, p 482.
† June 16th "Given them (Harry and Daniel) to keep their purses 2^s, Disbursed at Dalegarth 2^s"

comes to 4d. again. Another attendance at the great Cumberland Fair cost him 2s., " & given him for his paines at 12^d ye day 3s," adds his father with an unusual burst of generosity. Patient Daniel! Content to labour without gain (for there is no trace of salary or allowance made him), to be dressed less well than his elder brothers, and to have but infrequent, small sums with which " to keep his pocket." At the age of 38 he died of smallpox, possibly taken when cattle-buying, for the crowded fairs were dangerous places in time of infectious sickness * ; and his father lost him and his labour.

George, born 1667, was seven years younger than Daniel, as John (who died an infant) and Barbara and Mary came between. The entries concerning him give an impression of a lively, smooth temperament, with a head-piece good enough to make it worth while, in his father's estimation, to send him to college. He had several schoolmasters. At eleven he left the Rydal village school for Kendal, where Daniel was finishing, and after Daniel left, from June, 1680, to the close of the year, he was there alone. But a life in town lodgings for one so young could scarcely be advisable, and he was removed at the end of the year, to go to the Ambleside school, with his three next brothers, Michael, Richard and Roger, and was there taught by the curate. Here only the boys' dinners had to be paid for, instead of their complete " Table," *e.g.* :

" May 22. Sent by Jo Banckes to pay unto Mrs Forth in full of all Tableing and other Demands now due, for Daniel and George my sons .. 05 05. 00.

In 1686 George and Richard were sent to Sedbergh, to be under Posthumus Wharton.

In the summer of 1688 George was sent up to Oxford, but not to Queen's College, where Henry still was, but to St. Edmund's Hall. His letters to his father show a

---

See Edward Tyson's letters

calm undaunted demand for reasonable things, which none of his brothers could muster, a Greek Testament, or a Fee to enable him to enter and read in the College Library, or a desire to winter in Rydal (1691-2) after he has taken his degree and has two terms leave. This he did, and took his brother Roger with him on his return in March, having a bad journey with snow that took the horses up to their girths. George had a keen eye for advancement, and (4483) carried to the Master of Lincoln College in 1692 a pedigree which showed a family connection with Richard Fleming, Archbishop of York, and (when Bishop of Lincoln), founder of the College, hoping by it to be assisted to some gifts of the Foundation This proved in vain, and he had to fall back upon the ordinary path of ordination, with the assistance of such influence as his father possessed (5870), and on March 26th, 1695, he was collated by the family friend the prelate of Carlisle to the vicarage of Aspatria. But now his quick, ambitious mind caught at a strange project, and on October 6th he wrote to tell his father that he wished to go as chaplain with the East India Fleet (4856), a post which (along with a stipend of only £40) carried with it exciting possibilities. The last chaplain, for instance, brought home £3,000 (a sum to be at least quadrupled in modern values), and by an admiring University had been made Doctor on his return! Therefore George, with a confidence begot of sums given him of old to bet upon his cock, desired that his father should furnish money with which to engage in trade, as this was allowed by the Company. To this astonishing proposal we do not, unfortunately, possess the squire's reply, if he ever got it written; for two days later his relative Henry Brougham of Queen's College, wrote to Rydal discountenancing the "unaccountable" project, and George himself in another two days followed this up with apologies and repudiation. It was as well to get him in clerical harness, and his father apprised him in February next that the Bishop would expect him to be at his post in Cumberland by Easter (5156). In July, 1697, he was in Oxford again. He became chaplain to the Bishop and ended by being Bishop himself, and on his brother William's death in 1736, succeeded to his title as baronet.*

The church was no place for Michael, who left Hawkshead school in 1685. He was acting as his father's steward in 1690† but in 1693 at the age of 24 he obtained an ensign's commission in the regiment that was going to Flanders under Captain the Hon James Stanley, there to fight with William III's Dutch army against the French. For this he had to raise twenty men, and he soon obtained twenty-one volunteers, at whose head he marched to London, on roads almost impassable from snow.‡ He took part in the stirring campaign of 1693-4, of which he kept his father well informed, and obtained his lieutenancy; after petitioning for money (which he had previously asked for, for a horse) that would by enabling him to "look handsome" in the camp, assist his preferment. He was sent home as recruiting officer, when his father reported him as much improved (5842), stammering little, "neither swearing nor taking any tobacco, and very free from drinking, which are great accomplishments in a camp as well as a college"; this was written to George who was at Oxford with two brothers. With a fine set of northern recruits Michael left home again for Flanders, where he was engaged in the siege of Namur and wounded in the second attack of the town by the French. He writes home cheerfully on the day when the ball had been extracted from his shoulder, and expects under his good surgeon to be soon well. Home again with his Colonel at the end of 1695, he petitions his father from Lancaster

---

* Sir George Fleming, Bishop of this Diocese, died at Rose Castle, July 2nd, 1747, and was buried in the south aisle.—Hutchinson's *Cumberland*, II, 603

† See the Setling-Book.

‡ Letter from Warrington, March 5th, 1693.

for money for his recruiting service, and later announces from Kendal that he must give up some proposed visits, as he hears that some of the recruits are deserting, so he must get back to them, and march them to Lancaster.

These recruits were drawn apparently from the parts where his family was best known. He reports their behaviour in general as excellent, though two deserted to the French (4835), and a son of Mrs. Barnes (a Rydal name), had got dismissed by his captain in Flanders for extravagance and carelessness of his horse. Michael hopes he has been heard of at home.

" He came to me nakid and starving & I fitted him out at a cost of £5."

Later Michael was with the army as Major in Ireland.[*] He represented Cockermouth in Parliament in 1706,[†] and is said to have died in Hull, where his regiment was stationed in 1713 or 1714. He married Dorothy Benson, and had a son William, who eventually succeeded to the Rydal estate and baronetcy. The Bishop having lost his son in 1743

Richard (sixth living son), born 1669, followed Michael as steward of the demesne in 1693, and the neat little " Setling-Book " kept up to 1699 is his handiwork. He was fortunate enough in that year to marry Isabel Newby, heiress of Cawmire, in Winster, whither he removed. He died in 1717. His son Daniel died unmarried, and three of his daughters likewise. There is a monument in Grasmere to these aged spinsters, who seem to have made a home in Ambleside with their one married sister, Catharine, the wife of George Cumpstone.

Roger gave his father some trouble. Despatched to Oxford with George in February, 1693, it was difficult at first to find him a room in Queen's College. But this was

---

[*] See Sir Daniel's notes in his pedigree
[†] Rydal Hall Papers

done, and James (next in age) soon followed him there. In February, 1695, Sir Daniel sent money for the use of the two through George, who now required the fees for his degree of M.A (5842), and he adds :—

" If you think it best for Roger to come home with this bearer, I would have him do it, since he neglects his study so much. In his absence I hope your brother James will not miss himself."

He wrote at the same time a letter of admonition to James, saying that he had something else to do with his money than spend it idly in ale and tobacco, and bidding him to make a list of his and Roger's books, and to keep all things left behind by Roger carefully. But Roger did enter Holy Orders, and his father described him as " House hold Chaplain " at Rydal Hall.* He married after his father's death, one Margaret Moorhouse†, but in Bishop Nicolson's Diary for 1707 ‡ he seems to be moving among his brothers as a single man, while the wives of Henry and George are spoken of. He became vicar of Brigham ; and it was to his great-grandson that the baronetcy reverted on failure of the elder lines, and it continues in his line.

James, who was Captain of Militia, died unmarried. Fletcher, the youngest son, born on the mother's death in 1675, seems from the slight touches to be found about him, to have been a genial and loveable character. He was with his eldest brother William in London shortly before Sir Daniel's death,§ and after that event seemed to be in Rydal. He came into possession of half of Hobson's holding in Rydal, which he sold in 1714 ‖ He bought Fellfoot in Little Langdale, apparently about 1707. Also,

---

* Notes on the pedigree.

† Sep 29, 1702, Staveley in Kendal Register communicated by the late Mr J. A. Martindale.

‡ See *Transactions* C. & W A. & A. Society, N s. vol. iv.

§ Notes to pedigree, Rydal Hall MSS.

‖ Bishop Nicolson's Diary.

by his marriage with Elizabeth, daughter of Thomas Brathwaite, he acquired property at Storrs (known as Braithwaite Fold). Fell-foot remained his residence, and the Fleming crest of the coiled serpent on the front of the present house, with the remains of a raised plaster frieze in an upper and former guest-chamber, show that he decorated his house in the general style, though it could have no manorial pretensions. Remote as this dwelling appears to us now, he kept in touch with the times. Mr. Ben. Browne of Troutbeck wrote to his nephew, Mr. John Philipson, solicitor in London, in 1710.—

"Last Satterday Mr Fletcher Fleming sett fforwards of his Jorney towards London, and I think hee will be in London Tuesday night at the Bell Inn in Warwick Lane, and I with some other Company sett him through Lancaster wee parted with him last Tuesday at 3 or 4 o'clock in ye afternoon, as for the passage of our Travail and Mirth I suppose hee, when you meet with him will give you an account I pray God bless him for he is a worthy Gent^n and my very good Friend."*

He died in 1616 or 1617, and was buried at Grasmere. In his will he desires that instead of a funeral sermon, the preface to the Whole Duty of Man should be read by the minister, to whom the usual £1 must be given. His son Fletcher bought Rayrigg on Windermere in 1735, where the family has ever since resided.

Mary, the youngest daughter, born 1665, married first (*see* pedigree) Henry Bouch of Ingleton, who accepted a dowry from the father of only £500, being £100 less than went with her sister Barbara.

Sir Daniel died on March 25th, 1701, at the age of 68. He speaks to George (5842) in 1695, when urging him to make use of his time in Oxford, of the possibilities of his death, and his health may not have been good in later

---

* For this passage with other particulars I am indebted to the late Mr George Browne of Troutbeck

years. He led apparently a sedentary life, and made much use of his pen. Always a book-lover, he had bought books from his college days, when money was scarce ; and he continued to amass them to the end.* He corresponded with all who could furnish him with political information, and subscribed for the first news letters, written out by Mr. Joseph Williamson's clerks. These, with the printed ones that followed, were found among other papers at Rydal Hall in a state of confusion and neglect, by Sir Maxwell Lyte in 1882, and, being unique, were printed by the Historical MS. Commission † Sir Daniel likewise corresponded with antiquaries, county historians, map makers, and even with lesser schoolmasters, whose published books he criticized and recommended. He turned latterly to pedigree-making, his own family engaging of course his chief attention. He wrote down also the laws of the manor, as well as descriptive sketches of the counties over which he had ridden for so many years of his life. His MSS. were shown by his sons to Bishop Nicolson, on the latter's visit to Rydal in 1707, and two of them have been printed by the Cumberland and Westmorland Antiquarian Society.

It is satisfactory to note that there was no rancour in Sir Daniel's nature. He made friends with those whom he considered his enemies, as soon as the strife was over. He entertained his cousin, Lady Crossland, several times at Rydal, and also his cousin Collingwood. He was applied to by his arch-enemy Richard Harrison of Waterhead, Coniston, for a loan of £20 to £30 in 1667 for three months : the latter being pressed for money by Sir Jordan and Collingwood, and he attended his funeral. His daughter Catharine was godmother to Lancelot Harrison's son and heir.

With his family in general he was, unless a money-

---

* For particulars of these, see *Flemings in Oxford*
† Twelfth report, appendix, part vii

dispute arose, on excellent terms. His brother Alexander, after settling in Newcastle as a silk merchant, had died young, leaving his cousin Joseph Hudleston * (also in trade at Newcastle) his executor. With him Daniel had a law-suit from 1670 to 1673, alleging that Alexander had owed money to himself and his brother William, as well as to their mother. He enters £60 9s. received from the Hudlestons for his " charges " in his suit, as well as £4 passed on to his mother and brother. Daniel's remaining brothers died, like himself, at the turn of the century, William in the last month of the year 1700,† and Roger on the 3rd day of 1703. They were bachelors, as had been several in the older generation of the family. Roger had returned from London probably in bad health, and was content for the rest of his life with the quiet of Coniston Hall, where he and William were left alone after the deaths of their old uncle John Kirby and their mother, which occurred September 20th, 1680, and February 26th, 1681.‡ William had the family turn for saving; and amassed a good deal of landed property at the foot of Coniston lake, which he left to his nephew William, heir to Daniel. He seems to have been peculiarly kind to Daniel's children, " ye Major's man " (a name given him from his commission) being deputed often to " carry " them to and from Coniston or even to ride with the young ladies on their visits to distant relatives. It seems possible that the tradition lingering in Coniston as to " Major and Roger " may apply to the two bachelor brothers.§

Sir Daniel left as his executors his younger sons Roger, Richard, and Fletcher, with his unmarried daughter Alice. He left £10 to the poor of Grasmere, and £10 to poor tenants of Rydal and Coniston, etc., while six score of

---

* Second son of Andrew of Hutton-John, who married Dorothy Fleming.
† Buried December 23rd.—Coniston Register.
‡ For an inscription to their memory see *Flemings in Oxford*.
§ See *Book of Coniston*, W. G. Collingwood, p. 77.

his relations, friends and tenants (ten of Rydal among them) were to be chosen by his executors as recipients of a small bequest. The cash dealt with by them amounted to £6,396. 3s. 8¼d.

PART VII.

DE QUINCEY AND THE NAB.

De Quincey at Dove Cottage 1809. Marries Margaret Simpson of " The Nab " 1817. Edits " Westmorland Gazette " 1818-19. Writes " Confessions of an Opium Eater " 1821. Settles at Fox Ghyll 1821. Returns to Dove Cottage 1825. Goes to London. Dorothy Wordsworth's letter. Buys Nab estate 1829. Letter to Knight. Letters from de Quincey 1829. Further letters 1832. Eighth child born February, and Nab estate offered for sale September, 1833. Gives up Dove Cottage 1834. Hartley Coleridge at The Nab.

WHILE the poet Wordsworth enjoyed a peaceful tenancy of one old Rydal farmhold, another was connected with a literary man by ties of happiness, struggle, and pain. De Quincey indeed went in and out of two Rydal houses as master, but of The Nab he was for a time professedly owner. The story of that phantom ownership is here told for the first time, as the correspondence that reveals it was only lately found by the writer at Rydal Hall. It is at least an interesting episode in his life, and not only furnishes new details of his doings during several years, but throws a clearer light on his methods of dealing with money.

Wordsworth, a professed radical in his youth, retired to Grasmere to write poetry in 1800,* when the course of events in France had alarmed and disquieted his mind. Thither De Quincey followed him, first on a brief visit in 1807, which was succeeded by a longer stay in 1808-9;

---
* Actual date December 21st, 1799.

and when the poet left Dove Cottage in 1809, the younger man took up the tenancy of it. Kind Dorothy, the poet's sister, saw to the furnishing of it, bought pots and pans in Kendal and set village seamstresses to stitch curtains. Edward Wilson, the Grasmere carpenter, made shelves for his multitudinous books, the account for which stands at £7. 17s. 8d. in the ledger still preserved by his son. They were of deal, but the rest of the furniture was mahogany, which had been mentioned by De Quincey, and which Dorothy considered a prudent purchase, as it would sell for a higher price in case he left the cottage.

On November 19th, 1809, Dorothy* writes :—

"Our friend, Mr. De Quincey, is come to the cottage, rather I should say to Grasmere, (though we have already spent several comfortable evenings at the cottage), but he is with us at present, his servant arrived only the day before yesterday, and she is now busied in preparing the cottage for his permanent residence. He has been above a month with us, and is like one of our own family; so we have now almost a home still at the oldest and dearest spot of all. Mr De Quincey has an excellent library, far too large indeed for the house, though he will have bookcases in every corner. You may judge of the number of his books when I tell you that he has already received nine or ten chests, and that nineteen more are on the road. Some of these books must be kept in chests, on account of the smallness of the house . .
It is a great pleasure to us all to have access to such a library, and will be a solid advantage to my brother."

Thus De Quincey at the age of twenty-four settled in the Lake country as a man of leisure, not having yet finished the small fortune left him by his father, the Manchester merchant. His prospects of comfort and of congenial society looked promising. With the Wordsworths he seemed thoroughly at home ; and at their house he was frequently brought into contact with Coleridge, his first literary hero, as well as with Southey. To their children—and all children attracted him—he was passion-

---

* *Letters of the Wordsworth Family*.—Ed by Prof. Knight

ately devoted. It was doubtless for them that Wilson contrived the "Childers Carridge" that was charged to him 6s in this year. Later he came to know Professor Wilson (Christopher North) of Elleray, and Charles Lloyd of Brathay, with whom he took long walks in the hours of darkness With the two latter his intimacy grew. Perhaps with them his shy peculiarities of temper told less than when in the society of Wordsworth and Southey. De Quincey—whose tendency was to read and to dream, and in practical matters to drift—had already contracted the habit of opium-drinking, which drowned physical ills and gave him pleasant sensations. How long it was before the Wordsworths knew of this failing, identical with Coleridge's, cannot be said; but the eccentricities produced by it could not have been long or altogether hidden.

But besides these friends De Quincey made others, and of another class. He found congenial company in the Westmorland Statesman, who—intelligent, shrewd and humorous—knew how to talk to the courtly little gentleman without loss of dignity on either side. With the household of the Nab in Rydal an accidental reference shows that he was intimate as early as 1814; for it was on his return thence to Dove Cottage at three o'clock one Sunday morning, that he found Wilson—who had arrived at 1-30 a.m to pay him a visit—awaiting him, but asleep upon his bed * The story is characteristic of both men. But one wonders what kind of intercourse or talk was that, which so often drew the intellectual dreamer to the lonely farmstead and kept him there after midnight. We know the personages that sat around the hearth-fire of peat and wood within the low oak-raftered house. There was the old man, William Park, the holder of the place, vigorous but obstinate, and somewhat violent in temper it would seem. His idiot son might sit by, who was harm-

---
* Page's *Life of De Quincey.*

less indeed but still a terror to Grasmere boys, who gave him a wide berth on their way to the Ambleside school.* There was his son-in-law, John Simpson, a man it seems of intellectual tastes, who "in his long days, and sometimes nights, of solitary work, had made his own a good deal of the best literature of the country," according to his grand-daughter, who heard him recite in his old age, passages from "the Bible, Milton, Shakespeare, Pope's *Homer* and sometimes a whole *Spectator*," all in Westmorland dialect.† This side of his character must have created a bond with his fireside guest ; on another side he was easy-going, without judgment, and reputedly led by his wife. That wife, Mary, soon to inherit her father's estate, was a woman of a high and passionate nature, who was blamed, like her own heady son (perhaps present too) for subsequent misfortune. Then there was her daughter (at an earlier hour of the evening at least), sweet young Margaret, aged sixteen, who must have listened fascinated to the fluent talk of this stranger, and have brightened under the unwonted courtesy of his manner, so unlike that of her men-folk.‡ Finally, there was De Quincey himself, with his low stature and fine head, in love with Margaret and her shy looks.

The talk would be racy and radical in politics. It was a time when reform was in the air. And the need for reform in Rydal was pressing. The fetters of the manorial system, borne for centuries with ease, and later with simple patience, were now galling the statesmen. There seemed no redress from their grievances, and yet they hoped for it. The Rydal steward complained that there was at this time a sort of conspiracy among the tenants ; and certainly from 1806, when the highest known fine had been levied on them at the lord's death, a few of the

---

* From Edward Wilson, one of those boys
† Mrs Florence Baird-Smith Page's *Life* vol 1, p. 194
‡ Margaret had three sisters and two if not three brothers of whom William had a forge at Tongue Ghyll later

most prominent among them had ceased to pay their rent. William Park was one of these. It was a violent measure to take, and one quite hopeless, unless they could have secured a voice in Parliament that would demand some amelioration of conditions that were continually pressing harder. The village court was lost, by which the body of holders, claiming "custom," could have made head against their lord; and there was no other court in which the peculiar condition of their tenure, carried out by oral law only, could be rightly adjudged. An eminent counsel, when appealed to over Scott's case,* had advised the lord not to carry it to court. This may have given confidence to the tenants and raised their hopes of a favourable verdict in a distant and alien court; or perhaps they thought by rebellion to bring the lord to compromise. Possibly Park and the Simpsons believed that talk with this reputedly rich gentleman, who knew London and the world, might forward their matter. But the sword, long over-hanging, was presently to fall.

Before this, however, De Quincey had married Margaret. It was by licence, and the Grasmere register speaks of them as "both of this parish." Little Dora Wordsworth signed the register. It was a union entered into blindly on both sides. He was now thirty-one, and she twenty-one. Since 1813, his opium drinking had increased to an appalling extent, reaching he says 8,000 drops of laudanum per day; and though in prospect of his marriage, he suddenly and totally checked the habit, and could enjoy with his gentle wife something like a year of happiness, it set in again before long with force, and through 1817 and part of 1818, was at the old level, occasionally touching 12,000 drops per day.† How must his condition, drugged, wretched, and useless, have affected the young wife, now fast bearing him children? "She

---
* See chapter on Green-how Law.
† Masson's *Life of De Quincey*.

was a woman of a steady mind, tender and deep in her excess of love."*

And she had other cares, besides her husband's condition of mind and body. The question of means was not apparently considered on the marriage, and Margaret was simply taken to live among the crowding books of Dove Cottage. Every room was lined with them, and every chair piled with them, while the residue lay upon the floor. De Quincey was indeed looked upon as a man of property by the dalesfolk, but if he had cared to examine his financial position in 1816, he must have found that the little fortune which he had been spending and giving without thought, had diminished to a perilously low sum. At his best he understood money only as a scheme on paper, which had no more relation to fact than had his opium-bred dreams : while at his worst he was incapable of thinking at all of money. "Without the aid of M(argaret)," he says,† "all record of bills paid, or to be paid, must have perished ; and my whole domestic economy, whatever became of Political Economy"—a subject on which he had begun by dictation to her, to write—"must have gone into irretrievable confusion." But how little could poor Margaret do, by the sorting of bills, when there was no money with which to pay them ! By 1818, absolute want must have faced De Quincey, and he is found rousing himself from opium, by a brave effort, to endeavour to earn money by his pen, the only means open to him. He not only sketched one of his monetary *chimeras* for the benefit of his uncle, the colonel in India (while asking for a loan of £500) demonstrating that he could easily from this time forth earn a competence by writing for the Reviews and by editing the *Westmorland Gazette*, but he did actually conduct that paper for over a year. His connection with it has been dealt with by

---

* Page's *Life*, p. 200.
† Page's *Life*, p 202

Mr. Charles Pollitt, its late proprietor, in a pamphlet ; *
and in this he corrects some slight errors of the *Lives*.
It was on July 11th, 1818, that De Quincey entered on
his office, which he held under a committee of Tory
gentlemen who had started a weekly newspaper as the
organ of their party, at a time when Brougham's contest
of the seat held for long by the Lowthers had raised
politics to a high pitch of excitement For his editorship
he received £3 a week for the first three weeks ; but by
that time it seems to have been found necessary to engage
a sub-editor, owing to his distance from Kendal, and
possibly also to his unmethodical ways. He therefore
agreed to receive only one guinea for the leaders and
articles he wrote, while his subordinate who saw to the
business make-up of the paper took the remainder. This
arrangement seems to have been preferred by De Quincey
to giving up his mountain home, and living in Kendal.
Still, a letter written to his wife from a Kendal inn, shows
that he was at least occasionally detained there.† It
expresses home-sickness and anxiety about an illness of
baby Margaret , while he assures his wife that if she
cannot come to Kendal the following day, he will try to
be at Grasmere next week Margaret must have often
accompanied the chaise that bore him the seventeen miles
to and from his home , for many years afterwards he
recalls the drives downwards past Orrest Head, where the
road drops steeply through the woods of Windermere,
with her by his side, and her hand within his ‡

" Through many a score of nights—nights often dark as Erebus,
and amidst thunders and lightnings the most sublime—we descended at twelve, one, and two o'clock at night, speeding from
Kendal to our distant home twenty miles away."

---

* *De Quincey's editorship of the Westmorland Gazette* Kendal · Atkinson and Pollitt, 1890.

† Masson, p 68 ; Date not given.

‡ Given in his essay *The Saracen's Head*.

Perhaps his imagination, playing half remorsefully round the past, after his loving companion was lost to him, exaggerated the frequency of those nightly adventures, when they plunged down the road " often with the speed of a hurricane." Such journeys were liable to detention. It was necessary at least once for the editor to explain in writing to the proprietors that his failure to appear at the office before printing time was owing to the fact that a foot of snow had impeded his progress. Explanations also to the readers, as to the delay of writing on promised subjects, were frequent. He was indeed constant in apology and explanation; for De Quincey would not have been himself had he been punctual and prompt. We cannot indeed but admire the continued effort made by a man who had hitherto lived by no rule or limit of time, and often under the effect of drugs. However, friction increased between his chiefs and himself, until a climax came when, under date June 29th, 1819, they put into writing their displeasure at the loss and injury to the paper caused by his frequent absence from his post at a critical moment, and they expressed as well a desire that he should prevent the recurrence of such mishaps, due doubtless (they politely added), to the great distance of his residence from Kendal. This kind of remonstrance became too much for the sensitive and proud De Quincey, and at a special meeting of the proprietors on November 5th, 1819, his resignation was accepted. Thus his first and only attempt at editorship came to an end

That it was a failure cannot be said. Drudgery at a guinea a week (with hire of chaise deducted) could not keep De Quincey and his family; yet the period of toil was not wasted. It had roused a hitherto idle man to a sense of power: his capacity was proved; he could write, and he loved to write. That he was immensely interested even in the recriminating politics of the county, is evidenced by the excerpts given by Mr. Pollitt. Some of these passages—notably the one on Fox's party—show him to be already a master of prose; and singular indeed was the fortune of this provincial paper in that it introduced to the world at its start one who was shortly to become a shining light in the literary firmament. The germ of many a famous essay is to be found in the columns of the little news-sheet: notably his theory on the origin of the language of the district. Kant too he discoursed upon, Political Economy, Royalty, on its theoretic side, etc., or he would recount the story of a fire at Dove Cottage, fortunately discovered in time by himself as he toiled with his pen through the midnight hours. And whatever he wrote about, he promised his readers more of the same in the next issue; while he constantly proposed a fresh series that was not continued. Strangely enough, he suppressed local news, in favour of long reports from the Assize Courts. This bore fruit later in " Murder considered as one of the Fine Arts." He was, in fact, brimming over with literary energy and ideas, as is shown by a letter written to Wordsworth on June 14th, 1819.

Thus when De Quincey bid adieu to the Kendal printing office, his life-work was cut out for him. But further literary employment had to be sought, and after a visit to Edinburgh, where he was cordially received by Wilson and his friends; but obtained nothing certain, he returned home early in 1821, and thence travelled to London on the same quest. Success as a writer came; his *Confessions of an Opium Eater* that appeared in the *London Magazine* for September, 1821, made him all at once a famous man. But money flowed in slowly from these irregular sources; he was often terribly short, and miserable in the extreme. He speaks pathetically of his permanent exile from his home, saying :—

" My three eldest children, at that time in the most interesting stages of childhood and infancy, were in Westmorland; and so powerful was my feeling .... of some long, never ending separation from my family, that at length in pure weakness of mind, I was obliged to relinquish my daily walks in Hyde Park and Kensington Gardens, from the misery of seeing children in multitudes that too forcibly recalled my own."

His family was at this time settled at Fox Ghyll, Loughrigg, a cottage owned by Mr. Blakeney of Whitehaven, who had likewise purchased Fox How. The reason for the move seems merely to have been that Dove Cottage would not hold both books and babies, therefore the babies must go, even if a double rent be incurred, though his means and his capital were getting alarmingly low. The date of this change is not ascertained, but that it was accomplished before the close of 1821, is shown by a letter of the landlord to the poet Wordsworth, in which he remarks, under date April 25th, 1822:—

" I too regret the necessity of letting Fox Ghyll. I do not understand Mr. De Quincey; he has promised by two different Letters to pay his rent, but the Bill is not yet come to hand; it was to have been paid on the 15th. April. Next week I must write him, if it does not arrive."*

On November 19th of the same year, Dorothy Wordsworth wrote to Edward Quillinan:—

" Poor Mr. Blakeney is dead, so it is probable that Fox Gill will be to be sold, for Mrs Blakeney is not likely to come to it herself— Mr. De Q. is there, shut up as usual—the house always blinded—or left with but one eye to peep out of—he probably in bed—We hear nothing of him."

This clever descriptive touch of the house and its strange occupant, shows that De Quincey's morbid tendency to shrink from society could not pass unnoticed in the country as it might do in the town. The letter is followed up by another from Mrs. Wordsworth to the same

---

* Kindly communicated by Mr Gordon Wordsworth from the poet's correspondence, as are the following extracts

correspondent ten days later, when she apprizes him of the fact that :—

"F. G. may be purchased—yet it is not publickly offered for Sale. The Seer continues in close retirement."

De Quincey's fourth child, Francis John, was baptized from Fox Ghyll on February 28th, 1823. This is only the second entry to be found in the church register, but we know that besides William, little Margaret and Horace had been born to him, and that another followed at the end of the next year.

Sara Hutchinson writes to Edward Quillinan, December 8th, 1824 :—

"perhaps you may not have heard that Mrs Luff has purchased Fox Ghyll, but the question is, when will she eject the de Quinceys?"

And Mrs. Wordsworth, writing on December 10th, says ·

"Mrs Luff has really and truly purchased Fox Ghyll—the de Q s are to leave early in the spring i e. provided the O(pium) E(ater) arrives from London, whence he has been expected for weeks, and is able to move himself and family out of it—by the bye Mrs de Q. is confined of her 5th —Then her (Mrs L's) business of building repairing and ornamenting will begin"

There were eventually three more children, whose names and dates are set out in the following list :—

De Quincey.

1816. Nov. 15.	*William*	" my first-born child, the crown & glory of my life " [d 1835, not quite 18]
1817. Feb. 15.		married Margaret Simpson
1818	*Margaret,*	bap July 29. 1818 (called by Masson the eldest, after death of William)
1820	*Horace,*	" next after Margaret " Masson p 95 died in China, end of 1842.
1823	*Francis John,*	bap. Feb 1823 b at Fox Ghyll.
1824	*Paul Frederick,*	b. at Fox Ghyll Nov or Dec. baptized Ap. 29. 1827

1827	*Florence Elizabeth*, b. at Nab Cottage. bap Dec. 2 1827
1829	*Julius*, bap Nov 14 1829 [b either at Dove or Nab Cottage]
1833	*Emily Jane*, b Feb. 27. 1833.

Margaret and Horace were born at Dove Cottage, but only William, who was born at the Nab is entered in the church register. It will be noticed that two of the children were taken to the font in one year.

Page says that his two elder children, William and Margaret went to Edinburgh with him " shortly after " 1826 for a better education.

Florence Elizabeth married an officer who greatly distinguished himself in the Indian Mutiny. His daughter, Miss Florence Baird Smith, writing to Miss Armitt, December 11th, 1909, says :—

" My sister and I are not the only survivors of my grandfather. His youngest daughter Emily de Quincey is alive and the two children of his eldest daughter Margaret Craig "

De Quincey, already dubbed " the Opium Eater," from his astonishing " Confessions," * when writing to Wilson from London in February, 1825, advises him of the removal soon taking place, and tells him to address next either under cover to his wife at Rydal Nab, Westmorland, or to a friend in London, but preferably to the latter, since he did not wish to be tracked just then He speaks of being quite free from opium, but miserable in the extreme :—

" To fence with these (his ailments) with the one hand, and with the other to maintain the war with the wretched business of hack-author, with all its horrible degradations, is more that I am able to bear At this moment I have not a place to hide in sometimes I meditate I know not what . . . . With a good pub-

---

* " Confessions of an Opium Eater " appeared in *London Magazine,* Sep , 1821.

lisher and leisure to premeditate what I write, I might yet liberate myself after which, having paid everybody, I would slink into some dark corner, educate my children, and show my face in the world no more,"

And Wilson writes hoping that :—

" some beautiful things are winging their way hither at this time from Rydal Cottage."

De Quincey was in fact about this time in the direst straits for money. It was apparently a little later that his friend Knight, editor of the *Quarterly Magazine*, at whose house he might (but for his shyness) have been staying, found him in a miserable lodging, waiting till he could cash a large draft from his mother, which was to release him from pressing debts and permit his return to Westmorland. In an unpublished letter, dated July 16th, 1825, he implored Dorothy Wordsworth, in the most moving terms, to go and see his wife, about whose condition he is anxious. She is taking so much to heart his embarrassments, that grief in her present lonely situation may produce illness

" If that should happen, I know not what I must look for next; and I shall never have any peace of mind, or a happy hour, again."

He adds that he is now in a condition to extricate himself in 28 days.

Whatever response he received, he was able soon after, with lightened circumstances and heart, to return to his family, who had moved back in this year, 1825, from Fox Ghyll to Dove Cottage. It was at the close of the next year, when he was back in London, that kind Dorothy Wordsworth paid his wife a visit at Dove Cottage, as we know from her letter written to De Quincey, now back in London, to tell him of his family's welfare. The letter is dated November 16th, and though published already *

---

* *Letters of the Wordsworth Family*, edited by Professor Knight, vol. ii, p. 293.

will bear repetition in part here, giving as it does a somewhat pathetic picture of the patient wife, who was clearly no letter-writer herself, and was moreover never sure when she might hear from her husband. Dorothy's wise advice, that she and the little ones should join him to form one household, was not to be carried out for a long time.

"My dear Sir,
A letter of good tidings concerning Mrs De Quincey and your family cannot, I am sure, be unwelcome; and besides, she assures me that you will be glad to hear of my safe return to Rydal after a nine months' absence. I called at your cottage yesterday, having first seen your son William at the head of the school-boys; as it might seem a leader of their noontide game, and Horace among the tribe, both as healthy-looking as the best, and William very much grown. Mrs De Quincey was seated by the fire above stairs, with the baby on her knee. She rose and received me cheerfully, as a person in perfect health, and does indeed seem to have had an extraordinary recovery; and as little suffering as could be expected The babe looked as if it would thrive, and is what we call a nice child, neither big nor little

Mrs De Quincey seemed on the whole in very good spirits, but, with something of sadness in her manner, she told me you were not likely to be very soon at home. She then said that you had at present some literary employments at Edinburgh; and had, besides, had an offer (or something to this effect) of a permanent engagement, the nature of which she did not know; but that you hesitated about accepting it, as it might necessitate you to settle in Edinburgh. To this I replied "Why not settle there for the time at least that this engagement lasts? lodgings are cheap at Edinburgh, and provisions and coals not dear." Of these facts I had some weeks' experience four years ago. I then added that it was my firm opinion that you could never regularly keep up to your engagements at a distance from the press; and, said I, "Pray tell him so when you write." She replied "Do write yourself." Now I could not refuse to give her pleasure by so doing, especially being assured that my letter would not be wholly worthless to you, having such agreeable news to send of your family. The little cottage and everything seemed comfortable."

Dorothy proceeds to urge him a little further to settle

in Edinburgh, and in a postscript, written on a day subsequent, she adds :—

" I have been at Grasmere and again seen your wife She desires me to say that she is particulaty anxious to hear from you on her father's account "

This message is significant. Affairs had been going badly with Margaret's kinsfolk at the Nab how badly one may conceive, since De Quincey was being looked to for advice and help. Old William Park had died in 1825,* leaving his estate and scattered lands to his daughter Mary Simpson and her husband, who duly paid their fine of £12 6s 8d. with an extra £2 as " Income " fine. Trouble had begun to brew before the old man's death. For in 1820 the heads of the manor had pulled the rebellious tenants sharply up, and William was forced to pay his fourteen years arrears of rent. Next year compensation was demanded from him for cutting timber without the lord's leave This was a sore point Over and over again the Parks had struggled to maintain independent wood-rights. Removed from the close-set village houses and the Hall by fair slopes of meadow, they dwelt apart. The woodland strip behind them that clothed the sharp rise of Brockstone Rigg was all their own That they must suffer the felling of their trees for the wants of their neighbours by order of the lord's bailiff was injury enough ; but to ask that menial's leave to cut for their own wants was not to be borne So old William, who had watched the fierce battle of the trees fought between Mr. Ford-North† and the manor, rebelled, and (unlike his ancestors), persisted in his rebellion. Particulars of the law-suit that followed are not known. The manor won, on the plea, it is said, that though the tenant may use wood for needful repairs, always however

---

* See p 360
† See p 238-9

obtaining leave from the lord, it is not lawful for him to erect a new building without consent specially obtained And tradition, whispering still of the ruin of the Nab, points to the tall barn that abuts upon the road as the immediate cause of it.

The expenses of this law-suit, which was not settled until 1827, had then to be faced by the Simpsons. Now the ordinary statesman had no capital in money. A sum might be raised by a forced sale of cattle; but this was a ruinous policy: while by the sale of his land he would lose his means of livelihood and become an alien and a wanderer. Yet this was the position that faced John Simpson, when he applied to his son-in-law for help. The latter states that the manor authorities had offered to release the debt, by purchase of the Nab estate; but to sell to his enemies would naturally be too bitter, unless no other loophole of escape could be found. Simpson's financial position is hard to understand. Mr. Park of Hawkshead already held a mortgage on the estate for £500, which may have stood over from William Park's time; and by the end of 1828, when the expenses of the law-suit became pressing, he required a further sum (according to De Quincey) of from £500 to £800 to set him straight. It may be noticed that the latter does not at first in his letters mention the law-suit, but only the settlement of the daughters and the debts of a son. The scheme concocted for getting out of this position, was, as divulged by De Quincey's letters, a truly amazing one. It was that De Quincey should buy the estate from his father-in-law, giving him (nominally) £2,500 for it, while he himself, having no money, should borrow in order to purchase. The candid details of the transaction—that can only be described as dubious—do not transpire until letter 5 following. Letter 1 shows that De Quincey, now in Edinburgh, had applied to a firm of Manchester solicitors for a loan of £1,400, offering security for the same in the estate of The Nab. The firm naturally proceeded with caution. De Quincey's family, being a Manchester one, may have been known to them; and though the erratic Thomas was hardly to be trusted, his widowed and apparently well-to-do mother, now residing in Bath, stood as a comfortable surety in the background. They took the precaution to demand a valuation of the Nab estate, which was ultimately (Simpson's of £2,923 9s. 9d being rejected) made out as worth £2,288. 14s. by one J. Williamson. They wrote also to the steward of the Rydal manor, to make sure of the validity of John Simpson's claim to the estate through his wife. James Jackson's reply decries the estate and alarms the possible purchaser. He tells of the "various grievous Imposts" to which customary land is liable, and though admitting the estate to be capable of improvement, adds that if improved, the manor would exact still higher fines than at present. He himself would not give £1,000 for all Simpson's land within Rydal; and even with the freehold land outside its worth is no more than £2,000. He again admits however that if the customary land were broken up into small plots, it might find purchasers at exorbitant prices, "for the other day Wordsworth the Poet purchased a fancy piece of rock (subject to all the Inconveniences I have ment'd) at a price almost equal to what is given in large Towns for building Ground."* Then he goes on "De Quincey is a gentleman & Simpson, his father-in-Law, is a sober, regular man—rather too much influenced by his Wife to litigation, but I believe he is now sick of it." In Letter 2 the objection that the abstract does not go far enough back shows that neither De Quincey nor the lawyers understood the ancient form of customary tenure, by which a dalesman held his land— not by deeds—but by witness of the community at the

---

* This was "the Rashfield," for which Wordsworth had lately given £300, fearing that he might be turned out of Rydal Mount.

village court Parchment therefore is only to be found for comparatively recent transfers of land.

LETTER I.

FROM DE QUINCEY.

Edinburgh, 18, Pitt Street,
Sat December 6, 1828

To W A Duckworth Esq.
Messrs Duckworth and Denison
       Manchester

Sir,

Immediately on the receipt of your letter on the 18th ult , I communicated the substance of it to Mr. Simpson ; and yesterday morning, by way of reply, I received a letter and accompanying Valuation, which I transmit herewith, from Mr Bartholomew Sympson, Land Agent and Surveyor Mr B. Sympson, though bearing pretty nearly the same name as my wife's father (with the difference only of spelling his name with a y) is not in the remotest degree connected with him by blood or otherwise Mr John Simpson, my wife's father, is of an old Westmorland family, immemorially connected with the soil of that county, being of the class known locally by the denomination of 'Statesmen (i e Estatesmen) in contradistinction to the labouring part of the rural population This class are honorably distinguished from those who are obliged to personal labor, and indeed from the *corresponding* classes (in a money sense) of other parts of the kingdom, by good sense—thoughtfulness—gravity of character—and general respectability. They have landed estates all the way up from £40 or £50 a year to 4 or 5 hundred , and in some cases even more But, apart from the consideration which these estates give them, they make no pretensions to the accomplishment or rank of gentlemen. This explanation I make as some sort of answer to the question which you put on the punctuality and regular habits of Mr. J Simpson . he has all the good qualities of his order in an eminent degree is now upwards of 60 , has spent his life hitherto in the industrious cultivation of his estate (viz this estate in part acquired by marriage, and a patrimonial one in Martindale, of which I know nothing) ; has no habits of expense whatsoever , and undoubtedly never contracted one shilling of debt except in connection with the improvement of his estate and latterly some of no great importance (though distressing to him at the moment) arising out of the irregularities of a son now dead A more honorable man, or of stricter veracity and integrity, I have never known But *his* character, except as a collateral security for the payment of the interest, is of less importance—since his purpose is to sell the estate to me, on my raising by mortgage the sum which he requires, and continuing to pay to him and his wife during their lives, interest at the rate of 3½ per cent on the remainder of the price,—the purchase money being finally paid on the death of Mr J Simpson, of his wife, aged 58, and of her brother aged 51 The only burthen upon the estate is the £300 mortgage which I conclude I must have mentioned in my last letter To pay off this, and for other purposes connected with the settlement of three daughters I *now* find (by a letter received the very day after my last letter to yourself) that the total sum which he will want is £1300—and not £1000 as I had first said under a mistake

I remain sir
Your faithful servant
Thomas Quincey

LETTER 2.

FROM DE QUINCEY

Edinburgh
Sat Jany 24 1829

To W A Duckworth, Esq
Manchester

Sir

I am much concerned to find from your letter of the 17th inst., that the Title—as abstracted by Mr Walker, does not in all points meet your approbation For that part of your objections which applies to points connected with the local tenures, I hope that Mr Walker will by this time have given you sufficient explanations but for the other ground of dissatisfaction—viz. that " the Abstract does not go sufficiently far back "—I fear, from the knowledge I have of the carelessness in this particular prevalent amongst Westmorland 'statesmen, and from the imperfect legal assistance which they resorted to until very lately (often no better than the parish clerk, sexton, schoolmaster, etc) that so far the defect will be found to be irremediable. My wife, who is at present with me in Edinburgh, informs me that the *whole* of the Nab estate (the Estate in question)—as well freehold as customary— came to her maternal grandfather, Mr William Parke, by purchase from the Trustees of Mr John Parke his half-brother. Mr *W* Park was a younger brother (viz by a second marriage, but the eldest of that marriage) —hence the principal family estate (the Nab) went to Mr J Park the only son of the first marriage ; and William inherited only an inferior estate called Hart Head. Mr. John P left the Nab to Trustees with directions to sell it for the benefit of his widow and only daughter and thereupon Mr. W. P. my wife's grandfather became the purchaser Now at the death of Mr. J P —*his* branch of the family (the elder branch) was reduced to that only daughter above mentioned, whose only daughter died childless, and to a sister whose whole family perished at sea in coming from Antigua In the person of these descendents the elder branch of the family was finally extinguished From all which my wife's inference is this—that any other documents or records, beyond those in her grandfather's possessions, must now be irrecoverable.

With regard to the question you put to me on the nature of the contract between myself and Mr Simpson,—as I am exceedingly anxious to avoid all causes of delay which might arise from any want of precision or determinateness, you may rely on the following answers as conclusive —

1st " *is it intended that I shall be the purchaser immediately ?* " I answer *undoubtedly* unless it would materially forward the transaction to make the mortgage to Mr Simpson, and *afterwards* to make a conveyance to me of the estate so burthened , a point which I am not lawyer enough to understand. Presuming however that this process is either not a feasible one, or not attended with any advantages, then undoubtedly it is the wish of Mr. S. and myself equally that I should be the purchaser immediately

2 ndly " *and on what terms ?* " You notice the difference between the heading of the Abstract which states the purchase-money at £2923, and one of my letters which states it at £2500. The *latter* is the true sum Mr Walker, who is not confidentially acquainted with the transaction between myself and Mr. D. (and indeed in a recent letter to me confounds my wife with my mother, so that his information on this part of the case must be considered as liable to inaccuracies), has no doubt in saying £2923 been guided by the Valuation—having a general knowledge that Mr. S. has asked three thousand pounds for his estate of indifferent persons But to *me* he makes the price absolutely and irrevocably £2500 . and for this I have his written engagement. He thus considers himself as virtually bequeathing to my eldest son £400 , and at his own death he purposes to leave at least £200 more, or according to circumstances a larger sum, to the same person.

3 rdly " *Do I propose to pay Mr. S the balance of the purchase money beyond the amount to be advanced on mortgage ?* " I answer

No: it is the wish of Mr. S that this balance should remain in my hands until the death of himself and his wife, I paying interest on the balance during their lives, and at their decease paying up the £900 (i.e. after the deduction of my son's account) to the several parties mentioned in his will

With respect as to the advice you give me " to be satisfied with a contract from Mr. Simpson for sale of the estate subject to the mortgage for £1400,"—I refer myself of course entirely to your judgment, and abide by that recommendation.

      I remain, Sir,
        Your faithful Servant,
         Thomas Quincey.

There was nothing in all this to prevent the firm from procuring the £1,400, though the precaution was taken, when the transfer of the estate came to be made in a special manor-court, to admit—not Thomas De Quincey—but Gerard Pendlebury, the gentleman who lent the money. But before these leisurely assurances were complete, Simpson's difficulties had reached a crisis. An execution was taken out for the payment of the law-suit expenses, and he had to hurry off to Hawkshead to procure a further loan of £250 from the Rev. George Park * for a time, in order to prevent a forced sale. His wife meanwhile, excited and distressed by these difficulties, was so ill that her family supposed she might die

LETTER 3.
FROM DE QUINCEY.

        March 26, 1829.

To W. A. Duckworth, Esq.
 Manchester.

Sir,

Two days ago I had a letter from Mr. Simpson, which threw me into great anxiety; so much so, that at first I made up my mind to go down immediately to Westmorland—and thence to Manchester. However, on further consideration, I have thought it better first of all to acquaint you with the two facts which Mr.

---

 * The earlier of the two incumbents of Hawkshead of this name, and the holder apparently of the first mortgage, died about this time His son did not succeed to the clerical office till 1834.—M. H. B. Cowper, Hawkshead

Simpson's letter communicates   The first is—that he has been compelled to apply again to Mr. Park, who has advanced another sum of £250 upon mortgage. This, I presume, will make no difference in the affair depending between us ; and I mention it only in evidence of the state of distress which the long protraction of this affair has brought upon him   for he would not again have applied to Mr Park unless in circumstances of the last extremity   The fact is—he has been for some time summoned to pay the expenses of two suits at law into which he was hurried by the impatience and precipitancy of his late son and very much against his own wishes   These expenses, or rather the balance which still remained unpaid, amounted to about £200 or something more , and at length (payment having been of necessity repeatedly delayed) an execution was either really taken out, or Mr Simpson was made to believe so , and in his alarm, without further application to me, he obtained the sum I have mentioned from Mr Park

The other fact is more alarming .—Mrs. Simpson, who has long been unwell, has become so much worse in the course of one week —that, at the date of her husband's letter (Sunday last, March 15), serious fears were entertained for her life   Whether any medical man concurred in those fears I do not learn from the letter , but such were the fears of her family. The result of that event would of course be to throw void any papers which may have been drawn under the present circumstances , but a still worse effect would be—that, according to Mr Simpson's belief, his power of settling his estate for the benefit of his daughters and of a child of mine would be entirely defeated for want of his wife's concurrence

Such being the hazard, I write earnestly to know how soon the deeds of conveyance can be ready. And if there is any preliminary of any sort—which, by knowing it beforehand, I can forward— pray, have the goodness to let me know. For example, the form which it was necessary to obtain from Mr. Johnson and Mr Atkinson—had I known earlier that they would be wanted, I could have had provided in time for your call without putting you to the trouble of making separate applications, and with less (possibly with no) delay. My misfortune at present is, that Mr. Simpson believes that the transaction languishes in consequence of inattention or remissness on my part.—However, on looking back to the dates of your last letters, I venture to hope that— barring any such unfortunate event as Mrs Simpson's death— everything may now be drawing to an early conclusion : and to forward this as much as possible, I will keep myself in readiness to attend your call at any moment you may find it possible to name time and place. Meantime, believe me, Sir

Your most faithful servant,
Thos Quincey.

P S Have the goodness to address me for the present at
Mr. Porteous's
19 Duncan Street, Edinburgh.

After the urgent letter No 3, there is a lull in the correspondence, caused as we know by the transmission of £1,400 to De Quincey. The stress was now over, the loan shared, and the older debts paid. Simpson repaid a total £750 to his Hawkshead connection, who was clearly eager to close the transaction. He also hastily paid some lawyer's bill of £50 and received from his son-in-law £100, a comfortable sum to go on with. This made up £900, leaving £500 in De Quincey's own hands. That he kept it, instead of paying it to his father-in-law as further purchase money for an estate which they claimed to be worth £3,000, is a transaction which requires all De Quincey's casuistry to explain. No doubt he reserved it to pay the interest of the Manchester loan, without any regard for the ultimate paying back of that loan. He dreamed of finance as he did of other things; and it was sufficient for him that he had a comfortable sum in hand, without thought of the sure consequences that time would bring. With £500 loose cash—or £460 after his stated expenses were paid—all was relief and joy. He hastened to Grasmere and to his family, and took at least temporary possession of the Nab as master. This explains his invitation, otherwise puzzling, to his good friend Knight, to come with his wife and enjoy the delights of the country. It is written (July, 1829) in the highest spirits, and refers clearly to Nab Cottage :—

"And now, my friend, think what a glorious Eldorado of milk and butter, and cream-cheeses, and all other dairy products, supposing that you like those things, I can offer you morning, noon, and night. You may absolutely bathe in new milk, or even in cream ; and you *shall* bathe, if you like it. I know that you care not much about the luxuries of the dinner-table ; else, though our luxuries are few and simple, I could offer you some temptations—mountain lamb equal to Welsh ; char famous to the antipodes ; trout and pike from the very lake within twenty-five feet of our door ; bread, such as you have never presumed to dream of, made of our own wheat, not doctored and separated by the usual miller's process into insipid flour and coarse, that is merely dirty-looking white, but all ground down together, which is the sole receipt (*experto crede*) for having rich, lustrous, red-brown ambrosial bread ; new potatoes of celestial earthiness and raciness, which with us last till October ; and finally, milk in which you must and shall bathe."

The lake is of course Rydalmere, which Sir Charles Lloyd describes thus :—

" This Lake is unusually shallow by comparison with its neighbours ; but at the point I speak of it takes (especially when seen under any mode of imperfect light) the appearance of being gloomily deep two islands of exquisite beauty, but strongly discriminated in character, and a sort of recess or bay on the opposite shore across which the shadows of the hilly margin stretch with great breadth and solemnity of effect to the very centre of the Lake, together with the very solitary character of the entire Valley, in which (excluding the little Hamlet in its very gorge or entrance) there is not more than one single house,* combine to make the scene as impressive by night as any in the Lake Country "

It must have been during this short period of De Quincey's residence at the Nab that his boys, Horace and Francis, were sent to a school in Rydal taught by John Sproat, where they were school-fellows of little John Backhouse, who narrated this fact and remembered their names in his ninetieth year.†

---

* The Nab Cottage

† Born February 14th, 1819 ; died March 11th, 1909 Edward Wilson, still living (1909) was a school-mate also at Grasmere with some of the De Quinceys, and remembers having once seen the Opium Eater himself [E.W. died at Grasmere, April 9th, 1910 —ED].

But £500 does not last for ever, even if scrupulously kept for the doling out of interest, which clearly was not the case here. Some of it must have been used for the family's removal to Edinburgh, which at last was decided upon. The joint household arrangement at the Nab could not have proved comfortable, and Margaret would be thankful to be permanently fixed with her husband. The move was made, as shown in Letter 4, in 1831, though De Quincey did not finally give up Dove Cottage until 1834, having rented it for a period of 25 years * The simple appealing letter of Margaret has the throb of trouble under its haste, and it tells that by 1832, there was nothing left of the loan De Quincey was again penniless, except for his irregular literary earnings ; and he was clearly then seeking help from his mother. The letter (No. 5) he writes on his return is excited, yet lofty and indignant ; but in the next his pride is humbled into pure petition for time. The mother must have been weary of such applications ; but she appears to have written to the lawyers and finally, as their letter (No. 2) shows, have wiped out the debt of the interest up to that date.

LETTER 4
FROM MRS. DE QUINCEY

Edinburgh,
7 Great King Street.
Monday Night. Jan ye 9. 1832.

—Duckworth, Esq
    Solicitor
      Manchester.
Sir,

Yesterday I was greatly concerned to hear from Westmorland that my Father, Mr. John Sympson of Rydal, was in danger of falling into great trouble on account of the arrears of Interest due to Mr Pendlebury :

Mr De Quincey is at this moment in the South of England on

---

* From Edward Wilson.

that very business the principal purpose of his journey being to obtain the money necessary (seal) paying up everything due —last year it happened, greatly to our disturbance, that the heavy expenses attending the removal of our large family to Edinburgh and the extras which naturally belong to a settlement in a strange place, left us really without the means of discharging that debt But these expenses are now over, The last of them having been paid this Christmas They will not occur again— And by Easter at furthest I know we shall be able to send the money, even if Mr. de Quincey should not succeed in obtaining it sooner I do hope and trust, for the sake of my poor Father, that this plan will suit Mr. Pendlebury's convenience

From the love we all bear to the place, there need be no doubt that we will all of us make any sacrifice rather than endanger its loss Full interest shall be paid up for the time during which the arrears have been standing, and everything else shall be settled Nor shall any delay ever occur again

The information, which I am now noticing, ought to have reached me (I believe) some weeks ago but the person who was commissioned to call upon me with the intelligence, forgot or neglected to do so

For the future we should be much obliged to you if you would cause any letters on this subject to be addressed to us at this place.

    I remain Sir
      your obedient Servant
        Margaret de Quincey

LETTER 5.

FROM DE QUINCEY.

Edinburgh, 7 G t King Street
    Tuesday night Jan y 31—1832

Mess rs Duckworth, Denison
  and Humphrey,
   Manchester
Gentlemen,

Having returned home only on this afternoon, I had it not in my power to answer your letter of the 20 inst before

I now answer

First,—That I accept the terms there proposed I doubt not that the conditions were framed in a spirit of forbearance ; and I am obliged to you for them. But, considering the temper of indulgence which (I am sure) dictated them,—I regret deeply that they were not made more certainly effectual for their purpose; so that, in labouring for the end in view, I might have found my task a little more within the limits of ordinary means and opportunities Much may certainly be accomplished by those who are determined to do everything and forego everything but hope, and the spirit of hope, after all is a mighty assistance.

Secondly—With regard to the transfer of the Mortgage, I had an offer of that nature made some time ago by a man of property in Liverpool. He then made some few conditions which seemed to me objections: but in the summer I am to see him in Westmorland , and I will report his proposals fully at that time.

Meantime

Thirdly,—if this plan should for the present be defeated, I shall in that event, propose to you the reduction of the Mortgage by the whole sum, which it properly belongs to *me* to provide for. The total sum borrowed was £1400 Of this £750 went instantly to Mr J Simpson for the purpose of paying off the Rev d George Park , and £100 to the same Mr J Simpson for miscellaneous purposes. A £50 Bank Note was paid within 4 days from the 29th of April 1829 to Mr Francis Walker, Solicitor This payment was made under some great misconception of Mr. Simpson's meaning and wishes as afterwards stated by himself. How much was really due, I cannot pretend to know So much was certainly paid . and I understand that no part has yet been returned —These payments allowed for, there remains £500 . and that sum, with the exception of £30 paid at the time to yourselves, and £10 spent in journeys (viz Edinb to Ambleside, Amb. to Manchester,—and the same reversed),—i e in fact £460 I myself received by Mr J. Simpson's consent and wish —I make the statement simply for this reason—that, undertaking the entire interest myself and the entire expenses,—I might else be supposed to have received the entire £1400 whereas, the account stands just as I have here stated it. The distribution of the money, You will say, cannot concern Mr Pendlebury, nor affect his rights. Doubtless it cannot But it will serve very satisfactorily to explain and to establish the fact of my eager desire to diminish or to transfer a mortgage by which I am so great a sufferer. My own just share of the annual interest is £26 ; viz £25 on the account of the £500, and £1 as what might be regarded my share in the 50 shillings, paid annually for Mr Walker's £50 This is my just share— the rest belongs in no fraction of a farthing to me or mine. But what others cannot pay—under this existing arrangement I *must* Under a new arrangement, a new contract, and a new lender, I should have a right to prescribe new conditions—more reasonable, and better suited to the interests of my children   It may be judged therefore whether I am likely to be backward in releasing Mr. Pendlebury from his mortgage.

I remain, Gentlemen, Your obed t Serv.t T.Q

LETTER 6.

FROM DE QUINCEY.

Edinburgh,
7 Great King Street
Saturday, March 24, 1832

Mess.rs Duckworth, Denison
and Humphreys,
Manchester.

Gentlemen,

The time, fixed by yourselves, is now arrived. Yet, as the regular term for the payment of the Interest to Mr. Pendlebury does not come round until the 29th. of April, I do hope and trust that you will allow me the benefit of that small extension of the time originally granted   Any the very shortest delay, without an adequate purpose in seeking it, I assure you that I should think it both weak and unhandsome to ask. The truth is—a single day may make the whole difference to me of receiving or not receiving the requisite sum. In a matter, which to me involves the most serious consequences in one event, I venture to hope that you will not precipitate your measures: more especially as I hear that the interest of your own client would be too likely to suffer heavily from a sale of the entire property at a season so unfavourable beyond all precedent to such a purpose as the present.—Within the time I have mentioned I hope to be able to remit the entire amount of the arrears   And from that time forward I will make a provision for paying the Interest half-yearly with the utmost punctuality.

I remain, Gentlemen,
Your obedient humble servant,
Thomas De Quincey.

LETTER I.

TO DE QUINCEY'S MOTHER.

Manchester,
2nd. April, 1832.

Dear Madam,

We feel pleasure in complying with the request contained in

your letter of the 30th. ult : In Nov.r 1829 we received a letter from Mr Quincey stating that he had agreed to purchase his father in law Mr. Simpson's estate at Rydal for £2500 part of which he proposed to raise on Mortgage, and to allow Mr & Mrs. Simpson int.t on the balance during their lives, the principal or considerable part of it falling to his family at their decease   We advanced for a client £1400 on security of the estate   There is now 2 years interest in arrear besides upwards of £40 the expense of the security, Mr Quincey having only paid for the stamps. Under these circumstances in July last we gave Mr. Simpson notice to repay the Mortgage money or we should exercise the power of sale given us by the security   It is the fear of the estate being sold which makes Mr. Quincey anxious to raise a sufft sum to pay the arrears of int.t & expenses   Should he succeed we shall still desire him to find some other party to advance the money for him, for from what has passed we see no chance of his paying the future int. regularly.   Should you determine to assist him we shall be glad to forward your views by being the medium of paying the mortgagee his interest.

       We remain etc.
       Duckworth, Denison & Humphrey.

Mrs. Quincey
 Weston Lea
  Bath

Letter II.

TO DE QUINCEY'S MOTHER

        Manchester, April 27th 1832

Dear Madam,
 We are in receipt of your letter of the 23rd Instant inclosing a Banker's Bill specially endorsed to us for £180 intended by you to be appropriated by us as follows viz

to Gerard Pendlebury Esq. two years int . on £1400 advanced by him to your son Mr. Tho.s Quincey on Mortgage of an estate at Rydal	£140
to ourselves being the balance of our bill against Mr. Tho s Quincey	40
	£180

We will appropriate the money accordingly and for the present will not proceed to sell the estate at Rydal we trust however that the future int . will be regularly paid half yearly by Mr Quincey— if it is not our client will assuredly exercise his power of sale un-

less, which he would much prefer. Mr. Quincey can find some one who will take a transfer of the security.
     We remain etc
      Duckworth Denison & Humphrey.
Mrs. Quincey
 Weston Lea
  Bath.

NOTE.

These letters were found with the " Nab " Deeds at Rydal Hall.

But beyond? The case was hopeless The next interest remained unpaid; and after a year's delay, the Nab estate was advertised for sale at the Salutation Inn, Ambleside, in September, 1833. One final desperate effort to save the old homestead was made by a member of the family, William Simpson, who at the last hour signed a paper to say that if the sale were stopped, he would himself pay both principal and interest. But he could have had no power to fulfil his promise. The little estate, possessed by the Parks from time immemorial, passed to the Rydal manor, and the statesman with his family and personal belongings left the old home for ever.

John Simpson himself sought refuge with the De Quinceys at Edinburgh, and thither went also the idiot Park. An annuity with which the estate was charged for the latter's benefit (£12. 12s.) was paid regularly by Lady Fleming up to 1840, when presumably he died, for the reserved sum of £280. 6s was then paid over to John Simpson, his signature being witnessed by his grandchildren Horace and Margaret, the elders now of the homestead, for William had died in 1835, and the mother in 1837. It is comfortable to think that the old man's exile was cheered by the bright young daughters of his own daughter Margaret De Quincey, (Mrs. Craig).

With the rest of De Quincey's career Rydal is not connected.

The Nab was destined to be associated with yet another name of literary eminence. When it was necessary to find a home for the gentle, talented, but incapable Hartley Coleridge, the Wordsworths undertook to find him one in the quiet country where he had spent his childhood, and where he was well known and would be respected. Mrs. Wordsworth, who was wise and prudent, as well as kind, supervised the arrangements made for his comfort, and (after a time spent in Grasmere) placed him at Nab House with the tenants who rented it from the Hall. Here he occupied (as I am told by one who was taken in as a child to be shown his wastefulness in throwing away cheese which he did not like, into the grate) the front parlour to the left, and behind it there was a tiny bedroom partitioned off, where he slept. Such was the simple cheap style of living of these still secluded parts, that Mr. W. paid only a few shillings a week for his board and lodging.

He is still remembered by old men and women with great affection. His short dumpy figure was a familiar object to them as children upon the road between Ambleside and Rydal; and unlike the solemn stately Wordsworth, who passed them all unseen, and "bumming" his poetry as he went, he always noticed them, and would bar the way in play or sometimes chase them, to their great delight. Despite his powers of poetry-making, he was only a grown child himself.

Occasionally the road between the little town and the now dwindled hamlet of Rydal was all too long for him, (though perhaps, as a fellow-sufferer once said, it was not the length of the road, but the breadth of it that worried him,) when at times he returned belated and bemused, from an evening spent unwisely amid temptations unresisted. Once he turned aside, by Scandale Brow and threw himself down to rest in the log-house that then stood there. The farmer, coming round early next morning, not seeing the prone figure asleep in the hay, locked the place up, and Hartley, whose shouts, when he woke to the situation, could not be heard from the road, remained a prisoner for more than 24 hours, when the place was opened and he was found quite weak and spent.

But Hartley's brighter hours are well remembered too.

APPENDIX

THE BIRDS OF RYDAL

ROOK *Trypanocorax frugilegus* L Permanent resident Rookery at the Hall; and a few nests are annually built on Old Hall Hill, where the former seat of the lord of the manor stood

RAVEN. *Corvus corax* L Seen frequently, and nested undoubtedly in 1901.

CARRION CROW. *Corvus corone* L. Permanent resident Breeds in the deepest woods or wild tracts where trees grow I have seen several of these birds follow a Buzzard, hampering it; probably because the Buzzard occasionally takes its nest One new-made nest of the Crows' I subsequently found occupied by Buzzards

JACKDAW *Corvus monedula* L Permanent resident Frequent, breeding in old trees and in crags, as well as in chimneys

JAY *Garrulus glandarius* L Permanent resident. By no means rare, though kept down

MAGPIE *Pica caudata* L Permanent resident Not abundant and oftenest seen by White Moss

COMMON STARLING *Sturnus vulgaris* L A permanent resident; yet wandering flocks do leave the parish in the very worst of winter for flatter and fatter lands. But the return is always made by February, and no breeding species is more numerous, as it nests in the holes of woodland trees—generally taking there an old nest of some other bird—and in roof-spouts, holes of masonry, etc, in almost every house

GREENFINCH *Ligurinus chloris* L. Summer visitant Nests in secluded gardens and shrubberies Arrives at the latter end of March or early in April Leaves when the nest season is over, first for adjacent oat-fields, and then, apparently, for more distant ground The species is seen, however, occasionally in winter, but then only as a single bird or two, in company with Mountain Finches or Chaffinches It feeds its young on the tender green seed of the Wych Elm, which is already swelled by the middle of May. From its swarming in April over the Gorse bushes, I conclude it eats the young pods of this plant

HAWFINCH *Coccothraustes vulgaris* L According to the account given by the intelligent woodman of the estate, he appears to have found nestlings of this species, six or seven years ago, in the upper Hall gardens He carried them to a cage in his cottage, and a parent followed them this considerable distance, remaining in a tree over against the verandah in which the cage was hung, for the few days they lived In 1901 the fresh occupant of the same cottage saw a pair of Hawfinches constantly about, so in all probability they nested there

CHAFFINCH *Fringilla cœlebs* L Permanent resident Abundant at all times The occasional winter flocks seen—feeding, for instance (as I discovered them to do), on the minute grubs of the Spangle-gall in a season when these are abundant—may be immigrants from other parts

BRAMBLING *Fringilla montifringilla* L Winter visitant Comes in flocks, sometimes of a great size, when snow is on the ground, and the Beech harvest has been full

GOLDFINCH *Carduelis elegans* L It is reported not only as having nested in the neighbourhood formerly, but to have, within the memory of middle-aged men, resorted in autumn flocks to the lower pastures of Loughrigg I have never seen it.

LESSER REDPOLL *Cannabina rufescens* Vieill Permanent resident, in the sense that it nests in the district, though possibly not every year in this parish It is oftenest seen in winter, either singly, keeping up with a party of Bullfinches, or in a small flock, feeding on the Alder or Birch trees I once met quite an army, passing through the Fir-woods of the high ground between the Esthwaite and Langdale valleys

HOUSE SPARROW *Passer domesticus* L. Permanent resident, and abundant

CROSSBILL *Loxia curvirostra* L Occasional visitant, doubtless A flock of them remained in the Fir-woods of the heights round the Esthwaite valley all through the late summer and autumn of 1894 I first saw them on 10th July, 15 to 16 in number, and constantly afterwards ; and was told they remained through the winter after I left.

BULLFINCH *Pyrrhula europœa* Vieill Permanent resident. Most frequently seen in winter in small flocks when feeding upon the birch-seeds of the wood But a brood or two are hatched every summer in some secluded part of the parish A family of young birds is generally led to this garden in early July, where they are fed on various kinds of seeds—those of the Welsh Poppy, eaten green, the Melancholy Thistle, and the small *Viola cornuta* This bird in winter will take the driest of hard seeds, notably those of the late Blackberry flowers, that never swell to fruit, as well as Knapweed, Dock, and, I think, the dry seed of the Heather plant

REED BUNTING *Emberiza schœniclus* L Summer visitant Nests on the marsh at the head of the lake Appears from the middle to end of March 12th March, 1888

YELLOW BUNTING *Emberiza citrinella* L. Summer visitant to this parish, where it nests in a few spots on wild land I have never seen it here in winter, though small parties linger round the farmsteads of the upper Esthwaite valley regularly at that season.

SKY LARK *Alauda arvensis* L Summer visitant. This bird is practically absent from Lakeland, where, according to an old inhabitant, it once existed in fair numbers—a change ascribed to the lapse of old corn-lands into pasture and meadow But it is a remarkable fact that a few pairs return each summer to nest on the summit of our mountain range. It is to be heard singing, I am told, on almost the topmost height of Fairfield; and the farmer, whose sheep range over the slopes, has found its nest towards the top of the spur called Heron Crag—marked in the Ordance Map as Earring Crag Its choice of this exposed position, rather than the floor of the Fairfield basin, where Meadow-Pipits have their home, is hard to understand

PIED WAGTAIL *Motacilla lugubris* Temm Summer visitant. Numerous Nests in walls and sides of barns, and is particularly fond of a ruined building Appears in March (generally in the second or third week), and is then seen in companies upon a fresh-ploughed field or lake margin, which shortly break up into nesting pairs, but gather together again in autumn At this time I have frequently observed it rest upon telegraph wires on which House Martins were congregating, and fly round imitatively after these birds or follow them over the lake It sports also very prettily over the lake margins, and roosts in the reeds. Generally it withdraws in early October, but odd birds are often seen in winter A solitary bird lived in Ambleside through the mild winter of 1895-6

GREY WAGTAIL *Motacilla melanope* Pall Summer visitant Appears on the Rothay early in March Nests on the shores of the lake and on the streams. Withdraws in August and September, but odd birds are sometimes seen in November

YELLOW WAGTAIL. *Motacilla campestris* Gray. Summer visitant. I found the bird on 6th May, 1898, on the spot where I had always looked for it—the bit of flat about the river and Dunny Beck, where they flow into the lake. The site, however, is closely hemmed in and commanded by the noisy highway, and it did not stay. It is there again this year, I am glad to say. Mr Macpherson, in the *Fauna of Lakeland* conveys the impression that this bird is rare with us. It may be well, therefore, to note its stations hereabouts. All are of the same character. a flat alluvial meadow, situated at the junction of an affluent of some size with a lake. By the Troutbeck and by Burdhouse mouth, on Windermere; by the Rothay, on Grasmere; by Black Beck, on Esthwaite. The two stations I am best acquainted with are occupied year after year, and where the space is considerable, by several pairs.

TREE PIPIT. *Anthus trivialis* L. Summer visitant. Abundant wherever there are trees, even in the scanty fringe of those along the Rydal Beck, in the basin under Fairfield, 600 feet high; and so crowded is it on the limit of its range that while one bird may be seen in possession of the very last singing post (an old dwarf Ash) another beyond starts and concludes its aerial course of song from a wall-top or bank. It is also in the Junipers of Loughrigg. First singers heard from the 16th to 25th April. A beautiful though variable singer. Seems to sing best and most on the wing, in cold, wet seasons, while in heat and drought it keeps more to the boughs and sings in shorter strains. Nests generally in dry grass slopes, close to trees or wood. Possibly a second nester sometimes. Last seen 20th August.

MEADOW PIPIT. *Anthus pratensis* L. Summer visitant. This bird leaves us as regularly as the preceding species, though its method of autumnal roaming and its very occasional reappearance in a mild winter evidence a more partial migration. It comes, like the Pied Wagtail, in March, and often as a small band, but does not settle to its higher breeding-ground till quite a month later. It appears to have two characters of nesting habitat. one in the valley, upon a marsh or watery meadow; the other upon the high, bleak, and grassy slope of the mountains, where, however, a stream flows near. In the latter station it sings more freely than in the former. There is a colony of these birds in Rydal Head; and their range, bare and treeless, touches, almost overlaps, that of the Tree Pipits', which ascends to the highest bush of the vale ; so that the two species may be heard singing together The Tree Pipit far outnumbers it on lower ground In autumn it collects (like the Pied Wagtail) in lively parties, and lives upon the heather uplands, where, I believe, from its actions, it eats the minute green seeds of the plant. It disappears from the heights at the end of September or early in October.

TREE CREEPER. *Certhia familiaris* L Permanent resident Present in all the woods Will undertake a second brood as soon as the young of the first are self-supporting Has nested quite a number of times in a rustic garden summer-house

GREAT TIT *Parus major* L Permanent resident Numerous Nests generally in sides of barns or in high walls ; sometimes in holes of trees Eats Beech-mast (beginning quite early), as does also the Coal, but not, in my experience, the Marsh Titmouse. It breaks open the Hazel-nut in winter by blows that resound through the coppice. It eats the hard, green Yew-berry, rejecting the aril, also Sunflower seed, Knapweed, and Elderberry. It breaks the marble gall, I believe, for the grub inside

BLUE TIT *Parus cœruleus* L Permanent resident Very numerous Nests in walls, or—when they are to be had—in small pocket-holes of trees Searches house-fronts for spiders' eggs (possibly spiders too) in September, as does the Great Titmouse It is not so great a fruit-eater as that bird, but will eat Laburnum seed and seed of *Arundo Phragmites*, and of Alder. I have seen the hen, in the manner of the Marsh Tit, peck at a hole of an Oak tree to enlarge it, incited by its mate

COAL TIT *Parus britannicus* S & D. Permanent resident. General, though not so abundant as Great and Blue Nests in low walls, very occasionally in tree-holes Eats, besides Beech-mast, Alder and the seed of Conifers, when the woody scales have opened

BRITISH MARSH TIT *Parus dresseri* Stejn Permanent resident. Nests invariably in rotten or pollard trees The only bird I know that is partial to the Honeysuckle-berry ; and this it feeds upon—rejecting, as Titmice do in all fruits, the juicy outside and picking at the hard seeds within—from early August right on to November, when the second crop of flowers have set their seeds in a dry, juiceless skin. It will eat the Yewberry, and loves the Thistle seed, as well as Sweet Violet, Knapweed, and even Hogweed In late September I have seen it apparently busy with Rhododendron seed, then in a hard, green state. It breaks up the Cherry-gall for the grub inside

BRITISH LONG-TAILED TIT. *Ægithalus vagans* Leach Permanent resident Not very numerous It is fond of the Juniper as a nesting-place

COMMON GOLDCREST *Regulus cristatus* L Permanent resident Though in general a solitary bird, or in winter keeping up with the mixed parties of small birds that go about quiet places together, I once met a little flock of the species amongst the Juniper bushes of the fell. They prattled joyously, and even attempted to sing, though only January The song, minute as the bird, is regularly begun about the 17th February.

WAXWING. *Ampelis garrulus* L Occasional visitant Seen several times in winter by Mr Wykeham Martin

WHITETHROAT. *Sylvia cinerea* L Summer visitant Nests in waste corners of gardens and low coppice-woods In the latter station it is not infrequently the companion of the Garden Warbler

BLACKCAP. *Sylvia atricapilla* L Summer visitant. Rarer than the Garden Warbler, and hardly ever nesting in coppices as that bird does, but in shrubberies of gardens or parks Males arrive in the latter days of April, but in general it is a late nester, nests often not being begun before early June It is also capricious and often starts afresh 18th April, 1902, 14th September, 1894.

GARDEN WARBLER *Sylvia simplex* Lath Summer visitant. Tolerably frequent, nesting in large gardens as well as in close coppices Is stationed in the highest woodland (about 550 feet) on the Rydal Beck, as on the Stock Beck. Arrives (as far as can be told from the song) later than the Blackcap, varying from the 4th to 15th May Whether the cock takes part in the building of nest, as I have seen the Blackcap do, I am not sure, but I once found four collections of nest materials yet unworked, which I believed he had brought together; for he sang close by one, which caused me to find it, and seemed to be seeking a mate The nest is placed lower than the Blackcap's.

WOOD WARBLER *Phylloscopus sibilator* Bechst. Summer visitant Fairly abundant where there are trees of large growth Arrives about a fortnight later than the following species Forerunners appear in the last week of April, late comers first week of May. Nests generally on rocky braes below trees, though occasionally on a bank. Feeds its young on small caterpillars as well as insects 22nd April, 1893, 1st August

WILLOW WARBLER *Phylloscopus trochilus* L Summer visitant Abundant Arrives by twos and threes in the second or third week of April. Great accession of numbers about the fourth week, when singing is general. Nests wherever there is foliage of small trees. 6th April, 1893; 20th September, 1894.

CHIFFCHAFF. *Phylloscopus minor* Forst. Somewhat rare in the Lake country. It nests, however, in several woodland patches on the lower slopes of Loughrigg. One of these, by Fox Ghyll, in Rydal parish, it resorts to year after year. On 11th September I have seen and heard this bird at a spot above the Hawkshead valley where it never nests. As a friend has heard it there also in late summer, it may travel that way when migrating.

SEDGE WARBLER. *Acrocephalus phragmitis* Bechst. Summer visitant. Though its song is occasionally heard, in passing, at other spots, it probably nests nowhere but about the dykes of the marsh at the head of the lake. Arrives towards the end of the first week in May.

BLACKBIRD. *Turdus merula* L. Permanent resident.

RING-OUZEL. *Merula torquata* L. Summer visitant. Nesting occasionally in Rydal Head, or on Fairfield. This species, is, in fact, rare in Lakeland, where ground fruits such as belong to true moor-lands are scarce. I have seen it above Yewdale, and on Skiddaw.

REDWING. *Turdus iliacus* L. Winter visitant. Present in the old woods, singly or in considerable parties, when Holly, Thorn, and Ivy are fruited. I have known it appear (13th October) before the coveted harvest of Yewberries has been cleared by Throstles and other residents.

SONG THRUSH. *Turdus musicus* L. Resident, in the sense that odd birds may be occasionally seen in winter, even in times of severe frost. But the mass withdraws from these rocky lands (where no deep clay soils exist) in November. By early February they are back and beginning to sing.

MISTLE THRUSH. *Turdus viscivorus* L. Permanent resident. Is perhaps the first bird, except the Starling, to flock when the nest-season is over, and parties of 12 to 20 may be met with in early July, scouring the wilder lands for food. In winter, however, it feeds singly on the fruit of Thorn, Ivy, and Holly. The song is certain to be heard about the 22nd of January, but often begins earlier.

FIELDFARE. *Turdus pilaris* L. Winter visitant. Erratic in its immigration, which depends—along with the length of its stay—on the quantity of food in a neighbourhood, and on the weather. In times of snow large flocks remain wherever old

Thorns and Hollies are full of berries As I have seen Fieldfares in great numbers over a fell where Junipers were in fruit, I conclude they take this fruit likewise No bird has a more skilfully-managed commissariat, for the feeding of large travelling armies, than the Fieldfare, two and three birds moving as scouts backwards and forwards Its system of sentries and of signalling, too, while the main body settles to the feast, is a feature to admire. Odd parties may be seen till the latter end of April and even the 1st May At that time, though not heard to sing (which happens presumably when they break flock on their northern nesting-ground), they show musical susceptibility A concert of Starlings will draw them nearer, with many sounds of excitement I have known them in large numbers, along with Starlings and Rooks, to mob a Sparrow Hawk; when the volume of sound made by Starlings and Fieldfares in concert was astonishing, and quite beyond the needs of the occasion

REDBREAST. *Erithacus rubecula* L Permanent resident. As frequent by wood edges as in gardens Is an occasional, though rare, fruit eater Have seen it eat the Honeysuckle berry, peck at Crab-apples, and swallow a hard Yew berry This it seemed to do in emulation of other and larger birds (Great Tit, Throstle, Blackbird, etc), that were greedily devouring the fruit I am told of it swallowing a Cotoneaster berry

REDSTART *Ruticilla phœnicurus* L Summer visitant No species, whether migrant or resident, more numerous; yet so skilfully does it evade notice that few people are aware of its presence It nests generally in walls, both of the dusty highroad and the lonely fell, as high as trees grow, occasionally in a nick of rock or quarry, or in a heap of mossy stones Only once have I seen it in a cleft of pollarded tree. The nests are often, in spite of the extreme jealousy of the cock birds, not 120 yards distant The date of first arrivals varies, 10th or 11th April is not unusual, though early, (it was seen on the 3rd in 1892 by Mr White, and on the 6th by myself!), and 20th April is late. The general arrival and settlement takes place in the last week of the month, when the hens appear with the later males The song varies with the season. In some years, especially cold ones, it is rarely heard, in others, when the spring is hot, and when hens seem late in coming, it is loud and prolonged. Nesting is begun as soon as the birds are paired The early hens pretty often start their building on the 30th, and in about ten days' time will be ready to sit The cock, who rarely feeds the hen, sings at this time. She comes off early and late and at noon to feed, frequently calling, as if to bring him. Indeed, the penetrating "*Hweet*" heard everywhere in the first and second weeks of May, confounded with the Chaffinch's note, seems the invitation of the hens to their mates. This call is sometimes heard from the first arriving males while in ambush, and from the last wary travellers, who seem to be alone. In a softer tone, and followed by a Robin-like "Tit-tit-tit-tit," it is the well-known alarm signal of the nesting-time. The nesting operations occupy about 28 days, 14 for the sitting and 14 for the feeding-stage in the nest. The parents are highly nervous, and in quiet places often call the passer's attention by their cries of alarm. But in frequented places feeding is conducted with the utmost skill and secrecy, and it is the bird's caution as well as its speed of flight that enables its brilliance to pass unnoticed and its broods to emerge safely upon roads, like the Rydal one, noisy with traffic. In a nest close to the house, which was placed in a shadowy stable-side abutting the highway, I watched the procedure of food-getting. In order to reach the river-bank, where much of the ground food for the nestlings was collected, the birds kept first along the trees of the road bank, then they crossed the road to a garden hedge, which runs at right angles, and along this they sped swiftly to the river, practically unseen. Flies were collected nearer the nest and bits of gravel carried in. The blue eggs frequently number seven. The young often fly (possibly owing to the hen sitting before all her eggs are laid) in two instalments, and usually in the middle of June. The 24th is a late date; one noted 15th July, 1899, for the flight of the two last nestlings, must have been a second venture after accident to first. The young are fed for certainly ten days after flight, and though piloted to a safe distance from the nest at once, they appear to return to its neighbourhood each night to roost for some weeks longer, as the notes of the parents attest. The Redstart is sadly put out if one halts by his usual roosting station at dusk. From mid June to mid July the young families remain, gathering strength. Then they leave, and Redstarts are rare by the end of the month. Odd birds, possibly passing travellers, are occasionally seen or the call-note heard at the end of August. Last heard, 8th September, 1894.

WHEATEAR. *Saxicola œnanthe* L. Summer visitant. Nests in a few places only, on high and wild ground in Rydal Head and on Loughrigg. I have known it once to appear on the open fell above Lake Windermere on 29th March (where indeed Mr. White saw it on the 12th), 1893; but in general it arrives on the first days of April. In the bleak valley of Rydal Head it is still later in settling.

WHINCHAT. *Pratincola rubetra* L Summer visitant. The highway traffic seems to have banished this bird from the valley under Loughrigg, where it once had nesting-ground. It is now found in the wilder nooks and principally in Rydal Head, where there are several pairs Occasionally it may be seen on 21st or 22nd April, but 30th April or 1st May are the more usual dates of its arrival

HEDGE SPARROW. *Accentor modularis* L Permanent resident Nests most frequently in gardens, but in wild spots also Has two, or even three, broods Eats minute seeds, as of the Nettle plant, Welsh Poppy, Violet

DIPPER *Cinclus aquaticus* Bechst Permanent resident Nests on the Rothay and Rydal Beck Starts its autumn song shortly after the Robin, generally in the first days of September, though occasionally in August Continues until the nesting season is advanced Pairs often in January and builds in late February and March Is fond of the arch of a bridge to build in, to which it resorts year after year, or the face of a rock A nest built on the rock-face opposite this garden was used afterwards by a Wren, that contracted its too-large entrance I doubt if there are many second nests in these parts, where rivers and becks are apt to run low in the usually dry weather of early summer. The Dipper is on Rydal Mere almost a lake bird, at least in winter, when two or three are generally squirming in the shallows There it invariably flies to the feeding spot, and drops through the water like a stone

WREN *Anorthura troglodytes* Macg Permanent resident. Fairly numerous A frequent nester, and young may fly as late as 11th September

SPOTTED FLYCATCHER *Muscicapa grisola* L Summer visitant. Most abundant, nesting on every dwelling and out-house, and upon the broken and ancient trees of the woodlands Arrives generally from 9th to 11th May 5th May, 1893, 15th May, 1899: 23rd September.

PIED FLYCATCHER. *Ficedula atricapilla* L Summer visitant Fairly abundant in Rydal, where the ancient trees of the estate afford it nest room Numbers vary, as well as the nesting-ground, owing in some degree at least to other birds following it in its nest-hole and using it in the next season The Blue Titmouse will do this, and I believe the Great, but the Starling is the worst enemy A patch of woodland that was literally crowded by a colony of these gentle little birds in 1895, was in April, 1899, at the time of its arrival, fully possessed by Starlings, who completely occupied all the old trees. The spread of the Starling is certainly mischievous to the smaller woodland birds and likely to diminish their numbers. Single old cock birds begin to arrive from the 18th April, taking up at once their old stations, entering the old nest-hole, and singing for their mates. When the hen arrives (from three to six days later) singing abates and the two proceed to nest at once very quietly in the same hole. Later cocks arrive on the last days of the month, and through the first and even second week of May. Being probably young birds there is much more commotion while they try to procure both a mate and nest-hole; and their excitement on gaining the two is extraordinary. They fail, often, however, of one or the other, and many of the later comers appear never to establish themselves. The nest-processes occupy, from the sitting of the hen to the flight of the young, 27 to 30 days; the latter period being most usual. The eggs are often seven in number, like the Redstarts. The young are fed by the parents at least eight days after flight. They then retire into the deepest seclusion and silence, and are difficult to trace. Last sight I have had of them was on 18th July; last sound, 29th July. I have twice seen pairs toy and court while they were yet feeding their nestlings, but have never known a second nest. The food of this species is much of it taken from the ground, like the Redstart. It consists of small beetles, such as the Bracken Clock (*Phyllopertha horticola*), and *Lagria hirta*; Wolf Spiders, or *Lycosæ*, as well as flies, more particularly the large-winged, slow-flying ones that come from water. An abundant greenish river-fly often taken I am unable to name. The Pied Flycatcher has the pretty habit of hanging to its nest-hole, warbling, with fanned tail. Upon excitement it lowers and raises its tail slowly; also upon excitement and fear flickers its wings high.

HOUSE MARTIN. *Chelidon urbica* L. Summer visitant. Not abundant. Nests on the Hall and upon a few cottages.

SAND MARTIN. *Clivicola riparia* L. Summer visitant. Small bands in spring seem to be explorers for new nest-quarters, which are not to be had in the parish, and are rare all over Lakeland. Holes are sometimes bored in the low alluvial bank of the river, where it flows into Windermere, but I am not sure that broods are brought off there. Another station is by Wray, in a thin patch of gravel (the *Sammel* of the district) above a small quarry.

CHIMNEY SWALLOW. *Hirundo rustica* L Summer visitant Present, but not abundant, as farmsteads and rafters open to the air suitable for its nest-station are few

GREAT SPOTTED WOODPECKER *Dendrocopus major* L. Bred regularly in the Park a few years back Mr H E Rawson has taken young from the nest there. Mr Wykeham-Martin says, however, he never knew more than one nest in the season The present keeper has seen the bird but once, and in winter when a pair were at work on an old tree He shot one I have been unable to find it myself, nor has the squire seen it for eight or more years

COMMON CUCKOO *Cuculus canorus* L Summer visitant. Fairly numerous

COMMON SWIFT *Cypselus apus* L Summer visitant Has no nesting accommodation in the parish, but comes regularly from Ambleside to hawk over the river Pushes its excursions into Rydal Head, and probably to the tops of the range

COMMON NIGHTJAR *Caprimulgus europæus* L Summer visitant Nests on the fell slopes by a wood edge in several spots; probably drawn by *Typhæus vulgaris*, which burrows in great numbers, as well as the Dor beetle

COMMON KINGFISHER *Alcedo ispida* L Occasional visitant. Becoming possibly more frequent A year ago neither the keeper nor myself had seen it within the parish. Since then it has been even seen upon the lake by myself and the woodman. Years ago it attempted to nest in the bank at Fox How, but was flooded out. It quite regularly attempts to nest about the junction of the Brathay and Rothay, beyond the parish, and sometimes succeeds, I believe

WOOD OWL. *Syrnium aluco* L Permanent resident Abundant.

The Barn Owl *Strix Flammea* appears not to be present, as neither woodman nor gamekeeper have seen it It breeds, however, in the vale of Esthwaite and in Grisedale

SPARROW HAWK *Accipiter nisus* L Permanent resident. Succeeds in nesting here occasionally, though it is shot.

COMMON BUZZARD *Buteo vulgaris* L Permanent resident. Has nested for the last few years in the parish Its fine wild call may frequently be heard as it floats observantly above the rocky ground, or from (apparently) the last scattered trees on the precipitous Scar.

PEREGRINE FALCON *Falco peregrinus* Tunst Occasional visitant The Rev. E Reynolds, master of the foxhounds, meets with it on the fells from time to time. It formerly nested on

Dove Crag (just outside the parish), where, I am sorry to say, its last nest was harried.

THE MERLIN *Falco Æsalon* is not recorded for the parish I have seen a pair in March, 1887, on the small Grouse moor over Hawkshead Hall, where a friend later met with it

COMMON KESTREL. *Cerchneis tinnunculus* L. Permanent resident After the Buzzard our commonest Hawk. Its old nest-station on Gate Crag, after being regularly harried, has been vacated

COMMON CORMORANT *Phalacrocorax carbo* L. Occasional visitor Seen by myself 11th October, 1901, and by Mr. Granville Sharp in the previous year

CANADA GOOSE *Branta canadensis* L Resident According to common report this species was introduced on Grasmere Lake some years ago A pair now breed regularly every year on an island in Rydal Lake. With the goslings they spend the autumn and early winter between the two lakes, and after disappearing for a time from both waters, the solitary pair return to Rydal punctually at the beginning of April, when the *honking* of the male bird becomes frequent.

GREY LAG GOOSE. *Anser cinereus* L. Geese are heard flying north regularly in February and March Mr H. E Rawson considers them to be the Grey Lag

MALLARD *Anas boschas* L Permanent resident Nests on the islands and, I believe, in the steep wood. The keeper thinks that the drakes have a lighter body than the usual Mallard.

WIGEON. *Mareca penelope* L Occasional winter visitor I have picked it up dead on the marsh at the lake head, and the keeper has come across it once.

COMMON TEAL *Anas crecca* L An occasional visitor, only now, I believe At least, I have seen a pair but once. Mr Wykeham-Martin found a nest, however, on the lake

POCHARD *Fuligula ferina* L Winter visitor. Generally considered scarce, but has been frequent on the lake these last two winters. In the cold weather of February, 1901, their number, few at first, increased to 27 In January and February 1902, there were often more than 30 birds, probably the band of 33 or 34 first noticed on Loughrigg Tarn on 27th Nov., 1901 Like the following species the adult drakes are generally in a large majority

TUFTED SCAUP-DUCK. *Fuligula cristata* L Winter visitor This pretty little Duck is, next to the Golden Eye, our most frequent visitor, and never more frequent than in the early days of March, shortly before it leaves. Then two or three are sure to be found feeding at the head of the lake, in the neighbourhood of the Coots, who give to them maybe a protective, home-like feeling Larger, shyer bands, too, are seen, and these sail in a closer knot than any other Duck I know All the winter-coming water-fowl are erratic in their movements; constant on the lake one winter, scarce another; here one day, gone the next In fact, with many meres and tarns at hand, they roam, and their stay depends largely on the season's food supply The apt local name for this species is Whitesides

GOLDEN-EYED DUCK *Anas clangula* L Winter visitant Present every winter in varying numbers It appears neither quite as early nor stays so late as Mr Chapman reports it on the Northumbrian loughs. On the other hand, the parties seem larger here, and I have known thirteen in company Adult drakes, too, are frequent, either with the party or singly, and are sometimes seen three together. It is November, and sometimes late in the month, before they appear; and on the latest date I have, 21st April, the two birds, duck and drake, were decidedly paired

GOOSANDER. *Mergus merganser* L Occasional visitant. On 10th November, 1900, I saw a female or young bird of this species diving in the lake

COMMON HERON *Ardea cinerea* L Permanent resident Constantly on the lake, and last autumn (1899) a couple seemed to roost in the trees of shore or island But it has no nest station in the parish The well-known heronry on the island was deserted, according to Mr Jones Balme's report to Dr Gough, three or four years before 1876, when the birds took to a Larch plantation on the side of Loughrigg When this was given up I do not know. The birds nested in two fine Scotch Firs high on Silverhow, I was told, in the summers of 1897 and 1898; but this station likewise has been vacated

COMMON BITTERN. *Botaurus stellaris* L The Bittern I have no record of in the parish One was shot at the head of Windermere a few years back. Another was shot at High Cross Tarn, above Hawkshead Hall, by Mr James Cowper, who has the specimen stuffed

LAPWING. *Vanellus vulgaris* L. Summer visitant Nests still in one or two of the marshy hollows of Loughrigg Arrives on the Esthwaite Marsh in a large flock in February, but does not disperse to the higher breeding stations on the low fells till about middle of March. I have a note of its arrival on the marsh on 10th January, 1890; and was told of a flock on Grasmere Marsh on 14th January, 1900; but these too-early incursions are followed by withdrawals.

COMMON CURLEW *Numenius arquatus* L Occasional visitor only, as it no longer breeds on Loughrigg. Its quavering cry is heard in early spring, as it moves to its nesting quarters, on the rough heights (Black Fell, Hawkshead Moor, etc) round the head of Esthwaite Lake In the late summer of 1898, when I had word that it was unusually numerous on its breeding ground, it pushed the incursions it makes into the Esthwaite hay meadows (when these were shorn of grass) as far as this parish Nine or ten birds were about in the last days of July Farmers regard these incursions as a sign of bad weather, as they are more marked in a rainy season, when the fields are soft

COMMON SANDPIPER *Tringoides hypoleucos* L Summer visitor Several pairs nest upon the lake each summer. Last season (1899) they were so numerous that I met with six in one quarter mile of shore Several of the nests were placed at some distance from it One was in a patch of *Arum maculatum*. 15th April, 6th August

JACK SNIPE *Limnocryptes gallinula* L Winter visitant. On the marsh at the head of the lake Latest date on Esthwaite Marsh, where it also is regularly, 4th April, 1894 To the latter place comes the Common Snipe to breed. I cannot find it on the Rydal Marsh, though Mr. Wykeham-Martin says it nested there in his time Probably the noisy traffic of the adjacent highroad has banished it

WOODCOCK *Scolopax rusticula* L. Permanent resident. Breeds regularly in the deep enclosed woods; cocks may be seen "flighting" in the season from at least three different quarters of the parish Mr Wykeham-Martin has seen seven birds on the wing together I am told that it nests, too, in the woods above Grasmere The gardener at Silverhow, who sees it often, found two young birds drowned in the garden well in a dry season when the beck was empty

COMMON TERN *Sterna fluviatilis* Naum. Occasional visitant I picked up a dead bird on the west shore by Steps End on 22nd May, 1897; a straggler probably from bands migrating to their nesting-ground on the Cumberland coast.

BLACK-HEADED GULL *Larus ridibundus* L Winter visitant. and, indeed, at all seasons but the nesting After the nesting is over it swarms up the valleys from the coast, and stays as long as food-supply holds out It is here for the short season of the

Bracken-clock Beetle, vast numbers of which it must eat. On 9th July, 1899, I found a young bird by the lake shore so immature and weakly that it rose with difficulty, and was too feeble to move far. It must have been left behind from a moving flock

LESSER BLACK-BACKED GULL *Larus fuscus* L Passing visitant in spring A beautiful sight it is to see a pair of these Gulls drop and float side by side on the lake, while a third sweeps round with loud queer cries Odd birds are often present, too, after the nest-season, along with flocks of the former species, and spend their time floating on the lake snatching at the great flies Formerly they bred on islands of Windermere and Ullswater

HERRING GULL *Larus argentatus* Gmel Occasional visitant Seen sometimes in spring, like the above species

COMMON GULL. *Larus canus* L Winter visitant in small flocks. These are much larger in wild weather and in flood-times, when with the Black-headed Gull it haunts the flat land under Loughrigg.

GREAT CRESTED GREBE. *Podiceps cristatus* L. Occasional visitant. Seen in Rydal and Esthwaite.

RED-NECKED GREBE *Podiceps griseigena* Bodd Occasional visitant Seen by myself 6th March, 1900 The identification of this species (of which I took careful notes) was very kindly confirmed by Mr. H. E Rawson, who has skins of this species and one of the Sclavonian Grebe shot on Windermere

LITTLE GREBE *Podiceps fluviatilis* Tunst. Winter visitant. Frequents the river mouth and the shallower ends of the lake

LAND RAIL. *Crex pratensis* L Summer visitant to the few hay meadows.

MOOR HEN. *Gallinula chloropus* L. Permanent resident. Frequent by the lake at almost all times. I have seen its nest very cunningly constructed of Horse-tails, in a growing patch of which it was placed.

COMMON COOT. *Fulica atra* L Permanent resident, except in the early months of autumn, when the birds vanish for a time It is in the patches of Lesser Reed-mace (*Typha angustifolia*) that this bird chiefly nests It may be seen in times of flood hurriedly building its nest higher.

WOOD PIGEON. *Columba palumbus* L. Permanent resident Large travelling parties appear, too, in the winter to feed upon Holly and Ivy berries, as well as upon acorns and Beech mast. As I have seen them upon the Juniper Fell above the Esthwaite Vale (where the farmer says they come sometimes " in a cloud "), I suppose they also eat the " Savin " berry.

STOCK DOVE. *Columba œnas* L. Summer visitant. A small flock of these birds generally appear with Ring Doves in the first months of the year and remain about the Knott Wood and the high trees under the Scar. That they occasionally nest in the rocks of the Scar is certain, as the keeper found a nest there in 1895 or 1896.

RED GROUSE. *Lagopus scoticus* Lath.. The keeper has never seen it in the parish, though it is said to be in the Heather of Wansfell. There is a small preserved Grouse moor above Hawkshead Hill. But in general the character of our mountains on which the sheep graze in summer, does not favour the species.

BLACK GROUSE *Lyrurus tetrix* L. Occasional visitant. This species breeds on all the heights round the Esthwaite Valley, but has been only occasionally seen in Rydal by the keeper.

COMMON PARTRIDGE *Perdix cinerea* L. Permanent resident. Scarce. The keeper sees a pair occasionally on the breast of the Scar, above Hart Head; another in the park, whence they move into Scandale.

COMMON PHEASANT. *Phasianus colchicus* L Permanent resident. Extensive breeding is done at the park. The keeper tells me he has to protect the young chicks from Sparrow Hawks and from Jackdaws, which come upon them in a swarm. The Buzzards give no trouble.

[*Naturalist*, Aug 1st, 1902.]

INDEX

Accounts, 34, 242, 488, 502.
Adam Fisher, 389, 391.
Age-names of beasts, 268.
Agistment, 97, 242, 245.
Agricola, 11
Alchfrid of Deira, 24
Alf and Alfwin, 29
Alfward, King, 29.
Allom, artist, 435
Alnager, the, 193
Ambrose, John, 481, 487, 619, 664
———William, 503, 582
Amora de Lancaster, 168
Amounderness, 32, 33, 36, 48
Anlaf, King, 34
Anne, Queen, 650
Appleby, 640, 654
Archer, G, 624, 628-631, 637
Arnold, Dr, 450
Ashmolean, 583
Athelstan's treaty (A D 926), 31
Atkinson of Mallerstang, 631-634

Backhouse, James, 385
Baisbrowne Manor, 75
Banks, John, 242, 245-246, 365-368, 547, 556, 572, 590
Banner, 152
Bannisdale, 147.
Barns, construction of, 305
Barring out, 458
Barton parish, 3, 32
Barwise, Anthony, 524
Baxter, schoolmaster, 457-458, 461, 465
Beasts of the Forest, 160, 161
Beckermet, 216, 473, 479, 481.
Bedford, Duke of, 56
Bedford, Earl of, 55
Belle-Acqua, John de, 52
Bellingham, Alan, 52, 124, 271, 624-625, 631, 657
———Col, 503, 512-517, 524-525, 536, 544
———Henry, 184-185, 503
———James, 640
Bensons of Loughrigg, 205-6, 214, 218-19, 373, 379.
Bernicia, 21
Bier-law, man, 61, 104, 109, 125.
Bigg (barley), 250
Billetting rates, 513.
Bindloss, Agnes, 218, 475   *See* Agnes Fleming
———Dorothy,
Blackstone, Lady, 493, 495, 498, 529, 537
Bokland, 66, 68

Boon-service, 72, 92-93.
Border Warfare, Pt. I, chap xiii.
Borran or Burn, 11
Borrans field, 13, 14
Botchwood, 117.
Bouch, cousin, 595, 597, 617.
Boundaries, 32
Boundering, 63.
Bower, the, 313-317
Brathay, 24
Brathay Bridge, 589
———fishing, 273-4, 277-282, 284-285.
———Lake, 51
Brathwaite of Barnside, 503
———Gawen, Ambleside Hall, 525
———Thos and Reginald, 519, 540, 620, 624, 632, 638.
Breweresses, 122
Briggs, Col, 513, 517, 520
Brown of Troutbeck, 112
Brunanburh, battle of, 34
Brus, Margaret de, grants Rydal to Sir Roger, 171
———Peter de, 49, 51
Buckstones Jumb, 275
Bur stones for grinding, 427
Burh-gemot, 121

Calfgarth of Rydal, 321
Calgarth, 149, 150, 151, 181
Carlisle, Lord, 622, 626, 628, 653
Carriers in Rydal, 428-9, 451-454.
Cartmel Priory, 136.
Catmallison, 310
Cattlegate, 97.
Causeway foot, 371.
Caw-weel and bridge, Rydal, 39, 589
Celtic outposts near Rydal, 37, 38
Celts in Westmorland, 11, 19, 21
Chapels, 27, 28
Char, 277, 281, 286
———pie, 286-296
———potted, 296-301.
Charcoal, 113
Charles II, 619, 620, 624, 649, 652, 654
Clappers-gate, 6.
Clocks, 588.
Clothmills in Loughrigg, 200-204
Coaches, 301, 583-4, 657
Cock, J, 628-631, 639.
Cockermouth, 581.
Cock-pennies, 458-463
Cockstone, 51, 77.
Coleridge, Hartley, 471, 705.
Comet, A D 1680, 644-5
Common Field, Rydal, 101
Compounding Royalists, 525-526.

INDEX

Conishead Priory, 48.
Coniston, 465, 473, 475, 477, 537, 545, 547, 567, 673.
Constantine, King of Scots, 31, 34
Cooking utensils, 307
Corn mills, 403
Cote or Coat, 16, 17.
Cottages to have 14 acres attached, 89
——Elizabethan statute about, 90
Coucy, Lords of, 55, 137, 139, 151.
Court Baron, 124, 128
Court rolls, 97, 104.
Crosland, Sir Jordan, 532-534, 546, 551, 553, 557
Crow How, 235, 254.
Crowle, G , 579
Cumbria under Eugenius (A.D. 904), 31.
Curwen of Cark Hall, 487
Cuthbert, Bishop of Lindisfarne, 25.

Dacre, 31, 184, 207, 566
Dales, 59, 327.
Dancing-master, 469, 470
Danes in Northumberland, 30
Daniel Fleming, father of William, 545, 673
——son of William, 545, 547, 581, 558
——the great Squire of Rydal, part VI , &c.
——the third son of the Squire, 246
Davenant, Sir W , 593.
"Davids" Inn, 429
De Quincey, at Dove Cottage, 676, 680, 684, 687
——at Fox Ghyll, 684, 687
——children, 685-6
——edits *Westmorland Gazette*, 680-1.
——grandchildren, 704
——his letter to knights, 697.
——Margaret, 678-704
——— letter from, 699
——"opium eater," 679, 683, 685.
——Thomas, Part VII
Deira, 8, 21, 24, 630
Deer parks, Part I , Chapter 14
"Doll" Barbon, 483, 484, 532.
Doomsday book, 40, 41
Dorothy Wordsworth's letter, 238
"Down-house," 306, 317.
Druid Circles, 11.
Ducket, Sir Francis, 475
——J , 624, 625, 641.
Dunmail, King of Cumberland, 35
Dutch miners at Coniston, 482, 614
Dyes and colours of Kendal cloth, 207, 208

Eadwulf, Earl of Northumbria, 35, 36.
Eamont, 31
Edward I , 69
Edward, son of Alfred, 31
Edward the Confessor, 36

Eel-fishery, 276, 277, 279.
Egfrid, King of Northumbria, death of, 25.
Election expenses, 657
Elterwater, 51, 273
Eugenius, King of Cumbria, 31-34
Euthred [Ethelred I] slays son of Elfwold, 20, 29

Fairfield, 3
——meaning of, 194
Farmstead, plan of, 304-315.
——furniture of, 307-308, 310-312.
Farthingale, 592, *note.*
Feudal system enforced, 65.
Fidler's farm, 235.
Field-foot, 67.
Fines on cottage hearths, 106.
Flemings, 13-19
——in Rydal (A.D. 1409), 171, 176-187.
——*see* Pedigree
Fleming, Agnes, 218, 241, 257, 273, 482
—— her will, 257, 481, 558.
—— letters to son John, 223-225
——Alexander, 575, 576, 596, 599, 673
——Ambrose, 619.
——Anne and Bridget, 495, 532-533
——Anthony, 216.
——Barbara, 603, 607-609
——Hugh (1538), his wedding agreement, 215
——John, 177, 179, 186.
——Katy, 600, 602, 604, 605
——Richard, 219
——Roger, 572, 575, 577
—— letter about his "Ant," 573
——Sir Daniel, 1633 to 1701, 561.
—— at Rydal 1655, 563.
—— D L , 626-628.
—— dies March 25th, 1671, 671
—— his boys at home, 611-616.
—— his executors, 673
—— his marriage, 563.
—— his sons, 662-671
—— knighted, 652-653
—— life at home, 672.
—— M.P , 657-659
—— Sheriff of Cumberland, 622
—— under James II , 656-659
—— wife dies, 601.
——Sir Thomas, 169.
——Squire John, 473-486
—— his son William, 495, 498, 500, 508, 522-539
—— statesman, 442, 444, 447.
——"Will," 662, 664
——William, buys Grasmere advowson, 220
—— Buys other half of Rydal manor (1575), 219
—— marries Agnes Bindloss, 218

INDEX

Flemings rebuilds Coniston Hall, 217
Flemish weavers, 192.
Fletcher, Barbara, 561, 562, 601.
—— Bridget and Anne, 582.
—— Lady, 561, 580.
Flocks entailed, 257.
—— size and value of, Part III., Chapter IV
Ford-North, 238-9, 360, 609.
Forest silver, 95
Fox Ghyll, 51, 635, 684-685
Fox How, 450, 684
Frith and Frithmen, 62, 322.
Fuel restrictions, 106
Furness Abbey, 48.

Gales, 609, 610 *note*.
Gandy, Lady Vere, 607.
Gee, George, 448
—— Sir Orlando, 656.
Geldwether, 94
Genista tinctoria, 207.
Gilbert de Lancastre, 45
—— fitz Reinfred, 46, 47 seq
Gilmichael, 41, 65
Gilpin, Rev W, 208.
Girlington, Sir John, 506
Gist (agist), 97-100
Godwin, Earl, 36
Goloshoes, 598
Gospatrick, Earl, 40
Gown, the, 594, 595, 596.
Grasmere, 1, 8, 49-54, 68-69, 96, 128, 220, 474, 478, 481, 486.
Green-hew, 104, 109, 120, 343.
Gregory IX, 33
Gressum or fine, 74
Greystoke, Ralph of, 179, 184, 186
Griggs, 379, 386, 451
Grot-house at Rydal, 586.
Groves, 145
Gynes, Ingelram de, Lord of Coucy, 55

Hallan, 306, 307
Hallandrop, 308.
Hamelsate (Ambleside), 138.
Handicraft helps husbandry, 384, 428.
Handicrafts in Rydal, 303.
Hand-writing a rare art, 455
Hare and Hounds Inn, 426, 438, 441.
Harrison, steward at Rydal, 246, 252, 264, 437, 489, 493-494, 537, 541.
—— David, 391-393.
Harrisons, the, 429-433.
Harold at Hastings, 36
Hawkshead School, 456, 460, 463, &c.
Hearth tax, 430.
Heck, meaning of, 309, 315.
Henrietta Maria, Queen, 592.
Henry I, 43
—— II, 45
—— VI., 181, 182.
Herbert St. Derwentwater, 28.

Herdwicks introduced by Norsemen 37
Heriot, nature of, 82
—— cost of commuting, 87.
Hird, Hugh, the Troutbeck giant, 153, 154.
Hobson, Michael, 373-6.
Hoggart, Thomas, 403, 410.
Homespun, 609, 613, 615.
Hotham, Sir John, 52, 271
Howard, Viscount, 621-622.
Howgill or Holgill, 158, 167
Hubleshow, 127, 343.
Hue and cry, 123.
Hudleston, 673.
Hyde, Anne, 650.

Idiots provided for, 60.
Inglewood forest, 145-146.
Inquisition, 104, 124.
Inseygte (furniture), 215.
Interest on bills renewed 8 per cent, 372
Inventory at farm, 338
Ivy cottage, 399, 434, 437.

James II, 646, 659-661
Josie Eamontson, 491, 492, 496
Journeys to London, 301, 657, 659

Katie Benson, 488, 496.
Kelbarrow, 70.
Kellet Moor, for millstones, 418, 421
Kendal connected with Yorkshire for 1200 years, 44.
—— barony of, 6, 8, 46.
—— cloth, 195, 198
—— Lordship, 181.
—— Parliamentarian, 625-629.
—— surrenders Charter (A D. 1190), 654
Kentmere, 52, 205.
Kesslop, 589.
Kirkby Kendal, or Cherchebi, 41
Kirkstone, 11.
Knight's chamber, 230, 563.
Knots and ribbons, 591.
Knott, 9, 80, 86, 87, 117, 336-352.

Lancaster, Alice and Helwise de, 6, 7
—— heiresses, 46-49, 270-271.
—— House of, 180
—— Isabel de (A D 1409), marries Thomas le Fleming, 170, 171, 177
—— Margaret de, 52, 54
—— Roger de, 53, 77, 330
—— town, Charter, 654.
—— William de, land in Kendal, 46-48
Lancaster, Gilbert de, 45, 46
Langdale, 7, 53, 68, 69, 96, 330
Langholme islands, 27, 28, 64
Lawson, Sir Wilfred, 519, 521.
Le Fleming, 169, 171; Nos IV. and 1-11 in Pedigree.

Leaders, Northern, 536
Leech-gatherer, the, 3
Levens, 272, 330, 567
Leygate, 98
Lindesay, Walter of Warton, 49-51, 151
Little, John and Katey, 601, 608.
Lloyd, Charles, 677, 698.
Locker, the, 310.
Lodge in Rydal, 228, 234
Lord's oak, 232.
Loughrigg, 1-9, 53, 68, 70, 163, 330
——Brow, 51.
——Mills, 200.
——Tarn, 273.
Lowe, Ed., music-master, his letter to Barbara Fletcher, 562.
Lowther, Joan, 214.
——Lady, 518, 525, 539
——Lancelot, 215.
Lumley Fee, 124, 271.

Manor, definition of, 6.
——Lords of, 65
Manorial dues and fines, 71-80.
"Manto," the, 595, 608, 609, 616-617
Margaret, Countess of Richmond, 181
Marquis fee, 54.
Mere, meaning of, 58
Middleton, Lady, 645, 649
Military service, land tenure by, 133.
Miller Bridge, 51.
Millers, why called thieves, 405, 423.
Miller's thumb, 423
Millstones, transport of, 418, 422.
Money lending, 482.
Monmouth, Duke of, 658
Moot Hall, 128
Moot hundred and shire, 121, 123
Mourning, gift of, 596
Mowbray, house of, 45
Mulcture for millers, 404, 424, 426.
Muncaster, "Luck" of, 183
"Murray," from Lat. Morus Mulberry, 208
Musgrave, Sir Philip, 509, 620-622, 630-634, 640-641, 647-648
——Sir Chris., 653, 655-657, 661.
Music-master, 467, 468, 470, 562.

Nab, Scar, trees felled on, 238.
——Cottage, 356, Part VII., 675
——The, 352-360.
Needle-rest, 312.
Newman, Mrs. F. (the "Ant"), 573, 596-597, 599-601, 617.
Nicholson, hall carpenter, 577.
——Richard, 275.
Nigel de Albini, 45-47.
"Nightgown," 600
Norris, Sir W, 475, 480
Norsemen as colonists, 36
Northampton, Marquis of, 54, 215.
Numerals, Welsh, for counting sheep, 37

Oates, Titus, 624, 636.
—— ——his plot, 624-633, 644-645
Old Hall, 15-18, 35, 129, 170, 216, 220, 226.
——Orrest, 313, 315.
Orphans of Squire John, 485, 492-497, 518-519, 522, 532-533, 539.
Osred, 29, 30
Oswy, King of Northumbria, 24.
Otley, Rydal blacksmith, 395, 397
Otterburn, 178

Papists harassed, 643-646
Park, Rev G, 695
Parks at The Nab, 80, 81, 118, 352-360, 677-9, 689
Parr, Sir W of Kendal Castle, 54, 187, 215.
Paston letters, 182.
Pedlars, 600, 602-603.
Pedwardyn, 52, 54, 271
Pennington, Sir J., 183.
Philipson, Christopher, 155
Philipson's smithy, 394-395
Pigs for pin-money, 603
Plough common, 320.
Popish plot, 644-645
Priest's chamber, Rydal Hall, 484.
Primitive house, 305, 315.
Prince Rupert, 509-510

Quakers, 635, 637
Quillinan, Ed, 437, 684

Rake (path), 322
Rannel-balk, 311.
Ranulf Meschin, builder, Carlisle Castle, 43
Rash-field, 377, 385, 691
Ravenglass, 26
Reeve, 61, 62, 121, 125
Reinfrid, Gilbert, 46, 157, 160.
Rent in kind, 66, 67, 147, 177.
Restoration, 619, 621.
Richmond, Earl and Countess of, 56, 181
——fee, 56.
Right of Common, 102.
Ripon Cathedral, (A D 670), 25
Roman camp in Ambleside, 12, 13, 20
——roads to Ambleside, 12-18, 26, 27
——rule in Britain, 19.
Roses, Wars of the, 182.
Ross, John de, 54.
——Robert de, 52, 54.
Rothay, 7, 9, 10, 45
Routhamere, 7, 9, 51, 272.
Rufus, William, 42, 145
Rydal, a gateway of the mountains, 9, 12, 15
——Beck, 2, 4, 5.
——Cottage, home of Author, 386
——Deerpark, 106, 147.
——Demesne accounts, 242-245.

INDEX

Rydal, derivation of word, 17.
—— descends to Isabel le Fleming (A.D. 1409), 170-171.
—— granted to Sir Roger (A.D 1274), 171
—— House or Hall, 561, 569
—— Houses, Part IV, Chapter I, 302
—— Inns, Part IV., Chapter 6, 426
—— Lodge, 447, 449, 450
—— Manor boundaries, 1.
—— Mills, 412, 416, 422
—— Parish boundaries, 2, 3
—— —— three natural divisions, 4, 5
—— School, 456
—— Smithy, 304, 309
—— Township boundaries, 2.

Scandale beck, 1, 3.
Scots in Westmorland, 31, 515-517, 527-528.
Seaves, 311.
Sequestration at Rydal, 538-539, 544
"Setting-book," 243, 249, 264, 266
Sheep, price of, 262
Sheep-salving, 261
Shoe-makers, 598
Simpson, John, 678, &c.
Siward, east of Northumbria, 36
Sizergh, 495, 541
Skelwith Bridge Mill, 41
Skirwith manor, 241, 479, 508, 526, 545
Smith, Bishop, 580-581, 657-658, 661
Sole-foot, 306
Southey, 677.
Speke hall, 225, 475, 480, 481.
Stafford Visitation, 644
Stainmoor, 24, 32, 35.
Statesmen exterminated, 278, 374-375, 382, 386
Steady-stone, 62.
Stinted pasture, 61-62, 99, 101
Stirkland or Stircaland, 8, 41, 42, 45.
Stock Ghyll, 50
Strickland, James, 541
—— Ketel, 8, 42, 67
—— of Sizergh, 179-181, 187, 189.
—— Sir Robert, 532.
—— Sir Thomas, 541-542
—— Walter, 537-539, 543
Swan with two necks, 301.

Tabbie, 593, 595-596
Taxes for ever, called casts, 527-530
Terynllwg, 8, 24, 44
Thanet, Earl of, 655, 659, 660
Thingmount or Moothill, 38
Thompson, John, 363-364, 366.
Threshing at 2d. a day, 382.
Tilbrook, Dr, 434, 436-437, 449.

Tosti, son of Earl Godwin, 36
Township, 128
Trainbands, 622-3, 628, 632, 644
Treaty of Athelstan, 31.
Trespass, forest, 155.
Troutbeck, 50, 58, 76, 77, 96.
—— Mill, 411.
Tweng, William de, 53, 55.
Twenge or Thweng, Marmaduke de, 53-55, 271.

Uchtred, Earl of Northumbria, 35
Udall, carrier and publican, 377, 378 450
"Udalls" Inn, 450
Undermount, 370.

Valuation by John Banks, 244
Verjuice, 266
Verney, Lady, 571
—— Sir Ralph, 571, 580, 596.
Vill, the, 58, 66, 78, 121

Waberthwaite, 27
Wages, 251, 254, 261, 382, 401, 481-489, 613-614
Wainscotting, Rydal Hall, 584.
—— Grasmere Church, 585.
Walking silver, 94
Warrant, words of, 104
Warwick, King-maker, 181.
Westmorland, County formation of, 43.
Westmorland Gazette, 680-1
Whitefield, Sir Matthew de, 176
Whitfield, John, 636.
Wilfrid, St, 24, 25.
Will of Thos. Hudson, 388.
William III, 661.
—— Rufus, 42, 105
William the Conqueror, 36, 40
Williamson, Joseph, 622, 636-637, 641, 651-652.
Wilson, carrier, 377
—— Edward, 605, 608, 676
—— of Elleray, 677, 686-687.
—— parson of Grasmere, 511
Window Tax, 316
Winter, Ed, 553-554
Winterseeds smithy, 395.
Witherslack, 147, 167
Women work in fields, 254
Wool, price of, 191
Wordsworth, Dora, 679
—— Dorothy, 238-239, 676, 687-688
—— Mrs William, 685, 705
—— William, 673-677, 684
Wytheburn Court, 130.

Yeats (= gates), 97
Yeld, 93

TITUS WILSON, PRINTER, KENDAL